Letters and Memoir of Joseph Charles Philpot

Letters and Memoir of Joseph Charles Philpot

BAKER BOOK HOUSE
Grand Rapids, Michigan 49506

Reprinted 1981 by
Baker Book House Company
ISBN: 0-8010-7060-0

First published in 1871

PHOTOLITHOPRINTED BY CUSHING - MALLOY, INC.
ANN ARBOR, MICHIGAN, UNITED STATES OF AMERICA

Yours affectionately
J. C. Philpot

INDEX TO LETTERS IN MEMOIR

INDEX TO LETTERS

PREFACE

Reader, you will perhaps ask, What may I expect to find in this book? Is the master at home? Standing at the door, and placed here merely to show the way into the presence chamber, I answer, Do not fear to enter; but I warn you, you must not expect anything merely to amuse the imagination or excite the feelings, nor any novel expositions of the Scriptures of God; but I can say, you will surely find on the table the old wine of the Kingdom, set forth by a thoroughly honest and earnest man—made honest, not through the fear, or to gain the favour, of his fellow men, but by the indwelling of God's Spirit.

When he had completed his academical course, well furnished with human learning, and with a most active and energetic mind, he became a minister in the Church of England, and had before him the prospect of both honour and emolument. But after the probation of a few years, he found he could not remain there, for some of the rules and formularies of that Church compelled him to say and do what his conscience could not approve. He resolved, therefore, to quit his post, but his resolve was not lightly taken: it cost him much. He hesitated, and rightly hesitated, long before he left a people among whom he had zealously laboured, not without profit, and from whom he received many testimonies of affection and respect. But he could not remain where he was, for the arrow of conviction had entered into his very soul, and leaving behind him not merely worldly profit and honour, but, what was infinitely more, many loving hearts, he went forth not knowing whither he should go. But he soon found a place and sphere of duty. And what was the work assigned to him by God's Spirit, who divideth "to every man severally as He will"?

Past records seem to teach us that every man deeply taught of God has a special work assigned to him. That signal instrument of God's power and love, Luther, "the solitary monk who shook the world," was sent forth to teach the corruption and bondage of the human will, and to proclaim afresh the only sure refuge for the awakened sinner, the love and blood and righteousness of Jesus Christ, brought home to him by a loving faith, the gift of God. And what was the office assigned to the subject of the following Memoir? Mainly this, that the faith of God's elect, the faith that Luther set forth, cannot be acquired through the teaching of man, nor by any effort of man's will or intellectual powers ("the flesh profiteth nothing"!) but that it must be brought into the heart by God himself, and be felt and known there as an effective reality. In a word, that there must be a divine revelation of Jesus Christ in the sinner's heart—not that our departed friend meant that there must be some sensible apparition, some visible manifestation, for he again and again disclaimed that, but he held, with Hart, that,

"Something must be known and felt;"

that Jesus Christ must be so revealed as to be an object loved and longed for. This, I think, is a key that satisfactorily opens some of the utterances of Mr. Philpot that at first sight may surprise and offend. For instance, he writes to a friend, "I can find none in this place but Bible Christians." He meant to say that he did not think the reading so many chapters in the Bible day by day, or the learning and repeating of so many texts of Scripture, made a man a Christian. And is not this just what was said by Capito, one of the Swiss reformers in the sixteenth century? "It is not enough that ministers (or their hearers either) have often in their mouths the words 'Jesus Christ, our Saviour,' and other like terms; for the Gospel of the kingdom consists, not in mere words (though they be the words of the Bible itself), but in the power of God, which lays hold on the hearts of the faithful, changes them, renews them, and of poor sinners, as they were, makes them the children of God, and transforms them into men of heavenly minds, whose inclinations are no more carnal, but divine." Again, the same holy man writes, "whoever does not grow in the experimental knowledge of Christ, declines and falls back, or, rather, has never yet been in the right way." And how forcibly and feelingly was the great theme of Mr. Philpot set forth in the last prayer, and almost the very last words of Luther! "Oh, eternal and merciful God, my heavenly Father, Father of our Lord Jesus Christ, and God of all consolation! I thank Thee *that Thou hast revealed to me Thy Son Jesus Christ;* in whom I have believed, whom I have preached, whom I have confessed, whom I love and worship as my dear Saviour and Redeemer, whom the Pope and the multitude of the ungodly do persecute, revile, and blaspheme. I beseech Thee, my Lord Jesus Christ, receive my soul. Oh, Heavenly Father, though I be snatched out of this life, though I must now lay down this body, yet know I assuredly (blessed assurance!) that I shall dwell with Thee for ever, and that none can pluck me out of Thy hands."

Reader, do these words of the doorkeeper commend themselves to your heart and conscience? Do you desire truly to eat the flesh and drink the blood of the Crucified One? Then enter in, and may you find the provision made for you in this book profitable to your soul.

W. Clayton Clayton

Hampton Court, June, 1871

ADVERTISEMENT TO THE READERS

DEAR FRIENDS,

I feel that I cannot introduce this work to your notice without a few words of explanation and apology, not for the letters of my late dear husband, which, I am assured, stand in need of neither, but in behalf of whatever part I have had in the compiling and editing of them.

Anxious as I was that such a rich mine of experience and such useful teaching as the following letters contain should not be wholly lost to the Church of God, yet I was most unwilling from the first to have any hand in their publication; and it was, at last, at the pressing request of many of my late husband's dearest friends, and not till I had made many unsuccessful attempts to find one qualified to ease my shoulders of the load, that I at length consented to undertake it.

Thus left to my inexperience, and I may say incompetence, it was commenced with many doubts and fears; has been prosecuted amid great anxiety and most troublesome delays, and it is now with grave misgivings that I cast it upon the waters. But from the commencement a gracious God has raised up for me innumerable friends, who, by their munificence in contributing funds, by their kindness in giving counsel and advice, and by their readiness in sending me letters, have materially lightened my burden; and, indeed, without such assistance it must have proved too heavy for my unpractised powers. Still I am but too well aware of the many defects of the work I now publish. I feel that the Memoir of the life and labours of my dear husband is very incomplete; that the collection of letters contains much which, as being uninteresting to the general reader, might well have been omitted, and does not perhaps include some of his best correspondence; and, further, that the whole is marred by errors which, with the greatest care, I have been unable to exclude. One principle—and I feel sure it is a right one—has however guided me throughout, and may perhaps account for some deficiencies. I have attempted to portray our dear departed friend mainly by what he has left behind him, or, in his own words, "I merely furnish the thread on which to string the pearls." And as he was one who seldom spoke of his own doings, and almost never of his own feelings, I have experienced considerable difficulty in my task. I have preferred to let the letters tell their own tale, and am sure that the reader who studies them carefully, as tracing a "soul's growth in grace," will reap a harvest of useful lessons, and, I trust, may glean a few precious ears of Christian comfort. Notwithstanding all the errors arising from want of judgment and experience which disfigure the work, I feel confident that it contains the pure gold of the Kingdom, and as such the Lord will bless and apply it to the hearts of its readers. To Him be all the glory.

My most sincere thanks I owe to William Clayton Clayton, Esq., of Hampton Court, for invaluable assistance in the revision of the sheets; and to the many kind friends who have shown such readiness in contributing letters, and in affording me counsel and encouragement in my arduous undertaking.

I am, dear Friends,

Yours very faithfully,

SARAH L. PHILPOT

Croydon, August 14, 1871

MEMOIR

Joseph Charles Philpot was the third son of the Rev. Charles Philpot, rector of Ripple and vicar of St. Margaret's at Cliffe, near Deal, Kent, and was born at Ripple, September 13th, 1802.

On either side he claimed descent from French families of the Reformed or Huguenot faith, who, driven from their native country by the fierce persecutions of their Popish fellow-countrymen, had settled and become naturalised in England. His father, a clergyman in the Church of England, was a man of considerable talent; in youth he had highly distinguished himself at Cambridge, and in after-life wrote several learned but now almost forgotten works. He was greatly respected and beloved by all with whom he was brought in contact, no less on account of his kind and earnest disposition than for his sterling and honourable character. Though somewhat cold and distant toward strangers, he was kind and friendly to his parishioners; and though strict and unswerving in his duties as a father, he was most gentle and affectionate to his children. Mr. Philpot's mother was a woman of a very sweet but, perhaps, of a too indulgent and yielding disposition. She was the only daughter of the Rev. Peter La Fargue, rector of Greatford, near Stamford, a lineal descendant of a distinguished French family, who expatriated themselves for conscience sake. The head of this family had held a high position at the court of Louis XIV. Forced to flee to England by the Catholics, he utterly renounced the land of his nativity; and, in his fear lest some of his posterity might be sordid enough to embrace the Catholic religion, as a means of recovering the French estates, he burned the title-deeds of his magnificent château in France, and thus at a blow sundered all connection between his family and their native land. Mr. Philpot's maternal grandfather was the grandson of this refugee, whose portrait in full robes of office is still preserved by a collateral branch of the family. Thus, on both his father's and his mother's side, he was intimately bound to the Established Church, from which his conscience afterwards compelled him to secede.

Though little will be said in this Memoir of Mr. Philpot's father, for he died before those events which will most interest the reader took place, yet the influence which his example and teaching had upon his son was well marked, and indeed gave a tone to his whole character. He perceived in him, at an early age, high promise of those talents for which he was afterwards so eminently distinguished, and was induced to take especial pains with his early education. Being himself a correct and well-trained scholar, and a man of extensive information, he most carefully laid the foundation in the boy of those attainments which became so noted in the man. There can be little doubt that it was his father's influence which greatly fostered, if it did not altogether create, that intense love of reading and of gleaning scraps of information from every science or study, which, though modified in after-life, was always one of his leading characteristics. And at the same time, from an early life spent in the country fields and by the sea-shore, and from having his attention constantly directed to them by his father, he learned to take great delight in flowers, in plants, in birds, in fishes; and these objects never throughout life ceased to interest him. Nor was the moral effect which the early teaching of his father had upon him less marked in after-life. The father was what the world accounts a strictly honourable man, and strove to inculcate in his children, both by precept and example, those high principles by which he guided his own life. Before long, however, he, fully appreciating the benefits which his son would derive from a more extensive acquaintance and association with others of his own age and station than was to be found in a rural village, and having also his time fully occupied by the education of a younger son and the numerous cares of two parishes, determined to send him to a public school. Merchant Taylors' School was the one selected, and in 1811, when only nine years old, this beloved son was sent away from his home and placed among strangers in London. Being further advanced than most boys of his age, he at once assumed a somewhat high position amongst his playmates, and for some months his education progressed most favourably. But he was unfortunately seized ere long with a malady which at once temporarily incapacitated him from the continuance of his studies, and, indeed, had such an effect upon his constitution as he felt through all his life. He was hurriedly taken home and placed under the care of the family doctor; yet, with every care and precaution, his illness increased, and for long his life was despaired of; but he rallied at the point when his strength seemed almost wholly exhausted, and was slowly but gradually restored to a measure of health, though his constitution ever felt the results of his long sickness.

After this, his parents determined to send him away from home again; but this time he was placed at St. Paul's School, London, where he remained till he left it for the University. His career here was highly honourable, and he left after a six years' stay with the reputation of being one of the best scholars the school had produced.

As his father had destined him for the Church, it was desirable that he should take a degree at one of the Universities, and accordingly, in the spring of 1821, he went to Oxford to compete for an open scholarship. Though unsuccessful at his first attempt, yet his acquirements were most highly commended by the examiners, and he was shortly afterwards elected to an open scholarship at Worcester College. His residence at Oxford commenced in the following October, and for the succeeding five years he chiefly lived at that place.

It will be a good opportunity here to pause and view his moral character before the entire change that grace wrought in it was effected. From his own lips we gather that at this time, though he was not what is called a gay young man—not living an immoral life—yet that he was still utterly dead in sin, "without God and without hope in the world," looking forward to prospects in life, surrounded by worldly companions, and knowing as well as caring absolutely nothing spiritually for the things of God. But even then, so great was the contrast between his quiet and regular mode of life and the gay and fast life of many of the Oxford undergraduates, that he acquired the reputation of being a godly young man. Among his fellow-students he was generally popular; but, as was his wont in after-life, he made few bosom friends; some, however, he met with whose feelings and character were most congenial with his own, and for them he cherished a most ardent affection. One of his earliest friends has told us that his conduct was at that time singularly pure, that he was quiet and steady, abhorring all profanity and open sin. Yet he had plenty of confidence in himself, and was never led by others. He was a lively and pleasant companion, and was not only popular among the students, but earned the friendship and respect of the tutors, who were proud both of his talents and of his moral character.

The habits of work which he had acquired at school he carried with him to the University, and during the three years of his undergraduate life read with steady zeal. Moderation, however, guided his work, and he never allowed his health to suffer from too ardent application. He arranged his hours of work and relaxation with the same method which he observed in his later years, and making a point of taking a full share of daily exercise, permitted nothing to interfere with his custom. At the Universities the three years' study may be said, for the most part, to converge and culminate in the final pass examination; this, at any rate, at the time of which we speak—fifty years ago—was the chief goal of the student's ambition, and on this his eyes were steadily fixed through the long months of study; for as the position which his efforts might gain for him at that examination might greatly affect his success in after-life, it was incumbent on him, were he at all ambitious, to strain every muscle toward that goal.

It was in the Michaelmas Term, 1824, after three years of hard reading, that Mr. Philpot presented himself for his final examination, and his success answered his highest expectations, for of over a hundred students who went up with him, only four were placed in the first class (the highest rank), and of these he was one. He was now a graduate with a Bachelor's degree (B.A.), and as his scholarship must in time lead to a fellowship, he had only to wait for a vacancy to be appointed fellow of his College. He still, therefore, continued to reside at Oxford, and by taking pupils was enabled to earn an ample livelihood.

During his residence as a student at Oxford he suffered from a second most dangerous illness, an attack of inflammation of the lungs. The severe measures which it was the practice in those days to employ with the idea of subduing the inflammation, reduced him almost to death's door, and it was only a changed plan of treatment which, under the blessing of God, restored him again to health. His physician said at the time he had seldom seen a more severe case, and though he was mercifully preserved for a long life of usefulness, it was with a weakened constitution. All that painful susceptibility to constantly recurring attacks of bronchitis which proved one of the greatest trials of his life, was chiefly the result of this severe and indeed almost fatal illness.

In the autumn of 1825, however, about a year after he had taken his degree, an offer was made to him which induced him to change his plans, and took him away from the University for some time. An Irish gentleman, of wealth and position, came to Oxford with the intention of procuring a private tutor for his sons: by chance, or, as we rather should say, in the course of Providence, Mr. Philpot was mentioned to him, and an interview with him resulted in his engagement. In a worldly point of view this step must have then appeared disadvantageous to his interests, for it would in great measure sever his connection with the University, and thus, perhaps, interfere with his future prospects; but, now that one reviews it after an interval of nearly half a century, how plainly can he trace the hand of God in every step. It was this event, and the train of circumstances which followed it, that, under God's direction, led to the turning-point in his career, his call by grace, and ever afterwards he spoke of it as the most important event of his life.

Between his engagement and the assumption of the duties of his post, a slight adventure occurred to him which it may be interesting to some to read. Journeying home from Leicester, whither he had been called by business, his coach was delayed by an accident for two hours at Oakham, in Rutland. He took a walk round the town, and at length entered the only bookseller's shop which the town then possessed, to purchase a book to read on his homeward journey. The stock consisted chiefly of Bibles, church-services, and school-books; but at length his eyes lighted upon a book of hymns which he had never before met with; he purchased it, and walked into Burley Wood reading the hymns. He was much struck by the truthfulness and beauty of many of them, and took it with him to Ireland, where it formed his inseparable companion. The book was "Hart's Hymns." Little could he have thought then, when he purchased it, that he would one day prize them so much, and find them so precious on his dying bed; and little would he have believed it, had any one told him then, that in ten years' time he would be preaching in a Dissenting chapel in that very town, and listening to the singing of hymns from his newly purchased book.

In the spring of 1826 he went over to Ireland, and commenced his duties of tuition. The part of the country in which he was located, though not far from Dublin, was inhabited for the most part by the poor tillers of the soil, and there were very few families accessible with whom he could be on terms of intimate acquaintance; with the former, he had not as yet learned to feel that union of heart which he did when he was placed more in contact with them as a parochial clergyman, and afterwards as minister, and thus, necessarily, he at first missed the lively and congenial society which he had enjoyed so much at the University. Always fond of books and solitary contemplation, he doubtless did not feel the want of companions so much as many young men of his age would have done; and in after-days he did not fail to see in this separation from all his former associates the Lord's hand preparing to effect the work of grace in his heart. Mercifully, during this time of comparative solitude, his thoughts were directed in a great measure to the things of God, though as yet he knew but little of them, and his heart was thus being made ready to receive the seed which was soon to be sown there by the hand of God. Thus for a year his life passed happily and quietly, till in the early spring of 1827 the Lord sent upon him a most heavy and grievous affliction; he felt compelled to leave Ireland, and, abruptly resigning his post, he returned to Oxford, where he had been in the meanwhile elected fellow of his College.

It was this affliction which formed the turning point in his career. Every man must know something, more or less, of afflictions, but it is only the true child of God that ever feels their sanctifying influence, and is blessed with the sight of God's hand bringing good out of evil. He only who has experienced a deep and stunning affliction can realise how thoroughly it masters and absorbs the whole faculties, and throws a pall of gloom over every object in life. Man is short-sighted, and cannot look forward to the time when his wound shall be healed, and he shall enjoy renewed happiness. "Ah!" he cries, "let me die; life is not worth living; my sorrows are more than I can endure;" and then, when every hope is gone, and everything man clings to is torn away, and he feels the depths of despair, then is often the time the Lord chooses to show His face and to raise the poor grief-stricken man up and fix his hopes on Himself. It was thus that the Lord dealt with our dear friend when in Ireland, for under this heavy affliction He gave him first a true spirit of prayer and of supplication; it was then that He showed him what a guilty sinner he was in the eyes of a righteous God, and gave him power to pour forth from the bottom of his heart groans and cries for pardon and peace through the blood of His dear Son.

This period in a Christian's career is one that he always looks back upon with a grateful remembrance as the sweetest of those "evidences" which God has given him. Mr. Philpot was no exception to this general rule, and of the oft-repeated allusions which he made to it from the pulpit we quote the following:—

"In the autumn of the year 1825, I was residing at Oxford, earning a comfortable livelihood by taking pupils, and looking forward to obtaining a still higher grade in my College. But quite unexpectedly, just at this time, a very eligible offer was made to me, and a high salary held out as an inducement to go to Ireland for a short time for the purpose of educating, for the University, two sons of a gentleman of wealth and high position, whose country seat was not far from Dublin. Now, it was not to my interest to accept such an offer, as I was in good circumstances, and it was rather breaking my connection with my College, and so far somewhat interfering with my future prospects, to leave the University even for a short period; but no doubt the hand of God was in it, though I saw it not; for His thoughts were not my thoughts, nor His ways my ways. But I was tempted by the large salary, and went to Ireland in 1826, where I spent that year very happily and comfortably, for I had everything that money could buy, or heart could wish. But all this time I knew nothing experimentally of the things of God; for though highly moral, as far as regards man, and having a great respect for religion, the grace of God had not then touched my heart. But in the beginning of 1827, in the early spring, the Lord was pleased to bring upon me a very great trial and affliction, which I cannot name, but it was one of the greatest sorrows I ever passed through in my life, and it was in and under that affliction that the Lord was pleased, I have every reason to believe, to begin His work of grace upon my soul, and to do for me the things I have spoken of, in giving me the light of life, planting His fear in my heart, pouring out upon me the spirit of prayer, and communicating those other sealed evidences of the first kind which I have laid before you; for though not without a hope in God's mercy, I was not favoured, until some years after, with any special manifestation of Christ. Now when I came back to Oxford in the autumn of 1827, the change in my character, life, and conduct was so marked that every one took notice of it. I did not perceive myself, so distinctly, this outward change, though I well knew the inward; but it was very soon observed by others, and especially at my own College, and, in fact, very soon brought upon me a heavy storm of persecution, which, with other concurring causes, eventually drove me from the University. I have no wish to put myself forward, and the only reason why I have mentioned these circumstances is to show that wherever there is any real work of grace upon a man's heart, it will be made openly manifest; that others can see, as well as he can feel, that something has been wrought in his soul by a Divine power, which has made him a different man from what he was before. It might, perhaps, have been easy for you, and cost you little sacrifice, to make a profession of religion, but it was not so with me. As fellow of a college, and looking forward to the honourable and advantageous office of public tutor, it was no small cross for me to break off old friendships, and incur the dislike and contempt of the ruling authorities, and thus with my own hands pull down all my prospects of preferment and emolument for life. But there was a power resting on me in those days which made religion with me as everything, and the world as nothing. Thus I must testify, from my own experience, that if we lack this open evidence of a change having been wrought in us, we certainly are deficient in a very main particular."—*Sermon, "Evidences Sealed and Open," preached at Croydon, June 6th*, 1869.

"There are certain providential leadings, and there is scarcely any child of God who is not, more or less, acquainted with them. These providential leadings are often of the greatest importance as it concerns spiritual things. Nay, I may add further, that some of the most important events of our life were connected with apparently the most trivial incidents. The most important event of my life was my going to Ireland in 1826, when a young man at Oxford; I call it the most important event of my life, because it was in 1827, now twenty-two years ago, that eternal things were first laid upon my mind, that I was made to know myself as a poor, lost sinner, and a spirit of grace and supplication poured out upon my soul. I may have had doubts and fears since, as to the reality of the work of grace upon my soul; but I have never doubted, and never shall doubt, that if I possess grace in my heart, it was then first implanted. That important event, connected as it is with my standing before you at this moment preaching the word of life, depended upon a very simple incident. It was this. A gentleman sleeping in Oxford, instead of going off early the next morning, remained two or three hours later. That circumstance gave me an interview with him, which resulted in my going to Ireland. Upon that simple incident, then, of a gentleman staying a few hours in a town, hinged the whole work of grace in my heart.

"Now, when we are in these circumstances, we have no light upon them; but light is sown in the circumstances. When I went to Ireland, I had no idea that the Lord meant there to visit my soul with His grace; I went merely from carnal motives; but light was sown in that circumstance, and has since sprung up.

"I see now why I went to Ireland while a carnal young man at Oxford; I view now the hand of God in it; light shines upon that providential circumstance, and, though dark then, it is clear now."—*Sermon preached on Lord's-day morning, July* 15*th*, 1849, *at Zoar Chapel, London, and published in the Zoar Chapel Pulpit—"Seeds of Light and Gladness."*

"I have often thought of the way in which the Lord seemed pleased to begin His work of grace in my heart. I was at that time a young man at Oxford, not, indeed, what is called a 'gay young man,' not living an immoral life, but still utterly dead in sin, 'without God and without hope in the world,' looking forward to prospects in life, surrounded by worldly companions, and knowing as well as caring absolutely nothing spiritually for the things of God. Well, the Lord, in His mysterious providence, removed me from that place and took me to Ireland, contrary to the wishes of my friends, and shut me up, as it were, for more than a year and a half away from the society of the world, brought me into great natural affliction of mind, and then in that affliction of mind He was pleased, as I trust, to communicate His grace to my soul and quicken me into spiritual life. Now, I have looked sometimes with wonder upon the circumstance of His taking me from all my former companions, and putting me there in quietness and solitude. When life came, this quiet and secluded nook seemed to be like a little nursery, where the infant plant of grace might for a while be fostered, before I was thrust out into a rude world. It seemed to be a little spot where the Lord might not merely begin His work of grace, but strengthen it in some measure, that when I was thrown back amongst my old companions I might have power sufficient to resist their wiles, and that I might be separated, as indeed I most effectually was, from them. And thus looking at the Lord's dealings with my own soul, and at His way of working with others, I have sometimes seen what a concurrence there has been of providential circumstances, which, though they were not grace, yet were so necessary in the chain of Divine appointments, that could one link have been broken, the whole chain must have fallen to the ground."—*Sermon preached in* 1841, *June* 17*th*.

We have already said that Mr. Philpot abruptly left Ireland and returned to Oxford, now a fellow of his College; but it was impossible for him to resume the place with regard to his old friends and associates which he had occupied before he left. Apart from the changes which months of separation are calculated to bring about in even bosom friendships, he now found himself a changed man, and felt but little union of mind with the friends with whom he had once associated. Nor did they, on their part, fail to perceive the change which had come over their friend; naturally it was a change they could not appreciate, and his altered views and conduct soon began to draw upon him cold looks. Harsh words succeeded often to cold looks, and he began to be looked upon with distrust by many of his colleagues. He has left it on record how, soon after he first felt the weight of eternal things, ofttimes seated after dinner in the common room with the other Fellows, amidst all the drinking of wine and the hum and buzz of conversation in which he took no part, he has been secretly lifting up his heart to God. Amidst all this social intercourse, he longed in quiet solitude to pour out the feelings of his heart to God. He resolved, therefore, to take refuge in the duties of a parish clergyman, and accordingly, early in 1828, was appointed to the perpetual curacy of Chislehampton with Stadhampton (commonly called Stadham), two neighbouring villages not far from Oxford. At first he resided in his college rooms, riding over to his parishes as often as occasion required, for he still continued to take pupils in Oxford, and cherished hopes of obtaining higher preferment in his College; but several circumstances combined to incline him to leave Oxford altogether, and the declaration of the provost or head of his College, that his religious tenets must exclude him from all hopes of advancement there, decided him to reside permanently at Stadhampton, one of his parishes.

"When I first went to Stadhampton, in the year 1828, it was with the intention of riding backwards and forwards to Oxford, and thus maintaining my connection with the University, where I took pupils, and where I was looking for the highest offices in my College. But I soon found that there was no mixing together the things of God and man. Persecution from the heads of the College fell upon me, which much severed the tie, and broke to pieces the pleasing prospects I was indulging of worldly advancement. A great gulf seemed placed also in my feelings between my former friends and myself; and one day in particular, in the year 1829, as I was sitting on my horse near the College gates, it was so impressed on my mind that Oxford was no place for me, that I gladly turned my back upon it, and went to reside permanently at Stadhampton."—*Preface to Warburton's Memoir*.

As there was no parsonage at Stadhampton, Mr. Philpot was obliged to take rooms at a farm-house in the village, and here he continued to reside till his final separation from the Church in 1835. He had entered upon his new duties with zeal and earnest perseverance, and he soon gained the love and esteem of all his parishioners. His sermons, we have been told, even then contained a life and power very seldom met with in the Church of England; his church soon became thronged as each Sunday came round with people from far distant villages, chiefly poor labourers to whose needs his preaching was specially adapted. Amid all this popularity, much of it no doubt due to false enthusiasm and to a general craving after something new, the Lord greatly blessed his pulpit labours, and many of his congregation were at that time born again under his ministry. His residence on the spot gave him new opportunities of work and a more thorough acquaintance with his flock, though at the same time the situation of Stadhampton was so unhealthy that he never, during his residence there, enjoyed really good health. But, notwithstanding his weak and ailing frame, he zealously undertook much extra labour, both in the church, the school-room, and the cottage. His labours on Sunday were excessive. On each Lord's-day, before the morning service, it was his custom to spend some time at the Sunday School, teaching the children the word of God; from thence he would walk with them to the church, where he took the whole morning duty himself, and generally preached *extempore* for an hour. After the morning service it had long been the custom of the clergyman to take luncheon with the squire of the parish, but Mr. Philpot had not long held the incumbency when he was constrained from conscientious motives to break through this custom. It was a step which much offended the squire and his lady, and brought upon him great reproach; but he bore it all with uncomplaining meekness. After the afternoon service, he again went to the school, and had the children assembled all around him, to hear what they remembered of the sermon, and to explain to them what they could not understand of it; he then dismissed them with prayer. His day's labour was concluded by an exposition given on some portion of the Scriptures in his own sitting-room, where often quite a goodly number of his parishioners assembled to hear him. On Tuesday evening he held a prayer-meeting in a cottage at Chislehampton, and on Thursday evening he gave a lecture in the school-room at Stadham.

Daily, too, was he found labouring for the temporal good and comfort of his poor parishioners. He appointed visitors to distribute tracts, raised a fund to buy coals and other necessaries for the poor, and purchased large quantities of flannel and calico to make into clothes. He was unwearied in his daily walking from house to house to read and pray with his people; and many even now survive who remember the kindness and unpretending simplicity of his manner.

It was in the spring of 1829, whilst residing at Stadham, that he first became acquainted with the late William Tiptaft, who had lately been appointed vicar of Sutton Courtney, a neighbouring parish, and from this time dates the commencement of the life-long friendship which bound these two God-fearing men together. Mr. Philpot, it will be remembered, survived the friend of his younger days more than five years, though really a few months his senior; and it must be a great matter of congratulation to the Church of God that the account of the toils, the sufferings, and the upright and unselfish life of the one was preserved to posterity by the pen and labours of the other, and, indeed, formed almost his last work. It is from this memoir that Mr. Philpot's own account of the commencement of the firm friendship to which allusion has been made is quoted below, and there will be frequent occasion in the course of this narrative to extract further portions from that work:—

"About this time, then, I belonged to what is called a clerical meeting; a few of the evangelical clergy in the neighbourhood meeting together once a month at each other's houses for the purpose of reading the Bible, prayer, and religious conversation. Some time in May, 1829, I was present at one of these assemblings—I think, if I remember right, at Wallingford—and there, for the first time, I met William Tiptaft, who had lately joined the clerical meeting, through the introduction of Mr. Knight, vicar of Harwell, near Sutton Courtney, who was one of its leading members. He, as being a stranger, said but little at the meeting, nor did we come, as far as I can recollect, at all close together. We met, however, again early in the same summer, at another clerical meeting at Hagborne, near Sutton Courtney; and there, as we were walking out for a little air, after the main business of the day was over, he drew near and began to converse on the things of God. At that time I was further advanced, at least in doctrine and a knowledge of the letter of truth, than he was, being a firm believer in election and the distinguishing doctrines of sovereign grace, which I preached according to the ability that God gave. We therefore soon got on the topic of election, when I at once perceived that he had not been led into the grand truths of the Gospel, and though not altogether opposed to them, yet, like many others in his state, viewed them with a measure both of fear and suspicion. I was struck, however, even then, with his great sincerity of spirit, and the thoroughly practical view which he seemed to take upon all matters of religion, considering them, as he always did so markedly through the whole of his subsequent life, as the great, all-important one thing needful for time and for eternity."

Mr. Philpot happened to leave Stadhampton soon after this first interview, and did not again return until the end of August, 1829. During this very time, however, a great revolution had taken place in the views and feelings of William Tiptaft; gradually, as he himself has told us, had the scales fallen from his blind eyes, and gradually had he been led to know the blessed doctrine of the final perseverance of the saints, and the doctrines of predestination and election. (See *Memoir of William Tiptaft*, page 9.) Thus when he and Mr. Philpot again came together, to the ordinary bond of friendship to which similar tastes and congenial tempers had given rise, was added the still more lasting and still dearer bond of Christian union and fellowship. They soon found themselves almost the only ones amongst the labourers in the vineyard who were truly and sincerely fighting the good fight, and each strengthened the other by mutual prayer and exhortation to bear, without repining, the persecution which their own zealous efforts and consistent conduct were bringing upon them. It was at this time that Mr. Philpot first went over to preach at Sutton Courtney, the parish of his friend, the narration of which event is given below in his own words:—

"About this time, as I had returned to Stadhampton, and he (William Tiptaft) knew that my views were in full accordance with those he had just embraced, he wrote me a note to ask me to come over and preach for him on a week-evening, as he had recently set up a week-evening service, and I was, from my own engagements, unable to come for a Lord's-day. Not having heard of the revolution which had taken place in his views and feelings, I was struck with the change in his language from the usual cold, stereotyped, evangelical form, (as, for instance, the expression of his desire that 'If I came, the Holy Spirit would enable me to preach such truth as God might bless to his people,') and accepted his invitation. It was about the end of the summer of that year, 1829; and as we went into the churchyard, it was surprising to see the number of people coming along the various roads, or standing in groups waiting for the service to commence. The church soon became so filled that there was scarcely standing room in the aisles. The middle aisle which is unusually large in Sutton Courtney church, and was then in front of the reading-desk, was completely thronged, one might say, jammed with hearers—strange contrast to most of the country parish churches, which, even on a Lord's-day, present a miserable attendance. And of whom was the congregation made up? Almost wholly of poor men and women. Labourers were there in their smock-frocks and week-day clothes, almost as if they had just come out of the fields; poor women in their cotton shawls, with a sprinkling of better-dressed people in the pews; but a thorough plain and rustic assembly had gathered together to hear a sermon on the week-day evening—an event which had not probably occurred in that church or neighbourhood since the days of the Puritans. He read the prayers, and especially the lesson, which was a chapter out of the epistles, with all that loudness of voice, emphasis of accent, and earnestness of manner which were always such a marked feature in him; and it seemed to thrill the whole congregation, as he roused up the sleeping echoes of the old church walls as they probably had never been roused up before. I shall pass by myself, and my sermon, which, if I remember right, was from Isaiah xlv. 24:—'Surely shall one say, In the Lord have I righteousness and strength,' enabling me to show in whom were stored our righteousness and our strength, and that both were in Christ, and neither of them in ourselves. Though now so many years ago, I still retain some remembrance, not only of my text, but of my manner of handling it, and of the way in which I was listened to by the large congregation. As I was young in the ways and things of God, my sermon, doubtless, was neither very deep nor experimental; but I think it was a faithful exposition of the truth as far as I knew it, and most probably suited such a mixed congregation better than such a discourse as would meet my more matured judgment now. I slept at his house and stayed a day or two with him, if I remember right, during which we had much conversation on the things of God." —*Memoir of William Tiptaft*, p. 21.

The boldness of William Tiptaft in preaching these new views brought upon him no small share of persecution; his former evangelical friends were frightened at what they considered his new and extravagant tenets, and all the clergy of the neighbourhood turned their backs upon him. But Mr. Philpot still clave to him, and from the similarity of his views and feelings seemed on this account more closely drawn to him; and as the two friends lived only six or seven miles apart, they had frequent opportunities of personal intercourse. In the autumn of 1830, however, a circumstance brought them into closer habits of intimacy. The narrative is continued in Mr. Philpot's own words:—

"In the autumn of 1830 a circumstance brought me and William Tiptaft into closer habits of intimacy. In September it pleased the Lord to lay on me His afflicting hand. I had overworked myself in my parish, and having taken a severe cold, and increased it by going out one evening to my lecture at the school-room, was quite laid aside and unable to preach. My friend, hearing of my illness, came over to see me several times, and rendered me what help he could in my week lectures; but, finding my health did not improve, he kindly invited me to come and stay with him for a few weeks for change of air, as Sutton was drier and warmer than Stadhampton, where I was living. This invitation I willingly accepted, and went to his house, November 4, meaning to return home in a few weeks. He was, however, so kind and hospitable, and we got on so well together, that I was easily persuaded to remain with him the whole of the winter, especially as I still continued tender, not being able to leave the house all through December and January. During those winter months nothing could exceed his affectionate kindness and attention, waiting upon me like a brother. Being too unwell to get up to breakfast, he always brought it to me in bed, and afterwards assisted me to shave myself. We spent the morning alone in our own rooms, he giving up to me his airy and cheerful drawing-room; but in the evening we generally sat together, and either read the Bible or conversed—I think I may say almost always—on something connected with the concerns of eternity; for I may add that it was a solemn period with me at that time,* with many searchings of heart and prayers to the Lord as regarded my own state; for eternity was brought near, and I was made to see and feel that nothing short of Divine manifestations, and Christ revealed to the heart, could bear the soul up in the trying hour.

"In the beginning of February, 1831, I was able to leave the house, and take a walk under a sunny wall, where he would accompany me and suit his pace to mine; and as strength mercifully came with the advancing season, I was enabled to go to the church and hear him preach."

The reader will see from this extract that the afflicting hand of God had been again laid upon the subject of our memoir, and that for some months he had been confined to the house. In the early spring he found himself sufficiently recovered to leave his friend's hospitable roof; but his long illness had so worn out his strength that he felt wholly unfit again to take in hand the care of his parishes. He therefore went to reside some time on the south coast of England, spending the time chiefly with his mother. His father had died suddenly in 1823, when Mr. Philpot was still a student at Oxford, and his widowed mother had removed with her daughters to Walmer, which was not far from their former place of residence. The affection which he cherished for his mother had, if possible, received increase after her sad affliction; and accordingly, soon after his long illness, he hastened to seek in the affection and comforts of a home the repose and quiet that he needed for his restoration to health. His parishes he left under the care of a young clergyman—Mr. Charles Brenton, son of Sir Jahleel Brenton—who held the same views as himself, and whose help at this time he found very seasonable. In the summer of this year William Tiptaft had, in company with Mr. Bulteel, then a curate at Oxford, gone on a tour in the west of England, preach-

* "Up to that period I fear I was resting more on the doctrines of grace than on the Lord Himself; nor had I then been led into a knowledge of the evils of my heart. But in that illness I was made to see and feel that something more than doctrine and knowledge of the truth was required to bear the soul up in the solemn hour. Not but what I had tasted that the Lord was gracious, and had felt Him precious, and was blessed and favoured in the first part of my illness; for I well remember that, as I lay very ill in bed on my birthday, I was so happy in my soul that I said, 'This is the happiest birthday that I ever had.' But afterwards I was much tried in my mind, and brought low both in body and soul, and led down into the chambers of imagery as I had never been before."

ing the gospel in towns and villages, in churches, chapels, houses, or barns, or even in the open air. Over Mr. Bulteel, as a curate only, the episcopal authority had a greater hold than over William Tiptaft; and about the end of the summer, on account of his infraction of ecclesiastical discipline, the Bishop of Oxford had withdrawn his licence to his curacy. Mr. Bulteel at once announced his secession from the Church of England, and William Tiptaft seemed inclined to follow his example. At this juncture was written the earliest letter of Mr. Philpot's that has been preserved. In it he warns William Tiptaft against too great precipitancy in leaving the Church, and gives him a good deal of friendly advice.

"*Walmer*, *Sept.* 7, 1831.

"My dear Tiptaft,*

"You ask me to write you as long a letter as your own. Please to bear in mind that your writing is larger and wider than mine, and, therefore, because this sheet is not foolscap, do not think I am unmindful of your request.

"I trust you will deliberate much and long, and seek much the direction of the Spirit, before you venture on the step you meditate of resigning your living. You are placed in a very important station, and, according to your own testimony, have many opportunities of usefulness. You say your congregation is undiminished, that many come to hear you from distant parts, and that you have many spiritual hearers. You have no wish to remain for the sake of the loaves and fishes, and would willingly give up your house and furniture and live in any obscure place that you might be placed in. All those who have left the Church, agree in this, that a man should have a clear direction from the Spirit, and that if he leaves it without sufficient grounds, and seeing his way clearly, he will repent of it. Your eyes are partially open to see its defects, and most of your present intimates have either left her communion or are dissatisfied with what they see in her. All this works on your mind and perplexes you. Now, a good deal of what is merely carnal may here influence your mind. Your objections may arise, not from the teachings and leadings of the Spirit, but may be merely the workings of the flesh and the temptations of Satan, who would gladly see you removed from your present sphere of usefulness. I do not say you may not be under the leadings of the Spirit, but I say they should be very manifest and clear, much more so than they now seem to be, before you should take so important a step. My dear friend, do nothing rashly. Seek only to be led and taught of God. Cease from man—even spiritual men. They cannot direct you in

* Mr. Tiptaft was afterwards minister of the Particular Baptist Church at Abingdon, Berks. He died August 17, 1864, aged 61.

such difficult circumstances. I would not wish you to stay a moment if you were really led of the Spirit to quit the Church; but I am afraid of your acting on the suggestion of others, or from feelings merely carnal. The flesh, you know, is wondrously changeable, and can work just as well one way as another. It may work well to keep you in, and it may work to turn you out. All I would say is, seek earnestly the direction of the Spirit, and do not move till you see your way very clearly either by inward light and manifestation or outward providence. I think the Bishop will not bear with you much longer, and then you will see your way clearer. You may think me carnal, and so on, but I cannot be wrong in advising you to seek earnestly direction from the Lord, and not to move without it. It will be a heavy blow for Sutton and its vicinity if you leave. I feel very sorry to think that many who now can hear you will not then be able, and I think, too, of Stadham. May the Lord guide and direct you. Do not act precipitately, or from merely carnal feeling, but wait to have your way very clearly made out.

"I hope you will go over to Stadham, before you go away for a time. Can't you go over the day this reaches you? it is the usual lecture-night. I could wish that Brenton had more the gift of preaching, and could speak more to the comfort and edification of the people. His sermons are too dry and abstract, too much of the reflections of his own mind, and need simplicity of statement and application. They are good and true as far as they go, but they want that energy and speaking to the heart, and suiting it to the cares and wants of the hearers, which make preaching profitable. They require too much attention to follow, and a mind in some degree imbued with the truth, and able to catch it when obscurely stated, to be generally useful. I am thankful, however, for the seasonable help the Lord has sent me in him, and feel a confidence in him which I could not have done in another. Besides which, I trust the Lord will teach him, and apply the truth with such power to his heart that he will be constrained to speak it with power to others. Preaching without book, too, will, I think, be useful in leading him to greater simplicity of statement, and bringing him out of that essay style into which he has fallen. I fear I shall not be able to comply with the wishes of the Stadham people in taking a part of the service. In the first place, I need rest, especially during the winter, when each cold affects my chest; and, secondly, if I were sufficiently strong, I should not think it right to interfere with Brenton. I have left him there to be in my place, which he has kindly consented to occupy; and if I were to return, of course the whole would seem to revert to me, and he be only my assistant. I think it best to leave him in sole charge, and am thankful I can do it so much to my own satisfaction. His visits and conversation, and his lectures, perhaps may be more profitable than his preaching, and it may lead the children of God to pray for him, and so be beneficial to their souls and his. I was much pleased with a little note from Mrs. T., in which she expressed herself as thankful for Brenton's being there, and seemed to imply this was the general feeling. I am anxious to know all about them. When you go over, make a point of seeing some of them, and let me know how their souls fare. I am glad Mr. —— has come to hear you. There seems something like a shaking there. Few have, I believe, abused you more. His conversation was a tissue of oaths. I rejoice that Husband and you are so intimate. Your preaching at S. M. would, I am sure, give offence. The Pharisees can bear the Law better than the Gospel, and even the mild Husband now gives offence, and will do so more and more.

* * * * *

"Miss —— is, I fear, something like the robin spoken of in the 'Pilgrim's Progress,' who can eat sometimes grains of wheat and sometimes worms and spiders. I am quite sick of modern religion; it is such a mixture, such a medley, such a compromise. I find much, indeed, of this religion in my own heart, for it suits the flesh well; but I would not have it so, and grieve it should be so. We sadly want stirring up here. It is a trying situation to live altogether without spiritual society, and more worldly company comes to the house than is profitable to me, as I cannot altogether refuse to enter occasionally into their conversation. I think of leaving about the 16th or 17th, and going to London, and thence to Petersfield. I cannot yet decide where I shall go to spend the winter. I wish to go to Plymouth, and think it very likely I may decide to go thither. The back of the Isle of Wight would be better for my health; but I should have no society there, and no opportunities of hearing anything profitable. At Plymouth I should find many friends, and have the opportunity of hearing the word. My sister is now staying at Stoke. The climate, I am told, is very damp and rainy, which is bad for me. I trust I shall be guided right. I heard Fowler preach at the little 'Refuge' in Deal. Old John Kent, the author of 'Gospel Hymns,' was there, and I had the pleasure of shaking hands with him. He had heard and drunk tea with Bulteel about three weeks before. I do not think it likely I shall speak to the people at Deal; I do not see my way clear. I do not wish to give up Stadham and forget my licence, which I should in that case do. I trust I am not unwilling, should the Lord please, to forsake worldly honours and gain for Him; but I must see my way clear.

* * * * *

"I should wish to know on what plan Bulteel means to conduct his chapel. I do not like to promise beforehand; but if his intended chapel is on such principles as seem right and eligible,

I should be glad to contribute £5. I cannot afford more in my present circumstances.

"I shall be glad to hear from you shortly again, and let me hear something about my Stadham people. I am sure Brenton would be glad for you to speak to the people, but on Tuesday night, being harvest-time, he was most likely apprehensive of not getting a congregation. May the Lord teach you out of His Holy Word, and make your ministry profitable to all His dear children.

"Believe me to be, with true affection,

"Yours in the Lord,

"*To Mr. Tiptaft.*" "J. C. P.

It will be seen from this letter that Mr. Philpot was still residing at Walmer, and did not yet contemplate returning to his flock. But he did not forget them; though absent from them in body, he was present with them in spirit, and ever felt a lively interest in their spiritual welfare. This the reader will gather from the following two letters written to one of his parishioners about this time:—

"*London, Sept.* 23, 1831.

"My dear Mrs. Rackham,*

"Grace, mercy, and peace be multiplied unto you from God the Father and Jesus Christ our Lord. I take the opportunity of my friend and brother Mr. Tiptaft's meeting me in London to send you a few lines to express my remembrance of and affection towards you in the Lord. I trust, during the season that has past since I saw you, that you have been enabled to trust in Him, who of God is made unto us wisdom, righteousness, sanctification, and redemption. I hope the Lord has shown you more and more of His cleansing blood and justifying righteousness, and given you faith to look to the one and lay hold of the other. To feel our deep need of forgiveness and reconciliation is God's gift; to see that there is a Saviour provided, who by His life and death put away sin and brought in everlasting righteousness, is God's gift; to lay hold of and believe on this Saviour, so precisely suited to our lost and condemned state, is God's gift. The whole plan and scheme of redemption in its first devising, after-execution, and individual application to the heart and conscience of the child of God, is, from first to last, the work of God the Father, Son, and Holy Ghost. This is a truth of which we should be deeply and firmly persuaded. We must learn and feel our lost and helpless state as sprung from our Covenant Head, Adam, by natural generation. We must be deeply and inwardly persuaded that we are utterly dead and

* Mrs. Rackham died at Sutton, near Dorking, Surrey, March 25, 1857, aged 78. Her end was peace.

powerless in consequence of this original sin of Adam, in which we are involved by being in him at the time of his fall, and that we have neither will nor power to see, relish, or believe the things of the Spirit of God. This conviction, applied by the Holy Ghost to our hearts, will stir us up to earnest prayer that the eyes of our understanding may be enlightened, that we may have the truth, as it is in Jesus, applied to our souls with power and the Holy Ghost and much assurance, and that we may have an experimental divine faith in the Person and work of the Son of God wrought in our souls. I trust the Lord has shown you this, and thus stirred you up to true and earnest prayer that you may have the truth brought home to your soul by the Holy Ghost, and are desirous to experience all the powerful teachings of the Lord the Spirit, though the word of God in His hands should even, as in the Virgin Mary (Luke ii. 35), be a sword to pierce thine own soul, and divide asunder soul and spirit, and the joints and marrow, by discerning and revealing the thoughts and intents of the heart (Heb. iv. 12). I mean by this that through grace you are willing to have the secret chambers of your heart laid open to your view, and be stripped of your own righteousness, that you may learn only to glory in the Lord. We must come to this, if we hope to be saved, and earnestly seek the Spirit's teachings, whatever sharp lessons He may teach us, and however He may humble us in our own sight.

"Through mercy, my health is much recovered, though my chest continues weak, and is soon irritated by exertion; my general health is much restored, and I feel stronger and less nervous than I did at Stadham. The sea air has, through God's blessing, braced me, and, my chest excepted, I feel nearly as well, though not so strong, as before this attack. I was forced, by a concurrence of circumstances, to take an afternoon service a few Sundays back, as if I had not done so the church must have been either shut up or served by a carnal minister. I was much helped at the time, and preached for nearly three-quarters of an hour, but suffered from it afterwards, my chest being weak and heated for two or three days. I trust that, during the interval which I have allowed myself for rest, it may please the Lord so far to restore me as to allow me to preach once more in the pulpits I have, through His mercy and providence, occupied amongst you. I sincerely hope that during that time the Lord may teach and bless your present minister to the edification of many. Fail not to pray for him, that the Lord may speak in him and by him to the hearts of his people, and furnish him with food suitable to the weak and to the strong. I look to the prayer-meeting as a means of great good in the Lord's hands. May He give a spirit of grace and supplication to its members, and lead them privately and publicly to intercede with Him for a blessing for minister and people. Those who do not pray aloud in these meetings may plead earnestly with God, both at home and when assembled together, and these prayers He that searcheth the hearts will answer, if offered up by the Spirit that dwelleth in them. Pray also that your own eyes, and the eyes of the church at Stadham and Chisleton, may be enlightened to discern the devices of Satan, and that that cruel wolf may not be allowed to rend the sheep. A praying church and a watchful church must flourish. When it becomes cold and lukewarm, when prayer is restrained and it ceases to be watchful, then the great adversary gains an advantage, and everything that is miserable creeps in, to the grief of God's children, to the joy of the world, and to the destruction of souls. Do not be unmindful that you have a God to glorify by your holy life and conversation, especially as being the mother and mistress of a family, before whom you should let your light shine, that they may see there is a truth, reality, and power in religion, and that it is not a mere change of opinions. I was glad to hear Mr. B—— had borrowed a religious book of Mr. Brenton. In your conversations with him I would have you avoid all disputes about election and such doctrines, and speak rather of such subjects as our natural sinfulness and condemnation, the necessity of having Christ for our perfect Saviour, the efficacy of His blood and His blood alone, and the need of embracing this by faith, together with the necessity of being born again and being taught of God. Such subjects will either be so distasteful that he will cease to speak upon them, or will be of use to him. Disputes about election will only harass your own mind, and stir up in him a mere spirit of carnal reasoning which will only do him harm. Seek wisdom from the Lord to direct you, and speak in His strength only, and not your own. But a holy, self-denying, and separated life is the best preacher.

"I trust that, with respect to your temporal concerns, the Lord is teaching you the meaning of that text, Matt. vi. 33, 34. Read the whole of that chapter, from verse 19 to the end, and seek of the Lord faith to believe and feel it in all its truth and power. Read also what the Apostle says to Timothy, 1 Tim. vi. 6—16. Observe how God there tells us to be content with food and raiment, and declares that godliness with contentment is great gain. See what he says of those that desire to be rich; how that they err from the faith, and pierce themselves through with many sorrows, and bids the man of God flee these things, and follow after righteousness, godliness, faith, love, patience, and meekness; and bids him keep this commandment without spot, unrebukeable, until the appearing of our Lord Jesus Christ. There is much instruction in these words if the Lord is pleased to seal it home on your heart and make it a principle of action. Let me advise you, my dear Mrs. R——, to be much in reading the Scriptures. Be like the Bereans, and search the Scriptures daily, Acts xvii. 11, and like David, Psalm cxix. 11, 97, 105, 140, 162, where he expresses his delight in God's word. See also the character given of the righteous man, Psalm i. verse 2. Pray earnestly that the word may be wrought into your heart, that its precepts, truths, and promises may be the comfort of your days and nights, the motive of your actions, and the guide to all your ways. Remember that the Lord has helped you through many afflictions, and turned them into blessings; and so He will be ever with you to keep, guide, and bless you. Only trust in Him. Do not hanker after this wretched world, or desire its honours and riches for yourself or your children. Give them up to the Lord, and ask Him to put them into such situations of life as may be for their spiritual good and for His glory; and be willing that they should be poor and despised, if it be His will. Seek also earnest blessings for the church where you live and the Church of Christ in general, that the Lord may pour out His blessing richly upon it. Seek for a spirit of humility, faith, and love, and avoid everything that may produce contrary feelings in the brethren. Set your face against everything that is ungodly and profane, wherever you may meet it; and in the regulation and management of your own household act as a Christian mistress and a Christian mother. A Gospel practice is the only outward proof of a Gospel faith, and wherever the principles of God's word are wrought into the heart they must and will produce the fruits of holiness and godliness in the life and conversation. I hope Elizabeth is able still to attend the Sunday-school, and that her class is improving. I would not wish her to set the children too long lessons, as I would sooner they should learn accurately and well than much. And I would wish her to consider the different ages and capacities of the children, and set them their tasks accordingly. I do not like that they should learn to hate school, and what they are there taught, as it may have an unhappy influence all their days; and the way to teach them to love school and their teachers is by giving them to learn what they are able to accomplish easily, and by treating them with the greatest kindness and gentleness, and yet due strictness and severity, if needful.

"Believe me to be,

"Your affectionate Friend in the Lord Jesus,

"J. C. P."

"*Petersfield, Nov.* 17, 1831.

"MY DEAR MRS. RACKHAM,

"Grace, mercy, and peace be multiplied unto you through the love of God our Father and Jesus Christ our Lord. I thank my God that the word which I preached amongst you did not return unto God void, but was accompanied with the power of the Spirit to the heart of some, and amongst them, I trust, to you also. This gives me confidence in writing to you, and I hope I shall be enabled to say something which may profit and comfort you. It grieves me to think that the sheep of Christ amongst you should not be walking in that light and comfort which is their portion and privilege. It has pleased our heavenly Father, who does all things in wisdom and love, to unfit me for that work which once I performed amongst you, and which it is my desire again to commence when it shall be His will. But why should you not still enjoy what you once enjoyed? Christ is the same, and His Spirit is the same, and the Word of God is the same. I am afraid the children of God have been looking in times past too much to the instrument, and not been looking simply to Christ that they might be filled out of the fulness that is laid up in Him. And, therefore, I trust God is teaching them this lesson, to cease from man, and to wait only upon God. My desire is to labour again in the vineyard where I laboured in times past, and I trust in God's good time I shall be allowed once more to go in and out amongst you. God has wonderfully restored my health since I left Stadham, though I am by no means so strong as I was before my illness, and am obliged to continue indoors when the weather is at all cold. Sir William Knighton discovered, I think, the cause of my illness under God, and said it arose entirely from over-exertion and exhaustion of the vital energy. By rest, through God's mercy, it is recovering; and here, I think, we may see the good hand of God in afflicting me with illness at the time He did. If I had gone on as before, most likely when illness came my constitution would have sunk under it. I trust now, by resting some little time longer, I shall have recovered sufficiently to labour again in the vineyard of the Lord. By this dispensation also God may be teaching His children at Stadham, Chisleton, and Ascot to depend more simply on Him for His teaching. We know what the children of Israel said in the wilderness (Numb. xxi. 5), 'Our soul loatheth this light bread,' and so, perhaps, where the children of God hear the sound of the Gospel so continually, they may become indifferent to it, and not receive it with that sweetness and power which they once did; and God has various ways of training up His children, and His ways are most wise, deep, and unsearchable. Jacob once said (Gen. xlii. 36), 'All these things are against me,' when these very things were working together for his good. But afterwards, when he saw his beloved son Joseph (Gen. xlvi. 30), he could say, 'Now let me die, since I have seen thy face, because thou art yet alive;' and again (xlviii. 11), 'I had not thought to see thy face; and, lo, God hath showed me also thy seed.' And thus it is now; we cannot see the wisdom of God's dealings at the time, but can afterwards look back and see (Psalm cvii. 7), 'He has led us forth by the right way, that we might go to a city of habitation.' 'Those that sow in tears shall reap in joy.' The advice which I would give to the children of God at Stadham, etc., is to search the Scriptures much for themselves, and be much in prayer for themselves and for each other. If they cannot derive that benefit which they would wish from their present minister, let them pray much for him, that God would teach him, and speak in him and by him to their souls. You may call to mind that when I left Stadham for a little while in May, 1830, the children of God were much in prayer that when I returned I might be enabled to preach more to their comfort and edification. I think they acknowledged at the time that the Lord, in a measure at least, heard their prayers. Let them now pray in the same way for their present minister, and the Lord will hear and answer. I really do not know where I could get a more satisfactory person. You all know how much trouble and anxiety it cost me, when Mr. T—— left, to procure the aid of any one even from Sunday to Sunday, and scarcely any except my dear friend Mr. G—— preached to the edification of the saints. You should consider how much worse you might be off, and probably would be, should the Lord remove Dr. P——. I don't mean, my dear Mrs. Rackham, when I say 'you,' to admonish you in particular, but I speak to all the people of God who love to hear the sound of the Gospel. I believe that you love the truth, whoever preaches it, and desire to receive the engrafted word with meekness and humility.

"In all your various trials, both personal and domestic, and what regards the Church of God, put in practice the command of the apostle, Philip. iv. 6. If you do this, you will find the promise in the seventh verse made good, 'And the peace of God,' etc. Pray for yourself, for your family, for the children of God around you, for your present minister, for all saints (Ephesians vi. 18), and for me also—that my health, if the Lord will, may be restored, and that I may come again to you, when I do come, in the fulness of the blessing of the Gospel of Christ (Rom. xv. 29). Pray that I may come unto you with joy, by the will of God, and may with you be refreshed (Rom. xv. 32). Seek to be guided in all things by the Spirit; for 'as many as are led by the Spirit of God, they are the sons of God.' Meditate upon James i. 5; John xvi. 13—15; xiv. 13, 14; Luke xi. 13; xviii. 1; Prov. ii. 3—6; iii. 5, 6; Jer. xxix. 11—13. I could fill my letter with sweet and comfortable passages, as, indeed, the Word of God is full of comfort and instruction. 'Only believe; all things are possible to him that believeth.' If you are in trouble about temporal concerns, read over, and pray upon, Matt. vi. 25—34, and Jer. xlix. 11, and ask the Lord for faith to believe and live upon these promises. The Lord seems to have helped you in inducing Mr. and Mrs. B—— to continue with you. The Lord, in sending bread, does not promise there shall be no trials and crosses with it. The bread is to be eaten in the sweat of the face (Gen. iii. 19), and so those that do not labour bodily for it must often labour for it in their mind. We are obliged sometimes to 'eat our bread by weight and with care' (Ezek. iv. 16); but, if God will, our countenances, if we eat only pulse, 'may appear fairer and fatter in flesh than all the children which did eat of the portion of the king's meat' (Daniel i. 12, 15). With respect to placing E—— with Mrs. W——, I would have you do what you think right in your conscience. Do not for temporal advantages do anything which you think might hurt her soul. But I am not sufficiently acquainted with all the circumstances to give my advice. Seek the will of God in the matter, and act as you think right in His sight, without regard to man. Remember me very kindly to your nieces, the Miss R——s. I trust they are cleaving to the Lord through evil report and good report, and glorifying their Saviour in their life and conversation, separating themselves in heart and spirit from the world. The greatest kindness that you could do them is to tell them where they are wrong, if you see anything of that kind in them. 'In many things, you know, we offend all.' Give my Christian love also to Mrs. L——, and tell her to look to Jesus for strength in all things; and let her light shine in that wicked neighbourhood where she dwells, that they may take knowledge of her that she has been with Jesus. Remember me also very affectionately to Mrs. L—— and Sally N——, and bid them watch over their hearts and tongues where they live, that they may not speak unadvisedly with their lips. May the Lord comfort and teach them, and make them shine as lights in the world. Give my Christian love also to Sally and Nanny H——. I trust the Lord is with them, to comfort them, and to say unto their souls, 'I am thy salvation.'

"Your mind may, perhaps, be troubled by what you hear from Oxford about Mr. B.'s change of views. Let not that trouble you. You know what truth God formerly blessed to your soul; hold it fast. Remember you are a poor sinner who can only be saved by Jesus, and that the promise is given to those that believe in Him that they shall be saved. Cleave simply to this, that His blood cleanseth from all sin, and let nothing drive you from that. Avoid all questions and strifes of words, and look simply to Him that died on Calvary, and is now risen again to make intercession for His people, and to appear a second time for their salvation. I trust I do not forget any of the children of God, though I may not now mention them. I have spoken of those to you whom you chiefly know; but I send my love to all.

"Believe me to be,

"Yours in true affection,

"J. C. P."

Two months after the date of the letter to William Tiptaft, the latter was constrained by his conscience to secede from the Church.

His secession, while in the eyes of many it degraded him and rendered him a despised outcast, in no wise altered the feelings of love and friendship with which Mr. Philpot regarded him. He at least did not look upon his own church as the only way of salvation, and, indeed, was already beginning to doubt whether it were even the best way. He began to break away from all the prejudices with which the whole training of his life had surrounded him, and knowing that it was conscience and conscience alone which had driven Tiptaft to his final act of non-conformity, he acknowledged the uprightness of his course, and extended to him the hand of unaltered friendship as to one who had merely changed his sphere of usefulness. All this our readers will glean from the following letter written to Mr. Tiptaft as soon as the tidings of his secession could have reached the writer:—

" *Petersfield, Nov.* 28, 1831.

" My dear Tiptaft,

" When Brenton made me the offer of my coming to Stadham, it seemed to me, at first, the very opening I had been desiring and praying for. But since I have considered the subject more maturely, I have thought it best not to accept his offer. My desire is to do just what God pleases in the matter, and to be willing to go or stay just as He thinks best. At the same time, I find myself counting the weeks to next spring, and feel somewhat of what Laban said to Jacob, 'Thou sore longest after thy father's house.' But I think, all things considered, I am doing what is best in staying here. Though it has pleased God to restore me to much better health, yet it is not so far established as to enable me to face the fatigues and cold of the winter, and I could not think of turning Brenton out of his lodgings at this time of the year. Besides which, I trust I am not altogether without use here. If I did not think Brenton a child of God, and one who had the spiritual welfare of my people at heart, I would not stay away from them a day; but though he may not preach with power, or to much edification, I fully believe he declares the truth. I at times feel very anxious about them, and trust it may yet be the Lord's will that I may return to them. I am glad you are not likely to leave the neighbourhood of Sutton, as I believe you have been made useful there. You should take care to have your chapel sufficiently large to hold a good number, as it is likely to be much crowded. This step of yours is not likely to meet with the approbation of the vicar of Abingdon, nor, indeed, of many of our friends in your neighbourhood; but if the Lord gives you His blessing, you need not mind what is said or thought. . . .

" To make light of experience cannot be right, for all the power of religion consists in it, and I fully believe what you have often said, that where there is no experience there is no religion. I am sure, for my own part, that the only time when the truths of Scripture influence my mind and practice, is when they are felt experimentally in the heart; and, I am quite sure, if I knew more of the mighty operation of the Spirit in my soul, I should walk much more happily, humbly, and consistently. I fully agree to all you say about the work of grace in the soul, and earnestly desire the gift of the Spirit, that I may feel more and more deeply the things of Christ. God has given us His Son—in addition to that, He has promised to give His Spirit—to take the things of Christ, and show them to us, and if the possession of the Spirit does not distinguish the believer from the unbeliever, I know not what does.

"Though it may be a trial, it is perhaps best for you to have no friend with whom you may readily consult upon the matters that interest you, as it must throw you more immediately upon God to obtain wisdom and counsel from Him. There are many promises of this in the word of God, and I believe, where the eye is single, the path is not in many cases very difficult. Scripture speaks much of patience, and I suppose we must be still before we shall see the salvation of God. I observe in the Old Testament that the saints waited much and long for the fulfilment of God's promises, and that, generally, help was delayed to the last extremity, and then afforded promptly and effectually. I was much struck the other day with Proverbs xvi. 9; I found it very applicable to my own case, as I was much perplexed about coming back to Stadham. My inclination is to go there, but I certainly, at present, do not see the way clear.

"I often think of you and your great kindness to me last winter—indeed, I trust I shall never forget your unwearied attention to such an invalid as I was then. May the Lord richly reward you! I think I have, on the whole, enjoyed more of the power of the truth since I have been here than I had done for some time previously; but I daily feel how much I have to learn. What I need is the gift of the Spirit; this is the promise of the Gospel, and without it all that Christ did, taught, and suffered, is nothing to us. I trust the Spirit has not left my people at Stadham. I am sometimes apprehensive of their becoming lukewarm and dead. But the Lord must keep those who are faithful to His promises, and can keep them without human means.

"Your affectionate Friend,

"J. C. P."

In a few weeks the example of Mr. Tiptaft was followed by one of his most intimate friends, Charles Brenton, who has already been mentioned as taking duty for Mr. Philpot.

This step he took abruptly, to avoid reading the Church burial-service over a wicked man who had died without any sign of repentance. Mr. Philpot was thus at once obliged to return to his parishes—an event which occurred at Christmas, 1831, after he had been laid aside for a year and a quarter. This return to Stadham he regarded as a most direct answer to prayer; for while he had been away from his flock he had been much exercised in his mind about leaving the Establishment; but his great love for the people amongst whom he had laboured so zealously and with such good effect, and who, if he entirely left them, would be as sheep wandering without a shepherd, constrained him still to remain a member and minister of the Church, whose errors he felt more and more acutely every day.

While thus perplexed, calling earnestly on God to lead him aright, he was suddenly called back to Stadham by the secession of Mr. Brenton. From this he concluded that God had still more work for him to do there; and from that time he continued steadily and quietly to labour in his own sphere, avoiding all intercourse with the outside world.

While he was thus employed, William Tiptaft, who was eminently a man of action, had no sooner found himself free from the constraint of the Church than he set about building a chapel to preach in. Before the winter had passed, land was bought at Abingdon, where he had determined to fix his abode, and a chapel was built, the whole expenses being defrayed by himself. It has already been mentioned that his separation from the Church in no way affected the firm friendship which Mr. Philpot bore him; and as Abingdon is no further distant from Stadham than Sutton Courtney, they saw each other almost as frequently now as they had done when clergymen in the same Church. The views of William Tiptaft were identical with those held by the Particular Baptists, and he was soon on terms of intimate friendship with the leading ministers of that sect. The late John Warburton was then in the full vigour of life, and had for many years been pastor of the church at Trowbridge. A great friendship had already sprung up between this good man and William Tiptaft, and he assisted, with Mr. Hitchcock, in opening the new chapel at Abingdon, March 25, 1832. It was not long after this date that Mr. Philpot met John Warburton at the house of their mutual friend William Tiptaft, and heard him preach in the new chapel. He had already heard Henry Fowler, at the little "Refuge," in Deal, and had shaken hands with old John Kent, the author of "Gospel Hymns." He was now introduced to Warburton, and from this time dates a friendship which lasted between them till the death of the latter in 1857. Such an important meeting should surely be narrated in Mr. Philpot's own words:—

"It was then some time in the year 1833 or 1834 that Mr. Warburton came to Abingdon to preach at the chapel of my dear friend Mr. Tiptaft, whom I had intimately known for some years previously as a brother-clergyman, and whose secession a year or two before from the Establishment had not broken or impaired our union in mind and heart in the great things of God. I went over, therefore, to Abingdon, about eight miles distant, to see and hear Mr. Warburton. I was then, and had been for some time, a good deal exercised in my mind about eternal things, and went with many fears and under much bondage, both on account of my position in the Church of England, which I was then beginning to feel, and the state of my own soul, which was, as I have hinted, then passing through various trials. Though reared in the lap of learning, and instructed almost from childhood to consider mental attainments as the grand means of winning a position in the world, I had some six or seven years before been taught by the weight of eternal realities laid on my conscience to value grace as the one thing needful; and the trials and temptations I was passing through in a lonely village, separated from all society but that of a few people who feared God, had deepened the feelings in my breast. Under these circumstances I went to Abingdon, feeling my own want of grace, and therefore with more fears than hopes, as about to see and hear a servant of God so eminently possessed of it, and anticipating rather a frown than a smile both in the pulpit and the parlour.

"I afterwards learned that the poor dear man, having heard I was a man of great learning, was almost as much afraid of meeting the Oxford scholar as the Oxford scholar was of meeting him. But how much better grounded were my fears than his; and how much his grace outshone my learning!

"He received me, however, with much kindness, and talked pleasantly and profitably on the weighty matters of the kingdom of God. I heard him very comfortably in the evening; and next morning after breakfast he would have me engage in prayer, which I did with a trembling heart, but seemed helped to express simply what I knew and felt. We afterwards went inside the coach together to Dorchester, about seven miles off, conversing the chief part of the way, and there we parted very affectionately. I do not wish to speak of myself, but I afterwards heard that my feeble lispings had given me an abiding place in the dear man's heart, and laid a foundation for that friendship and union which have subsisted unbroken ever since between us."

He continued zealously to care for the spiritual and temporal welfare of his flock, quietly and unostentatiously doing the work which God had set him. Perplexed he still was with doubts whether he ought any longer to remain a minister in the Church of England; but God, he tells us, had so wonderfully strengthened him for his work, after he had been laid aside so long by his trying illness, that he did not as yet seriously think of relinquishing his cure. His labours at this time seem to have been abundantly blessed. His church at Stadham still continued to be crowded each Sunday by hearers from far-distant parishes, and even his week-evening lectures attracted large numbers of peasants, fresh from the fields, in their work-day smocks, so eager did his people then seem to hear the word of God. The harvest indeed was great, but the labourers few.

Knowing and feeling the errors of the Church, both in creed and practice, he tried as far as he possibly could to walk consistently in his own case; but he found himself called upon, as a clergyman of a parish, to perform duties against which his conscience rebelled. Thus, in 1833, he felt bound to refuse to send any children from his parish to be confirmed, and was in daily expectation that the bishop would severely reprimand him for this omission. Again, from the letter which we quote below, it will be seen that complaints had been made to the bishop about his speaking in the pulpit against the practice of many of the neighbouring clergy taking out shooting-licences. So that though he did not as yet see the way open for his voluntary secession from the Establishment, he felt that at any moment his suspension by the bishop for his outspoken truthfulness might drive him to join the ranks of the Nonconformists.

At the same time the persecution which his altered views had aroused long before had by no means abated, but after the secession of William Tiptaft rather increased. The clergy of the neighbourhood were scandalised that one of their own body, however false his doctrine, however strange his views, should encourage, nay, live on terms of dearest intimacy with a deserter from their cause, a renegade, an enemy to their religion—for such they regarded William Tiptaft. Cutting letters were written against our friend, harsh words were spoken of him, and lying tales were circulated. Doubtless his feelings were deeply wounded by these false slanders, and the sting of the reproaches must have caused him many a sigh; for his was a very sensitive nature, one that felt very deeply and acutely, though it concealed its grief from the eyes of others. But under all these trials God supported him and held him up, enabling him to bear them all with meekness, and to feel that they were part of the cross that was laid upon him.

About this time we hear of the secession of another clergyman, the Rev. Thomas Husband, who professed the same views, and was on terms of most friendly intercourse both with William Tiptaft and J. C. Philpot. Mr. Husband resided at Appleford, a village in Berkshire, not far distant from Abingdon, and his two friends often met each other at his house, where they had opportunities of sweet spiritual converse. The fact of so many faithful servants leaving the pale of the Established Church increased the perplexity of Mr. Philpot, and called up with renewed force all those doubts which had lately been somewhat lulled to rest. A letter of his, which is here inserted, will describe, more faithfully than can be done by another, the agony of doubt that clouded his mind at this time. It is the first of a series of letters written to Mr. Parry, of Allington, Wilts, to whom he had lately been introduced, and who became afterwards, one may say, his dearest and truest friend.

Mr. Parry had heard through William Tiptaft of the exercises of Mr. Philpot's mind about leaving the Church of England, and had been given a remarkable spirit of prayer that the latter might at once secede and come and minister to them at Allington. He could find no rest in his mind till he had driven over to Stadhampton to hear him preach, and had made his personal acquaintance. Acquaintance ripened into firm friendship, and they continued to correspond regularly from that time; and the long series of letters addressed to Mr. Parry forms one of the most important remains that our dear friend has left behind him.

"*Stadham, near Wallingford,*
"*Oct.* 11, 1833.

"My dear Sir,

"Grace, mercy, and peace be multiplied unto you through the experimental, soul-humbling, soul-melting, soul-rejoicing knowledge of the gracious and living Immanuel.

"I am thankful to the God of prayer for having put a spirit of prayer into your heart for such a hard-hearted sinner as myself, as I doubt not you mingled among your petitions for my coming among you sundry desires for my own experimental acquaintance with divine things. I cannot, however, see my way to come among you at present, as I am still ministering to the little flock amongst whom I have been going in and out for some time past. My connection with the Establishment is not yet broken, but I am inclined to think it shortly will. The Lord, in answer to prayer, brought me back in so remarkable a way not two years ago, and so wonderfully strengthened me for my work, after being laid aside by illness one and a quarter years, that I have always felt I could not leave until I should see the way very clearly. For these last few months past I have laid the matter before Him, and sought of Him wisdom and guidance, as the corruption of the Establishment in practice and principle has been much opened to my mind. I think I now see symptoms of my way being about to be laid open, and that I am very likely to be put out of the curacy. If this should be the case, my way is open at once, as it is my ministry here which chiefly detains me in the Establishment. A few days will probably decide, and, should I be removed from the curacy, my present intention is to remain here till the spring, (God willing,) and then go into Kent for a season, where my friends reside, and where I should have an opening to preach the word.

"There is not a soul upon earth to whom I have communicated these particulars, and therefore I beg you will for the present keep them secret. I have been informed upon the best authority that a complaint has been, or will be, laid against me before the bishop for certain comments which I lately made respecting the conduct of clergymen taking out shooting-licences; and if I stand to the ground I have taken, which I trust the Lord will give me grace to do, I think he will remove me. I would sooner be turned out than go out. Let them thrust me out of the land of Egypt and the house of bondage and my way is clear enough. No one knows what it is to give up a people who love you, and whom you love, and a situation where the Lord has blessed you, but those who have the trial. I can safely say that my return hither, Christmas 1831, was the directest answer to prayer I ever had in my life, and therefore I cannot leave until I see my way clearly opened in providence or grace. Be pleased to keep what I have communicated secret, as not a single person, not even my assistant, knows what steps are pursuing against me but the parties concerned.

"Let me have your prayers that the Lord will guide me aright, give me a spirit of faithfulness, joined with meekness and humility, and separate me in His own time and way from a corrupt system, and more especially that He would be pleased to take present matters into His own powerful hand, and lead the devices of men to accomplish His own gracious and eternal purposes. Oh! for grace to believe and love, to seek His will, to have the mind of Christ, and a single eye to His glory! Oh! for a heart to fear none, and to please none, but the risen Lord, and to taste His love, constraining the soul to love, delight in, and obey Him!

"Present my affectionate remembrance to Mrs. Parry; and believe me to be yours affectionately in Him who is the Lord of all.

"J. C. P.

"*To Mr. Parry, Allington.*"

Whilst his soul was thus tried, vexed with scruples as to whether he were right in staying in the Church, and yet sorely tempted by love of his flock to remain in it, his weakly body proved to him another great source of trial. He seems to have been far more subject at this time to chest attacks than even in the later years of his life. Stadham was situated in a damp unhealthy district; his labours were excessive, and he was often exposed to cold and wet in passing between his two parishes. The result was that he was frequently laid up with cold and inflammation of the chest, and each succeeding attack, even when he was recovered from it, entailed a long period of bodily weakness. Even when not actually laid aside by illness, his Sunday's work greatly affected his general health. He did not recover from the single sermon, to which he was now obliged to restrict himself on Sunday, till the following Wednesday, and was often quite unable to take duty at all. At this time his frail body must have been a special trial to him: if he left the Church he must give up his whole income, and rely solely on his own exertions for his daily bread; if his health were then to fail, there would be no Fellowship to fall back upon, and beggary must stare him in the face. Only strong faith in the God, without whose knowledge not a sparrow falleth to the ground, could have supported him under these anxieties.

Thus a year passed away; he was still expecting to be turned out of the Church, and, indeed, once received a reprimand from his bishop, but heard nothing more of it. Meanwhile, his soul was dark and dead; he seemed to have fallen into the Slough of Despond, and hope had not yet stretched forth her helping hand. The three following letters, written in this year, will be interesting on this account:—

"*Stadham*, *Feb.* 1, 1834.

"My dear Sir,

"I have been partly prevented from answering your letter earlier by a painful inflammation of the eyes, which has been upon me this last fortnight, off and on, and is not yet subsided.

"I could wish I could give a more satisfactory answer to it than I fear you will find this to be. But my own mind is very dark, and the arm of the Lord is not yet revealed to me. The affair which I communicated to you went off more quietly than I had expected. Either the bishop was not applied to, or did not think it worth while to interfere. Whilst that matter was pending, I was quite satisfied to leave it in the hands of the Lord, and was indeed more desirous to be removed than to remain. But I felt then, that if it was not to turn me out, it would more settle me than before. And so it has proved, my mind being now less at work upon leaving than it was at the time I saw you. Towards this place and people I can almost say, 'Reuben, thou art my first born; the beginning of my strength.' And thus I feel unwilling, I may say unable, to quit them without some clear direction in providence or in grace.

"And I think, if you knew what a dark, dead, ignorant, lifeless, corrupt creature I was, your desire to see more of me would be much abated. Often do I seriously doubt whether I was ever converted at all, so much darkness, corruption, and infidelity do I find in myself. And as to the ministry, I feel myself more and more unfit for it, as having so little light, life, and power in my own soul, and knowing so little how to deal with the souls of the heaven-taught family. And these, I do assure you, are not the common-place confessions which every one professes to make, but what I really see and feel in myself. And what a grievous thing it is for a church to invite a man to minister for a few weeks, to be satisfied with his gifts and graces, and then find they have saddled themselves with one who knows nothing of the things of God spiritually, and therefore cannot build them up in the experimental truth as it is in Jesus! The people here are ignorant, and do not discern my deficiencies so clearly, perhaps, as I do myself; and as they profess at times to obtain good, I am led on from time to time to preach to them. But, as to leaving them and undertaking a new work in a new part of the vineyard without seeing my way clearly marked out, it is what I dare not do. At the same time I adhere to what I have long felt and said, viz., that if I had more grace I should not remain in the Establishment. But this very want of grace, which keeps me in it, would render my ministry unprofitable out of it. In this day there is too much of the cry, 'Put me into one of the priests' offices, that I may eat a piece of bread;' and as it is like people, like priest, it is not very difficult for a man with tolerable gifts to secure himself a pulpit in a respectable chapel. But I trust this is far from my views and wishes. A minister to be profitable must be sent; and he that is sent will seek the glory of Him that sent him, and will desire, above all things, grace in his soul as a Christian, and grace as a minister, that the work of the Lord may prosper in his hands. And amidst all my darkness and corruptions I desire nothing more than to have light, and life, and unction in my soul, both privately and ministerially.

"This, then, you must accept as my answer to your very kind letter, that I do not see my way to leave my present post, and that I hope you will not delay on my account to settle over you such a minister as the Lord may send you. But should I come into your parts, and I consider myself at liberty to preach in chapels, and it meet your wishes, I should be very glad to accept your offer of preaching for a Lord's-day or so. But whether that time will ever arrive, or when it may arrive, I cannot just now say. I, the Lord, it says, will hasten it in His time. He is a Sovereign, and I would willingly see His sovereign hand and hear His sovereign voice directing me in the path wherein I should go. Brother Tiptaft I have not seen for some time, and am inclined to think he must be from home. I fear you will think this letter unsatisfactory. I feel it to be so myself, but I know not how I can write otherwise. Give my Christian regards to Mrs. Parry, and accept the same from,

"My dear Sir,

"Yours very sincerely and affectionately,

"J. C. P.

"*To Mr. Parry.*"

"*Stadhampton, Oct.* 1, 1834.

"MY DEAR TIPTAFT,

"I have been kept from writing to you sometimes from occupation, sometimes from sloth, and sometimes from the feeling that I could write nothing profitable. Every day, indeed, I seem to see more and more that I have little or no grace. And at these times, when I can draw to the throne of grace and ask the Lord to work in and upon my soul, I seem to have less grace than ever. At such times, and I have been occasionally favoured with a little earnestness, I feel everything in me so shallow, so unreal, so little like the mighty work of the Spirit on the soul. The fountains of the great deep are not broken up, and all my religion seems to consist in a little natural light, just as I know any point of history or language. These are my best seasons, at least in private, when, feeling I have no grace or religion, I ask the Lord to work on my soul. At other times, what with the workings of infidelity, unbelief, carelessness, pride, evil temper, and conceit, with all the silly, foolish, filthy, lustful imaginations which crowd in one upon another, my soul seems like the great deep, 'without form and void' (in the original, 'confusion and emptiness'), before the word of God said 'Let there be light.' In my ministry, if I am shut up and cannot come forth, I care more for my own failure than the want of profit to the people. And if I am favoured with a little liberty, my proud heart takes all the glory, and gives none to God. So that what can you expect profitable to read from so silly and graceless, so earthly and carnal, a creature as I am? When I am in my right mind I would gladly feel something—law or gospel, conviction or consolations, cries or praises; anything of God would seem better than my present dark, blind, earthly, graceless state. I feel I shall run on so to perdition, unless sovereign grace interpose, and lift me up out of this fearful state. And yet at times only do I feel this, and at other times am as careless as if all was a fable from beginning to end. And then infidelity, with all its subtle doubts and questions, will creep in, and turn my prayers into mockeries. Your heart, I dare say, will echo all this; but what evidence is that to me? I shall perish in my carnal state unless sovereign grace step in; and from that nothing can shake me. But I will not detail any more of my complaints. Only picture to yourself the proudest, hardest, most unbelieving and carnal person you can, and you have my picture.

"I enjoy the Pinnells being so near very much. I have seen them quite often, and we always speak on the best things.

"I scarcely expected by this time to have been curate here, as the bishop wrote to me about five weeks ago, reprimanding me for having had an assistant so long without his permission, and requesting an immediate answer, if I was able or willing to resume the whole duty immediately. I answered him very concisely, neither calling him 'My Lord' nor 'Right Reverend,' and, after having stated a few particulars, said I could not dispense with an assistant. Of course, I expected to hear in reply, of his intention to remove me; but no such answer has come, nor indeed any. I committed the affair to the Lord, and as fully expected to be turned out, as you do to return to Abingdon. But here I still am unmolested.

"Clamp and three others walked over here one Lord's-day. I had much conversation with Clamp, and felt my soul refreshed, and found a union with him. On Sunday, 14th ult., I preached at Kennington, and was favoured with some little liberty—at least, as far as I felt myself. G—— was there, who seems awfully departed from the narrow way; and though I knew nothing of the circumstance at the time, I have been told that the sermon fitted him exactly. But so it is. We can hear so well for others, and never hear for ourselves. Mr. Clowes has been down at Wallingford, and is coming again for three weeks, so that we shall see him. I feel much union with, and regard for him. Jones, Mr. P——'s butler, a man of some light, though little grace, heard Gadsby at Gower Street. He described the congregation as excessive, and mentioned, though not to me, an expression of Gadsby, 'There is enough filth in the hearts of the people here to make the very walls stink.' His subject was Isa. lxiii., but this was said in explaining Zech. iii. 3, 4.

"A notion has got abroad that in your new edition of 'Gadsby's Hymns' you mean to leave out all the experimental ones adapted to peculiar metres. This I have contradicted.

"The Miss G——s are come to live here. They contend for the inward power of religion, and have been led to see P——'s 'wood, hay, stubble.' Much, however, still remains to come down. They speak of his ministry as powerless, and of his people as dead. He used to call on them about once a week, and never once talked on the things of God. I tried to bring his people to a point, but they seem to me like stones. If we are dark and dead, we know it; but they seem satisfied with their ignorance, and much like the Laodiceans of old. Tysdale preached the charity sermons for me, but did not, I hear, enter very deeply into the mystery of iniquity or the mystery of godliness. S—— has been here lately. I liked him much. He has gone through Lam. iii. since we saw him, and spoke much of his dark paths. I took him to the Pinnells, who were much pleased with him, and were very kind to him. Pray come over soon after you arrive. I fear this letter will only carnalise you.

"Kind regards to Mr. and Mrs. Keal.

"Yours affectionately in Christ,

"J. C. P.

"*To Mr. Tiptaft.*"

"*Stadhampton, Dec.* 11, 1834.

"My dear Friend,

"Having a favourable opportunity of transmitting you a letter by a private hand, I sit down to write you a few lines.

"And, first, let me ask how the things of the Lord are going on in your soul? Are you, like most of us in these parts, saying 'My leanness, my leanness! woe unto me!' Are you putting your mouth in the dust, if so be there may be hope? Are you crying with Paul of old, 'O wretched man that I am! who shall deliver me from the body of this death?' Are you indulged with views of the atoning blood and justifying righteousness of Immanuel? Do you see yourself complete in Him, and is He to you the chiefest of ten thousand and altogether lovely? Or are you buried in your farm and worldly business, and find your soul as hard as a rock and as barren as the sand? Is your continual experience, 'The good that I would I do not, and the evil which I would not that I do'? And do you go about your farm restless, dissatisfied, weary of self, and yet unable to deliver your soul from darkness, guilt, and wretchedness?

"It is commonly said that a fool can ask questions which a wise man cannot answer, and I find it a great deal easier to ask persons about their souls' experience than to answer them myself. As to my own state, I have but little life, feeling, or power in my soul, and sometimes seem to have none at all, and to care no more for the things of God than a horse. The Bible seems at times to have neither food nor savour in it, and all its mysteries appear shut up from my view. The love of idols fills my heart, and I go a whoring after them all the day. No trifle is too foolish to engage my attention, and take off my thoughts; and my heart seems to be a sink of infidelity, lust, pride, filth, and obscenity. I am, indeed, kept from outward evil, but so very wicked and vile is my heart that I can throw a stone at nobody.

"Rumour brings strange things to our ears respecting Mr. ——. I fear he has departed from those things to which he once testified as the very life and power of inward religion and vital godliness. The last account represents him as renouncing baptism. These things must sadly trouble the church at ——, and shake the weak and unestablished, more especially, I believe, his doubt of the reality and power of his own religion. But we are to meet with everything to trouble and perplex us, and what is more trying than when 'a standard-bearer fainteth.' The fall of the officers is much more trying than the fall of the soldiers. 'Smite the shepherd, and the sheep shall be scattered,' was true of the great Shepherd, and is to a certain extent of the under-shepherds.

"The young gentleman who will convey this either to Allington or, at least, to Devizes is a son of Mr. L., of that place, and has, I trust, in him something good toward the God of Israel. He comes over sometimes to my lectures on a week-night, and seems really desirous after an experimental work upon his soul.

"How is your health? Do you sometimes murmur that you are not so strong and healthy as those around you; and does pain never depress your spirits, and almost make you say, 'I do well to be angry'? Oh, our hearts are strange compounds of rebellion, peevishness, and perverseness, and full of unkindness and ingratitude. It is well if we are sometimes melted down with a sense of our baseness and unkindness towards the great God who hath so blessed us. My health is always very weak in winter, and I stay pretty much at home; but I find the old corrupt, earth-loving nature as much at work as in the streets of London.

"Believe me to be, with Christian regards to Mrs. P.,

"Yours affectionately in Christ Jesus,

"*To Mr. Parry.*" "J. C. P.

The winter of 1834 passed by, and the spring of 1835 commenced; his doubts grew deeper, the errors of the Church seemed to him more and more glaring; but faith and resolution were bestowed where there was need of them, and in the March of that year he came to the final determination to secede from the Church of England. He had acquainted only two persons with his resolution, but on Sunday the 22nd he determined to give public notice of it from the pulpit. He chose as his text 2 Pet. i. 16, 'We have not followed cunningly devised fables,' and preached in his usual way, as though nothing were about to occur. But, when he had finished his sermon, words to this effect echoed from the pulpit, 'You have heard my voice for the last time within these walls. It is my intention to resign my curacy and withdraw from the Church of England, for I cannot longer continue in evil that good may come.' His congregation seemed struck dumb with sorrow and astonishment; the blow was so painful, and, at the same time, so unexpected, that the sounds of weeping were heard on every side; there was not one that did not feel it acutely, for he was beloved by all. Many had received much spiritual comfort from his ministry, while each and every one that knew him honoured him for his true and godly life, and for his kind and courteous character. They all felt that their parish was about to lose a true friend, and their Church a faithful servant.

The following letter, written to his sister after the event, will continue the narrative in his own words:—

"*Abingdon, March* 30, 1835.

"My dear Fanny,

"The tidings I am about to communicate may concern you more than surprise you. After many trials of mind about it, I have come to the resolution of seceding from the Church of England. In fact I have already resigned my curacy, and shall, in a day or two, give up my fellowship. I could have wished to have retained my income and independence, but, as I could not do so with a good conscience, I was compelled to give it up. The errors and corruptions of the Church of England are so great and numerous that a man, with a conscience made tender by the blessed Spirit, cannot, after a certain time, remain within her pale. And though I have thus resigned ease and independence I feel my mind more easy and at liberty, and trust I shall never come to want. My wants are now much less than they used to be, and I trust I shall be content with such slender fare as I may have to expect. Life is short, vain, and transitory; and if I live in comfort and independence, or in comparative poverty, it will matter little when I lie in my coffin. I trust, if I have health and strength given me, I shall not be a burden to my dear mother. Religion has, indeed, spoiled all my temporal prospects, and, doubtless, made the worldly and carnal think me a fool or mad. But, after all, the approbation of God and the testimony of an honest conscience are better than thousands of gold and silver. My resolution was rather suddenly executed. I had thought of giving my incumbent notice at Lady Day that I should resign the curacy at Midsummer. But it seemed to me inconsistent to tell my incumbent that I could not continue in the curacy but a certain time because I was doing evil. It was as though I had said to him, 'Will you allow me to do evil for three months to come?' So I resolved to resign it at once, especially as my assistant promised to undertake it, if required, for the ensuing quarter. I told only two persons of my intention, and having, on Sunday the 22nd, preached in my usual way, I added at the end, 'You have heard my voice within these walls for the last time. I intend to resign the curacy and withdraw from the ministry of the Church of England.' It was as if a thunderbolt had dropped in the congregation. I did not wish any excitement or manifestation of feeling, and therefore shut it up as quickly as possible. The people were much moved. And the next day some met, and said they could build me a chapel if I would consent to stay. To this, however, I do not feel inclined, though the people wish it much, and say it should not cost me a farthing.

"I think, God willing, at present of staying at Stadham till some time in June, and then I shall probably go to a place called Allington, near Devizes, Wilts, where there is a chapel in which I shall preach. The deacon heard me preach about one year and a half ago, and directly he heard I had left the Church he had his horse saddled and rode to Stadham to see me. I happened to be here whither he came. So I have consented to go to Allington for a few weeks.

"I am now writing a letter, which I mean to publish, to the provost of Worcester College to resign my fellowship, containing my reasons for seceding from the Established Church. It will be not more than twopence or threepence. If you should like to have some copies, I would desire the London bookseller to send you a hundred or so. It will be rather strong against the University and the Church of England system.

"I trust that my dear mother will not be much hurt at this step I have taken, and I sincerely trust I shall prove no burden to her. The disgrace and the sinking in life I do not think she will mind. The reproach of Christ is greater riches than the treasures of Egypt. At present I can speak nothing as to my future plans. I may spend some little time with you in Devon, and obtain that rest which I find necessary after preaching, and I trust the good Lord will never leave nor forsake me. He has many ways to provide for His servants, and can make the ravens feed them as Elijah of old. If I had health and strength, I might find support from preaching, or might keep a school. But at present I can say nothing, as I do not see my way as to anything. Sufficient for the day is the evil thereof.

"I have been staying here, at my friend Tiptaft's, since Saturday, and I shall stay a day or two longer. So that I do not know whether you may not have already written to me. Direct your letter Stadhampton as usual, and tell me what you have settled about going into Devon.

"This life is soon passing away, and an eternal state fast coming on. The grand question is, What do we know of Christ by the inward teachings of the Spirit? What true faith have we in a Saviour's blood and righteousness? What do we know of His having died for us?

"The time of the post going presses so that I will add no more than that I am, with love to my dear mother and all your circle,

"Your affectionate Brother,

"J. C. P.

"*To Miss Philpot, Walmer, Deal.*"

No longer now a member of the Established Church, he could not remain fellow in a University inseparably connected with that Establishment, and, from the letter just quoted, the reader will see that he had already written a letter of resignation to the provost of his College, in which he gave full and weighty reasons for the step he had taken, and freely criticised the errors of the Establishment he had just quitted. This letter he felt bound to publish, as his secession had made no small stir in the clerical world, and his motives had been much misrepresented in many quarters. While still in the Church, he had been acknowledged as a man of great ability, and many had looked upon him hopefully as one who would fight for their Church against the then prevailing inclination to Nonconformity. By his secession he arrayed himself on the opposing side, and it was expected, alike by his old and his new friends, that he would publish some reasons for the step he had taken.

No one could accuse him of seeking his own advantage, for his action cost him wealth and position. He would be no longer looked up to with vague reverence as a member of that powerful but strangely mixed caste, the English clergy; he would no longer receive a settled income from the Church, alike in health and illness; he would no longer be able to seek refuge in his fellow's rooms and fellow's stipend, should health fail him. He had given up every worldly advantage for conscience sake. To quote words of his which have often before been quoted, but which seem each time as fresh as ever, "Like Abraham he went forth, not knowing whither he went, but counting, with Moses, the reproach of Christ greater riches than the treasures of Egypt, and little foreseeing either what the Lord in His providence would do for him, or in His grace do by him."

Thus he published his letter, and the outside world read it. They could not understand his motives; they were beyond them. Yet they could not call him a knave, so they dubbed him a fool. The pamphlet had a large sale, and soon reached the fourth edition. Among the children of God it was read with interest as a faithful testimony; but amongst his old comrades in the Church it was hailed with sneers. Several replies to it were published, but they either totally misapprehended the gist of his arguments and misunderstood his motives, or only loaded him with vile abuse, not deigning to answer his assertions. His "letter" is read by hundreds now, but where are the score of "replies"?

Meanwhile Mr. Philpot remained at or near Stadhampton arranging his affairs before leaving for Allington, where he had determined to sojourn at least for the present. Some little money he had saved; but he was obliged to sell almost all his books. Of these he had a valuable collection; many of them were prizes he had gained at Oxford; many had been given to him by kind and affectionate friends; and all of them were dear to him as the companions of his solitude, for he was passionately fond of books. But he was forced to send them nearly all under the hammer, retaining only a few more dearly cherished than the rest.

He stayed some part of the time with William Tiptaft, at Abingdon; but at length, all his affairs being arranged, he said farewell to his kind friends at Stadham, and bidding them to continue steadfastly in the Lord, and promising to come again to them shortly, he went to Allington on June 5, 1835. For the present he went there chiefly as a Supply, to stay as long as he might suit the church, and the church suit him. He found, however, that the people heard him so favourably, and he himself was favoured with so much freedom, that he stayed there till the middle of July, and then only left them with a promise of speedy return. The three letters that are quoted here have reference to about this time.

"*Abingdon, June* 3, 1835.

"MY DEAR FRIEND,

"To avoid all mistake, I think it best to inform you of my intended movements. I hope, then, if the Lord will, to leave Abingdon to-morrow morning for Newbury. I shall sleep there, (God willing,) at Mrs. Merrewether's, where there will probably be gathered together a few friends to hear a few words as to the way of salvation and the work of grace upon the heart. The next day (Friday) I intend, if the Lord will, to leave for Marlborough, where I shall expect to find you or some one from you. I shall come by the Newbury coach, and get down where it stops, and stay there until I see or hear something of you. I am still very weak, and liable to take cold, and indeed have been unwell for three or four months.

"I hope and pray that I may not come amongst you in vain. How far our views and principles may coincide, I know not; but I shall, God enabling me, faithfully declare what I feel and believe to be true without fearing man. I am on the dark side of things, and more for confusion, guilt, and bondage than liberty, assurance, and freedom. Not that I object to the *realities* of these latter, but to their *counterfeits* so universally current. Neither do I wish to preach to a people who will not or cannot receive me and my doctrine. I come, therefore, to you, as a friend, for a few days, or a few Sundays, just as I and the church suit one another. If I do not suit them, I should be glad to leave Allington after the first Lord's-day. If they can hear me comfortably and profitably, I would not mind staying three or four. But I wish it to be understood that I come to see you as a personal friend, and only to preach as a friend staying with you—as a wayfaring man that tarrieth for a night. Expect but little from me, and you will be less disappointed, as I am a very poor creature in body and soul.

"If you could borrow something less open than a gig for me on Friday—such as a light covered cart—it might suit me better than a more exposed conveyance, though I believe your gig has a head.

"With Christian regards to Mrs. Parry, and all that love the truth at Allington,

"Believe me to be,

"Yours affectionately,

"J. C. P.

"*To Mr. Parry.*"

"*Allington, Devizes, June* 17, 1835.

"MY DEAR FANNY,

"As I promised to write to you when I was somewhat settled here, I sit down to fulfil my promise.

"I came here Friday, June 5, from Newbury, whither I had

come from Abingdon the day preceding. I was engaged to speak in the room of a Christian lady at Newbury, but as it was feared it would not be sufficient to hold all that were expected, she procured a chapel for me to preach in. This was amongst the General Baptists, who are Arminians in sentiment. When I, therefore, began to open up that God had a chosen and peculiar people, the whole place seemed in commotion. One man called aloud, 'This doctrine won't do for me;' and started out, and was instantly followed by five or six others. I was not, however, daunted by this, but went on to state the truth with such measure of boldness and faithfulness as was given me. Some of my friends in the chapel thought that the people would have molested me, but no one offered to injure me by word or action, and I came safe out from among them. The next day I came by one of the Bath coaches to Marlborough, where my friend Mr. Parry met me, and brought me safely here. I have already preached here five times, *i.e.*, twice on two Lord's-days, and once in the week besides.

"My services have been requested at Reading about the middle of next month for one Lord's-day, but the time is not exactly fixed; on that must depend a good deal when I shall come into Kent. Indeed, for some reasons, I would rather not come to Walmer at all this year. For, first, there is a great desire here that I should stay at Allington as long as I can. This is a neighbourhood remarkably favoured, and a great spirit of hearing abroad. It was supposed that there were 250 persons in the little chapel last Lord's-day in the afternoon, some of whom had come seven miles' distance, and others distances varying from one to five or six miles. There are also many of the children of God in this vicinity, who would gather under the banner of truth if faithfully displayed. I am very comfortable at Mr. Parry's; he is a very large farmer, and has a wife and four children. He is a very good and gracious man, and is the deacon, and, in fact, the sole support of the cause of God in the village. He has a very great desire that I should settle here awhile, as they are quite destitute of a minister. But I am in a strait betwixt two, having, for some reasons, a wish to return to Stadham, and yet finding difficulties in the way. I am praying for the Lord to guide me, as I scarce know what to do, or which way to take.

"I can say I do not at all regret leaving the Church of England, and feel quite satisfied and comfortable at having done so. My conscience is now at ease, which it was not whilst I was entangled in so carnal a system, and at times I see more of its awful mockery and the dreadful lies which are solemnly told the blessed JEHOVAH by His professed ministers. I do not fear but that the Lord will take care of me, and, indeed, have no reason to think otherwise as long as he gives me sufficient health and strength to preach. There are many places which would be glad enough to have me were I willing to go.

"My letters to the provost, &c., have had a great sale, but are now declining. They have, I believe, reached the fourth edition. Though the main sale may be over, yet straggling copies will yet sell for some time.

"I heard the other day from Wise, the auctioneer, of my books. The two cases had arrived from London; the sale was to commence on the 15th of this month, and to last three days. I hope they will go off well. Wise said in his letter that a great many persons had been to see them, and he thought the sale would excite some interest.

"I hope Mary Ann and the little boy are now doing well; if they go to Plymouth in the beginning of July, I fear I shall not see them. I do sincerely hope that I may be able to run down into Kent for a few weeks, as such a change and rest is good for my health; but I feel that I must go on working while it is day. The harvest is plenteous, but the labourers are few. It is a great thing to be engaged in the work of the Lord of hosts, and the desire of carnal ease and rest must be laid aside by him who would endure hardness as a good soldier of Jesus Christ. . . .

"There is no greater inheritance than to be a son or daughter of the Lord Almighty. 2. Cor. vi. 18. Gold and silver cannot purchase this; for Jehovah has redeemed His Church and people, not with corruptible things as silver and gold, but with the precious blood of Christ, as of a lamb without blemish and without spot. 1 Peter, i. 18, 19. To have an interest in the covenant love of the Father, the redeeming blood of the Son, and the sanctifying operation of the Holy Spirit, is worth a million of worlds. Without such an interest we must be eternally miserable, and with it eternally happy. This was all David's salvation and all his desire. 2. Sam. xxiii.

"Write soon, as I don't know when I shall be leaving this, and tell me your plans, and how you all are. My affectionate love to my dear mother, Mary Ann, and Augustus, and accept the same from,

"Your affectionate Brother,

"*To Miss Philpot.*" "J. C. P.

"*Exeter, August* 29, 1835.

"MY DEAR FRIEND,

"My present intention is to leave this place on Wednesday next, September 2, for Bath (God willing), where I mean to sleep, and leave next day for Devizes, where I shall hope to meet you, or Mr. Tuckwell if you are not well, with the gig. I could not trouble you to come to Bath, as there are coaches through Devizes, and the weather is uncertain. You speak of the baptising. But I have many doubts and fears respecting it.

First, I feel my miserable unbelief, sinfulness, hardness of heart, backslidings, ignorance of Christ, and manifold corruptions as most powerful obstacles in the way. Secondly, my poor, weak, shattered, tottering, cold-catching body fills me with many apprehensions. But I trust if I saw Jesus one side of the water I should venture through. I seem now to have missed the most favourable opportunity during the warm weather we have just had. But I would add that, if I am to go through the ordinance this year, it must not be pushed into the autumn. September 13 is the latest Sunday I could submit to it, and I do assure you I shall be very thankful to escape with a cold. I asked Mr. Warburton to baptise me if I should go through the ordinance, and should not wish any other. If, then, he is able to come to Allington on September 13th, I would, the blessed Lord enabling me, follow the example of the great Head of the Church, in passing through the waters of Jordan. You should, perhaps, write immediately to Mr. Warburton to invite him for that purpose, and to preach as well, as I could not think of preaching that day. I hope, however, the church will understand I should not at all alter the relation in which I proposed to stand to them. I should still be no other than a Supply, willing to go or stay as we mutually suited each other. I am daily more and more sensible of the desperate wickedness of my deceitful heart, and my miserable ruined state as a sinner by nature and by practice. I feel utterly unworthy of the name of a Christian, and to be ranked among the followers of the Lamb. And I have no wish to palm myself upon any church, any minister, or any Christian, as though I were anything. I am willing to take a low place; and whoever doubts my Christianity, only does what I do myself continually. Now that you are likely to see more of me, you will be sure to find out more infirmities and failings, both as a man and as a minister, than you have as yet, perhaps, discovered. A few weeks is too short a period to know a man. There is in most, and I am sure there is so in myself, much waywardness, selfishness, obstinacy, and evil temper, which is not at first developed. Persons, from a short and imperfect acquaintance, expect great things, which subsequent intercourse does not realise. And many are foolishly apt to imagine a minister is more spiritual than any one else, and in conversation is more profitable. As to myself, I disclaim any such remnant of priestcraft. I am very carnal, very proud, very foolish in imagination, very slothful, very worldly, dark, stupid, blind, unbelieving, and ignorant. I cannot but confess that I have a dreadfully corrupt old man, a strange compound, a sad motley mixture of all the most hateful and abominable vices, that rise up within me, and face me at every turn. So that, instead of expecting a profitable and spiritual companion for your fireside, you must make up your mind for a poor invalid, shrinking from every breeze, and a proud, presumptuous, hardened creature, that can neither be softened by mercies nor humbled by trials. But this I say, as I did once before, I wish to saddle myself on nobody. I wish to be independent of the deacons and members of the church, male and female; I mean so as not to flatter or please them. If they don't like me, or are not satisfied with my doctrine, experience, or practice, let them tell me so at once, and I will leave by the first coach. Or if they can't hear me to profit, and wish a more gracious and gifted man, I will give up the pulpit at the first warning. I don't want the canting speeches and honeyed looks of hypocrites and dead professors, whether Calvinists or Arminians. My desire is to feed the Church of God which He hath purchased with His own blood. Remember me affectionately to Mr. T., Mrs. C., your good lady, and all the church. If I lift up the sword, recollect it must go through friend and foe that are not on the Lord's side, and may He keep me from sparing any but those whom He loves as the apple of His eye.

"Yours affectionately, in the best of causes, and the service of the best of Masters,

"J. C. P.

"*To Mr. Parry.*"

He returned to Allington on September 3rd, and, according to the intention expressed in the last letter quoted, was baptised in the chapel there by Mr. Warburton, on September 13th. Meanwhile he did not forget his old friends at Stadham: the two letters which are introduced below were really meant for the perusal of all the friends there, and were intended for the comfort of each and all. Many of his old hearers at Stadham had left the Church at the same time with him, and had offered to build him a chapel there to preach in; but he felt that it was not God's will that he should remain amongst them, and with many sighs his friends were compelled to acquiesce in his decision. They formed themselves, however, into a church, and prevailed on Mr. Doe to become their pastor. James Brookland, who had been called under Mr. Philpot while still in the Church, was appointed deacon; and it was to him, for whom his late pastor felt great respect and affection, that these general epistles were addressed:—

"*Allington, Sept.* 23, 1835.

"My dear Brookland,*

"Grace, mercy, and peace be multiplied unto you through the knowledge of God the Father, and His Son Jesus Christ the Lord.

"I have been desirous for some time past to write to you, that those who profess to love and feel the power of experimental truth

* James Brookland died at Stadhampton, Jan. 28th, 1855, aged 55.

in Stadham and its neighbourhood may not think I have totally forgotten them: though I have been taken from you in presence, I trust not altogether in heart. And I shall rejoice to hear that you, who have separated yourselves from a carnal and corrupt system, are walking in truth, from tasting, feeling, and handling the sweetness and power of it in your own souls. I find the Lord daily to me far better than I could in any way anticipate; He has raised up for me kind friends, with whom I feel a spiritual union, given me a measure of acceptance among His people, and supplied my dark, foolish, ignorant, barren soul from time to time with thoughts, words, and feelings when I stand up in His name. But my cold, ungrateful, proud, presumptuous, deceitful, and rebellious heart only repays Him with deadness and coldness, worldliness, carelessness, sin, and corruption. Thus, I am driven to salvation by free sovereign grace as my only hope, and see in myself at times so few marks of grace, and so many of unbelief and carnality, that I feel I must be singled out as an especial object of discriminating mercy, if saved at all. Thus, I am taught that profession, knowledge, consistency, creature strivings, fleshly righteousness, and all the other trumpery of nature's forging, are useless and vain. I am brought to contend for the immediate, powerful, and supernatural work of the blessed Spirit on the soul. I am daily more and more confirmed in my views of the profession of the day, and can find but few in whom I can trace the powerful operations of the Holy Ghost. Broken hearts, contrite spirits, emptied, stripped, and humbled souls, I very rarely meet with; and thus I am led to insist much on the need of the mouth being put into the dust, and of being plunged into the ditch until our own clothes abhor us. But all this stripping and humbling work, I am led to see and feel, is of sovereign grace in the person, in the manner, in the time, in the means, and in the circumstances. I am brought to see and feel that it is not of him that willeth, nor of him that runneth, but of God that showeth mercy; that His elect family are the 'clay, and He the potter;' and that He works in them to will, and to do of His good pleasure; and thus I am brought to see these things, not as dry, dead doctrines, but as truths of inward and feeling experience; and I am convinced that, however painful the lesson is, there is no other way of learning truth but by a feeling sense of our deep need of it, and of its precious suitability to our lost and helpless condition. This also teaches me the shallowness and emptiness of professors and the religion of the day, and that, for want of being stripped, emptied, and wounded, they are mistaking husks for bread, and chaff for wheat, dross for gold, and the delusions of Satan for the truth of God. Your eyes and those of my dear friends in the neighbourhood, are, I trust, open to see these things; and if you have learned this in the school of experience, and not in your own judgment only, you have reason to bless

God who has thus kept you from the delusions of the day. About a week back I was privileged to follow the dear Lord through the waters of baptism, and never more sensibly felt my unworthiness than on that day. He was pleased to keep me from taking the least cold, to give me more confidence to step into His watery grave than I could have expected from my many bodily and spiritual temptations and exercises. Mr. Warburton preached, and baptised me with the greatest solemnity, unction, and affection.

"I am glad to hear that Mr. Doe is enabled to come amongst you, and that there is some prospect of having a place of worship erected where truth may be preached. I am daily more and more convinced that nothing is of the least avail but experimental realities, made known unto the soul by the unction and manifestation of the blessed Spirit. All forms, opinions, rites, ceremonies, and notions to me are nothing, and worse than nothing; they are the husks which the swine eat, not the food of the living soul. To have the heart deeply penetrated and possessed with the fear of Jehovah, to be melted and filled with a sweet sense of dying love and atoning blood, to have the affections warmed, and drawn forth under the anointings of the eternal Comforter, this is the only religion that can suit or satisfy a regenerate soul. But, alas! how dark, stupid, lifeless, trifling, and unfeeling are our hearts; every little trifle, every lustful desire, every covetous wish, every rising anger, every emotion of pride, carries the soul away at once, and makes it more like a devil than a saint; and then guilt, doubts, and fears set in like a flood, and hide from the soul all hope or evidence of grace. But, after all, by these things men live, and in all these things is the life of our spirit; by these trials and temptations, these ups and downs, we are experimentally taught to know ourselves and the wondrous riches of electing love, redeeming blood, justifying righteousness, quickening, upholding, and renewing grace; self falls lower and lower, and a triune Jehovah rises higher and higher in our eyes. Self is loathed, and Jesus loved; self is taught its weakness, foolishness, and sinfulness; and the strength, wisdom, and love of Jesus glorified. And thus, the sovereignty of divine grace, the emptiness of professors, the folly of free will, the deceitfulness and wickedness of the heart, the reality of vital godliness, and the blessedness of a free salvation are taught experimentally, and wrought into our souls as eternal realities. I am daily made more and more sensible of my unfitness for the work of the ministry; but the Lord is pleased sometimes to favour me with some liberty and enlargement of soul in contending for experimental truth; and glad should I be to be assured that I did not spend my strength for naught and in vain at Stadham, but that the Lord did indeed work by me to quicken and edify the souls of His dear people. May He be pleased to bless the little company who there are willing, from an experimental acquaintance with it, to contend for the power of truth. May He unite them in the bonds of love and affection, and keep far from them all jealousy, division, and disunion. You will have much to contend with from without and from within, from the world and from professors, as well as from yourselves. Many are watching for your halting, and saying, perhaps, of your little Zion (Neh. iv. 3), even that which they build, if a fox go up, he shall even break down their stone wall. May the blessed Lord keep you from disunion and division amongst yourselves, and may He shut out all jealousy and suspicions of one another, and unite you to contend as one man for the faith once delivered unto the saints.

"I have, through mercy, enjoyed of late better health than when I saw you in the summer, and have reason to bless God for the comforts and kindness which He daily bestows upon me in His providence. I am sure He is kind to the unthankful and to the evil, and is never weary with blessing the rebellious and ungrateful. If, indeed, we belong to His blood-bought family, well may we say, 'Happy art thou, O Israel: who is like unto thee, O people saved by the Lord?' It is uncertain when I shall see you all again in the flesh, but trust I shall ever continue to love you with Christian affection. Give my Christian regards to all the Christian friends who meet together to worship in spirit and truth.

"I shall be glad to hear from any of the friends that can write, as I wish to know how you are going on.

"I am, your and their affectionate friend,

"J. C. P."

"*Allington, Nov.* 12, 1835.

"MY DEAR BROOKLAND,

"To all that, under the blessed Spirit's teaching, experimentally and feelingly know the plague of their own heart, and something of the riches of a Saviour's blood, grace, mercy, and peace be multiplied from God the Father and the Lord Jesus Christ.

"An opportunity occurring to answer your letter, I reply to it sooner than I might otherwise have done; and may the eternal Spirit guide my pen to write a few lines on vital godliness and experimental truth to the comfort of any of God's quickened family who may hear or read them.

"Instead, then, of finding day by day the number of heaven-taught souls increase in my eyes, I seem to draw the circle narrower and narrower; and the more that I am led to see the nature and reality of true religion, and the great mystery of godliness, I seem to see more and more how few are experimentally led into it. Notion is the grand deceit with which Satan deceiveth the nations; the husks which the swine do eat he passes off as the bread of life. Dry doctrines, which only puff men up with pride and presumption, he palms off as the truth as it is in Jesus. A sound creed, a fluent tongue, a well-informed judgment, a ready gift in prayer, a consistent life, attendance on the means, a sanctified look, a knowledge of the Scriptures, pass off upon thousands as the religion that can save the soul.

I am quite convinced that very few persons have been taught by the blessed Spirit even the very first elements of religion, namely, repentance toward God and faith in the Lord Jesus Christ. A man that has repented toward God has had his back broken, his mouth has been in the dust, and himself plunged into the ditch till his own clothes abhorred him. The idol of free-will has been broken to pieces, self-righteousness stripped away, presumption plucked up by the roots, and hypocrisy torn off. Not but that these members of the old man will ever continue to trouble and plague the living soul, but they will be hated and disallowed. "What I do I allow not," said Paul of old. "God maketh my heart soft," says Job, xxiii. 16. And thus, when there is true repentance toward God, the heart will be softened down into meekness and contrition. But how few are lepers; how few have got the plague of leprosy in their houses, their garments, or their bodies. They have never had this spreading scab and quick raw flesh (Lev. xiii. 8—10) to eat the vitals of their fleshly religion, and to make them filthy and leprous from the crown of the head to the sole of the feet. A man must know something of this inward experience before he can be said to repent towards God. And, again, how few have the other element of true religion—namely, faith toward our Lord Jesus Christ. Acts xx. 21. Most persons' faith is an assent and consent to the mere letter of truth. They believe because they never disbelieved. They believe because their fathers told them so; because they were taught in the Sunday-school; because they have read about Jesus Christ in the Word; because they have heard Mr. So-and-So preach about it; because they have read a tract of Dr. Hawker's which explained the way of salvation; because they have heard others tell their experience; and because it is so wicked and dreadful not to believe in our blessed Saviour.

"Such are some of the lying delusions of the father of lies whereby souls are juggled into hell. A notional faith never did and never can save a soul. To be thus born of blood, and of the will of the flesh, and of the will of man, leaves the soul where it found it—an enemy to God, and the bond slave of the devil. And all this false notional and fleshly religion will be as stubble when the day cometh that shall burn as an oven. May the blessed Lord keep us from a notional religion, which will only leave our souls exposed and naked to His terrible wrath when He shall rise up to the prey. The only faith that can satisfy a living soul is that which is the gift of God, and springs out of the inward relation of Jesus Christ. How few have experienced that work of faith with power whereby they have come out of themselves as Lazarus came forth from the tomb. The question is, What has our religion done for us? Has it left us where it found us? Are we, indeed, new creatures; have we been inwardly and experimentally translated from the power of darkness into the kingdom of God's dear Son? We had better throw away our religion on the first dunghill we come to, to rot there in corruption, if we have nothing better than a name to live. We had better be open sinners than deceived and deceiving hypocrites. But I believe no living soul can be satisfied with a notional religion: though a miserable backslider, and driven into the fields to feed swine, he cannot feed on their husks, but sighs after the bread of his Father's house. The eyes being enlightened to see the nature of sin, the justice and holiness of God, and the miserable filthiness of self, the quickened soul can find no rest in anything short of a precious discovery of the Lamb of God; and the more that the soul is exercised with trials, difficulties, temptations, doubts and besetments of various kinds, the more does it feel its need of that blood of sprinkling that speaketh better things than that of Abel. What is a Christian worth without inward trials and exercises? How dead and lifeless are our prayers; how cold and formal when the soul is not kept alive by inward exercises. Where are the sighs, cries, groanings, wrestlings, and breathings of a soul that is at ease in Zion? The world is everything and Christ nothing, when we become settled on our lees, and not emptied from vessel to vessel; but inward exercises, fears, straits, and temptations, stir up the soul to cry, and pray, and beg for mercy. The certainty, the power, the reality of eternal things is then felt, when guilt, and wrath, and fear, and disquietude lay hold of the soul. Mere notions alone of Christ, false hope, a dead faith, a presumptuous confidence, a rotten assurance, are all swept away as so many refuges of lies, when the soul is made to feel its nakedness and nothingness, its guilt and helplessness before God. And thus all their inward exercises pave the way for their discoveries of Christ—those views of His blood and righteousness, that experimental acquaintance with His person, love, grace, and work, which is life and peace. May this be our religion. It is a religion that we can die by, but it is a religion which the profane and professing world hates and derides. If you and the other friends of truth who meet together at Stadham are enabled to contend for this religion, you will be hated and despised by those professors who never had their backs broken and their mouths in the dust; for you cannot sanction and uphold their religion, and will be constrained, as wine which hath no vent (Job xxxii. 19), to tell them faithfully your opinion of their state. You that contend for experimental realities are a city set on a hill: all eyes are upon you; the professor and the profane will alike watch for your halting. They would say of your little cause, "Raze it, raze it, even to the foundation thereof;" and much would it please them if you would say a confederacy to all to whom they say a confederacy. May the blessed Lord keep your steps. Oh, how weak and helpless we are: how fond of sin, how averse to God. If He does not keep us, we must fall. Our pride, presumption, hypocrisy, lust, covetousness, carnality, love of ease, and fear of the cross, must overcome us unless He is stronger than we, and prevails.

"It is very uncertain when I shall see the friends at Stadham and the neighbourhood face to face. I shall most probably winter here, and believe it is of the Lord that my steps were directed to this place, as it affords me a much wider sphere of usefulness, if the Lord bless the word, than I could have had at Stadham. If, indeed, the King of Zion was pleased to bless my weak ministry at Stadham, it will be proved by the people's abiding in the truth who professed to have been profited by it. By their steadfast perseverance in, and earnestly contending for, the faith once delivered to the saints, they will make it manifest whether they have been spiritually quickened, or have learnt their religion from man. And if the blessed Lord has indeed been pleased to raise up your little cause as a witness for Himself against corruption and error, He will keep it, He will water it every moment; lest any hurt it, He will keep it night and day. I hope you may soon see the foundation-stone of a house for His worship laid, and that He will create upon your assemblies a cloud and smoke by day and the shining of a flaming fire by night.

"My love to all that have been made honest, who fear God, have a tender conscience, and depart from evil.

"Greet the friends by name,

"Yours and theirs affectionately in Christ Jesus,

"J. C. P.

"*To James Brookland.*"

He felt so comfortable at Allington, and there seemed such a spirit of hearing abroad in that part of the country, that he was induced to stay there, at his friend Mr. Parry's house, for more than three-quarters of a year. He often preached at neighbouring places, and occasionally supplied for Mr. Warburton at Trowbridge; but as the winter approached he was again seized with an attack of inflammation of the chest, and was for some time prevented from leaving the house.

All through the spring, however, he continued to labour in the Lord's vineyard in Wiltshire, till, in June, 1836, he left them for Oakham. Mr. Tiptaft had been to Allington in the autumn of the preceding year, and had prevailed on his friend to preach one Lord's-day for him at Abingdon, and then to visit his relatives in

Rutland. While away from Allington, he wrote the three following letters to his friend Mr. Parry :—

"*Stamford, July* 18*th*, 1836.

"MY DEAR FRIEND,

"It being Monday, and I being, as usual, not fully recovered from yesterday's exertions, I will not promise to write at any great length. I arrived here on Friday evening last from Oakham, a distance of about eleven miles. Mr. de Merveilleux sent a fly for me, so that I arrived here without inconvenience, though the day was cold and rainy. I was very unwell during the first part of my stay at Oakham, having caught cold on my journey. Towards the end of last week, however, I rallied, and am now, through mercy, as well as I usually am. I preached at Oakham twice yesterday week, July 10th, and again on the following Wednesday, July 13th. Yesterday I preached twice in Mr. de Merveilleux's chapel here. The place was very full both times. Many, no doubt, were attracted from curiosity, my 'Letter' having been widely circulated in these parts, and my intention to preach having been made known through the newspaper, as well as by printed bills. The Baptist minister left his flock to visit his friends, and, there being no Supply, his congregation came to hear me. Many Church people, too, were present; and doubtless we had a sprinkling of gracious characters out of the country, for many miles round. I never feel at home amidst such a motley multitude, and such was the case yesterday. I attempted, with God's help, to cut down natural and to build up spiritual religion; but I fear Joseph Charles had much more hand in the sermon both times than the Spirit of the living God. At least, if they were as much dissatisfied with me as I was with myself, the children of God went grumbling home; and if the word came home to them with no greater power than I felt it myself, they went home as hungry as they came.

"I have received invitations to preach from Boston, Peterborough, Leicester, and Cambridge. All these invitations I have declined but the last, which I have accepted for Thursday, July 28th, on my way home to Welwyn.

"I found myself quite at home at Oakham, Mr. and Mrs. Keal having all the friendliness and hospitality of Tiptaft. I cannot say that I was much favoured in the ministry there, being, in my own feelings, shut up, except on the last time that I preached, which was on Wednesday last, when, the spring seeming to flow and the cruse to run, I was enabled, as I freely received, so freely to give. A great multitude, especially if in a strange place, usually shuts me up, and, instead of a sweet entrance into the word of truth, and a living experience, I seem able to bring forth nothing but a noisy stream of pulpit prattle and a tangled skein of unmeaning declamation.

"I find Mr. de M—— very kind; and, indeed, so vile and unworthy a wretch as I, who seem at times to be a burden to myself and to everybody else, finds everywhere kindness and attention. They wish me very much to come again to Oakham, and I have thought of the following plan, if it should be agreeable to the friends and yourself. Instead of going down to Plymouth, as I proposed, I would return to Allington from London, so as to preach on Lord's-day, August 14. Thus I would stay with you during August and September, and leave you during the month of October, which, in that case, I would spend at Oakham. The weather in October is not too cold, and the days not too short, to hinder my travelling at that time. I think such an arrangement might suit me, as well as yourselves and the friends at Oakham. August, I know, does not suit you so well, as it is so bustling a time; but it is hard to arrange any plan to which objections may not be raised. There is a great spirit of hearing at Oakham, and I have found myself well received by the people. On Wednesday evening last the congregation was larger than at Allington on the Lord's-day afternoon. Let me hear from you on this subject immediately, as I wish to write to Plymouth, which I cannot do till I receive your reply. I shall hope to spend the winter at your friendly and hospitable fireside.

"This dry weather, I suppose, stirs up the old man sometimes in your bosom, and you are thinking what will become of the sheep unless the turnips look better than they now do. I observed that the wheat crops in Berkshire, Oxfordshire, and Northamptonshire had a much better appearance than those in Wiltshire. But what will it signify to Joseph Parry, in a few years, whether the fly had carried off his turnips or not; and what will it matter to J. C. Philpot whether his chest was sound or unsound? But how much will it matter to each of them whether their religion was natural or spiritual, their faith human or divine, their hope a heavenly gift or a spider's web! But our blind, foolish hearts are so concerned about things which are but the dust of the balance, and so little anxious about our all in all.

"I hope that friend Stenchcumb was heard with profit, and brought you some of the good old wine, and that Tiptaft was favoured with a door of utterance and a door of entrance into your souls.

"I intend to leave Stamford, if the Lord will, on Wednesday, July 27, and proceed by Cambridge to Welwyn, where I hope to arrive the Friday evening following. On the succeeding Tuesday I shall hope to go to London, and it will depend on the arrangement that we may make whether I shall proceed to Plymouth or Allington. I would wish to consult the wishes of the friends, as well as my own; and though I cannot brook much thwarting or controlling, I feel desirous to walk amicably and comfortably with the people of God.

"I hope the friends are well, body and soul, and that the Lord has shone upon your assemblies. Greet them all with my Christian love. The children, I hope, are well. May the Lord stir up our fainting, stumbling souls, and lead us into all experimental truth. My affectionate remembrances to Mrs. P., Mr. and Mrs. T., Mrs. C., and all that have any care for, or any interest in, so poor a creature as

"Your affectionate Friend,

"*To Mr. Parry.*" "J. C. P.

"*Stamford, July* 25, 1836.

"My dear Friend,

"I fear I must make my usual excuse for a short letter, viz., that it is Monday, on which day, you know, I am fit for little else than to loll about and do nothing. Mr. Keal was over here from Oakham yesterday, and we talked matters over. The arrangement which I seem to have come to is to be at Allington before August 14th, so as to stay with you during that month and the following, and return, if the Lord will, to Oakham by the first Lord's-day in October. I must thus give up my visit to Plymouth, which will be a disappointment to my mother, as well as to myself, and deprive myself of that rest in which I usually indulge my poor body once a year.

"The opening for truth at Oakham and Stamford is very great, and persons come from distances which put your lazy Wiltshire professors to the blush. Twenty miles is not thought much of as a distance in this country. Yesterday morning was very wet, and this thinned down the congregation to what the Dissenters call 'comfortably full'; but, the weather clearing up, the afternoon congregation was overflowing. It appeared to me larger than on the Lord's-day previous. Through mercy, I was holpen with a little help, and the door of utterance was not shut so close as I often feel it, and thus I was enabled to deal out a portion to professor and possessor more than I sometimes can. On Wednesday next I intend, if God will, to leave Stamford for Cambridge, where I am to preach next evening. On Friday I mean to go to Welwyn, and on August 2nd to London, and hope to reach Allington August 12th, but will write to Mr. Tuckwell or yourself to mention when you are to send to Marlborough for me. Mr. T., it appears, was anxious to view my old haunts at Oxford, and went to spy out the nakedness of Worcester College. I doubt not he thought the inside quadrangle a pretty spot. My rooms were in the handsome range of building upon the terrace, to the right as a person enters the College. Well, they have pretty much forgotten me, and I them. Our tie has been broken through for ever, and I am satisfied it should be so.

"I am glad that you heard Tiptaft well, and that he found an entrance into your heart. You had, no doubt, much conversation together, and I dare say he asked many questions on many subjects. He will not lack information if inquiry can obtain it. I have found much kindness both here and at Oakham. Mr. Keal is a particularly friendly person, and we soon became able to converse freely. His wife is very much like Tiptaft in manners and disposition. If I consulted my own wishes I should go to Plymouth and rest, and return to Allington in September, as I originally proposed. But there seems a field of usefulness opened here, and my ministry appears to be received by the people of God. An old professor came about thirty miles to hear yesterday, and came to see me this morning for about three hours. I found him a man well and deeply taught in the things of the Lord.

"You will, perhaps, think that my coming into these parts may be the first step to my leaving Allington altogether. I do not anticipate any such conclusion. It may lead to my coming here occasionally, but I do not think it will have any other consequence. Both at Oakham and here they seem attached to the ministry of Tiptaft and Smart, and I think the utmost of their wishes is that we three should come as well as we may be able. Mr. Keal does not wish to hear any other ministers, and reads when one of us is not at Oakham. Mr. de Merveilleux engaged a minister, who proved to be a duty-faith man, and he was obliged to withdraw from his ministry; so that he usually reads in the vestry, and that to not more than twelve persons. Nearly all the congregation left with the minister, and took a room very near. Thus, as this is an infant cause, and there is much opposition both from Church and chapel, it needs a little fostering.

"I do not forget the kindness of yourself and Mrs. Parry amidst the kindness of my new friends, and I do not believe that I ever shall. Wherever a union is felt, through grace in the heart, it cannot easily be torn up. Jealousies may rise, and evil tempers may work, but I believe there will be always a revival of affection in the soul where a true union exists. I have sold nearly two hundred copies of my pamphlet here and at Oakham. Nearly all the influential people of this town are acquainted with my family, my grandfather having resided here many years. What a violent tearing asunder of all natural ties is produced by leaving the Establishment! Those who would have hailed me as a friend, would now turn from me as an enemy. I find more and more that to leave Babylon is to offend all that is respectable and worldly. Mr. —— would not be so angry, nor his friend Miss J., if I would uphold their system. Well, their hatred little troubles me. I fear my own vile heart more than their enmity, and if they knew as much of my vileness as I do they would find plenty of room to shoot their arrows at. I am quite aware of your kindness from repeated instances of it, as well as that of your wife, and hope that nothing may ever occur to interrupt our friendship. My kind regards to Mrs. Parry, and remember me very kindly to all inquiring friends. I am obliged to Mr. Tuckwell for his kind letter. I am, through mercy, pretty well, and beg to remain,

"Your affectionate Friend,

"J. C. P.

"P.S.—Shall I buy any of Huntington's works for you, as there is a cheap edition coming out, and you would find them profitable to read and lend?

"*To Mr. Parry.*"

"*London, Aug.* 6*th*, 1836.

"MY DEAR FRIEND,

"As the time of my return to Allington is drawing near, you are doubtless expecting a line from me to fix the precise day on which you are to send to Marlborough for me. I intend, then, to leave town on Tuesday morning next, if the Lord will, and do not think of stopping anywhere on the road before I reach Marlborough. Mrs. Merrewether, probably, and the friends at Newbury would wish me to stop one night there, and speak in her room; but I feel so unfit to preach anywhere, that necessity must be laid upon me before I can engage in the work. I believe, if it were left to me, I should never preach again—so much vileness, unbelief, and dreadful sinfulness do I feel working within. Those who say they always hate sin must have very different feelings from me, as the chief part of my burden is that I love it so much. I feel something like a man in love, who is prevented by a thousand obstacles from gaining what his heart is set upon. If he did not love the fair lass, his heart and affections would not always be roving after her, and he would little care whether she were dead or alive. But to feel the constant workings of passionate love and eager desire, and then to be prevented, cut off, and intercepted by a thousand difficulties, this will make a man miserable enough. Thus sin, that crafty and cursed Delilah, is loved to distraction by our old man. If we dared woo and win this beautiful Philistine, a match would be made, vows plighted, hands joined, and the marriage celebrated. But when a tender conscience, a godly fear, the wrath of God against sin, His presence in the soul, and a thousand other inward obstacles step forward and forbid the banns, and positively forbid a union, what a storm does it raise within! But if to press the hand and touch the lips of this accursed Delilah cause such guilt within, and force out such groans and sighs from a burdened conscience, it is our richest mercy that so many real friends come forward and prevent a complete union. These two things I know, that sin is sweet, and that sin is bitter. The honey and the sting are in the same bee, and, if you plunder the hive, it is a narrow escape if you are not stung to death. . . . I left Stamford, July 27, and arrived at Cambridge the same evening. On the following evening I preached at a chapel, about a mile out of the town, to a full congregation. If they felt as straitened as I did, they were shut up enough; and if they were as dissatisfied with me as I was with myself, they went grumbling home. On the next day I arrived at Welwyn. I found friend L. and his wife very kind, and was quite at home with the friends at Welwyn on spiritual things. I think them a people of the right stamp. I cannot say I was much at home in the pulpit on the Lord's-day. On the Tuesday evening, however, I spoke again and felt more of the springing well and flowing brook. The place was quite full on Lord's-day both times, and on the Tuesday evening there were not many vacant places. The friends thought the place was fuller on the Lord's-day than they had ever seen it.

"Friend Smart's house is roofed in, and, if the God of all comfort now and then visits it with His presence, will be a comfortable abode for him. The plan is simple enough. Two rooms, one on each side the street-door, will form his kitchen and parlour below, and there will be two bedrooms above. I told Friend L. that a third bedroom was wanting for the little handmaid, as he would wish to have a spare bedroom for a friend. On the day before I left, the foundation was laid for the washhouse, etc. The friends of truth are looking anxiously forward for his coming to settle amongst them, and the friends of the world are marvelling that so much has been done to carry on the cause, the downfall of which they prophesied.

"I am pretty well tired of London, though from my former residence of six years in it, and continual visits to it for nearly every year since I was nine years old, it is less strange to me than to most regular inhabitants of the country. It is some degrees warmer than the country, which, in some respects, suits me, though I find more excitement from its noise and bustle than is good for my head and chest.

"I hope I shall see Friend Smart before he leaves Wilts. You must do your best to detain him at Allington until I arrive, and as long after as he feels disposed to stay. I sincerely hope that the Lord may be with him to-morrow, and give the word that he shall preach a blessing and effectual entrance into your hearts. I do not know what you would do in this scene of bustle and confusion, where Mammon seems universally worshipped, and where Satan's seat seems above most places to be. I shall hope, if the Lord will, to find you, your wife, and children, well. Remember me affectionately to all inquiring friends, and

"Believe me to be,

"Your affectionate Friend,

"*To Mr. Parry.*" "J. C. P.

He came back to his old resting-place early in August, and remained there till the end of September; but he had been heard so well at Oakham and Stamford, that he felt anxious to return thither to preach to his friends there during the months of October and November. He found, however, that the climate of Lincolnshire suited him so much better than the cold bleak winds of Allington, that he was induced to stay the winter there. This year he escaped the illness which generally seized him with approaching winter, and he was enabled to preach to the people either at Oakham or Stamford every Lord's-day throughout the winter months. He was at the same time engaged in preparing for the press a sermon which had been preached at Stamford, October 23rd, 1836. The text was taken from Isaiah l. 10, 11, and it was so blessed to the souls of many of his hearers, that a universal desire was expressed that it should be printed. It was accordingly published in February, 1837, under the title of "The Heir of Heaven walking in Darkness, and the Heir of Hell walking in Light;" and the first edition of 1,500 copies was soon exhausted, and a second edition called for. It is to this sermon that Mr. Philpot alludes in the four letters to Mr. Parry, which are inserted at this point, and which were written during his stay at Oakham:—

"*Stamford, October* 24, 1836.

"MY DEAR FRIEND,

"I arrived here on Friday last from Oakham, and am, through mercy, pretty well.

"The friends at Oakham have much pressed me to stay the winter, to which I should not have any great objection, as the climate is mild, the friends kind, and the door for preaching wide. The last Lord's-day afternoon on which I preached being very fine (Oct. 16), the congregation was overflowing. A person at the door counted fifty who could not get in; and on last Wednesday evening, which was moonlight and a beautiful evening, we had considerably more than at Allington on the Lord's-day afternoon. I do not mention this as though it were anything, for novelty will bring a congregation; and I dislike a crowd, as it usually shuts me up, and seems to draw back anything like a flow of unction and feeling. I seem at such times lost in a flood of unmeaning generalities, and to have no power to dive into the depths of man's heart. Like a raw swimmer, I seem to be splashing in shallow water, knocking the waves about perhaps as I spread forth my hands to swim, and every now and then gulping down a draught of salt water or gasping for breath, but unable to dive into those dark silent depths of internal experience or the calm depths of a free-grace salvation, without which to preach is only to beat the air and to run as uncertainly; yet this I would say to the glory of God, that though wretchedly dark and barren out of the pulpit, I have not been altogether left to my foolish and empty self in it since I left Allington, but have at times found life, and light, and a door of utterance opened out of confusion and ignorance. Yesterday morning I felt myself favoured in some degree with an open door; but in the afternoon my old shackles were again put on, and confusion and perplexity seemed to fill my mind. The congregation was very large both times, the day being fine, and in the afternoon uncomfortably crowded. I feel, however, but little drawing towards Stamford, and should fear there is but little life in the place. I am much more at home at Oakham, and have usually more feeling and liberty in that pulpit than in this. . . . .

"Poor —— seems to display his weakness more and more. I can hardly think him sincere in all his admissions to you, but I believe the great key to his words and actions is to know that he has no fixed opinion to give, and no firm principles on which to act. A man that does not know his own mind must always be a puzzle to others, and I should expect fixedness as much from a weather-cock as from ——. A weather-cock, you know, will sometimes not turn for a week if the wind is still, and rust will make it at times wondrous steady; but a good stiff breeze will turn it round a hundred times a day. Let Master —— encounter what the sailors call a north-wester, or let 'a tempestuous wind called Euroclydon' beat into him, and I believe he would be in their case of whom we read that, 'when the ship was caught, and could not bear up into the wind, we let her drive.' If the —— friends had gone down to the sea in ships, and done business in great waters, they would have found out that their pilot looked too much to the chart, when he should have sounded, and if he had found it twenty fathoms should have gone a little further and sounded again, and if he found it fifteen fathoms, should have cast four anchors out of the stern and wished for day. But, instead of that, when the wind of Irvingism 'blew softly' he must needs loose the rudder bands and hoist up the mainsail to the wind, and make towards shore; and thus he fell into a place where two seas met—the sea of experimental Calvinism and the sea of Arminian Irvingism; and then need we wonder if he ran the ship aground, and whilst the fore part, *i.e.*, his head, stuck fast and remained immovable in the sands of unknown tongues, miraculous cures, and unfulfilled prophecy, the hinder part, *i.e.*, what the Lord had done in his heart, was broken with the violence of the waves? I can only say that it will be his mercy if he escapes safe to land on boards or broken pieces of the ship. As Master —— is so fond of spiritualising the word, he could not be offended at my tracing his experience in Acts xxvii., and I believe that my explanation is every whit as good as his interpretation of 'The Wall,' which he was so willing to favour you with.

"I hope that Friend Smart will furnish you with such savoury meals that you will go in the strength of that meat many days, and will not want to be fed again for some weeks to come.

"I wonder, indeed, that any persons are willing to be burdened with my company, as I am often a burden to myself, and am a wretched mass of vileness and corruption. I seem surprised at the priestcraft of the human mind, which makes people so fond of ministers. If they all thought of them as I do, there would be many sent to the right-about. They would see that they had a deal more of the devil in them than of the angel, much more of the flesh than the spirit, and more hypocrisy than humility. I wonder sometimes that persons can bear my rough remarks, and rude speeches, and doubts as to the genuineness of their religion; but I suppose they see enough carnality in me to serve as a nice excuse for their own. If the minister is so carnal, says Mr. Worldly-mind, surely I may be so too; and if the Reverend Dr. So-and-so is not always so spiritual, surely I may give my tongue a little licence. Thus people like the ministers to be carnal, that under this shed, as Friend Kay says, they may creep with their carnality, and think they will do exceedingly well if they have half the religion that the parson has. It is to some such feeling as this deeply lodged in the human heart that I am fain to ascribe the kind reception I meet with wherever I go.

"Your affectionate Friend,

"*To Mr. Parry.*" "J. C. P.

"*Oakham, Nov.* 14, 1836.

"My dear Friend,

"I hinted in my last letter at the probability of my staying the winter in these parts, and as the friends here, and at Stamford, are very urgent that I should do so, I seem inclined to listen to their wishes. I do not, however, think it right to decide upon a point which affects you as well as them, without first writing to you on the subject. I am encouraged to continue here a while longer, as the people profess to derive profit from my ministry. At Allington, you know, the winter congregation is often very scanty. I find the climate here and at Stamford much more suitable to my weak chest than the cold blasts which blow so chill and strong over your unsheltered downs. I hope you know me too well to think I have forgotten your unvarying kindness, or that I am tired, either of your hospitable fireside, or of the pulpit where, I trust, I have at times felt refreshings from the presence of the King of kings. I should be sorry, too, that you should think I have any intention of forsaking Allington, or that new faces and new friends have had the effect of dividing my regard for old ones. You recollect when I first came among you, I never promised to tie myself to Allington, and have always considered myself as a temporary Supply, who was at liberty to go away for a shorter, or longer time, or even altogether, without its being considered that I violated any engagement, or broke any promise. At the same time I feel a regard for Allington, and for some of the people who attend the chapel there, and, I need not add, for yourself. But, after all this preface, you will be saying to yourself, 'But how long does he mean to stay away? What does he call staying the winter? How long does he call "winter"?' Why, if we were to calculate very nicely, it might be winter at Allington, perhaps, when it is spring elsewhere, and the almanacks tell us that winter commences December 21st, and ends March 21st. And if my chest were consulted on the subject, and I do assure you that I am obliged to take its opinion much more than I could wish, it might say winter lasts from September to the beginning of June. I will not then take either Francis Moore's winter, or my chest definition of the same season, lest I should weary out your patience altogether. But I think it probable I shall continue in these parts during the months of December and January, and return to Allington about the beginning of February. In this case, I purpose to be at Oakham the three following Lord's-days, November 20th and 27th, and December 4th. I then think of returning to Stamford, to be there three or four Lord's-days more, and to return afterwards to Oakham. There is a great spirit of hearing both here and at Stamford, and persons come from considerable distances. I have been favoured at times with the Lord's presence in the pulpit, and as the people profess to hear me well on different occasions, I feel encouraged to continue a little while longer amongst them. If you cannot procure such Supplies as you can profitably and comfortably hear, I should recommend you to go on with reading. And I would counsel you to read sometimes Huntington, and at other times Webster, as the people seem to hear with profit.

"Tiptaft has been for five Lord's-days in London, and, according to his own account, got on better with the Londoners than he expected. I wrote to him a few days ago, and mentioned my plan of staying here a while longer, as well as suggested that he might pay Allington a visit. I get on but slowly with my pamphlet, and have a new work in hand, a sermon from Isa. l. 10, 11. This, however, I am getting on but slowly with, and find my quiet room at Allington more favourable to writing than this place, or Stamford, where there are so many things to distract the attention. I was surprised yet glad to hear that Friend Smart preached at Devizes, and I hope he shook the boughs with a firm and vigorous hand. I shall be glad to hear that the Lord was with him there as well as at Allington. For myself I go on in spiritual things much as usual, generally very dark and dead, and at other times favoured with desires and breathings after a fuller discovery and enjoyment of eternal things. I feel, however, that the old vile heart will turn up its mire and filth, and that no change of time or place can bring a clean thing out of an unclean. I need not say I meet with every kindness both here and at Stamford, and can only wonder what persons can see in me to call forth so much attention and regard. They do not, I believe, see me as I see myself, and it is my mercy that they do not know all the workings of a vile and depraved heart.

"I think, with one exception, besides twice on the Lord's-day, I have preached once in the week regularly since I left Allington. I have received an invitation from Boston, which I have promised to attend to for some future opportunity, besides one from Nottingham, Lynn, Woburn, and other places. But when I return to Allington, I shall hope to remain there quietly for a few months. I have through mercy been stronger, since I left Allington, in my chest and general health, and do not feel the cold weather quite so sensibly. This, I confess, is one reason why I am induced to spend the severe part of the winter here, as I do not forget my last winter at Allington, and how I suffered from the cold.

"Let me hear from you soon, and write me a good long letter. . . .

"Believe me to be,
"Your affectionate Friend,
"J. C. P.

"*To Mr. Parry.*"

"*Oakham, Dec.* 1, 1836.

"MY DEAR FRIEND,

"I am very sorry that my intention to continue here a little longer has so much hurt your feelings, and that you have found the old man so rebellious on the subject. I find it very difficult so to act as to escape censure from some one or other, and whichever way I turn I find difficulties. Ministers cannot always consult private feelings, nor, indeed, would they act right if they did so. Many motives sway their minds and influence their decisions, of which hearers have little conception. The hearer looks only to himself and his own pleasure in hearing any favourite minister, and never considers how far that ministry, which is profitable to him, may be so to others also. But the minister looks to where he has the widest door set before him—where he is most blessed himself, where the most evident blessing rests on the word, and where he feels most unction and power present with him. And thus he has many motives and leadings, of which the hearers know nothing. I feel, too, in my own case, as you yourself have so often remarked, that I require some time to make way into the understandings and affections of the people, and that it is not half-a-dozen sermons which will make my drift evident. To this let me add that I require a short time before I am at home in the pulpit, and that a little thing will shut me up, and stop the flow of utterance which I enjoy sometimes. I need not enlarge on this point, as you have often remarked the same, and said I need a little time before the people can receive my ministry and enter into my drift. I feel that hitherto I have been labouring at a disadvantage, and that I am only just now obtaining a footing in the understandings and affections of the people. This is one main reason why I have been induced to prolong my stay. I have felt desirous, too, of leading the people to contend for *right* things, for internals more than externals; and I have been anxious to demolish some of those mighty castles of letter religion which Satan everywhere builds up. I find I cannot accomplish my work in one or two sermons, and that I have to build up, as well as to throw down. These motives have weighed with me to continue some time longer, and I have been further induced by the often-repeated wishes of the people and my kind friends here and at Stamford. To this I must add that I have been so much better in health, and find the climate much more congenial to my weak chest than Allington. Thus, I can say it is from no diminution of either Christian affection or esteem that I have protracted my stay from your hospitable fireside; and I trust I need not add that it is no mercenary motive that weighs with me, as I have many expenses here, as travelling, servants at two houses, washing, wear and tear of better clothes, &c., which I have not at Allington. I hope I have said enough to set your mind at rest, and I need not hint that I am bound by no engagement to Allington, and have always considered myself as a Supply from week to week. Indeed, I may add that my strongest tie to Allington is my private friendship for you, though I admit that there are several in and out of the church to whom I feel a union, and whom I shall be glad to see again. I intend at present (D.V.) to return to Allington some time in February, if health and weather permit, and hope to stay with you for a few months, before I take a second flight.

"I am glad that Friend Warburton has paid you a visit, and that his word was blessed. John, with all his faults, has the right stuff in him, and will outlive a thousand May-flies, who flutter their hour in the religious world.

"I intend (D.V.) to leave Oakham for Stamford about Dec. 8, and shall stay until about Jan. 5, continuing there for four Lord's-days. I do not see that you should be anxious about having preachers. Your cause is small, and in winter the congregation is never very numerous. Let them hear Huntington or Webster, and I believe they will hear no such preaching as the former, let them go where they will. Stand firm for experimental truth; none but the chaff oppose it. I doubt not that many are glad that the troubler of Israel is many miles away from Allington, and that the Church ministers are not the only persons who are secretly rejoiced. I hope, however, if the Lord will, to trouble them again, and not leave them always to rejoice.

"My sermon advances slowly. I find that so much letter-writing as I have cuts up my time for it very much. It is quite uncertain when I shall be able to bring it out. I often find it irksome to write, and a thousand excuses rise up in my mind to defer it to another day, and thus I do not often set to work upon it. A person has offered to advance me £50 if I could put to press a volume of sermons; but I have no intention to do so. My other pamphlet I have laid aside for a long time.*

"I hope the Lord may lead us more and more to contend for *realities*—the things that accompany salvation. All things else are mere soap-bubbles, blown up by the breath of a child, which glitter for a few moments with the rays of the sun, and then burst for ever. If the people at Allington do not contend for realities, it shows there is a woful deficiency somewhere; for I am well satisfied that God will make all His people, great and small, contend for what they have tasted and handled. I look upon it, then, as a fatal mark, when men are contending for externals and doting about questions, whilst they neglect the weightier matters of the law. Contend for the power of eternal things, and the mysteries of vital godliness, and you will have the devil and his twin family of dead sinners and dead professors against you; but you will have the family of God, to a man, with you, and, above all, you will have God Himself on your side. Where now are all those that, in their day and generation, worshipped an unknown God, talked of an unknown Christ, and took into their lips the name of an unknown Spirit? In hell, is the answer; reserved in everlasting chains, under darkness, unto the judgment of the great day. And where are all those happy saints who saw, believed in, worshipped and loved a triune God? Safe with Christ; happily landed on the peaceful shore of eternity. A few years will put us amongst one of these two companies. Let us contend, then, earnestly and unwaveringly, for that truth which is able to save our souls. 'But foolish and unlearned questions avoid, knowing that they do engender strife.' Let us not have separated from ungodly systems and dead professors on account of doctrines only and outward ordinances, however true and scriptural; neither let these things, especially the latter, break the union between the family of God. I am a decided Baptist, but I can stretch my hand across the water to God's children, whose eyes are not open to see the ordinance, whilst there are thousands of Baptists to whom I would not willingly hand a chair. Write me a good long letter soon, as I like your letters much, and think you a very good scribe.

"Your affectionate Friend,

"*To Mr. Parry.*" "J. C. P.

"*Oakham, March* 3, 1837.

"MY DEAR FRIEND,

"The first edition of my sermon,† consisting of 1,500 copies, is already exhausted, and a new edition, with a short pre-

* This pamphlet still remains unfinished.

† "The Heir of Heaven," &c.

face, will appear in a few days. Fowler has had some orders for this also, so that it appears at present likely to sell. More than 500 copies have been disposed of in these parts, and many have read it who never heard me preach. It has made quite a stir at Stamford, and it is thought many more would come to hear me who have hitherto not done so. P—— of A—— refuses to sell it, as being 'contrary to the religion which it professes to illustrate,' and has returned all the copies. I have a notion the edge is too keen for his self-righteousness. A—— of O——, I have reason to think, is equally afraid of them. But all this will not stop their sale, and Tiptaft says he will sell them at his chapel. I think you gave too great an order when you wished to have 300. I felt my mouth opened the morning that I preached it, and some have preferred my oral to my written discourse, which is, of course, only a resemblance of it. I am glad you think it sounds like my own, as R. H. might think I have been dipping into the ample stores of Goodwin and others. I think I am too proud and independent to borrow of others if I had no other motives to restrain me, and would not readily send abroad into the light of day stolen goods. This I leave to those who have no mind, no original ideas, no real experience, no open door, no decided views for themselves. And I believe stolen goods are sure to be detected, sooner or later, though the fashion of them be altered and the marks cut out. Nothing but realities will ever stand the brunt of time and trouble. The plated goods wear, the mock lustre fades, the potsherd, covered with silver dross, betrays its base original. But gold may be beaten, bruised, worn down, melted, shivered into dust, and each little grain will still say, 'I am gold, do what you will to me and grind me down to powder.'

'True faith's the life of God,
Deep in the heart it lies,
It lives and labours under load,
Tho' damped it never dies.'

"Realities! realities! What is all the windy blustering noise of preachers worth who will not contend for realities from a real experience of them? Guilt, condemnation, dismal forebodings of judgment, fears of hell, a sight of one's own self—that hideous monster self—cuts out the way for realities. Real guilt needs real pardon, real weakness requires real strength, real wounds need a real cure, real trouble demands real consolation. A sense of one's own dreadful malady cuts to pieces all that empty, formal, superstitious, traditional religion, in which well-nigh all the churches and chapels of the land seem buried. And when a faithful warner comes, the cry is, 'Hast thou found me out, O mine enemy?' Oh, to be kept from myself; my vile, proud, lustful, hypocritical, worldly, covetous, presumptuous, obscene self. O self! self! Thy desperate wickedness, thy depravity, thy love of sin, thy abominable pollutions, thy monstrous heart wickedness, thy wretched deadness, hardness, blindness, and indifference; thou vile wretch, how thou dost make my sword droop and palsiest all my strength. Thou art a treacherous villain, and, I fear, always will be such! Do these exclamations find an echo in J. P.'s bosom? Is my heart a copy of his? Is it a looking-glass in which he sees his face reflected? What! no further yet in sanctification? Tell it not; publish it not.

"Such feelings, however, my friend, pave the way for sovereign grace to heal all, cure all, cover all, swallow up all. No half measures, no creature contributions, no a little bit here and a little bit there will do for those who feel so weak, so helpless, and so vile. A dose of evening prayer, or a regular chapter, or a three-times-a-day attendance at chapel, will not reach such a malady as those groan under who know themselves and toil in the deep slough of corruption and heart wickedness. Something deep, powerful, and effectual; something fully commensurate with the disease; something that goes to the very bottom of the case is required, and where that is not obtained, all seems wanting. Few know the up-stroke of the great A in religion who are thought wonderful Christians, and most professors can no more read the mysteries of vital godliness than Belshazzar could read the letters written by the hand upon the wall. . . . .

"Your affectionate Friend,

"*To Mr. Parry.*" "J. C. P.

He returned to Allington, however, in March, and stayed there during the spring and summer, and then having preached a few Lord's-days at Zoar Chapel, London, in September he went to Manchester to supply for Mr. Gadsby, taking Oakham in his way. Whilst at Manchester he engaged himself in preparing for the press a second sermon, "Winter afore Harvest," taken from Isaiah xviii. 5, 6. The sermon when preached at Oakham the previous August, had been greatly blessed to many of his hearers, and when published, according to a very general wish, it seems to have been equally blessed to the Church at large. The four following letters to Mr. Parry were written at this time:—

"*Stoke, Devonport, June* 3, 1837.

"MY DEAR FRIEND,

"I presume you are, by this time, expecting a letter from me and watching the movements of the postman more than usual. I am happy to say that, through much mercy, I arrived here safely, on the evening of the day on which we parted, about ten o'clock. I was a little fatigued with my journey, which, however, a night's sound sleep dissipated, and I awoke in the morning quite uninjured by my long day's work.

"I found my dear mother quite as well as I expected. She

seems much reconciled to her loss,* and feels that there are many alleviating circumstances connected with it. I find I have already derived benefit from the change of air, combined with the rest of body which I am able to indulge myself with. I do not think it at all likely that I shall preach here, as I am quite unknown, and mean to continue so if I can. The religion of the place seems to me to be chiefly Bible religion, of which there is a vast abundance of every kind and in every direction. I heard, last Lord's-day evening, John Hawker, a son of the Doctor. If his father were like the son, I would not give a shilling a year for a seat under him. Abundance of Scripture, a copious supply of dry doctrine, a tolerable quantity of pride, and enough presumption to stock half-a-dozen pulpits, seemed to me to make up the sermon. Among other things, he said, 'Sin! what is sin? I can't define what sin is! Sin is a principle. The Scriptures say it is a transgression of the Law, and that is all I know about it.' I thought if he had tasted the wormwood and the gall, though he might not be able to define the nature of wormwood or explain what gall was composed of, he could have told us what a bitter taste it had, and how many wry faces it causes in those whose mouths are filled with it. Like most ministers whom I hear, he and sin never seem to have fought with drawn swords. As usual, he was 'established in Christ'; far too established for a poor creature like me, driven up and down by every vile lust and abomination. I find hearers and preachers must be like mortise and tenon. Unless there be a fitting in of feelings there can be no union, and they are barbarians one to the other. I could see, plainer than ever, that dead Calvinism is the best weapon that Satan has to harden the hearts and sear the consciences of unhumbled professors. I find almost everywhere the same great mistake—Bible religion substituted for soul religion. Believe me, it is here and there only a pilgrim who knows anything of the latter, whilst thousands on thousands have an acquaintance with the former. As to myself, I often feel that hitherto I know nothing as I ought to know, and at present am only groping for the wall like the blind, and groping as if I had no eyes. I am full of confusion, and often full of condemnation, and still more often think, act, and talk as one without God in the world.

I find I can do very little to my intended publication, partly from indolence, partly from disinclination, and partly from weakness of my eyes. Of all places that I know, this is the worst for the eyes, from the dazzling glare produced by the limestone with which the streets are paved and the houses built. All persons, but especially strangers, complain of it. The beauty of the scenery here, the many lovely prospects afforded by a large harbour, enclosed by wooded heights and occupied by noble ships, and the many pretty walks in a rich country, have all tempted me to more

* The sudden death of Mr. P.'s only surviving brother.

exercise than at Allington, and I have already derived benefit from the change. The weather, too, has been fine and warm, and thus I have been able to walk out every day. I have not yet arrived to that degree of perfect sanctification to be dead to all the charms of nature and wonders of art, and can gaze with pleasure on a lovely expanse of blue sea, or on a noble three-decker lying at anchor, as the masterpiece of human skill and ingenuity. Though all things are deadening where God is not, yet I should feel happy to have no worse thoughts than those which arise in my mind as I view the beautiful arm of the sea in which my brother-in-law's noble ship stands out of the clear blue water as a moving fortress, weighing more, probably, than 2,000 tons, and yet moved by every wave, and swinging to and fro at every tide.

"I called on a friend at Exeter on my journey. I found they had had there a minister, but he was obliged to leave. He was one of your dead Calvinists, and had a great knowledge of the word, and a great aptitude at quoting it. But texts and chapters are a poor bulwark against sin. That giant easily runs his spear through such a wooden shield as a memory well stored with passages, and a prating tongue that can repeat them by dozens. A small portion of godly fear will do more against sin than a concordance, or even Bagster's Family Bible with a million of marginal references. A paper religion is a poor affair. The ten commandments, written by God Himself, could not stand a fall from the hand of Moses, and how can a paper creed stand when a stone decalogue was broken to shivers? The Law, written on fleshy tables of the heart, can alone endure both fire and water, and a living epistle, like a quick hedge, will last a dead letter out, as that will a dead hedge till it is rotten. But whereas two of your labourers could put up the one in a day, whilst the other requires months and years to make it a hedge at all, so a dead religion can be put up under a sermon, whilst a living one needs many revolving seasons to make it grow. It must be cut and pruned, and hoed and weeded, and plashed and well-nigh cut through, and laid flat, before it will become a fence to keep out intruders. A dead hedge needs none of this. A few dry doctrines for stakes, and an ample supply of cant and worldly policy for willow-poles to interweave the stakes with, and a hole dug in natural conscience, by the bar of Moses, are all that is needed for a dead hedge to be made up. It will last a few years, and is sometimes useful to protect the young quick from being nibbled off by goats, but its end is to be burned, and, sooner or later, it finds its way to the oven. I dare say you often think your religion, if it has life at all, is something like the hedge round the orchard, which you have spent so much money and pains upon. O for a little real, genuine, Divine, God-given, supernatural, eternal life. Nothing else will preserve soul and body from stinking with putrefaction in the nostrils of a holy God.

"I hope you find the coal-heaver improves as you dig deeper into him. I believe he will be known and valued, just as we know little or much of experimental religion. The world, profane and professing, knoweth not true Christians, because it knew not Christ. It can understand everybody but a gracious soul, and love every one but a child of God. And let me whisper this in your ear, that a sound creed, and a profession of experimental religion too, cannot open a man's eyes to see, nor his heart to love, the secret track of a living soul. Therefore, friend Parry, marvel not if Particular Baptists' churches and ministers hate you as bad as Wesleyans and Independents.

"I intend (D.V.) to be at Trowbridge, June 24, and come to Devizes by coach the following Monday, when please to send in the cart to meet me.

"Your affectionate Friend,

"*To Mr. Parry.*" "J. C. P.

"*Manchester, Sept.* 13, 1837.

"My dear Friend,

"I presume the harvest has found so much occupation for your hands, that it has left none for your fingers. The driving-whip and the pony bridle have been in such requisition that the ink has become mouldy in the stand, and the penknife covered with rust. As, however, you are at no time fond of writing, and as this uncertain weather must have given you more than your usual harvest occupation, I can readily excuse you. I believe, however, a letter from me finds a welcome at Allington, and therefore, without further delay, I send you a few lines.

"I have now fulfilled half of my engagement at Manchester, and have no reason to regret coming into these parts. I cannot, indeed, well say how I have been received by Gadsby's people, but I have reason to believe with some measure of acceptance. I judge more from the size and attentiveness of the congregation, and scattered hints, than from any positive direct testimony. North country people usually are not flatterers, and you know that I am not much of a vestry man, or a gadder about from house to house. A good many persons, methinks, who run about to pick up tit-bits of flattery, would not like to hear all the remarks made upon them even by their professed friends, and did every stick and stone which were hurled at them behind their backs fall upon their skin, they would be too sore to preach the Sunday following. As, however, the deacons have waited upon me to ask me to stay over another Lord's-day, it seems as though they were not fully tired of me. I declined their invitation, as I had previously promised to be at Stamford on October 1, and could not disappoint the friends there.

"I have some thoughts of publishing a sermon which I preached at Oakham on Lord's-day morning, August 20, from

Isaiah xviii. 5, 6. It is the same text that I preached from at Trowbridge, but I could not get into my subject as I did at Oakham, and most probably the printed sermon will differ from both. The text was opened to me one morning at Devonport as I was reading the chapter, and I saw in it a path traced out of which I knew something experimentally. I therefore took it at Trowbridge, but could not get into it, and as I felt a great desire to open up that line of experience at Oakham, I preached from it there, and was more favoured with an entrance into it and an utterance out of it than at Trowbridge. The people, I believe, heard it well, and as it seemed to me a path in which many of God's children walk, when I came here and found more than my usual leisure for writing, I felt inclined to put it upon paper. After I had written some pages, I mentioned my intention in a letter to Oakham, and have since heard from Tiptaft that the friends there had a wish to have the sermon in print before I mentioned the subject. Thus there seems a coincidence of inclinations unknown to each, and this has given me encouragement to persevere in my undertaking.

"I went last week to Liverpool by the famous railroad. We were just an hour travelling thirty miles. The last mile and quarter is by a tunnel carried all under the town, which occupied four minutes. During this part of the journey you have no light but that of lamps affixed to the carriages. I was pleased with my visit to Liverpool, and heard a minister there—a Mr. Kent—with great satisfaction. His congregation on the week night did not exceed twelve people. He is building a new chapel at the expense of £1,600, and wishes me to come and assist Gadsby in opening it; it will not be ready till November. I made myself known to him, and was very cordially received, and sat an hour with him the day following. We conversed very pleasantly upon experimental religion, and did not at all jar. He invited me to preach for him, but as I have declined all invitations, I was compelled to refuse. Many invitations have come to me from the neighbouring towns, in most of which some place in connection with Gadsby's is to be found. But I find preaching in this large chapel, twice on the Lord's-day and once in the week (Tuesday evening), quite as much as I can get through. Last Lord's-day I had a cold upon me, and found it hard work before I concluded the day, as I exceeded the hour both times. The congregation was very large, exceeding probably 1,200 persons, and I believe I exerted myself more than was needful, as a lower pitch of voice might have been heard all over the chapel. I have, in other respects, through mercy, been pretty well, though I think the Oakham air suits me better than the Manchester. I intend (D.V.) to preach at Leicester, September 28, on my way to Stamford, and mean to be at Stamford the three first Lord's-days in October, and at Oakham the two last in October and the first in November.

"I hope the Lord was with Smart, and that you and the friends heard him profitably. You are doubtless reckoning now upon Tiptaft's visit, and getting your appetites well sharpened up to the feeding point. He is an honest, sincere man, and such God will bless.

"My religion at times seems altogether gone, and at the bottom of the Kennet and Avon Canal. I have had some heavy steps along its banks, and sighs enough to ruffle its waters.

"I have not found many sinners at Manchester. They talk about trials and deliverances, but so few seem to have had a battle with Sin, or know what a giant he is. All seem to have buried him and preached his funeral sermon, and, like Giant Pope and Giant Pagan, he seems only able to grin at the pilgrims, and abide in his cave; but he and I cannot keep so far asunder. I know he has cost me a good many groans and sighs, and yet, to this day, he cleaves to me as the collar of my coat; yea, he is bone of my bone, and flesh of my flesh, and is not a neighbour but an in-dweller.

"I find Warburton's MS. will cost me a great deal of labour. Mr. J. Gadsby put it into the hands of a schoolmaster to copy and correct the bad grammar, but he has sewed so much gold fringe upon John's plain cloth, that my present employment is to rip it all off. He has altered John's plain, straightforward language, and made him talk like a schoolmaster, so that my present tedious task is to compare the two copies line by line, and word by word, and restore the original language. This, with numerous letters, and my sermon from Isaiah xviii. 5, 6, leaves me scarcely any leisure time for anything else.

"Give my Christian love to all the friends of Jesus, and believe me,

"Your sincere and affectionate Friend,

"*To Mr. Parry.*" "J. C. P.

"*Oakham, Oct.* 21, 1837.

"My dear Friend,

"I can readily imagine you and our mutual friend Tiptaft walking over the farm together, conversing, sometimes on things temporal, and sometimes on things spiritual, and on each and all finding your opinions not very far asunder. It will give me great satisfaction to hear that our valued friend has been blessed to your soul and to the souls of the people of God, and that your drooping hearts have been revived under him.

"I arrived here on Friday, and am, through mercy, well and strong in bodily health. I have recovered the fatigue of my Manchester labours, and feel better than I have done for some time. The spirit of hearing at Stamford increases rather than diminishes, and I have never yet seen the chapel so crowded as during this last visit. The beautiful weather and dry walking have, no doubt, lent their powerful aid. As there is such a desire after the word, I have felt induced to half promise that I will come again in the spring, for March and April, previous to my going to London in May, being the first of those months at Stamford, and the second at Oakham. I scarcely expect that this will please my Allington friends, but when I see the great thirst after the word in these parts it makes me feel willing to come amongst them. That I should come in March was Mr. de Merveilleux's proposal, and did not come from Oakham; and it was chiefly seeing the large congregations, and the great desire for preaching at Stamford, that induced me to think seriously of his proposal. How far the work may be of God I will not undertake to decide, and I am sure, so much do I feel of my own vileness and dreadful wickedness, that it astonishes me either to be ever blessed myself or to be blessed to others. I hope Tiptaft will go to Stamford when he comes into these parts, as there is a great desire to hear the truth. Mr. de Merveilleux proposes to build a gallery in his chapel, but I don't much encourage him to do so, as there is so little probability of constant preaching. He is somewhat better in health, but his chest is still very tender.

"I like one of the friends here, but it is young days with him, and he and Giant Sin have not fought many battles. He has never been dashed down by the giant seizing him by the collar of his coat, nor rolled over and over in the stinking ditch of loathsome nature. I wish that giant did not lay hold of me so often and so dreadfully bruise my bones. I could wish at times never to sin more, and not receive such cruel wounds; and at other times I think my conscience is altogether seared and I shall live and die a reprobate. I often see myself an outcast from God and man, and think I shall either be cut down by some sudden judgment or short disease, or die in sullen despair. I am sure I have no reason to love sin, as I have tasted the wormwood and the gall, but if I loved it not my conflict would cease. I am sure we pay very dear for the transient pleasures of sin, and they leave little else but ashes in the mouth after we have sucked the first fruit. Divine things leave no sting nor cutting remorse behind them, but are like the money we give to any of the Lord's needy family, which, though it may cost a momentary struggle, leaves no guilt and sorrow behind.

"They are looking forward here to Tiptaft's visit in January. Reading does here better than at Stamford, but it is very hard to carry a cause on, especially in its infancy, by reading. Persons are so accustomed to preaching from infancy that reading seems hardly worship at all, and this is much the case at Stamford, where there are many persons who would give up their seats at other places of worship, if there were constant preaching at North Street. Their cry is, 'What are we to do?' To which my answer is, that it is better to hear truth read than error preached. I may seem, perhaps, more drawn to Stamford than I was. If so, it is for two reasons:—(1) Because I have felt at home in the pulpit there; and (2) because I feel there is a desire after experimental preaching. Tiptaft was heard very well there the last time, and I sincerely hope he will go again.

"The Leicester friends wish me to preach there on my way, and I think I shall most likely comply. I wish to see Tiptaft before he leaves for London, and fully intend (D.V.) preaching for him on Nov. 19, and at Allington, Nov. 26. You will then have me for three months before I again start on my travels. I cannot expect you to enter into my feelings as a minister, nor can I enter into yours. Where I am well heard, and feel myself at home in the pulpit, there I like to go, and where I am shut up, there I feel unwilling to set my feet in the stocks. At Allington, however, I have felt at home often, and feel a union with some who worship there, never to be dissolved. Go wherever I may, I shall meet with no kinder or dearer friends than some there. I said at Leicester, speaking of my exercises in leaving the Church, that I had found kinder, better, dearer friends since I left it, and had had every want more liberally supplied, than when I was dependent. I am sure I have had more money to give away, as what comes in liberally opens the heart to go out liberally, whilst a certain small income pinches you up into dross. You know your income and dare not exceed it. Mine was one I could not sink if I would.

"*October* 22.—We have had two large congregations to-day, and this afternoon quite overflowing. I never saw the chapel fuller. I was not at home in the morning, but more so this afternoon. Mr. and Mrs. de M. and Miss L. came from Stamford. He seems quite decided on enlarging the chapel and building a gallery, and calculates on an accommodation for 150 being thus afforded. They think at Nottingham that ministers should leave it to God to sift tares from wheat. S—— has been preaching against baptism, and sprinkled openly six children. They wish me to go again to Nottingham, but I think I shall decline on account of S——'s errors and speaking against baptism. I might as well unite with free-will as infant sprinkling. Though not always prating about it, I cannot bear to have baptism spoken against, as a part of the faith delivered to the saints. I never saw an argument against it worth a straw. S—— thought the eunuch was sprinkled because he would not like to ride in his wet clothes! So Queen Candace's treasurer had not a change of raiment nor even a portmanteau.

"I shall hope to hear from Tiptaft whilst with you, and that when he has left you will favour me with a long letter. Give him my sincere and affectionate love. I earnestly desire that the Lord may bless him, and believe that He will. I have seen him taken and myself left; him a vessel of mercy and me of wrath. I hope when I have finished Warburton's MS. to go on with my sermon, which is at a complete standstill. There is great inquiry for the Appendix separate from the Barber's Block, which does not seem much admired.

"My love to Dredge and all Christian friends.

"Yours affectionately,

"*To Mr. Parry.*" "J. C. P.

"*Oakham, November* 8, 1837.

"MY DEAR FRIEND,

"If you measure me by yourself you will not conceive writing letters so pleasant a task as to expect two of me before I return to Allington. One, I believe, must satisfy you this time. I intend, God willing, to leave Oakham on the 15th, and hope to arrive at Abingdon that evening. I have been wanted to preach at Newbury, but I cannot fully settle when until I have seen Tiptaft. I am glad he was so well heard at Allington. You, I doubt not, had much pleasant conversation with him, and found in him a listening ear as well as a ready tongue.

"The spirit of hearing at Oakham, and the anxiety of the people, greatly induced me to remain so long here. As I was sitting in the pulpit the last Sunday I was there, and viewing the congregation and their eagerness to hear, I felt I was about to return to a comparatively thin chapel, and the desire to preach to a people so willing to hear arose in my mind. And this it was which led me to lend a more willing ear to Mr. de Merveilleux, when he asked me to return in the spring. The general impression here was that I meant to stay the winter, which I never thought of doing since last July. Our congregations here continue unabated, and as we have been favoured with fine Sundays, it enables the distant hearers to come. I don't think any hearers can be fair judges of ministers. They, of course, think of themselves, and if they hear well, and love a minister, they want to keep him all to themselves. He, on the other hand, where he feels life and a blessing to attend his ministry, is drawn to that place, and where he meets a hungry people, is willing to give them such food as he has. And I dare say we wanderers contract a roving disposition and like change. Popularity, too, has its dangerous charms, and large congregations please the carnal mind. But I think I am so well weighted and ballasted by temptations and sins, that popularity has less charms for me than many. A man full of evil, and that continually, has not much to be proud of, and his fear is lest God should stop his mouth or cut him down for his presumption. As a farmer you are not very proud of your diseased lambs, and as a preacher I cannot be very proud of my diseased prayers and sin-stained sermons. Neither can I boast much of my daily backslidings, hardness of heart, discontent, vileness, and abominable filthiness. I at times know not what will become of me, and fear I shall live and die a reprobate. I find sin has such power over me, and, though I call on the Lord again and again for deliverance, seem to be as weak as ever when temptation comes.

> 'O thou hideous monster, sin,
> What a curse hast thou brought in.'

I love it, I hate it; I want to be delivered from the power of it, and yet am not satisfied without drinking down its poisoned sweets. It is my hourly companion and my daily curse, the breath of my mouth and the cause of my groans, my incentive to prayer and my hinderer of it, that made a Saviour suffer and makes a Saviour precious, that spoils every pleasure and adds a sting to every pain, that fits a soul for heaven and ripens a soul for hell. Friend Joseph, canst thou make out my riddle? 'Is thy heart as my heart?' said one of old. 'Then come up into my chariot.' We shall quarrel by the way unless 'as in water face answereth to face, so does the heart of man to man.' Black men will not form a good regiment with white ones, and clean hands will not do to show dirty hands with. I believe I shall never live and die a Pharisee. I must come in amongst the sinners, the ragged regiments of adulterous Davids, idolatrous Manassehs, swearing Peters, persecuting Sauls, fornicating Corinthians, railing thieves, and self-abhorring publicans. Pardon, to the innocent, is a word of six letters—and that is all. Redemption, to the self-saved, is a Bible term—no more; and some of them say it is a universal term, and others a particular term; and the one quotes an Arminian, and the other a Calvinistic text, and with these sticks they belabour one another's heads. Whilst a lost, sin-bitten, bulrush, howling, half-desperate, ditch-plunged, black-hearted wretch, up to the neck in guilt, cries for its individual application as his only remedy and only hope.

"I at times quite despair of salvation, and then again am as careless as if hell had no wrath, and heaven no love; as if sin had no wormwood, and pardon no sweet; as if there were no God to mark evil, and no devil to tempt to it. So my friend you must not expect to find your winter fireside companion much grown in progressive sanctification and creature holiness.

"You say very little about my leaving you again in March; I suppose, from thinking me too obstinate and self-willed to listen to anybody's will and advice but my own. I shall hope, however, to have some pleasant conversations with you during the dreary months so rapidly coming on. I am glad to hear all your family are well, and desire my kind love to all the children. My kind regards to Mr. and Mrs. T., Mrs. C., and your kind lady, and believe me to be,

"Your affectionate Friend,

"*To Mr. Parry.*" "J. C. P.

He again returned to Allington for the winter, and stayed there to the end of March, 1838; but he still felt an ardent desire to preach again to the friends at Oakham and Stamford, and accordingly we find him staying at the latter place in April. At this time he appears first to have entertained the idea of fixing his permanent abode in that part of the country. Throughout the whole three years of his sojourning at different places as a Supply, he longed for a fixed and settled home, and for a people whom he could regard as his own especial care, and with whom he could be on terms of more intimate relationship than he had been with those churches who had engaged him only as their temporary minister. Accordingly, when the friends at Stamford, fearing lest he should settle at Oakham, invited him to come and be their permanent minister, and offered him a fixed stipend, he did not at once reject their proposals, but requested a little time to consider their invitation. At the same time, his approaching marriage with the eldest daughter of Mr. Keal, who was the chief (if not then the sole) supporter of the cause at Oakham, presented an additional inducement to him to fix his home in that part of the country. So that when he left his friends for London, in June, it was with the almost settled intention of returning in the latter part of the year to fix his permanent abode at Stamford.

"*Oakham, April* 30, 1838.

"MY DEAR FRIEND,

"I was sorry to learn, through a most kind and affectionate letter from our dear friend Dredge, that you were so much troubled at the mention which I made in my last letter of my intention to settle here. Believe me, my dear friend, that had it not been for my being under the necessity of fixing on some settled place of abode, I should have paused very long before I relinquished my post at Allington; and had I continued, as might, perhaps, have been best for me, unmarried, I should have felt very unwilling to leave that abode, which not only your kindness and hospitality, but also our union in divine things, rendered always so comfortable. I shall never forget that for nearly three years our friendship, instead of diminishing, has only kept continually increasing, and that during all that time no unkind word, or, I believe, even look, has passed between us. Whatever unkind thoughts or feelings Satan or our vile hearts have coined, they have mercifully been confined within our own bosoms. As you never thwarted or opposed me, and, indeed, were only anxious to anticipate my wishes, I cannot take much credit to myself for evenness of temper, as I know not how sullen and growling I might have been had you often trampled on my toes; and you are well aware that I have two or three corns which will not bear much treading upon. And as to my reception by yourself and a few others, as a minister, all

I can say is, that I most fully believe that both you and a few others thought by far too well of me, and were blind to great defects which I daily see and feel in myself. Nor do I ever expect to find, wherever I go, hearers, on the whole, comparable to a few at Allington, who understood, received, and felt my drift and line of things, so as in most things that we could see eye to eye, and feel heart to heart, with each other. I feel a real soul union to a few there, who, as our friend Dredge once truly expressed it, met together to worship God aright. And it was the desire of my soul not to read for reading's sake, nor pray for praying's sake, nor preach for preaching's sake, but to be so favoured with the presence and power of the blessed Spirit in each and all, that our souls might be refreshed thereby. And though, through weakness of the flesh, hardness of heart, deadness of soul, temptations of Satan, and withdrawings of God's presence, I was often bound, fettered, and shut up in heart and tongue; yet this I can say, to the honour and glory of God, if ever I felt my heart solemnised in prayer, or my soul enlarged and mouth opened in preaching—if all was not delusion and a subtle refinement of nature counterfeiting the operation of grace—I have felt both in Allington pulpit. I have felt something like what Bunyan mentions, 'Grace abounding,' section 282; with respect to the things I have there contended for, 'methought I was more than sure that those things which I asserted were true.' I was much pleased with friend Dredge's kind letter, and felt a real soul union to him. A few real, gracious, heaven-taught souls, how preferable a thousand times is their friendship to all the canting, whining, 'brother this' and 'sister that' of empty professors! . . . . .

"When a man begins to doubt, and fear, and question for himself, he will find similar exercises respecting others, and universal charity will wither away from the root. You and I, my friend, cannot say that sin has no dominion over us. Alas! Alas! We feel its power daily and hourly; and we sigh and groan at times to be delivered from the giant strength of those corruptions, which seem to carry us away captive at their will. Though sin is a sweet morsel to our carnal mind, it grieves our soul, cuts up our evidences, removes our landmarks, and often seems to make our salvation impossible. Oh, what snares and temptations does the cunning devil lay for our feet, and seldom do we see the snare before we feel the smart! And a preacher, too! Oh, I think if I were seen in my right colours, and if that window, of which the Wesleyans talk, were placed in my bosom, what filth and vileness would be seen. I am sure I must be a monument of grace and mercy if saved from the guilt, curse, and power of sin. Few know what sin is. Who would think one spark of fire, on which your little boy could tread and extinguish, could burn down your ricks, barns, house, and everything whither it could reach, or on which it could feed! Such is sin. 'Behold how great a matter a little fire kindleth.' We feel we have no strength against sin, and we are sure that the blood of Christ alone can cleanse from sin's guilt and filth, and His grace alone from its power and dominion.

"I arrived here on Friday last, and preached yesterday to two large congregations. I felt shut up in the morning, but more at home in the afternoon.

"As a convenient house does not offer at Stamford, we think of lodgings for the first year or so. I think most probably we shall be married in July. Give my love to friend Dredge, Mrs. Wild, etc. etc.

"Your affectionate Friend,

"J. C. P.

"*To Mr. Parry.*"

"*London, June* 4, 1838.

"Here at length, then, my dear friend, am I in this busy metropolis, where, as far as the eye seeth, well-nigh all are seeking their own, and not the things which are Jesus Christ's; and yet here, doubtless, there is a remnant, according to the election of grace.

"I was sorry to hear of your heavy loss of ewes. I dare say these trials in Providence, which you have lately so much suffered, have been both embers and bellows to the carnal mind, which is enmity against God; but sure I am that the letter of the word, as well as the universal experience of the living family, testify that providential losses and crosses are marks for, and not against, those that fear God.

"I preached twice yesterday to two large congregations; the evening one might be called overflowing, as the forms were filled up all the aisles, and many sat and stood upon the stairs of the galleries and the windows. I cannot say that I felt much at home in the morning, but had more of a door of utterance in the evening. But, indeed, I feel myself very unfit to preach either in London or anywhere, and would much sooner tarry at Jericho till my beard be grown. I hope, however, the Zoar friends did not think my sword had been lying, ever since I saw them, at the bottom of the Kennet and Avon Canal, and was covered, blade and handle, with a thick coating of rust. I felt, towards the close of my sermon, that I cared for nothing and nobody so long as I cleared my own conscience, and I desired that every arrow should pierce through the joints of the armour into the heart. That, however, I must leave in the hands of Him who hath twice said that power belongeth unto God. I was not so fatigued with my exertions as I expected, and feel to-day, notwithstanding my broken rest, pretty comfortable and strong. I have walked about a good deal to-day, and am just returned from hearing the Jew, who said some good things; but not exactly in our line. I intend (D.V.) hearing him again, as he preaches near here every Monday evening, and is very sound in the letter of truth, as well as preaches more experience than most of the London ministers. I see, from his preaching, how defective I am in bringing forward Scripture. He quotes it very much, and often much to the point. I intend taking the opportunity of hearing various ministers whilst in town, that I may feel more what it is to be a hearer, and what food and what preaching feeling souls need.

"I was pleased to hear, from Dredge's letter to S——, that he hears Kay so well. It will be quite a providence if you can have him occasionally, as you are likely to be so destitute. I believe him to contend for right things, and to bear many marks of Divine teaching. I do not, however, conceive that he will be permanently attended with crowded congregations.

"I find this busy city very distracting at times to my mind, and am too much carried away by its noise and glare. Yet I walk about its streets as one who has no communion with its busy crowds. I heard this morning old Mr. Wilkinson, near the Bank, preach. He appears to be a good old man, but is very smooth, and would by his preaching take in hundreds. He was speaking about the sin against the Holy Ghost, and almost intimated his belief that it could not now be committed. He is the last left of Romaine's school, and is sound in the letter of truth. The aisle was quite full, and I stood during the whole time. I find there are very few preachers that can really hit the right nail on the head. I saw in the old gentleman's sermon, this morning, abundant places for discrimination and separation from the vile, which he never alluded to. No one that I hear ever insinuates a doubt whether there be such a thing as a counterfeit religion and a false experience. The old gentleman would make the stockbrokers look about them if he talked about forged notes and dishonoured bills. The walls of his church form a part of Capel Court, where the Stock Exchange is situate, and many of his hearers are brokers there. I receive most days invitations to preach, but am compelled to decline them all, as having to speak two evenings at Zoar besides my labours on the Lord's-day. You are looking, no doubt, to Tiptaft's coming among you, and expecting much pleasure and profit both from his preaching and conversation. I shall be very glad to hear that the Lord has blessed him both in the pulpit and the parlour. As I have to speak this evening, allow me to wind up thus hastily by signing myself

"Your sincere and affectionate Friend,

"J. C. P.

"My Christian love to the friends.

"*To Mr. Parry.*"

"*London, June* 12, 1838.

"My dear Friend,

"I received your kind letter safely; and as the wetness of the afternoon allows me a leisure hour, I answer it thus early.

"I have now fulfilled half my engagement at Zoar, and have reason to be thankful for having been helped thus far. I have never, I think, more sensibly felt my unfitness and unworthiness for the pulpit than during my visit to town this time; and this not because I have been altogether left to my own miserable barrenness and nothingness, or because I have been more than usually shut up and restrained. No; I have reason to be thankful that I have been enabled to contend for the things of salvation with such a measure of utterance as is commonly vouchsafed to me. The morning congregation yesterday (Sunday) was very large, and besides the seats and galleries, the aisles were fully occupied, benches being placed up the middle one. I cannot say that I felt much at home. After service I received five different invitations to preach, viz.: at Dunmow, Essex; at Winchmore Hill; at a place on the road to Brighton; at Mr. Fowler's, Gower Street; and for the Aged Pilgrims' Friend Society. Of these I could only accept one, viz., the last, as I find that preaching twice at Zoar on the Lord's-day, giving an exhortation, as they call it—though I make a short sermon of it—on Tuesday evening, and preaching again on Thursday evening, is ample work for my weak chest. On yesterday evening, the congregation was very large, there being a row of standers as well as sitters up the middle aisle, and all the lobby and porch quite full too. Well, you will say, did not old nature swell up and puff at such a sight? Ah, my friend, I had ample valves to let out all this stinking gas. First, I felt that novelty and excitement would draw a congregation, where there was no power from on High; and that a man who would preach a sermon standing on his head, would draw ten times as large a congregation as I. Grimaldi turned preacher would fill St. Paul's to suffocation. Secondly, I felt my ignorance and want of experience, my deep pollution and sinfulness, and utter unfitness and unworthiness to be a teacher and leader of the people. I was enabled, however, to contend for the power of vital godliness, and the attending deficiencies and obstacles of the way, and endeavoured to show that it was no easy or common thing to be a Christian. I particularly aimed my shafts against those who, according to their preaching, were in the third heaven, and yet never spoke of trials proportionate to their faith.

"Mr. Triggs, of Plymouth, was my immediate predecessor, and I am told fills the chapel very much. They say there are but four or five ministers who fill the place, amongst whom they reckon Kershaw, Tiptaft, and my unworthy self. I had almost resolved that I would not break the bread at Zoar this time, but Justins pressed me so warmly, and saying that the friends wished me so much to do it, that I felt I could not decline. I think you know my aversion to putting myself thus prominently forward, and I can say I scarce ever felt more sensibly unfit and unworthy. But my frame was solemnized, and I was enabled to pray and speak with some simplicity. The galleries were nearly full of spectators, and I dare say some remarks which I dropped upon close communion did not suit many. One woman came into the vestry afterwards to set me right, which she failed in doing, though I received her experience, which she told me as a striking one.

"A lady at Kensington, a widow, who has an establishment for twenty-four young ladies, came to me in the vestry last Tuesday, and had an interview with me yesterday. I cannot narrate all her history, but it appears she has been under spiritual exercises for some years. About two years ago a friend put into her hand my pamphlet about the Church of England, which, according to her account, opened her eyes, and drove her out of the Establishment. Not able to find food amongst the Dissenters, she joined a party who met to read and expound the Scriptures. On discovering that some of the party lived in known and justified sin, she left them, and meditated returning to the Church; but a singular coincidence threw 'Winter afore Harvest' into her hands, which decided her never to go back; and learning from the *Gospel Standard* that I was to be at Zoar, she determined to come and see me, and take my advice what to do. Seeing me so young, and, as I suppose, ruddy as youthful David, she thought she could not open her mind to me, till I took a text which had been applied to her mind with power some years ago, and then she determined to come forward and ask my advice how to act. She said she did not mind losing all her scholars if she could but know where to go to hear and what to do. I liked some things she said; but she has been badly nursed. She is quite a lady in her manners and appearance, but says she cares not how mean and poor her companions are, if she could but hear truth. I could give her no advice but to seek counsel of the Lord.

Poor Fowler broke a blood-vessel again on Saturday, and of course could not preach yesterday. The deacons wished me to preach for him to-morrow, but being published here I could not. I thank you for your kind invitation for myself and fair companion, which I hope to accept in due time. I cannot fix exactly the time, as it will depend on our visit to Plymouth. I think of staying in town a week, and then of going to see my mother, but you may depend upon it I will endeavour to give you what time I can. I hope you will write often, as, believe me, I would sooner hear from you than most of my correspondents. I have written a short P.S. to Tiptaft. And now, my dear friend, with my Christian love to friend Dredge and all the friends, from

"Your affectionate Friend,

"*To Mr. Parry.*" J. C. P.

He was married at Oakham, July 24, 1838, and forthwith took his young wife away with him on a visit to his mother, then residing at Plymouth. A few days were spent in the metropolis on their way, whence they took boat round the south coast to their destination. His mother, long desirous of seeing her son married and comfortably settled, received his bride with all the warmth and affection of her loving heart, and her daughters most heartily joined in the friendly welcome.

Whilst staying here he did not once enter the pulpit, but took his place as a hearer under Mr. Triggs. He so strongly desired that his own preaching might be blessed and applied to the hearts of such of the Lord's people as might hereafter be his hearers, that at about this time he would, as often as occasion permitted, embrace the opportunity of sitting under a good and gracious man, and take his place in the pew instead of in the pulpit; thus, he thought, he would find out a hearer's needs, and would henceforth be able to speak more to their hearts from knowing, from self-experience, what were their yearnings, their wants, and their desires.

How deeply he felt his own deficiencies, and how earnestly he desired that the Lord would bless his preaching to the souls of His people, the reader will glean from the following letter written to Mr. Parry during the stay at Plymouth :—

"*Stoke, Devonport, August* 8, 1838.

"MY DEAR FRIEND,

"We arrived here safely, through mercy, on Thursday evening, after a rough passage. . . . I was not sorry to go ashore and leave the steam-vessel and all its disagreeable accompaniments behind. I was thankful, however, at the protection granted by an unseen Hand, when there were so many provocations of the great majesty of Heaven.

"I propose (D.V.) to continue here until about the 23rd inst., when I think of leaving, in order to be at Allington for the last Lord's-day in this month. This will enable me to be with you seven or eight Lord's-days before I take my flight to Oakham and Stamford. I have not heard from Tiptaft since he reached Oakham. I much fear he will not be better unless he consent to lie by for a time and give himself rest. I believe he will give up his Manchester engagement. . . . .

"I am well and deeply convinced that a man can neither distress nor comfort himself, bring his soul into bondage nor deliver it into liberty. The Lord killeth and maketh alive. I often feel as if I were utterly dead in sin and had never received a spark of divine life out of the fulness of the Godhead. I seem as dark, as blind, as earthly, and as sensual as any worldling. I know well that nothing can rouse me out of this state but trials and afflictions, yet my flesh cries out for a smooth and easy path. If I had not at times some breathings after the living God, I must conclude I had not a spark of vital godliness. I am glad to learn that you heard Tiptaft profitably, and hope that you found Smart's testimony blessed to your soul.

"I received a letter the other day from a gentleman, a hearer of mine, in London, in which he said that he had met a gentleman, a hearer of Mr. Huntington's, who expressed himself willing to take a chapel on his own responsibility, with the full conviction that I should raise and keep a congregation in the metropolis. I felt, however, little disposed to attend to any such intimation, knowing my ignorance and weakness, and want of sufficient grace and gifts, experience and power, for the great metropolis. I need to be taught much more deeply and powerfully before I can stand up as a leader of God's people. I am only fit for lispers and stammerers, and inquirers of the way to Zion. I know well what I want, but to get it is out of my power, and I should probably kick and rebel were it even now given me in the Lord's own way.

"I was glad to find that the Lord had opened your heart to sell your corn at a cheaper rate to your workmen than the market price. Nature and reason would sadly cry out against this, but the word of the everlasting God is on your side, and let God be true and every man a liar. Now don't expect any gratitude from those whom you have thus benefited; and if you want to know the reason, call into court a witness named Joseph Parry, and make him an evidence for the prisoners at the bar. He will tell judge and jury what an unthankful wretch he has been, and is, and will declare from his own experience that gratitude is an exotic plant that grows only in the courts of heaven, and that if ever he smelt the fragrance of that heavenly plant, a sprig of it was put into his bosom by the Holy Ghost.

"I hope and trust that friend Dredge and you are walking in sweet union and communion. It is good for brethren to dwell together in unity, though it is only the oil that was poured on the head of Aaron that can reach to the skirt of his clothing and glue together the hems of the garment. And I think and believe that you both would be well content with a name and a place at the Redeemer's feet, however higher others might aim and soar. I feel more united to him than ever. Give him my Christian love, also to Mrs. Wild and all the friends of truth from an experimental acquaintance with it in their hearts. Believe me to be,

"Your sincere and affectionate Friend,

"*To Mr. Parry.*" "J. C. P.

From Plymouth, after a three weeks' stay, they journeyed to Allington, where he was again to resume the duties of his preacher's office. Here, for two months, he ministered as formerly to the lovers of truth who assembled in that small but highly-favoured chapel, and thence returned to fix his home at Stamford. The friends there, neither very numerous nor wealthy, feeling that they alone could not support him in comfort, only asked for his services for alternate Lord's-days, and for one evening service a week, and at the same time expressed a hope that the Oakham friends would consent to compensate him for his services on the remaining twenty-six Lord's-days. To this proposal the latter gladly assented, and thus it was that he became joint minister of the two churches. Fixing his home at Stamford, he spent the greater part of his time there, and contrived, by visiting Oakham each fortnight from Saturday to Wednesday, to give the people there his services on alternate Lord's-day and Tuesday evenings.* Here he continued to minister for six-and-twenty years, till at length, in 1864, his failing health compelled him to seek a warmer air and drier climate nearer London.

But while making the churches at Stamford and Oakham his special care, he did not forget the friends who had received him with open arms when he came fresh from the Establishment, and who had listened to him with affection and welcomed him with Christian love when he had as yet no settled charge; and he made it his custom, when each succeeding summer came, to go on a tour visiting friendly churches, and exhorting them to continue steadfastly in the faith. London generally claimed a month or more of his services, and little Allington always claimed, and always received, another month; other churches were forced to be content with a single Lord's-day, or a week-day evening. But, wherever he went, his visit was always looked forward to with glad expectation, and looked back upon with sweet remembrance. He was one of the four or five ministers who alone could fill the chapel in Great Alie Street, London, and when he was advertised to preach there, there was seldom, even at week-day-evening services, a spare place to be found in the whole chapel; the gallery stairs were crowded by hearers, and not a few were forced to go away, unable to find within sitting or standing room. At Allington, where he had first been kindly listened to when but just freed from the trammels of the Church, his visit was, if possible, regarded with still greater eagerness; not only was the small chapel crammed in basement and gallery, but the aisle was crowded with hearers, and the small plot of ground in front, where they lay the bones of those dear departed ones who have so loved to sit within the chapel in their life, was filled with men and

* During his fortnightly stay at Oakham he was most hospitably entertained by his father-in-law, Dr. Keal, who set apart a room in his house as a study for his own especial use.

women from far distant parts of the neighbourhood, forced to be content with some few words which every now and then floated out through the open windows. The congregation there was gathered from miles around; rough Wiltshire peasants came trudging in from places ten or fifteen miles away, sometimes with their hardy wives, not unfrequently with their children; small farmers drove over in their spring carts across the Wiltshire downs from their far distant farms, and brought their wives and friends with them; and the wealthier came in their phaetons and sociables to join the poor in the worship of God, and hear the words of His servant. And the Lord was pleased to bless his preaching and his prayers to the hearts of many who came to hear him. God had given him gifts, and abilities, and had crowned them with grace; he, as a faithful steward, did not wrap them in a napkin and bury them for safety; but while health and strength permitted he used them for the good of God's people, and made the children of God bless and praise His holy name that He had sent them comfort and exhortation through His servant.

Mr. Philpot's letters to his friends have hitherto been inserted by way of tracing his history down to this time, and our narrative has only been, to use one of his own phrases, the thread on which the pearls are strung. He had been passing through a period of trial and a time of uncertainty, and the letters in which he poured forth his inmost feelings, it was felt would best describe the Lord's dealings with his soul. Being, too, almost our only source of information as to his actions and feelings at this important period of his life, when the seed of grace was sprouting up into full leaf, it would seem as unfair both to their author and to his readers to cull only so much as bears upon his own matters as to insert them with the bulk of his correspondence.

But now that he had obtained a fixed home, round which his earthly hopes centred, his life was less a life of uncertainty. The excitement and interest which his secession from the Church had aroused, had either passed off or had subsided into a fixed love of his character and esteem for his Christian principles. Other churches which had earnestly called upon him to be their minister found themselves forced to be content with an occasional visit from him, and were obliged to give up all hopes of ever obtaining his constant services. Henceforward, during the greater part of the year, we find him quietly and unobtrusively ministering to his two congregations at Oakham and Stamford. First, then, the chief events which came during the quarter of a century that his home was there fixed to disturb his quiet life will be briefly sketched, and the collection of his letters will be reserved for the end of the volume. Inserted, however, in this place is a letter which was written to Mr. Parry after his two months' stay at Allington.

"*Stamford, Dec.* 24, 1838.

"My dear Friend,

"I had been for some time daily expecting to receive a letter from you, and I think, had not your last arrived when it did, I should have written either to you or to friend Dredge to express my wish to learn how matters were going on among my friends in Wilts. You had no need to reproach yourself for having displayed coldness when we parted, as I perceived no such manner; and if I had I should have known that our friendship rested on too firm a basis to be shaken by such a trifle. I am usually much averse to displays of sentimentalism, and would rather meet and part with friendship in the heart than friendship in the hand, tongue, or face. So I hope your conscience will be at ease on this score.

"We may now, I suppose, consider ourselves pretty well settled, though our constant journeys backwards and forwards to Oakham have a great tendency to unsettle us. We go there every alternate Friday, and return the following Wednesday, thus spending five days in every fortnight there, and the remaining nine here. I preach here every Thursday evening, and at Oakham on every alternate Tuesday, making it more laborious than I have been accustomed to for some years. I find, however, through mercy, my strength equal to my day, and have not enjoyed better health for some years. I am glad to find from your letter that you seem to see your signs more than you often have done, and feel the flowings-out of love and affection to the Friend of Sinners. I believe, previous to such a clear and full revelation of Christ to the soul as sets it at full liberty, there usually is such a view of Him through the lattice as causes the affections to flow forth. The Beloved puts in His hand by the hole of the door, and then the bowels are moved for Him. This makes us rise up to open the door, but the Beloved withdraws Himself, and though we call He gives no answer. I believe there is much of this preparatory work before deliverance comes; and though the stall-fed oxen and fat bulls of Bashan must always have oil-cake, and turn away from a nip of wiry grass under the hedge, the famishing calves can eat it with a very good appetite.

"The preaching is usually well attended at both Stamford and Oakham, and I have found it at times good to preach. I will say, however, that I have usually found myself more at home in Allington pulpit than in any other, and think that perhaps I felt myself more unfettered there, as being more accustomed to the people, and able to run on as the thoughts and words came. The people here being less accustomed to my manner and drift, I think cannot follow me so well, and this sometimes checks me in my career. I think I have been heard best on the week evenings, when there is usually a good congregation, as many, perhaps, as there used to be at Allington in the afternoon. I am glad to hear good tidings of Dorcas. I received her experience as a divine one as soon as I heard it, and believe it will stand for ever and ever.

"We had a collection yesterday at our chapel here for the poor, and though the day was wet, and the chapel thin, we collected £23 odd. We are to have a collection at Oakham for the same purpose next Lord's-day, and I hope we shall raise as much there. They call me a good beggar, but I do not consider myself one, and hate to stand pleading for money out of the pockets of skinflints. If I can say a few words in season to God's princely family, it is all well; but I cannot bear to flog the blood from the back of misers. Let their money perish with them; for if they have not a heart beyond their money, they have no treasure in heaven. A covetous Christian is as great a contradiction as a drunken Christian or a Christian adulterer, and the one is as far from heaven as the other. But the old leaven sticks close, and needs the sword of the Spirit to be thrust under the plaster to tear it off. . . .

"I find religion very up-hill work, and am more and more dissatisfied with myself. I seek sometimes to commence at the very beginning, and come to God as if I never came to Him before. I feel like a person who has been badly educated, and who, conscious of the defects of his education, goes back to the very first elements, and seeks to learn them perfectly and understand them thoroughly. And as to my preaching, I am often sick and ashamed of it, so little do I know aright, and so little calculated to point out the way to Zion. It is, however, through ignorance we learn knowledge, and through foolishness wisdom, according to those heavenly paradoxes which you like to hear set forth. If you have not read Huntington's 'Destruction of Death by the Fountain of Life,' you will find it a profitable piece to read in the chapel. The observations about Adam in the beginning might be omitted. There is such a fulness and depth in Huntington's writings that two or three close readings are hardly sufficient, even to inform our understanding, and for spiritual profit and edification they will bear being read again and again. . . .

"Your affectionate Friend,

"*To Mr. Parry.*" "J. C. P.

But while confining his services in the pulpit to two small churches, he began, first about this time, to serve with his pen the whole Church of God in every part, and it was not long before he came more fully into notice as a writer than a preacher. His first publication, "The Letter to the Provost of Worcester College," had sufficiently vindicated his title to a clear and truthful style of writing, and, what was of far more importance, had shown that he had both the power of grasping the most difficult problems, and of making himself easily understood to his readers. The *Gospel Standard*, a monthly publication which had been lately started at Manchester, by the late William Gadsby, as the organ of the Particular Baptists, gave this little work a most friendly reception. "We look upon it," it said, "as a masterpiece, every letter of which ought to be printed in gold, and placed on the table of every conscientious man in the kingdom." We have before alluded to the numerous replies which the letter to the provost had called forth; some of these were manifestly written in a spirit of prejudice, and were only loaded with such senseless abuse as their opponent could well afford to pass over in silence; but there were others who, while treating him in a more Christianlike spirit, yet totally misrepresented his views, and even called his sincerity into question. It was in answer to the latter that Mr. Philpot felt himself bound to publish a second pamphlet, entitled "Secession from the Church of England defended," which forms a valuable supplement to his first defence. Next appeared the two sermons before alluded to, "The Heir of Heaven, &c.," and "Winter afore Harvest," both of which have been much blessed to the doubting, fearing family of God. By this time he had become universally recognised as one of the leading ministers of the Particular Baptists, and as such the reader soon finds his name appearing in the publication already then well known as the expositor of their views—the *Gospel Standard*. At first it was only as a writer of letters to the editors that he contributed to its pages; but these letters, written generally on some doctrinal point, and subscribed with his name, carried with them almost editorial authority. Still was the old cry raised against him, that in his writings, as in his preaching, he was too particular, too severe; some complained that, standing, as it were, on a height alone, he used his efforts to prevent all others from attaining to the same eminence by remorselessly cutting down their every means of support, and hedging about their way with fresh difficulties. If the reader will refer to his correspondence with "a few wretched men," in the fourth volume of the *Gospel Standard*, he will see how thoroughly Mr. Philpot turned the weapon of these complainants against themselves, and how completely he beat down their arguments. By degrees, however, his name began to appear less frequently subscribed to letters to the editors, and yet one generally failed not to recognise his clear and refined style in some one or more unsigned articles in each number of the *Gospel Standard*. From a friendly writer of letters to the editors he came insensibly to enrol himself as one of those whom he had formerly addressed, and to form a portion of the "editorial we." His new occupation entailed upon him a considerable amount of labour, though at the same time, of a kind for which he was undoubtedly well qualified. His fellow workers wisely allotted to him the task of writing reviews of books, a portion of their office at once difficult and invidious. To themselves they, for the most part, reserved the selection of pieces for insertion, though, as we have gleaned from letters of the late William Gadsby, which are still extant, they not unfrequently called upon him to aid them in their decisions; and at times, too, they kindly relieved him of a portion of his duties in writing some few of the reviews. It is gratifying to remember with what love and deference conjoined the first editors and originators of the *Gospel Standard* received him, then almost a tyro in the art of writing for the press, as one of themselves. At the same time, the event proved that they had been wise and discriminating in their choice; nay, it was surely God's hand which led them to receive thus early as an apprentice the man who afterwards, under God's guidance, conducted the magazine with such success as master-workman. The first review which Mr. Philpot wrote, as joint editor, had for its subject John Warburton's "Mercies of a Covenant God," and was inserted in the *Gospel Standard*, April, 1838.

On Mr. Gadsby's death, Jan. 27th, 1844, more work still was thrown upon his shoulders; and, though Mr. M'Kenzie still maintained his post as the chief editor, Mr. Philpot seems to have had the greater share of the work. At length, on the death of the former, Aug. 12th, 1849, he became sole editor of the *Gospel Standard*, and continued so for over twenty years, till the day of his death. No one who has not had some experience in literature can form any idea of the amount of work which the editing of a magazine like the *Gospel Standard* entails. The pieces selected for insertion have to be culled from hundreds, each of which must be carefully read over before it is rejected; the chaff has to be winnowed from the grain, and where there is a great outward resemblance between the golden wheat and the worthless chaff this task is by no means an easy one. And in addition to the writings of others, the wish of the general readers of the *Gospel Standard* was generally gratified by the insertion of some lines from the editor's own pen, either a few pages of "Meditations," or a review, or an address. This, then, combined with the labour of revising proofs, the reader may well imagine formed no sinecure, and only a strong love for the welfare of God's church could have induced him to sacrifice so much of his time for a moderate remuneration; and, indeed, had it not been for the strict method with which he apportioned his time to his various tasks, he could not have undertaken alone the arduous work of editing the magazine.

He was, indeed, very methodical and careful as to the employment of his time, and had he not been so he could never have got through so much editorial work and general correspondence as fell to his lot. It was his custom every morning to read for an hour after breakfast his Hebrew Bible, and from eight to nine o'clock in the evening he devoted to his Greek Testament. His love for languages made these two hours very enjoyable to him, and he allowed, if possible, nothing to curtail this pleasure. The greater part of the forenoon, when his mind was fresh and unwearied, was devoted to his editorial work, and to the revision of his printed sermons. In the middle part of each month this part of his work was especially onerous.

The hour before dinner he set apart for his daily walk—an enjoyment which he seldom allowed himself to forego. It was one, too, which was very necessary for him, not only as imparting renewed vigour to his often overtasked energies, but as giving him a quiet time for thought and meditation. His love of solitude has been already alluded to; but solitude to him was not only an enjoyment, it was a necessity. Every one who has to say and write many original things needs hours of quiet and undisturbed thought. Some men have the power of retreating into solitude, so to speak, even when surrounded by the hum of conversation, and of absorbing themselves in their own meditation amid the noise and prattle of a family. But to a finely-strung mind like Mr. Philpot's entire solitude was necessary. He must have his own sanctum to think alone in, and must have his solitary walk to gain still further abstraction. Many a sermon and "meditation," which are now read with delight by God's people, are the fruit of his quiet lonely walks. His afternoon he usually occupied in calling on the members of his flock to converse on the things of God, or read and pray with them. His evening was employed in further literary labour, and in writing letters to his numerous friends and correspondents. The day was commenced and ended with family prayer. Such is a short sketch of the routine of his duties during the many years he lived at Stamford. It was, however, varied by his fortnightly visits to Oakham, and by his yearly tour among the friendly churches.

Thus, though his labours in the vineyard were directed by strict method, and each recurring year brought the same pastoral cares for his flocks at Oakham and Stamford, and the same general work for his friends abroad, yet was his life no time of ease and quiet; it was ever being ruffled by recurring trials, not the less deeply felt because they were but little seen by the outward observer. At one time he was attacked from without by cruel and harsh words, and by unchristianlike misrepresentations, which we would now willingly bury in oblivion; at another from within, by long wearying illnesses, almost more trying than the former, because they debarred him from his beloved labour in God's vineyard.

In 1845 the Lord permitted him to pass through one of the most heavy and cutting trials that it was his lot to experience. To this we need make no further allusion than to say that he endured the scourge in the truly meek and humble spirit ever so precious in the sight of God, an assertion which his friends at Stamford and Oakham would fully confirm.

In August, 1847, worn out by continuous preaching, his health succumbed to an attack of chronic inflammation of the lungs. He was persuaded by a kind friend, who generously defrayed all expenses, to try the air and water-system of Malvern. Entering a hydropathic establishment, he submitted himself to what is called the water-cure; but this, so far from restoring him to health, only aggravated his disease. After a month of semi-starvation, varied with daily douches, packings, and incessant baths, he left Malvern far weaker than when he first consulted hydropathy; but though weakened in body during this stay, his soul was many times refreshed by the Lord's presence. A month's stay with his mother at Plymouth, under an altered plan of treatment, restored him to a measure of health and strength; but it was not till the spring of 1848 that he was sufficiently recovered to resume his ministerial labours, though he was able to use his pen during the greater part of his eight months' illness.

He was enabled to preach again in April, 1848, but at first only one sermon on the Lord's-day. From this date to the summer of 1864, though often laid aside by repeated illnesses brought on by cold and over-exertion, he continued to labour as before for the Oakham and Stamford churches.

As years went on he had some thought that he would in the end be obliged to leave the cold and bleak town of Stamford for some warmer locality; but it was not until the year 1864 that he found himself forced to come to a final resolution. In the summer of that year, while on a visit to London, under the roof of his kind friends Mr. and Mrs. Clowes, he was seized with a severe attack of illness induced by unremitting exertion. He was attended by Dr. Corfe, who strongly advised him to give up the ministry and remove his home to a drier and warmer part of the country. After some period of uncertainty, Croydon was at length fixed upon as a place which offered the most suitable form of climate, together with that indispensable privilege, the opportunity of attending the means of grace. No one who has not known what it is to break through old ties and long-standing connections, and to transplant himself in old age from a field in which the best years of his life have been well and happily spent, can realise the grief and trouble that Mr. Philpot felt in carrying out this resolution. The bond of union and affection which existed between him, as a faithful pastor, and the kindly churches to which he was attached, was not one which could be torn asunder without causing many tears and much sorrow, and these were not only for the flock which looked forward with apprehension to the future, but no less for the shepherd who had watched over them for so many years. Willingly would he have shortened his life in their service had it been his own to give; uncomplainingly would he have borne renewed illnesses brought on by exertions in their behalf; but he felt, and rightly, that it was not only to his own immediate flock that he was sent, but that his work was equally for the whole Church. We have only to refer our readers to the letters addressed to two of his oldest friends, which are inserted below, and to the farewell sermons (Nos. 80, 81, and 82 of the "Gospel Pulpit") which he preached to his churches, to assure them with what doubts and regrets the course he pursued was environed, and after what earnest prayers and supplications it was accomplished.

"*London, August* 3, 1864.

"MY DEAR FRIEND,*

*　　*　　*　　*　　*

"These continual attacks warn me that I cannot go on labouring as I have done. I cannot sacrifice my health and life, as I certainly shall do if I continue my ministry at Oakham and Stamford. I have a wife and family to think of, and I may add, the Church of God generally, besides the two causes where I have laboured so many years. But I feel convinced I cannot go on as I have done. The climate, too, is too cold for me in winter, and especially in spring; and as every attack weakens me more and more, I am less able to endure it. I shall much feel leaving my people and the friends with whom I have been connected so many years, and no other cause would have induced me to do so. But again and again, and especially of late years, I have been laid aside for weeks together, and it is but a gloomy prospect to look forward to a succession of attacks of a similar nature. At present, my heart, though weak, is not diseased, nor is emphysema in itself a fatal malady; but I have to consider the probable consequences of my repeated bronchitic attacks, and their effect on my constitution. And if these consequences are likely to be very serious, no people could require of me that I should sacrifice not only health, but life itself, for their sake. I should not lay down the ministry if I ceased to minister at Oakham and Stamford, except, perhaps, for a few months this winter and spring, to recover my health, nor should I attach myself to any other people. But occasionally, as the state of my health permitted, I might supply at Gower Street, or any other place. I wish to make it a matter of prayer that the Lord would direct my path; nor do I wish to come to a hasty decision; but, as my year is up at the end of October next, and I cannot stay another winter at Stamford, it is in my mind not to go on beyond that time.

"I have no doubt that my dear friends at Oakham and Stamford, and you and your dear wife amongst the number, will feel much grieved at the decision to which I have been compelled to come. But I have been almost practically useless for some time, and every attack lasts longer and leaves me weaker. I shall have

* The account of his illness, and the opinion of the medical men who had attended and were attending him, is here omitted.

to sacrifice a good part of my income at the very time when I want it most; but I do not wish to be a burden to the friends who have hitherto for so many years liberally ministered to my necessities. Indeed, I am in a strait, and much tried and exercised in my mind, as the step is so important in every way. I have great need of faith and patience, as the trial is exceedingly heavy, spiritually and temporally, in body and soul. None but the Lord, to whom I look, can do me any real good, and He alone must guide, support, and be with me.

"Croydon is the place to which we shall probably move, as there is a chapel of truth there, and the soil and situation are dry and warm. This last attack has much pulled me down, both in flesh and strength. Dr. Corfe advises me to go to Allington for a little change, though I should prefer to come home.

"Our united love to your dear wife, our children, &c.

"Yours very affectionately,

"J. C. P.

"*To W. T. Keal, M.D.,*
"*Oakham.*"

"*London, Aug.* 4, 1864.

"MY DEAR FRIEND,

"I feel that I must write to you on a subject which, I am sure, will much try, not only your mind, but the mind also of many of my dear friends and hearers; and nothing but necessity would compel me to do so.

"I have for some time been convinced that the state of my health, and the repeated attacks of severe illness which I have now had for several years, quite unfit me for the labours which I have undergone at Stamford and Oakham for nearly twenty-six years. I came to London very weak, but was in hopes that the change, as in former years, would do me good. And this was the case for the first two or three weeks; but the Lord was pleased to let a cold fall upon my poor weak chest, and the consequence has been one of my attacks of bronchitis, which has quite laid me aside. Dr. Corfe has attended me, and carefully examined my chest, &c., and says I am not fit for continuous work, and that the climate of Stamford is too cold for me. I will endeavour to procure his opinion in a written expression of it, but I am quite convinced, from a feeling sense of my great bodily weakness, that he is right in his judgment. What, then, must I do? Must I go on till health and life fail together, or adopt such means as, with God's help and blessing, might to some extent preserve both? I have a family to think of besides myself and the Church of God generally; and am I called upon to sacrifice all to the people amongst whom I have so long laboured? I do not see that I am; nor could my friends, though they might be sorry to part with me, demand such a sacrifice. Besides which, my long and severe illnesses make me almost practically useless for weeks and months together; and if this is to increase, I am only a burden to the friends and no benefit. I am much tried on the subject, and am begging of the Lord to guide and direct me; for it is a most important step for me, as well as the people.

I seem, then, brought to this point, that I must resign my pastorship of both my churches at Stamford and Oakham; and, as my year expires in October next, *then* to leave, as I cannot stay at Stamford another winter and spring. You, and my dear friends and hearers, will think this a very hasty and precipitate step, and that I ought to have given you a longer notice. And so I would, had there been any other reason than the state of my health. I shall have to make a very great sacrifice of income, which I can ill afford; but this will prove my sincerity, and that I am not leaving my people for interested motives.

"I am very unwell, and deeply tried. The Lord appear for me in this most painful trial. My love to your wife and the friends.

"Yours affectionately in the truth,

"J. C. P.

"*To Mr. Lightfoot, Stamford.*"

Towards the end of September he came home to take his final farewell of his two beloved flocks. It was very sad parting. Many of his poorer people had looked upon him as their only friend and adviser in heavenly things; they had known him in the vigour and prime of life; he had grown grey amongst them; a family had grown up around him; and they had never, through these long years of service, had cause to murmur against him; for ever kind and gentle, he was never anything but just and true. On taking leave of one of his dear friends at Stamford, she said to him, "What shall I do without you?" His answer was, "You have your Bible; read it, and pray over it." This was his advice to all. He was but the servant; while they had the Master to look up to and cling to, what need had they to fear? It was the same which he had given on another similar occasion, when, thirty years before, he was obliged to leave his flock at Stadhampton. It was a sad lot that twice in the course of his life he had to tear himself away from friends who loved him and whom he loved, to leave old ties and to cling to new ones; but it was God's will, and as such he submitted cheerfully to it. But each time going among new faces, he drew around him earnest and sincere friends, and while he did not forget his old affections, the Lord raised up for him new ones, as happy and as true as the old.

At length, a home prepared for his reception at Croydon, he preached his farewell sermons to sorrowing congregations, and then he left them. But before he left, the kind friends both at Stamford and Oakham presented him with handsome testimonials of their appreciation of his labours amongst them. From the former he received a silver goblet, together with a purse of gold; from the latter, a handsome sum of money, presents especially useful to him at that time, amid the expenses of moving from his old home and entering a new abode.

His physician had not miscalculated when he had assured him greater freedom from illness in a healthier locality. During his first winter at Croydon he did not suffer from his usual attack, and so far was his health improved that he was encouraged to look forward to resuming his pulpit labours at the approach of summer. He found in Mr. Covell a warm and sincere friend, one with whom he could converse with pleasure and profit, and he regarded his frequent visits with great appreciation. In the Croydon hearers he found a friendly and earnest flock, who gave him a cordial welcome whenever he came amongst them. It was his delight, whenever his health permitted, to seat himself under Mr. Covell as a hearer, and sometimes he even found himself strong and well enough to take part in the service, an assistance which both the pastor and his people highly valued.

He still continued to visit his old friends in London, at Allington, and at Stamford and Oakham, during the summer months, and was, by God's blessing, enabled to preach to them, even in the last summer which he spent on earth. But it was noticed by some that his strength was gradually declining. His mental powers were still as strong as ever, and, indeed, may be said only at length to have arrived at full maturity. But his bodily powers were evidently failing. He was more easily fatigued by exertion than he had been but a year or two back. He was forced gradually to shorten the extent of his daily walks, and was often obliged to rest himself while out. It was, indeed, wonderful that one who had been attacked so often by severe illness yet retained strength enough to reach almost to the Psalmist's span of life: or was it not that God having yet work for him to do would not take him to Himself till he had finished it, and could say, with Simeon of old, "Now lettest Thou Thy servant depart in peace!"

During the month of August, 1869, when fulfilling an engagement at Allington, his health gave way, and he had a slight attack of his old complaint, caused more by overwork than by cold. From this he recovered, and he laboured with his pen, as usual, until November 21, when he took cold, and gradually a more severe attack of bronchitis than usual came on, attended with great shortness of breath. On Thursday, the 2nd of December, he felt too ill to leave his bed, and in the evening his eldest son, Dr. Philpot, was written for from London; but, as he had so frequently suffered from these attacks, no serious apprehensions were entertained as to his recovery. He refused to have any further medical advice, but when urged on Tuesday, the 7th, he consented that his dear friend and ever kind physician Dr. Corfe should be requested to call as he passed through Croydon on the Thursday.

From Sunday, the 5th, he suffered at intervals from shortness of breath, which he patiently endured, saying frequently, "O Lord, pity my case;" and "Gracious Lord, mighty to save!" He could not lie down or rest on his right side, and scarcely slept for two nights; but on Tuesday night the bronchitis was so far better that he was able to lie down, and obtained some refreshing sleep, so that on Wednesday morning it was hoped he would recover from this attack, as he had done from so many previous ones. The event proved, however, that it had been too much for his strength. About seven o'clock that evening he appeared very much exhausted, his strength gradually failing, and towards midnight it was evident he was sinking. His children were then called round his bed to take a last farewell of their loved and honoured father. He was perfectly conscious, knowing them all, and calmly bidding them good-bye. His dear wife asked him if he suffered pain. He answered, "No." To his children he said, "Love one another." "Be kind to your mother; she's been a good wife to me, and a good mother to you all." "Follow on to know the Lord." After sending his parting love to various friends by name, and "The friends," his son said to him, "If you have anything to tell us, will you say it now, dear father?" After a pause he said, "Let Covell bury me." The question was asked, "Where?" He answered, "In the cemetery here." After a pause he said, "Goodness and mercy hath followed me all the days of my life." After another pause, during which time his lips moved as if in prayer or in praise, he spoke about his will, and again said, "Goodness and mercy." More was not audible, but his lips moved for some time. He felt the absence of his youngest son (it being too late to summon him from London) and twice he left a loving message for him. The staircase clock striking two, he opened his eyes, and looking at the bedroom dial, said, "I am long going." Then at intervals were caught these last words, "Better to die than to live!" "Mighty to save!" "Mighty to save!" This he said several times. "I die in the faith I have preached and felt." "The blood of Jesus Christ cleanseth us from *all* sin." "O, *if* I could depart, and be with Christ, which is far better!" "Praise the Lord: bless His holy name." His dear ones watched his strength gradually ebbing; and, just before he departed, he looked up earnestly, then closed his eyes, and said, "Beautiful!" His dear wife, who was close beside him, asked, "What's beautiful?" He made no direct answer; but presently said, with his failing voice, "Praise the Lord, O my soul!" These were his last words; and soon after this he gently passed away, at half-past three on the morning of the 9th December, 1869.

He was buried in the Croydon Cemetery, on Thursday, Dec. 16th, by Mr. Covell, assisted in his sad office by Mr. Godwin and Mr. Fred. Marshall, ministers of God's word, who ranked chief amongst the friends of the deceased. As with prayer when living he had entered his new abode but five years before, so with a mournful prayer was all that remained of him on earth borne from it on its way to man's last resting-place. He was followed to the grave by his two sons and a nephew, and by his ever-kind physician, Dr. Corfe. A knot of friends, too, who had once known and revered him, assembled at the door and walked in mournful procession behind the mourning coaches. Wet and stormy as was the day, numbers from all parts of the country had come to see him laid beneath the ground. After a solemn service in the cemetery chapel he was borne forth to the grave. The storm of wind and rain, which had before somewhat abated, now burst forth with renewed force; but it did not deter his friends from pressing round to catch a last glimpse of the coffin that contained all that was left of their dear friend. As it was lowered into the grave Mr. Covell said:—

"Know you not that a great man and a prince is buried this day, proving that all flesh is grass, and the glory of man is as the flower of grass? The gold of acquired literature that our dear departed friend possessed, and the silver of human eloquence to speak it forth, now lies silent in the dust; but John said he 'heard a voice saying, Write, Blessed are the dead which die in the Lord: Yea, saith the Spirit, for they rest from their labours, and their works do follow them.' It is done; the conflict is over; the spirit has fled. Let Zion's children weeping kiss the rod, and gird on their robes of deepest sackcloth. As the husbandman sows his seed in hope of a fruitful crop, so we commit our friend's body to the dust, in sure and certain hope of the resurrection to eternal life. And while we say, 'Earth to earth, and dust to dust,' yet this mortal and corruptible body shall at the archangel's trump be raised immortal and incorruptible, and soul and body be reunited, and be for ever with the Lord, singing 'Salvation to God and the Lamb.'"

Mr. Godwin uttered a solemn benediction, and the mourning friends dispersed.

The funeral address which Mr. Covell spoke was, at the time, so applied to the hearts of the mourning friends, and withal has been felt to be so excellent and true, that this memoir would be incomplete without it. These are his words, as extracted from the *Gospel Standard*:—

"What a solemn reality is death! It is enough to make the infidel and the sceptic alike tremble, and blush, and be filled with confusion; for, apart from the blessed consolations of true religion, there exists nothing which can inspire one with a holy confidence in meeting with the grim tyrant. Man dies by various diseases; but few people find the real cause. If men would but turn to Holy Writ, they would find 'sin entered, and death by sin, and that death has passed upon all, for all have sinned.' And so, dear friends, nothing but death will remove sin from the child of God. Death, as I have said, is enough to make the scoffer and the mere professor tremble. A sound creed, a consistent life, being the member of a church, will avail nothing at death. Death sweeps all these away; but a living union to the blessed Son of God will enable the believer to swallow up death in victory, and to hail the approach of the grim tyrant as a release from the troubles and trials of earth to the joys and serenity of heaven. Look to it, sinner! Look to it, mere professor! Thou art united in the bonds of a living faith to the Redeemer, or to the world. Death will dissolve all partnerships—the partnership of the husband with the wife, the parents with the children, the brother with the brother, the friend with the friend, the holy with the unholy; but with a living union to the Son of God there is no separation. The death of our dear friend is a warning voice, speaking to all the children of God. It is a warning voice, telling us to have our loins girded, our shoes upon our feet, and our lamps burning, like servants waiting for their lord; and when He shall appear, we shall have nothing to do but to obey his summons, and say, 'Come, Lord Jesus!' What a union is that which exists between soul and body! The soul is immortal, the body is of the earth, and both are held together by the breath of our nostrils, which, if suspended for one moment, dissolves the union. How slender is the thread by which we are bound to life! Sleepless nights, weakness of body, the care of physicians and friends, are all terminated by the suspension of breath. What may have been with us a struggle for months, nay, years, is terminated by death in one moment. Death is a blessed exchange for the true Christian; but let the mere professor turn from his perversity, and let him pray God to enable him to consider his latter end. In the case of our dear friend death put him near to Jesus Christ—the best position he ever had. How many sicknesses, how many recoveries and relapses he had are known to his friends, but death terminated the work in an instant; and from that there is no relapse. He can become sick no more; his racking cough has ceased to trouble him, his weakness has left him. Oh! what a friend to him was death! On earth he had in his own soul the substance of future joys, and he realises now the truth of the Scripture and the declaration of God, that He will satisfy the desires of the righteous: He shall no more travail with pain, he shall suffer no more corruption; and thus, I repeat, death proved his best friend, in carrying him into the arms of the Son of God.

Our good friend had three birthdays, and these all must experience if they ever reign with God in heaven. The first was, when he was born into a world of sin and sorrow, and when the hearts of his parents were filled with gladness; but he was conceived in sin, and shapen in iniquity. The next birthday was when he was born of the Spirit, and was made alive to God by Jesus Christ. The last birthday was on the 9th of December, when he dropped this mortal flesh, and the heaven-born spirit ascended to the Father of Mercies and the God of Love. He was at the first birth led captive by the devil; sin ruled, and ruled so as to lead him captive by its power, and conquered him by its prevailing influence. At the next birth sin became a servant, for the master was the love of Christ, which led him to aspire to eternal things. At the last birth, sin was nothing, for, despite its power, he entered into glory, and into the never-dying love of Christ. You all know what it is to have the first birth; would to God that all had felt the blessed experience of the second! If there are any here who have not known what it is to be born of the Spirit, I beseech you to consider the matter. You have come here to follow the remains of our dear friend to the tomb; but what an unspeakable mercy it would be were you able to follow him in faith, to follow him in truth, to follow him to eternal glory, to walk in the footsteps of the dear departed. The Holy Ghost tells us, 'Whom He did foreknow, them He also called.' Then the first step to heaven is being called—called from darkness to light, and from the power of Satan unto God. When God said, 'Seek ye My face,' the heart's response of our dear friend and brother was 'Thy face, Lord, will I seek.' His next step was repentance for sin. 'Oh!' he used to say, 'what a filthy thing is sin! What mischief there is in it!' And so, like our dear friend, we should be animated by a hatred for sin and turn from it. But our trust must not be in ourselves. Like our dear friend, we must look to God to free us from sin, and say, as he often said—

'Other refuge have I none,
Hangs my helpless soul on Thee.'

He knew what it was to have peace in his conscience, and peace in every respect, because he knew what it was to be reconciled to God by the death of His Son. Not only did he have faith, but the witness of the Holy Ghost. 'The Spirit itself beareth witness.' He had the witness in his heart: 'For if we believe the testimony of man, the testimony of God is greater;' and 'There are Three that bear witness in heaven—the Father, the Word, and the Holy Ghost; and there are three that bear witness on earth—the Spirit, the water, and the blood.' The Spirit bore witness to his heart that he was a child of God. Blessed man! Happy man! He has now entered into glory, and realised what his soul longed to obtain. But we are told of the 'fruits of the Spirit,' and those fruits in him were humility, meekness, and other Christian graces, whereby the world took knowledge of him that he had been with Jesus. These were some of the steps in which he walked Zion, ward, until at last he reached the destined place, singing, 'To Him that loved me and washed me in His own blood, to Him be glory, might, majesty and dominion.'

"Let us look at him in his earthly career, and see what the

grace of God made him. I am not here to extol the man, but I am to extol the faith in which he lived, and in which he died. He was a man of like passions with ourselves, and had feelings and infirmities appertaining to sinful flesh; but what he was besides, was by the grace of God. He would say, 'Not to myself, but to God do I owe everything;' and it was that grace that made him the man he was in all his relationships in life; and 'if any child of God lack grace, let him ask of God, and it shall be given;' for our Heavenly Father has no partiality: nor is there in His character a shadow of turning.

"If we look at our departed friend as an editor, we shall find him exemplifying, in his own life, those Christian graces for which he was so distinguished. How many pens were employed against him, and how many bitter words were used! As far as they touched himself, he passed them by: but when doctrine was assailed, with what vigour, a masterly vigour, did he tear the arguments to pieces, expose error, and defend the truth! As an editor, he had opportunities of glorifying his own name; but, except when absolutely necessary, his name never appeared. He sank his individuality in the ennobling principles for which he contended. If we look at his writings, and his meditations, we look at something that will speak even now that he has gone. How ably he exposed error, how aptly he answered perplexing questions, how he made difficult things plain, I need not say. Thousands living have been benefited by him, and, perhaps, it is not too much to say that thousands now dead have in their time been the same.

"If we look at him as a preacher, how bold he was in declaring truth, how masterly was his manner of dealing with Scriptural passages! Thousands have hung upon his lips. It was but to proclaim his name, and the edifice in which he was to preach would be filled.

"If we look at him as a Christian, we shall find him very low in his own esteem. If you had seen him as often as I have, you too could have borne testimony to the tears and the sorrows he manifested for sin. And yet, as I have said, he had an inward peace in believing which stamped him as a true child of God.

"As a husband, how kind, how affectionate he was! The bereaved knows that, and for her our deepest sympathies are excited in her sad affliction.

"As a father, O how anxiously and constantly did he strive for the temporal and spiritual welfare of his children!

"As a friend, I can bear testimony, from a long intercourse, to his courteous and affable manner. It might have been somewhat hard to find a place in his heart, but, once found, confidence was not easily destroyed. It must ever be a source of satisfaction to me that he declared that he enjoyed my ministry. Again and again has he expressed how thankful he was to God for bringing him to Croydon.

"His labour now is o'er, and earthly things with him have come to an end. He is now absent from the body, but he is present with the Lord, and is singing the song of Moses and the Lamb. So may we be followers of him who, through faith, now inherits the promises, and may the desire come from the inmost depths of our soul, 'Let me die the death of the righteous, and let my last end be like his.'"

The truthful estimate which his dear friend Mr. Covell gave of Mr. Philpot's character, in the address just quoted, needs but little amplification: those who lived with him in his own house, who saw him alike in his joys and in his sorrows, who ministered by his sick bed, and saw his patient sufferings, who were with him in health, and experienced his kindness, and bowed to his wise and just decrees, can add but little more. Retiring as he often was with strangers, to them he was everything that heart could desire: strict, but kind; distributing friendly cautions and mild reproofs, where there was need of them, but never withholding praise when praise was due. Over his children, while yet young, he exercised a just but kind authority; when grown up he made them look upon him rather as a friend—a friend, too, of such sort as they can never replace; taking pleasure in their joys, and sympathising in their sorrows. Wisely in them did he implant both respect and love, so wisely that obedience to him became at once the highest of duties and the best of pleasures. Though by natural disposition reserved, especially in the presence of strangers, yet where he saw one whose character he could admire, and whose conversation he found edifying, reserve was soon broken through, and he became the kindest of friends and the best of companions. Possessed of great insight into character, he could read, almost at a glance, the minds of those with whom he was brought in contact: and thus, perhaps, it arose that some have blamed him as cold, proud, and reserved; while others have felt for him the deepest love, have delighted in his converse and companionship while living, and have shed tears over his grave when dead. Happily, the latter were numerous among God's people; the former class could almost be counted: they were few, and for their opinion he cared but little. He could afford to hear a few harsh words, could bear a few cruel calumnies, where he found love and esteem so general.

Many of his choicest friends have remarked that conversation with him was singularly edifying; he could not bear to give his time to that which was only trifling. In speaking upon Scripture, or of experience of the power of the word upon the soul, he was truly at home: ever instructive and excellent, one could not but be struck with his marked clearness in discriminating a real spirit-wrought work of grace upon the soul, and the devil's counterfeit of the same. At the same time, his conversation was cheerful, his intercourse sincere and confidential, and his advice on divine subjects so clear and decisive that one felt he could rely upon it. He was most tender and sympathising towards the afflicted and bereaved, as many can testify whose beds of sorrow he has comforted, or into whose aching hearts he has whispered the words of hope and consolation. With them there was nothing which lay in their path too small to reach his open ear or touch his feeling heart.

Amid this earnest care for the welfare of God's people he did not forget their temporal benefit. No one will ever know the sums that he expended in charity, because the heart which gave, and in many cases the hand which received, have passed for ever from this earth. But many have heard of his free-handedness, and some still live who have experienced it. He was systematic in his almsgiving, would thoroughly know the character of the recipient before he gave, but nothing delighted him more than to help the temporal needs of the poor saints on earth. From the first he took great interest in the Aged Pilgrims' Friend Society, and gave that estimable institution, not only his own support, but prevailed on many of his friends to add theirs also to the good cause. He often preached on behalf of this Society, and obtained goodly collections in aid of its funds, and he was enabled himself to distribute among those poor Christians whom he could recommend a portion of the funds which were contributed by his means. This he did by receiving the votes of those who subscribed through him, and those which his own preaching gained for him, and by conferring them on those poor friends whom he knew from experience to be deserving objects of the charity. In this way he generally was successful in placing on the list of pensioners one or more "aged pilgrims" each year.

Amongst his own people he was a most kind and affectionate pastor, gentle and forbearing almost to a fault, ever ready to praise, ever loth to reprove. In his intercourse with them he had the simplicity of a child, and in their church meetings would often say with the greatest humility, "My dear friends, exercise your own judgment; I have only one voice amongst you." Ever careful and judicious in receiving church members, he would have them first well proved, and known and commended to the people, so that when he had once received them he could walk with them and hold them up firmly and affectionately. The earnest solicitude which he manifested for the best interests of the people, whose pastor and friend he had been for twenty-six years, when he bade them farewell at their last church meeting, will never be erased from their memory. Speaking in the words of the Apostle, 1 Thess. ii. 13, he appealed to their conscience:—"For this cause, also, thank we God without ceasing, because when ye received the word of God which ye heard of us, ye received it not as the word of man, but, as it is in truth, the word of God, which effectually also worketh in you that believe."

His forbearance and meekness under afflictions, both temporal and spiritual, have already often been alluded to in the course of this narrative. Under one particular trial it was said to him, "How can you bear this as you do?" "I am fully assured," he replied, "that if the enemy could make me return as I have received, the Lord's honour would be tarnished, and it would weaken or belie my ministry. I do ask the Lord, as did the Psalmist (xli. 10) to raise me up, that I may requite them; that is, by prayer for my persecutors I may heap coals of fire upon their heads, and the Lord may bless me by turning it into my own bosom."

A few words regarding Mr. Philpot's character as a preacher. His chief distinguishing mark was his simplicity; he so adapted his words and his arguments that the most simple-minded among his hearers, and even children, could listen to him with interest. He had a most remarkable talent for applying similes and analogies from nature and from the affairs of every-day life to heavenly things. And by this means he made the most abstruse points in our most holy faith easily comprehended to the simplest intellects. But he rarely spoke from the pulpit of doctrinal points or entered into those questions in theology which have caused such feuds and divisions in the church in all ages. Valuing above all things the heaven-taught experience of each true Christian, he preferred to treat rather of experimental than doctrinal truths. For this he has often been severely censured, but inconsiderately and without true cause. He made it his mission to cheer the poor downcast family of God, rather than to trouble their minds and hedge their path with abstruse difficulties. The mere professor can, and often does, know the points of the Christian belief perhaps more accurately than the true child of God, just as the Pharisees of old were best versed in the minutest regulations of the Mosaic dispensation; but it is the true heartfelt experience, the love he feels toward God, the sweet manifestation of God's presence that he enjoys at times, which form the salient point of distinction between the real Christian and the barren professor. It was this point on which Mr. Philpot especially insisted, and following it up in his preaching, he was able to cheer onward the one, and cut away the false props of the other, perhaps more successfully than any minister of God's word had done before. This will account for the murmurs which often arose against him, and to which frequent allusion has been made in the preceding pages. Many, like "the few wretched men," rose up in arms against what they called his pride and self-sufficiency; but those who had felt the work of grace upon the heart like himself, formed a truer estimate of his character as a preacher and as a man. Before leaving this subject, one can hardly refrain from a few words as to his talent for *extempore* preaching. This was very extraordinary; his mind was so clear, and he had so well arranged what he was to say, that he seldom lost the thread of his argument or wandered from his text. At the same time, his words were so well chosen, his sentences so simple and concise, and his arrangement of his subject so lucid, that his sermons were often published even without a verbal emendation; and they lost but little of their original power when read aloud to other congregations.

The points which distinguished his preaching he carried, for the most part, also into his writings, with the exception that the care that he was enabled to bestow upon them, and the undisturbed quiet in which he thought over and wrote them, gave him the opportunity of being, if possible, more logical and correct, while they did not interfere with his usual simplicity of demonstration. In these he allowed himself to treat more of doctrinal truths, especially in his work on the "Eternal Sonship," and in his meditations on "Our Most Holy Faith." This too, rightly, because people can give more earnest attention to that which stands in black and white before their eyes, than to those sentences which flow from the lips of a fluent preacher.

There now only remains to give a short account of Mr. Philpot's literary labours. From the time of his settlement at Stamford up to within a week of his death, with health never strong, and often in spite of severe illness, he engaged himself unremittingly in literary pursuits. His connection with the *Gospel Standard*, and the load of work which it threw upon his shoulders, has already been described; but toilsome as this was, he did not flinch from engaging his pen in other labours. Of these, the revision of his sermons was the most important. Those two, to which allusion has already been made, "The Heir of Heaven," &c., and "Winter afore Harvest," published as they were at the special request of his friends, and written from memory months after they had been uttered from the pulpit, are not so characteristic of his style of preaching as many of his later ones. It is in these, and especially in those of them which were addressed to his dear churches at Oakham and Stamford, that we can now best realise and recall what he was as a preacher.

It was not vanity in his case which first led to the publication of his sermons; it was only a very general demand for them amongst the people of God, which induced him to consent to it. This feeling, expressed as soon as he became at all widely known as a preacher of God's truth, first met with a response in the summer of 1840, during which year nine sermons of his preached in London, at Allington, and at Leicester, were taken down by Mr. J. Paul, and published in the series known as the "Penny Pulpit." The publication of these was continued at intervals during the years 1840 to 1844, fifty-six sermons in all appearing in this series. They were for the most part short, often not extending over more than eight pages, nor had they in many cases the advantage of revision by their author; but, incomplete as they were, they met with such general favour that many of them passed through several successive editions, and thus an opportunity was given to Mr. Philpot to revise and correct them.

It was the style of the preacher, no less than the weighty truths which he uttered, which secured for his sermons such approbation, for they were one and all so simple and uninvolved that they were easy of comprehension to the most untaught reader, and at the same time, were well fitted for the reading-desk in chapels which at times could not obtain the services of a minister.

In July, 1843, a fresh series of Mr. Philpot's sermons appeared in the "Zoar Chapel Pulpit." Some of these were identical with those which were then being introduced in the "Penny Pulpit," but the former series continued to be published for some years after his sermons ceased to appear in the latter. These were all revised by the author, but as they have now been long out of print, they are, in compliance with a very general demand, being reprinted in the series known as the "Gospel Pulpit." This last series is the one in which the most complete, and perhaps the best, of Mr. Philpot's sermons appeared. The "Zoar Chapel Pulpit" had been discontinued in 1851, on the death of the reporter and publisher, and during the following six years, only a few sermons appeared, in a new publication, the *Gospel Ministry*. But in 1857 an arrangement was made with Mr. Ford, of Stamford, to report and publish a sermon on the first day of each month. This series, the "Gospel Pulpit," was commenced in November, 1857, with the sermon entitled, "The Spirit of Power, of Love, and of a Sound Mind." The rapidity with which the first few hundred copies of this sermon were sold quite astonished the publisher, and a second edition was hurriedly printed, to disappear almost as quickly.

A success so obvious encouraged Mr. Ford to continue the series, which had been inaugurated almost as an experiment; and at the commencement of each month a new sermon was issued from the publisher's office. By degrees the monthly sermon came to be looked upon by many as an institution, and, going hand in hand with each month's *Gospel Standard*, was soon looked forward to by many of the friends with similar interest and expectation. Thus directed by the same master hand, these two friendly publications held on their course together, until the mouth which uttered the one, and the hand which penned the other, were silenced by the cold grasp of death. Then it was found that God, in His providence, would raise up others to carry on the *Gospel Standard*. "But what," asked many anxious friends, "what will become of the sermons?" A few MS. sermons remained in the reporter's hands, which Mr. Philpot had not revised, and these were first published untouched; and then, as has been already mentioned, it was proposed that the "Zoar Chapel Pulpit" series should be reprinted. These are now appearing, and in God's providence will appear for some months and years yet to come, and then, if we may look forward so far into the future, there are still in our possession a few MS. sermons, taken down by various reporters, which may prolong the series till our material is quite exhausted. We have thus briefly sketched the history of Mr. Philpot's published sermons up to the present time, and have even presumed to carry it on hopefully into the future.

Though many admire the freshness and vigour of the earlier sermons, for our part we incline to the opinion that the last series contains the best ones; and it is in the very last numbers of the "Gospel Pulpit," in those few sermons which he preached in the summer months of his declining years, and which were the fruit of a whole winter's meditation, that we must look for those points by which he was most especially characterised in his office as preacher. On the whole, no one can deny that his utterances of the last twelve years, taken down by the accurate pencil of Mr. Ford, and all of them revised and most carefully reconsidered by himself, form a most valuable mine of experimental truth and teaching; and biassed as we are by our great love for his name, we think we are justified in expressing a sincere belief that they will be read, pondered over, and cherished, long after the present generation has passed away.

The nature of Mr. Philpot's duties, as editor of the *Gospel Standard,* together with the revision of his sermons, left him but little time for other original works. In two cases, however, a series of his editorial articles, originally written for the *Gospel Standard,* were, in accordance with a general wish, republished under his name. The first of these, entitled "The True, Proper, and Eternal Sonship of the Lord Jesus Christ, the Only-begotten Son of God," appeared in 1861, and was almost the only work which was contributed by him to doctrinal controversy. For our part, we must say we do not regret that he did not devote more of his time to controversial writings; though ever ready to come forward as a champion of God's truth when any essential point of faith was involved, he will be remembered with far greater love and admiration as he strove with earnest zeal to "bring again that which was driven away, and bind up that which was broken, and strengthen that which was sick" amongst God's sorrowing family on earth. But, standing alone as it does, it is sufficient to vindicate his claims as a controversialist, and its success in virtually closing the protracted controversy which gave rise to it, proclaims the blessing which God associated with it.

"The Advance of Popery in this Country, viewed under both its Religious and Political Aspect," was the second work reprinted from the *Gospel Standard,* and it appeared but a few months before his death. The subject was one in which he had always felt a deep interest. His essay on it cost him hours of laborious research, brought into requisition all his vast stock of learning, and called for the most careful exercise of his now fully-ripened judgment. Its success was commensurate with its merits, and its wide circulation was most gratifying to him, as showing how generally his labours had been appreciated.

Just before the publication of "The Advance of Popery," &c., appeared one of his most interesting labours, "The Memoir of William Tiptaft," his dear friend and fellow-labourer, excellent as a biography, because he so completely merged his own individuality in his description of another. It was a truthful and unbiassed account of the dead, by one who, as his dearest friend, was the best qualified to write it, and we can hardly tell whether the absorbing interest which it excites is most due to the work and character of Tiptaft himself, or to the charm with which the pen of the writer invested them.

Many of God's servants have, in the course of a long and active life, preached many more sermons, and written more voluminous writings than our dear departed friend, but he, like the poor woman who anointed the Lord at Bethany, "hath done what he could" (Mark xiv. 6). Those energies and those talents which his Father in heaven had given him he devoted fully to the service of his Master. Many have left behind them a greater name, but few have left so sweet a memory in the hearts of their friends. A child of God could hardly wish for a more blessed lot than to be, like him, engaged in his Master's service till the summons came which should take him from earth and land him amidst the saints in heaven. For the blessings which his toil and tribulation have conferred on the family of Christ be given praise and gratitude from us—where they are due—to the Lord God of Sabaoth.

LETTERS

LETTERS

I—To Mr. Parry

Stadhampton, April 19*th,* 1834.

My dear Mr. Parry,

Our mutual friend Tiptaft informed me a few days ago of his visit to Allington, and of your wish to hear from me. So dark, ignorant, and benighted is my mind, that if I were to give you a view of what is doing in the chambers of imagery, it would afford you but little pleasure or profit. The first time that I saw you, as we were standing in the churchyard together, I think I observed that I knew more of the dark than of the bright side of religion, and I feel it to be so still. I cannot, like some professors, make to myself wings to soar when I please to the third heaven, nor kindle a fire and compass myself about with sparks, and then walk in the light of it. I am obliged to come to this: "Behold He shutteth up a man, and there is no opening." "When He hideth His face, who can behold Him?" Some of our professors here can always lay hold of the promises, and so strong is their faith, that they neither doubt nor fear; but this is a religion which I cannot come up to. And when I see that this faith of theirs is the work of man, and born of the flesh, I tell them that I would sooner have my unbelief than their faith. Not that I think unbelief and darkness good things, but this I learn from them, which few know in our day, that faith is "the *gift* of God"; and this, too, I know, that the feeling sense of our own helplessness and unbelief, is the necessary, yea, the only preparation of the soul for the inward discovery and manifestation of Christ. We have, in our day, too many spiritual thieves and liars. They first get their assurance by climbing over the wall, and then "boast themselves of a false gift," which, as Solomon says, is "like clouds and wind without rain," *i.e.*, has all the appearance of watering our souls, and then goes off without giving them a drop. From such a religion may the Lord keep us. It is better to be of a humble spirit with the lowly, than to divide the spoil with the proud. It is better to sigh and mourn over a heart full of unbelief and corruption, than to take to ourselves one promise which the Lord does not apply. Many will tell us to believe, and say, "Ye are idle, ye are idle," who have never been in the iron furnace, nor sighed out of the low dungeon. I believe, for myself, that the souls which can really and spiritually rejoice in the Lord are very few, and that their experience is very much chequered with seasons of darkness and distress. And as for that religion which tells us we must rejoice, because believers are told in the Bible to rejoice always, it savours to me too much of man's power and free will to be of God. The religion which I want is that of the Holy Ghost. I know nothing but what He teaches me; I feel nothing but what He works in me; I believe nothing but what He shows me; I only mourn when He smites the rock; I only rejoice when He reveals the Saviour. I do not say I can rise up to all this, but this is the religion I profess, seek after, and teach; and when the blessed Spirit is not at work in me, and with me, I fall back into all the darkness, unbelief, earthliness, idleness, carelessness, infidelity, and helplessness of my Adam nature.

Religion is a supernatural and mysterious thing. It is as much hidden from us, until God reveals it, as God Himself, who dwelleth in the light which no man can approach unto. It is the work of the Holy Ghost from first to last; and no text is truer than this: "No man knoweth the Son, but the Father; neither knoweth any man the Father, save the Son, and he to whomsoever the Son will reveal Him." He will have mercy on whom He will have mercy, and He will have compassion on whom He will have compassion; and these favoured objects of mercy, and these alone, know the only true God, and Jesus Christ whom He hath sent; and that happy soul which is thus experimentally taught of the Holy Ghost, and brought into a heavenly fellowship with the Father and the Son, will enjoy for ever the Triune Jehovah, when professors, high and low, doctrinal, experimental, and practical, Calvinist and Arminian, will be cast into the blackness of darkness for ever. A man thus experimentally taught will be humble and abased, will be swift to hear and slow to speak, will have a tender conscience and a godly fear, will seek rather to please God than man, and would sooner speak with God for five minutes than with a frothy professor for an hour. This religion I am seeking after, though miles and miles from it; but no other will satisfy or content me.

I cannot say I am at all nearer leaving my post here than when I last wrote; indeed, whilst I am heard with acceptance, and have nothing to perform which presses on my conscience, I cannot move till I see my way. I am praying to be delivered from a carnal system, but my way out seems at present hedged up. Let me have your prayers that I may see my way clearly, and neither run before I am called out, nor stay after I hear the warning voice. I can't move just when and as I please, but must wait for the pillar and the cloud.

Give my Christian regards to ——, and believe me to be,

Yours affectionately, in Jesus Christ,

J. C. P.

II—To Mrs. Rackham

Stadhampton, Dec. 12, 1834.

My dear Mrs. Rackham,

Having an opportunity of sending a letter to town, I avail myself of it to redeem my promise of writing to you. You are now, doubtless, thoroughly settled in your new abode, and in some measure reconciled to your mode of life. The noise and bustle of Rochester must have seemed very strange to you at first, and I dare say you have often turned in thought to your former quiet abode, where almost the only noise was from the brook that ran by your window. But if faith is in exercise, the hand of God will be seen in this change. And besides, what really matters it where we spend the few years of our pilgrimage below? God is to be found, known, loved, and served as much in all the stirring noise of a town as in the seclusion of a country village. His abode is in the heart, according to His promise, "I will dwell in them, and walk in them," 2 Cor. vi. 16. Thus, also, He speaks in the following passages, to which you can easily refer: Exodus xxix. 45; Leviticus xxvi. 11, 12; Isa. lvii. 15; Zech. ii. 2. But you will say, "Would indeed it were so with me! would I could have the Lord God to dwell in me and walk in me!" If we look to our own fitness, we must say with Solomon of old (1 Kings viii. 27), "Will God indeed dwell on the earth? behold the heaven and heaven of heavens cannot contain Thee; how much less this house that I have builded?" If God indeed dwells with any soul, it is only through the Son of His love that He does so. As to us, "all our righteousnesses are as filthy rags, from the sole of the foot even unto the head there is no soundness in us, but wounds, and bruises, and putrefying sores." "As a fountain casteth forth her waters (Jeremiah vi. 7), so we cast out our wickedness." And in our hearts—I speak from experience—there is nothing to be found by nature but pride, unbelief, worldliness, idolatry, infidelity, and sensuality. It is a cage of unclean birds, a nest of scorpions, and often seems to realise John's description of Babylon (Rev. xviii. 2), "the habitation of devils, and the hold of every foul spirit." In ourselves, then, we shall ever be vile and sinful, and utterly unfit that Jehovah should dwell in us and walk in us. If we are acceptable to God at all, it is only so far as we are "accepted in the Beloved." The Holy Ghost describes the Church (Ezekiel xvi. 5) as "cast out in the open field, to the loathing of her person, in the day that she was born." This is our state by nature. But then it adds, verse 8: "Now when I passed by thee, and looked upon thee, behold, thy time was the time of love." There is nothing beautiful or comely in man to attract the notice of the Lord. No; on the contrary, he is vile and loathsome in His sight. Love, on the part of God, is free, as He says (Hos. xiv. 4), "I will love them freely." And it is from this free, eternal, sovereign, and unalterable love on His part, and not from any goodness or fitness on theirs, that He spreads His skirt over any poor soul (Ezek. xvi. 8), and enters into covenant with it. But you, or rather your unbelieving heart, will say, "This is not for *me*." But, why not for *you?* Are you not a poor, helpless, sin-burdened creature? Are *you* not without hope, and without help? Well, these are the persons for whom this free salvation is appointed. "He hath filled the hungry with good things, and the rich He hath sent empty away." "The wine and milk of the gospel is without money and without price." If you are weary and heavy laden, Jesus speaks to *you*, and invites *you* to come to Him, Matt. xi. 28. I know well what an unbelieving heart is, and how it always takes part against us, and writes up bitter things; but still I would encourage you "to hope," like the father of the faithful, "against hope;" yea, "to hope to the end for the grace that is to be brought unto you at the revelation of Jesus Christ," 1 Peter i. 10.

Your trials, doubtless, are many, and I dare say at times you are well-nigh ready to sink under them. But these are the appointed lot of the true children of God. There is a needs-be for all their temptations, crosses, and afflictions, as Peter speaks, 1 Peter i. 6, 7. It gives me pleasure to learn that you have met with a profitable ministry. I hope your present minister will *wear well.* It is one thing to hear profitably for a short time, and another to find a living spring in the minister's soul for a long time together, so as to minister grace and good to the children of God. I should advise you to be slow in forming any connection, either with a church as a member of it, or with professors in general. The best are the hardest to find out, and the most obtrusive are likely to be those whose religion lies more in word than in power. If the Lord sees good He can raise up for your comfort Christian friends, but it is best for a stranger like yourself to wait, than form acquaintances which you must afterwards give up. We are going on here much as usual. "My leanness, my leanness, woe unto me!" seems to be the general cry. But, indeed, from the shortness of the days and my liability to cold I have not been able to see much of the people lately. S. Hall seems to be a little revived from her deadness, though she is still full of complaints, and often speaks of you with affection. Indeed, I trust we all remember you with affection, and regret your departure. You mention, I think, in one of your letters, your thanks to me for having taught you much of the evil of your heart. I could wish I had been enabled to have taught you as much or more of Christ. We have two lessons to learn, one full of pain, the other full of pleasure. The first you have been learning, hitherto, in a small measure. The second, which consists in the experimental knowledge of Christ, is that which you have still to learn. And as you learn to know the cleansing, healing, purifying efficacy of His blood, love, grace, and righteousness, so will your heart rejoice with joy unspeakable and full of glory. Whatever some may say about experimental ministers building up their people in doubts and fears, I do not believe it is so. They are no enemies to gospel joy, if it be joy of the right sort and obtained in a right way. They are, indeed, enemies, and so may they ever be, to rotten hopes and false assurances; but when they see a heart truly broken and contrite, they love to see it healed by the great Physician. Though I have advised you to be slow to form religious friendships or even acquaintances, still if you can in your vast population find a few humble souls who are experimentally taught sin and salvation, it would be profitable for you sometimes to converse with them. Our cold, dead heart needs refreshing, and "as iron sharpeneth iron, so a man sharpeneth the countenance of his friend." But seek the Lord in solitude, as David of old; "commune with your own heart upon your bed, and be still." The food which Christ gives is called "hidden manna," and the new name written on the white stone, no man knoweth, saving he that receiveth it (Rev. ii. 17). One spiritual believing view of Him in secrecy and in solitude is far better than to talk of Him with the tongue, and to hear of Him by the hearing of the ear for a twelvemonth. He will give you such visits as He sees good for you, and I believe you will generally find them before trouble, or in trouble, or after trouble.

Our assemblies at church and lecture have been fairly well attended of late, especially the latter. What we need is to be endued with power from on high. We need showers of blessing to make our hard hearts soft and our barren hearts fruitful. When He is present with us, all is well; when He is absent, all is ill. Believe me to be, my dear Mrs. R.,

Your sincere and affectionate Friend,

J. C. P.

III—To Mr. Parry

London, June 7, 1839.

My dear Friend,

I have felt desirous for several reasons to write to you before the time arrives when I hope to see you again in person at Allington. I cannot, however, precisely fix the time when I intend (D.V.) to visit my Wiltshire friends, owing to a cause which I doubt not you will be sorry to hear. Coming up outside the coach from Welwyn has been the cause, under God's designing wisdom, of giving me a severe attack on my chest, such as you have witnessed at Allington in times past, and from which I have been for some time mercifully free. I was able to preach twice last Lord's-day at Zoar; but in the evening with great inconvenience, through hoarseness, which, indeed, I sensibly felt in the morning. I have been confined to the house ever since, and, indeed, for most of the time to bed, but am, through mercy, slowly mending. I have been obliged to write to the deacons at Zoar to decline preaching in this week and on Lord's-day next. It gives me pain thus to disappoint them as well as the congregation, which is so usually large and crowded; but I have no alternative, as I am utterly unfit at present to preach. My wife's uncle is attending me, and says I am better to-day.

I spent a few days at Welwyn very pleasantly with friend Smart. We walked, and talked, and confessed, and got on without one jarring note. He is truly a gracious man, and, in my judgment, much improved. Without losing any faithfulness, boldness, or decision, he has become more softened in manner and expression. He preached a very sound, blessed, and experimental sermon. The collection was £27 18s. 6d., which I consider very handsome for so poor a people. The chapel, I believe, never was seen so full as it was all three times.

I trust our friend Tiptaft was better when I left Stamford. He finds that most beneficial which his hearers would willingly not have so—cessation from preaching. Those only who are engaged know what a trying thing it is to the health and constitution, and how it acts on mind and body. I have felt sometimes most desperate rebellion against it on this score. But our nature is so desperately crooked and rebellious that it will quarrel with God Himself if He comes across our path or thwarts our carnal wishes. Surely those who speak of growing sanctification know nothing of that leprosy within which is always breaking out in thought if not in actual word or deed. I am well convinced that we are incurables, and that even the great remedy unapplied is like untasted medicine at the bedside of the patient. I am baser and blacker than ever. I seem, at times, the very prince of hypocrites and impostors, as I feel so unlike everything a minister and a Christian should be. I am like a watch gone down, and need a heavenly hand to put in the key, and I find that there is no such thing as winding one's self up by prayers, reading, meditation, &c.; and I find also that the Heavenly Engineer does not just wind up in twenty-four hours, and then leave the machine to go; He puts in the key by littles and littles, and no sooner does He take out the key than I stop. Neither do I find that illness sanctifies the mind or creates religion. I am stupid and carnal, ill or well, unless the blessed Lord makes me to feel otherwise.

Friend Justins has just been here, and expressed the disappointment of the friends last evening. This being the case, I cannot refuse to speak next Lord's-day, and therefore have promised to do my best. I don't know that I would do it for any other place or people, but they were quite crowded last evening, and will probably be more so on Sunday. A man must pay dearly for being followed, both in his soul and body.

Believe me to be,
Your affectionate Friend,
J. C. P.

IV.—To Miss Richmond

London, June 22nd, 1839.

My dear Miss Richmond,

I am sorry that it will not be in my power to accept your kind invitation, and that of the friends, to come to Stadham, as my engagements have been made for some time, and I have already refused several invitations since I came to town. It would, indeed, give me pleasure to see my old friends at Stadham and the neighbourhood, and converse with them on the things that belong to our everlasting peace, and the many and various ups and downs that we meet by the way.

I find myself in the old track still, nor can I get into a smoother road. But in my right mind, and that is a rare mind to be in, I feel it is a better and safer path than the vain confidence of puffed-up professors. It is easy for a dead unfeeling soul to presume, but it is hard for a living God-fearing soul to believe. Servants ride upon horses, a vain thing to save a man, whilst princes walk as servants upon the earth. Surely, there are many whose excellency (in their own estimation) mounts up to the heavens, and whose head (not their heart) reaches unto the clouds, and yet they shall never see the rivers, the floods, the brooks of honey and butter, but the heaven shall reveal their iniquity, and the earth (God's children) shall rise up against them (Job xx). The whole testimony and spirit of the word of everlasting truth is to put down the mighty from their seats, and exalt them of low degree; to fill the hungry with good things, and to send the rich empty away. Thus the lame take the prey, the blind see out of obscurity and out of darkness, the lepers are cleansed, the deaf hear, the dead are raised up, and the poor in spirit have the gospel preached to them. But if we are never feelingly and experimentally lame, blind, leprous, deaf, dead, and poor, surely we can have no meetness for, nor interest in gospel blessings.

I trust I learned lessons in your little village, which have been, and are now, profitable to me since I have been brought out more into the public ministry of the word; and the experience I there had, often in sickness and sorrow, of the deceitfulness, hypocrisy, pride, presumption, vileness, and desperate wickedness of my heart, as well as of God's mercy and goodness, have, I trust, in some faint and feeble measure qualified me to testify of the inward evils of the heart in others, and to contend for a free-grace salvation, experimentally made known. I am now in this large metropolis, where I believe amidst all its wickedness and abominations God has a living family, and the chapel where I preach, though large, is very fully attended. Amidst the many scores of ministers, there seem to be few indeed who are privileged to undo heavy burdens, and let the oppressed go free. Most are grovelling in the dregs of Arminianism, or soaring aloft in the regions of letter Calvinism. Few, it appears to me, feed the flock of slaughter.

I have heard very recently from Oakham, and am glad to say that Mr. Tiptaft is better. Preaching, however, so much injures his health, that he has been compelled to give up for a time. Both he and the people feel much his being thus laid aside. As to my own health, it has been, through mercy, considerably better than when I was at Stadham, the damp situation of which never agreed with me. I have enjoyed, too, better health since I left Allington, and suffer now less from preaching twice than once when at Stadham.

I am glad to hear that Brookland has been promoted from the barn to overlook his fellow workmen, and sincerely hope the Lord will make him faithful to his earthly master. He will have many temptations to be otherwise, and Satan will lie hard upon him to cast him into a snare, and thus thrust him down; and then the ungodly would shout. I understand Mr. Kay was lately at Stadham. I hope the Lord was with him to bless the word.

Remember me affectionately to the friends who worship in your little place. Greet them by name. Were I to mention some and omit others, the latter might think I had forgotten them or neglected them, when I had not. I remember most with Christian affection, and should be glad to see them once more in the flesh.

Yours, very sincerely, for truth's sake,

J. C. P.

V.—To Mr. Parry.

Stamford, Sept. 5, 1839.

My dear Friend,

You will no doubt wish to hear how we are, and how we arrived safely, through mercy, at our destination. We arrived in London on the same day we left your hospitable abode. I went on the following day to see my friend Justins, whom I found in great perplexity, from not being able to procure a minister for the Thursday evening; their supply having left them the day preceding. The old man said he had been praying the Lord to send him a minister, and laid hold of me as an answer to his prayer. I fought off as much as I well could, till I could resist no longer, and consented to preach for them, upon which he said he would do his best to make it known, and would publish a few handbills.

Well, to my surprise, and, I believe, to that of the deacons, when Thursday night came there was quite a large congregation, the body of the chapel and galleries being comfortably full. I trust the Lord was with me, and, I hope, enabled me to tell them a little of what true religion was, and how the soul came at it. I felt gratified to see such a congregation, as the notice was so short, and there was no other means of giving it publicity than what Friend Justins adopted.

There were two very good congregations, morning and afternoon, on last Lord's-day, and the friends seemed glad to welcome me home.

I presume that J. Kay arrived safely on Friday. It is my sincere desire that the Lord may come with him and bless him, and make him a blessing. He may talk about golden and wooden trumpets, but "Who hath made man's mouth? Or who maketh the dumb or deaf, or the seeing or the blind?" (Exod. iv. 11). One word spoken by God Himself to the soul will wound or heal, kill or make alive, when all the words of human wisdom and power will fall useless to the ground. If God chooses to speak by and through a man, who or what shall hinder? And if He will not speak by him, who or what shall make Him? No one contends more for this than J. Kay, and those that honour God He will honour. Preaching is a mysterious thing, and God's mode of blessing souls through such weak, ignorant, defiled, worthless creatures, as some of us feel ourselves to be, is a mystery of mysteries. I have not been able often to receive a testimony of being blessed in preaching, from a feeling of my ignorance and vileness. If I knew more, felt more, prayed and read more, believed more, and were more diligent, fervent, jealous, watchful, humble, separate from the world, and so on, I think I could believe in the blessing more. But when I feel so dark, stupid, blind, worldly, foolish, sinful, and guilty, I find it hard work to receive any testimony of being made a blessing to any of God's elect. Yet, if I were all I wished to be, I might soon burn incense to my own drag, and, instead of wondering how God could bless me, might fall to wondering how He could not bless me for being so diligent, prayerful, watchful, and so forth. Thus, God will take care to secure to Himself all the glory, and in our right minds we are willing to give it Him.

My dear wife is busy getting the house in order. We have a servant whom we much like, being very steady and quiet. So we have everything, as far as this world goes, to make us comfortable. But what is all this in the absence of divine consolations? I feel still tried about my religion, and spend most of my days in Doubting Castle. I seem to want the right marks, and more decisive and continual testimonies to my adoption into the family of God. I do not at all regret my journey into Wilts, as I never felt, I think, more union to the friends than during my last visit.

Though my heart is not a very capacious one, I think some of my Wiltshire friends have a place in it. I have only to find fault with their kindness and esteem, both of which are indeed undeserved. But those who have warm friends, have generally bitter enemies, and so I have proved it. The friends here, I understand, find fault with me for being absent so long, and hope I shall not be away next year for so long a period.

Give my affectionate remembrance to J. K., friend Dredge, Mrs. Wild, and all friends. We beg our united kind regards to Mrs. Parry, Mrs. C., Mr. and Mrs. T., and all those friends for whose kind attentions we desire to be grateful.

Your affectionate Friend,

J. C. P.

VI.—To Mr. Isbell *

Stamford, Sept. 17, 1839.

My dear Friend,

I feel I have need to apologise for neglecting to answer your last friendly and experimental letter before. I have had, however, many hindrances, some of an external, and others of an internal nature. What with travelling, preaching, and moving from place to place, I have had my time much occupied. These external hindrances, however, have not operated so powerfully as internal ones. Sometimes unconquerable sloth and lassitude, arising, perhaps, much from over pulpit exertion; at other times, deadness and coldness of heart; at others, the feeling I could write nothing worth sending; and at others, fears of writing hypocritically and deceitfully. I must throw myself, therefore, on your kindness to excuse my apparent, but not real, neglect and forgetfulness.

What a mass of filth and folly, blindness and ignorance, deceit and hypocrisy, carnality, sensuality, and devilism are we! Prone to all that is ill, utterly averse to all that is good, bent upon sin, hating holiness, heavenly-mindedness, and spirituality, what earthly wretches, guilty monsters, abominable creatures are we! And if our minds are sometimes drawn upwards in faith and affection, and we pant after the living God, how soon, how almost instantly, do we drop down again into our earthly self, whence we are utterly unable to rise till the Blessed Spirit lifts us out again! What fits of unbelief, shakings of infidelity, fevers of lust, agues of carelessness, consumptions of faith, hope, love and zeal; yea, what a host of diseases dwell in our poor soul. "Who healeth," says David, "all thy diseases." Well, then, the soul must have

* Mr. George S. B. Isbell was minister of a Particular Baptist Chapel at Bath. He died March 6, 1860, aged 45.

many, and I am inclined to think there is some analogy between the body and soul in their diseases, and that a scriptural and spiritual parallel might be drawn between them. Some I have hinted at above, and blindness, deafness, dumbness, paralysis, leprosy, &c., are scriptural analogies. But they all admit of a twofold cure, that wonderful medicine which John saw run from the wounded side of the Redeemer, blood and water, the one to heal, the other to wash; the one to atone, the other to cleanse—justification by blood, Rom. v. 9, and sanctification by the washing of regeneration, and renewing of the Holy Ghost. I feel I have but little religion, but I feel, also, that many who think they have a great deal, have none at all. I have been cut off from what they worship and idolise. "Tekel" and "Ichabod" have been written in my conscience on scores of things set up by hundreds for religion. I cannot build up the things I have destroyed, lest I make myself a transgressor; and thus naked, empty, and bare of creature religion, human faith, fleshly righteousness, and outside sanctification, I stand often in my feelings, devoid of religion altogether. If I am only to believe when faith is given; hope, when the Spirit casts forth the anchor; love, when divine affection is shed abroad; pray, when a spirit of grace and supplication is poured out; be holy and spiritual when heavenly-mindedness is communicated,—what am I, and where am I, when divine communications are withheld? A desolate being, without religion. O tell it not in Plymouth, publish it not in the streets of Devonport, that there can be such a wretch as to have no religion but what, when, and how God gives! Why, Methodist, Ranter, Baptist, Independent, Calvinist, and Hawkerite will all hold up their hands in pious dismay, and cry, "Lives there such a man who only sees when he has light; hears when words are spoken; runs when he is drawn; feels when divinely wrought upon, and speaks when he has something to say? Where, then, is all our religion, our family prayers, and personal piety, progressive holiness, preaching, reading, prayer-meetings, love-feasts, Calvinism, religious privileges, and morning and evening portions? Breathes there a wretch whose grand aim, prayer, and desire it is to be the clay, and have God for his Potter?" Aye, more than one, or a dozen, or a score, I trust of such wretches still cumber the ground, and spread dung upon the pious faces (Mal. ii. 3) of creature religionists. It is, indeed, an unpardonable offence to be nothing; and a spiritual beggar and bankrupt is as much despised and hated by the rich Laodicean church of our day as a shiftless, tattered and torn ragamuffin by a purse-proud, turtle-fed alderman. As to the religion of thousands, I have been scraping it off for about nine years, and it sticks to me like pitch still. Oh, when tarred and feathered, I was a delightful young man, so sweet, and holy, and spiritual! but when sickness, and temptation, and doubts and fears, and gusts of infidelity, and boiling corruptions, and a deep-growing conviction of the worthlessness of all but divine teaching, and heaven-sent religion, began to scrape away the feathers and show the naked skin—and as I was scraped myself I began to scrape others—oh, then I was of a bad spirit, and in the eyes of some, a very devil. And what is my trespass, and what is my sin, that they so hotly pursue after me? That I make the creature nothing, and Christ all in all. May I be more vile than thus, and drop daily into nothingness, and rise up in Christ as my wisdom, righteousness, sanctification, and redemption.

I understand you have been at that great ice-house, Exeter—that abode of deadness, ignorance, and heresy. I should be glad to hear your message was blessed in that city of churches, where the power of vital godliness is so little felt and known. It gives me pleasure to hear that my relations sit under your ministry, and that you call occasionally upon them. May the Lord bless the word to their souls. My chest has been suffering pain from over-preaching, but is, through mercy, better. You, perhaps, have not yet found the bodily as well as mental fatigue and labour of preaching. It will surely come if you labour hard and often. I would say, do not anticipate it unnecessarily; my friend Tiptaft is nearly laid aside from this cause.

May the Lord guide and lead you, plant His fear deep in your heart, give you many sweet testimonies of His favour, and bless you, and make you a blessing.

Your affectionate Friend,
J. C. P.

VII.—To Miss Philpot *

Stamford, Oct. 16, 1839.

My dear Fanny,

I was indeed deeply surprised, as well as gratified with your letter, and cannot but receive your testimony to the reality and power of the blessing you have received. It is indeed wonderful that any guilty wretch of Adam's fallen race should receive such a blessing as a revelation of the mercy and love of God in Christ Jesus, and to us a wonder of all wonders that any of us so alienated from the life of God should find any blessing at His hands. I have no doubt you have often perceived how slow and backward I have been to speak or write to you about religion. And what chiefly kept me back was that I could not receive your religion at that time as divine. I always thought you far removed from insincerity and hypocrisy, but still there was in my mind

* Mr. Philpot's sister, who afterwards became the wife of Mr. Isbell. She died at Plymouth, August 11, 1870.

something wanting which prevented me from receiving it as a divine work, and arising out of heavenly teaching. But I cannot but fully receive your present testimony, as the spirit and savour of it has much rested on my mind since I received your letter. May you enjoy the sweetness of it for a long time, and may the chilling blast of winter and the nipping frosts of temptation be held back by the hand of the Saviour from your soul for some time to come. You must expect persecution from a world lying in wickedness and a world lying dead in profession, and your own corrupt, deceitful, treacherous heart will cause you many a pang. Hart says—

> "When the pardon is signed, and the peace is procured,
> 'Tis then that the conflict *begins*,"

—not "ends" as most think. And this great change of heart and spirit will effect a corresponding change in your life, and this will draw down persecution; as Paul says, "Every one that will live godly in Christ Jesus shall suffer persecution;" because your life and conversation will bear witness against the evil of theirs, and this will stir up their carnal enmity against you. I hope the Lord, who has dealt so graciously and mercifully towards you, will keep you separate and peculiar, lead you up into much and sweet communion with Himself, deaden your heart and affections to the things of time and sense, and make you a pattern of faith, love, and good works. I would not have you battle and argue with Mrs. R., it will only make you barren, lean, and dry. Let her see by your spirituality of mind, devotedness of life, tenderness of conscience, simplicity, and godly sincerity, that you possess a treasure obtained not in the congregation of the dead, but where God is worshipped in spirit and truth. If she be a heaven-taught character she cannot resist heavenly evidences, and I should not marvel if, after a time, she too had her eyes opened to see the corruptions and formality of the Establishment. Persons often fight for a while against convictions, especially if they oppose strong prejudices or the worldliness and pride of our heart, but are obliged after a time to bend to the force of truth. I resisted convictions about the Church of England as long and as much as I could, and could not bear to hear her spoken against, but I was obliged after a time to feel those convictions were right, and that I must obey them.

I can hardly gather from your letter whether Mrs. R. is staying at your house, or living near so as often to come in. We breathe out no curses against the Establishment, but simply proclaim her corruptions. As for myself, it is very rare that I mention her name, or say anything about her, having far more important work to do than batter her walls. Nor would I lift up a finger to pull her down, nor do I covet any of her possessions. If we act conscientiously we must prepare ourselves for persecution.

It must have been a trial to you to have refused standing proxy for Mrs. W. You acted quite right, however, in refusing to go if your conscience witnessed against it. And, indeed, how could you promise for yourself or another that the child should keep all the commandments, and such vows as are made at the font by the sponsors. It would have been awful mockery in you, having an enlightened conscience, to make such promises as you knew no flesh, especially in an unregenerated person, could perform. May the Lord make and keep your conscience increasingly tender, may He bring you again to His blessed feet, and preserve you from backsliding in heart and life from Him. The children of Israel, after they had passed through the Red Sea, soon forgat His works, and their next step was to make an idol and bow down before it.

I heard from Mr. I. this morning, and felt a sympathy with his letter. He speaks of sending me some hymns to read. If so you might send them in your parcel to L. When the penny post comes into operation I shall hope to correspond with you more frequently. You will be increasingly anxious for our dear mother's and sister's spiritual welfare. Oh, what a mercy it is to escape the wrath to come! What a terrible weight of wrath will consume all that know not Jesus and the power of His resurrection! May we have our evidences again and again renewed. Pray for me that I may be blessed indeed. My chest is rather better. I have now less pain in it. I was afraid at one time I must for a time give up preaching.

You will find Huntington's works profitable to read. Some of them are published cheap, as "The Kingdom of Heaven taken by Prayer," and "Contemplations on the God of Israel." The last is a very sweet production of his pen. Hart's Hymns, too, are a choice treasure for a child of God, who knows his own grief and his own sore. But, after all, the Word of God, under the teachings of the blessed Spirit, is the most profitable companion for a living soul. It is said of Jesus, "Then opened He their understandings that they might understand the Scriptures." Blessed instruction is it when He that hath the key of David opens His own word, and opens our heart to receive it with heavenly unction and divine authority! When He puts His hand in by the hole of the lock, and moves our hearts to hear His voice speaking in the Word! You will, no doubt, attend as much as you can on Mr. I.'s ministry which the Lord has blessed to your soul. Under the word you will find many secrets opened up, many mysteries of godliness as well as of corruption discovered, and will be sometimes wounded and sometimes healed, sometimes rebuked and sometimes comforted, sometimes cast down, and sometimes lifted up. The life of faith is a strange, mysterious life to lead, and contains many lessons of a painful, and some of a very pleasing nature. Well may it be said, "Who teacheth like God?"

I will add no more for the present than our united love to our dear mother, Mary Anne, and yourself.

Your affectionate Brother,

J. C. P.

VIII—To Mr. Parry

Stamford, Oct. 17, 1839.

My dear Friend,

We were expecting a letter from you for several days, I had almost said weeks, before it came, and were disappointed at seeing the postman so continually pass our door without entering our gate. I was anxious to know how friend Kay was heard, and perhaps a little jealous feeling intruded itself lest his larger foot should have obliterated my footmark. I am glad you have heard him profitably, and that his testimony has found an entrance into your conscience. Comfortable hearing is not always profitable hearing, and often that which condemns us does us more real and lasting good than that which encourages us. To hear others on whom we can depend speak of their manifestations and enjoyments, whilst we ourselves are dark and dead, writing bitter things against ourselves, and cutting ourselves off from eternal life, often stirs up much jealousy as well as self-pity and rebellion. But sometimes it gives us encouragement to feel that they too had to grope for the wall before they got in at the gate, and this stirs us up to cry, seek, and pray, and say, "Hast thou but one blessing? Bless me, even me also." If you read or hear the experience of gracious men, such as enters with power and conviction into your heart, you will always find that they wrestled much and long before they won the prize. And this encourages us to wrestle too, and so run that we may obtain. I could wish that our dear friend Mrs. Wild had obtained a blessing as well as E. Pope and some others, whom I may call choice feeders. It is most desirable to relieve friend Tiptaft of the burden he has borne so long and so cheerfully, yet those who would push J. Kay out should be well persuaded he is called to the ministry, lest in their anxiety to befriend one party they really injure the other, and act against God's Word. I know it is W. Tiptaft's opinion that he will never hold a body of people together, and, I presume, he speaks from what he had seen at Abingdon. I gather from your letter that the chapel at Allington is not crowded. I am convinced that a door of utterance, and some measure of what is popularly called "a gift," is absolutely needful for a preacher who is to be useful or generally acceptable to God's family. And, indeed, it might be asked, why should a man mount a pulpit at all unless he can teach the church of God; and how shall he teach, if not abundantly supplied with spiritual feelings, thoughts, and words? The scriptural qualification of a minister is, that he should be "apt to teach." A certain measure of divine utterance is therefore absolutely needful for a minister of truth, and I will defy any one to point me out a minister widely or abundantly blessed who is destitute of such a gift as renders him acceptable to God's family. I am speaking all along of a divine gift, for all that falls short of this is wind and vanity. I am glad to hear W. Tiptaft means to come for a short time to Allington at the end of next month, and could wish for your sake that he had accepted a longer invitation. He writes word to Oakham that he is stronger and better.

I received a remarkable letter on Monday from my elder sister; I say remarkable, for I was as much surprised at its contents as if she had written it in Greek. It was written under the powerful influence of a divine manifestation, and carried with it to my mind all the savour, reality, and power of a heavenly blessing. In fact she could scarcely write from her feelings of joy and praise, which she was afraid would be too much for her weak body. She has been under soul concern for some years, but there was always to my mind something wanting, and I could not receive it as a divine work. It appears she has been more tried lately, and sought much of the Lord to manifest to her if she were a child of His. She especially implored Him to make it plain under Mr. Isbell's ministry one evening, but she could get nothing till towards the end of his sermon, when he suddenly changed his subject, and began to read Isaiah lvii. She says, when he came to verse 10 the veil suddenly dropped from her eyes, she had a view by faith of the Saviour and entered into the strait gate after so long groping for the wall. She hurried home, fell upon her knees, and could say without a doubt, "My Lord and my Saviour." She has been full of praise and blessing ever since. I never saw such an alteration in my life. Her letter to me is full of power, and I can scarcely believe she wrote it, so different is it from anything I ever heard her write or speak of. She is a very sincere person naturally, and has always been afraid to profess anything, and has never been among experimental people to pick up canting whine. I know her so well that it must be either a strong delusion or a divine work, and I dare not say it is the former, lest I do despite to the spirit of grace. It is fully received by Isbell, from whom I have since heard, as a divine work, and he appears to have been much led out in private prayer for her previously. The savour has been on my mind nearly ever since, and has continually occupied my thoughts. I trust it has stirred my spirit up, and led me to offer up many fervent supplications by night and by day, that I too may enjoy a blessing. She writes at present in the full assurance of faith, calls Jesus brother, and says, whatever comes she is sure she is safe. I am astonished at her language, and the way in which she expresses herself, which puts me in mind of some of Huntington's correspondents.

Mr. Isbell is the person who writes in the *Gospel Standard* as G. I., Stoke. I think him a well taught, and much tried and exercised young man, and is, I have felt, encouraged to believe in God as one who hears and answers prayer. Oh, it is a good thing to wait upon the Lord, and, like Paul, to serve the Lord with all humility of mind, and with many tears and temptations! What a dread sovereign is He! How fearful in justice, and yet to His own how abundant in mercy!

My chest is, through mercy, better. It has been very unwell, so much so that I thought I must diminish for a time my pulpit labours.

I have been expecting a letter from friend Dredge; but I know that he cannot sit down like many and write, whether he feels or not. He must have something like a springing well before he can lay hold of the pump-handle. I am glad he gets on well with Kay, and goes about with him to the various villages and towns, where there is a door opened for him to preach. Your Wiltshire professors will have a good opportunity to put J. Kay into the balance; but, perhaps, like the man who laid hold of a warrior in the wilderness, you may find he has caught you instead of your taking him.

I am sorry the bookseller's delay prevents your accumulating a store of agricultural knowledge. You will find some useful hints in the book, I doubt not; but, like other precepts, they must be obeyed to know their value. At the same time, I should be sorry if Loudon took you away from Huntington, or that you preferred reading his Cyclopædia to the Word of God. I wish I had more appetite for the blessed truths of God, and could search and read the Scriptures more. How sweet, how suitable, how wise, how heaven-tending, how world-deadening is the Word of God! What rich treasures of truth are there stored up, and when we read them in God's light, and feel them in God's life, what a penetrating power is there in the truths there revealed! "Then opened he their understanding, that they might understand the Scriptures." Blessed opening, when He that hath the key of David puts in His hand by the hole of the door, and opens our heart to receive His own Word. Then when we go to the Word of Truth, after it has come to us, our fingers drop with sweet-smelling myrrh upon the handles of the lock. It is said that "the dead shall hear the voice of the Son of God, and they that hear shall live." Oh, to hear the voice of the Son of God in our hearts! Surely it shall make our dead hearts, cold frames, withering hopes, drooping love, dying faith, languishing prayers, and fainting minds live; yea, revive as the corn, and grow as the vine. What is all religion without a Divine beginning, middle, and end, commencing, carried on, and accomplished with a heavenly power, supernatural life, and spiritual unction? Well may we be ashamed, sick, and sorry of all our thoughts, words, and works, all our knowledge and profession that have not stood, or do not stand, in the power, teaching, and wisdom of God. All our talk has been but vain babbling, our prayers lip-service, our preaching wind and vanity, our profession hypocrisy, our knowledge the worst kind of ignorance, and all our religion carnality or delusion, if they have not been divinely communicated. Sir Isaac Newton, the wisest philosopher, is said to have remarked to one who congratulated him on his knowledge, "I have been like a little child on the sea-shore taking up a little water in a shell when the vast ocean of truth lay undiscovered before me." Much more may a spiritual man feel how little, how nothing, he knows of the unsearchable riches of Christ, and the boundless stores of wisdom hid in them. As J. Kay somewhere quotes, "It takes a man twenty years to become a fool." Look back, and see how, with Hart, you can say, "His light and airy dreams I took for solid food." What has become of the tons of instruction you have heard in your chapel from the old Supplies? Surely they have all vanished, like the gas from a torn balloon; and all the "preliminary remarks," as well as the "concluding observations," have been to you as the morning cloud and early dew. I believe we must learn to be ashamed of our religion as well as of our sins. I see such hypocrisy, presumption, deceit, and falsehood in my profession, that I am obliged to confess it continually, and seek pardon for and deliverance from it. Anything does us good which racks us off from our lees, stirs us up to cry and pray, leads us to search the Word of God, and makes us earnest and sincere. I am so rarely sincere, so seldom in downright earnest, and am so lukewarm, and cold, and careless, and carnal, and sensual, that I have reason to take a low place. Some professors are always, as they think, sincere; but those who think so are the most remote from spiritual sincerity, and know it not as God's gift and work. If they knew their own hypocrisy it would make them cry for sincerity, and they would learn that to be sincere brings with it a daily cross, and very often a furnace.

My love to J. Kay and the friends.

Your affectionate Friend,

J. C. P.

IX—To Miss Philpot

Oakham, Monday, Nov. 18, 1839.

My dear Fanny,

I was glad to hear that the good Lord was still dealing graciously with you. I also received a letter and package of hymns, &c., from Mr. I., which I hope shortly to acknowledge. I have read the hymns, and think they have many beauties; but there are roughnesses which need polishing, and in some instances false rhymes, which, if possible, should be altered. I think I prefer the first, entitled, "The Bloodhound," to any. There are, I think, too few for publication, unless through the medium of some periodical, as the *Gospel Standard.* His MS. would appear diminutive indeed in print, and the expense would be nearly as great as a larger volume. Purchasers like some quantity as well as quality, and so few would hardly find a sale beyond his own congregation and immediate friends. If he would go on composing more, and polish what he has already written, I think it would be a preferable step to a hasty, perhaps premature, publication. A certain amount of poetry is absolutely requisite in hymns, the want of which, as in the case of Herbert's (of Sudbury), is a positive impediment to their wide diffusion, in spite of choice experience and sound doctrine; whilst Cowper's and Kent's owe much of their circulation to the sweetness of the poetry. It may be said these are carnal embellishments, but it may be replied that we may as well write in prose if we set aside the main essence of poetry, and by choosing that mode of conveying our feelings and ideas we tacitly assume that we take with poetry that which belongs to its essence. Hart, the first of hymn-writers, had an especial gift for that work, but next to the experience and blessed unction that rests upon them, I admire the beautiful fulness of every line where every word conveys an idea, If I did not like much of Mr. I.'s hymns I should not advise him to go on writing more. I hope to write to him more at length on this and other subjects, but don't know whether it will be just at present.

I felt your letters profitable to my soul, and this induced the desire of sending some extracts to the *Gospel Standard*—only initials—and I have erased or altered anything of a family nature. May the promise spoken to your soul be fulfilled. My faith cannot rise so far. But continue in prayer and supplications, my dear sister, for all whom you believe that promise to encircle, and for me also, that I may have the love of God shed abroad in my heart, and the atoning blood of Jesus sprinkled on my conscience. It is not always those that manifest enmity are farthest from the kingdom of God. Pliables are sometimes worse than opposers. Rachel envied Leah's fruitfulness, which, if it stirred up her enmity, also awakened her desire, and she in time had a similar blessing, though she paid for it with her life. Nothing is impossible with the Lord, and nothing can frustrate His designs; no, not our dreadful corruptions and wretched unworthiness. You were not suffered to fall into those outward sins which many of God's elect have been betrayed into before called by grace, but if sin could have defeated God's purposes of mercy towards you, you would never have had the blessing. You will have to learn many painful lessons of inward corruption, and will have to wade through depths of which you have little present experience. When the flame of indwelling sin is stirred up, and Satan blows the coals, and the blessed Lord hides His face, you will find that a Christian soldier has to "fight with hell by faith," as Hart says. But whatever trials and difficulties you may be called upon to pass through, faithful is He who hath called you, who also will do it.

Like yourself, I have been often much exercised upon family prayer. I cannot think written prayers acceptable to God, who as a Spirit must be worshipped in spirit and in truth. And if prayer be the cry of a child to his father, it should come freely from the heart, and not according to a written form. If a child were to ask for bread from its parent according to a paper put into its hand, it would seem more to be at play than really in want of food. I certainly would not advise you to act contrary to conscience, or any way seem to mock God. But could you not offer up a few words yourself, *extempore*, as it is called? There is nothing to forbid a female praying amongst females, for we read (1 Cor. xi. 5) of a woman praying, *i.e.*, publicly, though not before males, for then she is to keep silence, 1 Tim. ii. 12; 1 Cor xiv. 34. A few simple words might be more blessed to the rest and would relieve your conscience, for then you need only utter what you feel. What is called "a gift" is not needful so long as a person does not break down, and can express his wants in simple language. But I desire to leave the matter entirely to yourself, and may you seek counsel and direction from the Wonderful Counsellor.

You will find that many who have heard of your having received a blessing will very narrowly watch your conduct to detect some inconsistency. Those especially who go to the same chapel will minutely examine your dress, looks, and very gestures to find some flaw inconsistent with Christian perfection, for many believers, as well as unbelievers, form an idea that such is the state of one who has received a blessing. And marvel not if some of that mire and mud which is so liberally bespattered on Mr. Isbell should be thrown at you, for similar doctrines and experience will call forth similar enmity. Satan, too, has his baits skilfully prepared and set. You will not find yourself dead to the lust of the flesh, the lust of the eye, or the pride of life. And Satan has temptations, too, as the angel of light, and can instil presumption, hypocrisy, spiritual pride, Pharisaism, and a host of other evils. But He that has called you to be a soldier, will teach your hands to war and your fingers to fight, and greater is He that is in you, than he that is in the world.

What a wonderful revolution is effected by divine teaching and heavenly visitations! The soul is brought to live in a new world, and breathe a new element. Old things pass away, and behold, all things become new. New desires, feelings, hopes, fears, and exercises arise, and the soul becomes a new creature. The world appears in its true colours, as a painted bauble, and as its pleasures are valued at their due worth, so its good opinion is little cared for or desired. But what complete dependents are we on the bounty and love of God, and on the divine operation of the blessed Spirit, to feel or realise one grain or atom of heavenly things! And how unable to believe, feel, taste, handle, or enjoy the smallest particle of eternal realities, except from spiritual manifestation of them! Of reading as well as of making many books there is no end, and much study is a weariness of the flesh. It is not advisable for children of God to read much of the writings of fallible men. Their writings often confuse the mind, and lead to controversies and vain jangling, or at any rate tend more to impart that knowledge which puffeth up, than that love which edifieth. Not but that a sound, savoury, experimental author is sometimes profitable, especially at those seasons when we cannot read the sacred Scriptures from distracting thoughts. But when there is an appetite for God's word, far more weighty, powerful, heavenly instruction is to be derived thence than from any writings penned by man. And why need we go to cisterns when we have the fountain? All that is good in human writings has been got from the Bible, and why need we obtain that at second-hand which we can have immediately from the same source? And the pen of man has been far more frequently wielded to propagate or support error than the cause of God and truth.

We return to S. to-morrow, yesterday being my Lord's-day here. We like our new house much, and have a very steady, confidential servant, whom we like much. My love to our dear mother, M. A., and her little ones. My very kind regards to R. and Mrs. R., whom I so well remember from almost her infancy.

Your affectionate Brother,

J. C. P.

X—To Mr. Parry

Stamford, Nov. 29, 1839.

My dear Friend,

Knowing you are one of those who do not grudge postage when a letter comes from a friend, I answer your letter earlier than I otherwise should have done, especially as it contains some questions which require an immediate reply. . . .

I can well sympathise with you in your various do bts and fears. I often feel as if I had not one grain of religion nor spark of divine life. I am often groanless and sighless, and as reckless as if there were no heaven or hell; and then wake, as it were, out of my sleep and sigh out a desire. But I cannot swim in ——'s vessel, nor any such smooth-sailing craft: I, like a shipwrecked mariner, must be picked up out of the deep unfathomable sea, or perish. My sister's deliverance for a while much stirred up my mind, but, alas! I am got pretty much into my old spot again. An extract from two of her letters will appear in the *Gospel Standard* for next month. Some may quarrel with it, and others doubt it, but let those who quarrel and those who doubt bring forward a better one of their own. I should myself be well satisfied with such a one, and if similarly favoured would fight for it against flesh, devil, conscience, law, the world, the Pharisee, and the Antinomian, professor or profane, God's children and the devil's. And I find we need hold fast what we have, however little, for doves will pick at it as well as rooks, and sheep will nibble as well as goats. But he that has God's testimony in his soul will stand by that, and that, too, will stand by him when all other witnesses fail or bear testimony against him. When we first start we are like a child learning to run alone. We lean on a chair, or get hold of somebody's hand, but by-and-by, when we have had some tumbles, and fallen sometimes over a friend's foot, and sometimes through an enemy's push, and sometimes slipped down through our own corruptions, we learn to walk alone, hanging only on free grace and divine teaching.

People are looking to me to teach them, and what can I teach them but this, that we are fools and God only wise, and that, therefore, none teacheth but He and like Him? And this makes people angry who have not yet learnt their folly. People are crying up religion all over the country, and there is not one of a thousand who has yet learnt the first lesson—to be nothing. Some extol faith and some works; some are preaching free-grace and others free-will, but of all this noisy crowd, how few lie at Jesus' feet, helpless and hopeless, and find help and hope in Him! I wish we lived nearer, that we might sometimes compare notes, and talk over some of these hidden mysteries.

The review of Hawker and Huntington has stirred up the wrath of many, but I believe experimental Christians will not very much quarrel with it. I wrote it out of my own heart and described my own feelings. Many, I believe, have given up the *Standard* in consequence. William T.'s letter is much liked at Oakham. I think "a Traveller" (J. H., I believe,) has written well, and touched some strings that will vibrate in feeling hearts.

Mr. R—— is discontented at my drawing away his hearers, and says he has lost his very best. Mrs. ——, once a lost one, but now reformed if not regenerated, begins to find, I believe, that all he could do was to build her up in presumption, and the trowel having got into a chink which he did not sufficiently plaster up has made the whole coating tremble. When it has all come down she will begin to learn a little of what religion is. I can't help picking away at every piece of untempered mortar, whether Pharisaism or Antinomianism, presumptuous confidence or feigned humility, and directly it is all down I want to fall to and build it up again with better materials. But I am a sad and bungling workman, and sometimes, perhaps, stick the pick into sound mortar whilst aiming at the rotten, and at other times put up a plaster of road mud instead of well-tempered cement. But my way is to keep picking at what I find in myself rotten and unsound, and not to put on any cement that does not satisfy or heal my own soul. Sometimes guilt makes one's hand shake, and, anon, recollection of inconsistencies makes the uplifted blow come down more softly, and then doubts and fears of presumption make all the cement fall out of one's hand. So that I find that to pull down aright as well as to build up aright. Hart, in his "Preface," that invaluable piece, has hit the right nail on the head, where he advises "no one to trust the directions of his own heart or of any other man; therefore let the Christian ask direction of his God." I find myself more and more brought off from looking to or leaning upon man, as I see and feel all are liable to err, and that none can teach but God.

Mr. Isbell has written to me some very nice letters lately. He speaks very highly of W. T.'s letter in this month's *Gospel Standard*. Remember me affectionately to him, your wife, and children. My kind love to Dredge, Mrs. Wild, E. Pope, the Canning's women, &c., &c. I have few friends, after all, better than my Allington ones.

Your affectionate Friend,
J. C. P.

XI —To Miss Philpot

Stamford, Dec. 24, 1839.

My dear Fanny,

I received safely your packet yesterday, and was much interested in J. G.'s letter to G. I., and think with a little revising it will do very well for the *Gospel Standard*. Surely every quickened and regenerated vessel of mercy is a fresh proof of that sweet passage, "Where sin hath abounded, there did grace much more abound." And those that owe all they are and all they have to sovereign, distinguishing, superabounding grace must sing to the praise of the glory of His grace wherein He hath made them accepted in the Beloved. Well may we hang solely and wholly on grace, for the past, the present, and the future, and whilst others spin their spider-woven garments out of their own bowels, may the grace of the Three-One Jehovah be all our hope here and all our song hereafter.

I am not surprised that you feel your ignorance. This is far better than boasting of your knowledge. You will see one day, if not now, that it was your mercy your head was not stored with knowledge, as it makes the change more striking and evident. By feeling your ignorance, too, you are made more dependent on divine teaching, and will be kept from sacrificing to your own drag, and the cry of your soul will be, "What I know not, teach Thou me;" "Open mine eyes, that I may behold wondrous things out of Thy law." I have long been deeply convinced of the necessity of divine teaching, and have at different times, and do still from day to day, put up many earnest petitions for the blessed teachings of the Holy Ghost. The promise stands fast for evermore: "All thy children shall be taught of the Lord." And Jesus Himself has put His own blessed seal upon it where He says, "It is written in the prophets, And they shall be all taught of God. Every man therefore that hath heard, and hath learned of the Father, cometh unto Me," John vi. 45. This is the "unction from the Holy One, whereby the children of God know all things;" "the anointing which teacheth of all things, and is truth, and is no lie," 1 John ii. 20, 27. You will find it good to read much of the blessed word of truth. It is, when applied by the eternal Comforter, "spirit and life" (John vi. 63); and the leaves of this tree are for medicine, and the fruit thereof for meat, Ezek. xlvii. 12; Rev. xxii. 2. "For all Scripture is given by inspiration of God, and is profitable for doctrine, for reproof, for correction, for instruction in righteousness." By continually reading the word you will make up for a defective memory, and let none despise having the word of truth stored up in the mind, as the blessed Spirit will sooner or later apply to the heart many passages which at present may be only in the memory. "Let the word of Christ dwell in you richly in all wisdom," Col. iii. 16. "This book of the law shall not depart out of thy mouth; but thou shalt meditate therein day and night," Josh. i. 8. See also the following Scriptures: Deut. vi. 6—9; xvii. 18, 19; xxx. 11—14. Compare with Rom. x. 6—10, Psalm i. 2, 3; cxix. 97, 99, 103, 115, 130, 148.

You have received such encouragement to pray that I doubt not you still persevere in making your requests known unto God. I have not been blessed with that spirit of prayer nor assurance of an answer that you have been favoured with. My earnest desires and breathings have been more for a blessing on my own soul. I feel my daily need of visitations and manifestations from the Lord. Jabez offered a sweet prayer (1 Chron. iv. 10): "Oh that Thou wouldst bless me indeed, and enlarge my coast, and that Thine hand might be with me," &c. To be blessed *indeed* is the soul's desire of one taught of God, and the application of His love and blood to the conscience is a blessing indeed. And to have His guiding, directing, supporting, upholding hand with us, what more can we desire? And to be kept from evil that it may not grieve us: what tender conscience does not desire such a blessing too? I am not surprised Mrs. —— is cold. Expect many such chilling looks from former friends. There can be no real union with, nor cordial approbation of persons that condemn us. "Can two walk together except they be agreed?" To be brought out of Egypt condemns those that are yet in the house of bondage, well pleased with the leeks, onions, and garlic. Such coarse fare pleases well an earthly appetite, however little suitable to those that have tasted the hidden manna. You will find your motives misrepresented, your words misinterpreted, your actions narrowly observed, your gestures, dress, and general appearance strictly scrutinized. I am sorry to hear your health continues weak, but it may be a blessing to keep you more at home, and thus in some measure preserve you from the keen eye of saint and sinner, professor and profane. May the Lord in His own time and way bless the word to our dear mother. Encourage her to seek for mercy from Him who is merciful, yea, rich in mercy. And as the Lord enables you, continue in prayer and supplication for her, and may I add, for me also, that the Lord would bless me indeed, by the manifestations of His love to my soul.

I seem to think that in hearing Mr. Isbell you are somewhat under the influence of excitement, at least it struck me so in your last, from the feeling you express of expecting to hear a scream or a shout under his preaching. The Lord does not usually work in that way—witness yourself—when He speaks with power. He was neither in the storm, the earthquake, nor the fire, but in the still, small voice. The waiting prophet did not wrap his face in his mantle, nor go out of the cave during the raging war of elements, but when he heard the still voice of love and power, he went forth and stood in the entering-in of the cave. Excitement is frequently substituted for religion as among the Wesleyans and Ranters.

[*The remainder of this letter is lost.*]

XII—To Mr. Isbell

Stamford, Jan. 9, 1840.

My dear Friend,

I have been expecting to hear from you every day, to obtain permission to send J. G.'s letter to the *Standard*. But as you do not write, I presume you are waiting a reply to your kind letter. Indeed, I am at times fit to write to nobody from darkness of mind, and carnality of heart. It is mostly ebb-tide with me, and when the tide turns and begins to flow, I am too much engaged with opening all the gates and sluices to sit down and write. I have often been most able and willing to preach and write when opportunity did not serve. And when the season has come, the thoughts are gone, the feelings flown, the dew evaporated, the warmth extinguished, and the food got cold and tasteless. Sometimes when walking or when dressing I have felt zeal, life, power, ideas, words, so that I could have with boldness set forth the word of life, or penned down truth with what seemed at the time vigour and decision. But when I have afterwards been in the pulpit, or taken my pen, not only has the power and feeling flown, but the very train of thought, the texts of Scripture, the light thrown upon them, and all clearness of idea, have fled, too, and left me shut up, embarrassed, confused, and almost worthless. I have spoken on a text sometimes in a way that has been a wonder to myself, and then, perhaps, in another place from the same words have been so shut up that I could scarcely muster an idea, or utter a sentence that to me seemed to the point; and have wondered the people should ever hear me again. Many of the Calvinist ministers could preach the same sermon from the same words to any congregation. But it is not so with me. I am dependent on the Lord for every sermon and every occasion; and find a different vein of thought, or different mode of expressing myself, which varies with the congregation. Nor can I write when I please, nor express my thoughts and feelings when I wish. Some of my correspondents shut me up, and the ink freezes, as it were, in my pen; whilst to others I feel handling the pen of the ready writer, and can freely turn out the thoughts of my heart as my hand moves along the page. "Can two walk together except they be agreed?" enquires the Holy Ghost; and the experience of all honest men answers "No." Dissemblers and hypocrites can walk together; and so can enemies of truth, like Herod and Pontius Pilate, run in couples like bloodhounds to hunt down the precious life. My experience for these last seven or eight years has been to keep much to myself, and to have nothing to say to men with whom I do not feel a cordial union. Some call this pride, others bitterness of spirit, but I have never reaped anything from false unity without spiritual union but vexation and trouble. Bastards and servants can never be anything but spies (Gal. ii. 4) and enemies. Ishmael will mock Isaac, though born in the same house, nor can any wisdom of man reconcile the two seeds between whom God has put enmity. And however distasteful and wearisome the company of worldly men is to me, I honestly confess that the presence and conversation of a moral man, who does not absolutely pain me by his worldliness, is more tolerable than the smooth cant of a hard-hearted professor. I hope always to avoid the company of either, but I would sooner ride 100 miles inside a coach with one than the other. Nor have I ever found it wise to tell to such the feelings of my heart. If one dances, like Michal they despise, and if one is cast down, we are as a lamp despised in the mind of him that is at ease. With them the prophet is a fool, the spiritual man is mad, and though they smooth their tongues, and their words are softer than butter, they only do it that they may the better bend their bow and shoot in secret at him that is perfect. I was once for loving everybody that talked about Jesus Christ, but I have learned a different lesson, and find my affections now flow in a narrower channel, and, I believe, all the deeper from its contracted width. "As many as walk according to this rule, peace be on them, and mercy, and upon the Israel of God." And what rule is that? "A new creature in Christ Jesus." So says the Spirit by Paul, and so answer I, "Amen." But not new creeds, ye letter men; nor "new lives," ye reformed but not regenerated sinners; nor "new tongues," ye glib talkers. To all that come short of the new creature we must answer to their question, "Is it peace, Jehu?" "What peace so long as the whoredoms of thy mother Jezebel and her witchcrafts are so many?" But in this warfare we shall have no better treatment than those who have gone before us. If they hated the Saviour, they must hate the saved, and if they called him Beelzebub, how much more those of his household?

I have heard from friend —— on his brother's marriage. He seems much pleased and gratified with all he heard and saw. You would perceive he is not a man of strong mind, nor deep experience; yet, I trust, a sincere lover of truth and the possessor of it. But he is not what a friend of mine calls "a front-rank man." He will support another better than advance, and follow better than lead. Such, however, are useful when they know themselves and their own weakness, which I trust he does; and are content to boil the camp-kettle, or scrape lint for the wounded, rather than head the forlorn hope. He had been set up, before I knew him, by those who sought to build, but who knew neither how to dig the foundation nor handle a trowel; and, I believe, was much cut down before cut to his right dimensions. Alas! alas! how many in a church would squeeze up to nothing if grasped by the hand of the Spirit. And many others, were they put into the hydraulic press, as the Americans do their bales of cotton, would shrink into woefully small dimensions. You may depend upon it, that with all the light in our day there is very little grace. Most are boasting themselves on a false gift, and are potsherds covered with silver dross. The best taught are crying, "My leanness! my leanness! woe unto me!" and mourning over their barrenness and death. The professing church is in the Laodicean state of saying: She is rich, and increased in goods, and in need of nothing. She feeds on doctrines without knowing or caring to know their power, and rests on the general security of the Elect without feeling or desiring to feel her own. Antinomian presumption is the hydra of our professing day, the damning sin of Calvinists, as self-righteousness is of Arminians. The millstones are not wider apart than in the days of Hart, and the path between them is still what the vulture's eye hath not seen. If temptations, doubts, fears, crosses, and afflictions keep us from crying, "Peace, where there is no peace," it is far better for us than being at ease in Zion. Our flesh loves ease and carnal security, and absence of trials produces and brings that which the flesh loves. But in such seasons, when all is dead within, how soon does all the power of religion evaporate, how cold are our prayers, how dark and hidden is the word of truth, how pointless and worldly is our conversation, how vain and flesh-pleasing are our thoughts, and how feeble are our pulpit ministrations! Religion becomes a burden, and everything connected with it a task; whilst all the time we are sensible we are not what we were before, and yet, like a dreaming man, can tell neither what we are nor where we are. But when the entrance of the word of reproof or of promise giveth light, a ray is cast over the path we are in, our backslidings reprove us, our leanness rising up in us beareth witness to our face, and we cry, "Bring my soul out of prison; deliver me for Thy mercy's sake; visit me with Thy salvation, and lift up the light of Thy glorious countenance upon me." But we soon start aside like a broken bow, and go a whoring after our idols under every green tree. Like the wild ass of the wilderness we snuff up the wind at our pleasure, and in our occasions who can turn us away.

You ask how I was convinced of believer's baptism? I don't know that I can add any more to what I mentioned in my note. When the subject first arrested my mind I turned from it with enmity, as I saw it was like a man with a saw coming to cut down my apple-tree which bare the golden apples. This was evident, that if believer's baptism was the only Scriptural one, I must relinquish my connection with a system that was based upon infant sprinkling. But this I had neither inclination nor faith to do, especially as my health was indifferent, and all my income derived from the Establishment. Still, however, as I read the Scriptures I could see neither precept nor example of any other baptism, and together worked with this the awful mockery of the Church of England's service for sprinkling infants, which, however, I escaped, as having an assistant who did that as well as all the other formal work. Some friends of mine, too, at this time seceded from the Establishment, and were baptized, and as I still maintained equally friendly relations with them, we sometimes conversed upon it, and my convictions were still more strengthened till they outgrew and outweighed all bonds and shackles, and forced me out of Babylon. I was baptized by Mr. Warburton about six months after I left the Establishment, and have never swerved from believing it to be a Gospel ordinance, though I feel little disposed to make a Shibboleth of it, or make it a prominent topic of my ministry. The way in which many Baptists bring it forward I much object to, as though it were the all in all, and the grand turning point, whereas I rather regard it as an ordinance to be obeyed from divine teaching and love. "If ye love Me keep My commandments." But some of my dearest friends and best hearers are not Baptists, nor has this come in as a bar or a stumbling-block between our friendship and love. I cannot, however, agree with Mr. Triggs, or the late Mr. Fowler, to make it an indifferent thing, and in our zeal for spiritual substances to set aside the Lord's clear command, and His apostles' undoubted practice, as nullities and shadows. Jesus is a lawgiver to His chosen, and they honour Him little who despise His precepts. That is an awful word, Matt. v. 19, and you are well aware of the difference between transgressing through weakness, and neglecting through contempt, or despising through hardness of heart. And I dare say you have felt the keen edge of the verse I have quoted, in the expression, "And shall teach men so." I have sometimes derived comfort from this thought, that wherever I have transgressed I have not taught men so, and have neither justified to myself nor to others any deviation from the strait and narrow path. And here I draw a distinction between the opponents of baptism and the neglectors of it. S—— has preached against, and, I believe, ridiculed believer's baptism. I would not, therefore, pass by an opportunity of correspondence without telling him of his error. This produced some warm defensive language, and when I stated in my reply that I did not, perhaps, bring forward baptism once a year in the pulpit, he could not understand how I could be faithful in so doing, when I opposed him for denying it. He could not see the difference between a man's not seeing a truth and opposing it. Had you, for instance, been silent on the subject I should not have brought it forward; but had you opposed it I should soon have defended it, and I think this is a very intelligible distinction. If your church be not a Baptist church you will find that to bring baptism forward will set it all on fire and prove a bone of contention. But I would not have you the less bring it forward if the Lord has laid it upon your soul, and the most powerful sermon you could preach upon it would be to submit to it yourself. The very storm, however, might winnow out some of the old chaff, of which, I doubt not, you have more than you wish. You have probably found ere this that old members of churches are not usually the most spiritual or teachable, and that your chief hopes rest upon those whom the Lord has given you as seals of ministry. And you may find baptism to give the old members more offence than your other preaching, as being a more tangible point, and as affording them a rallying spot of ground whence they may discharge their artillery against what they call your bitter spirit, &c. It may therefore be a turning-point with you, and yet should not be so brought forward, but simply as a truth taught you by the Lord.

It is good for us to have little to do with men. I have had, I think, sufficient reason to be shy of most ministers, nor are there above half a dozen to whom I feel any union. The review of Hawker and Huntington in the *Gospel Standard*, generally ascribed to me, has made many very angry, who never knew the experience therein spoken of, and therefore their language is, "Master, in speaking thus thou condemnest us also!" Truth, however, will stand when the world is in a blaze.

Your affectionate Friend,
J. C. P.

XIII.—To Mr. Tuckwell *

Stamford, January 16, 1840.

My dear Friend,

I felt much interested in your account of your trip to Plymouth. You need not have felt such trepidation at calling on my mother and sister, as they are plain people, and would be glad to see any friend of mine. I am glad you liked my sister's conversation. Whatever others may think I care not. I myself fully receive it as a divine work, and those who doubt or disbelieve it, let them produce a better. I mean as to the feelings produced by a visit from Jesus; and if any cavil, and say there was not this preparatory work, and that preliminary hell and damnation terrors, all I can say, "Who shall limit the Holy One of Israel?" As Hart says in his golden "Preface"—in my opinion the most weighty piece of writing ever penned by man after the blessed Scriptures—"The dealings of God with His people, though similar in the general, are nevertheless so various that there is no chalking out the paths of one child of God by those of another; no laying down regular plans of Christian conversion, Christian experience, Christian usefulness, or Christian conversation." I heartily assent to what I have thus quoted, and though I believe there is no revelation of Christ without previous condemnation by the law, who shall define the necessary degree of depth, or the indispensable period of length? Who shall take the compasses and scale, and mark out a circle for the Almighty to move in, or a line to walk by? Let the measurer first cut and clip all the trees of the forest into a certain prescribed figure and uniform symmetry. Let him examine an unknown leaf from some Indian forest, and say, "This is not a leaf at all; it is not jagged, nor scolloped like the only leaf I admit as my standard—that of the oak; and therefore I cast it from me as a base counterfeit, a vile imitation, the work of some ingenious artist." You would say to such a critic in vain, "Why look, sir, is it not green? Does it not spring from a branch? Does it not fulfil all the functions of a leaf? Does it not, by its minute pores and vessels, give out all the superfluous moisture of the sap, and at the same time inhale the oxygen of the air, which, by combining with the sap, becomes nutriment to the tree?" Still he would answer, "I don't care what it does. I say it is not jagged nor scolloped, nor like an oak leaf, and therefore away with it."

* Joshua Carby Tuckwell. Died at Allington, Devizes, September 8, 1867. See obituary in *Gospel Standard*, April, 1868.

Apply this to the case in hand. I believe my sister has not felt the terrors of the Law, as many have; but if she felt lost, guilty, condemned, without hope or help, she had a work of the Law in her conscience. But I look more to the deliverance, and the effects produced by it. Who shall say, in reading her simple statement, that her leaf is not green? Does it not give out, and take in, as the leaf does—give out the flowings of love and contrition, and take in out of the fulness of the Saviour? Deliverances, my friend, are the grand evidences to look to. No other evidences will satisfy a needy, naked soul, and they are what a wise man will chiefly look to in estimating others. He will not, indeed, pass by, or think lightly of the sighing of the prisoner, but he will consider the knocking off the fettered captive's chains a better evidence than his lying in the dungeon. And whatever some may think about the most searching ministry being that which deals chiefly with dark evidences, I have not the least doubt that that ministry will be the most cutting, and at the same time the most establishing, which deals most in deliverances. This is a very different thing from the flighty, dry, letter ministry of preaching assurance and comfort. Deliverances imply trials, sorrows, and temptations. Troubles and deliverances are the scales of a balance; when one is up the other is down. But they who are all for darkness and unbelief have no balance, but a scale-pan detached from the beam; and they who are all for assurance, have the other scale unhooked from the beam also. They are thieves and deceitful weighers, who have stolen the scale, and left the beam behind them; and, being partners in the robbery, one rogue has taken away one scale, and his accomplice the other. The honest man holds the beam with the scales attached to it, and he puts the light-hearted and untempted into the scale of trials. They cannot make it move a peg; they are found wanting. He then puts the mourners into the scale of deliverances. The beam trembles, but does not move. It is worldly sorrow that works death. They are light weight too. But a living soul tempted will at one time weigh down one scale, and a living soul delivered will at another time weigh down the other scale, and thus be full weight in each. When I get into figures and comparisons I am like a trained horse getting upon the turf. Away he goes, and there is no stopping him till out of breath. The first horse I bought had run a race a week or two before I purchased him, and when I got him upon a down I had hard matter to hold him.

I am glad you get on pretty well with the reading at chapel. An exercised soul in prayer, who is enabled in simple language to pour out his feelings and desires, is worth all the prating, starched-up, letter parsons in the world. My soul has been softened with a single sentence of living prayer out of an exercised child of God, when a long sermon, well dovetailed and jointed, from a letter preacher would have filled it with barrenness and death.

I am, through mercy, pretty well. My chest still at times continues to give me pain, and is, I think, weaker this winter than it was last. I still, however, continue to preach twice on the Lord's-day, and once in the week, and usually to good and listening congregations, which increase rather than diminish. My ministry is too cutting to please the generality, and, I think, many are wounded who have the root of the matter in them. I trust I am not become mealy-mouthed or a man-pleaser, though my flesh would gladly lean that way. I think, however, they give me credit for seeking their spiritual good, and that I do not speak in bitterness and enmity to wound their feelings. But it is hard for those to relish faithfulness who have been used to flattery. I hope my valued friends who attend Allington Chapel are well. Remember me to them in Christian affection, such as E. Pope, the Cannings women (including Dorcas and her sister Sally), Mrs. Wild, Mr. and Mrs. P——, Mrs. C——, and all my other sincere and steadfast friends.

Yours affectionately, for truth's sake,
J. C. P.

XIV —To Mr. Parry

Stamford, Feb. 6, 1840.

My dear Friend,

The cheapness of postage increasing my correspondence my time scarcely admits of my writing so often or so long to my friends. In this, however, as in other cases, I feel a certain degree of self-denial and exertion necessary to prevent my friends thinking me guilty of neglect. We should all like the miserly plan of receiving letters without answering them. I call it miserly, for the essence of a miser is to receive as much and pay as little as he possibly can. In all friendship, forbearance, self-denial, and exertion are needful to keep it alive. He that will make no sacrifices, use no self-denial, and employ no effort in behalf of his friends, will soon find himself without them, and thus reap the just reward of his indolence and self-indulgence. A certain degree of communication and friendly intercourse is absolutely necessary to keep spiritual friendship and affection alive. Communication by bodily presence, or by letter, is the oil poured from time to time into the lamp which keeps it alive. I have generally found that, as I ceased to see or write to my friends, coolness arose, which increased with neglect, till at last I seemed to care as little about them as if I had never known them. These remarks, the truth of which you will, I believe, acknowledge, I trust will stir you up to put them into practice and use that small quantity of self-denial which is needful to pay as well as to receive.

Afflictions and trials are the appointed lot of all, elect and non-elect. Solomon observed this in his day (Eccles. ix. 2) and Job before him (v. 7; xiv. 1). So that crosses and losses are no distinguishing mark of divine favour nor yet of divine wrath, though the elect and non-elect draw just opposite conclusions from them. The elect often fear they are tokens of wrath, and the non-elect hope they will be a satisfaction for their sins. The great question is, what do they for a man's soul? Is any humbling of heart, breaking down of pride, deadness to the world, earnest fleeing to a throne of grace produced thereby? It is good to have a deep and feeling acquaintance with the malady, to groan and sigh under a body of sin and death, to be cut down, cut up, and cut off—but why good? Is it good in itself? No, not at all. It is only good so far as the soul is led thereby to the cross of Jesus, to taste and feel His blood and love. Everything that brings us there in faith and feeling is good; everything that keeps us away is bad. Since I began this letter I have received one from our friend Dredge, in which he mentions the trial you had at Allington with S. Poor fellow! he must have been miserably shut up, not to be able to fulfil his engagements and come all that way for nothing. I don't understand it: when God raises up a man to preach His word, I cannot understand his being totally shut up. Warburton speaks of it twice having happened to him, but one of those times was in early days when there was a special need of his being humbled. Such a thing has, I should imagine, never happened to him for these last twenty years. I never heard of such a thing occurring to Huntington, nor do we find it happening to Smart, Tiptaft, or others. Most complain of great deadness at times and shutting up in feeling, as though they could never preach again, but when the time has come they have been mercifully helped through. Friend Dredge, however, gives a right account of him, and speaks of many sweet marks of grace and godliness in him. I don't see that the Allington hearers and friends have any reason from this circumstance to write bitter things against themselves, as though they had shut him up, and that it is a mark of the Lord's displeasure and absence from them. Warburton and others have found liberty there, though he felt bondage; and we know not what secret need there was for him to be humbled thereby, or what spiritual profit to him or them is to spring out of it. "Judge not the Lord by feeble sense," &c.

Poor C. seemed to have had a roughish journey to Wincanton, and his fellow-traveller came in a storm and went away in one. O what trials the poor fellow must have had when he got home, and how the devil would set upon him that he was no minister, and only a deceiver and deceived! If it were bad for you it was a great deal worse for him, and yet I most fully believe good will come out of it. Storms and roaring waves sometimes cast upon the shore valuable treasures hid in the sands, and thus, spiritually, tempests and roaring seas often bring to light secret treasure. I have a strong suspicion that my Allington friends must tread the old track of reading and praying amongst themselves, as there is little prospect of their having a man to go in and out before them, and like many a labourer in these hard times they must satisfy themselves with long fasts and short commons.

I am sorry to find —— is still such a trial to you in every respect. I expect for you nothing but sorrow and trouble till he is no more seen. Yet if spiritual profit arise from it to your soul; if it wean you from the world, give you an errand to a throne of grace, make you helpless and hopeless, and through all this a heavenly smile break through the cloud to ravish your heart, you will not think you have one trial too many. We are poor judges of our own conduct, and even if in the wrong are ready to justify ourselves.

I was much pleased with friend Dredge's letter, and see him a very altered man from when I first knew him. I have seen him more softened and brought down, and less harsh in his speeches. Faithfulness is one thing; harshness is another. A man can't be too faithful, but he must speak the truth in love if he speaks aright. Paul, even of the enemies of the cross, speaks with weeping. But it is, indeed, a most narrow line, and most of us err through softness and compliance rather than severity and harshness, and, I believe, severe faithfulness is far better than compliant softness. Our friend's faithfulness makes him so hated, and sorry should I be to see him softened down to put bitter for sweet and sweet for bitter. But his enemies treasure up his hard speeches and turn them against him, and say, "Here is Dredge's religion." I like the way in which he talked to ——, and it was more likely to find an entrance into his mind than if he had harshly cut him off.

I heard from Smart this morning. He wishes me to pass through Welwyn for their anniversary, but I scarcely think I shall be able. I would stretch a point, however, to please a friend.

I am more and more satisfied with my sister's religion, and believe it will swim when thousands will sink. She has been brought more into darkness and conflict lately, and says what pleasure she found in reading my "Heir of Heaven." A lady who has been staying with them some time—a great professor—has been a wonderful trial to her. To save my hand, which is rather fatigued, I got my dear wife to copy a part of her last letter, which, I think, shows life and feeling:

"Mrs. —— has been a terrible sore to me, and I believe if I had been a worm and she could have put her foot upon me and crushed me she would; she has goaded and worried my soul, as a bull-dog would do a sheep. Even now I dread her coming into the house, and my whole frame is in agitation when she speaks upon the precious word, and what she takes to herself. She has no doubt of her salvation, and all Mr. I. preaches upon to the comfort of the Lord's dear ones she says she participates in. She has none of the doubtings and fears, no inward corruptions, no hidings of the Lord's face, no want of communion with Him, no lack of prayer does she say or appear to feel. And I am sure Mr. I. does cut down root and branch; so much so, that unless quite dead to the word, no one could hear him without being brought down into the dust. There could be no towering of the head, no watching or 'being constantly on the watch to detect errors in *others*' (as she unwittingly told me she did), were she brought to see her own nakedness before the Lord. Still her visit has been in love; it has taken me much from man's knowledge, made me look more entirely to the Lord for teaching and strength. Some of the Sabbaths have been, indeed, days of rest and peace to my soul, softened down quietness, a resting in the Lord, a peace and sweetness I would not part with for worlds (but without any rejoicing).

"I read, last week, your 'Heir of Heaven,' and it was a blessed sermon to me. My mind had been very wretched; no prayer, no understanding of the word; all was dark and miserable. I could not go up to the chapel on Sunday. Mr. I. came in in the afternoon. I had been poring over some chapter in Isaiah; all was a blank, and I said so to him. Very soon after Mrs. —— came in and began to talk to him on various portions of Scripture, and he partly expounded two of the chapters in Isaiah I had longed to ask him. Thinks I, this is very singular: here is one with a vast deal of Scriptural knowledge running from one part of the Bible to another, grasping at the meaning, and here am I, a very fool, hardly knowing one text from another, sitting by without a word to say. Blessed Lord, how hast thou dealt with me, a cobweb in Thy sight, and left Thy creature without a certain assurance of Thy love to her? Then Mr. I. spoke upon the chapter above named; in an instant a ray of light darted into my soul. I was sure I felt the rain of heavenly light was coming upon me, and as she rose, *courteously* thanking him for the pleasure she had had, and saying she would go home and *consult* her *Bible*, thinks I, you know not the instrument you have been in the Lord's hand of sweetness to my soul, and I never did enjoy a more blessed evening, quite alone in the house, if I can call it being alone. The 40th Psalm was deeply entered into, and I was again directed to the 14th of John; all entered into my inmost soul, and I did love the dear Redeemer and thank Him for His visible mercy to me. The same peace lasted several days, during which I read your sermon; but, alas! there was to be an end, and for several days I have been without a word to say to the Lord. Very miserable, no reading reached me, and I dare not kneel down lest

I should mock the Lord. To-day I have had a little comfort and been able to feel that the Lord is still my rock and my strength."

I need not apologise for the length of this quotation, as I think you will consider it the best part of my letter.

Give my Christian love to all the friends, and believe me to be,

Your affectionate Friend,

J. C. P.

XV—To Miss Philpot

Stamford, February 18, 1840.

My dear Fanny,

I am always pleased to hear of your spiritual state, and to find that He who hath begun a good work in you is still fulfilling it until the day of Jesus Christ. A life of faith in the Redeemer is not one of continued, nor indeed frequent enjoyment. There is an enduring hardness as a good soldier of Jesus Christ; and soldiers, you know, have often to fight and receive painful wounds. Our carnal nature is not sanctified by grace, but remains in all its unmitigated venom, and in all that mass of depravity, filth, and corruption, into which the fall of our first parents precipitated it. Satan is a powerful, as well as a most wily enemy, and is continually prowling about either to wound or ensnare. We are told "to fight the good fight of faith," and that "we wrestle not against flesh and blood (*i.e.*, not against flesh and blood *only*), but against principalities, against powers, against the rulers of the darkness of this world, against spiritual wickedness (or 'wicked spirits,' *margin*) in high places."

The strength of Christ is made perfect in weakness, His victory in defeat, His grace in subduing sin, His free payment in bankruptcy and insolvency. Here, then, is the life of faith, and a struggling, battling, wrestling, and sometimes despairing fight it is. We would fain have it otherwise, and be wise, and strong, and holy, and full of joy and triumph; and, could we gain our wish, we should take the crown from the Redeemer's head, and put it on our own.

Surely free grace is a sweet theme to all the ransomed family of God; but what makes it sweet but sheer necessity? If there were no sins to pardon, no backslidings to heal, no wounds to cleanse, no broken bones to restore, no aggravated iniquities freely to blot out, free grace would be but a name, a sound in the ears, a Bible word, the article of a sound creed; but not a felt, tasted, and enjoyed possession, sweeter than honey or the honeycomb in the soul. How long you heard the doctrines of grace at Eldad and Mount Zion chapels, but they only reached your outward ear as, perhaps, a pleasing sound, but without making heavenly melody in your heart, altering the current of your desires, thoughts, and affections, making you a new creature, and setting up the kingdom of God in your soul.

Many hate and revile me for speaking and writing against "dry doctrines." By "dry doctrines" I mean the intellectual, speculative, notional, dead, and dry knowledge of certain truths as they stand in the letter of God's Word. They are not dry in themselves, but rich, unctuous, savoury, and full of marrow; but as merely lodged in the speculative brains of natural men, they are dry to them as destitute of heavenly application.

I always suspected you overrated ——'s religion; but, not knowing her since her profession, I felt unwilling to hint anything to her disparagement, and wished to leave it more to your own discernment. You need not envy her her clear head, strong memory, inquisitive mind, and good understanding. One grain of Divine teaching is more valuable a million times than the highest human attainments, though they weighed tons in the opposite scale. One smile from the Fountain of bliss, the God of all grace, and Father of mercies, is an earnest of an eternal inheritance, incorruptible, undefiled, and that fadeth not away. And what are the best and brightest of human attainments? Alas! they are linked to life's short span, and the stroke that snaps the thread of life crumbles all natural attainments into the. . . . . .

[*The remainder of this letter is torn off.*]

XVI—To Mr. Isbell

Stamford, Wednesday, Feb. 26, 1840.

My dear Friend,

I think in writing letters I sometimes feel as a self-justiciary does. Being sensible of my defects, imperfections, and shortcomings in them, I offer or promise to write again, hoping I may then send something better worth reading, yet I fail again like the character alluded to, and then I am almost sorry I ever promised to write. Some such feeling I am now sensible of, and, therefore, hope you will throw a mantle of love over all that you see foolish or deficient.

I felt much the savour in your last letter but one, I mean that containing Mrs. B.'s experience. I hope you will not deny me what I am about to ask—viz., to insert it in the *Gospel Standard.* I would omit the name, and would leave out all personal allusions, and anything that might painfully particularise you or her. But I mean not only that part which contains her experience, but what you have said of yourself also; of course, omitting everything strictly personal. A free letter to a friend is often far more sweet and profitable than a set piece, however well written, and I believe the private letters of gracious men have been much blessed, as Huntington's, Romaine's, Newton's &c. Some letters of Warburton's, Tiptaft's, and others have been blessed in the *Gospel Standard.*

I fear —— is an unhumbled man, and mistakes what the world calls "spirit" for gospel boldness and faithfulness. Bunyan in the "Holy War" represents the ejected servants of Diabolus returning into the city of Mansoul, and hiring themselves as servants under assumed names. For instance, "Covetousness" hires himself under the name of "Prudent Thrifty;" "Lust" and "Licentiousness" under the names of "Gallantry" and "Good Breeding;" "Carnal Security" under the name of the "Assurance of Faith." I don't know that these are the exact names, but such is the idea of this deep observer and graphic delineator of nature and grace. So I think pride and self-importance have hired themselves to —— under the names of "Gospel Boldness" and "Spiritual Faithfulness." I dislike exceedingly the bold, arrogant way in which he calls himself a minister of the Gospel, knowing, as I do well, how in L. and N. he starved the living family, and amused or bolstered up dead Calvinists. I do not say he is not a good man; I do not say he is not a minister of Christ; but I see in him a spirit in my judgment very different from what I observe in those whom I love and honour as such.

You will find, I fear, your visit to Ireland a painful one. You know what enmity is in the heart against all light which forces the Cross into view. When persons breathed a word against the Establishment formerly, I felt the bitterest enmity rise up, and I wanted to put them down—stop their mouths, or keep them in any way from broaching a subject so painful to flesh. But still light would break in and work in my conscience. The burdens of a liturgy and the awful lies which I was compelled to tell a heart-searching God pressed me sore. There was no use my fleeing to this or that explanation. I stood before a holy God, and told Him with lying lips a senseless babe was born of water and the Holy Ghost, when I knew the blessed Spirit had no more regenerated the child than He had regenerated the font. I thanked him for taking a dear brother to Himself who I knew died under His eternal wrath. But some might say—"How did you know either the one or the other?" "How did I know there was a God at all but by faith in His Word?" and by the same faith that I believed in Him did I believe that His enemies were not His friends, nor carnal children living members of the true Vine. I twisted and turned every way, but I was here held fast. It is a lie, and the worst of lies, as being a lie unto God. "Thou hast not lied unto men, but unto God," Acts v. 4; and, therefore, far more aggravated. Let this be laid spiritually on the conscience, and a living man whose heart has been made tender must leave, come what will. I saw a gloomy prospect before me. My health so weak that I could only preach once a day, with no other service or using my voice, and hardly recovering the effects till the following Wednesday. All my independence, which kept me comfortably, gone at a stroke, and I felt most unwilling to burden my mother, whose income is small. But I cast myself into the waters and found standing-ground. My health after a time so improved that I now stand two full services, rarely preaching each time under an hour, and often to a crowded congregation, with one and sometimes two services in the week, when I preach at least an hour. I found friends raised up, pulpits offered, my wants freely supplied; greater liberty of soul, and more utterance and power. Two years after I left (which was in March, 1835), my elder brother died, almost suddenly, which gave me a little present property and a prospect of more. See how the Lord has fulfilled to me his promise, Mark x. 29, 30. Oh, my unbelieving heart! which pictured a thousand gloomy things never yet realized, as sickness, poverty, and almost a parish workhouse! And here I am better, or certainly not worse, in worldly circumstances, with a free unfettered conscience, improved health, kinder and more enduring friends, and a much larger field for my ministerial labours. I have been several times invited to settle in London, where I generally go to preach once a year, and should there have a congregation exceeding probably 800 persons, and many, if not most of those, not carnal, dead, bowing and curtseying Papo-Protestant parishioners, whose formality and ignorance made my heart ache, but a living, discerning people. Have I not made a good exchange? an easy conscience for a galled one, liberty for bondage, worship in the spirit for worship in the form, and a living people for dead formalists. Oh, how the Sacrament so-called used to gall me! At the head knelt my carnal Pharisaical squire, with his pleasure-loving, God-hating wife, who was so filled with enmity against me that she would never hear me preach. I was compelled to tell them individually and personally that Christ died for them and shed His blood for their sins (I believing all the while particular redemption), of which I put the elements into their hands, saying, "Take, eat this," &c. Lower down knelt a man generally suspected of having once committed murder, and near him the most hardened Pharisee I ever knew in my life, whose constant reply to my attempted warnings, &c., was "I dare say it be as you says." I was so cut up and condemned that at last I could not do it, and employed my assistant to perform the whole, but then I had to kneel down with these characters, which was as bad; and so I found myself completely hedged in and driven from every refuge, till at last, like an animal hunted down to a rock by the sea-side, I had only one escape, which was to leap into the water, which bore me up and afforded me a sweet deliverance from my persecutors.

Lying reports have been circulated that I wish to return, and some that I have actually gone back, but I have never repented leaving for five minutes since I came out of her walls. I am convinced she is corrupt, root and branch, head and tail. . . .

I was long held by the example of others, but what is that? Am I to commit adultery because David so fell; or deny Christ because Peter so acted? "Every man shall bear his own burden." I cannot in death or judgment hide myself under another's garments, as the Papists think of entering heaven in the habit of Dominic or Francis. I stand before Him whose eyes are as flames of fire to search out the secrets of my heart. And what is this poor vain world with all its gilded clay, painted, touch-wood honours and respectability, and soap-bubble charms? What is all the wealth of the Church (falsely so-called) piled up in one heap, compared to a smile of a loving Saviour's countenance? And we must follow Him, not in respectability and honour, with maces and organs, and greetings in the market-place, and "Rabbi, Rabbi," but in contempt and shame, hated by the world, despised by professors, and condemned by well nigh all.

You will find poverty and wretchedness enough to break your heart in Ireland. What a pity that so rich and fertile a county as Meath should have a population well nigh famishing! Devonshire peasantry complain of poverty, but what is theirs to Irish misery? . . . . .

My pen has run on at a great length, and I have much to ask you to excuse. I generally write freely, and, therefore, often foolishly; but, I trust, as sincerely as a desperately deceitful heart permits. You will long to return to your own country and people. There seems in Ireland to be such a conflict between Popery and Protestantism that it nearly absorbs all other considerations. My recollection is, that the outworks were so vigilantly guarded that the citadel was neglected. The heavy blows the Establishment has since received have probably driven in her champions from attacking the Catholics to defend their own emoluments, and united, as in England of late years, parties once quite discordant, as the Evangelical and Orthodox. When parties thus unite to defend a system in the maintenance of which both are deeply interested, it usually detracts from the spirituality of the one without altering the carnality of the other. In my remembrance the Evangelical clergymen (so-called) in England, were quite separate from the Orthodox (so-called equally falsely), but they have been united within these last ten years. I had but one pulpit besides my own open to me in the Establishment in my neighbourhood, and that was more as an accommodation for the person than love to the truth, as he preached it, and, I believe, knew it not. I and another clergyman, a notorious adulterer, almost a *taurus publicus* in his parish, were the only persons the bishop refused to bow to at his visitation. And did I mind his public slight? No. I saw and felt he was dead before God, and that it was for Christ's sake I suffered reproach, being classed with a man known everywhere for the basest immorality. And now, through mercy, I am free from all their shackles, the iron of which entered into my soul.

Write to me as soon as you return, and give me a full account of your voyage, and how you got on with your host. I have not heard from my sister since I wrote to her. I like much of what you said in your last letter but one. It describes much of my feelings. I insist upon an experimental knowledge of Christ in the soul as the only relief for poverty, guilt, leprosy, bankruptcy, and damnation. This is, I believe, the true way of preaching Christ crucified, not the mere doctrine of the Cross, but a crucified Jesus experimentally known to the soul.

Your affectionate Friend,

J. C. P.

XVII —To Mr. Wm. Brown *

Stamford, Feb. 19, 1840.

My dear Sir,

Hearing a good account of your experience and ministry, I feel desirous to invite you for three Lord's-days, in August next, to preach among my people at Stamford and Oakham, where I statedly labour. . . . I sincerely hope you may be induced to comply with our wishes. It is not every minister whom I would admit into my pulpit, nor the friends willingly hear. We look more to experience, feeling, unction, and power than eloquence or abilities. An honest, sincere, God-fearing man, who knows divine things by divine teaching, and who will neither stretch himself above his measure nor crouch beneath it, but simply stand up as he is, will suit them better than a pasteboard giant or a lord mayor's show champion. . . . I shall say no more; you know the man and his communication.

I hope you may be induced to accept the invitation in the same spirit that it is given.

Wishing you every New Covenant blessing,

I am yours sincerely, for truth's sake,

J. C. P.

XVIII —To Mr. Wm. Brown

Stamford, March 4, 1840.

My dear Sir,

I hope the Lord may incline your heart to accept my invitation to come and supply for me at Stamford and Oakham, and that He may come with you to bless you.

* Mr. Brown was for some years minister of the Particular Baptist Church at Godmanchester; he afterwards removed to Brighton, where he died, December 10, 1867, aged 55.

My people, especially at Stamford, are very young, and for the most part weak and feeble. They love, I believe, however, clean provender (or, as the margin reads, "savoury"), winnowed with the shovel and the fan. Experimental preaching alone suits them, and, indeed, I would not knowingly introduce any other than an experimental preacher into my pulpit. I am deeply conscious of my own baseness, ignorance, blindness, and folly; but my malady is too deeply rooted to be healed by dry doctrines and speculative opinions. The blood of the Lamb, spiritually and supernaturally sprinkled and applied, is, I am sure, the only healing balm for a sin-sick soul. "No man can call Jesus Lord, but by the Holy Ghost." And all our knowledge that does not spring from the teachings of that holy and blessed Comforter I must cast aside as a thing of naught. A childlike spirit, a thinking meanly of ourselves, a panting after God, an insatiable desire after the waters of life, a conscience exercised upon good and evil, a love of the holy Lamb of God, and an abiding affection to His people, I look upon as more satisfactory evidences of grace than a sanctified countenance and a fluent tongue. We live in a day of great spiritual light, but it is to be feared of little spiritual life. I feel increasingly disposed to turn away from the opinions of men and seek spiritual knowledge at the fountain head. But, unless a man comes nowadays with a Shibboleth, he is almost set aside as a man of truth. He must use certain words, whether Scripture or not, must preach in a prescribed manner, as well as with prescribed matter. He must not vary from a certain mould, and if he dares to use his own way of setting forth truth, in his own simple language, and as he simply feels and has felt, many can hardly tell whether he is right or wrong, and the majority perhaps set him down as wrong altogether. I dislike, amazingly, the artificial mode of setting forth truth by which, when you hear a text given out you know all the divisions and mode of handling it before they are mentioned, and can tell the end of every sentence nearly as soon as you hear the beginning. It smells too strongly of Dr. Gill and premeditation to suit me, but some cannot eat the dish unless served up every day in a plate of the same pattern; and, like children, when a differently shaped or differently painted cup comes on the table, cannot drink, as being so occupied with the novelty. But God will bless His own truth and His own servants, and when He thrusts forth His own stewards, will not send them forth as apes and imitators either of Huntington, Gadsby, or Warburton. They shall have their own line of truth and their own method of setting it forth, and they shall be commended, sooner or later, to spiritual consciences as men taught of Him. My pen has run on, as it often does, according to the flow of my own thoughts.

Believe me, I shall be glad to hear from you your willingness to come. If I did not esteem you as a man of truth I should not ask you, as I feel responsible for the supplies. My love to the Brighton friends.

Yours sincerely, for truth's sake,
J. C. P.

XIX —To Miss Philpot

Stamford, Mar. 31, 1840.

My dear Fanny,

Though you might feel your letter was written in a presumptuous spirit, I cannot say that I perceived any trace of it, but thought it, like your other letters, breathed a tone of sincerity and humility. It is well, however, to be of quick understanding in the fear of the Lord, and to condemn ourselves when we feel guilty, for if we judge ourselves we shall not be judged.

I fully agree with Mr. Isbell that Hebrews x. and xi. refer not to the elect, but graceless professors; nor do I see any great difficulty in what is said of their attainments, though the language is very strong. I fully agree with you that the saints sin wilfully if by that expression is meant "deliberately." When David wrote to Joab to set Uriah in the fore-front of the hottest battle, and retire from him, that he might be smitten and die, he certainly acted in the most deliberate manner. Consider his writing the letter, signing, sealing, and sending it off to the camp. What room there was for conscience to work and check his meditated crime! So when Aaron made the golden calf; what an interval of deliberation was there between breaking off the golden earrings, and fashioning it with a graving tool!

David's numbering the people, in spite of the remonstrances of Joab, was clearly a deliberate sin; and so was Abraham's, in twice denying his wife. The conclusion, therefore, is inevitable, that as the saints sin wilfully, *i.e.*, deliberately, the Apostle in Hebrews vi. cannot mean such transgressions as all saints more or less fall into. My own conviction is that by "wilful sinning" the Apostle means wilful and deliberate apostacy; and that by falling away, Hebrews vi. 6, he means falling into open apostacy. For he speaks of treading under foot the Son of God, and "counting the blood of the covenant an unholy thing," and "putting the Son of God to an open shame." Now to sin is not "to tread under foot the Son of God," and still less "to count the blood of the covenant an unholy thing;" for when a saint falls into sin, even with his eyes open, when he awakes out of his delusive dream, he longs for nothing so much as to feel the atoning blood of the Saviour applied to his conscience. Nor in the greatest hardness of his heart does he ever tread under foot the dear Son of God, but shudders at the thought. And the Apostle adds even "wilfully" to apostacy, as Peter openly apostatised, but not wilfully, as Judas did. I acknowledge the words of the Apostle respecting the attainments of apostates are very strong, and that there is much difficulty in many of his expressions. But I think they all may be explained of such a natural work as counterfeits the operations of the blessed Spirit. It says, for instance, that they were "once enlightened." Now, this may certainly signify light in the head as distinct from grace in the heart. In the time of the Apostles there were gifts of tongues, &c., as pointed out in 1 Cor. xii. Now it seems probable that these outward gifts were bestowed upon characters devoid of grace for the benefit of the Church, and therefore Paul (1 Cor. xiii.) supposes he may have all these gifts and yet be nothing. I think, therefore, that such expressions as "tasting the heavenly gift," and "being made partakers of the Holy Ghost," refer not to inward regenerating grace, but to such outward gifts as were then common. That they "tasted the good word of God and the powers of the world to come," I think may be explained by their having such an acquaintance with it as amounted to a taste only in the mouth, without an eating, feeding upon, or digesting it. We know there are natural joys in professors, as well as natural convictions, and the power of Satan working as an angel of light upon a deluded heart is wonderful indeed. All this may amount to a taste where there is no real feeding on the flesh of the Son of Man. You will also observe that faith, hope, and love are not once mentioned as existing in such characters, nor is anything said of repentance, regeneration, godly sorrow, filial fear, contrition, humility, or patience. Nay, the Apostle compares them to earth that bringeth forth thorns and briers, and is nigh unto cursing, whilst he expressly says that he is persuaded "*better* things, and things which accompany salvation," of those to whom he was writing, plainly implying that such things as he had previously spoken of did not accompany salvation. These "better things" and "things which accompany salvation" are "love" (ver. 10), manifested by its work and labour; "hope" (ver. 11), as an anchor of the soul, sure and steadfast, entering within the veil (ver. 19); and "faith" (ver. 12), whereby the promises are inherited. These are graces in opposition to gifts. A man may fall from the latter, but not from the former.

Again, if you refer to the connection of Hebrews x. 26, I think it is plain the Apostle refers to apostacy. He says (ver. 23), "Let us hold fast the profession of our faith without wavering;" implying there was a danger of letting go even the profession of faith. And he adds (ver. 25), "Not forsaking the assembling of ourselves together," &c., which it appears many then did, for fear of persecution; and then adds, "*For* if we sin wilfully," &c., connecting the wilful sin for wilful apostacy with ceasing to hold fast a profession, and forsaking the assemblies of saints. He also adds the pangs of remorse in such (ver. 27), and styles them "adversaries." Now, to fall into sin, or commit it in a measure wilfully, *i.e.*, deliberately, is a very different thing from being an adversary of Christ, despising his Gospel (as implied ver. 28), treading under foot the Son of God, counting His blood an unholy thing, and doing despite (literally, treating with insult and contempt,) unto the spirit of grace. The sin of the Corinthian (1 Cor. v. 1) was not so much as named among the Gentiles, and was a complication of adultery and incest. Of course, his taking his father's wife was a deliberate act, and not what is commonly called "a fall." And yet, when he repented after his being put out of the Church, and manifested repentance, he was to be forgiven and comforted, 2 Cor. ii. 6—8. Peter sinned wilfully when he withdrew himself from the Gentile converts for fear of the Jews (Gal. ii. 12), and therefore Paul withstood him to the face, and reproved him before them all. "There is," says John, "a sin unto death," 1 John v. 16. This, I believe, is wilful apostacy, or the sin against the Holy Ghost; but he adds, "There is a sin not unto death:" such are the falls and backslidings of saints. I have here, according to your request, given you a mere sketch of my views on this subject, which cannot be fully entered into without considerable space, and, after all, there are great difficulties in the passages. I have thought, sometimes, there is a purposed ambiguity to stir up the souls of the saints who need continual warnings of this kind to preserve them from declensions. God preserves all His saints, but He does so by means of promises, precepts, warnings, exhortations, threatenings, awful examples, &c., which serve as hedges against their falling away. He does not keep them from falling as a man puts a plate on a shelf, but as a mother warns her child of a deep well in the garden, and not to go too near it. I fear you will not find my exposition very satisfactory, but it may be a clue to further thought on your part.

I have received both Mr. Isbell's letters, and was much interested in his account of his visit to Ireland. He found things much as I expected. The Evangelical clergy are a dark tribe as to any internal acquaintance with the things of God. The little they know is chiefly in the letter, and they are not sound even in that.

I have a high esteem for Triggs. What a revolution, that the daughter, wife, and mother of a clergyman should like to hear a poor mason! I am sure, if we have satisfactory evidences that it is a real work of the blessed Spirit, we may well say with Hart, "Then grace is grace indeed." Oh, who is beyond the reach of sovereign, matchless grace? What a sweet way of salvation! How safe and secure to the elect! If our mother feels her deep need of the Saviour's blood to be sprinkled and applied to her conscience, she has every encouragement to cast herself at His feet. Who were farther from God than we in our affections and desires?

But He is found of them that sought Him not. It will be a blessed link in the grand predestinated chain that you left Walmer, that barren and icy land, to settle at Stoke, should the Lord's grace and mercy be clearly manifested in the remnant of our family. You are certainly highly favoured in having Mr. Isbell at Stoke.

You do wisely, I think, to mix but little with those who attend at the same place. To see occasionally a tried and exercised soul is profitable. "They that feared the Lord spake often one to another." "As iron sharpeneth iron, so a man sharpeneth the countenance of his friend." To visit the poor, also, of the flock, removes the imputation of pride which is easily affixed to too great seclusion.

You seem to begin to find the believer's path more rough and thorny than you at first anticipated. I have little opinion of those who find it a smooth and flowery road. As Berridge says:—

"The strait and narrow road they missed
That leads to Zion's hill."

There were little need of promises and such other encouragements as the word of God is full of, if believers were not brought into such straits and difficulties as to continually need them. Our heart is full of unbelief, infidelity, worldliness, pride, presumption, hypocrisy, and every other hateful sin. Where these evils exist they will manifest themselves, and it is this warfare between flesh and spirit which makes true religion such a continual scene of changes. What deadness is often felt, what darkness of soul, what coldness and hardness of heart, what disinclination, yea, what aversion to the things which belong to our peace! Thus guilt comes in and the conscience becomes defiled therewith, and we cry out, "Woe is me! My leanness, my leanness! Woe unto me! My soul cleaveth to the dust; quicken Thou me according to Thy word. Wilt Thou not revive us again, that Thy people may trust in Thee?" Some of God's people are not exposed to gross temptations, but, as Newton says of himself, they suffer by sap and mine. The fortress of their heart, that is, is not assailed by storm, but gradually undermined by the slower process of coldness, deadness, disinclination to spiritual things, and a miserable, careless, carnal, worldly, slothful state, which benumbs all the spiritual faculties.

I am very pleased to hear my brother-in-law is so affectionate to dear Mary Anne, and allows her to go to chapel; and I am very glad she has an inclination to go and hear the word of truth. May the Lord visit her soul with His own rich mercy and love, and that will abundantly satisfy her soul! You must expect to bear a cross if you are on the Lord's side. The carnal mind is enmity against God, and you know from personal experience what dislike and contempt the carnal mind has to dissent; and you well remember what a character was entertained of Mr. Isbell, even by yourself, before you knew the meaning and power of what he preached. You need not marvel, then, if you are despised and hated, as well as slandered and misrepresented. It is the usual lot of those who follow Jesus in the regeneration. Yea, He has promised a blessing on all such reviled and slandered followers of Himself. Matt. v. 11, 12; John xx. 18—21.

S—— sends her love to our dear mother, yourself, and Mary Anne, in which I heartily join.

Your affectionate Brother,

J. C. P.

XX—To Mr. Fowler, of Woburn

Stamford, April, 1840.

My dear Friend,

I consider it the part of a friend to act as you have done in asking me for an explanation of what you consider me to err in, instead of following the multitude to do evil in spreading my supposed errors behind my back and concealing them to my face.

I am glad you have asked me for an explanation of my meaning, as it allows me to clear up a point on which I think you misunderstand me. What were my words? "There are but two healthy states of the soul—hungering and feeding, &c. All other states are maladies and sicknesses." Is this new or strange doctrine? My friend, what are we by nature but one mass of malady and disease? But this malady and disease are not seen nor felt but by the entrance of divine light and life into the soul. The entrance of these heavenly blessings brings what I may call a principle of health into the soul, which, as Hart sweetly says, "lives and labours under load." And it is the working of this healthy principle, this new and heavenly nature, under the blessed Spirit's operations, in which the greater part of experience exists. Darkness, deadness, aversion to all good, headlong proneness to all evil, pride, unbelief, infidelity, lust, covetousness, enmity to God and godliness, what are those but maladies and diseases? Sorrow of heart for sin, breathings after God, hatred of self, living desires towards the Lord of life and glory, separation of spirit from the things of time and sense, faith in exercise, hope casting forth its anchor, love drawing forth the affections; these, when felt, are states of health, that is, the healthy man of grace seems for a while (alas! for how short a while!) lifting up his head amidst diseases and sickness. Is this inconsistent with sound doctrine or sound experience? You and I would often much sooner read the *Examiner* than the Bible, and would sooner talk on indifferent subjects with our wives than seek the Lord's face. Is this deadness and coldness, and miserable aversion to all good health or sickness? I feel it to be my malady, not my health. But again I feel what a base wretch I am. I hate myself for my base lusts; I sigh after the Lord to come down and visit my soul; I feel a little spirituality of mind, and taste a sweetness in the word of God. Is this a sick or healthy state of soul? I call my soul sick when sin reigns and rules; I call it healthy when grace more or less predominates. I may use wrong expressions, but you are not one who would make a man an offender for a word. Now let us come to experimental preaching. Does he preach experimentally who traces out the workings of corruption, or he who traces out the workings of grace in and under corruptions? I believe the latter. You know much of the workings of pride, lust, and covetousness; and you know something of godly fear, self-loathing, and contrition under them. Which am I to enter into? You are dead, cold, and lifeless. Am I to describe deadness, or trace out life working under deadness? Am I to describe pride, or the self-loathing of the soul when pride is discovered? Am I to say to my hearers, "You are cold, dead, hardened, unbelieving, proud, lustful, covetous. All these are marks and tokens of life"? Or am I to say, "Life struggling against death, godly fear leading to self-abhorrence, groans and sighs under a guilty conscience, cries for deliverance, pantings after God, and so on, are marks of life"? There is a precious experience, and there is a vile experience, and he that would be God's mouth must take the one from the other. I believe that to preach the corruptions of our nature apart from the workings of grace in them and under them is to build up bastards. One is preaching the remedy without ever entering into the malady, thus bolstering up hypocrites and making the heart of the righteous sad. The other is this—to set forth corruption in all its workings towards evil, and leave out the workings of godly fear, in and under corruption. If I feel dissatisfied, burdened, grieved for my wicked and wayward heart and life, the very feeling marks the existence of life. But is a minister to build me up in this, that I am to take deadness as an evidence? Let him tell me to feel and hate myself, for it is a mark of life, and I may get some encouragement. But to tell me that deadness (that is, deadness unfelt) is a mark of life, is a pulpit lie fit only for the twice dead. You might write to me that you are quite tired of all religion, that you hate going to chapel, that you rarely pray, scarcely ever read the Scriptures, never feel a sigh or a groan, nor any pantings after Christ. Well, I should answer, I know what you mean, for I am too like you. But do you mean to bring this forward as Christian experience? If you do, you are deceived. For if it be experience, the more of it the better, for we can never have too much experience, and to find it in its perfection I must go to the dead Pharisee or the twice dead professor. But tell me of some revival, of some brokenness, of contrition, of some glimpses of mercy, of some workings of life within, and I will say this is experience, and the more we have the better. I find the experience of the Scriptures that of mourning, complaint, sorrow of heart, pantings after God, hoping and trusting in His mercy. David in Psalm li. does not describe the workings of his lust towards Bathsheba, but cries and groans, "Cast me not away from Thy presence, &c." If the experience of corruption be good, why should not the practice of it be good too? If to have eyes full of adultery be experience, that is, Christian experience, why should not hands full of adultery be Christian practice? But, on the other hand, if to sigh and cry to be kept from evil is Christian experience, then to be kept from it is Christian practice. What I call experimental cant is this. Professors without life say, "I am so dead, I am so dark, I am so unbelieving." "Are you ever otherwise? Are you resting upon that as an evidence? Is that your state for months together?" I would answer, "Then it is to be feared that you are a bastard and not a son." I once heard a person give a long description of what a proud, covetous, lustful, slothful, rebellious heart he had. Among other things, he said that he never saw a farm, or a nice field, but he coveted it, or a carriage in the streets that he did not want to possess it. This I suppose he called experience. I do not; for if it be, Nabal and the rich fool are the most experimental saints in the Bible. Suppose I coveted Woburn Abbey, and the titles, estates, and power of the Duke of Bedford, would you call this Christian experience? If so, there must be a throng of experimental saints every day in the week that the abbey is shown. But suppose I were to walk in the park, and feel that I would sooner have Christ in my heart than a thousand dukedoms; suppose under that feeling I panted after Christ as the hart after the water brooks, and suppose that I dropped a penitential tear over my proud, covetous heart that ever coveted such toys, I might call that Christian experience. If pride, lust, and covetousness are experience, then the greatest sinner is the greatest Christian. See, my friend, on what a shore error in this momentous matter leads. Had this person told us of his covetousness, and the checks, the sighs, the deliverances he experienced out of it, I should have called it experience; but to set forth corruption separated from the workings of grace under it, I call a mistake altogether. Who paints corruption like Hart? But who paints more strongly the working of grace in corruption? I believe the malady is to be described, but never apart from the strivings of godly fear, faith, &c., under it. Why do we preach experimentally? To find out the feelings of living souls and cut off dead professors. But to trace out sin without godly sorrow, guilt, or condemnation under sin, is to preach the experience of the dead, not of the living.

I meant no more than this, and if you have understood me otherwise, it must arise from my want of expressing myself clearly. I believe I have advanced nothing here in which you will not agree.

If there be, I shall be glad to explain myself more fully, either by word when we meet, or by letter. Remember me affectionately to Smart, who, I suppose, is with you. I hope he and you will not set me down as wavering from the truth.

Yours sincerely and affectionately,

J. C. P.

XXI —To Mr. Parry

Stamford, May 12*th*, 1840.

My dear Friend,

* * * * *

I am sorry our dear and highly-esteemed friend Dredge should be so hurt at my piece on "Strict Communion." Did he not always know that I held and practised it? and what is to hinder my public defence of it when called upon to do so? I did not seek nor volunteer the controversy, but was called upon by name to defend it, nor could I shun it consistently with faithfulness. Will not friend D. defend and contend for his views of truth, and am I not at liberty to do the same? I love and esteem him far more than I do hundreds of strict Baptists; but I am not to love and esteem his errors. And I say deliberately, that were the question ever to arise whether I am to part with a friend or truth, I would not hesitate to part with the former. For truth, hitherto, I have had to part with the kindest friends after the flesh, as well as all my prospects in life, an independent income, good name and respectability. I hope I shall not now be left to swerve from it, even though to defend it wounds kindest and warmest friends. A living soul cannot long fight against truth; its keen edge must sooner or later enter the conscience, and be well assured if there be an abscess anywhere it will pierce it, and let out all the blood and matter.

I have felt myself of late very jealous of doctrinal errors, seeing to what consequences they lead, and that they usually are connected with delusion in experience and inconsistency in conduct. It is a mercy to be well guarded by having the loins girt about with truth. Friend Dredge will see by Tiptaft's letter that both he and J. K. are of the same mind with us. His opposition produces no unkind feeling in my mind, but it will not move me a jot to swerve from truth. Let him search the Scriptures, like the noble Beræans, whether these things are so. I was forced into the controversy, and being in it was bound to defend the side I believe to be true as well as I could. Nay, more, I feel disposed to go on with it if needful, and not to shrink from the combat.

I have had an attack of my old complaint, which has confined me to the house, and in great measure to bed, since Friday. I could not preach yesterday. The day being wet, the disappointment was not so great, though some had come fourteen miles. Mr. Morris read a sermon of Huntington's; I am very sure a hundred times better one than I could have preached, but you know reading is rarely relished like preaching.

I shall be glad to have a friendly chat, or rather a series of them, with you. An author is once said to have published a book with this title (*i.e.* translated) "Upon everything in the world and something besides," I think this might almost serve for a title to our conversation. I could very well wish to pass through London altogether and miss Zoar. It is a trying place to preach in, and I often feel I have no business in the pulpit at all. I was sorry to see the word "anniversary" used for the Welwyn preaching, as I have so often declined preaching at anniversaries, and this lays me open to the charge of inconsistency; neither can it be an anniversary, as it is on a different day from that of last year. Friend —— will not find me making baptism a bone of contention, publicly or privately. When attacked I defend myself, and when called upon for my reasons I give them; but I never wish to introduce strife or needless contention. Can friend Dredge say I ever cut him off because he was not a Baptist? Can he say I showed more favour to Mrs. Wild and others? Can he bring forward any sermon, or any speech, in the pulpit or out of it, wherein I condemned the non-Baptists? I believe if I have erred it has been more in the other way. He has, therefore, no reason to say I have cut them off. I have a firm conviction in the matter, one formed before I knew him, and for this belief I have my Scriptural grounds. If he can, he is at liberty to overthrow them, but if he cannot, he will do well to follow the advice of Gamaliel (Acts v. 39). If I could go through the world nipping a piece of truth off here, and clipping a corner off there, how many arrows should I escape from without? A faithful man like him should not complain of faithfulness. If he or any one can with meekness of wisdom show my arguments false, let them do so; but let them beware of opposing truth because it cuts them. I hope, however, he will have some of the mollifying ointment fall upon his eyes and into his heart, and that will set him all right. I am happy that our highly-esteemed friend Mrs. Wild is not angered by my remarks on strict communion; I am sure she is a worth a thousand rotten Baptists.

Kay seems to have wielded the sword pretty freely and forcibly at Allington. But if he cuts off seeking and seekers, what becomes of his experience for a good many years? But, after all, his sword can never cut out that text from the mouth of the blessed Lord, which has been the support of thousands, "He that seeketh findeth." I believe the following verse is the key to his text, Luke xiii. 25, "When once the Master of the house is risen up, and shut to the door," &c. This is spoken of foolish virgins who find, too late, there is no oil in their lamps, of a deathbed natural repentance, and tallies with Prov. i. 24—32. But it was never meant to cut off spiritual seekers and groaners, who put their mouths in the dust, if so be there may be hope. For if so, it would cut off the whole family of God at one time or other of their experience, for all are seekers before finders of the pearl of great price, though in the first manifestation of the only true God He is found of them that sought Him not. But the finding of guilt through the finding of the Book of the Law hid in the temple, makes the finder of a heart-searching God to become a seeker of a Saviour from the wrath to come, and thus these texts become reconciled. "What comfort can a Saviour bring?" &c., says our great experimental authority. "O, beware of trust ill-grounded," &c. Hart will not allow a man to be healed before he is wounded, to be saved before he is lost." What can wounded folks do but *seek* for healing, and what can lost souls do but *seek* salvation. To discourage such is to act differently from the great Shepherd, who came to seek and to save that which was lost. Yet to set them down safe as seekers before they find Him of whom the prophets have spoken, Jesus of Nazareth the Son of God, is certainly as great an error on the other side, and this Kay, perhaps, was anxious to avoid, and so, instead of hitting the narrow channel, ran aground on one of the sand-banks, where a buoy had been fixed but escaped the eyes of the pilot, seeing breakers on the other side of the vessel. Well, all of you came safe to land whom God had quickened, though the steersman pulled the helm the wrong way and drenched all who were heavy laden with doubts and fears. I dare say the salt water made you all cry, "Lead me to the rock that is higher than I." The pilot, however, seems for the present to have lost his commission, and another hand has got hold of the helm. May the God of Israel guide his hand and show him the narrow channel, and may he remember he has a precious freight on board, even if one pew could hold all the living souls in the chapel, and I believe there are more than that there. I am glad to hear that the Lord is with him, and that he is so well heard. May the Lord make one heart and one mind to be in us that love His truth.

Your affectionate Friend,

J. C. P.

XXII —To Mr. William Brown

Allington, July 27, 1840.

My dear Friend,

May the Lord go with you to Stamford and be your rearward. You know enough of the ministry to be deeply sensible that only in the Lord's light do we see light, and only in His life do we feel life. To be a daily pauper living on alms is humbling to proud nature that always is seeking to be something and to do something. "Though I be nothing" was Paul's highest attainment in the knowledge of self. Much pain in wounded pride and mortified self should we be spared, were this self-nothingness wrought in us. "Venture to be nought," says Hart. But it is like a man casting himself into the sea from the forecastle, that he may be buoyed up by an invisible arm. If you can venture to be nought in your meditated journey it will save you a world of anxiety and trouble. But proud, vain, conceited flesh wants to be something, to preach well, to cut a figure, and be admired as a preacher. With all this there is at times a hatred of such base feelings, and a willingness to be nothing that the Lord may be all in all. But doubts whether the Lord will be with us, whether He can condescend to bless such base wretches, and whether we have not presumption enough to damn thousands, will all at times work with earnest desires and breathings that He would bless us indeed, and that His hand might be with us, and that He would speak in us, and by us, and through us, to the hearts of His chosen.

Yours faithfully, for truth's sake,

J. C. P.

XXIII —To Mr. John Hards, Walworth

Allington, August, 1840.

My dear Friend,

I have thought that some of those sermons that I preached at Zoar, which I should myself most wish to have been published, were not, whilst others, in delivering which I felt less favoured, have been printed in the "Penny Pulpit." I certainly felt my soul opened and my tongue loosed to set forth the various wiles of the crafty adulteress in hunting for the precious life, the last evening that I preached at Zoar; but as I cannot now call to mind what I delivered on that occasion, I fear it would be useless to attempt it. I might, indeed, were I so disposed, trace out the workings of this base adulteress; but I could not say it should resemble the discourse I then delivered, except in the general drift. Here the painstaking ministers, who lay out all their discourses by rule and plummet beforehand, have the advantage of us, who are compelled to trust to the Lord for His supplies of wisdom and utterance at the time. The text occurred to my mind as I was getting up on Tuesday morning, and I saw that there was a view of experience in it suited to the occasion, as well as to the daily feelings of living saints. I, therefore, was encouraged to take it with me into the pulpit, and the Lord, I trust, set before me an open door, for He shutteth and no man openeth, and He openeth and no man shutteth.

I was certainly gratified at seeing so large a congregation as was then gathered together, more especially as no notice had been given on the previous Thursday of the alteration of the evening to the Tuesday. Having so many discouragements from my own fearful heart and unbelieving nature, and so much opposition from the professing church, as well as the world, I need occasional liftings up, lest I should sink into utter despondency that the Lord had not called me to the work of the ministry; dark in soul, dead in desires, cold in affections, earthly in appetites, barren in heavenly fruits, and everything but what I wish to be, and I feel I should be; I need many tokens for good to persuade me that I am in the King's highway of holiness, where none but the redeemed walk. Many think that a minister is exempt from such coldness, deadness, and barrenness, as private Christians feel; and the hypocritical looks and words of many of Satan's ministers favour this delusion. Holiness is so much on their tongues, and on their faces, that their deluded hearers necessarily conclude that it is in their hearts; but, alas! nothing is easier or more common than an apostolic face and a Judas heart. Most pictures that I have seen of the "Last Supper" represent Judas Iscariot with a ferocious countenance. Had painters drawn a holy, meek-looking face, I believe they would have given a truer, if not so poetical a resemblance. Many pass for angels in the pulpit who are devils and beasts in heart, lips, and life, did all come abroad which is transacted at home. It is our mercy, if we only feel and groan under corruption inwardly, without it breaking forth outwardly, to wound our own souls, grieve the people of God, and gladden our enemies. Let God but take the cover off the boiling cauldron of our corrupt nature, and the filthy scum would turn over in the sight of all men.

I am glad you felt satisfied with my refusal to attend the anniversary, to which I was, through you, invited. I see no warrant for them in the word, but rather the contrary. "Ye observe *days,* and months, and times, and years, I am afraid of you," &c. (Gal. iv. 10, 11.) They are generally money-getting contrivances, and more fit for apes to play their mimicry at in the pulpit, than for ministers of truth to attend. Many places which hate me for the truth's sake, are desirous to deal with me as the monkey did to the cat, when it made use of its paw to pull the hot chesnuts out of the fire. I may preach and bring down all the hatred of professors; but as long as I can get a few sovereigns for them they munch the chesnuts, and abuse the hand that procured them. So I am resolved not to attend such places and seasons unless I well know the people and am certain they are striving, not only for the faith of the Gospel, but also among themselves to support the cause and pay off their debt. This is the case at Welwyn, where I have preached these last two years. Mr. Huntington, I believe, found that many wished to use him as a means of getting money, who hated his preaching; he, therefore, declined such invitations.

I understand that Mr. W. has declared his renunciation of that abominable error which he held in denying backsliding, but as I have not read his letter to Mr. A., I cannot say how true this rumour is. We feel ourselves to backslide too constantly and too basely every day, to deny it. We must give the lie to all our feelings, our sighs, our groans, and our tears, as well as to the word of God, if we deny the backsliding of believers.

May the Lord smile graciously upon you, and be the light of your countenance.

I am, my dear Friend,

Yours affectionately, for truth's sake,

J. C. P.

XXIV —To Mr. Wm. Gadsby

Stamford, Sept., 1840.

My dear Friend,

I was truly sorry to hear of your serious injury, and wish it were in my power to render you some assistance. Were we Arminians I could supply you with abundance of precepts and counsel to act faith, exercise patience, and cultivate resignation under your present affliction. But all such counsel you would value at its due worth; and I believe were all the property of Manchester of equal value with such advice, it would puzzle all its accountants to find how much it was worth less than O. My desire, then, for you is, that you may feel yourself the passive moistened clay in the hands of the heavenly Potter, and experience His blessed fingers moulding you to His divine will. If a sparrow cannot fall to the ground without Jehovah, much less the body which lodges the ransomed soul of William Gadsby. But what can old nature do under pain and confinement but murmur, rebel, argue, question, and find fault with the garden walk, and the slipping foot, and the fragile limb, and the splints, and the bandage, and the aching back, aye, and the Sovereign Ruler of all things Himself, who appointed this among the all things that are to work together for your spiritual good.

I have been long searching ineffectually for something good and holy in self, but after much investigation I have been obliged to come to Paul's conclusion: "I know that in me, that is, in my flesh, there dwelleth no good thing." But to be a pauper, and live all one's life upon alms; and they, too, to be rarely given, and usually not before the eyes fail with looking upward, how galling and mortifying to the proud spirit of a rebel! And then to have such long seasons of neither food nor famine, without either begging or receiving; but to be borne down by a heavy mass of carnality and death, well may the soul thus situated cry aloud—

"Needy, and naked, and unclean,
Empty of good and full of ill;
A lifeless lump of loathsome sin,
Without the power to act or will."

Wishing you a speedy recovery from your present state, and that the Lord may favour your soul with many sweet visitations from Himself,

I am, my dear Friend,
Yours affectionately, for truth's sake,
J. C. P.

XXV.—To Mr. Parry.

Stamford, Sept. 28, 1840.

My dear Friend,

I was sorry that you should think I cut you off so short by sending only a note, but I wished you to write to Mr. Isbell without delay, and thought a few lines would be sufficient. But, indeed, it is now much with my writing, as Warburton sometimes says of his preaching, it seems "going spark out."

* * * * * *

My wretched helplessness and beggary were never more painfully felt by me, and my most miserable impotency to all that is good seems to run through all I am and have, all I think, say, or do. I feel, too, more of a bankrupt in the pulpit than, I think, I ever before experienced, and seem to have nothing, and be nothing that is holy, heavenly, gracious, or spiritual. Were I not kept and held in I should feel disposed to run away from the work altogether, so burdensome do I at times feel it to be. But the Lord can and will keep us to the work, whether we will or not. I found this the case at Stadham. I could not leave it though I wished to do so, and now only wonder how I stayed. I think were I then as rebellious and flesh-indulging as now, I should soon have bid farewell to the damp green, and the miry roads, and the unhealthy village; but, go where we will, we carry with us the body of sin and death. The load of our nature's evil is so unalterably fixed upon our shoulders that nothing but the icy hand of death can loosen it; and were we to sally forth in a fit of rebellion, and rush to the ends of the earth, the old man, with all his diseases, would still be part and parcel of us. We are continually praying to have the fear of God in our hearts, and this very godly fear causes all our trouble. Had you no inward principle of godly fear you could soon slip your neck out of the collar by filling your pulpit with a parson. My daily and hourly idolatries, sins, and pollutions, my ignorance, folly, and blindness, my pride, presumption, and hypocrisy, my utter insolvency and impotency would give me no pain, and cause no sighs had I no internal principle, whatsoever it be, which discovers to me these evils, and causes me to feel pain under them. I was thinking this morning of Tiptaft's words, "Lord, grant that we may not sin cheap." If that prayer be answered it will cut us out abundance of trouble; for, as we sin every moment, we shall pay dear for it every moment. A dear bargain costs us sometimes, in earthly things, a good deal of pain and annoyance; but if we are never to sin cheap, our dear bargains, spiritually, will be always causing us pain and sorrow. . . .

Were you to get a minister whom neither you nor the people could hear, and you Allington folks are somewhat nice in your hearing, you would be worse off than you are now. The way to heaven is not to be lined out like a railroad, but traced through all its windings like a path through a wood. I don't know whether I would not sooner hear doctrine preached than a cut-and-dry experience, so regularly laid out as though the all-wise and wonder-working Jehovah must needs move in a line chalked out by a worm. He never made our natural faces alike, nor created two flowers nor two leaves precisely similar; nor do I believe that we can find two vessels of mercy dealt with precisely in the same way. And yet there is a blessed family likeness running through all the quickened elect race, whereby all are brought spiritually and savingly to know the only true God and Jesus Christ, whom He hath sent. Were there not these family features, there would be no use in experimental preaching, and it would no longer be true that, as in water, face answereth to face, so the heart of man to man. I hope the Lord may bless Mr. Isbell's ministry to your soul and the souls of the people.

You have probably heard that Mr. Gadsby has broken his leg by falling down whilst walking in his garden. The church at Manchester has written to me to supply for a month; but the friends here are unwilling to let me go, and therefore I have been obliged to decline. It is feared he will be laid aside three months.

I am sorry to find Mrs. P. continues indisposed. The afflictions of our wives are our own, and must always be keenly felt by those who have any affection for their second selves. . . . .

If farmers were now to have no reverses I hardly know what would become of them. They would ride over everybody's head. Ballast is a very painful thing to carry, but what vessel could sail safely without it? Not the farmers, when the gale of prosperity so swells their sails. But, I doubt not, that you find temporal prosperity is but a poor balm for an aching heart. Guilt and fears of perishing eternally, with the heavy load of a wicked heart, are not to be allayed by wheat selling at forty shillings a sack. But with all your ballast and heavy weight you have not an ounce too much; you would not walk steadily without it. What has kept us both, ever since we knew one another, steadfast to experimental religion but having so many bruises, wounds, and putrefying sores, which need mollifying with Gospel ointment. You would have been long ere this satisfied with dry doctrine, if your weights and burdens had not made you feel your need of Divine power and heavenly manifestations. Probably you would have been shooting arrows at Huntington as an enthusiast, and at Hart's hymns as of too gloomy a cast, and have been despising Warburton as always muddling in corruption, unless you had had the top of the boiling pot of your own heart lifted off. Were we walking together by the side of your canal I could talk of many things more freely than I can write. Give Mr. Isbell my love and sincere desires that the Lord may be with him. My love to the friends, especially Mrs. Wild, E. Pope, and Mr. Dredge.

Your affectionate Friend,

J. C. P.

XXVI.—To Miss Philpot.

Stamford, Oct. 28, 1840.

My dear Fanny,

I should feel sorry if you thought that there was any cause in youself which has made me neglectful of my promise to write to you a long letter. Believe me that it is not so. The cause is in myself alone. Sometimes other occupations, sometimes preaching engagements, sometimes travelling backwards and forwards to Oakham have been hindrances; but frequent as well as more powerful obstacles have arisen from my own slothfulness, leanness, and spiritual helplessness and inability. The apostle says of himself, "The good that I would I do not, and the evil that I would not that I do;" and again, "When I would do good evil is present with me." Such were the complaints of this man of God, the highly-favoured vessel of mercy and ambassador of peace and salvation. He was not "a saint," in the Popish and Protestant-Popish sense of the word, that is, a man universally and perfectly holy, one elevated, as it were, on a pedestal above human passions and creature infirmities. But he was "a saint" in the only true and scriptural sense—*i.e.*, one sanctified by God the Father, and separated in His eternal decree, sanctified by God the Son when He bought him with His own precious blood, and sanctified by God the Holy Ghost when He regenerated him and made him a new creature in Christ Jesus. And one evidence of his being thus sanctified was, that he groaned in the body, being burdened. Sin was, in him, an indwelling principle, which continually put itself forth in thoughts, words, and actions, contrary to that new living and holy principle which the Blessed Spirit had implanted. So that, not absence of sin but the groaning of the living soul under it is the evidence of saintship. Sin, in our carnal mind, is like the blood that circulates through the arteries and veins of our body. I cannot prick any part of my body with a pin where blood will not flow from the wound. Nor can I put my finger on any spot of my carnal mind where sin is not, and whence, if pressed by temptation, sin will not gush forth in a larger or smaller stream. And, to pursue the figure a step further, as blood is the element that nurtures our bodies, so sin is the nourishment of our carnal mind. Humbling thought! that what God hates, what made the Son of God bleed and die, what fills hell with miserable beings to all eternity, dwells in our carnal mind, and fills and occupies every part of it. But it will not destroy nor separate from the eternal love of God those whom Christ has redeemed by His blood. "Now, therefore," says Paul, "there is no condemnation to them that are in Christ Jesus, who walk not after the flesh, but after the Spirit." And he asks triumphantly, "Who shall separate us from the love of Christ Jesus?" Not even sin shall effect this separation, nor undo the finished work of Christ upon the cross.

I was sorry to hear of Mr. Isbell's temporal and spiritual troubles. I should think that the anger of the old members of his chapel had a deeper root than that of baptism and strict communion. His faithfulness in turning up the deep corruptions of the heart, and insisting so strongly on Divine manifestations, is much more likely to have drawn forth their enmity, and have made baptism and strict communion merely a pretext. It is a tangible thing, and affords them some standing ground to accuse him of departing from their original church order whilst to find fault with his faithfulness would be to accuse themselves.

You will, with the rest of his hearers that are attached to his ministry, be glad to welcome him home from Allington. I think it most probable that Mr. Isbell may meet my friend Tiptaft at Exeter, and I hope the interview may be pleasant and profitable. I have not seen Mr. Ireson since he returned from Plymouth, but I understand that he was gratified with his visit. His usual manner is very reserved, and I should think his silence arose more from what he felt in himself than from anything he saw in you or others. When our own conscience points out anything as inconsistent, we easily believe that others see that which we so keenly see ourselves. But their eyes are fixed upon something which we do not ourselves perceive, and which, perhaps, they view as more objectionable and inconsistent than those things which we ourselves feel. A conscience made tender by grace is a blessed gift of God, but it produces daily and hourly matter of self-condemnation. "The fear of the Lord is a fountain of life to depart from the snares of death." Snares of death surround and beset our path. Some arise from the world, some from Satan, some from the people of God; but far, far most from ourselves. The fear of the Lord is a fountain of life which detects and manifests these hidden snares, and by its bubbling up as a living spring in the heart it brings the soul into the presence of God, and thus strength, wisdom, and grace are communicated to flee them when perceived before fallen into, or deliver our feet out of them when unhappily entangled.

I have read Mr. Isbell's sermon, which he preached at Saltash, and which you sent me. I think it is a very good one.

I am glad that Mr. Smart's sermon was made profitable to you. He has a deep insight into the corruptions of the heart, and of salvation through the glorious atonement of the Lord Christ.

I am sorry that any among you should be stumbled by my delay in baptising and forming a church. I am waiting for materials before I begin. There are many here, I believe, quickened souls, but hardly advanced enough for baptism; and, as to myself, I believe I could not, with any safety, baptise, as the immersion in cold water for so long a time, and partial exposure of my body to that cold would probably be very injurious to me. But several have expressed a wish to be baptised. I expect Mr. Warburton next year, who will probably be requested to baptise, as he did when here before. To wait does not imply I mean to defer it altogether. A beginning has been made already, Mr. Warburton having baptised two of my hearers when here last year, who would be members of the church when formed. The formation of a church will bring with it many troubles. Satan will blow the embers of pride and jealousy, envy, suspicion, and contention, and love will be hardly strong enough to endure the flame that will be created. I have found it so painfully wherever I have been. At A—— one of my warmest friends, and, apparently, attached hearers, seems now quite alienated from me on account of my defence of strict communion in the *Gospel Standard.* I hope never to give up truth, whosoever's friendship it may cost me, and to care neither for frowns or smiles in defence of the Gospel. You must expect many hard speeches and unkind words from professors of truth as well as from the world. This we are not at first always prepared to expect, or, indeed, well able to bear. Rebuffs we expect from the world and enemies of truth, but from those who profess to be people of God we as little anticipate unkindness as feel able to bear it. But all these things, however painful to the flesh, work together for spiritual good. They drive the soul more simply and more earnestly to the Lord, wean it from idols, and draw it off from leaning on Assyria or Egypt, finding that to do so is to lean on a broken reed, which runs into the hand and pierces it. You will find it, I believe, your wiser, safer, and happier course to keep clear of party spirit, and to turn a deaf ear to all the whisperings, surmises, and tales that too often form a large portion of the conversation of the Lord's people when they meet together. Were they to talk more about the Lord and what He has done and is doing in their souls, and less of religious tittle-tattle, they would leave each other's company more profited and edified. We read in Malachi that those who feared the Lord spake often one to another, and that the Lord hearkened and heard; but this implies that He heard with approbation. I fear, however, that He hears with similar approval few conversations now among those who profess to fear His great name. The exaltation of self seems more the object than the exaltation of the Lord of life and glory. . . . Our united love to our dear mother, Mary Ann and her children, and accept the same, my dear Fanny, from

Your affectionate Brother,

J. C. P.

XXVII.—To Mr. Parry

Stamford, Feb. 26, 1841.

My dear Friend,

I desire deeply to sympathise with you in your present distress. I believe you will find it hereafter to contain in it the root and seed of the best of blessings. I know that it is useless to try to comfort you, that being the Lord's sole prerogative. He alone can bring your soul out of prison, and I believe He will do it to the glory of His holy name. If the Lord had meant to have destroyed you, He would never have thus applied His holy Law to your conscience, but would have let you gone on in delusion and been in peace and quiet. I believe the soul is often quickened before the Law is experimentally known, and this, perhaps, is your case. Look at all the saints of God as Hart, Bunyan, Huntington, Barry. They have all passed under the bond of the Law before solid deliverance came. The Lord is able to deliver. He heareth the cry of the prisoner and preserveth those that are appointed to die. Jesus is just such a Saviour as you want, mighty to save, able to save to the uttermost all that come to God by Him. You have never been in such deep waters before, but when the Lord shall bring you out, your joys will rise as high. My dear friend, can you not cast yourself at a throne of mercy and grace? Can you not confess how base you have been and are? Can you not groan forth your soul to the Lord, and seek salvation, mercy, and pardon from Him? You condemn yourself as a presumptuous wretch. Indeed, indeed, we have, all that know our own hearts, reason to cry and groan under the sin of presumption. But did you ever take up religion as a matter of gain or ever were allowedly a hypocrite? I never heard you boast of things beyond your experience, or talk of liberty and assurance when it was not given you. I would fain encourage your poor drooping soul to wait at mercy's doorposts till light appear. Thousands have been saved out of as deep waters as you are now wading in; and why not you—oh, why not you?

I would advise you, my dear friend, in your present state to have nothing to do with the chapel service, as Satan is sure to employ it as a weapon against you. Let Mr. Dredge and Mr. Tuckwell carry it on as well as they can.

I cannot suffer a post to elapse without dropping you a line, but hope to write again in a few days. I will not ask you to write, but shall be glad, and indeed very anxious, to hear from friend Tuckwell how you are in soul matters. My dear friend, is there any limit to the Lord's power and love? Oh, may He quickly appear!

Your affectionate Friend,
J. C. P.

XXVIII.—To Mr. Parry

Stamford, March 2, 1841.

My dear Friend,

As I wrote you so hasty a letter the other day, I feel disposed to drop you a few lines of sympathy again without waiting for an answer to my last.

I fully believe that you will one day, if not soon, see and feel that the present fiery trial through which you are passing contains wrapped up in it a spiritual and eternal blessing. "I will bring the third part through the fire;" "I counsel thee to buy of me gold tried in the fire." Are not these the words of Him that cannot lie? The Lord has seen good for your profit and His own glory to plunge you into these waves of trouble; but He that has thrust you down can, and doubtless will, one day lift you up. What has produced your trouble? Not the commission of some outward sin to disgrace you before men; not any providential reverses; but the application of the Word of God with power to your conscience. But why should God apply His word to your soul unless He had a gracious purpose in it. The Law was never applied to the conscience of a reprobate. The Lord suffers such to glide smoothly on till they drop into hell. You have often sighed and panted after a divine deliverance into the light, life, liberty, joy, and peace of the Gospel. But, perhaps, you little thought that you should be plunged into such terrors, fears, and alarms as to be, as it were, without hope; and that this should be the way to know Christ and the power of His resurrection. But when the blessed change shall come you will see and feel how needful all this work was to endear the blessing. I dare say you think that you are not a common sinner, but a Gospel sinner, a presumptuous hypocrite that has rushed into religion of your own accord. I think, my dear friend, few know you better than I do. Our long and unreserved intimacy has, of course, made me well acquainted with you spiritually as well as temporally. I will not allow that you have been a presumptuous Gospel sinner; I know better. I have never seen allowed, indulged presumption in you. Like myself, you have a vile, presumptuous, hypocritical heart, but it has been with you as with Paul, "That which I do I allow not." You have had more or less of a tender conscience. You have had at times some seasons of solemn prayer to a heart-searching God; you have felt a knitting of soul to the people of God; you have esteemed such as Mrs. Wild, Dorcas, Edith, &c., as the excellent of the earth. I will not say anything of outward sacrifices, as none can take such evidences that know themselves. But I would appeal to inward feelings and Scriptural evidences. But you say, "They are all swept away, and I cannot find in myself one evidence." No; if you could there would not be such a thorough sweeping of the house. But cannot you cast yourself as the vilest, the worst, the basest of wretches, at the feet of sovereign mercy? Oh, my friend, is your case, however seemingly desperate, beyond the reach of Jesus' arm, or the efficacy of His atoning blood? Is He not mighty to save; and has He not saved, pardoned, and blessed thousands as black, as guilty, as helpless, and as hopeless as you feel yourself to be? I know that you cannot lay hold of any truth of this nature. But your fear, and guilt, and terror, and despair do not alter the case, nor render Him less able, less willing to save. He is able to save *to the uttermost* all that come unto God by Him. You are not beyond "the uttermost," nor ever will be. Many now in glory have sunk as low, many lower than you. Look at Barry, and Huntington, and Gibbs, and Wade; all have sunk below a hope in God's mercy, and all have been brought out to praise His glorious name.

A well-taught and well-exercised man, who could go in and out before the people would be very desirable for you at the present juncture. I think you will find a suitable letter in the *Standard,* which was written to me by "a Sinner Saved" (A. Charlwood, Norwich), in December number. You will see there what a state of despair he was in for five years, and what a deliverance he enjoyed. He now seems to live in the enjoyment of pardoning love. The first letter in this month's number, signed "G. M." (George Muskett), is from the young man whom he mentions as his minister, and who seems to be a well-taught man.

I will not weary you, my dear friend, with more now. May the Lord bring you out of prison, smile into your soul, and set you at happy liberty. Who can tell the boundless riches of His grace to the vilest of the vile?

Accept my affectionate sympathies and prayers for your deliverance.

Your affectionate Friend,

J. P. C.

[For the convenience of our readers, and in justice to Mr. P.'s esteemed friend and correspondent Mr. Brown, we must give the following letter before we insert Mr. P.'s answer to it.]

April 24, 1841.

My dear Friend,

I received from Mr. —— your sermon on "Heb. iv. 12," yesterday. One thing in it struck me as wrong, and this is my apology for addressing you. The paragraph I allude to is this: "A natural man has but two things, a body and a soul: but a spiritual man has three things, the third being superadded in regeneration, body, soul, and spirit." You have omitted to mention the old man as dwelling in the unregenerate, as also in the regenerate. If we admit the new man of grace was superadded in regeneration, must we not likewise admit the old man of sin was superadded at the fall? "The seat of natural religion is in the soul." But who occupies that seat? In the soul of a living man two armies are felt, as in a field of battle. The flesh and the spirit, lusting and striving against each other. The soul, like the earth spoken of in the Psalms, trembles, shakes, and melts when these conflicts are going on. Where there is no spiritual life the old man reigns unmolested; the strong man armed keeps his goods in peace. Thus I think it is evident the dead have three things: the body, the soul, and the flesh—or carnal mind, or old man, as I think it is thus variously termed in Scripture, while the living of course have four. I know there are many who would be glad to find Mr. Philpot in error, though in the most trifling degree, and I deem it the part of a true friend to mention what is thought to be wrong, instead of speaking of it to others.

I remain your sincere Friend,
William Brown.

XXIX—To Mr. Brown

Stamford, April 26, 1841.

My dear Friend,

I am obliged to you for your kind letter in which you point out what you consider an error in my sermon from Heb. iv. 12. I am not convinced that it is an error, and will give you my reasons why. I read that "God made man upright" (Eccl. vii. 29), "in his own image, after his own likeness" (Gen. i. 26; James iii. 9), which is declared to be (Eph. iv. 24), "in righteousness and true holiness." Man, therefore, as he came from the hands of his Maker, was perfect, upright and innocent, not indeed spiritual, but fully possessed of all natural perfection. In this state he had a perfect body and a perfect soul. But this perfect man had these two things, and these two only. So far, we are, doubtless, agreed. But we now come to the fall, and the entrance of sin into this pure, perfect man. This was a principle foreign to his original state, and introduced into him by Satan, in the shape of a serpent. But can this be called a third constituent part of man? I think not, and illustrate the case thus:—My hand, say, or my foot is now free from disease, but I lean my hand on a wall and a serpent bites it (Amos v. 19). By that bite venom is infused into my previously healthy hand, which is absorbed, and diseases first my hand and then my whole body. All my bodily juices become depraved, and through the powerful effects of this venom I sicken and die, not one organ of my body escaping its destructive influence. I consider this an illustration of the entrance of sin into the soul and body of man. Sin I view as the disease of the soul. But would it be correct speech to say of a consumptive patient that he had lungs and tubercles? of one afflicted with blindness, that he had a lens and opacity? of a paralytic that he had a brain and extravasation? And would it not be more correct to say "tuberculous lungs," an "opaque lens," and a "diseased brain"? The disease, and the part afflicted with it are not two distinct things in the same way as the body is distinct from the soul, or even the brain from the liver. A diseased limb is still a limb, and the disease is a departure from original health. So I look upon sin as the disease of the soul, and not a thing distinct from the soul. If you say the new man of grace was superadded in regeneration, it does not thereby follow that the old man of sin was superadded at the fall. If so, who superadded it? Surely not God, who cannot be the author of evil. Then, it must be Satan, and what is this but to make Satan a creator? For if it be a distinct principle superadded and distinct from the soul, it would seem as much created as the soul. Body, you must admit, was created, soul was created, and now your third superadded thing, called flesh, or old man, if it be so distinct from the soul that he is in error who says, man is not made up of three things, must have been created likewise, and you make Satan, a creature, to be a creator. But take my view, Satan, as a crafty serpent, full of all venom, infused a sinful thought into Adam's mind. This venom coursed, as it were, through all its faculties, and he became dead in sins. His posterity being in his loins became infected in him, as a consumptive mother brings forth a consumptive child. Is this unscriptural? "You hath he quickened who were dead." What was dead? was it not the soul dead God-ward. "The whole head is sick, and the whole heart faint." "From the crown of the head," &c. Is not a totally diseased body here used figuratively of a totally diseased soul? "Their mind and conscience is defiled" (Titus i. 15). Are not mind and conscience faculties of the soul, and defilement a disease?

"God gave them over to a reprobate mind," margin, "a mind void of judgment," perhaps more literally, "undiscerning" (Rom. i. 28). "Having the understanding darkened, being alienated from the life of God through the ignorance that is in them, because of the blindness of their heart" (Eph. iv. 18). The mind is here represented as undiscerning, the understanding darkened, the soul or affections alienated from the life of God through ignorance, and the heart blinded. Are not these diseases, or diseased states of the soul? The mind is void of judgment—it formerly possessed it; the understanding is darkened—it formerly had light; the affections alienated—they were formerly fixed on God so far as a creature could know him, such as Adam; and the heart blinded—which formerly saw. Are not all these diseased, depraved, superinduced states, and so represented? But this language would not suit with the flesh as a superadded distinct creation. The flesh cannot be darkened, for it was never light; nor can it be *alienated*, for it came in as an alien; nor blinded, for it was born so. If I, an Englishman, settle in France, and become naturalized there, I am *alienated* from my native country; but he who comes, as a Frenchman, into this country, and remains such, is an *alien*, and cannot be said to be *alienated*. So if Adam's natural affections were originally fixed upon God, and by the introduction of sin into them they became turned away from the Creator to the creature, they may be said to be *alienated;* but if these corrupt affections were superadded, as members of a distinctly created old man, they came in as aliens, and, therefore, cannot be said to be alienated. In natural religion, of which I consider the soul the seat, as distinct from the spirit (for they are often, as I have said, used synonymously) and the body, what fears, hopes, desires, believes, prays and loves? Does not the soul do these things? Are they not the natural exercise of the faculties of the soul on divine objects? How do I believe there was such a man as Julius Cæsar? By my mind, or soul, or understanding, call it which you like. So natural men in the same way believe in Christ. A truant child fears to be punished. Where does he fear? Is not fear some expectation of evil, and pain, in other words, an exercise of the mind? So natural men fear God. Thus I conceive all natural religion, which I conceive the Sword of the Spirit to separate between, is the exercise of the faculties of the mind naturally upon divine things. It is, therefore, called in the New Testament ψυχικός which literally may be translated, were there such a word, "soulish," *i.e.*, relating to the soul (1 Cor. ii. 14; James iii. 15; Jude 19.), translated in these passages "natural," and "sensual."

Viewing sin, then, as a disease of the soul, I do not consider myself in error in saying a natural man has but two things. I do not say the Church of England is any authority, but she takes the same view in her IX Article, where she says of original sin, that "it is the fault and corruption of the nature of every man"—"the infection of nature." And I consider that the Scriptures speak of the old man and flesh, and so on, distinctly, sometimes, as Eph. iv. 22, Gal. v. 17, as we speak of fevers and consumptions as certain distinct things from a consumptive or feverish patient, whereas they are certain states of the body. But spirit is clearly superadded, born of the Spirit, as flesh is born of flesh. If my views are wrong, I shall be glad to be shown so, as I wish not to be in error in any point.

I shall hope to see you when you come to L——, as Mr. —— promised to bring you down to Stamford. We can then, if agreeable, talk this matter over. My love to Mr. Gadsby.

I have felt this spring a trying time to my chest, and feel very unfit for my Norfolk journey.

My kind remembrances to Mrs. ——

Yours sincerely, for truth's sake,

J. C. PHILPOT.

XXX —To Mr. Parry

Oakham, Oct. 4, 1841.

My dear Friend,

. . . I should rejoice should it please the Lord to bless D. S——'s ministry to your soul; to wait for a deliverance amid many sinking fears whether it will ever come is trying work. Fear, guilt, bondage, and self-pity are painful companions. Hope delayed makes the heart sick, but there is no doubt a needs-be for the delay. It says, "He brought down their heart with labour; they fell down, and there was none to help." But it is not a little labour that can bring the heart down. The word implies long-continued toil, and that they became faint and weary with perpetual exertion. Could you see matters in a right point of view, you would doubtless feel that your present state of soul trouble is far preferable to carelessness and carnality. In those wretched states of mind, deliverance is not desired nor sought after; but you feel that you must perish without it. It is a good thing to be crying for mercy, and sighing forth the desires of the soul, for the promise-keeping God has given many sweet promises to those who seek His face.

I trust that my late visit to Allington may be manifested to have been of the Lord. I felt more, I believe, of the power and presence of the Lord than I have often felt before during my former visits. I am much obliged to you and Mrs. Parry for your kind hospitality.

Your affectionate Friend,

J. C. P.

XXXI.—To Miss Richmond.

Stamford, January 28, 1842.

My dear Friend,

I feel so unable to give wise and spiritual counsel that I hardly know what to write in answer to your letter. My carnal mind would advise one thing, and my better judgment another. I feel for you temporally and spiritually, and should be sorry to hear that you were obliged to give up your school, and leave Stadham; but I have usually found whatever perplexities and difficulties occur in our path, that they are such more from our own crookedness and waywardness, than from what they are in themselves. The path is straight enough, but our eyes look crookedly at it, and then the road appears to be crooked. Were our eye single, the path would be plain and clear; but the films of self-seeking and flesh-pleasing darken in our view the path itself. We often know not how to act, not because the right way is difficult to find, but because the road is too rough and thorny for our tender and ease-loving feet. But it is in this way, I think, that the Lord tries the strength and reality of faith. He brings the soul, as it were, to a certain point in the road, where he sets this question before it, "Wilt thou serve Me or thyself? Wilt thou act with a single eye to My glory, or please thy flesh?" All looks dark and gloomy; no possible way of deliverance appears, and there is nothing but the naked word of God, lying with more or less weight upon the conscience. Now if the soul is secretly strengthened to stand on the Lord's side, and not hearken to the flesh, deliverance will sooner or later come. But if the flesh be pleased, bondage and the rod will follow. See this in the case of Abraham (Gen. xxii.), Moses (Heb. xi. 24—26), and the three children (Daniel iii.). These would not consult the flesh, but acted in faith, and to them all deliverance came.

Your present difficulties seem to be two: 1. Whether you should teach the Church catechism; 2. Whether you should have with the children what is termed "family prayer." The first seems to be the more easy to answer. In the first place your own convictions, and in the second, the word that you received, as you believe, from the Lord* seem quite sufficient to decide that matter. You would be rebelling, not merely against light in your judgment, but also against the special word of promise in your soul were you to draw back to consent to teach the children the catechism. You know that whatever they are in Covenant purposes they are not manifestly "members of Christ, children of God, and

* "Be thou faithful unto death, and I will give thee a crown of life," Rev. ii. 10.

the inheritors of the kingdom of heaven"; still less were they made such when sprinkled at the font. I cannot see how you can swerve here without positive sin.

As to the other point, I cannot speak so decidedly. Family prayer might be preserved, and yet not a form persevered in. You might offer up a few petitions in the presence of the children, in which you might keep your conscience clear of, at least, wilfully mocking God. Their inattention is not your sin, and I think a few simple words might be offered up by you which need not pain your conscience, and which would yet preserve you from the imputation of utterly neglecting any recognition of God in your family. I do not think that you could conscientiously teach them or hear them what is called "say their prayers" individually; but I do not see that you are called upon to prevent or forbid them doing so, if they had been taught so to do before they came to you. I cannot say how I should act under similar circumstances; but I seem at present to feel this, that if I had a pupil who had been taught to pray before he came under my care, I would not forbid him, though I would not hear him. I could not make the child understand why he should not say his prayers without leading him to believe that there was no such thing to be attended to as prayer, because I could not make him understand the difference between carnal and spiritual prayer. If I were to teach him, or hear him say prayers, I am so far mocking God, and sinning against light, but the child has not my knowledge, and does not at any rate wilfully mock God thereby.

But indeed it is a most difficult point, and one on which special light is needed for our individual guidance. I can only refer you to the "Wonderful Counsellor," out of whose mouth cometh knowledge and understanding. You need much wisdom, much grace, much faith, much strength, which the Lord only can supply you with. May you be much at the throne. "If any man lack wisdom," &c., James i. 5. The Lord is able to deliver you, and amply provide for you temporally as well as spiritually. "It is better to suffer than to sin." The Lord can send you children from most unexpected quarters, or so turn the hearts of the parents that they shall disregard what in your mind is burdensome. A lady who keeps a school at K——, and is a member at Zoar, was very fearful of losing her school when she joined the church, but her school has never more flourished. So full of unbelief are our hearts, so able to deliver is the Lord.

I am sure that it is our wisdom, as well as our mercy, when we can act as conscience bids. None were ever eventually losers by making sacrifices for Christ. With all my unbelief, I must say that He has been faithful to His promise, Mark x. 29, 30.

I shall be glad to hear from you again, and hope that the Lord may direct you in all things.

I was very sorry to hear of poor Brookland's heavy affliction in the loss of his little girl. Give him my love and sincere sympathy in his heavy trial.

My love to the friends; greet them by name. My kind remembrances to your sisters.

Believe me to be,
Yours very sincerely,
J. C. P.

XXXII—To Mr. Parry

Stamford, March 24, 1842.

My dear Friend,

I should be sorry if my delay in replying to your letter should seem on my part a mark of neglect or of coldness. Most of my hindrances in answering the letters of my friends arise not from them but from myself. But were I to enumerate all the obstacles that daily and well-nigh hourly occur from that moving mass of carnality and helplessness which I carry about with me, and under the load of which I often groan, being burdened, my letter would be all preface, and, like some sermons that I have heard, consist almost wholly of introduction.

It seems scarcely possible for me to tell you how unlike I am everything I wish to be, and how like to everything which I wish not to be. I would be spiritually minded, would read the word of God with delight, would approach the mercy seat with freedom of access, would look back upon the past without sorrow, and to the future without apprehension. I would never throughout the day forget, "Thou, God, seest me"; I would not occupy nor interest my mind in anything earthly, sensual, or devilish; I would be continually fixing my eyes on the cross of Immanuel, and be living upon His grace as freely, sensibly, lovingly, and savingly revealed. This is *what I would wish to be;* and as to *what I would wish not to be,* I would not be a miserable idolater, raving and roaming after some dunghill god, nor a wild ass of the desert snuffing up the wind, nor a peevish rebel, nor a sullen self-seeker, nor a suspecting infidel. If not all these in open, daring, unchecked practice, I am it all in inward bent and wretched feeling. A friend of mine brought me word the other day that some of the Bedfordshire Calvinists had spread a report that I was turned Baxterian or Fullerite. Had I no other preservative, I think my daily and almost hourly sense of my miserable helplessness and thorough impotency to raise up my soul to one act of faith, hope, or love would keep me from assenting to Andrew Fuller's lies. Nothing suits my soul but sovereign, omnipotent, and superabounding grace. I am no common sinner, and must therefore have no common grace. No texts have been much sweeter to my soul than Jer. xx. 7, "Thou art stronger than I, and hast prevailed;" and Rom. v. 20, 21, "Where sin abounded, grace did much more abound," &c. In truth I find religion to be a very different thing from what I once thought it. There was a time when, in all apparent sincerity, I was looking to my spirituality and heavenly mindedness as evidences of my standing, instead of being a poor needy suppliant and starving petitioner for a word or a smile from the Lord himself. It seemed more as if my spirituality were to take me to Christ, than that my miserable poverty and nakedness were qualifications to bring Christ down to me; but all these idols have tumbled into ruins. I am now in that state that Immanuel, the God-man mediator, must have all the glory, by stooping down to save, bless, and teach an undone wretch, who has neither spirituality, nor piety, nor religion, nor anything holy or heavenly in himself, and whose chief desire, when able to breathe it forth, is to be but the passive clay in the hands of the Divine Potter, and sensibly to feel the almighty, though gentle, fingers moulding him into a vessel of honour meet for the master's use.

You speak of "going down 'Lumber Lane,'" I alas! seem to live in it. When we go down a lane, we may hope to get to the bottom of it; but I seem to have my house there, and besides all the mud in winter, and all the dust in summer, there are tall thick hedges made of thorns which shut out the sun. But I am glad to have that in me which hates "Lumber Lane," and longs after green pastures, still waters, and the warm sun.

Yours affectionately

J. C. P.

XXXIII—To Miss Richmond

Stoke, Devonport, July 19, 1842.

My dear Friend,

It will not be in my power to visit Stadham for a Lord's-day on account of my other engagements; but I hope (D.V.) to be at Abingdon on Lord's-day, August 28, when I shall hope to see my friends from that place. As my time is so limited I greatly fear that I shall not be able to visit it for a week evening, which I should like to do, did circumstances permit, feeling an interest in the place and in the cause of truth therein.

But what with weak bodily health, and what with similar or greater soul indisposition, I feel very unfit in every way to accept any engagement of a preaching nature. Many times I feel fit neither for the Church or for the world; being too barren and unprofitable for the former, and having too much light and sense of the evil of sin to join the latter. My own evil heart is more or less my daily burden, and hinders me in everything which would think, say, or do in the name of the Lord.

Sin, in some shape or other, is continually haunting me; and

I find the truth of what Paul says, "When I would do good, evil is present with me." But by this I am taught to prize the atonement which the Son of God has made by shedding His own precious blood, that it might be a complete propitiation for sin; nor can I find the least relief from the guilt, filth, or dominion of indwelling sin, but by faith going out towards and laying hold of the blood and righteousness of Jesus. Here, sometimes, the poor and needy soul is enabled to cast anchor, and only, so far as it does this, can any true or solid peace be tasted. A child of God can never rest satisfied with the knowledge of sin. He cannot rest in a spiritual discovery of the disease. No; he must have some experimental acquaintance with the remedy, "The blood of Jesus Christ cleanseth from all sin." Sweet words, when any measure of their truth is experimentally felt. "*All* sin" is a very comprehensive word. The horrible aboundings of iniquity in our carnal mind, the vain imaginations, polluting thoughts, presumptuous workings, vile lusts—what can cleanse our consciences from the filth, guilt, and power of those hourly abominations, but the precious blood of Christ as of a Lamb without blemish and without spot? Yet often in our feelings we are, as Berridge describes:—

"The fountain open stands,
Yet on its brink I dwell."

We lack the power to wash therein and be clean. And this makes us add—

"Oh put me in with Thine own hands,
And that will make me well."

I am glad to hear that the Lord deals kindly with you in providential matters, and, in spite of all your unbelief and distrust, still brings you pupils. What a mercy it is that though we believe not He continueth faithful. Did the blessed Lord change as we do what would become of us? but with Him there is no variableness, neither shadow of turning.

My love to the friends,

Yours very sincerely, for truth's sake,

J. C. P.

XXXIV.—To Mr. Isbell

Stamford, November 24, 1842.

My dear Isbell,

You must not expect me to answer your letters with much regularity or expedition. I have many hindrances to regular correspondence with my friends, of which the chief perhaps is the want of what David felt when he penned Psalm xlv. Were I, like him, bubbling up some good matter, I should have more of the pen of a ready writer. One said of old, "Behold, my belly (Hebraism for "heart") is as wine which hath no vent; it is ready to burst like new bottles." His heart was all in a ferment with the things of God, and he would fain speak that he might be refreshed. Blessed speaking, preaching, and writing when such is the case. But oh, how rare with me to be thus alive in the things of God! How rarely do pen and tongue move with spiritual readiness and divine unction! Carnal fluency in the pulpit or in the parlour may and often does exist with much barrenness and leanness of soul. The liberty of the flesh in handling divine matters is very different from the liberty of the spirit. The latter may exist where the tongue is tied, and *vice versâ*.

I am glad you desire to see your way made plain before you leave ——. I think —— might prove a much more trying spot. The old garment and the new patch never coalesce; and there you would have to take to an old church as at ——. I consider myself favoured in having had new ground to till here and at Oakham. My best people are, like myself, seceders. I remember reading, I think in Anson's voyage, of the effects of a long calm at sea. Corruption and sickness were the consequence, and they gladly hailed the whitening surf at a distance as the herald of a breeze. So a calm in a church may not be the most desirable thing. If it teach you patience and forbearance, meekness, gentleness and love, it will be a blessing eventually. —— may be to you a Southsea Common to make you a soldier. I do not mean to say I understand the use of arms, but if I know anything of drill I learned it in my seven years' exercise at Stadham. I was raw indeed when I went there, but had many trials and few friends or counsellors in them. I often acted very rashly and hastily, and frequently mistook my own spirit for the Spirit of the Lord. You will find it your wisdom never to allude to church or personal matters in the pulpit. Leave them all in the vestry with your hat and gloves. A pulpit battery is usually more destructive to the assailant than the assailed. . . .

Our love to Fanny and our relatives,

Yours affectionately and sincerely,

J. C. P.

XXXV

Stamford, April 24, 1846.

MY DEAR SIR,

Few greater afflictions can befall the people of God than the removal of a faithful and beloved pastor. It generally happens, if he has been long going in and out before them, at his decease the candlestick is removed with him; I fear that this may prove to be the case at —— with the spiritual hearers of the late

Mr. ——. Affection and respect cannot be transferred to a successor as easily as a pulpit, and even if truth be preached the ear is become so habituated to a certain mode of stating it that even a gracious man has to contend with difficulties and, I may almost add, prejudices, who succeeds to a much-esteemed minister.

I am sorry to hear of your trial. I feel so many evils daily, and sometimes hourly, working in my heart, and see so many traps and snares laid for my feet in every direction that my wonder is, not that any fall, but that any stand, nay, I am confident that all must fall were it not for everlasting love and almighty power, "kept by the power of God through faith unto salvation."

Like yourself, I have been much puzzled by men and things, in the professing world; but where I find a great assurance and unwavering confidence, unaccompanied by godly fear, and the other fruits and graces of the spirit, I cannot receive it; I therefore set it down for presumption or delusion. The Blessed Spirit is not the author of confusion inwardly or outwardly; where He works faith He works sorrow for sin, deadness to the world, tenderness of conscience, brokenness of spirit, humility, simplicity, sincerity, meekness, patience, spiritual affections, holy and heavenly desires, hope and love toward the Lord and His people. Where we see, then, these fruits and graces of the spirit lacking, or sadly deficient, there we must conclude that faith, the root from which they all grow, is lacking or deficient likewise. There is no monster in the kingdom of heaven. I mean such as have little hearts and large heads, active legs and withered hands, nimble tongues and crippled arms, such monsters are more fit for a travelling show than the Church of the living God. Little things, or rather such as are so called by dead professors, for nothing can truly be called little which God does for the soul, and what is wrought in the heart and conscience by a divine power, far excel all great and high speculative notions. To fear God, to tremble at His word, to be little and lowly in our own eyes, to hate sin and ourselves as sinners, to pour out our hearts before the Lord, to seek His face continually, and to lead a life of faith and prayer, to be dead to the world, to feel Jesus at times precious, to behold His glorious power, atoning blood, and justifying righteousness, and dying love by the eyes of living faith. These realities are almost despised and overlooked by many great professors in our day; but they will stand when pretentions to greater things utterly fall. It seems to me a day of small things generally in the Church of God. We may therefore usually suspect greater things, unless they are attended by strong evidences of their being of heavenly origin, as well as accompanied by the fruits and graces of the blessed Spirit.

I fear with you that the gospel sun is set at ——, it was so at Providence Chapel, London, when Mr. Huntington was removed. A minister whose years are prolonged generally buries his best people, and the others mostly follow him; the rest are often dispersed by providential dispensation, and their places are filled with those who knew not Joseph; then truth declines in its purity and power, till place and people at last become like the salt which has lost its savour, fit only for the dunghill. I hope this may not prove to be the case at ——, but it is the history of many places where truth was once preached in purity and power.

Remember me affectionately to the friends, and believe me,

Yours sincerely, for truth's sake,

J. C. P.

XXXVI —To Mr. Godwin

Allington, June 20, 1846.

My dear Friend,

I can only write a few lines to say that (D.V.) I will come to Pewsey on Friday. I wish much to see you, and should like to have a little more time with you than I fear I shall have.

I am, through mercy, pretty well, though somewhat fatigued with the heat, travelling, and pulpit work. I preached on Tuesday at Malmesbury, on Wednesday at Hawkesbury Upton, and last evening at Clack. I did not reach Allington last evening until a quarter to twelve o'clock. I have to preach (D.V.) three times this next week: at Calne, Tuesday; Devizes, Wednesday; and Pewsey, Friday. This would be nothing to a strong man, but it tries my weak frame, and sometimes I can hardly tell what it is all for, and why I should drag my poor body and often-tempted soul here and there. I felt much life and liberty in my soul last evening, but have generally been barren since I left home. We have often to labour in the dark, and sow the seed without knowing where it falls.

The friends here are pretty well. Mr. Parry seems weak in body; he says he had a sweet lift at Weston.

Yours very affectionately,

J. C. P.

XXXVII —To Mr. Godwin

Stamford, Nov. 27, 1846.

My dear Friend,

I am glad you did not stand upon ceremony with me, and wait till I answered your first letter. I seem slower at writing letters than ever. Unless the heart inditeth a good matter the tongue is not the pen of a ready writer; and my heart just now seems to be inditing ("boiling or bubbling up," margin Ps. xlv. 1) anything and everything but a good matter. Everything vile and abominable I feel at work within me, and the more I sigh and cry the less help do I seem to find—

> "how long
> Deliverance shall I seek,
> And find my foes so very strong,
> Myself so very weak."

It much casts me down and burdens me to feel so much of the power of temptation and so little strength against it. But I must bear my own burdens and carry my own perplexing trials. You well know how powerless is an arm of flesh to relieve and deliver. Whatever I may suffer this must still be my feeling; "Hast thou not procured this to thyself." I read part of Jer. ii. at Oakham chapel, on Tuesday evening; what a picture is there of my heart, lips, and life.

I have been obliged to decline going to Zoar again. I have felt at times as I like to feel in that pulpit, and as I have not often felt except at Allington, sometimes at home, and more than once at Pewsey. My dear friend, you know the feeling I mean—not what is called liberty, that is, a flow of words, but a solemn, sweet, spiritual feeling, better experienced than described.

As editors of the *Gospel Standard*, we have erred often and shall, doubtless, err again. But are not our motives in the main sincere, and for the glory of God and the good of the Church? I am sure it has caused me little else but anxiety and labour; and I would gladly lay down my office to-morrow, if any one whom I could depend upon would take it off my hands. I have had many bullets shot at me, my dear friend, but am alive to this day, and can tell you earnestly that I am more afraid of myself, my lusts and passions, and strong and horrible corruptions than of any body in the whole world. Self is and ever will be our greatest enemy; and all our enemies would be weak as water against us, were we not such vile wretches in ourselves.

You were exercised about your preaching when you were here the Lord's-day; but I believe it was blessed to the people. Our own feelings are not always to be the best judges whether the Lord has blessed the word or not.

Yours very affectionately,
J. C. P.

XXXVIII—To Mr. Godwin

Stamford, Jan. 13, 1847.

My dear Friend,

I think sometimes that no one professing to fear the Lord can be more tempted, tried, and exercised, than I am with sin. Unbelief, infidelity, and blasphemy, obscenity, and powerful lusts, are continually worrying my poor soul. At times, I feel quite cut up and cut down with the power and prevalence of these monsters. When entangled and cast down by these sins I have cried to the Lord sometimes for an hour together with tears, groans, and sighs to pardon, pity, and deliver. But still the conflict continues; and if for a few days the wild beasts lie a little still they soon wake up as bad as ever. You and friend ——, and a few more seem similarly exercised; but none seem so weak against sin, and so madly bent upon backsliding as I. It has done me good sometimes to have known a little of his and your inside. I must have often cut myself off had I found no travellers in the same path. And yet, perhaps, this knowledge of sin and self has enabled us to dig more deeply into men's hearts. At any rate, it seems to have stripped me pretty well of self-righteousness, and natural notional religion, and has made me try to strip others bare too.

I am glad to hear that the Lord should bless my poor labours to any of His children. I feel unworthy of the least of His tender mercies.

Yours very affectionately,
J. C. P.

XXXIX —To Mr. Beecher

Oakham, April 26, 1847.

My dear Friend,

I was glad to read your experimental letter, as I have many trials and temptations, both as regards myself and the ministry; and a word of encouragement is now and then desirable.

No one can know the mighty power of sin and the horrible love that there is to it in our carnal mind unless he has been beset by some temptation, and that at times night and day.

In this school have I learnt to my shame and sorrow what I am as a fallen sinner. Nay more, our very slips and backslidings are mercifully overruled to show us what we are, to hide pride from our eyes, to make us loathe and abhor ourselves in our own sight, and to make us put our mouth into the dust and say, "I am vile." We have no stone to throw at the vilest and worst, and can feel for and sympathise with the tried and tempted of God's family.

The Church said of old, "Thou hast showed Thy people hard things; Thou hast made us to drink of the wine of astonishment," Ps. lx. 3, 4. And to know and feel painfully and experimentally what we are, is, indeed, a draught of the wine of astonishment.

I am truly glad that what I was enabled to speak at Zoar, when you heard me there, was blessed to your soul and made a word in season.

It seems that I must travel through temptation in order to

preach it; and thus some of the Lord's family derive profit and comfort from my services.

May the Lord hold us up under our various trials, temptations, and besetments, for we have abundant proof that we cannot stand without Him.

May His precious fear be manifestedly in our hearts as a fountain of life to depart from the snares of death. Grace, grace alone can suit and save such. Nature's strength, wisdom, comeliness, and righteousness, have received their death-blow, and we dare not glory in self any more.

I am glad my little productions have been blessed to your soul.

I am yours affectionately,

J. C. P.

XL —To Mr. Grace *

Great Malvern, Aug. 19, 1847.

My dear Friend,

I am much obliged to you for your kind and affectionate letter, and for the unpublished letter by Huntington which it contained. It is a very acceptable gift for the *Standard*, and I will (D.V.) take an early opportunity of getting it inserted.

I feel with you that no man's writings (always excepting our favourite Hart's hymns) seem to possess the savour, unction, and power of Huntington's. I think I may say I scarcely ever take up his writings without some sensible feeling being communicated. I do not mean to say always, or often, deep and lasting; but something that is brought to my conscience, as of God speaking in the man. I might say, "Where is the man in England that can write a letter from a real divine experience, such as you have sent me of his? If there be such a man, I have never yet heard him preach, nor seen his letters. He was, indeed, "beloved of God," and, therefore, "abhorred of men." In divine things I feel myself a fool by his side, and to know nothing as I ought to know. But it is our mercy that the fountain is still the same, and that Jesus says, "If any man thirst, let him come unto Me and drink."

The same blessed Teacher of the Church of God who instructed Huntington is able to instruct us, and make us useful in our day and generation. This is a poor wretched world, and it will be our mercy to get safely and honourably through it. Trials, temptations, exercises, and afflictions we must expect ever to have; and, indeed, without them there is very little going on of a Divine and spiritual nature in our own souls, or little profit attending our ministry.

* Mr. John Grace was a Minister of the Gospel at Brighton. He died March 3, 1865, aged 65.

The family of God are, for the most part, a tried and tempted people, and an unexercised minister is to them rather a plague than a profit.

We have both suffered much from the hands of friends. God grant it may prove a blessing to our souls.

I am here for the benefit of my health, which has suffered from too much preaching. My medical advisers recommend perfect rest for a time, and promise restoration with due care. I think I feel, through mercy, somewhat better.

Yours affectionately,

J. C. P.

XLI—To Mr. Godwin

Great Malvern, Aug. 20, 1847.

My dear Friend,

I hope I may say I am, through mercy, mending somewhat under the treatment I am passing through here. The doctors give me encouragement to believe that I shall eventually recover; but they say it will be a work of time, and that I must give up all ideas of preaching for a considerable period. I think they consider me in a very critical state, and that I might soon go into a consumption if I go on preaching. They say that my lungs are not diseased, but would soon become so if irritated, and that, if not arrested now, irritation would pass on into disease. I need not say that it will be a trial to me to give up preaching for a time; and no doubt it will be a trial to the people at Oakham and Stamford also. How mysterious are all the Lord's dealings, and how unable are we at the time to fathom them! I have never, I think, yet been in a trial in which I could at the time see the hand of the Lord. When seen, it has been afterwards. My enemies, no doubt, will rejoice and see judgments in it, but I hope the Lord will support me under, bless me in it, and bring me happily out of it.

I am here surrounded by the world, not a child of God to speak to. For nearly twenty years I have not seen so much of worldly people. But through mercy, I feel at times a different spirit from them, and their presence and conversation which I am almost obliged to listen to, is a weariness to me. I have a good bedroom fitted up as a sitting-room, and there I mostly pass my time when not walking or at meals. Sometimes I feel as carnal and as Godless as any of the poor wretched creatures around me; but the Lord often favours me with a spirit of grace and supplications in my walks and on my bed, and I am often crying to Him, "Bring me near to Thyself," "Keep me from evil," and so on. But patients will stop and speak to me, and my mind often gets carnalized by their conversation, though it generally is upon our bodily ailments. I am not here by choice, and shall be glad to get away.

Yours very affectionately,
J. C. P.

XLII—To Mr. Godwin

Stamford, Oct. 18, 1847.

My dear Friend,

Knowing that I am poorly, you will not expect a long letter from me. Still I will (D.V.) try and write a few lines.

As regards my health, I am much the same; if anything, perhaps, a little better. But all serious affections of the lungs are in themselves so perilous, as well as uncertain, that I cannot say much about my health. My mind much fluctuates upon this point. Sometimes I feel as if my race were run, and at other times I think I may recover. The Lord has brought me through some severe illnesses, and can through this if it be His gracious will. I am very sure I deserve, as well as need, very heavy strokes. Gentle taps are not enough for me; nor, indeed, will heavy stripes do me any good unless in a special manner sanctified and blessed. At present I can see but two fruits of my affliction: 1. Chastisement, and that deeply deserved; and 2. A deliverance thereby from a temptation which has long beset me, and caused me some groans and tears. When I say "a deliverance," I mean in a good measure, for the tail of the torch burns yet. I cannot say much about the dealings of the Lord with me during this illness, as I have felt generally stupid and hard; but the other day my heart was in some measure melted and softened toward the Lord in my walk, which is, you know, a sweet feeling while it lasts, makes all afflictions bearable, takes away the strong heart, fills the eyes with tears, and the heart with tenderness, meekness, patience, resignation, and love.

I understand that some of ——'s hearers are rejoicing at my illness, and expressing their hopes that my mouth is for ever stopped. This is no new thing. Psalm xli. 8 has been much in my mind, and I have sometimes breathed forth the cry, "Raise me up that I may requite them," not with anger and evil, but with what will grieve them more, declaring the goodness of the Lord to my soul. But is it not a horrid spirit, and one to be found almost only in professors? Who have slandered and persecuted me most, the world or professors? As a proof, the *Stamford Mercury* last week, mentioning my illness, spoke of me with kindness and respect, whilst those who profess so strict an adherence to the precepts of the Gospel, seem almost as if they thirsted for my blood.

I am glad you felt so at home at Allington. I believe it was mutual, for friend Parry mentioned how well you were heard, and what power and savour there was with the word. I have myself had most peculiar feelings in that pulpit, such as I have rarely had elsewhere, and much resembling what you describe—tender and soft, and a liberty of heart as well as of lip. I felt quite rejoiced there was such a mutual feeling at Allington, as I have a love and union to both, and I have thought sometimes I knew more of each and felt more towards each than they perhaps to one another. I mean more in a way of intimacy and friendship, for you were never brought much together.

Amid all the strife and confusion, what a mercy to feel a little real love and union to any of the Lord's family! I feel convinced that there cannot be this without real soul humility. Pride, self-esteem, and self-righteousness are brothers and sisters with strife, jealousy, and enmity.

Yours very affectionately,
J. C. P.

XLIII —To Mr. Godwin

Stamford, Nov. 5, 1847.

My dear Friend,

I hope I may say I am gradually mending. Still, it is very slow; indeed, scarcely perceptible, and the time of year is against me. The inflammation, I hope, is slowly subsiding, but until that is fully removed I cannot recover strength, nor can I preach without danger of bringing it on again.

It tries my mind to be thus laid aside in many ways. I hope I may one day see more clearly the hand of the Lord in it. My mind just now is very dark and confused, and I can scarcely trace one grain of grace in my soul. But I at times know something of what you say in your letter—of crying to the Lord to teach, lead, and guide me, for I am sure no one ever needed it more. O, how dark our mind is without His light, and how dead without His life! My religion is reduced to a very small compass, I can assure you, under these feelings.

Poor Dredge made a happy end, and was buried at Allington. My letter was read to him just before he died, and he sent me his dying blessing. . . .

Yours very affectionately,
J. C. P.

XLIV —To Mr. Godwin

Stamford, Nov. 24, 1847.

My dear Friend,

I was truly sorry to learn that you had been so seriously ill; but at the same time was equally glad to hear you were better. . . . In the autumn of 1822 I had, when a youth at College, a most severe attack of inflammation of the lungs. Indeed the physician said that few survived so severe an attack; but I soon got round again when the inflammation was subdued. You must expect to be very weak for some time; but I trust, through the Lord's mercy, we shall see you by-and-by in the vineyard again. You have long enjoyed that great blessing health, and will doubtless learn to prize it more than you have yet done.

As to myself, I believe I may say I am better, and feel stronger and healthier. Still the inflammation is not wholly gone, and till that is fully subdued I cannot regain much strength.

I hardly know what to say about my soul. I seem such a strange being. Some days I am so earnest after the Lord, so prayerful and tender and pleading with Him to appear, as if I would and could take no denial. I have lain awake half the night and been pleading with the blessed Majesty of heaven for His sweet visits to my soul; and yet have, perhaps, the next day, for hours together, dropped into such a stupid, careless, insensible state that I seemed to have no more religion than a horse. To-day, for instance, had a person overheard me pleading with the Lord in the Park he might have thought how earnest I was, but this evening it seems as if there were not a desire in my soul after the Lord at all. To be taught, to be kept, to be blessed, to have the veil taken away, to have the Lord come into my soul to take full possession of me, how earnestly do I sometimes plead with the Lord for half an hour together. But it seems to pass away too much like the early cloud and morning dew. . . .

Yours very affectionately,

J. C. P.

XLV—To Mr. Godwin

Stamford, Dec. 23, 1847.

My dear Friend,

I have been very poorly with the influenza, and, indeed, kept my bed nearly four days. I am now, through mercy, better, but still tender against the cold. . . . In my illness I seemed to have little else but the workings of my most miserable self, with little power to read, or pray, or think upon anything spiritual or divine. O what a poor, helpless, miserable wretch is man, especially when he has a burden to-carry, which he can neither bear patiently, nor cast upon the only Burden-bearer! In these seasons the question with me is, not how much grace I have, but have I one grain? For I am very sure I can neither see nor feel one. O how my heart wanders, wanders, wanders from the Lord! and how unable and how unwilling to return! And if for a few moments brought to His feet how hard, how impossible, to keep it there. As Berridge, I think, says, "Just like an eel," how it slips, and twines, and twists away out of one's hands. I had just a little touch yesterday morning from reading the account of my old favourite Hannah (1 Sam. i.). I could see how long that tried creature mourned over her barrenness, and what a long row of fine children her rival had; and what taunting looks she could aim at poor Hannah, and how the poor barren wife felt it all; and how conscience gave her many a secret lash that her barrenness was a plain proof of the Lord's displeasure. But where did the poor thing go but where you and I, dear friend, for many years have been obliged to go—sometimes driven and sometimes drawn? To the mercy-seat, perhaps in her feelings for the very last time. And we know that she did not go in vain. I was glad her case was recorded in the word of God; and have not thousands (dead and alive) felt communion with Hannah?

I am sorry to say that my younger sister, Mrs. W., is very poorly and in a very precarious state of health. I have great apprehensions about her. What a world of trial and sorrow we live in! I scarcely ever heard of greater grief than she felt at the loss of a child, about three years old, last year. She hardly had her senses for the first month. I fear it has ruined her constitution.

Yours very affectionately,

J. C. P.

XLVI—To Mr. Grace

Stamford, January 13, 1848.

My dear Friend,

I hope that by this time you are fully recovered from your fall, and have had additional proof that, if a sparrow cannot fall to the ground without your heavenly Father, much less the body of John Grace. How much better, my dear friend, to fall from a scaffold, and break a couple of ribs, than fall into sin and break all your bones.

There is no guilty conscience, nor hanging down of the head, heart, and hands before God, nor rejoicing in the Philistine's camp, when we have only broken a rib or a leg. The dreadful consequences of sin, external or internal, I need not tell you.

I am sorry to have cast any doubt upon the previous non-publication of the letter of Huntington, and have, I hope, set the matter right in the forthcoming *Standard.* The great similarity of thought and expression to what I have met with in his published letters led me to believe I had seen it before; and I was not willing to give occasion to those who seek occasion to bring charges against the *Standard,* in order to wound and injure its reputation and influence, and that of its editors.

I am glad you like the writings of Rusk. I myself have the highest opinion of them, and think them most scriptural and experimental. Few writers, it appears to me, dive so deeply into the mysteries of nature and grace, and bring forward Scripture so closely and pertinently to clear up and prove every point and well-nigh sentence. He often describes the very feelings of my heart. He was, I believe, a poor sailmaker, and lived in Rotherhithe. He was a constant hearer, if not a member, at Mr. Huntington's chapel; and, after his decease, heard first, I believe, Mr. Robins, and then Mr. H. Fowler. He died a few years ago; and, I think, there is some account of his death in the *Spiritual Magazine*, some years back. I know a person who knew him well. Mr. Gadsby bought all his MSS. two or three years ago, amounting to seven or eight good sized volumes, and we hope to insert them gradually in the *Standard*.

Send me, when you can, more of Huntington's letters.

Yours affectionately,

J. C. P.

XLVII—To Mr. Godwin

Stamford, Feb. 9, 1848.

My dear Friend,

If I delay much longer to write you will think I have fulfilled the old saying, "Out of sight out of mind," or that something has occurred, as illness, to prevent me. I am glad, however, to say that neither of these causes has prevented; for, as regards the former, I can say, I never felt a better union with you since we first knew one another; and, as regards the latter, I am much as when you left Stamford.

I hope, my dear friend, your visit here was of the Lord. I am sure that our friends heard you with sweetness and power—much more than they ever did here before, and I hope we may one day see more clearly that you came with a message from God by the fruits and effects following. We sometimes do not hear for years, and perhaps never, of any blessing that may have rested on our ministry. We could not bear much of either—for, or against. To hear too much, or to hear too little of what God may condescend to do by us might not suit our pride or our despondency. I have sometimes thought myself a wonderfully great man, and sometimes felt myself one of the poorest noodles that ever stood up in a pulpit.

My dear friend, how much I feel as you describe; and it is, in my right mind, one of my greatest griefs and troubles that I am so earthly, sensual, and devilish. I remember, as I think I told you, somewhere about this time twenty-one years ago, when eternal things seemed first laid with weight and power upon my soul, that, for many months, two subjects only occupied my mind —a temporal trouble that I was passing through, which cost me almost rivers of tears and sighs, and the solemn things of eternity. I may one day open up a little of what I then passed through, when I have often wetted the pommel of my saddle with tears amid the lonely valleys of the Wicklow hills, or galloped half distracted along the seashore, where no mortal eye could see or ear hear me cry and groan, sometimes from natural trouble, and sometimes in pouring out my soul before the Lord. I did not then think I should ever be the carnal and careless wretch which I often now feel to be. I once told friend Parry, when I first went to Allington, that "I often had no more religion than a horse." Friend P. could not then receive such a speech, though since he has often found himself in the same plight. Next to the cutting feelings of a guilty conscience I feel my own carnality my greatest burden. Oh, what a cumber-ground! Oh, what an unprofitable wretch! Oh, what a fruitless branch do I feel myself to be! with just enough feeling to sigh a little after the Lord as I lie awake in the dead and still night. As Hart says:—

"Fickle fools, and false to thee."

And again—

"Only wise by fits and starts,"

I think I feel a little stronger these last few days. I get out and walk, which seems to do me more good than anything else; George Isbell and I walked to Tinwell to-day, and I felt all the better for it when I came home. The fresh air seemed to revive me. He is but middling, and much harassed with different things.

My poor sister, Mrs. Watts, is, I fear, very ill, and much tried both in mind and body. I hope the Lord may appear for her. . . . I wish you could drop in that we might have a little talk as we had when you were here. I much enjoyed your visit and company. I have not had your depths nor heights, but I know scarcely another man that I can travel so well with in spiritual things. Your letters seem sometimes written out of my heart. I am, you know, a black man, and I must have an Ethiopian companion. I once made great attempts to be holy, and was getting on pretty well, with, however, some terrible inward pullbacks sometimes, till the winter of 1830-31, when it all went to wreck and ruin. Death stared me in the face and I used to count how many months I had to live. How I used then to roll about on my midnight bed, with scarcely a hope in my soul, and turned my face to the wall like good old Hezekiah! Some have said and thought that I stole my religion from books. But I preached experience before I knew there were such men as experimental preachers, or such writings as experimental books. I never stole a searching ministry from any one, for I did not know there were such ministers. But I was searched, and I searched others; and I actually thought when I left the Church of England that all the Baptist Calvinist ministers were in that line of things. And I believe, in my conscience, that at my Thursday evening lecture at Stadham, when I was in the Church of England, I used to preach at times more searchingly than I have done since. For why? Because I was being searched myself. But I must not run on any more like this, for if I do you will begin to say, "What is my friend J. C. P. about, praising himself so?"

My friend, I have sometimes gone into the pulpit full of confusion, and sometimes as guilty as a malefactor, begging mercy, cut up with guilt and shame. Where was my 1st, doctrine, 2nd, experience, 3rd, practice, then? And after preaching at Zoar I have almost roared aloud in the cab with real sorrow of heart, and just stopped while the wooden pavement was passed over, lest the cabman should hear me. There was not much self-applause for a nicely divided sermon then. To my mind, what we read together in ——'s sermon, cuts up experimental preaching root and branch. Where was your nicely divided doctrinal sermon, the first evening you preached here, when the friends heard you so well? I know for myself that when I preach doctrinally it is when my soul is not exercised; and when I am in that carnal state I sometimes hate myself for every word that I say, and hate and am condemned for my prating chatter. To preach what is called "a great sermon," condemns me inwardly as a presumptuous wretch; and my carnal liberty and great swelling words about Jesus Christ trouble me more than darkness and bondage. In my right mind I would rather stumble on with a little life and feeling in my soul than preach the greatest sermon in the world without it, and I know that my friend T. G. is of the same mind. How little godly fear can a man have to say inwardly, after preaching free grace, "Well done I." But I shall tire you with my chatter.

Yours very affectionately,
J. C. P.

XLVIII—To Mr. Godwin

Stamford, March 9, 1848.

My dear Friend,

When I tell you that my poor sister, Mrs W., is dead, you will not be surprised at the paper on which I write. She departed on Lord's-day morning last about 8.30. She was a great sufferer both in body and mind, believing herself to be a reprobate and filled with condemnation and despair. We have, however, some hope that her poor soul is not lost, as three times on the night before she died she said, "I am going to God above," and, I believe, never spoke after, being insensible all the night. My sister, Mrs. Isbell, said that her convictions of sin were very deep; all her sins of childhood, &c., were laid on her conscience, and her distress of mind was very great, being fully persuaded hell was her portion for ever. She was a remarkably sincere and honest person naturally; and, I think, the most reserved character almost that I ever knew. So that, knowing her disposition, and what she passed through, we cannot but hope that a sense of mercy at last reached her soul, and that she felt she was going to God above. My poor mother is at present calm and resigned, though she was her favourite child, from whom she has scarcely been ever separated, and her life was almost bound up in hers. But I have often observed, and no doubt God has wisely ordained, that old age blunts and dulls the feelings so that aged parents do not feel the loss of their children as younger ones do. . . . .

O, my friend, what is all preaching or all the gifts in the world unless the power of God accompany it to the soul? I am at a point here. We want the mighty power of God to be felt in the soul, and without that all is nothing. What two sermons Wm. Tiptaft preached here last Lord's-day! as regards gift what most professors would despise, and perhaps ridicule, but what weight there seemed to be in them to exercised souls.

I cannot say much about soul matters just now. We want a little flowing in before there can be any flowing out; and where this is not the case the pen or tongue move in vain, or like Pharaoh's chariot wheels drive heavily.

Yours very affectionately,

J. C. P.

XLIX—To Mr. Isbell

Stamford, March 16, 1848.

My dear Isbell,

I am truly glad to learn that my dear mother and sister have been supported under this heavy trial and affliction; and I hope they may still find that as their day so is their strength. It is a great mercy to be supported in and under the first outbreak of trouble when the heart is too full to find relief in giving vent to its feelings. The grief afterwards may be more poignant but is more endurable.

I think that we are warranted in indulging a good hope that our dear sister's poor soul is at rest. Having sunk so low and been so near despair, putting away all hope, I think she would hardly have uttered the words which her nurse and husband heard, had not some divine intimation of mercy and acceptance reached her soul. There at least I wish to rest; and, indeed, have found my mind to lean upon it as a support. We might, indeed, have wished for earlier and clearer tokens, but these are not always vouchsafed. We are apt to forget, or rather hard to believe, that salvation is all of grace from first to last; and that the Lord in all His dispensations is and will ever manifest Himself as a Sovereign. I have often thought of the dying thief. What a display of grace! One short prayer, one believing look, one act. O what a mighty act, of living faith upon the crucified Son of God, and his soul was fit for paradise. What a death-blow to works and work-mongers! Simeon Stylites on his pillar for thirty-seven years, and the thief on the cross—how different their religion! Of the latter I would say with Hart—

"Be this religion mine."

When I have sometimes felt my miserable carnality and earthly-mindedness, so that it has seemed impossible for me to be either going to or to be fit for heaven, I have, as it were, fallen back upon the dying thief. Where was his fitness, externally or internally? I have thus seen what grace can do by what grace has done; and I neither expect nor desire to be saved in any other way than the dying thief.

We may know, or think we know, a great deal, but really and truly in what a narrow compass does all vital religion lie? I am tried because I am day after day the same carnal and earthly wretch. No better, no better; nay, never shall be in myself anything but a poor, filthy, fallen sinner. I have long believed the doctrine of the non-sanctification of the old nature; but am now compelled to believe it whether I would or no. I might as well doubt whether ink were black, or snow white, as doubt that my fallen nature is incurably corrupt. I must, therefore, ever despair of salvation from self or from anything short of the blood of the Lamb; and all teaching or preaching, dreams or doctrines, that lay the least stress on creature doings or duties, piety, or holiness, I look upon as I should a zealous defence of perpetual motion, squaring the circle, or aërial navigation.

I have attempted to speak a little here on the Oakham Lord's-day, confining myself, however, at present to exposition and prayer. I do not think what little I have hitherto done has at all hurt me. Still I hope to move cautiously, and not to attempt too much at first. I find this cold, damp weather, much against me, and I am anxiously expecting the advent of a warmer and drier season.

I wish you could get a little rest. I think when medical advisers of acknowledged skill recommend rest, it is desirable to attend to their directions. I know, indeed, that it is a trial to be silent, but you know the adage, "for want of a nail the shoe was lost." . . . .

[*The remainder of this letter is missing.*]

L.—To Mr. Godwin

Stamford, April 4, 1848.

My dear Friend,

I hope I may say I am better. I preached here last Lord's-day morning, and went up and prayed in the meeting in the afternoon, and did not seem much fatigued by the exertion. As all tell me how much better I am looking, I cannot help believing what they say. I think, too, that I am getting flesh on my bones, which is perhaps more favourable than mere face looks, which vary from day to day. . . . I would not have troubled you with all these details about my poor worthless body if I did not believe you wished really to know how matters stood with me.

I did not feel as I could wish on Lord's-day. William Tiptaft has been here, and other supplies, and they have quite daunted me as a preacher. I never heard William Tiptaft preach so well and with such weight and authority as this time. He was, indeed, most searching, and made such appeals to the conscience, that at times it seemed quite to thrill through me. O what a poor, ignorant, unprofitable, carnal wretch do I see and feel myself, compared with some that I know! I see them growing in grace, and in the knowledge of the Lord Jesus Christ, and preaching with power and savour, whilst I feel a miserable cumber-ground, going back whilst they are going forward. I think once I had some life and feeling in my soul, and in the ministry; but now I seem to be destitute of all I value and esteem, as the only things that make and manifest a minister and a Christian.

But I can assure you, my dear friend, that I find it a much easier thing to get guilt on my conscience than get it off again; and more easy to talk about and lament one's darkness and deadness than get life and light into the soul. I told the friends on Lord's-day why the Lord had afflicted me, though I could not enter into all the circumstances of the case. I can see mercy in it and mingled with it, and hope I shall one day see it more clearly. . . .

I have written to the friends at Eden Street to decline going there this year. I have two reasons for so doing.

1. My health, which is not sufficiently re-established for the exertion, anxiety, and excitement of London.

2. As I have been so long laid aside from my own people, I think it hardly right to leave them just as I am getting a little better. . . .

Still, I hope to pay my Allington friends a visit in August.

Since I wrote part of this I have been among some of the friends, and to my surprise learnt that I was very well heard on Lord's-day. I kept mumbling on with my own path, temptations, helps, and hindrances; and I suppose it suited some poor bewildered creatures. How different is preaching from what I once thought it was! All my vapouring knocked into nothing; and poor J. C. P. mumbling and stumbling like a fool.

Yours very affectionately,

J. C. P.

LI—To Mr. Parry

Stamford, April 15, 1848.

My dear Friend,

I hope I may say I am through mercy better in health. I have partially resumed the work of the ministry, having commenced to preach once on the Lord's-day. I seemed shut up and embarrassed the first Lord's-day that I spoke here; but had somewhat more life, liberty, and feeling at Oakham. I seemed favoured with a little of the spirit of prayer whilst going there by the coach, and also in the morning before preaching. It is a mercy to feel the heart sometimes a little softened and humbled, and life and power to accompany the word. I was in hopes that my long affliction would have done my soul more good, and produced more solid, spiritual, and visible fruit, internal and external, than I have yet experienced from it. It seems to be indeed a sad and lamentable thing to be continually chastened, and yet be after all an unfruitful branch and a vile cumber-ground! A sickly body and a dreadfully diseased soul make a daily cross, and one sometimes hard to be borne. I cannot throw aside my religion, and yet how hard it is to keep it. To think, speak, act, and live as a Christian; to be one inwardly and outwardly; to be a true follower of the Lamb whithersoever He goeth; to walk daily and hourly with godly fear in exercise; to conquer sin, master temptation, and live a life of faith in the Son of God—if this be true religion how little I seem to have of it. I never could boast much of my exploits and attainments, or the great things I have done or mean to do; but now seem less disposed to do so than ever. Nothing short of an almighty miracle of mercy and grace can suit or save me. We often prate and prattle about sin and grace, faith and repentance, and Christ, and so on, when we really know scarcely what the words mean. Many painful lessons and humbling cutting strokes are needed to teach us the A. B. C. of vital godliness; and perhaps all that we may know in this life about eternal things may be no more than what a babe a few days old knows of this life. It breathes, and cries, and sucks, and sleeps; and as regards divine things we may never here do much more.

I hope that the Lord may own and bless T. G.'s word among you this time as he did before. I am very sure that all preaching without the power and blessing of the Lord upon it will be but empty breath. I never saw the littleness of man so clearly, and my own littleness in particular. My friend will believe me when

I say I never felt so much my miserable ignorance, unfitness and insufficiency for the ministry. Indeed, I am and have nothing.

I hope Mrs. Wild will be comfortable at Allington. You must not, however, expect too much from one another. Man is a poor fallen creature, a selfish wretch, a very monster of iniquity. At least, I am. Nor does grace always reign even where it dwells. I very much esteem and respect her, and perhaps think better of her than she does of herself. But there is truth in what W. T. says, that Christians are like cabbage-plants which flourish best when not too near. I am afraid of everybody, and afraid of none so much as of myself. No one has ever so much tried me, so much plagued me, or so much frightened me as J. C. P., and no one, I am sure, but myself knows what reason I have to be afraid of him. . . .

Yours very affectionately,

J. C. P.

LII.—To Mr. Godwin

Stamford, May 12, 1848.

My dear Friend,

. . . . I am much as I was in health, and do not seem to gain much strength at present. I still continue to preach once on the Lord's-day, and for the last three weeks have also spoken here on Thursday evenings. The friends at Oakham all seemed to hear well on Lord's-day. The day was fine, the congregation large, and I was enabled a little to speak on some vital things. My dear friend, we must plough pretty deep, if we are to get at the heart and conscience. Skimming the ground over will not do ; but to be learning every day how vile we are is trying work. My preaching seems shut up into a narrow compass—sin and grace. I can assure you that when I was laid aside I seemed to have lost completely the power of preaching, and felt as shut up spiritually from a door of utterance as I was naturally. This made me a better hearer, for so far from thinking I could preach better than the ministers who supplied for me, I actually felt that I could not preach at all ; and according to my feelings had not ten words to say upon any text, good or bad. I cannot describe how entirely all preaching gifts, if I have any, were as much taken away as if I had never opened my mouth, and I felt that even were I better in health, I could not get into a pulpit. I think I can see now this was not a bad thing for me, for when I heard T. G. and others, I was not measuring my abilities with theirs, and thinking how the great Mr. I. would handle the text, but I really felt I could not preach at all, even as to words and gifts, much more power and savour. But I think I may tell my friend that since I have been able to stand up a little in the Lord's name I have not always been shut up, and have sometimes gone beyond the time when for my poor body's sake I ought to stop. Last

Lord's-day morning I felt such a vile sinner that I could hardly help telling the Lord He would do right if He stopped my mouth. But it was not so, as I believe I may say without boasting (and how can such a vile sinner boast?), that I was well heard that day, and that the friends seemed melted and blessed. O that God's mercy and goodness would constrain me to live to His glory, would overcome that raging love of sin that so ensnares and captivates me, and make me and manifest me a Christian indeed. I cannot, oh, I cannot subdue and mortify my pride, and lust, and unbelief, and infidelity, and a thousand other monsters that, like the beast in Daniel's vision, are opening their mouths and saying, "Arise, devour much flesh."

Yours very affectionately,
J. C. P.

LIII —To Mr. Godwin

Stamford, May 18, 1848.

My dear Friend,

I believe you have long found, by painful experience, that it is impossible to do any thing according to the word and will of God without trouble before, in, or after. To serve God in any way is a bitter-sweet. Sometimes conscience, sometimes Satan, sometimes the world, sometimes an evil heart, sometimes foe, and sometimes friend cause trouble. If we are let alone to have our own way, and sup up the east wind, that brings trouble; and if the Lord exercises our souls, that brings trouble. I do not mean to say that my troubles are so wonderfully deep and many, but pretty well all day long there is something as it were knagging and gnawing within. Love of sin, my poor body, family cares and anxieties, and a wicked, unbelieving heart, keep me from much rest or peace. I cannot, like the ungodly, rest in the world, and I cannot often rest in the Lord. O, the amazing power of sin! I am sure that very few know its mighty power. I sometimes walk in the streets feeling and saying to myself, "Death in me, death in me;" and yet sin is active, strong, and lively as if I were to live a hundred years. It is really dreadful how eye, and ear, and tongue, and heart, are all alive after sin, like fishes after a May-fly. I keep preaching man's dreadful corruption, and that nothing but grace through the blood of the Son of God, made known to the soul by the power of the Holy Ghost, can save such miserable sinners. My dear friend, we must plough deep, or we shall never get at the heart of the living family. I find that the worse I make them out to be, the better it suits them; and the more I draw from my own likeness, the more I hit theirs. But I cannot bring all out, only a hint now and then to the wise. A frail tabernacle and a wicked heart will I believe be more or less my daily plague till they are both laid in the grave.

I hope the Lord's-day at Allington and Tuesday at Calne may be days of blessing to your soul and those of the people. I trust I have had good times at both places. I cannot at present preach more than once on the Lord's-day, and I am afraid I can venture to do no more should I come to Allington in July. Preaching tries my chest almost more than anything, and a little extra exertion would soon, I think, make me as bad as ever. . . . We have to live and learn; sometimes more of ourselves, sometimes more of others. To be quiet and meek, to think little of ourselves, to prize grace in others, to think very highly of and to cleave close to the Lord Jesus for every thing, is far better than striving who is to be the greatest. Give my love to Mr. Warburton and any enquiring friends of the seed-royal at Calne. I wish you a real good day there.

Yours very affectionately,
J. C. P.

LIV —To Mr. Godwin

Stoke, Devonport, Aug. 4, 1848.

My dear Friend,

We arrived here safely, through mercy, on Tuesday evening, and found my mother looking pretty well. Friend D. is supplying at the chapel, but is not very well attended. I was there last evening, but there were very few hearers. Truth is pretty much fallen into the streets, as regards these three towns, with a population more than eighty thousand. It seems strange that there should be so little concern about their never-dying souls, until we feel what careless hardened wretches we ourselves are, except at times and seasons when eternal things lie with weight and power on our consciences. When my poor soul gets a little revived out of its dark and dead state, I wonder at my own previous state of carnality and worldliness. I need not then go far to find the cause of all men's carnality and carelessness, for where should I not, and where, indeed, do I not get when the Lord does not revive my poor dark soul? If we had no gracious dealings from the Lord, either in judgment or mercy, we should soon be a great deal worse than the professors whom we are so loud to condemn. A sense of these things stops my mouth, and makes the stones drop out of my hands, which, in times past, I have been ready enough to throw at others. I cannot say what I should not do, or what I should not be, were I left to myself; for I never hear of evil or error committed by professor or profane which I do not find working within my heart, and a great deal worse too; for no man ever did, or ever could, carry out in word and act what our imagination can breed and sit upon till hatched, like a hen upon its eggs. It is a mercy when our eggs prove addled, or are crushed before they are hatched, for, depend upon it, an adder would come out of every one of them. What a mercy it is to have our hard hearts softened and blessed at times, and to hate and abhor those vile things which at other times our fallen nature so lusts after. What a paradox are we! What a bundle of contradictions! We love what we hate, and hate what we love; we follow what we flee, and flee what we follow. Sin is our sweetest, and sin is our bitterest morsel; God is our greatest friend and most dreaded enemy. But I must not run on with my contradictions, or I shall fill up my sheet with them. You have got both the riddle and the key locked up in your heart.

As there was a very great attendance at Allington I was induced to preach twice on Lord's-day. I think I never saw the chapel so crowded. It was, I think on the whole, my best day; but I have not been much favoured at Allington this time. I had so many outer court hearers that they seemed almost to stifle any soft or tender feeling; and I was several times led rather to hammer away at Wiltshire profession than feed the lambs.

I am much as I was in health. That great blessing, good health, I never expect to enjoy again. I only could wish that my various trials, exercises, and afflictions were more blessed to my soul, but I have lived to prove that nothing but almighty grace can do the soul good.

Yours very affectionately,

J. C. P.

LV—To Mr. Godwin

Stamford, Feb. 23, 1849.

My dear Friend,

It is a mercy amidst all one's coldness, deadness, and hardness sometimes to feel a little revival, and to be blessed in speaking to the Lord's people. It encourages us to go on in spite of all opposition within and without. I think more of the value and blessedness of the preached gospel than I once did. It often stirs up prayer, shows where we have been wandering, revives the soul, points to Jesus and His precious blood, and encourages us to believe that where sin did and does abound, there grace does much more abound. And, I believe, where the preached gospel is little valued, it arises from deadness and carnality. It is, I believe, a great mercy when the heart of the preacher is enlarged and his mouth opened to set forth the truth as it is in Jesus, and the ear and heart of the people enlarged and opened to receive and feel it. It will detect many snares, make the soul cry at times, "Search me, O Lord, and try me," and give now and then a little strength to fight against besetting sins and temptations, as well as lead the poor soul at times to the fountain once opened for all sin and uncleanness. I once thought I really should get better before I died; more holy and pure, and strong and spiritual. But I find that these things are only at times and seasons, as the Lord is pleased to work in the soul to will and to do of His good pleasure; and that left to ourselves we are, and ever shall be, sinners of the deepest and blackest dye.

But religion and experience and all that regards the mark of grace in the soul will ever be a mystery; and we not only can know only just as much as we are divinely taught, but seem only then to know it when under the feelings and influences. I can recollect having seen and felt such and such things, and may, perhaps, be able to describe them; but how different this is from being under their power and influence. Then they seem to be really known, and only really then. . . .

Yours very affectionately,
J. C. P.

LVI—To Mr. Parry

Stamford, March 8th, 1849.

My dear Friend,

You will be very sorry to hear that our poor friend M'Kenzie is dangerously ill. He broke a blood-vessel on Saturday last, and brought up much blood, and had a return of the same on Monday. The doctor says it is from the lungs, which makes it all the more dangerous. He may not be immediately removed; but I should greatly fear the ultimate event, as such attacks generally terminate in consumption even when not quickly fatal. The Lord, however, mercifully blessed his soul, after the first attack, with His presence, and that, after all, is everything. Our time here must at the very longest be short; and what is the longest or most prosperous life without the Lord's blessing. When we feel what vile sinners and dreadful backsliders we are, and have been, it almost makes us despair of a blessing. Indeed, we could not entertain the least hope of one were it not for free and sovereign grace; but that opens a door of hope for the vilest and worst. How valuable, how indispensable a blessing seems to be when sickness makes death stare us, as it were, in the face. How empty and worthless really are all human cares and anxieties, as well as all human hopes and pleasures, when viewed in the light of a vast and endless eternity.

I have not been very well of late, having suffered from my old complaint, cold on the chest. I generally suffer from it every spring, especially when the winds are cold and searching. It much confines me to the house at present; but I still go on preaching as usual. I never have been attended better since I was settled here, and especially since the weather has been dry and fine. We have many country hearers; and short days, bad weather, and dirty roads are hindrances to their attendance.

I do not see any probability of my being able to be at Allington more than the three first Lord's-days in May. Poor M'K.'s illness will make a sad gap in the supplies. He was to be at Leicester in April, and to follow me at Eden Street Chapel in August. What they will do at the latter place I know not. I should not be surprised if they should wish me to stay another Lord's-day, and then it will be, perhaps, a question with me whether I ought not to stay in preference to coming down to Allington. When I dropped a hint of coming to Allington on my way to Abingdon for August 12, I of course could not contemplate such an event as M'K.'s illness. Ministers have to consider not merely their own feelings and wishes, but the good of the churches.

Mr. H. has already applied for me to help them at Leicester, and I should like to do so, if I could see my way, or procure an acceptable supply here. I find it more difficult now to leave home than ever, there being a greater unwillingness among the people that I should go from home. Churches, like individuals, are selfish, and rarely consider or consult each other's profit and convenience.

How our friends and acquaintances seem continually falling around us! R. Dredge lies in Allington graveyard, and J. M'K. may soon be numbered among the departed. Such things have a voice, could we but hear it, and be stirred up by it. It seems to say, "Be ye also ready." But what can we do to prepare ourselves for the solemn hour? Nothing. The God of all grace can alone, then and there, by appearing to us, and for us, enable us to say, "Come, Lord Jesus!" But it is a mercy when deep and solemn considerations about death and eternity have some effect in loosening the strong bands of sin and the world, and lead on to that spiritual-mindedness which is life and peace.

I doubt not that the low price of corn, conjoined with the bad yield, sometimes tries your mind. But you will have enough of "the thick clay," doubtless, to carry you honourably through. And why need you covet more? We shall always have enough for wants, but never for covetousness.

Yours very affectionately,

J. C. P.

LVII—To Mr. Tiptaft

Oakham, March 26, 1849.

My dear Tiptaft,

I consider poor Mrs. C.'s case a very trying one, and one very difficult, indeed, to pronounce any decided opinion upon. Say, for instance, that we gave it as our decided advice that she should stay away from the chapel; *that* would seem shunning the cross. Say, that we advised her still to go, and she should lose her life in consequence, painful reflections might be cast upon us. Such dreadful brutality we rarely hear of—indeed, I might say, such murderous proceedings. I think, however, there is a decided difference between doing evil, and forbearing to do well. Thus, I think, she might resolutely deny to go to church, whatever the consequence. *There,* I think, my mind is pretty clear. But whether she might not abstain for a season, during his present dreadful madness, I might call it, from going to chapel, is another matter. Christians when persecuted in one place, might flee to another. Here was an allowed declining persecution by flight; but, on the other hand, God, we know, can make a way of escape even by persons persevering to go. Look at D. C. of A——, how her husband stood with a knife at the door the morning she was to be baptised, to stab her, and how she crept out at the window, was baptised, and how all was overruled, as we hope, for his eventual good. A leaf which fell into my hands this morning gives an account of a poor woman much in Mrs. C.'s situation. I think much must depend on the state of her mind what she feels led to do, what promises the Lord has applied to her soul, what faith and strength she has in exercise, how her own conscience is exercised in the matter. It is so hard to lay down rules of action in these matters, for what one can do another cannot. Peter, who once denied his Master, could afterwards be crucified with his head downwards. Nicodemus comes first by night, and afterwards goes boldly into Pilate's presence. Elijah flees before Jezebel, and then meets Ahab in Naboth's vineyard. David kills Goliath, and then flees before Absalom. Thus, good men act differently as faith is weak or strong; and we would not counsel any man to walk on the waves unless we knew he had Peter's Master near, and Peter's faith in exercise. Thus I feel slow to offer advice, or give counsel in this painful and difficult matter. We feel, however, encouraged to hope the Lord will appear for her from the promise He has given her.

We had a church meeting here yesterday. Two candidates were fully received, Miss B., from M——, and Mrs. L., from K——. They were both well received, but the latter particularly. Oh, with what sweetness and power did she speak! I never myself was so melted with hearing an experience, and I am sure there was not a dry eye amongst us. I did not know I had such a hearer. She has been, and is, a most deeply-tried woman; bodily pain, tic douloureux, till lately, deep poverty, and soul trouble have sunk her very low; but lately she has been so much blessed in her soul, especially yesterday fortnight and the following Tuesday. Besides this lately, she was much blessed in her soul some years ago. I do not think we ever had a candidate before the church so much *in* the present savour of things. Others may have as good an experience, but they did not come before the church in the savour, blessedness, and power of it. It seemed quite to encourage me in the work; she could speak of what she had felt under this and that preaching, and how it abode with her and what it did for her, so clearly and sweetly. She has great trials about coming to chapel, having opposition at home, and an afflicted body. She has been a hearer eight or nine years.

R. S. has been blessed again in her soul. She thought she was dying, but had no fear. She has a great desire to see you. Some of the friends, I think J. C. among them, have seen, and think well of her.

Mrs. L——'s testimony has much encouraged us all. I felt I should not care for the speeches of a hundred enemies if the Lord would condescend so to bless the word.

If spared, I hope to baptise the three candidates (D.V.) April 8th. Mrs. L. spoke how she heard you on baptism. What a power there is in true religion, and what can be compared to it! but how it is got at only through trials and exercises! My heart cleaves more and more to the *power*. All without it is worthless—a mere tithing of mint, anise, and cummin. Mrs. B—— of K—— speaks highly of Mrs. L.'s consistency.

Yours very affectionately,

J. C. P.

LVIII —To Mr. Godwin

Oakham, April 24, 1849.

My dear Friend,

. . . . We were well attended at Leicester. Many, I am told, could not get into the chapel in the evening. I hope it was a good day, as I had a spirit of prayer on the Saturday, and a text came with some sweetness to my mind; and I had some liberty and sweetness in speaking. There is quite a spirit of hearing there.

I baptised here the Lord's day previous, and the candidates were, I hear, much blessed in their souls. One was so blessed in her soul that she could not sleep that night, and could do nothing but bless and praise God for two or three days. So that we have some little evidence that the Lord has not forsaken us, whatever men may say or surmise. Indeed, it matters little what men may say or think for or against us. If God be for us it matters not who is against us; and if God be against us, it matters not who is for us. My mind is much more here than it used to be. Everything cries aloud, "Cease ye from man," who cannot make one of his own hairs, nor ours, black nor white. How much better is it, instead of seeking man's smile, or fearing man's frown, to be committing our way to the Lord, to be seeking His presence and smiles, to desire to know and do His will, and live and walk in His fear! What support under trial, deliverance from temptation, comfort in affliction, submission in sickness, or peace in death, can man give us? What blind unbelieving fools, then, to be looking so much to the creature and so little to the Creator!

We have a poor girl dying in this town; and it is, indeed, marvellous to see what a work God has done for her soul. I saw her in her trouble and distress, and have seen her since the Lord blessed her soul, which He has repeatedly done. All fear of death is gone, and her soul seems filled with peace. She has had convictions for years, and been a constant hearer, but nothing decided till lately. What a wonderful thing grace is, both in its Fountain and streams! Well may we contend for nothing else, for what else can save, suit, or bless a poor guilty, fallen sinner?

I am much as usual, sometimes feeling very poorly, and then again a little better. Our poor clay tabernacle, what a burden it is to us from sickness and sin!

Yours very affectionately,
J. C. P.

LIX—To Mr. Parry

Stamford, June 2, 1849.

My dear Friend,

I reached home safely, through mercy, on the Friday, to dinner, and found my dear wife and little family pretty well.

I preached at Wellingborough, Thursday evening, 24th ult. If "like priest like people," be a true saying, I should fear there was not much life, power, or feeling in the congregation; and I felt but little in my own soul. My words seemed to rebound upon me almost as if I were throwing balls against a brick wall. Good, however, might still be done, as our feelings are in these matters by no means infallible marks. I should be sorry to set up my feelings as a tribunal from which there is no appeal; though we cannot help being to a certain extent guided and influenced by them. I consider this a nice and difficult point. I have generally found that when I have gone contrary to my feelings as regards men and things, I have erred, and more or less suffered in consequence. We may be thus slighting the secret leadings and impressions of the Holy Spirit. But, again, we may be under wrong impressions which a subsequent experience may correct. In this, as in all other matters, wisdom is profitable to direct. In all our movements and actings we need grace to teach, guide and direct; and without it we are sure to err.

My visit to Allington seems now almost like a dream. I would hope, however, that all the effects have not so passed away. A minister should leave a sweet savour of heavenly things wherever he goes. If he do not he will make the people worse instead of better. When the Holy Ghost makes our bodies His temple He will cast forth some rays of His indwelling presence. Christians will either spiritualize or carnalize each other—will stir up one another to good or evil. When we are ourselves a little spiritual, we are grieved to see the children of God, and especially those whom we love, worldly and carnal. This makes us get away from them, and in solitude seek the Lord, feeling no pleasure nor rest out of Him. Time and experience correct many errors, and especially in religion. I am daily more and more convinced that it is a secret work carried on in private between God and the soul. The conscience is the grand battle-field where the conflict is fought. Condemnation and justification in all their various branches and workings are there felt and known. And unless we live much alone and are more or less continually engaged with this inward communion of heart our religion withers away. "Commune with thy own heart on thy bed and be still." I only wish I could live a more separate life, and have eyes, ears, and heart more separate from the world lying in wickedness. The friends here consider me looking better than when I left; and, indeed, I feel so myself. It always suits me best when I can get air and exercise. But I often find when I am, as it were, congratulating myself with being better, and so forgetting to die daily, I get a pull-back; and so now some of my old pains and sensations admonish me not to be high-minded but fear. Like slipped greyhounds, how madly and eagerly we rush afield when the hand that checks seems a little to slacken its hold! But evening comes and the old collar is slipped over our necks; and perhaps a rating or a beating is added for our wild roamings. A head-ache or a sinking market, or a sense of guilt and bondage, or a solemn view of eternity, or a remembrance of past backslidings and sins, or a slip with the tongue or feet, or some unaccountable depression of spirits—each or any or all put the feet in the stocks. I am well persuaded that without exercises the soul cannot be kept alive—that is, in a healthy or spiritual sense. He that began must carry on; He that kindled must keep alive; He who is the Author must be also the Finisher of faith. This we are well persuaded of in our judgment; but we have to learn it in daily experience. And, I believe, it is often to us a cause of inward condemnation that we are what we are; that we have not more life and feeling, more prayerfulness and watchfulness, more knowledge of and communion with the blessed Jesus. We condemn graceless professors, and would rather open our lips no more upon religion than speak like them; and yet how much we really resemble them. Indeed, we differ from them only as far as our souls are kept alive by exercises, and gracious influences and operations. All things that we see and hear, the very necessary business of life, and all our relationships in the world, only tend to deaden and harden. And though we can leave neither our families nor the world, and must continue in the calling where God has placed us, yet we shall ever find it our wisdom and mercy to live much alone as regards our souls. In this point you are much favoured. You have fields and downs, quiet meadows and lonely walks, where you may think, meditate, and pray. And as these fields have formerly witnessed your sighs and tears, so may they witness your blessings and praises till the green sod covers your body in that little spot, which many gracious feet have trod, and where sleep our friends, R. D., poor farmer Wild, and others, that we have been united to in life, and from whom we hope death will not separate us.

We may have worldly troubles, and worldly mercies, and our hearts may be often depressed by the one, and carried away by the other; but, after all, there is nothing really enduring and satisfying but grace in its Fountain and in its streams.

Yours very affectionately,

J. C. P.

LX —To Mr. Godwin

Stamford, June 7, 1849.

My dear Friend,

It seems that troubles and trials still await me, and what is to be their end or issue I know not. * * I was thinking the other day that either Satan must hate me very much, or that there must be something in me very wrong, for many seem to rise up against me. . . . .

And having so much besides in me which causes condemnation and fear, and the Comforter who should relieve my soul being far from me, makes me wonder how the scene will end. What adds to the trial is my public situation as a minister and editor of the *Gospel Standard*. Were I obscure and unknown, like many private Christians whom I envy, how many trials should I be free from! But so many eyes are fixed upon me, some for good and some for evil. I have so many enemies as well as friends; and I find it so difficult, either by pen or tongue, to express myself so as to be free from misunderstanding, misrepresentation, or cavil, that my way seems completely hedged up. But in the midst of all these trials I trust there are some mercies. The Lord has not withheld that spirit of prayer and supplication which I trust He first gave me more than twenty years ago, and to His throne of grace He from time to time draws me. And I have still encouraging testimonies that the work is going on at Oakham. A woman came to see me on Tuesday afternoon who has been a hearer ever since the chapel was opened. The Lord quickened and blessed her soul many years ago, but for the last seven or eight years she has been in a lukewarm profession, with only just enough life to keep her out of the world, and burdened with its cares and anxieties. But within these last few months the Lord has set to His hand the second time, and wrought very powerfully and blessedly in her soul, first bringing her to the deepest self-abasement and sorrow for her long state of backsliding, and then manifesting His mercy and love to her soul. She could hardly speak for tears and blessing the Lord for His mercies. It was not altogether under the word, though she said she has heard with new ears the last few months; but it seems that the work was helped on by the word. She will (D.V.) come before the church at our next meeting, when I doubt not she will be well received, and I hope to baptise her on my last Lord's-day at Oakham.

I am, you know, slow to receive what are called blessings, especially when said to have been under my preaching; but these cases at Oakham have been so clear, and there has been that savour and power attending the testimony which the friends have given, that I could not but believe them, they have come with such weight to my conscience.

Amidst all this, when I look within I feel much to condemn me. My past backslidings rise up to my view, with many sins and temptations, besides my continual propensity to carnality and folly. And then, when these attacks come from without, it makes me sink, as if the Lord had a strong controversy with me, and that after all my enemies might be right and I might be fearfully and perhaps wholly wrong. Why have *I* so many opponents? Other ministers pass along untouched, but book after book comes out against me, as if they would sink me outright. If this be the price paid for many hearers such as at Allington and elsewhere, methinks it is very dear. When, after hearing Mrs. L.'s testimony at the church-meeting at Oakham, I was walking from the upper vestry, I think, to the pulpit, I felt and said to myself, "If the Lord bless so my word to the people, let me go on preaching, I shall not mind a hundred ——s." But, alas! how soon the heart sinks again when trouble arises, and I could not help wishing I had lived and died in the Church of England. I thought I might have been quiet there, and need not have preached at all. I was struck last evening with Psalm xi. I cannot say that either it was applied to my soul, or that I would or did call my adversaries wicked. But the drift of the Psalm struck me as peculiarly forcible. We must be tried if we are the Lord's, and when our trials bring us to His feet, we may hope they may do us good. I do not wish, however, to burden you with my trials, though I know and feel you are and always have been a kind and sympathising friend.

I hope the Lord may be with you at Allington this time, and bless you in your own soul and in the ministry of the word to the hearts of the people.

I think (D.V.) of going to Lakenheath for Lord's-day, Aug. 12th. You know how desirous they have been for me to go there, and having that day to spare, I seemed led to spend it in that way.

I had a pleasant and I hope a profitable visit at Allington this time. But if I had my encouragements there, and many hearers and friends, I have had since and have now my ballast. . . .

Yours very affectionately,

J. C. P.

LXI—To Mr. Godwin

Oakham, June 19, 1849.

My dear Friend,

. . . We had a church meeting here on Lord's-day, and received two candidates for baptism. They were both well received, being well known to the friends and hearers almost ever since I came to Oakham; but one gave a blessed testimony, being now in the sweet enjoyment of the love of God, so that she could speak of the Lord having blessed her soul not once or twice, but again and again even to last Tuesday. She has been a backslider in heart many years, though a most consistent woman; but with what self-abhorrence does she now speak, and did, at the church meeting, with the tears of sorrow and love mingled together.

I went to K—— yesterday, and saw both her and the woman whom I baptised last, who so melted us all at the church meeting before I left home. I found also two other gracious persons there—constant hearers at the chapel—one a woman whose soul the Lord wonderfully blessed some years ago in a severe illness, but now much tried and harrassed. Since the Lord has revived the work here I have seen more of the friends, and believe when you come here you do not preach to stocks and stones. Amidst all our darkness and bondage, there is, I believe, life and feeling in the souls of some, and I am sure next to feeling life in his own soul, there is nothing so encouraging and so drawing, as it were, life out of him, as seeing there is life in the hearers.

I certainly felt some life and power when in Wilts, but since then seem to have well-nigh lost it all. On Lord's-day morning I really could not find one grain of grace in my soul, and I think sometimes I am one of the greatest hypocrites that ever walked, and all I feel and talk about is but pretence. Sometimes my mind is filled with infidelity as if the Bible and religion were all an invention; then again with unbelief as to my own state and standing, and then with all manner of hypocrisy and falsehood. So that when one's poor soul gets a little respite from the devil's snares in one way—lust and filthiness—there are snares and temptations on the other. There is either filthiness of the flesh, or filthiness of spirit, and we hardly know which is the worse.

But these things we must know experimentally, that we may dive into people's hearts and penetrate beneath that crust of self-righteousness and ignorance which hides so many from themselves. Men's motives, and thoughts, and feelings, are laid bare to us by knowing ourselves, and we are sure there is nothing really good in any but what God himself puts there by His grace; and thus whilst we value at its due worth all human pretensions we put a great price upon everything commended to our conscience as really of grace; and thus by these exercises we can not only draw a clearer line between persons in a congregation, but also more sift and separate the hearts of God's people and speak more to their comfort and encouragement.

Yours very affectionately,

J. C. P.

LXII.—To Mr. Godwin

Pentonville, July 17, 1849.

My dear Friend,

. . . I never came to London more unwillingly. I left Oakham very poorly, and weak in body, and tried in mind, and called myself a thousand fools to have made the engagement. But hitherto the Lord hath helped me, and I hope the poor and the needy may have reaped some little benefit from my trials and exercises. I hope the Lord was with me on Lord's-day, and I was enabled to speak pretty plainly upon the difference between exercised and unexercised persons, whether ministers, deacons, or hearers. I see this, that we must give up all idea of being what is called generally useful. There are very few children of God anywhere, and of these very few who are really tried and exercised, and know what they hear. There are but few who are really panting after heavenly blessings, or know the difference between the letter and the power. A doctrinal sermon about Jesus Christ will suit them far better than a real experimental one fetched out of the furnace. However, all we can do is to deliver our conscience, and speak what we know and feel to be true, and leave it in the hands of the Lord, who has promised that His word shall not return to Him void. There may be a few poor needy souls to whom it may be blessed, and that is all our reward and comfort as regards the ministry.

I think I have not felt so strong in speaking for months, I might almost say years, as I felt on Lord's-day. Though the place was very full, my voice seemed to ring through it like a bell. The preceding Lord's-day it seemed like speaking through water. But I had some life and feeling on Sunday; and that, you know, makes a wonderful difference even with our natural voice. What poor creatures we are without the Lord! and with Him we seem able to thresh the mountains. It seemed to raise up a little gratitude that the Lord had so far restored my health and enabled me to speak.

I hope you have found the Lord with you at Oakham and Stamford. I hope there is a work going on at Oakham, and that we shall have more come forward to declare what God has done for their souls; but it will be sure to make Satan rage, and stir up new trials and temptations.

Yours very affectionately,
J. C. P.

LXIII —To Mr. Godwin

Pentonville, July 24, 1849.

My dear Friend,

. . . I believe on the main points of experimental truth and vital godliness we see eye to eye, and feel heart to heart, and this makes us cleave to each other in affection and esteem. I am quite sick of the generality of Calvinistic professors, and I believe we may read their character in Ezekiel xxxiv., especially the ministers', 2—4, 17—22. But I leave them. Time and circumstances will make many things clear which now are dark and mysterious, and I wish neither their company, nor their standing, nor their spirit. When J. O——'s letter came out against me, these words were almost continually in my lips, "O Lord, fight my battles, and bring me off more than conqueror." All their strife and bitterness only give me more errands to a throne of grace and stir up my soul, which is so sadly prone to rest on its lees. J. O——'s scurrility, pride, and bitterness, seem to excite general disgust. Are these the fruits of Gospel liberty, and such manifestions as few have been favoured with since the times of the apostles? Judge such men by their fruits; and what is their religion really worth? The blessed Lord did not speak in vain, "By their fruits ye shall know them." Men may come in sheep's clothing, whilst inwardly they are ravening wolves. "Not every one who saith Lord, Lord," &c.

I am glad you saw Mrs. ——; she is a choice and well-taught woman, and I think I never call upon her without seeing the grace of God shining forth in her; and I think I could show you some who attend the chapel at Oakham, who can give as good an account of themselves as she, particularly some who have joined the church lately.

It is a consolation and encouragement to me to believe and feel that the Lord has a people at Stamford and Oakham to whom, from time to time, He blesses the word. Men may rage and storm and try to crush me as a worm under their feet; but if the Lord bless His word through me, what more, as a minister, can I desire?

I am well attended here. I think I never saw the chapel fuller than on Lord's-day evening. They were standing wherever they could, in the aisles and about the doors. But it was not a good day with me either time, and I seemed to have neither life and feeling in my soul, nor a door of utterance with my lips.

I believe your remarks about the real hearers are quite true. It is not the great body of seat-holders, but the unknown in holes and corners. Our hire, like Jacob's, must be "the speckled and spotted," "the brown and the ring straked;" all the snowy fleeced are Laban's.

Yours very affectionately,
J. C. P.

LXIV —To Mr. Godwin

Stamford, Aug. 31, 1849.

My dear Friend,

I was so poorly on Saturday night, and coughed so much during the night, that I almost despaired of being able to preach at all. I was sharply tried, for as I seemed to see the Lord's hand so plainly in my going to Lakenheath, it would have been very trying and mysterious if I could not preach, and I knew it would not only be a disappointment to the congregation, but would open the mouth of my enemies. I got up, however, and when, soon after breakfast the gigs and vehicles came pouring in, I felt I must preach, or at least make the attempt, come what would. I think if ever I looked to the Lord alone for strength and help, I did that morning. When I went up to the chapel it was so crowded I could scarcely get through to the pulpit. I read and prayed very short, and my cough kept interrupting me, so that I quite dreaded the sermon; but when I came to preach I found my voice strengthened, and I was mercifully helped through, beyond my expectation in every sense of the word.

There were persons there from twenty miles' distance, and the number of the vehicles very far exceeded that at Allington. I preached again in the afternoon, and my voice seemed clearer and stronger than in the morning. The people were standing back nearly as far as the trees, and yet my voice seemed able to reach them. On Tuesday evening I preached again to a full chapel. I came home on Wednesday. Tiptaft preached for me on Thursday, but I was so unwell I could not go out to hear him. I preached, however, on Lord's-day here twice, and had so good a congregation that I thought there was some mistake, and that there was an impression Tiptaft was to preach.

I hope I may one day see clearly why many painful things have been permitted. I think, indeed, I am getting more light upon them. The Lord has delivered me from some very trying temptations, and seems of late to be drawing me nearer to Himself. When we are under guilt and condemnation, all things seem against us, and there is a fleeing when none pursueth. All things in providence and in grace have a veil over them, and we see nothing clearly. But as the Lord draws us out of these feelings by drawing us nearer to Himself as the God of all grace, light begins to dawn upon the soul, and many perplexities are cleared up. It is a blessed thing to be drawn out of the world and things hateful and evil by tasting that the Lord is gracious. It is the power of sin which wants breaking; and this can be only by being brought under the power of grace. I have had many trials, afflictions, persecutions, and temptations; and I hope these have all worked together for my soul's profit. It is not often at the time that we see the good of our trials and afflictions. But what poor useless beings we should be without them—a burden and a nuisance to the children of God! I was thinking the other day that there were only two things really worth living for; to be blessed ourselves, and be made a blessing to others. Without this, what is life? To eat so many pounds of bread and meat, drink so many tumblers of water, sleep so many hours—is this life? But to be blessed and made a blessing, to have the hope of immortality in one's breast, and for some of God's children to bless the Lord that we ever lived—this is worth living for, and dying for too. Let us live twenty years longer it will only be the old scene over again, and we with less strength to bear it. The world, sin, and Satan will not change. But if by living we are made instruments in the Lord's hands of spiritual good to His people, this will be a blessing for eternity. This may reconcile us to our trials, if through them we are made a blessing to the heirs of glory.

Yours very affectionately,
J. C. P.

LXV—To Mr. T Beecher

Stamford, Sept. 18*th,* 1849.

My dear Sir,

From various causes I have not been able to attend earlier to your kind and friendly letter.

I think sometimes that Satan, seeing the Lord has blessed my ministry, is doing all he can to overthrow it. The doctrine and the experience cannot be overthrown; and therefore attempts are being made to overthrow the author. And what more ready way than to say that he borrows what he preaches? But surely they ought to point out whence it is borrowed. I have not read nor, indeed, seen poor old Osborne's book, but I am told it is a shameful production, and full of scurrility and abuse. But how little he can know of me, or of my experience. When he was at my house he seemed to have no inclination to talk upon experimental things, nor did he ask me one word about my experience. Nor do I believe he has read any of my writings. The poor old man was annoyed and disappointed because I would not praise up his writings, which I could not do when I found him so different a character from what I anticipated. And when the remarks in the *Standard* appeared, it incensed him all the more. I believe, therefore, in my own mind, his letter to me was written altogether out of spite and revenge. It is not likely, therefore, that God will own and bless a book written from such motives and in such a spirit.

I cannot now sit down and write you an experience spread over more than twenty-two years. My experience is incorporated in my sermons. And if you cannot see nor feel that to be genuine and my own, it is not all I can write could do it. I have felt guilt and bondage; have had sweet and blessed views of Christ; have seen His glory by the eye of faith; have felt Him precious to my soul; and, did time and space permit, could tell you where, when, and how. But you will find my experience in my sermons, for I feel what I preach, and preach what I feel; and this makes them blessed to God's children, and stirs up the malice of Satan. If I were to be satisfied with a dry doctrinal religion, I should be let alone. But because I contend for the power, some seem almost as if they would pull me to pieces. And if I know nothing of experience, why do I contend for it? Why did I not stay in the Church of England, where I might, but for conscience sake, have been this day, without let or molestation?

But I hope the Lord will bring me safely through all this strife of tongues. I mean to keep quiet (D.V.) and let them say what they will. All their attacks only give me fresh errands to the throne of grace.

Yours very sincerely,
J. C. P.

LXVI—To Mr. Parry

Stamford, September 20, 1849.

My dear Friend,

It is a mercy that where the Lord has begun a good work He will carry it on, and bring it to perfection.

If it were not so, what hope could there be for such poor, dark, dead wretches, who can no more revive than they can quicken their own souls? And when we have no trials or temptations, or at least not heavy ones, how soon we sink down into carnality and death. I dare say you find that nothing past, either trials or mercies, can do for the present; and that you need the Lord to set to His hand as much as if you had never known and felt anything of a vital nature.

I am, through mercy, better than I was after my Abingdon

visit, but not so well as I could wish. I was remarkably well this time last year, and I then thought I was almost as well as before my illness in 1847. But I fear this will never be the case, and that I shall never know good health again. I still, however, continue to preach as usual, and walk out most days when the weather is tolerably fine. At present we have been mercifully preserved from cholera, having had only one case in the town, and that caught passing, it is supposed, through London. At a village near Oakham it has been rather severe. I hope the Lord may mercifully preserve us and our families from that dreadful disease, which has already carried off so many thousands. It has been very bad at Plymouth and Devonport; but through mercy those dear to us have hitherto escaped at Stoke. I think our government very culpable in not having a day of national humiliation. Ahab and the city of Nineveh are quite scriptural precedents. As we are afflicted naturally and nationally, why should we not repent naturally and nationally? Some of my friends do not see with me in this matter, but I think my views are scriptural.

Poor dear M'Kenzie is at rest. There will appear (D.V.) a short account of his last days in the next *Standard*. He is taken away in the prime of life and, we might say, usefulness. Truly may we say "God's thoughts are not our thoughts," &c. His death throws more labour and responsibility upon me; but for some time before his death I had most of the *Standard* work to do, and I have long had to endure the chief responsibility. I hardly know where to look for help in his room; and must, I suppose, for the present, at least, bear the undivided burden. It is an office that requires some judgment and experience, as well as some degree of literary qualification, and it is hard to find all these in one individual.

My mind has of late been more settled. That matter troubles me but little now. I believe it is a legalized Gospel such as the Galatians were bewitched with; and we see from it similar fruits "biting and devouring one another." I hope to go on in my own path not moved by what is said for me or against me. It is through "evil report" as well as "good report" that ministers must pass. It is a mercy when the former does not cast down and the latter does not puff up.

You have had most beautiful weather for the harvest, and I hope have had a good crop. But prices are ruinous to the grower, and I fear will continue so. All things seem out of course. Thousands cut off by cholera, illness generally prevalent, much distress everywhere. And abroad still greater calamities. What a mercy amidst all the turmoil and strife to have eternal things to look to—a kingdom that cannot be moved! In twenty years it will probably little signify to you whether wheat sold in 1849 for 20s. or 40s. a sack; but it will much matter whether your soul is in heaven or hell. When the cold winds off the downs are whistling over your grave, or the warm sun sleeping on it, what will it matter whether sheep sold badly or well at the fair. Could we realize eternal things more we should be less anxious about temporal things, 2 Cor. iv. 18. It is only our unbelief and carnality which fetter us down to the poor things of time and sense. "Lord, increase our faith."

Through mercy we are all well, and this is a great mercy, for the town is full of sickness, chiefly small-pox, and many, especially children, have died. I consider ourselves favoured in having a healthy locality to dwell in.

Yours very affectionately,

J. C. P.

LXVII—To Mr. Godwin

Oakham, March 25, 1850.

My dear Friend,

My silence, I can assure you, has not arisen from want of friendship and affection. Since I have had so many enemies and so many treacherous friends, I have only more valued and cleaved to my few real friends. But writing is to me a great burden generally, and thus I keep putting it off till at last conscience compels me to make the attempt. But this morning, something I hope more than conscience, urges me to drop you a few lines in answer to your kind and affectionate letter. . . . .

I am glad you were comfortable at Leicester. Preaching is very pleasant when the Lord is present, but when all is dark and barren it is indeed hard work. I often wish I was anything else, or that I had more grace and qualifications for it. I had but a poor day yesterday, and seemed unable to get at anything that had dew and savour in it. I have so much opposition without and within. On the one side the Pharisees, and on the other the Antinomians; who are the worse, I can scarcely tell.

And then so much opposition within, so many temptations, lusts, and follies, so many snares and besetments, and a vile heart, dabbling in all carnality and filth. I am indeed exercised "by sin and grace" as you say. I liked the expression, it suited me well. Sin or grace seems continually uppermost—striving and lusting against one another. What workings, checks, lustings, sorrowings, fallings, risings, defeats, and victories. What a battle-field is the heart, and there the fight is lost and won. When sin prevails, mourning over its wounds and slaughter; when grace and godly fear beat back temptation, a softening into gratitude. Thus I keep hammering on at the old strain—soul exercise; and this sometimes meets with the experience of the poor and needy, and we see eye to eye and feel heart to heart in the things of God.

I have never wished nor cared for my sermons to be published, but if the Lord condescend to bless them, to Him be all the glory. I have never lifted up my little finger to spread or circulate them after I have corrected the proofs to prevent errors. Nor do my friends take any trouble about them more than myself. None of my people recommend them or circulate them. They are what they are; and are cast upon the waters and left to the Lord to do as He pleases with them.

Thus, if they are blessed it is of Him. And I think, sometimes, how hard the devil has been trying for years to poison people's minds for fear any good should be done by them.

I baptised Miss N. on the 17th.

Yours very affectionately,

J. C. P.

LXVIII—To Mr. Godwin

Oakham, Dec. 30, 1850.

My dear Friend,

You must not measure my feelings towards you by the frequency of my letters. Letter-writing to me is usually quite a task; unless there is something which I much wish to communicate I go to it as a schoolboy to his book. But I have felt for the last few days desirous to drop you a few lines.

I hope on the whole we had a pretty good day yesterday. I felt a little of the spirit of prayer on Saturday evening, and I trust we had a good morning. One of the friends, with whom I have a good union, told me afterwards what a spirit of prayer she had had through the week that we might have the Lord with us yesterday, and she had found her prayer answered. Our old friend at Trowbridge says when he is shut up the friends often hear him best. That, however, is not my experience, nor do I think it is yours. When I have some life and feeling in my soul I generally find it is so with the Lord's people; and when I am dark and shut up they are often so too. At those seasons I can get into nothing and describe nothing, and therefore how can I reach their hearts and consciences? The well is deep and I have nothing to draw with; and then what water is there for minister or people? I do hope there is some little work going on here. One candidate was well received, and we have two others coming forward whom I feel some union with.

At Stamford, too, I had more life and feeling on the 22nd—more than I have had since I came home. I told the friends I hoped it might be the dawn of a better day, that was the meaning if not the words. I am, I hope, also somewhat better in health, and have less irritation about my chest. The Lord is good if we could but trust Him.

You are, I dare say, exercised about your Liverpool engagement. Well, you don't know what you are going there for. It is not the seen but the unseen whom the Lord often blesses—some poor creature, cut up with sin and sorrow, who has neither pew nor seat, place nor name, among the great folks. Look at our large towns, Sheffield, Birmingham, Bristol, &c., what a state they are in. The only time I ever was at Liverpool, and heard preaching, there were less than twenty present; that was on a week evening. But there may be scattered individuals, who may creep in, whom you don't know. I believe you would sooner be going among our friends in Wilts.

To by far the greater part the Gospel, it is to be feared, is but the savour of death unto death. I am more and more convinced of this. We, who know a little of ourselves, need not wonder that men are what they are. What are we ourselves when left to our fallen nature? When I have felt my own carnality and aversion to spiritual things, I have ceased to wonder at the general ungodliness. . . .

Yours very affectionately,

J. C. P.

LXIX—To Mr. Godwin

Stamford, Feb. 7, 1851.

My dear Friend,

Before the February number of the *Gospel Standard* came out I saw that had I laid myself open to attack upon the point which you so kindly and faithfully name, and sent a partial correction to the office; but the letter being delayed to the morning mail, the *Standard* was already on the printing machine.

My meaning was that the body of Christ was not natural in the sense of deriving any taint of corruption through natural generation. I did mean that it was not animal, nor strictly identical with ours; but that it was sanctified in the very moment of conception, and was therefore intrinsically holy. I have thought that the supernatural generation of the dear Redeemer's human nature is too much overlooked. My mind was drawn to it many years ago, chiefly through Irving's heresy about Christ's "sinful flesh." And what I wished to convey was that the human nature of Jesus was and is "holy, harmless, undefiled, and separate from sinners." And this because begotten in a spiritual, supernatural way. Indeed, what but a holy nature could be taken into union with the Son of God?

When upon my bed I had, as I hope, a revelation of Jesus, I saw, by the eye of faith, most distinctly, His two natures in a way that I cannot describe, which has always made me so firm a contender for them.

I shall hope (D.V.) to explain my meaning more fully in the next number. I was wrong in using the words natural and spiritual. Meanwhile I thank you for your kind and faithful letter, and will (D.V.) look into the subject more closely.

Yours affectionately,
J. C. P.

LXX—To Mr. Godwin

Oakham, Feb. 24, 1851.

My dear Friend,

I am glad you are coming our way, but am sorry your stay will be so short. It generally takes a little time before we get into the marrow of anything. The bone, you know, lies pretty deep in the flesh, and the marrow deeper still. We want an evening together, and a little oil on the heart and tongue, such as we had, I hope, once before at my house.

* * * * * *

At present we are very comfortable here as a church. We had a church meeting yesterday, and received two candidates, and had a very comfortable meeting indeed. I never saw a better feeling among the friends; and the simple tale that one poor old woman told seemed to melt our hard hearts. I have not seen so many tears shed since Mrs. L—— came before us. We are very full, too, as a congregation, and I hope the Lord is sometimes with poor vile us.

I am called, "the blind leader of the blind"; but if I am blind, I have, I am sure, some who can see and feel too, and some who will shine as the stars for ever and ever. Nor am I blind to my own sins and follies, ignorance, unbelief, and helplessness; nor am I blind to the blessedness, grace, and suitability of the Lord Jesus Christ. And in standing up before the people, I feel a sincere desire for their soul's profit; and as far as the Lord enables, labour for their edification and consolation without fear or flattery. Herein I have through mercy the testimony of a good conscience.

My dear friend, I was not in the least hurt or offended with your kind letter about the review. I know you are a sincere friend, and that what you say or do you do out of real affection. I should be a poor proud wretch, worse than I am, if I could not take advice from friends. I know how many enemies I have, and how many are watching for my halting; and there is so much hypocrisy in men that I am weary of most professors. How true is Micah vii. 2, 3, and there is such cursed pride, envy, and enmity in the heart! I see it in myself and in others too. O what a wretch is man, and the best of men!

Yours very affectionately,
J. C. P.

LXXI —To Mr. Godwin

Oakham, March 25, 1851.

My dear Friend,

I should have answered your kind and friendly letter before, had not my time been so much occupied.

I have been down to Stoke to pay the last mark of respect and affection to my poor dear mother. She died early on Thursday morning, the 13th inst. I left home on Monday, slept at Exeter that night, and reached Stoke Tuesday evening. I found Mrs. Isbell better than I expected, and more calm and collected. On Wednesday morning her remains were committed to the earth. She was buried in the new cemetery at Plymouth (Dissenters' side), and Mr. Isbell performed the ceremony. He did it very well, reading 1 Cor. xv., and making some remarks on her character, &c., closing with prayer. It rained nearly all the time, and therefore we were not long at the grave. My mind was in a whirl from the time that I heard of her death; and what with so much travelling I was so confused that I could not realise that she was dead. Indeed I seemed hardly able to believe it till I saw the coffin with her name on the plate let down into the grave. She was in her 79th year, and had suffered much from rheumatism in her hand and limbs. Her last malady was influenza and bronchitis, from which she suffered much. Mrs. S——e, whom I think you know, has a good hope of her—indeed, has no doubt of her state. She knew more of her feelings and experience than any one, as my poor mother was much attached to her, and could converse more freely with her than almost any one else. She had once a sweet manifestation of the love of God to her soul, on which she seemed to hang, but was for the most part much pressed down with a sense of her unworthiness, and fears of being deceived, and being a hypocrite. She was always to me a most kind and affectionate parent; and I do not recollect that we ever disagreed once in our lives. When I left the Establishment she felt it; but said her house was open to me, and that I might go and live with her. And, I can assure you, I have sometimes wished I had done so, and thus lived a quiet obscure life, without the troubles and trials which I have had in occupying a more prominent place; but God has fixed the bounds of our habitation, and it is folly to think of carving out our own path. The weather being so wet and cold, made the journey more trying, and has made me feel quite poorly and out of sorts. My poor mother's death will be much felt by Mrs. Isbell, who was much attached to her.

I baptised three persons here last Lord's-day and hope the Lord was with us. . . . All here is labour and sorrow. Our own sins and the sins of others will always make it a scene of trouble. "O thou hideous monster, sin," &c. What a mighty power it has

—a power which grace alone can subdue. It seems sometimes subdued, and then rises up worse than before. Well may we cry out, "O wretched man that I am," &c.

Yours very affectionately,
J. C. P.

LXXII—To Mr. Godwin

Oakham, April 7, 1851.

My dear Friend,

It was my intention (D.V.) to write to you to-day, even if your kind letter had not met me here on Saturday.

I feel for you in your troubles, especially in *one* which I know presses you sore. My dear friend, most of us have to learn Micah vii. 4, 5, in painful experience. It is bitter work, especially where there is soul-union. I do hope the Lord will appear for you in this trying case. Oh, how He can soften hearts, melt away bitter feelings, and subdue that demon of hell—cruel suspicion. My dear friend, how should I get on with you, if I could not depend upon your friendship behind my back, as well as before my face? It is because I believe you to be a man who truly fears God, and a sincere, affectionate friend as well, that makes me cleave to you. We have all great faults and failings before man, as well as awful, damnable backslidings and sins before God; and I dare say my friend T. G. has his as well as others theirs. I do hope it may please the Lord to make this crooked thing straight.

I have not been well since my return from Stoke. The cold, wet weather seemed to try my chest, though, through mercy, I was preserved from cold. I should be glad to slip out of my London engagement, my chest being unfit for the exertion, heat, and mental labour and exercise which I have at Eden Street. What a life of toil, sin, and suffering! And all cannot subdue those dreadful lusts, which swarm like ants in an ant-hill on a summer's day. I have had two desires uppermost in my mind for years, one that I might not leave my wife and children destitute, the other that I might make a good end. The one has, by my poor mother's death, been in good measure accomplished. The other remains with the Lord. But, indeed, it must be all of grace, and no common grace, for I have been, and am, no common sinner. I am beset with temptations on every hand, and my vile heart will still meditate villainy.

I hope we had a pretty good day yesterday. In the afternoon I felt some little life and liberty. The day was fine, and we were well attended. As far as I can see and feel there is much more right and real religion in the country than in London. We know some in Wilts, and there are others in Berks, and a few, I hope, in Rutland and Lincolnshire, who, in my mind, outweigh those whom we see in town. They have more life, and feeling, and simplicity, and tenderness about them. But I hope the Lord will bless you among them in your own soul and ministry. It is a day of very small things, really and experimentally. There is much talk and noise, much light in the head, but little life or grace in the heart; and matters seem getting worse. I had more life and feeling ten years ago at Alie Street, and I have heard you and Tiptaft say the same. I had scarcely a barren season at Zoar in 1841, and I could no more preach those sermons now than I could fly. I had a large congregation at St. Ives, but I hardly know what to make of things there. The anointing oil seems much lacking. How easy to talk, preach, pray, and hear without the only thing which makes them a blessing. Alas! I see the nakedness of the land when I am a poor naked thing so often myself. Like a barren woman, I complain of the barrenness of others. God alone can make the barren woman keep house, and be a joyful mother of children.

Yours very affectionately,
J. C. P.

LXXIII—To the late Mr. Duncan Mathieson

Stamford, January 28, 1852.

My dear Sir,

I have, indeed, reason to bless the Lord for the way in which, in His mysterious providence and grace, He has condescended to spread and bless my little productions. And this because I have never attempted to spread them myself, and have no pecuniary interest in them. It is indeed mysterious that they should have reached your remote district, and especially so that your first knowledge of them should have come through such a remarkable channel.* A few days before your letter came to hand I received one from a clergyman in Herts, who had been under great distress of soul. Change of air was recommended, and he went to Ramsgate. Going one morning to bathe, his eye glanced in at a shop-window, in which the "Heir of Heaven" sermon was exposed for sale. He was struck with the title, and went in and purchased it. It was made a blessing to his soul. He was led to procure my other writings and sermons, and speaks of them as being blessed to him. How mysterious are the dealings of God! Feeling my own dreadful sinfulness, it makes me wonder at His free, sovereign, matchless, superabounding grace. Of all men I was most unlikely to be made useful to the Lord's family. Until I went to college in 1821 I actually never knew there was any such thing as religion professed beyond the mere

* The Duchess of Gordon.

Church of England formalism in which I was educated. There, by the conversation of a fellow-student, my judgment was convinced, but my heart untouched; until in 1827, in a solitary part of Ireland, in the midst of a deep affliction, the Lord was pleased, I trust, to quicken my poor dead soul. This entailed the overthrow of all my University prospects, which were good, as in human learning I had in 1824 taken what are called high honours; and, indeed, my heart was devoted to books and the acquisition of earthly knowledge. From 1828 to 1835 I was a minister in the Establishment, residing chiefly in a lonely village, where I had much sickness, and learnt, I hope, in soul some of those lessons which are embodied in my ministry. As my conscience became burdened with the unscriptural character and services of the Church of England, I was compelled to leave it. My path has been, and is, one mainly of trial and temptation, having a heart so evil, a tempter so subtle, and so many crosses and snares in which my feet are continually caught and entangled.

But I hope that my trials and temptations are mercifully overruled for the benefit and edification of the Church of God. We are overrun with a shallow, superficial ministry, which is destitute of all life, savour, and power. The trials and exercises of the family of God are untouched, or, if alluded to, are trampled down with contempt. A dry, dead-letter scheme of doctrine, as mathematically correct as the squares of a chess-board, prevails, where what is called "Truth" is preached, and to move texts on the squares as pawns or pieces is the art of preaching. Where heart and conscience are not reached, where the inward conflict is not opened up, where the sweet and savoury Gospel is not preached with the Holy Ghost sent down from heaven, there the flock of slaughter cannot feed. Ezekiel xxxiv. is a true picture of the false shepherds.

How simple is truth! Man's misery, God's mercy, the aboundings of sin, the superaboundings of grace; the depths of the fall, the heights of the recovery; the old man and the new; the diseases of the soul, and the balm of a Saviour's blood—these lessons learnt in the furnace of inward experience, how different from the monkish austerity of the Puseyite, the lip service of the Pharisee, and the dry Calvinistic formulary of the kirk!

A friend of mine, now departed, was called, in the providence of God, to Glasgow. Thence he wrote to me that he had wandered from church to chapel, and, I think, the same at Edinburgh; but all was dead joy. At last he used on the Lord's-day evenings to leave the town, sit on a hill-side, and there pray and read—drawing sometimes from his pocket one of my little sermons. He would have rejoiced to find a few there with whom he could have united. When I sent forth my little productions I had not the remotest idea of their being so widely spread, or that the Lord would condescend so much to bless them as, I trust, He has done.

With the sermons which have been taken down I have had still less to do; but as they have obtained a wide circulation, and are read in many little chapels where there is no minister, I think it right to revise them before they go forth.

May the Lord lead us more deeply into His most blessed truth! What are all the gilded toys of time compared with the solemn, weighty realities of eternity! But, alas! what wretches are we when left to sin, self, and Satan! How unable to withstand the faintest breath of temptation! How bent upon backsliding! Who can fathom the depths of the human heart? Oh, what but grace, superabounding grace, can either suit or save such wretches?

Tender my love to all in your circle who bear me in their heart. I deeply need their prayers. The Lord keep and bless you.

Yours, I trust, in the best bonds,

J. C. P.

LXXIV—To Mr. Godwin

Allington, June 4th, 1852.

My dear Friend,

I think sometimes when I am gone and carnal feelings buried in my grave, my writings and sermons will be more understood than they are now; and I hope I have a place in the hearts and affections of some of God's people.

You may depend upon it there are some of the right sort of people at Oakham and Stamford. I felt once at the ordinance at Stamford much as you did—as if I could take the friends all into my arms and heart.

I must not complain of my Allington visit thus far. I had a good day the first Lord's-day, and we had a very full chapel.

I am glad you have felt at home at Stamford and Oakham. It is miserable dragging work when there is death without and within. It is sweet and blessed to have one's soul watered whilst watering others. I hope we have had some right feeling in the chapel since I have been here. We went up to Shaw Farm last evening. We had a comfortable visit with the old lady (Mrs. Wild), and more conversation on the things of God than usual. We see well eye to eye. Providence, too, seems more smiling than at Stowell, and, therefore, less unbelief and repining. I enjoy the pure air from the downs, and they say I look better than when I came. This quiet life, retired spot, and walks by myself, suit me well; much excitement would soon kill me. I suppose I must try and fulfil my London engagement, but it will be hard work.

Yours very affectionately,

J. C. P.

LXXV—To Miss Richmond

Allington, June 9, 1853.

My dear Friend,

I hope, if the Lord will, and health and strength be given, to speak a little at Stadham on Thursday evening, the 23rd instant, on my way home. If your sister at Sutton Courtney would do me the kindness of meeting us with her sociable at the station, we could spend an hour or two with her before proceeding to Stadham; and I think Mrs. Philpot would like to see the place where her uncle was when in the Church of England.

It is some time since I was at Stadham, and I hope the Lord may bless the visit among my old friends. We hope that amidst much weakness and ignorance He did bless us in times past, and He is the same gracious God now as He was then—"the same yesterday, to-day, and for ever." And we, too, are the same poor and needy sinners who only see light in His light, and without whom, indeed, we can do nothing. Many years have passed away since I first came to Stadham, and we have seen many changes in ourselves and others; but the foundation abideth sure, and if we are indeed built on that we are safe amidst all trials. You have seen two sisters who married with every prospect of worldly happiness widowed and bereft, and thus have in your own family the strongest testimony how fleeting and vanishing all dreams of earthly comfort are. How good it is when these painful lessons produce spiritual abiding profit!

But, alas, we are slow and dull learners, and need line upon line, line upon line, here a little, and there a little, and, after all, often seem as if we knew nothing as we ought to know.

If salvation were not wholly of grace what hope could we have? In this bottomless sea of mercy poor sinners can cast anchor when there is any discovery of this superabounding grace to their hearts.

Yours affectionately,
J. C. P.

LXXVI—To Mr: Godwin

Stamford, Dec. 30, 1853.

My dear Friend,

You seem favoured with two great blessings—health of body and health of soul. Such blessings are they that without them life is not life. I wish you may long enjoy both, and be made a blessing for many years to the Church of God.

I am, through mercy, better. I preached at Oakham in the morning last Lord's-day, and spoke in the afternoon from the chapter nearly three quarters of an hour. We had our annual collection for the poor, and got £26 7*s.* 3*d.*, the largest collection for fifteen years. I urged them to liberality on account of the dearness of provisions and fuel, and the severity of the weather, and they came forward most liberally.

But I think, my dear friend, we have both seen much of a God of providence. I told them at Oakham on Lord's-day that I have sometimes thought I could write a "Bank of faith," for money has come in just as wanted. What I want most is grace, spirituality of mind, fear of the Lord, tenderness of conscience, and power against besetting sins.

Yours affectionately,
J. C. P.

LXXVII.—To Mr. Godwin

Stamford, March 25, 1854.

My dear Friend,

I have at length made my arrangements for going out. I think the friends here would hardly like my being absent from them five Lord's-days running, especially when I shall soon (D.V.) be leaving them again.

They have been particularly kind and liberal this winter, providing Supplies to give me a little rest, and I should not like to seem ungrateful to them now that the Lord has in some measure restored me. I think, therefore, I must come some other time, if spared, to Woburn, than the Lord's-day that you have named. The Eden Street friends were unwilling to let me off, so they proposed my coming for the Lord's-days as usual, and procuring supplies for the Tuesdays. But I declined their kind offer, as it is the heat and crowd on the Lord's-day and the two services which try me most. I have, however, offered to go for one Lord's-day, the last in July; but have, at present, received no answer.

Mrs. S. gave a sweet and blessed testimony before the Church. I never heard a sweeter account of the love of God shed abroad in a poor sinner's heart. But it was fresh and warm in her soul, and therefore came forth sweet and savoury. I understand she has been much tried about it since.

I am (D.V.) to baptise three candidates to-morrow, and hope we may have a good day. I expect we shall also soon have a baptising at Oakham, as we have received one candidate and another is coming forward.

I have been applied to about the propriety of breaking up the church at C——, and reforming it. There are, I believe, not more than four or five members left, the others having withdrawn on account of F.'s bad conduct, and as the present members seem to have sanctioned his evil ways, it has been thought an advisable step to break up the church, and so remove the reproach, and then form a new one. My own mind is in favour of it, as I think there will be neither peace nor prosperity whilst the present church continues. But the question arises, "Who has a sufficient authority to do so?" A Supply hardly seems to have sufficient authority to do it. For, if one Supply may do it, why not another? And then you may establish this principle, that a Supply may go and break up a church, like Eden Street or Allington, where there is no pastor, whether the church agree to it or not. So that, whilst I think it would be best for the church at C—— to be broken up, I hardly see how it is to be done, or who has authority to do it in a scriptural manner. Turn the matter over in your mind, as I dare say they will ask your opinion about it. I think it must eventually be done; but I believe it can hardly be done in a right way before they get a permanent minister.

Monday, March 27.

I had a hard day's work yesterday, and having a bad cold, was almost knocked up before I had finished. The baptistery here is most inconvenient, being so long; and the women were all much agitated, and I had almost to carry them through the water after I had baptised them to the further side, and the lattice under my feet quite slippery. I hope, however, we had, on the whole, a good day. I am quite poorly to-day, and, therefore, am not much fit for writing; but it is a mercy I was brought through yesterday, and did not disappoint the candidates and the people.

Mrs. Philpot is, through mercy, better in health. Amidst all our trials and afflictions we have our mercies and favours. My chief burden and trouble is sin, which haunts me night and day. O what an enemy to the soul's peace!

Yours very affectionately,
J. C. P.

LXXVIII—To Mr. Grace

Hartley Row, Hants, Aug. 22, 1854.

My dear Friend,

I am much pleased with Miss H——'s letters. There is a freshness, a simplicity, and a *naïveté* about them which, with their slightly foreign English, are very characteristic. I like the absence in them of that almost conventional language which has become almost the common epistolary style of gracious persons. I shall better, perhaps, convey my meaning by quoting the remark of a friend, that "nearly all the letters in the *Standard* might have been written by one person." Like a clear brook, Miss H——'s letters allow you to see through the water to the bottom. Her very ignorance, in some points, pleases me, as it shows she is struggling upwards and onwards for divine light. A few sincere simple souls, thirsting for divine teaching, open a minister's heart and mouth, whilst heady, high-minded, carping, cavilling hearers only bar and close it. Mr. Beeman always wondered what Mr. Huntington could see in him to like. It was his humility and his seeing nothing in himself.

I am sorry to hear of your trials and afflictions. But what would you be to the Church of God without them? An unexercised, untried minister is of little use to the suffering Church of God, Hart's "noble army of martyrs." I wish you well under them, and I wish you well through them, and I wish you well after them, and then you will say, "It is well." I was glad to see you in town, and believe we could have found matter for conversation had your visit been longer, as I felt free to talk with you, and believe that on most points, and on all important ones, we are well agreed.

You occupy an important position in your large town, and feel, doubtless, that all your sufficiency is of God. Without Him the wisest and strongest labour in vain, and with Him the worm Jacob can thresh the mountains.

Accept the best wishes and sincere Christian love of

Yours affectionately,

J. C. P.

LXXIX—To Mr. Grace

Stamford, Sept. 11, 1854.

My dear Friend,

I am much obliged to you for your kind and acceptable present, which came safely to hand.

I much like what I have read of the Doctor's Letters. They give us W. H. not as the controversialist, though in that a good soldier of Jesus Christ, but as he was in his secret chamber. There is an infinity of admirable touches whereby the secret work of the Spirit on the heart seems in some respects more effectually traced out than when drawn out in a clearer, more systematic manner. Some of his hints and directions are much to the purpose, and bear a stamp of genuine godliness. It may be taken up, too, and laid down at vacant moments without, as in systematic writings, losing the thread, and may thus lie on the table side by side with the Bible and Hart's Hymns, as the ready reckoner lies on the desk of the man of business.

I hope the Lord was with you in your late tour. We should be very happy to see and hear you here when you come again into these parts. It is a mercy to be blessed with will and power to labour in the vineyard. There is certainly in our day a spirit of hearing in many places, and we have reason to hope that among these thick boughs there must be some fruitful branches.

Things, perhaps, are not so bad as some think, though not so good as most imagine. But that the life of God is low, even where it exists, is, I fear, too true.

Wishing you the enjoyment of every covenant mercy,

I am,

Yours affectionately and obliged,

J. C. P.

LXXX—To Mr. Godwin

Stamford, Sept. 27, 1854.

My dear Friend,

I desire to sympathise with you in all your trials and sorrows, which the Lord has laid upon you so very heavy and severe. But I see in them marks of a kind and gracious Father's love to make you more useful to the Church of God, and establish you more in the truth and blessedness of the Gospel. Whatever men may think or say about you, they cannot say that yours is the bastard's portion, and that you have all that the carnal heart can wish for—you are plagued all the day long and chastened every morning. But what a mercy that you are not left either to hardness of heart or to rebellion under your afflictions, but are favoured with a spirit of grace and supplications, and prove from time to time that the Lord is a God that heareth and answereth prayer! I hope it may please the Lord when this affliction has worked out its destined end and brought forth the peaceable fruit of righteousness, to remove it in some measure. I say "in some measure," for I never expect poor Mrs. G—— will have much health in this life. It will be a daily cross for you both till her poor frail tabernacle is laid in the grave to wait the sound of the great trumpet on the resurrection morn, and then she will have a new and glorified body, fit companion for an immortal soul, and each as full of glory as they can hold. But she had better be tried in mind and afflicted in body, and have grace in her heart, than be mistress of Woburn Abbey and be called "Your Grace."

I am going (D.V.) to Leicester, Friday next, for Lord's-day and the Tuesday after.

I am much as usual in health. I did not come home very well, but feel a little stronger since I returned. Few places suit me better than my own home.

I am afraid our friends at —— are in a good deal of trouble and confusion. I hardly know what advice to give them. When churches get wrong it is like family troubles, which persons out of the family are very sorry for, but cannot interfere in. We can only give them kind and scriptural advice, and there we must leave it. I dread church troubles, as there never is an end to them, and they break up all peace, confidence, and union. We are, through mercy, pretty comfortable at present at both places.

I hear the old warrior was well heard at Leicester. The place was very fully attended, and many came a long way.

My dear friend, we have all our trials and sorrows. The great question is, what they are doing for our immortal souls? That is the main thing after all, for they must come one day to an end.

Yours affectionately,

J. C. P.

LXXXI—To Mrs. Peake

Stamford, Nov. 9, 1854.

My dear Friend,

You have given me, in your kind and affectionate note, so friendly and cordial an invitation, that I cannot feel it in my heart to decline it. I shall have, therefore, much pleasure in staying over the Wednesday, and will make my arrangements accordingly. I have for many years seen much difficulty in maintaining Christian intercourse with those towards whom we feel spiritual union. It is usually only at rare seasons that true spiritual communion is obtained with them; and without this, social intercourse rather damps than maintains our union. This feeling has long influenced me in declining much visiting among the friends, beyond those friendly and pastoral calls which the Lord may make mutually pleasant and profitable. But one may err on the right hand as well as on the left; and Christians may keep themselves too widely apart or be too intimate.

Any profit that you may derive from the ministry is wholly of the Lord's mercy and grace. This is my increasing feeling. What the Lord blesses is His own truth. Pure water in a horn, is better than foul water in a golden cup. My desire is to preach God's pure unadulterated truth, and leave the blessing of it to Him.

Yours very affectionately,

J. C. P.

LXXXII—To Mr. Grace

Stamford, Feb. 1, 1855.

My dear Friend,

I am exceedingly obliged to you for your kind present of the fourth volume of the invaluable "Posthumous Letters of William Huntington," and for your friendly and affectionate letter. I have been reading some of his most sweet and savoury epistles this morning, and find them instructive, edifying, and profitable. They contain the cream and marrow of vital godliness, and real, genuine, heartfelt religion unmixed with that controversial spirit which sometimes mingles with his other writings. What I admire most in them, next to their sweet savour, is the way in which he draws up the living water from his own experience, and that past as well as present. I should much like to make them better known through the *Gospel Standard*, and put down a few thoughts which have occurred to my mind in reading them. What an awful lack is there of such preaching now! I look round and see so few men qualified to feed the Church of God. We are over-run with parsons, but, O dear! what are they? I cannot but attribute much of the low state of the churches to the ministers who rather preach them dead, deaf, and blind, than stir them up and ministerially quicken, enlighten, and enliven them. I am sure that the life of God much consists in, and is much manifested by, the breathings, cries, and longings of the soul after Him, and that by these that coldness and deadness are sensibly relieved which many so much complain of.

With you, I admire above all others Hart's blessed hymns. I should be glad to help in their circulation, and I think a notice in the *Standard*, or short advertisement might help this. As all his hymns are in Gadsby's Hymn Book (with one or two omissions), our friends are pretty well furnished with copies, but I will mention the cheap edition to them.

Do you not think the churches should use prayer and supplication at this momentous crisis? The Lord's hand seems going out against us at home and abroad. How paralysed and dislocated all the men of war and counsel seem, and none able to stand in the gap. Mr. Huntington was a true lover of his country, and lived in still darker times than our own. With what boastings was the war entered upon, and now what despondency. How few acknowledge that the Lord reigneth!

I desire to sympathise with you in your trials and afflictions, but they are all in due weight and measure.

Yours affectionately,

J. C. P.

LXXXIII —To Miss Richmond

Stamford, March 6, 1855.

My dear Friend,

I am much obliged to you for your kind communication of the closing scenes of our lamented friend Brookland's earthly life. I perceived, when I last saw him, the inroads which his complaint had made on his appearance and constitution, and was therefore the less surprised to hear of his decease. He was a man so thoroughly sincere, and indeed so scrupulous to say nothing of himself but what his conscience could fully bear witness to, that we can receive with implicit credit what he said in those solemn moments. In those who have walked many years in tribulation's thorny road, and have at various times been favoured and blessed, we do not expect such a what is called triumphant death-bed as in those who are removed in their first love. The promise is that in Jesus they shall have peace. Their experience of the deceitfulness of their own heart has stripped them of lying hopes and a false peace; and therefore when we see them in the enjoyment of peace with eternity in full view, we cannot but believe that the peace of God is keeping their heart and mind through Christ Jesus. This our dear departed friend seems to have felt and enjoyed. I attach more weight to this, and his holding up his hands at the last, than what you mention of a more visionary nature. He was, as you justly observe, a firm friend to, and unbending pillar of, truth; and his quiet demeanour and consistent conduct for many years recommended and adorned his profession. Being so long afflicted with a complaint from which recovery was hopeless, we need not wish him detained here below. Among the blessings of the realms above, is that "the inhabitants thereof shall no more say, 'I am sick.'" Those only who have a sickly tabernacle can fully prize such a promise. Our dear friend, we fully hope, has entered into the enjoyment of it.

I am at present but poorly myself, having an attack of influenza on my chest. Truly this is a dying world. On Saturday last, my friend Mr. Harrison, of Leicester, was removed from this vale of tears. In helping to move a tree, he received a blow on the chest which produced inflammation of the heart, under which he sank. He was one of the kindest, sincerest friends that I was ever blessed with. How all these dispensations speak to us with a loud voice, "Set your affections on things above, not on things on the earth!" Twenty-four years have passed away since I spent the winter at Sutton Courtney, and nearly twenty since I left the Establishment. Mrs. Lowe, H. Witney, and poor Brookland, with many others, who used to hear my voice, have been removed from time into eternity, and these departures of our friends all seem to say, "Be ye also ready." But the Lord Himself must be our help, and hope, and all. To Him, and to Him alone, must we ever look, for there is salvation in no other. He is the way, and the truth, and the life, and no man cometh unto the Father but by Him.

Yours affectionately,

J. C. P.

LXXXIV—To Mr. Godwin

London, August 16, 1855.

My dear Friend,

I believe you will be pleased to hear that through rich mercy I have been brought through my labours here much better than I anticipated. I came up with many fears and faintings but have broken down neither in body nor mind. I found more exertion needed than at Eden Street, but I think what tried me so much at Eden Street was the foul air. I had all the windows opened at Gower Street round the gallery, and therefore felt not the least bad air or closeness.

We had great congregations, and I hope I was faithful to them. I did not feel all I could wish, far from it; but I must not complain. I see and feel my great, great deficiency and shortcomings as a minister. I felt Tuesday evening before the Lord, O that I could preach better—with more power and savour, and be more blessed to the people. I always seem to come so short of what I want spiritually to be. I am coming short all the day long and sinning with every breath I draw. What a debtor to grace! What else can I preach to poor guilty sinners?

Gower Street was the first London pulpit I ever stood up in, as I preached once for Mr. Fowler, August 8, 1836, just nineteen years ago. I am much pleased with the chapel, and hardly know whether to be more grateful to the Lord for the chapel, and bringing me through, or to Him for putting it into the heart of Mr. and Mrs. Clowes to take us in. Their rooms seem to suit my health, so that I may say that on the whole I have not got through my London labours so well for some years. I hardly dare say much, as I may fall ill when I return home, but as far as present feelings go I seem better than these last two or three years. I always much dread my Abingdon Lord's-day both for body and soul. There are many gracious well-taught people there, and they come many miles, and I feel my weakness in every sense of the word.

I hope the Lord will come with you to Gower Street. What an affliction you have; but ballast we must have to sail steady. We do not like trials and troubles, but what are we without them?

Yours affectionately,
J. C. P.

LXXXV—To Mr. Grace

Leicester, September 26, 1855.

My dear Friend,

I shall be most happy to see you at Stamford in October, but I cannot by any means consent to your being a hearer, for which I will give you three sufficient reasons: 1. The rest will do my body good. 2. I am afraid your being there might shut me up. 3. My people would be much disappointed. I am to them but an old song; but the Lord might, and I hope would, bless the word by you. I hope Mr. P. delivered my message *verbatim et literatim.* "Tell Mr. Grace I shall be happy to give him a seat at my table, a bed at my house, and a door into my pulpit."

I was glad to hear that Mr. H—— made a good end. The Lord is faithful to the work of His dear Son on the cross, and the work of the Holy Ghost on the soul. Clouds and darkness may surround the work on the soul as they do His eternal throne, though He himself dwelleth in the light which no man can approach unto; but at evening time it is often light. Grace is undying, and that is the mercy for the living family of God.

I am preaching here to large congregations.

Grace be with thee.

Yours affectionately,
J. C. P.

LXXXVI—To Mr. S

Oakham, October 30, 1855.

Dear Friend,

I am sorry I cannot accept the invitation contained in your kind and affectionate letter. My will is good to labour in the vineyard; but I do not possess the health and strength needful to carry out my will. My chest being weak and tender I can only just manage, with the Lord's help, to go in and out before my own people. Besides which, the winter season is fast advancing, during which I rarely go from home, except backwards and forwards here, which, indeed, is my second home, naturally and spiritually.

Apart from my own bodily comfort I have often much desired better health, that I might labour more in the Lord's cause. But He knows best what to do with, and what to do by us, and what we cannot alter, it is our wisdom and mercy to submit to.

I have no doubt that you find it hard work to carry on the cause of truth at L——. But if this make you feel more deeply your need of help from the Sanctuary, it will work together for your spiritual good. Those causes, or rather those people, usually flourish best where there is much opposition and many painful trials. These show how far we are sincere in our love to the truth, and give an errand to the throne. We soon sink down into a cold, careless state, when there are no trials; and, therefore, we may say of them that they are blessings in disguise.

Yours affectionately,
J. C.P.

LXXXVII —To Mr. Grace

Stamford, November 19, 1855.

My dear Friend,

I received quite safely both your kind letter and the book. I have not had much time as yet to read the latter, but like what I have seen of it. It is wrong to use such a term, but it has almost amused me from its pithy quaintness and dry expressions. It much resembles a book you are probably unacquainted with, a great favourite with Dr. Johnson, Burton's "Anatomy of Melancholy." The short Latin quotations were then the style of the age, as Latin was then as generally understood as French now. But apart from this there are many useful hints on experimental subjects.

I have lately adopted the plan of making a few short comments in a familiar manner as I read the chapter, and find it puts a life and interest in that part of the service of God. Our hearers are many of them exceedingly ignorant and want a little instruction, and things stumble them which a word of explanation might remove. A poor woman whom I knew was troubled that Peter should have had wicked Judas for his son (John xiii. 2), and a man, how there could be calling without repentance (Rom. xi. 29). Two words would have removed these stumbling blocks. Many a poor child of God has got a real blessing from a verse in the chapter or a line from the hymn when all the sermon was an empty sound. What we need is the blessing of God, and if that is not sought or wanted, preaching is but a worthless noise.

Yours affectionately,

J. C. P.

LXXXVIII —To Miss Richmond

Stamford, Jan. 15th, 1856.

My dear Friend,

I am much obliged to you for your kind and sympathising letter, and the invitation therein contained.

I am much pleased to learn that the Lord has graciously turned your captivity. It much resembles a manifestation which I was once favoured with when the Lord Jesus was so presented before the eyes of my enlightened understanding, and I had such a view by faith of the two distinct natures in one glorious Person. It was on my bed one morning during a long illness. I can, therefore, quite understand your feelings and experience. It will give truth a deeper place, and a firmer hold in your heart; and though it may be often disputed or doubted, hidden in darkness, and buried in confusion, still it will afford you some standing-ground which you had not before.

It is a very blessed thing, and a high favour to have clear and spiritual views of the Person of Immanuel. It gives faith a firm foundation to rest upon, and makes Jesus all in all. We are exceedingly obliged to you for your kind invitation, but all our family are now with us, and we cannot leave them to servants.

Yours affectionately,

J. C. P.

LXXXIX.—To Mr. Grace

Oakham, Feb. 22, 1856.

My dear Friend,

I cannot call to mind any distinct promise to review (my usual way of noticing) Huntington's letters. I may possibly do so, but much must depend on how I am led in the matter. I cannot write a review, unless the subject be one which I feel I can handle in a manner edifying to the Church of God. I take a book more as a peg on which to hang an essay on a subject which I think I can write upon feelingly and profitably, than to commend or censure the book itself. Now it may be a most excellent work, but unless I can produce out of my own mind, independent profitable matter on the same or some allied subject, I cannot review it. A review to me is almost like a text. It must come to me, not I go to it, and therefore I can no more promise a review, except conditionally, than I can promise to preach from a given text. Whether good or bad, the reviews cost me much time and thought, and are written with great care. I have a large well-instructed and critical circle of readers, besides many cavillers and fault-finders; and I must not attempt subjects which I cannot handle, or not handle scripturally and experimentally. I may, if not just at present, take up the "Posthumous Letters," and the best time will be when the angel troubleth the waters.

I feel much as you do about the truth of God. It is dear to me, and I can neither buy nor sell it as men would have me. It is to be bought without money and without price, and to be sold for neither. It alone maketh free. How can it then be parted with? Many of God's children are weak in judgment, and soon drawn aside, which should make us doubly desirous to contend earnestly for the faith once delivered unto the saints. I am, through mercy, a little better, and have resumed preaching, but my chest is still tender. That and my own heart are my two greatest trials.

Yours affectionately,

J. C. P.

Oct. 13, 1856.

XC.—To the Deacons and Members of the Church of Christ assembling themselves for the worship of God at Gower Street Chapel, London. Mercy, Peace, and Love be multiplied.

My dear Friends,

Having taken into serious and prayerful consideration the expression of your desire that I should come among you for a season, with a view to a settlement as pastor over you in the Lord, if approved of by you, I have been obliged to come to the resolution to decline the proposal.

Two obstacles have, from the first, presented themselves to my mind, which I feel would be insuperable unless specially removed by the Lord Himself.

1. The first is the delicate state of my health, in consequence of which I am sometimes laid aside from the public exercise of the ministry. This, which is much felt by my own people in the country, would be a serious objection in London, and with a large and more mixed congregation. Besides which, my general delicacy of health, and susceptibility to cold, would much hinder those pastoral visits, that attention to the sick, and interment, when needed, of members of the church, which would reasonably be required of a settled minister. Nor can I reasonably hope that, after so many years' duration of ill health, it is likely to improve with advancing life.

2. But, secondly, I have felt that after having been settled over two churches and congregations for about eighteen years, among whom I trust the Lord has blessed my labours, I could not dissolve that connection unless I had some clear intimation that such was the will of God.

My own people, both at Stamford and Oakham, have deeply felt even the idea of my leaving them, and have expressed their apprehension that such a step might, at least at one of the places, issue in the breaking up of the cause altogether.

Unless, therefore, I clearly saw my way, and unless the pillar of cloud went more manifestly before me than it does, I feel I could not take a step so important as that to which you invite me.

There are, indeed, many circumstances, both as regards you and myself, which would have made your invitation acceptable to me had these obstacles not intervened. But I am very certain that to undertake such an important charge, without clearly seeing the will and hand of God, would issue in sorrow and disappointment to both you and myself.

I am, my dear Friends,

Yours affectionately in Christ,

J. C. P.

XCI.—To Mr. Crake *

Oakham, Nov. 24th, 1856.

My dear Friend,

It is, I believe, twenty-four or twenty-five years since we first became acquainted, and you have, invariably, from the first, shown me great affection and respect; much more than I receive from most, and certainly more than I deserve. I thank you for your kind expressions of esteem and affection contained in your last kind letter, and I am obliged to you for pointing out the erratum to which you refer. I have taken the opportunity of mentioning it in the forthcoming *Standard*. It is remarkable what mistakes compositors continually make, and what is more remarkable still is the way in which they escape the most practised eye. Every line of the review is read by me at least three or four times before printed; and yet, with all my care, no sooner do I receive the work than some obvious mistake is almost sure to meet my eye. So it must have been in this instance.

I have had a lingering attack, and am not yet restored to my usual state of health, though I preached yesterday and do not feel to-day any inconvenience from it. It is true I only preached once, and not long or loud. I hope this illness has not altogether been unprofitable to me, as during it I have had many seasons of prayer, meditation, and reading the word with sweetness and feeling. There must be times, especially in a minister, for laying up as well as laying out. There is a trading in divine matters whereby the soul becomes enriched with heavenly treasure. Seclusion and solitude, of which I have had much, are favourable seasons for confession, meditation, and self-examination; and when the mind is solemnized with the weighty matters of eternity, prayer and supplication are made to the Lord for those blessings that we feelingly stand in need of. Much of my time, at various seasons during my illness, has been so spent. And there has been joined with it, at times, careful study of the word of God, especially some of the epistles of the New Testament. The mind and judgment need to be informed and established in the truth of God; and a minister or writer who does not give his mind to the revelation of God's truth, and does not take solemn delight and pleasure therein, will not much feed the Church of God. Here I see many ministers deficient in our day. There is so much gossiping and visiting from house to house, not as godly instructors, but for mere society's sake, that precious time is wasted, and the mind dissipated until the soul becomes like the garden of the sluggard.

* Mr. Jesse Crake, of Eastbourne, formerly of Clifton, near Abingdon. He died Jan. 1869. See Obituary in *Gospel Standard* for July, 1869.

My delicate health, it is true, in a good measure, keeps me from these things, and thus it may be, for this and other reasons, a blessing in disguise. . . . . . .

Yours affectionately,
J. C. P.

XCII—To Mr. G. Tips, of Rotterdam

Stamford, October 30, 1857.

Dear Friend and, I trust, Brother in the Lord of Life and Glory,

I received and read with much interest and pleasure your gratifying letter, the whole of which I was able to make out with tolerable facility. But, though I understand enough of the Dutch language to be able to read it, I am not sufficiently conversant with that tongue as regards its idioms and grammar to be able to write it. I therefore avail myself of your kind permission to write to you in my native tongue, which it appears you understand, and in which I hope to express myself in a manner intelligible to you and easy to myself.

The information which your truly interesting and spiritual letter contains, that very many of my sermons have been translated into Dutch, and widely circulated among the tried and afflicted people of God in your country, humbled and melted my soul before the Lord, and I was enabled to praise His holy name for His great goodness and wonderful condescension in making use of so sinful and unworthy an instrument as myself to spread abroad His gracious and glorious name, not only in my own country, but in a foreign land (2 Cor. ii. 14). It also led me to supplicate His gracious Majesty that He would still go on to make use of me as an instrument in His hands to spread the gospel of His sovereign, distinguishing, and superabounding grace. What made the matter more surprising in my eyes, and showed me more clearly that it was the Lord's own work, was this circumstance, that I had no hand in the matter, and knew nothing of the work that was going on until the pleasing intelligence reached my ears. And it has been the same in this country, for with the exception of two or three little publications sent abroad by me twenty years ago, I have never had any hand in spreading my own sermons in this land, but have left the matter wholly in the hands of the Lord, as feeling if they were worthy to live and be spread, it would be done, and if not, let them die.

It may, perhaps, not be uninteresting to you and the readers of the sermons in Holland to learn how they first came into public notice in this country. You are, perhaps, aware that I was brought up in the communion of the Church of England, our great national establishment, and was educated at the University of Oxford, where, to speak with all humility, I distinguished myself by my knowledge of Greek and Latin literature. I was ordained to the ministry in the Church of England in the year 1828, being then not quite twenty-six years of age. At that time I hope the Lord had, about a year and a half previously, quickened my soul into spiritual life, and taught me, by His spirit and grace, something both of sin and of salvation. But my eyes were not then open to see the errors and corruptions of the National Church. I was much afflicted with illness in the years 1830 and 1831, and, as eternal things came to lie with greater weight and power on my heart, and the Lord's work was deepened in my soul, I became led to see more clearly and feel keenly the errors and evils of the Church of England, and after some years of trial and prayer to the Lord to lead and guide me, I was compelled, in the spring of 1835, to withdraw myself from its communion, though obliged to relinquish at the same time a comfortable independence which I had in it, and at the same time to renounce all my prospects of future advancement, which were much bound up in it. At that time I was in a most delicate state of health, without any property, or the prospect of any; but, like Abraham, I went out at the call of God and conscience, not knowing whither I went, and I was enabled, through rich grace, to esteem with Moses the reproach of Christ greater riches than the treasure of Egypt. A door, however, in answer to the prayers of a spiritual friend, was soon opened for me to preach the gospel out of the Church of England, and since that period my ministry has been among the Particular Baptists—a religious denomination in this country called by that name, as holding the baptism (that is, by immersion, as you have well preserved the word "doop" and "dooper" in your translation) of believers only, and also holding that the Lord's Supper is, by apostolic practice, restricted to baptised believers, holding those particular doctrines which are generally termed the doctrines of grace, and which were so clearly laid down by your forefathers at the synod of Dort (Dordrecht).

Since the year 1837 I have been in the habit of going to London once a year in the summer season for the purpose of preaching the gospel, as well as to other places, where I proclaim the word of life, though my stated residence and ministry are chiefly at the town whence I date this letter, and another about twelve miles distant.

In the summer of 1839, being then in the metropolis on my annual visit, I preached a sermon at Zoar Chapel, Great Alie Street, London, which has lately been translated into Dutch by J. Nieuwland, and published by J. Campen of Sneek, in his "Eerste Zestal Leerredenen, von J. C. Philpot," from Psalm cvi. 4, 5, under the title "De begeerte des harten van elken wedergeborene."

This sermon was taken down entirely without my knowledge, and printed in a publication called, "The Penny Pulpit," but I saw neither the MS. nor the printed sermon till it was put into my hands. This sermon, however, which was, on the whole, a faithful report, had a most rapid and amazing circulation, the sale having reached, I believe, nearly twenty editions. This circumstance, of course, encouraged the printer to work a mine which seemed likely to yield him such profit, and thus, since that date, it has gone on, Mr. Paul and other publishers having availed themselves of my visits to London to take down and publish the sermons which I have been enabled to preach there, so that they now amount to a considerable number, and many of them are out of print (uitverkocht), and cannot be procured. They have also been taken down at other places, and published in the same way. In all this matter I have taken no steps to have them reported, or to forward their sale; nor do I derive any pecuniary profit from them. But in order to secure myself from the unavoidable errors which would arise if I did not look them over, I make it a point to revise them before they are published, and thus they have all passed under my eye.

I have looked over those which you have kindly sent me through Mr. Bayfield, and as far as I have had time and opportunity to examine them, they appear for the most part faithfully and ably translated. The idiom of the two languages so much differs that it is not possible always to preserve in Dutch the exact structure of the English sentences, in which much of the force and clearness of the English language consists. Nor is it possible in *extempore* preaching (all my sermons being delivered completely *voor de vuist*) to give that clearness and precision of thought and expression which can be communicated to a written discourse. Yet, as far as the Lord enables me, I do what I can to make them clear, distinct, and forcible, that the trumpet may give a certain sound (1 Cor. xiv. 8). The sermons, I know, are much read in this country, and by all classes, both rich and poor, educated and uneducated. Knowing therefore how much the truths I preach are opposed to the carnal mind, and how gladly many would make me an offender for a word, I bestow what pains I can to cut off occasion from those who would seek occasion to wound, through me, the truth of the gospel. At the same time I bear in mind that whatever the sermons are, much more dwelleth in Christ, for "it hath pleased the Father that in Him all fulness should dwell" (Col. i. 19); and it is declared that "God hath blessed us with all spiritual blessings in heavenly places in Christ" (Eph. i. 3). It will be, then, our wisdom and mercy to be ever looking unto this blessed Jesus (Isa. xiv. 22; Heb. xii. 2); and to be living upon Him, as the apostle declared that he did (Gal. ii. 20). It is in this way that we receive out of His fulness (John i. 16), feed upon His flesh, and drink His blood, and thus dwell in Him and He in us (John vi. 56). We should be much in prayer and supplication to the Lord for His own teaching and blessing. This is the direction given to us by James (i. 5), and the same apostle describes to us the blessed nature of that wisdom which is from above, and which, with every other good and perfect gift, cometh down from the Father of lights (James iii. 17; i. 17). The promise is, "All thy children shall be taught of the Lord, and great shall be the peace of thy children" (Isa. liv. 13); and the Lord Himself tells us what the effect of this divine teaching is (John vi. 45). To come unto Jesus for salvation, for pardon, for peace, for sanctification, for victory over our besetting sins, is the fulfilment of the declaration that every man who hath heard, and who hath learned of the Father, cometh unto Christ (John vi. 45). It is not a name, or a sound creed, or a mere calling Jesus "Lord," that can or will save the soul from death and hell. There must be a living faith, a good hope through grace (2 Thess. ii. 16), and a spiritual love, that shed abroad in the heart by the Holy Ghost (Rom. v. 5), in order that the soul may be saved and blessed. Thus, it is not merely the soundness of his creed which distinguishes a Christian, but that work of the blessed Spirit upon his heart, whereby he knows the truth, and finds to his soul's joy that the truth maketh free (John viii. 32).

There is a blessed unity of spirit amongst all who are truly taught of God. They are loved by the same everlasting love, and redeemed by the same precious blood, are justified by the same righteousness, are led by the same spirit, and are travelling toward the same happy and heavenly home. They all, too, speak the same language; for though in their time state one may speak English, another Dutch, and another German, yet they all speak a pure language, according to the Lord's own gracious promise (Zeph. iii. 9).

I much thank you for your kind invitation to come to Rotterdam, but I cannot accept it, as I am so much engaged in the work of the ministry. Besides which my health is delicate, and has been so for many years, so that I cannot go about as many do who are more favoured with bodily health and strength. But the Lord has been pleased to spread my writings amongst those who know and love His truth, and I hope that they have been blessed to many.

My friends in England greatly rejoiced in the circumstance that my sermons had been translated into your native language, and spread amongst the believers in Christ Jesus in Holland. Many wept rejoicing tears over your letter, which I translated into English, and inserted in the *Gospel Standard.* As this periodical circulates nearly 10,000 copies, it made your letter widely read. I have been requested to insert in the same periodical my answer to it, but have not at present done so. It is a blessing to be fellow-helpers of each other's joy, and fellow-labourers in the service of the same blessed Master. As there is a commercial connection between Holland and England, each interchanging with the other the commodities of life, so there may be, with the help and blessing of God, a spiritual exchange of those heavenly wares, the possession of which makes the owner rich indeed. If anything spoken by my mouth, or written by my pen, has been blessed to my believing brethren and sisters in Holland, to the Lord be given all the praise, honour, and glory. It does not, it cannot belong to me. Everything worth having, knowing, or enjoying is the pure gift of God, and to Him be rendered everlasting praise by the suffering saints below and the glorified spirits above.

My Christian love to your wife and all who love the Lord and His truth.

Yours affectionately in the truth of the gospel,

J. C. P.

XCIII —From the *Gospel Standard, Dec.* 1, 1857 *

Good News from a Far Country.

I always feel a great unwillingness to obtrude myself on public notice more than absolute necessity may require, and have, therefore, considerable hesitation in bringing the following letters before the readers of the *Gospel Standard;* but, as most of my friends, who have read them, have felt much interest in their perusal, and have rejoiced with me in the glad tidings communicated, I have been induced to comply with their expressed wishes to make them more widely known; and I hope in doing so I desire to seek the glory of God. Apart from all personal considerations, it may rejoice our hearts to see that the Lord has a people in other countries as well as our own. Of course, where self is in question, it is extremely difficult to judge righteous judgment; but, as I had not the least hand in the matter, and well know that the truths which I endeavour to set forth are only acceptable to the poor and needy children of God, I may well hope that the translation into Dutch of my sermons, and their great circulation in Holland, afford some evidence that the Lord has a people there who love and fear His name. A few words, however, of explanation may be necessary to give a clearer understanding of the circumstances under which the first of the following letters was written.

I received some time ago a very kind and friendly letter from a minister in London, mentioning that he had, in the providence of God, a short time before, visited Holland, and that at Rotterdam he had met with a Dutch gentleman, who asked him if he knew me and could furnish him with my address. On his answering in the affirmative, the gentleman showed him several volumes of my sermons which had been translated into Dutch, and which,

* This letter is here inserted from its interesting connection with the letters from Holland, to which the preceding (No. XCII.) was an answer.

he said, were much read and valued by the children of God in Holland. In my answer to his letter, as he had mentioned he was likely soon again to visit Rotterdam, I begged him to mention to his Dutch friend that I should be happy to receive a letter from him. The first letter, which I have translated from the Dutch as faithfully as the two languages, so different in idiom, admit, it will be seen was sent to me in consequence of this reply.

The second, which was written in English, was sent to me by one of the publishers of my sermons in the same country, and has no connection whatever with the first letter.

I cannot but say that I felt both humbled and softened in my soul at the receipt of these glad tidings, and was enabled to bless and praise the Lord's gracious name for His kind condescension in making any use of one so unworthy to take even His name into his polluted lips. Though my prayers and supplications have been up to the Lord, that He would bless me to the souls of His saints, yet I never sought even here, still less in a foreign land, to spread anything that fell from my lips or pen, knowing well how much the pride of the flesh and self-exaltation mingle with such matters, and being perfectly conscious that it is with the Lord alone to bless whom and what He will bless. My feeling has ever been this—if anything spoken or written in the Lord's name be worth living, He will make it live; if worth spreading He will make it spread; if not let it all die and come to nought.

I felt also, as an additional reason for bringing forward the first letter, that it would be read with interest as unfolding a little of the present religious condition of Holland, and though a dark cloud of unbelief and infidelity broods over that land, yet there are evidently bright gleams that break through.

J. C. P.

Stamford, Nov. 18th, 1857.

XCIV—To Mr. R. Healy *

Stamford, Feb. 25, 1858.

My dear Richard,

I was glad to receive a few lines from you, and still more pleased to learn that you were once more enabled to set up your Eben-ezer to the love and faithfulness of a Covenant God. Amidst all our miserable departures and wanderings from the only real Object of our soul's desire, and amidst all our temptations and trials, He remaineth still "the same yesterday, to-day, and for ever." When we get into a low place, and think over our dreadful backslidings, we expect stroke after stroke of chastisement; but

* Mr. Richard Healy, of Hooby Lodge, near Oakham. He died December 30, 1866. See his obituary in *Gospel Standard.*

the Lord's thoughts are not as our thoughts, nor His ways as our ways. Hart says—

"I looked for hell, he brought me heaven."

And so when the poor guilty, self-condemned soul looks for a stripe, comes a kiss, and for a frown, a smile. But it is this undeserved mercy, this unlooked-for and almost unhoped-for grace that so melts the soul into penitence, love, and obedience. O what poor nothings are we; how devoid of all power, and sometimes of all will, to look unto our best our only Friend—the blessed Jesus, whom we do love with all our heart and soul, and yet can, and do, so basely and foully forsake! O how I have sinned against and before His blessed Majesty. It makes me weep sometimes to feel how I have sinned in His holy and pure eyes; but all I can do, and that only by His grace, is to look again and again to His atoning blood—that precious blood which cleanseth from all sin. I believe you, as Mr. Huntington says, have passed the line; you will no more taste the gall and wormwood of unpardoned sin, but will, doubtless, have your measure of trials, temptations, sorrows, and afflictions. Without these your soul would soon cleave to the dust, and would seek its home and happiness here.

We were all much pleased to hear of your dear wife's safe deliverance. It is a most trying time for a husband. I can well enter into your trials and exercises about it. We know what we deserve, and feel if the Lord took away the wife, or sent a deformed child, we only had what we fully merited. But He is better to us than all our fears; He dealeth not with us after our sins, nor rewardeth us according to our iniquities. May our desire be to live more to His praise and glory. I hope I am slowly mending, but only slowly. I feel the cross and the separation from the friends. So much illness is a heavy trial and depresses my mind, but I hope I am learning some lessons in the furnace.

Yours affectionately,
J. C. P.

XCV —To Mr. G. Tips

Stamford, June 29, 1858.

My dear Friend,

I think if you knew how much my time is occupied with attending to the numerous claims made upon it, you would readily accept my apology for the lengthened delay in replying to your letter according to my promise; but, as I am about to leave home for London on my annual visit to the great metropolis, I will not delay my reply any longer.

I hope that the blessed Lord, who has called you by His distinguishing grace, who has planted His fear in your heart—a precious new Covenant blessing (Jer. xxxii. 40)—who has convinced you of your lost and ruined state by nature, and given unto you to believe in the Son of His love (Phil. i. 29, Eph. ii. 8), is also carrying on His divine work in your heart (Phil. i. 6), and making you meet for the inheritance of the saints in light (Col. i. 12). It is a most rich and unspeakable mercy that those whom Jesus loves He loves to the end (John xiii. 1), and that His sheep shall never perish, neither shall any one pluck them out of His hand. This is the grand security of the saints of God; for their inherent sinfulness and weakness are so great, Satan is so crafty and so strong, sin so powerful and deceptive, and the world so entangling and alluring, that but for the special and unceasing grace of God, they must perish, and concerning faith make sure and awful shipwreck. But the members of the mystical body, of which Jesus is the exalted Head (Eph. i. 22, Col. i. 18), can no more perish than He can, for they are united to Him by an act of sovereign grace, given them in Christ Jesus before the foundation of the world (Eph. i. 4), and thus being constituted members of His body, of His flesh, and of His bones (Eph. v. 30), the members can no more perish than their Head. Would you willingly suffer the tip of your little finger to be cut off, or to perish of mortification? Would it be a complete body if any member were absent? The high priest under the law was to be "without blemish." He was to have no member deficient, and none superfluous (Lev. xxi. 17—21). So it is with the blessed Jesus, the great High Priest over the house of God (Heb. x. 21). His body is a perfect body, as set up in the mind of God, as the Holy Spirit describes Psalm cxxxix. 16. Before an architect builds a house, or any other structure, he has the plan carefully drawn out in his mind, and then upon paper. Whilst the building is going on, the bystanders have a very imperfect conception of the plan of the architect and the beauty of the building, but he knows where every stone should be placed, and when the whole is completed, it is but the execution of his original design. So in grace; the Church of God is compared to a building (1 Cor. iii. 9, Heb. iii. 6, 1 Peter, ii. 5). These stones of which this spiritual house consists are "living stones," that is, stones made alive unto God by His regenerating grace; and by their union and communion with the Lord, and with each other, grow up into a holy temple in the Lord, being built together for a habitation of God through the Spirit (Eph. ii. 21, 22).

Amidst all the errors that abound, and all the declensions from the faith, experience, zeal, hope and love of those great and godly men who once formed the bulwark and the glory of your country, it is a mercy that the Lord has yet a seed to serve Him in your native land. Those very universities and schools which were founded for the purpose of becoming fountains of truth, to spread their healing streams over the land, have now become springs of deadly poison and error. It is something like what is described of the star called Wormwood, which holy John saw fall from heaven, burning, as it were a lamp, and falling upon the rivers and fountains of waters (Rev. viii. 10, 11). When the springs are poisoned at the fountain head, they must carry death and destruction wherever they flow. But there is a precious promise given to the believing disciples of the blessed Lord, that if they drink any deadly thing it shall not hurt them (Mark xvi. 18). Thus whilst the children of the wicked one greedily drink down the poisonous cup that is filled with the vine of Sodom, and the fields of Gomorrah, whose wine is the poison of dragons, and the cruel venom of asps (Deut. xxxii. 33), the children of God reject the deadly draught, and can only drink the pure blood of His grape (Deut. xxxii. 14). The wise mother of King Lemuel gave her son gracious directions when she bade him to "give strong drink unto him that is ready to perish, and wine to those that be of heavy hearts" (Prov. xxxi. 6). It is when we begin to feel the misery into which we have been cast by sin, and thus become ready to perish, and of heavy hearts, that the pure wine of gospel grace is suitable to our lost condition. As the holiness and justice of God are discovered to the conscience, and we are made to see and feel the depths of the Adam fall, we look out of ourselves for a salvation which we could not find in our fallen nature or in our deeply corrupt and unbelieving heart. When, then, we obtain by living faith a view of the Son of God as a Mediator between God and men, when we see by the eye of faith the blood of the cross, and the full and complete atonement which He, as the Lamb of God, made for sin, then we heartily embrace Him as "of God made unto us wisdom and righteousness, and sanctification and redemption" (1 Cor. i. 30). We see and feel that there is salvation in Him and in no other (Acts iv. 12); and as this salvation is seen to be worthy of God and suitable to us, as it answers all the demands of God's holy law, and glorifies it by rendering it an obedience as far excelling ours as heaven excels earth, and God surpasses man, we embrace it as our justifying righteousness and covering robe, from the eyes of Him who, out of Christ, is a consuming fire (Heb. xii. 29).

These doctrines, however they may be neglected or despised, are the doctrines, according to godliness, which God has revealed in His word of truth, and which He makes known by a divine power to the hearts of those who fear His great and glorious name. Because men of corrupt minds, destitute of the truth, and supposing that gain is godliness (1 Tim. vi. 5), have perverted the truth of God, their wicked and erroneous perversions do not at all impair Divine revelation. They have not succeeded in polluting God's pure word, or shutting it up from the people. They may, and do, deceive themselves, and their wretched disciples; but they never can, never will, deceive the elect of God (Matt. xxiv. 24). All who are taught of God, will escape their bewitching errors, for to them there is given an unction from the Holy One, and they know all things. This anointing which they have received from the Lord abideth in them; it teacheth them of all things, and is truth and no lie, and the effect of it is to cause them to abide in Christ (1 John ii. 20—27). I hope that my dear friend feels more and more his weakness and helplessness, and is enabled to look more believingly and steadfastly to the Lord Jesus Christ. You will never find anything good in yourself, for the apostle's own testimony is, "I know that in me (that is in my flesh) dwelleth no good thing." . . . . . As my sermons are often read in congregations where there is no preacher, and as those who know and love the truth are, for the most part, poor and illiterate, I have to guard against using such words and expressions as are beyond the reach of uneducated people. Being myself an educated man, naturally fond of literature, and not unacquainted with both some of the ancient and modern languages, I find it difficult always to suit my expressions to my hearers. But I hope the Lord has given me a desire to "condescend to men of low estate," and made me willing and desirous to speak in that simple, clear language which suits all classes, being neither too high for the low, nor too low for the high. My desire is to exalt the grace of God, to proclaim salvation alone through the blood and righteousness of the Lord Jesus Christ; to declare the sinfulness, helplessness, and hopelessness of man in a state of nature, and to describe, as far as I am able, the living experience of the saints of God in their trials, temptations, and sorrows, and in their consolations and blessings. All this brings with it labour and trial; but I do not know what else we have to live for in this world but to advance, as far as we can, the kingdom of Christ, the glory of God, and the well-being of the saints of the Most High; and if the Lord has, in His providence and grace, called me to the distinguished honour of ministering in His holy name, it should even be my object, as I hope it really is, to proclaim His grace and glory, and to seek so to do it that it may be owned and blessed by God the Holy Ghost to the souls of the saints of God.

I never sought the position in which I find myself placed, and the thought of that is sometimes a comfort to me. My natural desire would be to lead a quiet, obscure life, as I know both the perils and the trials to which a more public and prominent situation exposes a man. Many eyes are upon him to watch his movements—some waiting for good, and some for evil; some as friends, and others as foes; some as "helpers of his joy," and others hinderers, and, as far as permitted, persecutors, because he preaches a gospel which they hate.

The struggle between truth and error, free grace and free will, Christ and Belial, heaven and hell, is still going on in this country as in yours; the strong man armed is keeping his palace in many hearts, nor will he give way until one stronger than he comes upon him, takes away all his armour wherein he trusted, and divides the spoils. If we are on the side of Christ, we must expect much opposition from without and from within; many afflictions, trials, and temptations, to prove the reality and strength of our faith, as well as those communications of wisdom and strength out of His fulness, without which all our own strivings are worthless and useless.

It rejoices me to find that there is in Holland a poor and afflicted people that trust in the Lord, and know and love His truth. I have read with much pleasure and interest the prefaces prefixed to the various issues of my sermons, especially one by den Heer A. P. du Cloux, which has given me a greater insight into the character and condition of the people of God in your country than anything else which I have seen on the subject. In spite of all the miserable Socinianism and Infidelity which, from Germany and France, have flooded your unhappy land; notwithstanding the Atheistic influences of the first French Revolution, from which we, as an insular nation, were in some degree preserved; notwithstanding the state of theology in the universities and schools, one cannot but think that a country which produced so many martyrs to the Spanish Inquisition in the time of the Reformation, and has since given birth to such gracious and eminent divines as Herman Wilsius, Hoombeeck, &c., cannot be abandoned of God. Nothing can be sounder than your old Dutch confession of faith, or the articles of the Synod of Dort, and you, as a nation, are blessed with one of the most faithful and admirable translations of the word of God from the original languages that any Protestant nation has been favoured with. The blessing that has rested upon our English translation is inexpressible; nor is it possible that so great a gift as the Scriptures, in the Dutch language, can have been given to you, as a nation, in vain. Though divine matters may be at a low ebb with you as regards spiritual experience, and vital godliness, and though schools and universities, professors and preachers, may be enemies to Christ and His gospel, yet you have, as a nation, beyond almost any in Europe, the elements of a gracious revival. You have a large measure of civil liberty, toleration, a free press, an admirable translation of the Scriptures, and a sound confession of faith. You have the memory and example of godly ancestors, whom all the power of the Spanish monarchy could neither daunt nor crush; and you have as their descendants, a scattered people who know and love the gospel. How differently are you situated from the neighbouring countries of Belgium and France; and though, perhaps, one is apt to attribute too much importance to one's own labours and productions, I cannot but hail the favourable reception and the large sale that my sermons have met with in Holland as a tokèn for good. For I know who they are, for the most part in this country, who read them with interest, pleasure, and profit, and that they generally are those who know and love the truth of God as applied by the Holy Ghost to the soul. I come before my own countrymen as one known to them for more than twenty years, speaking in a language which is familiar to them; but I come before my friends and readers in Holland as a foreigner, unknown to them by name or character, and having the disadvantage of speaking in an idiom not altogether agreeing with their own. To what then am I, under the blessing of God, to attribute their favourable reception, but to the force with which they commend themselves to men's consciences? I may, perhaps, here quote the words of Heer A. P. A. du Cloux: "Shall I recommend these sermons? No, they recommend themselves." I was also struck with a remark in the same preface, that whilst the poor and afflicted family find the truth in other men's writings, they do not find their life in them, and that is just what they find in mine. My aim and desire have been to put into them, so to speak, the life of God, and the true experience of a living soul; and seeing that many of my readers in Holland have found that life in them, does it not show that they must have themselves divine life to find and feel it there? I also hail with great pleasure the fact that ministers of God's word in your country have been found willing to translate and recommend the sermons. There is so much miserable jealousy in the human heart that I cannot but think grace must have overcome their pride and prejudice against the writings of a stranger, and made them willing to listen to a voice from beyond the sea.

And now, my dear friend, accept my thanks for your affectionate and welcome letter, and

Believe me to be,

Yours affectionately, in the bonds of the gospel,

J. C. P.

XCVI—To Mr. Copcutt, Yonkers, New York

Stamford, Sept. 20, 1858.

Dear Sir,

I am much obliged to you for the interesting account which you have given of the removal from this vale of tears of both your parents, and hope the God of all grace will give you power to follow them as they followed Christ. Your deceased mother was one of the most remarkable women of whose experience I ever heard or read. I was much struck with one expression concerning her in a letter which I received from one of her family, "That she lived for no other object but the salvation of her soul." The Lord had separated her in a remarkable manner, not only from the profane world, but from the professing world. No doubt she saw the necessity of it, and that it was bearing the strongest testimony against it; but it did not diminish her affection for the real saints of God, or make her less kind and affectionate to her own family. And now your aged father is gone, as we hope, to join her in that blessed land where sin and sorrow are alike unknown, and where the Lord Himself wipes the tears from off all faces. As you cannot hear the pure gospel, and have no confidence in the ministers by whom you are surrounded, I think you do well to be separate from them, and follow out your mother's plan and read the Scriptures and the writings of sound authors. You cannot do better than read the writings of such gracious men as Bunyan, Rutherford, Erskine, and especially Mr. Huntington. These men had the Spirit of God, and were taught of Him to preach and write. They had tasted, felt, and handled what they wrote, and, so far as we are taught by the same Spirit, we shall see eye to eye with them, and feel a dew, unction, and power attend their writings to our soul. It must be a very trying path for you to walk in, as it must bring down upon your head much reproach and misrepresentation. But if you are favoured with the testimony of God in your own conscience, and have some manifestations of His presence, it will amply make up for any reproach that may assail you. It is a great mercy to keep close to the oracles of God and to a throne of grace, to distrust our own wisdom and our own way, and to seek divine teaching. The great difficulty and snare in standing separate is, lest it should foster a self-righteous or censorious spirit, into which we may easily fall unless preserved by the special grace of God. You will probably, therefore, have many deep discoveries of the evil of your heart, and many temptations spread in your path; that you may learn thereby that you are internally as sinful and as deeply fallen as any of those from whom you have felt compelled to separate. When separation is a necessity, as appears to have been the case with your late mother and yourselves, the Lord will support you in it, and give you the testimony of His Spirit. Otherwise separation from the Church of God is a great evil, and very much to be dreaded. Being so imperfectly acquainted with the state of things in your country, I am not able to say how far I myself should walk in that path. It is my privilege and mercy to find here in this land saints of God with whom I can unite, and, indeed, feel that they are profitable companions, and such as I should wish to live and die with. But if my lot were cast in a land, or in a spot where there were scarcely any of the manifested saints of God, I should desire to worship God in my own house, or where I could meet with two or three of the living family, with whom I might take sweet counsel in the things which belong to our eternal peace. It is not separation that will do us any good unless we have good grounds for separating; and it will be tried over and over again how far our walk in this or that point is consistent with the will and word of God. Our own conscience, our doubting mind, the word of truth, our great adversary, the opposition of enemies, the suspicion of saints, will all in various ways try those movements which seem different from the usual course of the Lord's family. And as you will have to die alone, and salvation is a personal matter, it will be well for you to consider how far you are influenced by the fear and grace of God, or how far you are acting merely out of respect to your mother's example. You must feel at times your isolated condition, and long for the ordinances of God's house, and especially for the gospel as preached with the Holy Ghost sent down from heaven. I hope the Lord may guide your steps, and seal His own instruction upon your heart.

We hear in this country of what is called the great revival in the United States; but those who know the work of the Spirit have much difficulty in receiving it as the work of God, knowing how much of the flesh there is in these matters, and what error is maintained by those who are first and foremost in such revivals; it will do much if it spread a healthier tone of morality amongst those who profess to be converted by the grace of God, and lead them to exemplify in their life and conduct the precepts and the practice of the gospel, which they profess to receive by the power of God. But if it be mere fleshly zeal it will end as it began, or worse, according to the true proverb as quoted, 2 Peter ii. 22.

I am much obliged to you for your kind invitation to visit your country; but there are two insuperable obstacles: 1. My health, which is very delicate, having a tender chest which could neither bear the winter or the summer of your latitude; besides which, I am a most wretched sailor, and could not, unless compelled by the most powerful necessity, face the storms and waves of the wide Atlantic. 2. The second objection is my numerous engagements in this country, not only as the pastor of two churches, and as preaching to various congregations, but as conducting the *Gospel Standard*. But I am equally obliged to you for your kind invitation, and, though personally unknown, respect and esteem you for your dear mother's sake, and your kind liberality to the saints of God. I am much interested in the Aged Pilgrims' Friend Society, as, I believe, it affords relief to many saints of God—some of them personally known to me and others by report. I have received two contributions from Australia, so that even distant lands concur in sending help to the saints of God in this country as they did in Paul's time to the saints in Judea.

Please to present to your sisters my Christian regards and affectionate respects for their parents' sake as well as their own, and accept the same from

Your sincere and obliged friend,

J. C. P.

XCVII —To Rev. W. Parks *

Stamford, Nov. 20, 1858.

My dear Sir,

I am much obliged to you for your kindness and courtesy in sending me your pamphlet upon Chastisement. I like it very much, and think it is a very clear and faithful testimony against that error, which I fear is making great and fearful progress.

Controversial writing is at times as needful for the Church of God as that which is more purely doctrinal and experimental. Each has its distinct and peculiar advantages; for truth requires to be set forth in its purity, experience in its divine reality, and error and heresy laid bare in all their naked deformity. Most errors have in them a dash of truth. The potsherd must be covered with silver dross, or its earthen nature would be discovered at once. But the grand deception is to draw natural inferences from Scriptural premises—which inferences are distinctly opposed to Scriptural conclusions. Thus, for instance, the carnal mind draws this inference from the blessed truth of salvation by grace, "Then the more I sin the more will grace abound," which conclusion is the very logic of hell, and as distinct from that drawn by the spiritual mind as Belial from Christ. So, because the advocates of non-chastisement see in the word that God has put away all the sins of the elect in and through the blood of Christ, they logically but erroneously infer that God sees in them no sin to chastise. Horrible conclusion!

Of course I cannot altogether sympathise with you in your present position; but I am glad to think there is any one in the Church of England who preaches truth and opposes error.

I am, dear Sir, yours very sincerely,

J. C. P.

XCVIII —To Mr. Parry

Stamford, Jan. 4, 1859.

My dear Friend,

Since I last wrote to you I have been very unwell; indeed, I have been confined to my bed for the last ten days. I was obliged to be blistered, which was the cause of a good deal of suffering and annoyance; but through mercy the congestion has been much removed, and I have been able to get up once more from my bed of sickness. As you know so well both the bodily and mental feelings of a sufferer under illness, I need not say much upon that point; and you are partially acquainted with the trial of the weight of the chapel being on your shoulders, as

* Mr. Parks was Rector of Openshaw, and died October 2, 1867, aged 58.

well as the bodily and spiritual experience to which I have alluded. One thing is certain, that all who are journeying heavenward are passing more or less through a path of trial, suffering, and exercise; and I need not tell you how the weak and coward flesh shrinks from the weight of so heavy a yoke. I find it often difficult to know what good I get from the cross; and you know there is such a thing as braying a fool in a mortar. I hardly know at times whether I am that fool who has been so often brayed, or whether I have learnt anything to profit. But I think I can say this; if I ever have learnt anything worth knowing, or got anything worth keeping, it has been through the furnace. That is the place where no self-righteousness, vain confidence, or fleshly faith can stand. They are like putting a piece of lead into the fire, which melts as soon as it feels the flame. But truth, salvation by grace, the blood of the Lamb, and the work of the blessed Spirit upon the heart, will stand the hottest flame, and shine all the brighter for it. I feel much convinced in my own mind that nine-tenths of what is considered to be religion is nothing worth; and I believe that you have come much to the same conclusion. How many forms, rites, and ceremonies which are thought so highly of sink into rottenness and death when they are viewed in the light of the Spirit; and perhaps an opposite temptation springs up, which is to think almost too little of the means.

My illness has very much thrown back my meditated publication upon the Sonship of Christ, and I hardly know when I shall be able to take it up again. A good part of the address was written in bed, and most of the sermon No. 22, which is just come out, was revised there also. I understand that they have an increasing sale, and that the publisher has been obliged frequently to reprint the back numbers.

Our friend —— would tell you how many of the ministers who have been thought men of truth are entangled in the error of denying the Eternal Sonship of the adorable Redeemer. How much we are sunk into the state which Mr. Huntington foresaw as coming upon the churches; and those who live will probably see matters get worse and worse. To deny vital fundamental truths is the first step to apostasy; for when men get indifferent to the truth of God, and view vital truths as mere opinions, the next step from this indifference is to depart from them; and as they go on they get from bad to worse, till the truth is altogether given up, and error after error greedily drunk in. There are two things for which a child of God should cry most earnestly; one is to be kept from evil, and the other to be preserved from error. Some are more tempted to one, and some to the other; but both are equally dreadful traps of Satan, and indeed I hardly know which is the worst of the two; but how we see in the New Testament times the prevalence of both in the churches! See what characters there were as drawn by the pen of Jude, and again what erroneous men as depicted by the pencil of holy John. Now I believe we have just such characters in the churches, only they are covered over with a decent profession. What need we have to be ever upon the watch-tower to be studying the word of truth, and to be begging of the Lord to give us His Holy Spirit to lead us into all truth, to make and keep our conscience alive and tender, and grant us everything which is comprised in the prayer of Jabez. With every kind wish for the new year,

Yours very affectionately,

J. C. P.

XCIX.—To Mr. Grace.

Stamford, Feb. 4, 1859.

My dear Friend,

I am always glad to have a few lines from you, though I cannot call myself one of the most punctual of correspondents. But I know that both your precept and practice combine in seeking to maintain that pregnant exhortation, "Let brotherly love continue;" which it never can if suspicion be allowed to mar it.

We shall be glad to see you if you can contrive to give us a look in by the way; but should have been better pleased if you could have contrived to have given us a week evening at the chapel. I believe our friends love real experimental truth. In fact, what else can really satisfy a soul which has been made alive unto God? How many, alas! in our day seem to amuse themselves with religion instead of its being their most weighty concern, to which all others must be subordinate. But the fact is, that the natural, legal conscience, wants soothing into quiet like a fractious child; and religion in some shape or other is taken as a kind of "Daffy" to quiet the uneasy babe. There are very many whose consciences would loudly remonstrate against having no religion, for as some are born poets, others musicians, others artists, so many are born religious; and these turn as naturally and as instinctively to religion as a person born with an ear to music takes to playing a musical instrument. It would be a great mistake to call such persons "hypocrites" in the strict sense of the word, as they are to a certain extent sincere, and do not put on religion as a mask to deceive others. It is of these persons that the great mass of hearers in all denominations is composed; and when, from various causes such embrace doctrinally the truth, they take their standing amongst professors of the doctrines of grace. But all this while their heart and conscience are untouched by the finger of God; no life has been communicated to their dead souls, nor has divine light penetrated into their consciences. In one sense they are the most hopeless of hearers, for they are accustomed so to hear everything which convicts or comforts the child of grace with an unfeeling heart that they seem almost beyond all conviction.

How we are brought by everything that we see without or feel within to be deeply and firmly convinced that salvation with everything which that term embraces or implies is wholly of free and sovereign grace! The helplessness, the ignorance, the unbelief, the darkness, the carnality and death of the heart of man, as sensibly and inwardly felt, preached to us in a way that no preacher can match our case and state by the Adam fall. And as the precious truth of God is opened up and applied to the heart by a divine power, there is a pulpit, and more than a pulpit, within, which proclaims the beauty and blessedness of salvation by grace that touches every secret string of the conscience. Every minister who hopes to be made a blessing to the Church of God must know something of Paul's experience, 2 Cor. iv. 13. It is by possessing the same spirit of faith which dwelt in the bosom of David and of Paul that any minister can be useful or acceptable to the Lord's family.

I am glad to find that the Lord continues to be with you at Brighton. I have always viewed it as a very important place, and we have reason to believe the Lord has many of His dear people there. Sussex has been for many years a highly favoured county; but you justly observe that men may hear the truth preached in its purity for years, and yet if the Lord do not apply it to the heart it has no real entrance, and men will readily turn away from it to error or empty sound.

I hope the Lord will be with you in your journeys.

Yours very affectionately,

J. C. P.

C

Stamford, April 5, 1859.

MY DEAR FRIEND,

I was glad to receive a few lines from you, and to find that your poor body was so far strengthened as to be enabled to use your pen. When I saw you at R.'s so brought down in body, I hardly expected that the Lord would raise you up to your present state of health. But He killeth and maketh alive both body and soul, and can and does at His sovereign good pleasure both pull down and raise up.

You have known much of these dealings of the Lord, both with your afflicted body and your exercised soul; and I dare say have found that there is a blessing in both, and that each of them is a part of the Lord's sovereign work, and that the one is quite as needful as the other; indeed, that they are both so connected that they cannot be put asunder.

I am sure that every soul which knows and fears the Lord must be sensible how it wanders and departs from Him when He does not put forth His power and His grace to hold it up and hold it in. And I dare say that my dear friend finds that illness and weakness are not only very hard for the flesh to bear, but that they give rise to many peevish, murmuring, and fretful feelings, all which very much tend to darken the mind, confuse the judgment, bring guilt upon the conscience, open a door for Satan's accusations, and cause the Lord to hide His face. When the Lord puts a soul into the furnace it is to take away the dross and tin. But how can these be taken away unless they are first discovered and brought to light, and thus separated from the gold? It is very perplexing to the mind of a child of God to find so much of the old man at work under trial and temptations. On a sick bed he would fain be spiritual, prayerful, and heavenly-minded, especially when he feels how soon life with him may come to a close. How full then he must be of self-condemnation to find so much sin still at work and so little grace. But here is the furnace which discovers the sin, and as it is hated and confessed there is a taking of it away; and when the Lord once more discovers Himself then the gold shines brighter than ever.

I wish for my dear friend much of the Lord's supporting presence, and that she may feel it is well with her, come what may, that she is safe in the Lord's hand for life and death, time and eternity.

Accept my best love.

Yours very affectionately,
J. C. P.

CI—To Mr. Grace

Stamford, June 18, 1859.

My dear Friend,

It is a great pity that those who are opposed to baptism should have taken such high ground. It is very rarely that I feel my mind led to say anything upon the subject—not that I do not hold it with a firm hand, but because my mind seems taken up in preaching with matters so much more important, and in which the life and power of godliness consist. The people of God, especially those who are tried and exercised, want some solid food for their souls, and many of them come very much cast down by temptation and sorrow. Such persons want to hear something that may be as a blessed balm to their hearts, and everything but Christ and His blood in the blessed power and experience to their souls is viewed by them as worthless.

Ordinances are good in their place, but let them not occupy

that pre-eminence which nothing can claim but the Saviour and His finished work, and the teachings of the Holy Ghost by which He is made known.

Yours affectionately,
J. C. P.

CII —To Mrs. Peake

Hampstead, July 22, 1859.

My dear afflicted Friend,

I sincerely desire to sympathise with you under your truly distressing bereavement, and hope that the Lord may support your soul in this season of grief and sorrow. When I saw your poor dear husband in town I could scarcely indulge a hope that his life would be spared. Still I could not have anticipated his removal from this vale of tears so suddenly as it has pleased the Lord to take his soul unto Himself.

I do not pretend to offer you any consolation in this most distressing hour, as I know that grief must and should have its way, and that nothing short of the immediate support of God can bear you up under your load of sorrow. You may say with Job, "The thing that I greatly feared is come upon me." And when I recollect what I have seen you to feel in the anticipation of the event I hardly dare paint to myself your feelings under the dreadful reality. Still, all is not unmingled grief and sorrow. You have a sweet persuasion that he is safely landed in that happy spot where he has often longed to be. Our dear friend, Mrs. Keal, mentioned in her letter the words which he spoke to you in the night, and I hope that the sweet assurance which they conveyed may impart a balm to your troubled spirit. You did not indeed need any such testimony, as you knew well the ground of his hope. Yet it was a ray of parting light, and as his poor mind seemed to have been allowed to lose its balance it was a great mercy that he was enabled to leave a dying testimony, to which you will be enabled sometimes to look in sweet confidence that he entered the open heaven which then seemed revealed to his eyes and heart.

I do hope and pray that the Lord may support you under this most heavy trial, and make it a most gracious means of bringing you nearer to Himself—that He may be Himself your husband, according to His promise.

Your most affectionate Friend,
J. C. P.

CIII —To Mrs. Peake

Allington, Aug. 20, 1859.

My dear bereaved Friend,

Nothing but extreme pressure of writing has prevented me dropping you a few lines of sympathy and affection. Pardon the unintentional neglect. The Review and Sermon have demanded much time, even to the suffering of health.

My intention is for the Obituary of your beloved husband, and my dear and valued friend, to go into the *body* of the *Gospel Standard,* and not on the wrapper. I hope it has intrinsic merit sufficient to justify its insertion there; but I would strain a point to place it there, from my esteem and affection for you both. Therefore dismiss from your mind any fear on the subject, as far as I am concerned in the matter.

You will long feel your loss, and probably more and more increasingly. A woman in losing her husband loses almost her earthly all, and you have lost a beloved spiritual companion, as well as a partner in life. But you have a sweet and blessed balm in the thought that he is only gone a little before, and thus you mourn not as those without hope. This, with the consolations of God to your own soul, will be your best cordial in this vale of tears. But grief must have its way, and it is desirable that it should flow and not be repressed too violently. I hope you may derive benefit from your sojourn at Y——, and I think it was quite wise seeking a little change of scene and air, after so much fatigue, and anxiety, and grief.

I have been attended here with more than my usual congregation. Mr. Parry stabled yesterday forty-five horses, which had brought hearers from all parts.

* * * * * *

Believe me to be yours very affectionately,

J. C. P.

CIV —To Mr. Grace

Stamford, Sept. 6, 1859.

My dear Friend,

I thank you for your kind letter and offer to take a number of copies of my meditated little work on the "Eternal Sonship of the Lord Jesus Christ."

I am sorry to say that my mind has been so much taken up with preaching and travelling that I have not been able to give it that attention which it requires before I can send it forth. A subject of such importance requires great quietness of mind, seclusion, prayer, and meditation, which I cannot give it when wandering about on the King's errands. I must return to the quietness of my own home, and get my mind, with God's help and blessing, into a frame suitable to the subject, as I wish to enlarge what I have already written, to digest the materials more thoroughly, and to arrange them more orderly than I have yet done. Writing is not altogether like preaching. I often take my pen in my hand and cannot write a single line. The spring does not rise, and, if this be not the case, the stream cannot flow. There is no use forcing the subject. It must come freely into the mind and flow freely from the pen. Unless some savour or unction attend what is written, it will never touch the hearts of God's saints, and there will be a want of freedom in the communication itself. On such sacred subjects great caution and holy wisdom are needful, and a close adherence to the very words of inspired truth or some expression may be dropped contrary to the mind of the Holy Ghost.

I was glad to learn that you had been so well heard in Berks and Oxon. There are many gracious people in that neighbourhood, and I should think that I had on the 28th ult., at Abingdon, one of the choicest congregations that met together anywhere that day, for we had a gathering of the Lord's people for many miles in all directions. I have been a long time from home, all July and August; have seen many people, and preached to large congregations. There certainly is a great spirit of hearing in many places, but I fear that vital godliness is, for the most part, at a low ebb. It is rather difficult to reconcile the two things, as a spirit of hearing is generally connected with life and feeling in the soul; and I cannot doubt that there are many saints of God up and down the land, though one finds few whose souls are much favoured and blessed.

* * * * * *

Yours affectionately,
J. C. P.

CV.—To Mr. Brown.

Stamford, October 3, 1859.

My dear Friend,

I desire sincerely to sympathise with you under your present heavy trial, especially as I have had myself some experience both of bodily affliction and also of being laid aside from the ministry. At the same time I cannot but concur in the prudence, and I might add, in the necessity, of the step which you have taken. Both you and Mrs. Brown have long suffered from the malaria of Godmanchester, and have clearly proved its injurious effects by being so much better in health when removed from its noxious influence. It is not, then, a sudden whim or fancy, but, unhappily, a sad fact, against which you have struggled again and again with the same result. Illness and weakness of body, we well know, are in themselves heavy afflictions, and when to them is added trials of mind, it is laying on a load at the very time when we are least able to bear it. At the same time, the very feeling of the people at Godmanchester shows a most sincere attachment to you. They could not bear to lose you, and were, therefore, angry both with you and the assigned cause for your departure. The air which they had breathed from infancy might be health to them, as Cowper speaks of the east wind to the waggoner, but death to you. The very atmosphere (Southport, Lancashire) which you are now inhaling with pleasure, and I hope with advantage, to recruit your frame, would not at all suit me, as I found three years ago the northern air was too chilling for my chest. But I well know how apt we are to make our own feelings a standard for others. But enough of this. I do most sincerely hope that you may soon be restored to your beloved work, for I am sure that you will feel being laid aside to be a heavier trial in reality than it appears in prospect. You will see the importance and the blessedness of the work as you scarcely ever saw it before; the weight of the ministry will rest with heavier pressure upon your mind, and, like Jeremiah, you will feel a fire shut up in your bones which would fain find vent. You must not expect to be favoured with many such Lord's-days as the first that you spent at Southport. Murmurings and fretfulness may arise in your mind at being laid aside, and when you look round and see the ministers of Satan full of health and strength, and you who would gladly speak in the name of the Lord laid aside, it may stir up many hard thoughts and unbelieving reasonings why it should be so. I do hope that the Lord may enable you to open your mouth, if not so fully or so widely as you could wish, yet with a sufficient testimony that He is with you in the work. There are, I believe, many little causes in Lancashire where, when your health is recruited, you may speak. But the Lord knows best what to do with us.

The lines which you quote from Milton's sonnet I have often thought of, for they are most expressive of the posture of a Christian. I have thought sometimes that ministers of Christ are too much engaged in spending without getting; and I am well convinced that so much preaching is not good for the soul unless the Lord be in a very special manner with the preacher. We have to receive before we can give; and if there be no reading, meditation, prayer, waiting upon the Lord, and passing through trial, exercise, and temptation, and being supported and blessed in and under them, there will be nothing, as it were, laid up in the heart to come out of the mouth. It is this want of reading, meditation, and spiritual exercises which makes the ministry of the day so lean, and to wear out so soon, and become a mere irksome series of unprofitable repetition. I do hope that the blessed Lord will in this affliction be pouring into your soul the riches of His grace, that you may see more and more of the beauty and blessedness of the Lord Jesus Christ, be led more and more into the fulness and depth of God's truth, so that when you come out of this furnace it may be like gold purified in the fire. The friends both here and at Leicester testify to the sweetness and savour which attended your testimony in your last visit at both places. O, it is by these things that men live, and in all these things is the life of our spirit! Our coward flesh shrinks from afflictions, but they are our best friends, and we learn nothing truly profitable but in and through them.

Yours affectionately,
J. C. P.

CVI—To Mr. Brown

October 31, 1859.

My dear Friend,

I still desire to sympathise with you in your present painful trial, and if I can do so better than some others, it is because I have had some experience of it, both in body and in mind. I remember feeling once so much the cares and anxieties of the ministry as to wish I had never opened my mouth in the Lord's name. But soon after this I was laid aside for some months by illness and great bodily weakness, and then I felt that the cares and burdens of the ministry were preferable to being laid aside from it, for, if there were trials in it, there were also secret blessings. But in all these matters the Lord is a Sovereign, and does not consult our wishes or feelings, but His own glory, though at the same time, with all that wisdom and grace which shine forth so conspicuously in His blessed character, He overrules these trials to our eventual good. To use Mr. Newton's figure, the mower is not idle when he is whetting his scythe, though he is not cutting down the grass; and so the Lord may be whetting your scythe, though at present you are not mowing the field. It is with the soul as with the body. When we are asleep, and even resting after dinner, we are only gathering up strength for renewed exertions; and we know that our success and power in the pulpit depend much upon what we are out of it. If there be no prayer, no reading, no meditation, no exercise of mind upon the things of God, there is nothing gathered up which may be drawn out of the heart and mouth when standing up before the people. A rain-water tub, a tank, a pond soon become exhausted; but a brook, a river, a springing well, ever keep flowing on. And so, where the life of God is in the heart of a minister, it will not run itself out, but, like the well of water spoken of by the blessed Lord, will spring up into everlasting life. You must not think, then, and I hope that Satan will not tempt you to believe, either that all your work is done, or that you are doing nothing by being laid aside, I sincerely hope only for awhile. As you sit upon the shore, looking out on the ever-restless sea, and inhaling the breeze which you find so beneficial, you may be secretly lifting up your heart to the God of all your mercies, and be deriving strength and consolation out of the fulness of the incarnate Son of God at the right hand of the Father. His eyes are ever upon the righteous, and His ears open to their cry; and He knoweth the way that you take. I need not recommend you to cast all your care upon Him, as He enables you to do, and beg of Him to do that which seemeth good in His sight. He can raise you up and strengthen your frame, which, no doubt, has been much debilitated by your long long residence in the malaria of Godmanchester; and though the effects of the present change may be slow, they may not be less sure. I believe the damp air and soil of Stadham, where I was for nearly seven years in the Church of England, has affected my health up to the present hour, and, therefore, I know what injury a bad climate may work in undermining strength, or rather, weakening the body so as to lay it open to the attack of other diseases.

I hope the Lord may guide you in this matter, and give you the wisdom which cometh from above. I am, through mercy, pretty well, and still hobbling on in the work of the ministry.

Yours very affectionately,

J. C. P.

CVII —To Mr. Parry

Stamford, Dec. 21, 1859.

My dear Friend,

I was intending to write to you soon, even if I had not received your kind and friendly letter, but I have been much occupied with the *Standard*, &c., and, indeed, have hardly been adequate for much mental exertion. I took cold at Oakham, and I rather neglected it, instead of sending for my medical attendant, who now knows pretty well the nature of my attacks. This has been rather more severe than usual. I was obliged to have a blister, which always much pulls me down, and I have been and still am very weak. But I hope, through mercy, that I am slowly recovering, but it is usually some time before I am able to bear exposure to the air, or the exertion of preaching. Last year I was wonderfully favoured, not being laid aside a single Lord's-day; but with my tender chest I could hardly expect to be again so favoured. Quite providentially Mr. Brown, of Godmanchester, has been in the neighbourhood, and has been supplying for me the month of December; but I fear we shall be destitute for the coming month, at least at Oakham. The friends, however, are very considerate, and seem quite willing to have reading during the time that I am laid aside. We cannot choose our own crosses, or I am sure I should not choose mine; but as we all must have our trials, and cannot choose what they shall be, it is our wisdom and mercy to submit to the will of God, and beg of Him to sanctify to our souls the troubles and afflictions which He himself lays on. I dare say you recollect that it was just about this time twenty-four years ago when I had a similar attack on my chest, and was unable to preach for some Lord's-days. Poor Mr. S—— was called in, and, I believe, thought me very ill, but I have lived to see both him and others as strong laid in their graves. You had poor old Mr. Slade to preach for you, and I remember well my text when I got out to preach again was "Gird thy sword upon thy thigh," &c.; but, instead of experiencing that sweet liberty which I anticipated on my first coming out, I was very much shut up, and had hardly anything to say. I have been but dark in my present illness. The poor body seems to sink under the weight, and the mind to sink with it.

It will be a very poor Address, I fear the worst which has appeared for some years. But I had to write a good part of it in bed, and being so weakened with the blister, &c., I felt quite unequal to any sustained mental exertion. People who read the Reviews and Addresses think, perhaps, that it is very easy to sit down and write them off; but they require an amount of thought and care that few persons are aware of. My desire and aim is to write something that shall be spiritual, experimental, edifying, and instructive to the Church of God. But very often I am not in a frame to write anything of the kind, and take up my pen, and can hardly write a single line.

Being also weak in body, much mental exertion wearies and fatigues me, and I am obliged after writing a few pages, to lay my pen down and rest. So altogether it is hard work. Still, I do not repine, nor do I wish to throw up my work. No task or office can be so honourable as to write or preach for the glory of God, and the good of His people. I hope I can say with a clear conscience that this is my desire. There is something very precious in the truth of God, something very blessed in the person of Christ, His atoning blood, finished work, and dying love. There are no subjects of meditation so sweet, so blessed, or so profitable. My mind runs out after a thousand things, and thinks over a variety of subjects, but there is no real profit in anything but the blessed things of God. But to get at them, and still more, to get into them, we need much of a spirit of prayer, and, above all, a spirit of faith to be mixed with the word. I am well convinced that carnality, sloth, and carelessness, will never do us any good. They are like the weeds that run over the garden or the farm, where the more they are neglected, the more they grow. But prayer, watchfulness, and meditation are means in the Lord's hands of keeping under these weeds, and keeping alive the crop of grace. You, as a farmer, have been distinguished as a clean one. I could not but contrast the lands you lately occupied with those of your neighbour, when I was at Allington last year. I fully believe any one of common observation could see where one farm ended, and the other began. So it is in grace, the heart cannot grow a large crop of weeds, and a large crop of wheat.

I hope the Lord may be with you on the coming Lord's-day. It is many years since it has been a merry Christmas to me, nor do I ever wish to spend one amidst the mirth of fools. Still, we wish you and yours everything that can be desirable to make it a happy Christmas, and if the Lord be pleased to sanctify it by His Spirit and grace, nothing will be wanted to make it happy.

Yours very affectionately,

J. C. P.

CVIII—To Mr. Brown

Stamford, Jan. 9, 1860.

My dear Friend,

I was glad to receive your kind and friendly letter, and to learn from it that you had safely arrived at Brighton, and were comfortably accommodated. To be released for a time from the strife of tongues is a sensible relief to the mind that is worn and jaded by struggling under a load of contention. It is to the mind almost like the pure breeze that blows over the wide expanse of the sea, and comes in a friendly guise to cool the heated brain, and brace the languid nerves. You need rest and quiet, and to get away from the depressing influence of Godmanchester air. You are almost like the poor weary London citizen who comes to Brighton, not only to inhale the sea air, and the buoyant atmosphere of its breezy downs, but also to get away from that load of care and business which is heavier than London air, and denser than London smoke.

I sincerely wish that the blessed Lord may enable you to leave in His hands all your trials, concerns, and cares; and if you could but calmly and quietly lay them at His feet it would be better for both your body and soul. I have no doubt that the anxiety and agitation of your mind has had much to do with your illness. The Godmanchester air first depressed your body, and then your spirits; upon them thus weakened came your trials and troubles there, and all these acted upon your bodily and mental frame till they brought you down as low as you were before you left for Southport. I have no doubt that as your bodily frame gets strengthened and recruited, you will find your spirits and nerves strengthened in equal proportion; and as we are strangely constituted, if body and mind be in good measure invigorated, you will have more strength to bear up under your present load of trial. This view of things does not in the least interfere with or militate against that peculiar strength and blessed support which grace alone can give; and they are easily distinguished by a discerning mind; for whatever strength may be connected with returning health, deliverance from trial is as far off as ever unless the Lord specially bless the soul with His manifested favour, and the consolations of His presence and Spirit. We have still the same need of prayer and watching for answers; the same patience, the same faith, the same hope and love. No one that knows anything of the blessing which maketh rich can substitute for it any amount of natural comfort, mental confidence, or animal spirits. They are distinct things, but as we find by experience that temptations and afflictions act upon the mental and bodily frame in weakening and depressing it, so it is a favour when body and mind are strengthened to endure them.

If I am restored again to preach it will be to go again amongst a people who sympathise with me in my present affliction, and who will, I believe, generally hail my reappearance amongst them with pleasure and affection, and their chief trial at present is my being laid aside.

It is a mercy when our trials, of whatever nature they may be, lead us to cast our burdens on our only Burden-bearer. He is able in His own time and way to deliver and to support till deliverance comes. At Brighton you will have the comfort of Mr. Grace's society and conversation. We desire our love to yourself and Mrs. B——, and also to Mr. and Mrs. Grace.

Yours affectionately,

J. C. P.

CIX.—To Mr. Parry

Stamford, Jan. 17, 1860.

My dear Friend,

I was very sorry to hear of Mrs. ——'s alarming illness. I do hope that it may please the gracious Lord to raise her up, for she would be very much missed among you from her kindness and liberality; but if such be not the will of God, I do hope that the Lord may be pleased to reveal a sense of His love and mercy to her soul. We have deep and daily proof that it is not a profession that can save or bless the soul, and that there must be that divine work upon the heart and conscience, whereby the soul passes experimentally from death unto life. It is not for us to decide how much or how little grace and faith are necessary for salvation, nor how clear and full a hope of confidence it may be blessed with. But we know that the Lord must communicate some sense of His goodness and mercy to take away the guilt of sin, and the doubts and fears that haunt the mind. It is a very great point to be made spiritually sincere before God; to be convinced of sin by the Holy Spirit; to have some experimental discovery of the Lord Jesus Christ to the soul, so as to raise up a living faith, hope, and love in Him. I think I know what true religion is or should be, and I think I can recognise it where the blessed Spirit has wrought it by His own divine power. There are those whom I know, of whose grace I have not the least doubt; and there are others of whom I dare not say that they do not possess the grace of God, but it has not been so manifested to my conscience as to remove all doubt about it.

You may depend upon it that when illness is very severe, the poor soul needs divine support, which often consists in keeping it simply to rest upon the faithfulness and mercy of God, without any of that earnestness and activity of spiritual feeling which many persons look for. You have often been much and deeply exercised in your own soul about your state and standing before God, and have at times sunk very low through doubt and fear. But the Lord has from time to time been very gracious to you, and given you some manifestations of His love and mercy which have cheered and revived your cast-down spirit. This experience, both of judgment and mercy, makes you look for it in others who profess the truth, and has taught you the emptiness and worthlessness of a mere profession.

If the Lord has shown these things in any measure to our consciences we cannot but contend for them. We may lament our own wretched coldness, deadness, and darkness in the things of God, and may see and feel ourselves very far from the enjoyment of the precious truths which we profess; but at the same time we cannot join hand in hand with those who we feel are out of the secret, and are satisfied with a name to live while dead.

But I need not go on writing in this strain to you, as from our long friendship and intimacy, and your knowledge of my preaching and writing, you are well acquainted—perhaps more almost than any other man, with my views and feelings upon the things of God; and, I believe, in these matters we have been led much to see eye to eye, and I trust to feel heart to heart.

I have been very unwell; indeed, I may say that I have not been so ill for many years. The attack has made my chest very tender and susceptible of the least cold, but what I feel now is chiefly debility, though cold, most probably, would have the effect of bringing the congestion back again. It is a trial to me and to my people to be thus laid aside; and I am almost afraid it may interfere with my engagements in the summer. I can hardly expect to get out much before April, and having been laid aside so long, I am afraid it would hurt the minds of the friends if I were to leave them much in the summer as I have hitherto done.

As we get older we may expect to see greater and greater changes. Old friends will drop off by death; we shall ourselves, if spared, begin to feel more and more of the infirmities produced by illness and age; and we seem to live in very trying times when we may expect great changes, and, perhaps, great calamities in the Church and in the world. How grievous it is to see error so spreading, and minister after minister drinking it in. How few faithful experimental men of God there are! and in what a state for the most part are the churches of truth.

I am glad that you liked the Address. Others have expressed a similar feeling. Where it was deficient was toward the conclusion, as I ought to have said more to encourage the saints of God amidst all their trials and temptations. But I was too ill to take up that part of the subject. And, therefore, it might have seemed more deficient to me than to others. I am well convinced that in this there is a very great departure from the power of the Gospel. If there were more of the life and power of God in the soul, there would be more power and godliness in the life. The one flows from the other. I only wish that I could feel more of the life and power of God in my own heart, and could manifest it more by my life, and conduct, and conversation. In the providence and grace of God I have become fixed in a very important and responsible position, for which I need the continual supplies of His grace. I consider that the *Gospel Standard* is a very important work, as having so wide a circulation among the churches, and I could wish it filled with the life and power of God, so as to exercise a divine influence wherever it goes. Besides which my sermons are much read and sought after, and these I wish to be impregnated with the life, and power, and grace of God, so as to reach men's hearts and consciences. Time with us all here must be short, and we should do what we can to serve our day and generation; to live as far as we can to the glory of God and the good of His people, and not lead useless, selfish, unprofitable lives, as if money were our God. All Christians have their place in the mystical body, and their place to fill in the Church of God. You have yours, as connected with the cause of truth, at Allington; to bear and forbear, and to manifest our love to the Lord, and to His people, in various ways as I believe you do.

* * * * * *

Yours very affectionately,
J. C. P.

CX—To Mr. Tips

Stamford, Jan. 24, 1860.

My dear Friend,

I received your New Year's gift, and wish that I could return you a fitting present by clothing my letter in a poetic dress. But it would take more time than I could conveniently spare; besides which, I feel myself better able to express my thoughts and feelings in simple prose.

You express a wish that I should return a speedy answer to your New Year's affectionate salutation. But it has pleased the

Lord to lay upon me a severe illness, which has lasted from the latter end of November, and is not yet removed. I am, however, through mercy, slowly improving in health, and hope, with God's blessing, after a time to be restored to the work of the ministry.

Trials and afflictions are the appointed lot of the family of God, and if we belong to that favoured number we shall certainly have our share of them. Some of these afflictions are of the body, others of the mind; some are connected with the family, others with our circumstances in life; some come from the temptations of Satan, and others from our own evil hearts.

The blessed Spirit in the Scripture compares these trials and afflictions to a furnace in which gold and silver are refined (Isa. xlviii. 10; Zech. xiii. 9), the object of God being to try our faith (1 Pet. i. 7). The Lord, therefore, bids us buy of Him gold tried in the fire (Rev. iii. 18), and compares Himself to a refiner and purifier of silver (Mal. iii. 3.) Now what is the first effect of the furnace when the impure metal is put into it? It begins to soften and melt by the application of the fire; smoke is seen gathering over the refining pot; scum and dross work up to the top. But where all the time is the pure metal? Out of sight, for it is hidden by the scum and foam. But when that is taken off the pure gold appears. Now nothing but the heat of the furnace could have separated the pure metal from the dross. So it is with the spiritual furnace. Nothing but the heat of the flame can separate true faith from false, and the life of God in the soul from a mere fleshly religion. But when we are in the furnace it is like what we see in the purifying of the gold. The dross and scum of our evil hearts at first alone appear; the pure gold of faith, hope, and love, which are God's gift, is hidden from view. But after a time, when the Lord is pleased to take away the dross, then the pure gold of faith shines more bright than ever. I hope that my dear friend to whom I am writing is well convinced that all true religion is the gift and work of God, as we read every good gift and every perfect gift is from above and cometh down from the Father of lights (James i. 17). God is too pure, just, and holy a being to look with satisfaction upon our obedience or anything done by the flesh. This He shows us by the teaching of His Holy Spirit; for we see light in His light, and it is by the shining in of divine light that all things are made manifest (Eph. v. 13). When Isaiah saw his glory in the temple he cried out, Woe is me for I am undone; because I am a man of unclean lips, and I dwell in the midst of a people of unclean lips (Isa. vi. 5). When Job saw God he abhorred himself, and repented in dust and ashes (Job xlii. 5, 6), and the comeliness of Daniel was turned in him unto corruption (Dan. x. 8). Now these Scripture instances show us what the saints of God saw and felt concerning themselves when they had a spiritual view of the glory and majesty of the Lord God Almighty. It is plain, therefore, that men who think highly of their own goodness have never had such a view of the purity and holiness of God as His saints have as recorded in the Scriptures. Therefore they see no danger; they fear no ill; they have no sense of sin; nor can they have any repentance of it. But those who are taught of God have been made to see and feel the exceeding sinfulness of sin; they have fled for refuge from the wrath to come unto Jesus the only Mediator between God and men. To his exalted Person at the right hand of God they look; before His throne of grace they bow; under His atoning blood and justifying righteousness they shelter themselves, and in Him they thus find rest and peace. The ever-varying, ever-restless sea rolls between us; but if we have a living union with the Lord Jesus Christ it may separate but it cannot divide. We speak two different languages, but I hope we can also speak the one language of Canaan. We may read the Bible in two different versions, but it is the same holy inspired Scripture which speaks to us as by the mouth of God, and we trust we have one and the same Father, one and the same elder Brother, and one and the same Spirit as our Guide, Teacher, and Comforter (Eph. iv. 4—6). The chief thing to press after is an experimental knowledge of the Lord Jesus Christ, to know the efficacy of His atoning blood, and to enjoy union and communion with Him. He is the Vine, we are the branches; without Him we can do nothing. But if we abide in Him, and He abides in us, then we shall bring forth much fruit. Our chief desire should be to know Him and the power of His resurrection, that we may be found in Him, not having our own righteousness which is of the law, but that which is through the faith of Christ, the righteousness which is of God by faith (Phil. iii. 9, 10). To do this we must cast aside our own righteousness and be clothed in this which is perfect. But we shall always find sin to be our worst enemy, and self our greatest foe. The carnal mind is enmity against God (Rom. viii. 5), and not being subject to the will of God it will be ever rebelling against him. We need not fear anything but sin; nothing else can do us any real injury. But sin can and will make God hide His face, will grieve the blessed Spirit, will darken our evidences, and give room to the accusations of Satan. It will be our mercy if we are found often seeking the Lord's face, confessing our sins, reading His holy word, and striving to obtain some manifestation of the Lord's mercy, goodness, and love. The Lord Jesus has promised to manifest Himself to those who love Him and keep His commandments (John xiv. 21), and it is by these manifestations that we come to know Him experimentally and savingly. The Lord Himself has told us what eternal life is, that it is to know the only true God and Jesus Christ whom He hath sent (John xvii. 3.) If we know by divine teaching the only true God we shall fear and revere His holy name; and if we know Jesus Christ whom He hath sent, we shall love Him with a pure heart fervently. You have the Holy Scripture in your hand, a treasure of which the blind Papists would willingly deprive the Church, and in that you can read the mind and will of God, and learn from it the way of salvation. The Lord Himself bids us search the Scriptures, and tells us that they testify of Him (John v. 39). You have a throne of grace which is ever open, and to which we are invited to come boldly, that we may find mercy and grace to help in time of need.

I was in hopes, from what you said to my young friend Mr. P——, that you would visit England last autumn. I hope you may be induced to come over this summer, and to come to see me. I shall be pleased to have a letter from you when convenient. And now, dear Friend, accept my Christian love for yourself and your dear wife, and all that love the Lord whom you know.

Yours, in the Lord Jesus Christ,

J. C. P.

CXI —To Mr. Tiptaft

Stamford, Jan. 25, 1860.

My dear Tiptaft,

Mrs. Keal has forwarded to me this morning a letter received from you, in which you are so kind as to offer to come and help me for two Lord's-days. It would very much gratify both myself and the friends if you could do so.

I am thankful to say that through rich mercy I am much better than when I last wrote, the congestion being very much removed, and what I now chiefly feel is great weakness and general debility, from being brought down so low and kept on such scanty diet. None but those who have been in a similar furnace know how trying to the mind illness is, and one of its chiefest trials is perhaps least observed, or, at least, less spoken of, than other attendant circumstances, which is the prostration of mind which it produces. Many people think that illness is the best time for religion, and for being prayerful and spiritually-minded; but this is a great mistake. When the illness is severe it takes such possession of the whole mind, and at the same time so enfeebles it, that it has not power to act as in health. I have often found that when the main force of the illness is over, and I am beginning to recover, that that is a good time, if the Lord is pleased to draw the soul upward to Himself, to read, pray, and meditate. But when illness is severe the soul needs divine support, patience, submission, resignation, and to lie passive in the Lord's hands, believing He doeth all things well. It is then we need special support, so that the mind may not be distracted, but rest upon the Lord's goodness and mercy, and what we hope has been felt in times past. I remember what poor Thomas Copeland once said to me in his illness. "People" he said, "think that illness is a good time to seek God; but they will find when they are very ill that the illness itself occupies all their thoughts and feelings." At the same time there are times and seasons in illness when the weight of bodily affliction seems partially removed, and then if the Lord be pleased to work by His spirit and grace there is a drawing up of the soul unto Himself. Certainly one thing trials and afflictions produce if they are in any measure sanctified; they show us the impossibility of being saved but by an act of free distinguishing sovereign grace; they make us cast ourselves wholly upon the blood and righteousness of the Son of God, and to rest satisfied with nothing short of its application. Sin also is seen to be exceedingly sinful, and the recollection of past sins grieves the conscience. Nothing has tried me more than the recollection of my sins and backslidings since I made a profession. These have been much more grievous in my eyes than any sins which I committed in the days of darkness and death. But I believe it is good for us to see and feel the weight and guilt of our sins and backslidings so as to break to pieces our self-righteousness. A man does not know his own temptations so as to say "I am not tempted with this or that propensity"; I may be wrong, therefore, when I say that I am not much troubled with self-righteousness; for I see and feel in myself nothing but sin; and what is more trying still, my carnal mind is just as sinful, polluted, and corrupt as ever it was in my life. I do see the deep necessity for every child of God to walk much in godly fear. Sin and Satan are never off their watch if we are. Sin is like a spring which can only be kept from expanding to its full length by continual pressure. Take away or relax the pressure, it expands in a moment to its full length. The fear of God in the heart is the pressure upon the spring; and if that relax or let go, sin extends itself in a moment, and who can tell how far it will go? As Francis Spira said, "Man knows the beginning of sin, but who bounds the issues thereof?" It is much easier to check sin in its first movement than when it has gained strength. If the egg be not crushed it will break out into a viper. What should we do without free grace, the atoning blood of the Lamb, and the work of the Holy Spirit to make the gospel precious to the soul.

I hope I have learnt some of these lessons in my affliction. But how soon is all forgotten? Religion is a daily, one might say an hourly, work; and only He who began can keep alive His work upon the heart.

The friends here, I believe, are all pretty well. Mr. Peake's legacy of £50 is (D.V.) to be distributed to the members of the Church at Oakham next Lord's-day after the afternoon service, by W. T. K., and R. H., junior. It will amount, I believe, to about £2 each, as all receive who feel they can do so with a good conscience.

As they have had no preaching at Oakham since Dec. 18th, they will be much pleased to see you.

Yours very affectionately,

J. C. P.

CXII—To Mr. Brown

Stamford, Feb. 1, 1860.

My dear Friend,

I am glad to find that through the rich mercy of the Lord, you have derived benefit from your sojourn at Brighton, and I hope that it may be permanent when in the providence of God you shall have turned your back upon that bracing air. We are strange creatures, and body and mind have so close and intimate a connection, that the very blowing of the sea-breeze upon the face not only cheers and braces the languid body, but acts in a corresponding way upon the burdened mind. Few things make cares sit more heavily than to stay at home by the fireside and nurse them. Not that relief is obtained from care and anxiety by any such natural means, but there seems more strength to endure them when the poor body is in some measure braced up. I could wish that your path were more free from perplexity, anxiety, and care, but no doubt He who sees the end from the beginning, and all whose ways are ways of mercy and truth to those who fear His name, sees that these cares and perplexities are for your spiritual good. This world is proverbially "a vale of tears;" thorns and briers spring up on every side, because the very ground on which we tread is under the curse; and as followers of the Lord the Lamb, we may expect not only the world's portion of sorrow but the Church's. And, indeed, though our weak flesh often staggers and sinks under the load, yet as the blessing of God, for the most part, only comes in this way, we are made willing to endure the affliction from the benefit connected with it. I have no doubt the farther we go the more we shall find of trouble, anxiety, and sorrow, both to body and soul, so as to be made willing at last to lay down our poor, worn-out frames in the dust, as being only full of sin and corruption. This seems to be the conclusion to which the Lord usually brings all His redeemed people, to be willing to depart and be with Christ as far better than continuing in a body of sin and death. We need something to wean us from life, and to deaden and mortify us to the charms of the world and the pleasures of sin, which are but for a moment. Christ is not to be found in the path of carnal ease and worldly joy. It is in tribulation and trouble alone that He is really sought and really found. We cannot choose for ourselves what that trouble shall be; but its fruits and effects must be good if they lead us up to the Lord Jesus Christ, or bring down any measure of blessing from Him.

There is so much of seeking and serving the Lord with half a heart; so much mingling of the flesh with the spirit, and trying to unite the manna of the wilderness with the flesh-pots of Egypt! But we may be certain that when the taste is vitiated with the onions and the garlic, there is no relish for angel's food. This, then, is one of the benefits of sanctified affliction, that it purges the appetite from delighting in the gross food of Egypt, to give it a taste for the bread which came down from heaven that a man should eat thereof and not die. But what is most puzzling to a spiritual mind is that the carnal mind still continues so base, so foul, so dark, and so dead, under any or every discipline. If I know anything of the life of God in the soul and of the operations of a living faith, I am also a witness to this solemn fact, that the carnal mind is still enmity against God, that it is not subject to the law of God, neither indeed can be. I am well convinced that there must be a measure of inward holiness communicated by the good Spirit of God, for "without holiness no man shall see the Lord." But I am equally sure that there is no sanctification of the body of sin and death, and that we only enjoy real sanctification of heart as the Lord is pleased to communicate it by His Spirit and grace.

I am glad that you felt yourself at home at Chichester. The Lord has a people scattered up and down this land whom He loves and who love Him; and though the Church is sunk into a very low spot yet the Lord has not left Himself without witness. He has still a people who fear His great name, and whom He will not suffer to be overcome by the Antinomian spirit of the day, for He causes His fear to work too deeply in their souls for them to be overborne by it.

Yours affectionately,

J. C. P.

CXIII—To Mr. Tiptaft

Stamford, Feb. 3, 1860.

My dear Tiptaft,

I am very glad that you have felt led to render us some assistance in our time of need; I have no doubt that the friends both here and at Oakham will be much pleased to see and hear you again. Mr. K. was here last evening and brought over your last letter. What you say in it about despair I can well go along with. To be abandoned to it, and that at the last, is more dreadful than tongue can express or heart can conceive; but I believe all must have some taste of it to make them in earnest about their souls and flee to Christ's blood and righteousness as what alone can save. Presumption and despair are indeed two wide extremes, and yet they touch so closely that as Hart says of two other extremes, "There's scarce a hair's-breadth between." And I suppose there is no living soul who has not been tempted with both, and that not once or twice, but many, many times in his Christian course; nor can one hardly tell which is the more distasteful to his soul, for if he hates the false joy of presumption he also dreads the deep feelings of despair. I am sure that it is good for the soul to be exercised in the things of God, and except being carried away by the power of sin there is no worse state for the soul than to be at carnal ease. But how impossible it is for us to produce any right or spiritual feeling! All is a sovereign gift, even to read the word with a believing heart or any softened feeling, or to lift up the soul even for a few moments to the Lord in real earnest desire for His presence and power to be felt, and His blood and love to be made experimentally known. To believe in the Lord Jesus Christ is thought by many a very simple and easy thing, and so it is when the Lord moves by His spirit and grace upon the heart; but to believe in spite of unbelief, infidelity, and the misgivings of a guilty conscience, is no such easy matter.

I much like the letter of Ridley which Mr. V. sent you. It will, I hope, be inserted in the *Gospel Standard*. I thought it gave a very sweet account of the manifestation of the Lord to His soul. I should not think that there are many engine-drivers who could write a letter like his.

We are expecting (D.V.) Mr. Taylor to preach here next Thursday, and at Oakham the following evening. He very kindly wrote to offer his services for those two evenings on his way to London. I have also written to Mr. Kershaw to give us, if he can, a Lord's-day, after he has been to Nottingham, and if he cannot to come over for a week evening.

I cannot say very much about myself as regards the poor body. I do not seem to be gathering at present much strength. What I feel almost as much as the bodily weakness is that it seems to have so unfitted my mind for any continuous exertion, so that I can scarcely attend as I should do to the *Gospel Standard*, &c. Still we cannot choose our own trials and afflictions. What adds to its weight is the care of my two churches and congregations; for though the Lord has been very kind in raising up Supplies, yet still it is a trial both to them and me to be so long laid aside. Mr. J. T. Smith has very kindly come over from Peterbro' for several Thursday evenings, and his preaching seems acceptable to the people.

What is there to be compared with a blessed manifestation of the Lord Jesus Christ to remove all guilty fears and to enable the soul to lie down in peace? I believe that the Lord for the most part will make His people thoroughly weary of this life before He takes them out of it. Sickness of body, trials in providence, afflictions in the family, and above all, the wearing conflict under a body of sin and death with a blessed view of a glorious immortality sooner or later will make them willing to depart and be with Christ as far better than living in this vain world.

I hope the Lord may come with you.

Yours very affectionately,

J. C. P.

CXIV—To Mrs. Oyler

Stamford, Feb. 6, 1860.

Dear Friend,

I am much obliged to you for your kind and affectionate letter, and the interest which you express in my health and welfare. I am thankful to say, through mercy, that the complaint under which I was labouring has been very much subdued, and I hope, with God's blessing, I may after a little time be restored to my usual health. But at present I am suffering under weakness and debility produced by the length and severity of the illness. I have found it a furnace in which much dross has been discovered, but, I hope, a little of that precious faith which is as gold tried in the fire, and whereby alone the soul cleaves affectionately to the Lord Jesus Christ as its only help and hope. Almost, if not quite, all I have learnt that has been for the good of my own soul, or for the profit of others, has been learnt in the furnace of affliction. It is there that we learn the necessity as well as the nature of a religion which is wrought in the heart by the power of God. Divine realities are then wanted—not shams or shows; and when the Lord is pleased to discover to us His own purity and holiness and our sinfulness and vileness, He makes us feel our need of atoning blood and justifying righteousness, and that these two rich blessings must be made known to the soul by a divine manifestation. As then He is pleased to reveal and make known the person and work of His dear Son, He raises up and draws forth a living faith in and upon Him which works by love and purifies the heart.

If, then, you have derived any benefit from what you have heard or read of mine, give God the glory. Compare it with the Scriptures, the experience of the saints, and what you have felt in your own soul. There is no teacher like the Lord, and no real blessing but what cometh down from Him. Ever seek His face, and to know Jesus for yourself and the power of His resurrection.

I sincerely wish you and yours every new Covenant mercy, and am with kind love to your partner,

Yours affectionately,

J. C. P.

CXV—To —— ——

Stamford, Feb. 7, 1860.

My dear Friends,

I write to you both, for I feel that I must, with my own hand, acknowledge your most kind and liberal present; and I trust it has produced in my heart thankfulness to the God of all my mercies, as well as real gratitude and affection to yourselves. I am almost ashamed to confess it, and yet as your most unlooked-for present has come as a secret yet sweet reproof from the Lord, I feel I must acknowledge a little—and oh, but a little, of my poor unbelieving heart. I was then foolish enough, and worse than foolish, sinful enough, to begin to fret and murmur, not only at the length and severity of the affliction, but at the long doctor's bill which I should have to pay, and other expenses attending illness. I felt then when I received your kind present that the Lord was still mindful of me—that He was what He always has been, most kind and gracious, and as I write to acknowledge your kindness my heart is softened and my eye moistened with a sense of His goodness and mercy to me, a poor vile sinner. I do not wish you to think that I could not have easily paid all these expenses to which I have alluded, but I see that the Lord knoweth all the secrets of our hearts, and is very pitiful, and is full of compassion to our inmost thoughts and wishes. I will (D.V.) in a few days, by the help of my dear amanuensis, to whose love and kindness in my late illness I owe so much, write more fully to my dear friend Mrs. ——, but I could not forbear to write myself a few lines to both my dear friends, as an acknowledgment of their kindness and liberality.

Yours affectionately in the Lord,

J. C. P.

CXVI—To Mrs. Peake

Stamford, Feb. 15, 1860.

My dear Friend,

We have been both, and still are, in the furnace of affliction, and it is this whereby we learn to sympathise with those who are afflicted. The blessed Lord Himself, as the great High Priest over the house of God had to learn sympathy with His afflicted people by being Himself "a man of sorrows and acquainted with grief;" and there is no other way whereby we can sympathise with Him and with each other.

Since I have read the letters which your late beloved husband addressed to you before and after your marriage, I can more see and feel what a bereavement you have had by losing him. Knowing how much in many things you outwardly differed, I did not know, or rather did not sufficiently bear in mind, how closely you were united in heart and affection naturally, or in mind and spirit spiritually. But his correspondence with you has shown it me as I never saw it before, and I must say I much admire the general tenor of his letters to you, and considering how you stood toward each other, and the strength of his natural affection, I have been struck with what I may call the *purity* which breathes through his letters, and the absence of much that might naturally have been expected in a correspondence of that kind. It has much raised my esteem of him as a man who lived and walked much in the fear of God. And considering how hastily many of them must have been written, and their number, I have been surprised at their variety and the uniform goodness of style and expression in one who had received so little education. No doubt I look upon it with a more favourable eye than would be the case with a stranger; but I do think when the work comes out it will be well received by the friends and valued as a memorial of their departed friend.

If I expressed my surprise at your being present at the meeting when the distribution was made, it was not that I felt any measure of disapproval. I was rather glad that you were able to be present, but feared you would be too much overcome to do so. No doubt, for a long time, perhaps even to your dying day, you will feel your loss, for there is something singularly "desolate" in the case of a widow from whom her earthly prop has been removed; but I have no doubt you will see mercy in the end. In reading the experiences of some of the most afflicted, and yet the most favoured of the Lord's people, I have observed that many were widows. If I remember right, Lady Kenmure, to whom Rutherford was so much attached in the Lord, and to whom he wrote some of his choicest letters, was a widow. Writing to her in one of his letters, Rutherford, who himself was a widower, has these words, "And albeit I must, out of some experience, say the mourning for the husband of your youth, be by God's own mouth the heaviest worldly sorrow (Joel i. 8), and though this be the weightiest burden that ever lay upon your back, yet ye know if ye shall wait upon Him, who hideth His face for awhile, that it lieth upon God's honour and truth to fill the field and to be husband to the widow." I have used his words as being so much more forcible and expressive than my own; and it much corresponds with what you yourself have said about the void made by your bereavement, which you feel none but the Lord can fill. If you wish to read the whole letter you will find it Letter xix., Second Part.

I feel very grateful to my dear friends at Oakham who have borne so kindly and considerately with my absence from them, and not murmured at the want of preaching. Here they have been more favoured, as there has been only one preaching Lord's-day since my illness when they have been altogether without a minister.

Yours very affectionately,
J. C. P.

CXVII.—To Mrs. Pinnell

Stamford, Feb. 17, 1860.

My dear Friend,

I was very sorry to hear through a letter, received to-day from Mr. Tiptaft, that my dear friend Mr. Pinnell did not improve in health so much as his friends could desire; but I was very much pleased to hear through the same channel that he is very happy in his mind, and bore his illness with much submission and patience, and was otherwise favoured in his soul.

It must be a great trial to you to see him brought down so low, but at the same time a great consolation to find him in so happy a state. The long illness of poor dear John must have long weighed heavily upon his spirit, and the suddenness of his death, though not unexpected, must have been a very great shock. I do hope it may please the blessed Lord to spare him a little longer for your sake, and that of his family. Otherwise, there is not much here to live for, as each year would add more and more to his cares and anxieties. Should it please the Lord to take him to Himself it will be to you an irreparable loss; but hitherto you have seen His kind hand stretched forth in every time of need, and He has promised that as our day is so our strength shall be.

Now that this winter has been so severe, and his dear father is laid on a bed of sickness, you will see the wisdom and mercy why poor dear John was removed at the time that he was. You have quite enough on your hands with Mr. Pinnell's illness, and how greatly would poor John's continuance have added to your anxiety and care. Had there been any hope of his life being spared it would have been different; but that being hopeless, his removal was only a question of time, and the sweet assurance that you have of his safety softened the blow and mingled mercy with it.

No real blessing is obtained but through trials and afflictions, not that they in themselves can do us any good; for, if not sanctified by the blessed Spirit, they only cause murmuring and fretfulness. Nor can we choose our own afflictions, and what are chosen for us seem to be the very last that we should have selected had the choice been left to us.

Few things can be more trying to an affectionate wife than to witness the illness of a beloved husband; and we know that when the master of the house, especially where there is business, is laid aside, there is little else but disorder and confusion. You say very justly that mothers are hardly fit to manage sons and daughters, especially when grown up. They rarely have the authority which a father naturally possesses, and their attempt to exercise it, instead of producing quiet submission, often rouses angry feeling. But even here, as in everything else, the Lord is all sufficient, and can give to weak mothers a strength and authority which they do not naturally possess. Every family should strive for the benefit of each other and the whole, for union is strength, and few sights are more unseemly than to see division where there should be nothing but love and union.

It is now many years since I first knew you both. Many trials have we seen since that day. You have had many family cares, and Mr. Pinnell has had his cares and anxieties in business, besides family afflictions common to you both, and, no doubt, at times painful spiritual trials and temptations. How good the Lord is to support the mind under the weight of trials and afflictions, and whilst He gives enough to make us sail steadily over the sea of life, yet He never lays upon us more than we can bear. By these trials and afflictions He stirs up a spirit of prayer in the heart, gives us to cease from all human help and hope, and teaches us to look wholly and solely to the Lord of life and glory for salvation and all. Here, I can truly say, I hang all my hope, and the more I feel the weight of affliction and trials the more I feel to hang upon the blessed Lord as upon a nail fixed in a sure place. We are so apt, when things go well with us in nature, to forget the Lord, and live to self. In order, therefore, to bring us near to Himself, He lays His chastening hand upon us, and by these means brings us out of self to rest more in Him. I am still an invalid, nor do I seem at present to gather up my strength. The severe weather has been much against me, as it keeps up the irritation in the chest; and till that is removed I cannot hope to make much progress. It is a mercy, however, that I am able to attend to my necessary writing, though I am laid aside for the present from the work of the ministry.

Please to give my sympathising and Christian love to Mr. Pinnell, and my sincere desire that he may experience more and more of the blessing which maketh rich. My love to Mrs. R. and all your family.

Accept the same from

Yours very affectionately,

J. C. P.

CXVIII.—To Mr. Brown.

Stamford, Feb. 21, 1860.

My dear Friend,

I am glad to learn that you continue, with God's help and blessing, to improve in health, and are deriving such benefit from your sojourn by the seaside. This improvement seems to afford the strongest evidence that it is the malaria of Godmanchester which has been the cause of much of your illness. I understand that you do not contemplate returning until next month, and I think you act wisely in so doing, as there has been much flooding of the waters in the low countries, and until the March winds shall have a little dried the meadows and dissipated the mephitic air, it would be hardly safe for you to return. It is a remarkable circumstance in all diseases caused by malaria, that the constitution never seems so to recover from them as to be proof against the influence of the same air. The Lord has hitherto appeared for you in opening doors for you to preach, and giving you acceptance amongst His people. This must very much relieve your mind, and convince you that you are not yet thrown over the wall, like a weed plucked out of the bed of a garden, which is, perhaps, one of the most painful feelings that a minister, as a minister, can well feel. Sussex is a highly-favoured county. It will be twenty-two years next July since I preached for good old Mr. Pitcher, and slept at his house. He told me some of his temptations and experience, and I believe we felt a mutual union which has never been dissolved. I much admired his simplicity and godly sincerity, and am glad to hear that he still continues to bear fruit in old age. How faithful the Lord is to His people, and how those who sow in tears are sure to reap in joy! Those who fear God and pass through many mental exercises, trials, and temptations, mainly in consequence of that fear being rooted deeply in their heart, shine all the brighter when the Sun of Righteousness arises upon them with healing in His wings, while those who seem so full of confidence often concerning faith make awful shipwreck. The sovereignty of God is as much displayed in the experience of His people as in their original choice. I see more and more that not only will the Lord have those whom He will, but He will have them in His own way. My desire is to be wholly and solely His, for Him to make me what He would have me to be, and work in me by His holy Spirit everything which is pleasing in His sight. At present I do not seem much to improve in health; but what I chiefly feel is debility, and this, I think, will be the case till I can take more food and get into the open air.

* * * * * *

What a world of sin, sorrow, and confusion this is! Satan, I see, is continually stirring up error and evil on every side. What need we have of grace every moment, and what poor, helpless creatures are we without it! I feel compelled to look more to the Lord than ever I did in my life, and to hang more and more all my hopes upon Him and Him only.

Yours very affectionately,

J. C. P.

CXIX—To Mr. Grace

Stamford, April 2, 1860.

My dear Friend,

I feel a desire to have some little memoir of the late Mr. Vinall in the *Gospel Standard,* and it has struck me that you could furnish me with some account of his experience. I have not quite decided in my own mind how I should do it, but I think that I should like to review your sermon, and in that to introduce some trustworthy account of his experience, and the general character of his ministry. I think no person could furnish me with better information upon these points than yourself. All I want is certain leading facts—elements as it were—which I could work up in my review, so as to be trustworthy, and such as would be acceptable to his numerous friends. You know very well that my heart has always been much with the real Huntingtonians. I say "real" because I have no union with the mere nominal followers of Mr. H——. There is, or rather was, a blessed life, feeling, and savour in those who were partakers of the same grace and spirit as the blessed coalheaver; and I know not where to look for men of similar depth of experience and sweet unction of utterance.

Yours very affectionately,

J. C. P.

CXX—To Mr. Godwin

Stamford, April 3, 1860.

My dear Friend,

Through mercy, I hope I can say I am progressing in health, and, for the first time since the end of November, went today out of my garden-gate, and took a turn up and down the Terrace. I feel also stronger in walking than I expected I should after my long confinement, and I hope now, with God's blessing, if I get no relapse that I may be restored once more to my pulpit and people. It has been a long and heavy trial to me, and I doubt not, I may add, in a measure to them; though the pulpits have been well supplied, especially here where there has been as much preaching as if I had not been laid aside at all.

I hope I may not lose the life and feeling which I have had for the most part through the affliction; but I have often found that as the body got stronger the soul got weaker, and that the sickness of the one was sometimes the health of the other. I could wish that my soul was always alive unto God—with no darkness, deadness, coldness, unbelief, or worldly-mindedness. But alas! I find that I have still a body of sin and death which will make itself felt, and which seems to suffocate by its pressure all spiritual good. But the blessed Lord has said, "Because I live ye shall live also;" so that wherever He has communicated life out of His own fulness He will maintain it in spite of sin, hell, and death. What a mercy this is for the living family of God.

I hope the Lord may be with you in your visit to Leicester. You will preach to a large congregation, and we hope that there are amongst them some of the royal family.

Yours very affectionately,
J. C. P.

CXXI.—To Mr. Grace.

Stamford, April 10, 1860.

My dear Friend,

I received your parcel quite safely and much prize Miss V——'s kind present. Have the kindness, when you see her, to present her with my Christian regards and thanks. I have no doubt I shall find it very useful as a book of reference, and a good companion to his invaluable commentary. The advantage of such books is that they lead us to the Scriptures, the fountain head of all truth, and pack together in a small compass the chief outlines on almost all subjects of divinity. I use such books not as masters but as servants; not as teachers, but as pointing out the road where I may get the true teaching; not as guides, but as direction posts. It is a mercy to be taught of God the truth for ourselves, so as to know it by an inward testimony, and thus be able to exercise a spiritual judgment in the things of God (1 Cor. ii. 9—12; 14—16; Heb. v. 14.) For want of this divine teaching many men take up with the authority of some great writer, and without the least power to exercise any judgment of their own become his disciples. This is the great danger of using commentators, or, indeed, adopting any one author as our guide. I love to read the word of truth by and for itself, and to have it opened up to my heart and conscience with a divine power. Then it does me good, becomes my own, and its effects are gracious, spiritual, and experimental. But if I read the Scriptures only in the light of Dr. Gill or Mr. Huntington I merely get my teaching at second hand, which will neither benefit me nor any one through me. I believe that if the Lord has a work for a man to do, either by tongue or pen, He will give him not only a sufficiency of grace, but an original gift to set forth the truth; and by this, among other marks, the servants of God are distinguished from mere apes and imitators. God Himself asks Moses, "Who hath made man's mouth?" And surely if the Lord sends a man on His errands He will put a word into his mouth. It was so with the ancient prophets, whom the Lord always furnished with a word to speak to the people; and where this is not we may doubt if the Lord has sent a man to preach in His name. Not but what I think that a gracious gift may be improved by exercise. The apostle bids Timothy "not to neglect the gift that was in him, but to give attendance to reading, to exhortation, to doctrine," or, as the word should be rendered, "teaching."

Yea, he bids him "Give himself wholly to these things, that his profiting may appear to all."

Yours very affectionately,
J. C. P.

CXXII.—To Mr. Godwin

Oakham, May 9, 1860.

My dear Friend,

I was much concerned to hear of the sad calamity which has fallen upon our dear friends at Allington; but it is a most merciful Providence that neither life was lost, nor limb injured. . . .

Through mercy I was enabled to preach here twice last Lord's-day. The weather was beautiful, and we had a very large congregation. I hope the Lord was with us, as I was helped through the morning sermon, but felt rather jaded before I got through the afternoon. It is a mercy to be raised up thus far, and I find my health and strength in good measure returning now that I can get my usual walks. . . .

I sincerely hope that our dear friends who have been burned out of their house and home will be enabled one day to see the hand of the Lord in it. It is not often that we can see His hand at the time, especially when lying under the afflicting stroke; but in due time the Lord's hand is seen, and a blessing in disguise manifested thereby. There is no use for a child of God to think of making his home in this fallen world. Poor Job at one time thought that he should die in his nest, and multiply his days like the sand. But how soon did the Lord burn him out of his nest, and made him even curse the day of his birth. Wherever I look around I see afflictions scattered, as it were, by the hand of God upon all.

I feel it a mercy to be raised up thus far, and except being rather more weak, and having lost some flesh, do not find myself much the worse for my long illness. The friends were surprised, at Stamford, at the strength of my voice the first time I preached there. I hope I shall not lose all the feelings which I had during my affliction; but I find that when the weight is off there is a springing back to the old spot. Nothing seems to put us or to keep us in our right place but trials and afflictions. Like the ballast on board a ship, there is no sailing steadily unless there be ballast in the hold. It seems hard to the flesh that it should be so, but the Lord knows best how to deal with us, and He will take care that none of His children shall want a cross, and that of His own laying on. But the blessing makes the cross not only endurable, but, in our right mind, even acceptable.

I hope the Lord will be with you this time at Allington, and that our dear friends may receive strength and encouragement under the ministry of the word. It is trials of this kind which make the consolations of the Gospel suitable and precious. My kind love and affectionate sympathies with them in their troubles. The loss which may have been sustained is of little value compared with the loss of the soul. . . .

Yours very affectionately,

J. C. P.

CXXIII —To Mr. Tips, of Rotterdam

Stamford, June 26, 1860.

My dear Friend,

I am glad that the Lord was pleased to give you and your friend a favourable voyage home, and that you found your dear wife and family in the enjoyment of that greatest of all temporal mercies. It gives me pleasure also to learn from your friendly and affectionate letter that you bear in remembrance the days which you spent at my house. There is no bond like a spiritual union, for that endures when all others sink and die. All natural ties must end with this life, but spiritual ties are for ever. Before your visit here you only knew me by having read my sermons; but now you have seen me, conversed with me on the things of God, and have heard me preach the word of life. You will now read the sermons with more interest, and seem to hear me preach them. The sermon which you heard me preach in the morning is just published, and if I can I will enclose it in this letter.

Through mercy my health continues pretty much as it was when you were here; and I hope it may please the Lord to preserve it for my own sake and that of others. I am going to-morrow, if the Lord will, from home for six weeks, half of which I am to be in London, and the other half in Wiltshire, one of our southern counties where there are a good number of the Lord's dear family. The work of the ministry is a great work to be engaged in, and none can be fit for it except the Lord is pleased to make him fit. "It is not by might, nor by power, but by my spirit, saith the Lord of hosts." "Paul may plant, and Apollos water; but it is God who giveth the increase." The blessed Lord has said, "Without me ye can do nothing;" and this is what all His dear people are fully convinced of; for they find and feel that in them, that is, in their flesh, dwelleth no good thing; for to will is present with them, but how to perform that which is good they find not.

Yours in the Gospel,

J. C. P.

CXXIV—To Mrs. Pinnell

Bath, July 27, 1860.

My dear Friend,

I much regret that I shall not be able this time to accept your kind invitation to come to Westwell, as I must reach home by August 10th. I should otherwise have had much pleasure in once more visiting you all, and renewing our friendship and spiritual intercourse. The time of the year naturally reminds you of that solemn scene which I witnessed when poor John passed away from this vale of sickness and sorrow to be at rest on that happy shore where sin no more defiles, and pain of body or mind are alike unknown. Viewing the peculiar severity of the past winter and spring, his poor dear father's long and trying illness, the incurable nature of John's disease, and the sweet hope you entertain of his eternal salvation, could you have wished him a longer stay here below? And as to the manner of his death, though solemn to the spectators, it was not painful to him, and was much more speedy, as well as easy, than a more lingering mode of departure. When faith can look through and beyond the dark cloud of sight and sense, it sees mercy and goodness in those things wherein the unbelieving heart does but murmur and rebel. But whose voice should we listen to? That of sense and nature, which always disbelieves and opposes the way, word, and will of God; or that of faith and grace, which believes, and submits, and speaks well of the Lord and His dealings? With many trials, you and dear Mr. Pinnell have had many mercies. In fact, your very trials have been among your mercies, and if not, the very chief of them have made a way for the choicest to be made manifest. "The Lord trieth the righteous." Their trials are as much appointed them as that righteousness in which they stand, and whereby they are justified. And if the Lord Himself try them, then the nature, season, duration, and all attending circumstances of all their trials, are determined for them; selected by infinite wisdom, decreed by unalterable purpose, guided by eternal love, and brought to pass by Almighty power. To believe less than this is secret infidelity, and will always issue in murmuring, rebellion, self-righteousness, and self-pity. But with faith (at least when in exercise) there will be submission and resignation to the will of God, and clearing of Him, and so condemning ourselves. Still, nature will feel and carnal reason will work, and then, under their wretched influence, there will be a going over the same useless and miserable ground. "Why this, why that? Why was dear John not spared as a prop to the family? Why cut down like a flower when other young men are going about in full health and strength?" So reasons, so murmurs nature, and then comes self-pity and that worldly sorrow which works death. May you and dear Mr. Pinnell be graciously delivered from all such subtle attempts of the flesh to wrest the sceptre of sovereignty from the grasp of Jehovah, and to say to Him when He exercises it contrary to our fleshly will, "What doest Thou?"

I am glad to hear that Mr. Pinnell is recovering from his long illness, though by slow steps. As life advances, bodily infirmities must be expected. He has had a long lease of health, but the longest lease runs out, and it is kind to send notice to quit some time beforehand, that expectation of renewal may be cut off. It is grievous to cleave to earth when nearest to leaving it; and illness and afflictions are mercifully sent to unloosen those ties which bind the heart to the perishing things of time and sense. All is fading and vanishing away but Christ and His salvation. May our desire be to know and love Him more and serve Him better. I am staying here with Mrs. Isbell, my poor widowed sister, who, though much shaken in body and mind, is quite as well as I could expect.

Yours very affectionately,

J. C. P.

CXXV—To Mr. Tanner *

Stamford, August 22, 1860.

My dear Friend,

I have been glad that you have been able in some measure to overcome the restraint which you have felt, I think I may say without reason, in writing to or conversing with me. I am sure there is no reason why you should feel it, though I believe there may be something in my natural manner which prevents persons whom I really esteem and love from speaking to me as freely as they do to others. I have seen for many years so much profession in people and so little vital godliness that it has made me suspicious of nearly all, and I have received so many wounds from professing friends that it has made me very cautious in what I say, as I have found my words caught up and turned against me. The only thing that I want to see in persons who make a profession is the fear and grace of God; and though there are great differences in my feeling for and affection towards such, yet I hope I can say that I truly desire to esteem and love all who fear and love God. In the very first teachings which I had of the wisdom from above, the value and blessedness of the grace of God as a felt experimental reality were deeply impressed upon my heart; and as the necessary consequence of this the real emptiness of everything else. Thus I do not value persons on account of what they may possess of natural gifts or abilities, but what they possess by the teaching of God in their soul. I cannot

* Mr. Joseph Tanner, minister of the Gospel at Cirencester. Died February 16, 1867. See obituary, *Gospel Standard*.

express in the limits of a letter what my feelings are upon this subject, and upon one very closely allied to it, viz., the indispensable qualifications of a minister of Christ; and what I must see in and feel towards a man before I can recognise him in my own conscience as a Christian or as a minister. From having read my writings in the *Gospel Standard* and elsewhere, you know more of my mind in these matters than I can know of yours; but I must say that all I have seen in or heard of you has led me much to esteem you, and that I felt much union of spirit with you in the little conversation that we had the other day at Calne.

* * * * * *

Yours in the best bonds,

J. C. P.

CXXVI—To Mr. Grace

Stamford, August 31, 1860.

My dear Friend,

I cannot recollect ever to have seen, or even to have heard of, the work which you name, by Francis Cheynell, and should be much pleased to have a copy of it, but I should be very glad to purchase it, instead of, as you seem to intimate, receiving it as a gift; though I know your great liberality of heart, and what pleasure it gives you to manifest it to your friends. Is there not some intimation of this liberal heart as the effect of the Gospel Isa. xxxii. 8?—for the liberal there is surely not what is understood in these days by the term as opposed to conservative, for the word means generous, noble, princely—a disposition very different from many of our so-called liberals. Mr. Huntington was a remarkable example of this liberal spirit, and the promise was verified in him, for by liberal things liberally ministered to him he stood and maintained his position in almost a princely manner compared with the blue apron and the black coal-sack.

I am much obliged to Mr. —— for his kind message. I have always held him in honour for his steadfast maintenance of sound doctrine. If we view religion as a body, may we not say that the doctrines of the Gospel are the bones, experience the flesh, and the blessed Spirit the life of both bones and flesh? The doctrines of the Gospel support all sound experience, but at the same time are so clothed with it that they are not visible except through the medium of the flesh. But in the body the flesh could not stand without the support of the bones. So in religion what would experience be unless supported by sound doctrine? But again, take the flesh from the bones and you have nothing but a dry skeleton. So take the experience of the truth from the doctrines of truth, and you have nothing but what Mr. Hart calls dry doctrine. Again, without the blessed Spirit, what is either doctrine or experience but a lifeless lump? The dead Calvinists have the bones without the flesh; the Arminians have the flesh without the bones; the daily experimentalists, for such there are, and such there were even under Mr. Huntington, have bones and flesh without life. But the living family of God have bones and flesh and life, for they have truth in doctrine, truth in experience, and truth in life and power; and thus religion with them is a living body. Of course I use it merely as a figure, and figures are necessarily imperfect; and as I have dictated just what has occurred to my mind, it may not be able to bear the test of rigid examination. Therefore receive it as I send it, and if you do not accept the figure, I believe you will accept what I mean to represent by it. One effect of this late controversy has been to show me the necessity of bringing forward into prominent view the grand leading truths of our most holy faith. I have been perfectly surprised, I will not say at the ignorance of private Christians, but even of some who are accepted as servants of God, upon that great leading point of vital truth, the real Sonship of our adorable Lord. Some have said they had never heard of the doctrine before, and others have expressed their regret that I should trouble, as they call it, the Church with it, and have called it my hobby. Is not such ignorance perfectly astounding when the true and proper Sonship of the blessed Redeemer, through the whole of the New Testament illuminating its pages with a sacred light, forms not only the fundamental article of a believer's faith, but occupies nearly the whole of John's blessed Epistle?

I very much like your remark that anything that sets forth clearly the eternal Sonship of our blessed Lord, creates a glow of love to His glorious Person. It is precisely what I have felt myself in reading such works written by men of God as set it forth. I think you have Dr. Hawker's works. If you possess Palmer's edition of them in ten volumes, published in 1831, you will find at the end of vol. iii. a blessed work of the good old Doctor entitled, "The Personal Testimony of God the Father to the Person, Godhead, and Sonship of God the Son." I think it is one of the best works that ever fell from the Doctor's pen, and must convince anybody who is willing to be convinced what his views were on that important point. Mr. ——, in the *Earthen Vessel* for August, has made mention of this work, and quoted a number of passages from it which must fall, one would think, with crushing weight upon those who would deny that the Doctor held the truth of Christ's real Sonship. There is one feature in the eternal Sonship of our blessed Lord, to which, I think, due prominence has hardly been given, viz., that without it you may have a Trinity but not a unity in that Trinity. It is most true that we cannot comprehend the mystery of the subsistence of three Persons in one Godhead, but yet we see that the unity of Deity requires a mutual and eternal relationship between them, or else they would be three distinct Gods. We can see by faith, and, I believe, we have both felt far more than we could ever express, in seeing the blessed relationship which Father, Son, and Holy Ghost have to each other from this mutual intercommunion in the one undivided essence. There is a most unspeakable blessedness in beholding by faith the Father as the eternal Father, the Son as the eternal Son, and the Spirit as the eternal Spirit. This mutual relationship must be eternal and independent of any acting of the Persons in the Godhead out of themselves toward man; and must, therefore, exist independent of any fore-view or fore-ordination of the Son of God as mediator. To my mind, then, to make the eternal relationship of the three Persons in the sacred Godhead dependent upon any covenant act of grace is, if I may use the expression, to break up the most blessed Trinity, for it destroys the eternal relationship which Father, Son, and Holy Ghost have to each other prior to, and independent of, any purposes of grace to man. According to their view our blessed Lord would never have been the Son of God if man had neither birth nor being. What was He, then, in those eternal ages before man was formed out of the dust of the earth? Was he not, then, the Son of the Father in truth and love? How derogatory to the Son of God and to the Father to deny that eternal and most blessed relationship which subsists between them from all eternity, and to make the very name and nature of Son depend upon the actings of that grace which Father, Son, and Holy Ghost felt as distinct from their mutual love and eternal intercommunion. But I forget that I am writing a letter and not a book, so please excuse the length of my thoughts on this most blessed subject.

I am now writing a very long letter to a Scotch minister upon the subject of the Law not being a rule of life to a believer. I did not wish to have any controversy on the subject, and kept silence as long as I possibly could, but he has plied me with letter after letter until I have been obliged at last to give him an answer. I shall keep a copy of it, and may perhaps put it in the *Standard*. Both Mr. Huntington and Mr. Gadsby have written most fully, clearly, and blessedly on the subject, but their works are not accessible to all who love the truth; and sometimes a short syllabus is useful to those who want to have a scriptural and experimental summary of the truth in a short and readable form. This was the reason why our reformers drew up in their time many Catechisms, that the people might be instructed in the truth in a simple compendious way. Great ignorance prevails amongst our people in many places, for very few ministers are now able to set forth the truth with clearness, and thus, like children, they are tossed to and fro with every wind of doctrine.

I spent a few pleasant days at Nottingham, preaching there twice, and speaking the intermediate evening at Wilford.

I leave home (D.V.) this day week for my journey to Abingdon, and thence to Bath, where my poor sister has all the weight of Mr. W.'s chapel upon her shoulders; so I am going there to give her a Lord's-day.

Yours very affectionately,

J. C. P.

CXXVII.—To Mr. Tanner

Stamford, Sept. 5, 1860.

My dear Friend,

You will not expect me to write you a long letter, but will be waiting to learn whether I object to preaching in the Temperance Hall instead of your little chapel. As a rule I generally feel more comfortable when I speak to the people in their usual place of worship, as a strange place and a mixed congregation often seem to rob me of that life and liberty which I like to feel in the best of all services; but for two reasons I should prefer speaking in the Temperance Hall:—1. On the ground of its accommodating more people; and, 2, as giving better ventilation; for small chapels, especially in the evening, when lighted with gas and crowded with people, much try my weak chest. I think, therefore, that upon the whole, if the Temperance Hall be not too large or too hard to speak in, I should prefer preaching there.

My sincere desire is, that the blessed Lord may come with me and anoint both my heart and lips with the unction of His grace. What we all need so much is that anointing of which John speaks as teaching of all things; for I am very sure without this blessed unction of the Holy Spirit we are and have, know and feel nothing in the true sense of the word. There is a power in divine realities when experimentally felt beyond all description, and if we know anything of this in our own souls, all but it seems light indeed. A man may have much knowledge, great acquaintance with the Scriptures, and a sound creed as regards the letter of truth, and yet be utterly destitute of that kingdom of God which is not in word but in power. It is for this power in their own souls, and as resting upon their ministry, that the servants of God should especially strive with the God of all grace.

I am very sure, whatever people may think of me, that in myself I am nothing but sin, and filth, and folly; but I hope the Lord has given me, in His sovereign grace, a knowledge of and a love unto His blessed truth; and my desire is to live and die in the sweet enjoyment of it, to proclaim and defend it as far as I am enabled by tongue and pen, to live under its liberating, sanctifying influence in my own soul, and never say or do anything which may cause it to be evil spoken of. That is a most blessed promise, "Ye shall know the truth, and the truth shall make you free."

Yours in the hope of the Gospel,

J. C. P.

CXXVIII —To Mr. Parry

Cirencester, Sept. 15, 1860.

My dear Friend,

As I am sure that you will be very desirous to know how I am, as you left me here so poorly yesterday, I avail myself of Miss Tanner's pen to drop you a few lines. I wish with all my heart that I could send you a better account of myself, but I felt so very unwell through nearly the whole night that I came to a decided conviction in my own mind that I should not be able to take my journey to Bath to-day; for even were I well enough to travel, I felt convinced I was not fit, or indeed able, to preach to-morrow, as I am almost bent double with lumbago, besides the cold on my chest. Mr. Tanner and I talked the matter over many times through the day, and after much conflict of mind, on account of his Alvescot engagement, and his burden of standing before the Bath congregation; he at length was most kindly induced to go down to Bath this afternoon, to preach for me (D.V.) to-morrow. It was a very trying night, and has been a very trying day with me, not so much on account of my illness, though that is a heavy burden, as on account of disappointing the Bath congregation, putting a heavy burden upon poor Mrs. Isbell, and the uncertainty whether she could procure a minister at so short a notice.

It has, therefore, greatly relieved my mind that Mr. Tanner is gone down; but it has been a day of great exercise to his mind. I felt placed in a difficult position, as I feared to say anything that might lead him wrong, as I consider an engagement once made should not be departed from upon light grounds, and I always feel much afraid of wounding men's consciences, or leading them in any measure to do what might afterwards be a burden to their minds. I hope that the Lord will be with him in a marked manner, and raise him beyond all fears of man. I feel for him as well as for myself. No man need envy the position of a minister, especially if called out into any prominent position. I should not have three-fourths, I think, of my trials and burdens if I were only a private Christian ; but what tries my mind just now is to be laid aside when I have such important engagements before me. I have written to Trowbridge to tell them that I cannot come. I do not know who is supplying there to-morrow, but I hope I have given them sufficient time to detain their Supply for Tuesday evening.

How full all things here below are of trial and disappointment. It seems as if the Lord would mar every plan and baffle all our schemes. It is possible that some at Bath or Trowbridge may have been looking forward too much to my coming there, and fixing their eyes more upon the man than his Master. God is a jealous God, and He will not give His glory to another. My desire is to lie submissively at His feet, and be resigned to His most holy will. I have never yet got any real good to my soul but in the path of affliction and trial. This, you know, long has been my doctrine, and I have had to learn it for the most part by painful experience.

I hope that you arrived safely at home, and found some sweet savour upon your spirit from your visit here. It is poor hearing when nothing is carried away. The gleaners in the harvest-field would not be satisfied to carry home ears out of which every grain of corn had dropped; and those who glean in the fields of Boaz, and are privileged to glean among the sheaves, may well be dissatisfied unless they carry some corn home.

Yours very affectionately,

J. C. P.

CXXIX—To Mr. Parry

Cirencester, Sept. 26, 1860.

My dear Friend,

I need not tell you what a trial and exercise of mind this affliction has given me, and how sorry I have been to be obliged to disappoint the people at Bath and Leicester. . . . It would be a very gladdening sight to see men raised up by the power and grace of God, able to preach the Gospel with the Holy Ghost sent down from heaven. But the Lord knows best. He will carry on His own work in His own way, for His footsteps are in the deep waters; He will work, and none shall let it. I must be content if I can submit to be laid aside, at least for a time, for I do not see much prospect of being able to resume the ministry for the present. The Lord knoweth best how to deal with me, and what to do by me. My earnest desire is, that it may be for my soul's lasting profit and for His own glory. The Lord will take care that no man shall glory in the flesh. It is very easy to say, as thousands do, "Thine is the power, and the kingdom, and the glory;" but how few there are who can submit that God should have what they tell Him belongs unto Him. He will, however, make all His people see that to Him belongs all power, by stripping them of all their own strength; that His is the kingdom, and that He will give it to whomsoever He will, and that His is the glory which He will not share with another. But when the Lord is carrying into execution His secret counsels, they are so contrary to the will of the flesh, and so opposed to our thoughts and ways, that we can hardly see His hand in them. Our flesh murmurs and rebels under the heavy strokes. It wants ease, indulgence, and self-gratification, not to be mortified and crucified. If we were wholly left to ourselves, we should choose greedily and eagerly the way of destruction. It is a mercy, then, that the Lord does not leave us wholly to ourselves, but brings down the heart with labour, so that we fall down and there is none to help. People may talk about crying and praying to the Lord, but to be made to cry and pray, really and truly, out of a believing heart, is one of the most trying spots into which the Lord can bring a soul that He has made honest before Him. It is not a little thing that will make us truly pray and cry to the Lord, and often when we do so the Lord seems deaf to the voice of our supplications, and we can get no manifest answer to our petitions. We often have to keep praying and crying on without any testimony that the Lord hears. This is very discouraging, and seems, at times, as if it would, if not stop, at least damp all the prayer of the soul. But it will be our mercy if we still call upon His name and seek His face, and a greater mercy still, yea, the greatest of all mercies, if He bow down His ear and give a manifest answer. You and I have been at this work, at various times, for a good many years, and I hope we may prove that praying breath is not lost breath.

I do not know at present how my place will be filled at L——. I feel much for ——, who is placed in a trying position, and whom I much esteem for consistent conduct and the way in which the cause has lately been carried on. There is a large congregation there, and, I believe, many good people. I have been there almost every year for nearly twenty years, and it much disappointed me not being able to go this time, according to my engagement. It has made me feel as if I never would make engagements again. . . . .

Yours very affectionately,

J. C. P.

CXXX

Cirencester, Sept. 28, 1860.

MY DEAR TIPTAFT,

I was in hopes that I should have been able to see you this week under my own roof, but I was so very unwell a day or two before I proposed to leave, that I felt myself quite unable to take the journey. I still hope, however, if the Lord will, that I may see you before you return. It has been in many respects a very trying dispensation to me to be laid aside just at this peculiar season. I always feel it a great trial to be laid aside, even when I am at home, not only on account of the personal suffering, but also because it so disappoints my own people. But it is much more trying when I am obliged to disappoint congregations from home, as I have been compelled to do under my present affliction. I wish I could see plainly and clearly the Lord's hand in it. I cannot doubt (it would be infidelity to do so) that there is a purpose to be accomplished in it, but at present I cannot penetrate into the mystery. I only hope that the affliction may be sanctified to my soul's good, so that, should it please the Lord to raise me up again, I may have reason to bless His holy name for the present trial. I have reason to hope that my illness last winter was blessed to me, and to others through me; for I certainly had more life and feeling in my soul, and, I believe, in my ministry, as the fruit of it.

But though we prize spiritual blessings above all others, yet our coward flesh shrinks from the trial of affliction through which the blessing comes. God, however, has joined them together, and they cannot be separated. I believe I can say I never had a single spiritual blessing which did not come either in or through affliction or trial; and I also know that we are not fit for spiritual blessings, except by being made so through the furnace. There seems to be no real, earnest cry, or longing desire for a blessing from the Lord Himself, except we are humbled and brought down into some pressing necessity. I have always found that this has been the spot where the most sincere and earnest cries and prayers are made to the Lord, and where the Lord Jesus Christ is made precious to the soul. These afflictions and trials strip, as it were, the world and worldly things off our backs, as well as all our own wisdom, and strength, and righteousness, and this makes us long for spiritual blessings, such as to be taught of the Lord Himself, to have His strength made perfect in our weakness, to be washed from all our sins in His atoning blood, and to be clothed with His glorious and perfect righteousness. And these prayers and desires are not mere words or formal expressions, but the real breathings and earnest desires of a soul which stands feelingly in need of them all. I know this has been my experience since I have been under my present affliction; and, therefore, I do not speak of things at a distance, but near at hand. Hezekiah, on his bed of sickness, could say, "By these things men live, and in all these things is the life of my spirit."

I could wish, if it had been the Lord's will, to have spoken at Bath, Trowbridge, and Leicester, of some of those divine realities which I trust I have seen and known for myself. But it was not to be so, and it becomes me, if the Lord enable, to submit. I am sure I fully deserve to be entirely cast out of His hand, and never again to be made use of, either by tongue or pen; so that if I were to look to myself I should not have far or long to search for the cause of my being laid aside, for I am sure I deserve nothing but the Lord's anger and displeasure, and that for evermore.

Whatever ground others may stand upon, there is one on which I can never stand—no, not for a single moment—and that is my own righteousness. And if we are to have some standing-ground—or how else can we stand for time or eternity?— what rock can there be for our feet but that which God laid in Zion? Being driven from every other standing-place by the law of God, the convictions of our own conscience, and a view of our dreadful sinful heart, we feel compelled to show to others, when called upon to do so, the peril of standing upon such a sandy foundation as self; and having seen and felt something of the blessedness and suitability of the Lord Jesus Christ, we can hold Him up to others as a sure foundation, if the Lord be pleased to reveal it to their hearts.

We had a very good congregation at Abingdon on the Tuesday evening. I felt in a solemn frame of mind, and I hope we had something of the power and presence of the Lord; I think I never knew the Abingdon congregation to listen with so much stillness and attention as on that evening. On the Lord's-day there is usually a good deal of crowding, and this sometimes takes off from the attention; but this year was the quietest and least excited congregation that I have known for several years.

The Temperance Hall was well filled. It was thought about or over four hundred people, and, I understand, if it had not been for a tea-meeting among the Independents we should have been overflowed. I hope I felt some life and liberty in speaking. It is one of the nicest places to speak in (not a chapel) that I was ever in. There is no ceiling, but it is open to the roof, very much like the college halls at the university, which makes it very airy and pleasant, without draught. There is no pulpit, but a raised platform, like that at Birmingham, and a kind of sounding-board behind, which throws the voice well out, so that there is no need of exertion.

I hope the Lord will be with you and the people at Stamford next Lord's-day.

Yours very affectionately,
J. C. P.

CXXXI—To Mr. Grace

Cirencester, Oct. 1, 1860.

My dear Friend,

You have probably heard that I am detained here by one of those attacks upon my chest to which I have now for many years been so subject. Indeed I have been so very unwell as not to be able to take my journey home. I find it a great trial and exercise of mind to be again laid aside by illness, and what makes my illness so trying is, not so much the personal suffering (though that is not slight) as being obliged thereby to disappoint congregations. This has been the case in my present illness as regards Bath, Trowbridge, and especially Leicester. But we must bow before the sovereignty of God, who orders all things after the counsel of His own will, and accomplishes His own purposes in His own manner. Trials, sufferings, afflictions, vexations, and disappointments are our appointed lot; and, though grievous to the flesh, yet when they are sanctified to the soul's good are made to be some of our choicest blessings. But when we are in the furnace we rarely see what benefit it is producing, or what profit is likely to arise to ourselves or to others out of it. Our coward flesh shrinks from the cross, and until submission and resignation are wrought in us by a divine power, and the peaceable fruits of the Spirit begin to show themselves, we cannot bless the Lord for the trial and affliction. It is true that our trials vary as much as our outward circumstances or inward feelings, and each, perhaps, thinks his own trial the heaviest. But, no doubt, infinite wisdom appoints to each vessel of mercy those peculiar trials in nature or degree which are required to work out God's hidden purposes. "What I do," said the Lord to Peter, "thou knowest not now, but thou shalt know hereafter;" and thus time and larger measures of light and grace may show us the reason as well as the needs-be of many afflictive circumstances, which, when we were passing through them, were to us an insoluble enigma. Nay, as out of the bosom of the darkest cloud the most vivid flash of lightning usually shines forth, so out of our darkest hours the brightest light sometimes gleams forth. Those especially who stand up in the Lord's name, if they are to preach with any profit to the tried and exercised family of God, must themselves be well acquainted with the path of tribulation; for how else can they go before the people, or cast up the king's highway, or take up the stumbling-stones? Levity, carelessness, and indifference, with a general hardness and deadness in the things of God, soon creep over the mind, unless it be well weighted with trials and afflictions; and when this spirit prevails in a man's mind, it will manifest itself in his ministry, to the deadening of all life and power in the preaching of the word. In this way we become surrounded with a host of men whose judgments are informed in the letter of truth, but who know little or nothing of its life and power. Not that trials and afflictions have in themselves any power to produce spiritual life and feeling, as they rather work rebellion and death; but the gracious Lord condescends to work in and by them, and to communicate of His grace to the soul that lies at His feet burdened and exercised.

What a mercy it is to have any divine life in the soul, any grace, or any marks of grace; to be made to see and feel the emptiness of the world, the sinfulness of sin, the evils of the heart, and, above all, to see and feel the preciousness of Christ in His bleeding, dying love! There is a reality in the kingdom of God as set up in the heart; and there is a suitability and a preciousness in the Lord Jesus Christ which may be felt, but can never be adequately described. The Lord knows how to support the soul in trials and afflictions; how to draw forth faith, hope, and love upon His most gracious and glorious self, and to give us eventual victory over every foe.

I hope that you have found the Lord with you in your present journey. It is a mercy that the Lord has not left Himself without witness, and that He still has a people whom He teaches by His Holy Spirit to fear, revere, and love His great and holy name. There are some of these, I believe, where you now are, and amongst them our esteemed friend under whose roof you now are. The Lord bless your visit and your mutual conversation on the things which concern your eternal peace. There will come a day when the children of the kingdom will no more be divided as now, even by local distance, when no long journeyings will be needful to bring them together, and, above all, when there will be no divisions and no differences.

Remember me, with all Christian affection, to Mr. Pickering and the friends at Bottesford who may inquire after me.

I am,
Yours affectionately,
J. C. P.

CXXXII—To Mr. Tanner.

Stamford, Nov. 14, 1860.

My dear Friend,

I hope that by this time both you and your dear wife are in some measure reconciled to the departure of your dear son to a foreign shore, and are enabled, in some measure, to see the Lord's hand in it. Time has a wonderful effect in healing grief and soothing sorrow, at least where that sorrow does not arise from sin and guilt, for that is a wound which time can never heal. . . .

You will be glad to hear that, through mercy, I am better than when I left you, and have been enabled to preach on the last two Lord's-days. I still continue, however, weak and tender, and have my fears whether I shall be able to continue preaching throughout the winter. How various are the trials and afflictions of those who desire to fear God, and walk in His ways. But though they may differ in nature and degree, yet they are, for the most part, as much as they can well bear. The Lord, indeed, is very gracious in not laying upon them more than they can bear; but He will give them all enough to find and feel that this world is full of sin and sorrow; that their own hearts are full of evil; and that nothing but the pure, rich, free, superabounding grace of God can save or bless their souls. It seems as if we needed day by day to be taught over and over again our own sinfulness, weakness, and helplessness, and that none but the blessed Lord can do us any real good. Religion is not like any art or science which, when once learnt, is learnt for ever; but is a thing which we are ever forgetting, and ever learning over and over again. Nor can we make any use of our knowledge, experience, or faith. It is like a well that is of no use unless water is drawn out of it by the hand of another. We may have a certain knowledge, both of ourselves and the Lord Jesus, and have had raised up from time to time a living faith in Him; but we cannot make any use of our knowledge or our faith, at least so as to do us any sensible good. The clay cannot mould itself into a vessel; it requires a potter's wheel and a potter's hand. So we are but the clay, and God must be our potter, for we only are what is pleasing in His sight, as we are the work of His hand. It is a great lesson, and yet a painful one, to be made nothing; to feel one's self weaker than the weakest, and viler than the vilest; to be a pauper living upon daily alms, and to be made often to beg, and yet sensibly to get nothing.

People think sometimes how highly favoured ministers are; they view them almost as if they were angels, and were possessed of a faith far beyond the generality of God's people. But if they could see them as they see and feel themselves, they would find that they were men of like passions with themselves, and often in their feelings sunk down lower than many of their hearers; more tried and exercised, more assailed with temptation, and, but for God's grace, more prone to fall. In fact, it must be so. It is necessary that those who stand up to preach to the hearts of others should have a deep acquaintance with their own; that those who have to preach trials and exercises should be well acquainted with what they speak; and that those who set forth the Lord Jesus Christ should know something experimentally of His beauty and blessedness, grace and glory. Unless ministers are well exercised in their own minds they are pretty sure to drop into the spirit of the world, and to depart in their feelings from the life and power of vital godliness. We must be *in* a thing that we may speak feelingly *of* it. You can now tell what a father feels when a son leaves his house for a foreign land; and those who have to pass through a similar experience will at once know that you were in it. So, therefore, unless a minister be feelingly in the things of God by a daily experience, he cannot speak of them with any life, power, or freshness. The life of God must be kept up in his soul, or he cannot be a breast of consolation to the family of God. Now this sometimes makes us very rebellious, that we should have to go through so many trials and temptations to be able to speak a word in season to others. We naturally love a smooth and easy path, and would almost sooner forego the blessing than get it in God's way. But He gives us no choice in the matter; for He leads the blind by a way that they know not. . . .

I hope your dear wife and daughters are as well as when I left you. My love to them, with every kind wish on their behalf. Accept the same from

Your affectionate Friend,

J. C. P.

CXXXIII.—To Mr. R. Tyrrell

Stamford, Nov. 21, 1860.

My dear Friend,

I am obliged to you for your kind letter and your liberal offer to take twenty copies of a sermon from Isaiah xvii. 10, 11, if I could bring it out in a similar way to "Winter afore Harvest." My time is so much occupied with the *Gospel Standard*, and a little work which I hope soon to bring out upon "The Eternal Sonship of our Blessed Lord," that I almost fear whether I should be able to comply with your request. But as my sermons are frequently taken down here by a very excellent reporter, and published once a month, I may, with God's blessing, be perhaps enabled to preach again from the same text at my chapel here, when it could be taken down. But though I may take the text, I am utterly powerless to preach from it, except so far as the Lord is pleased to give me thoughts and words, and to communicate a divine influence to my heart and mouth. Before I preached from that text in London I had spoken from it last year at Oakham; and I was particularly favoured on that occasion, so that, I think, I spoke from it with more power and enlargement of heart and mouth than I did this year at Gower Street. It is surprising, as all experimental ministers know, what a difference there is between the same man at different times; how sometimes he is so shut up that he has scarcely a thought in his heart, or a word on his tongue; and, at others, has his soul filled with a sweet influence, which communicates a flow of spiritual ideas and suitable expressions, even to his own amazement. When I was in London I was very weak, and poorly, and had, if I remember right, on that Lord's-day a severe cold and cough. But the Lord was better to me than all my fears, and brought me through the day, and especially the evening, far beyond my expectation. I do not usually care to have my sermons taken down, but there were two which I preached at Gower Street this year under a peculiar influence, one on the evening of Lord's-day July 15th, from Acts xx. 24, and the other on the last Tuesday evening, July 17th. Perhaps the congregation did not feel them as I did, but they were the two sermons that I should much like to have had taken down, for I was very much favoured in delivering them. What I said on those two occasions has quite passed from my mind, nor can I now recall them; but I should have been glad to leave them as my living and dying testimony to God's truth.

It seems to me that we live in a very awful day, when the shadows of evening are being fast stretched out, and the sun has well-nigh gone down upon the prophets. This awful error of denying the true and essential Sonship of our blessed Lord has taken a deep root in the minds of many doctrinal ministers and churches, and, I fear, has penetrated more into experimental churches than is generally thought to be the case. How, then, can we expect that the Lord should bless those who deny His only begotten Son? But no doubt there is a purpose to be accomplished in all this. It will make a wider and more decided separation between the letter ministers and those who know the truth by sweet experience; and as the latter are enabled more clearly and more experimentally to hold up the blessed Son of God, as the object of the Church's faith and hope, those who know and love His name will cleave with more affection to the men of truth, and be separated more widely from the men of error. All this brings down great hostility upon the head of those who contend earnestly for the faith once delivered to the saints—and I have had a large measure of it; but what is this compared with the testimony of a good conscience, and the conviction that one is labouring in the cause of God and truth?

I was pleased to hear the account that you gave of the good old woman who was blessed in reading "Winter afore Harvest." I have had many sweet testimonies of the Lord's having blessed that little work both to the quickening of those dead in sin, and to the comfort and consolation of some in bondage and distress, through the guilt of sin and the power of temptation. Letter men and presumptuous professors may fight against living experience, the reason being for the most part that it condemns them; but it will have a voice in the consciences of God's people; for it often meets their case, opens up mysteries which have often tried their minds, and casts a clear light upon the path in which the Lord is leading them.

May our desire be to know more of divine things by divine teaching; to see and feel more of our own weakness and helplessness; to have a stronger faith in the blessed Lord, and to have clearer and sweeter manifestations of His love, and blood, and grace. This will produce a separating influence from the world, will give more strength to fight against sin and Satan, and will eventually bring the soul off more than conqueror, through Him who has loved it with an everlasting love.

Yours in the best bonds,

J. C. P.

CXXXIV —To Mr. Parry

Stamford, Dec. 3, 1860.

My dear Friend,

You will probably have seen by the *Gospel Standard* that I have been in some measure restored from my late illness; but it is a great trial to me, and no doubt to the people also, that I should be so weak and tender, for it makes my preaching so uncertain, and has such a tendency to scatter the congregation.

Were I in the full enjoyment of health and strength, and above all, were the Lord to favour me with His presence and blessing, I should not lack a congregation either here or at Oakham; and, indeed, I might say, if I were favoured with the strength of body enjoyed by so many ministers, I should, as far as I can judge, find hearers in other places. But no doubt there are wise reasons why I should not be thus made use of, for we know however dark and mysterious things may appear to our mind, the Lord cannot err in His dealings with His children. It is my earnest desire that my long affliction may be deeply blessed, not only to my own soul but for the good also of others, and that will throw a blessed light upon the whole path from beginning to end. You may depend upon it that in my solitude, for I spend most of my time alone, many thoughts pass through my mind with many exercises on various things. I have thought sometimes that there are few temptations, and especially inward temptations, that I have not experienced and been exercised by; and I have felt and found in them that none but the Lord Himself can deliver me out of them, or overrule them, for my spiritual good. When we are passing through various temptations we cannot well speak of them, but when we are in some good measure delivered from them, then we can trace them out and speak of them as things painfully known. I am well convinced that no man knows anything to any real profit, except what he is taught in his own soul. All true religion must be got from the Lord, and that only will stand which He Himself has wrought with a divine power in the heart. This, I trust, was shown me many years ago, and impressed upon my heart so that I have never been able to take up for myself, or preach to others, any religion but that which cometh down from above, from the Father of lights, with whom is no variableness, neither shadow of turning. And I believe also that true saving religion must be got in the furnace, and for the most part through trials, temptations, and afflictions. At any rate, I am sure that such a religion not only shines brightest, but wears best and lasts longest. Nor, indeed, have I any union or communion with any other religion, though I could only wish I had more of it in my own soul.

I am sorry to hear so sad an account of poor Mrs. T——. I do hope that the Lord may appear for her and bless her with some manifestation of His pardoning love. It is a mercy that she is delivered from trusting in her own righteousness, and is enabled, however dimly, to look to the atoning blood, finished work, and glorious righteousness of the blessed Lord. I have often thought what sweet and blessed words those were which dropped from His sacred lips when upon earth, which I need not quote at length, for you will find them, John iii. 14—16. It is not our knowledge, or wisdom, or gifts, or abilities, or usefulness, or anything of the kind that can save us, but looking unto the Lord

Jesus Christ, and being blessed with a living faith in Him. Many a poor creature who has scarcely been able to say anything during life, and been seemingly outshone by great professors of religion, has received that into his soul, dropped into his heart, as it were, from the mouth of God, which has saved him with an everlasting salvation, whilst the other has sunk into eternity without hope. So I would encourage every poor, tried, tempted soul still to look, and still to long, still to seek, and still to knock till the Lord appears, for it is in this way that deliverance is obtained, Christ revealed, mercy manifested, and pardon sealed upon the heart.

O that I could be both as a Christian and as a minister, what I see and feel a Christian should be, for I feel to come sadly short of even my own standard of one or the other! There is a general complaint of the low state of things in the Church of God. But if ever there be a revival out of it, I am well convinced through what means as an instrument that revival must come. It must be through a pouring out of the blessed Spirit upon the ministers. It was so on the day of Pentecost; for the disciples were bidden to tarry at Jerusalem until they were endued with power from on high; and we find that it was through this power being then given them that God wrought in the hearts of His people.

I was glad to hear that poor old Sarah Giddings is so favoured. She is another testimony that your prayer under the apple-tree was accepted. Surely we can both look back to my coming to Allington as a marked event in our lives, for we have known both the dead and the living to have testified that the blessing of God rested upon my testimony in the little chapel. It is not a little temporary excitement, or what is called hearing well, that proves a ministry to be owned of God, but that it abides in the heart, stretches through life, and reaches down to the very swellings of Jordan. I hope I can say, to the praise, honour, and glory of God, that some of those who have been blessed either in hearing my voice or in reading my sermons, have borne upon a dying bed their testimony that God had blessed the word to their souls. I am sure I feel in myself one of the most unworthy of all men that the Lord should condescend to speak in, by, and through me, to the hearts of His people; but I know that He will send by whom He will send, that He chooses His own instruments, works in His own way, and does His own will. Oh, that He would bless and favour my soul with His manifested presence, keep me in His fear all the day long, sanctify to me all my trials and afflictions, bless me in life, be with me in death, and land me safe in a happy eternity!

I hope that those who follow you may never sell the truth out of the chapel, and that they would rather convert it into cottages than let error come within the doors.

My daughter is still at Leicester. I miss her, as I find her very useful as a secretary. I told her when she accepted the office that she would find it no sinecure, and I believe she has proved my words to be true, though nothing can exceed her kindness and readiness to help me in my correspondence and occupation in carrying on the *Standard*. As a specimen of the work which she had to do I dictated a letter to a Scotch minister, which filled six sheets of the largest sized note paper. Several friends wish me to put it in the *Gospel Standard*, and I think I probably shall do so. It is on the subject of the law not being a believer's rule of life. Our friend William Tiptaft invited him to preach at Abingdon, and there he got into conversation with him and J. Kay upon the subject of the law, and the Scotchman was so shocked by the views which were expressed by our friends on the subject that he fairly took flight and would not preach, though engaged to do so. He wrote in consequence to W. T. upon the subject, but could get no answer from him. So at last he wrote to me several long letters begging most earnestly for answers. So I was compelled to take up the subject, though I could scarcely afford the time. And when I had written it it struck me it might do for the *Gospel Standard*, as many children of God who are sound in the truth, though they cannot explain their own views, can understand them when they are put forth by others; and as those friends who saw the letter wished me to put it into the *Standard* it seemed to concur with my own feelings, and therefore I probably shall do so. . . . .

Yours very affectionately,

J. C. P.

CXXXV—To Mr. Grace

Stamford, January 2nd, 1861.

My dear Friend,

* * * * * *

The address, too, requires some thought and labour, as not only must it be in great degree original, that is to say, not a repetition of former addresses, but in some way adapted to the readers of the work. It is more easy to see how such things should be done, or to criticise them after they are done, than to do them. The difficulty is to write with some sweet savour upon the spirit, and whilst all appearance of teaching is laid aside, yet to speak with that degree of authority and power which becomes those who stand forward to instruct or admonish others. I have no doubt you understand my meaning, as it is so analogous to preaching. If a man cannot preach with some authority and savour he seems little qualified for such an office; and yet the assumption of any undue authority would be felt by the people as unbecoming his position. But it is the Lord, and the Lord alone, who can commend both what we speak and what we write to the consciences of His people; and there is in truth, as applied to the heart by the power of God, a weight and an authority which is not to be found in any assumption of the priestly office.

I am more and more convinced what error there is in the professing Church, and how we seem fallen on those evil days when perilous times were to come. I used, some years ago, in reading Mr. Huntington's writings, to wonder at two things: 1. The erroneous men that he had to deal with. 2ndly, his severe language against them. But I can now see that we have just the same men in our day, and just the same errors, and though I would not use Mr. Huntington's language because I have not his experience, his discernment, or his authority, yet I can see that such language was, in a measure, deserved, and that it was zeal for his Master and for the truth, that made him so denounce error and erroneous men.

I preached here on Christmas-day and did not suffer any injury, though the thermometer was lower than it has been for many years. I feel it to be a mercy not to be wholly laid aside, as it keeps the people together, and, I trust, is sometimes made profitable to their souls as well as giving me the opportunity to preach what extends to a wider circle than my own congregation. How very differently the Lord, for He is the author of all good, deals with different instruments; and yet how His wisdom is displayed in the various circumstances of His all-wise arrangement. You, for instance, are favoured with a good measure of health and strength, and have a regular and large congregation; whilst I am for the most part but a poor invalid shut up in a narrow corner of the land. And yet we hope we are both filling up the exact position which the Lord has designed, and so far as He is making use of us are qualified to do the work which He has appointed us to do. It is a blessed thing when we can feel nothing in ourselves, but all in Him, and are blessed with a single eye to His glory and His people's good. We have just entered upon a new year, and who can tell whether we shall see its close? I wish for myself that I may live more to the Lord's praise during the year now present, if my life be spared, than I did through the year just passed. And yet I am very sure if I am left to myself I shall spend a worse year as regards living to the Lord than I did during that now for ever gone. We have seen in one sense the best of our days, for youth is departed from us; and though you enjoy a larger measure of health and strength than myself, yet every coming year will rob you more and more of both. I do earnestly desire for myself that my last days may be my best days, and that when my sun sets it may not go down in a cloud, but shine the brighter before it passes altogether out of sight. But this, like every other gift, must be all of superabounding grace, for, indeed, nothing short of that can bless us in life or death.

I have read the sermon which Mr. —— lately preached at your chapel. It is not marked by any great depth of experience, nor does it bear the stamp of great ability of mind, but there is something very sound, savoury, and sweet in it, and in many points I could see with it very nicely eye to eye, and feel with it, I trust, heart to heart. Amongst the men of experimental truth how few we have who are gifted with any great ability to set it forth. Sermons sometimes come across me which are preached by men ignorant experimentally of the truth, and scarcely sound, indeed, even in the letter; but as regards clearness and force of language, and ability in putting forth their views, they seem to me far to outshine the experimental ministers of our day. This cannot be because the subject of experience is not calculated for clear and vigorous expression, for where do we find more beautiful writing than in the works of Mr. Huntington and the poetry of Joseph Hart, not to mention the Pilgrim of the immortal tinker? With what power, too, our esteemed friend Mr. W. Gadsby used to preach! So that there is nothing in experimental preaching which is unsuitable to clearness of thought, vigour of language and force of expression. Besides which, there is in it a sweet savour and a blessed unction when God speaks through the lips, which is true eloquence, for it reaches the heart and produces an abiding effect upon the soul. It is true that God by the "foolishness of preaching saves them that believe;" but the Apostle does not mean that the preaching itself is foolish, but that the effect is so far beyond the cause that it may be considered in that sense a foolish, because in itself a weak instrument. Please excuse my running on at this rate, but very often in dictating letters I think aloud instead of writing, and thus sometimes may burden my friends with unprofitable thoughts.

Yours very affectionately,

J. C. P.

CXXXVI —To Mr. Parry

Stamford, Jan. 11, 1861.

My dear Friend,

You will be desirous, I have no doubt, to hear how I am this severe weather. I may well call it severe, for we have not had a winter for some years during which the thermometer has been so low; and at present there does not seem much prospect of an alteration. I am thankful, then, to say, that though I feel the cold, yet I am quite as well as I could possibly expect, and, indeed, I may say, much better than when I saw you last at Cirencester. I preached last Lord's-day in the morning, and think that I should have stayed for the afternoon had I not made arrangements to come home. The weather was so extremely severe that we had not our usual congregation; still there were quite as many as could be expected, considering that very many of our friends come out of the country, and no doubt they felt a little uncertainty whether I should be out to preach in consequence of the extreme severity of the weather. . . . You know that for many years I have taken an interest in agricultural matters, not only as having friends amongst the tillers of the soil, but as feeling its general importance to the whole country. It has struck me, therefore, that this severe frost may be mercifully sent to dry and pulverise the hard clays after they have been so saturated with last year's continual dripping; so that if the Lord be pleased to give us a suitable spring, and a warm and dry summer, we may see the benefit of what now pinches our frames, chills our blood, and nips our fingers. What a deep fund of unbelief and infidelity there is in the heart of man, ever ready to start up like a wild beast from its lair and seize hold of any coming forth of the life of God in the actings of faith! I have sometimes thought that it is scarcely possible for any amongst the living family of God to have a heart so full of unbelief and infidelity as I carry in my bosom. But I know this, that the grace of God, and the grace of God alone, is able to subdue it. My wonder is, not that all do not believe, but that any do; it is not the multitude of unbelievers which surprises me, for this I know all men are, but that any should, by the power of God, have their unbelief subdued and overthrown, and the grace of faith communicated and kept alive in their breast.

We are entered upon another year. The last, as you will remember I said in the pulpit when I was at Allington, was an eventful one, and we do not know what circumstances lie hidden in the bosom of 1861 to make it even more eventful than 1860. We are no longer young. Our families are growing up around us; they are the generation that is pushing us out of our place, as a young healthy shoot pushes off and displaces a decaying one. We feel, and that more deeply and more sensibly every day, that we are passing away out of this time state; and when we look around what is there abiding? for we all seem like the passengers by a railway, all of whom are journeying by the same means of conveyance, and though each drops off from the train at different stations, yet all eventually come to a terminus where they leave the line. As then we see and feel that all is passing away, what a mercy it is if we can look beyond this vain scene to that which abides for ever and ever! "We have no abiding city here," is a lesson which the Lord writes upon the heart of all His pilgrims; and as it is more deeply engraved upon their breast, and cut into more legible characters, they look up and out of themselves to that City which hath foundations, of which the maker and builder is God. You, no doubt, feel something of this from day to day, and so far as you do, it will keep you from looking forward too anxiously to, or thinking too much of, the house which they are building for you at Allington. It is very blessed when we can use the favours of God in providence without abusing them; can see His kind hand in the gift and not make an idol of it; can bless Him for His providential mercies, and yet feel that without Himself they are not only worthless but miserable. How many have lived all their lives in beautiful houses, have never known a day's hunger, have eaten of the fat and drunk of the sweet all the days of their life, have lain down at night in a luxurious bed, where they have felt neither cold nor frost; and yet at last when their mortal career has come to a close have made their bed in hell! When I say this, I may add that I sincerely hope that you may have a comfortable house, that your life may be spared long to live in it, and health be granted that neither house nor life may be a burden. But with all that, I wish for you, and I wish for myself, a house not made with hands, eternal in the heavens, with which we may be clothed when the earthly house of this tabernacle is dissolved and reduced to its native dust. Even the troubles and trials which we meet with in the way are so far made blessings as they become thorns to prevent us settling down in our nest and counting our days as the sand. How often the very circumstance on which we most set our heart is made to be the source of the keenest trial! And how many have built houses, and either not lived to go into them, or have soon yielded up their breath when they have taken possession of them. Poor Mr. M——, no doubt, promised himself many years of enjoyment in his new house; but the Almighty Disposer of events had ordered it otherwise, and whilst he suffers a Sally Durnford, and a Nanny Benger to creep on to the extreme verge of life, mows down in the prime of his years the father of a family, and the possessor of the finest farm, perhaps, in your county. What lessons such things would teach us if our eyes were more open to see, our ears to hear, and our hearts to feel their solemn import! But I am well convinced that however enlightened our judgments may be, it must be the immediate power of God to lay these things with any real weight and profitable influence upon the heart.

I am sorry to hear so unfavourable an account of poor Mrs. T——. May the gracious Lord condescend to support her mind under her bodily affliction, and, above all, to give her a blessed token for good, and a sweet testimony of her interest in the love and blood of the Lamb. This may be delayed, as it was with poor Mrs. C——; but delays are not denials, and God is faithful to His promises, as well as to His own work of grace upon the heart. He will never despise the work of His own hands, but will graciously perfect that which concerneth His people. And what can concern them so deeply as the salvation of their immortal soul? What are all concerns to this grand concern? If that be right, how can anything else be wrong? If that be wrong, how can anything else be right? She has lived to an advanced period of life, has no anxiety about leaving children behind her to battle with a rough, ungodly world; and her only earthly tie, besides the natural clinging to life which all have, is a kind and affectionate husband. So that if the Lord be but once pleased to smile upon her soul, and give her a testimony of His pardoning love, she may look up out of her affliction and say, "Lord, now lettest thou thy servant depart in peace, for mine eyes have seen thy salvation."

You will find more and more, if your life be spared, that there will be a gradual dropping off of your members; and you may expect well-known faces gradually to disappear from the pews. But the Lord is able to give you fresh accessions, both of members and hearers, and thus fill up your number, and, it may be, put fresh life and feeling into your midst. May He do this if it be His will for His great name's sake.

In speaking about the future, I feel myself compelled to do so with a great degree of hesitation. Still, it is necessary, for the sake of others as well as one's self, to make arrangements for the coming summer. I think, then, if life be spared, and health be given, of going to London for the last three Lord's-days in June; and in that case I should like, if spared, to come on to Allington for the first three in July. I should be glad to give you four Lord's-days, but I fear I shall not be able, as having been so often laid aside, I feel it necessary not to be away so much from home.

Yours very affectionately,

J. C. P.

CXXXVII—To Mr. Tanner

Stamford, January 31, 1861.

My dear Friend,

The end of the month is with me usually the little leisure season that I am able to enjoy, and during that brief respite I endeavour as much as I can to pay off those arrears of correspondence which I am almost sure to contract. I therefore embrace this opportunity to send you a few lines in answer to your last friendly and affectionate letter.

You will be pleased to hear that I am much better than I was when I was under your hospitable roof, and have been enabled, with God's help and blessing, to resume my ministry. The weather here, as over all England, was extremely severe; but yet I did not feel it nearly as much as I did the preceding winter, and went out and preached upon Christmas Day, when the thermometer was not many degrees above zero. It was in many respects a singular providence which tethered me so long at your house, but I have often viewed it as a display of the kindness of the Lord that, during my illness, I was brought under a roof which afforded me such a suitable and such a comfortable abode during that season of affliction. I hope never to forget the liberal and unvarying kindness displayed both by yourself and your dear wife and daughters, which, though they could not remove, yet much alleviated the affliction. Why it pleased God to lay me aside on that particular occasion I have not yet seen; but no doubt there were reasons known to Him who is wise in counsel and of infinite mercy. I have thought sometimes of the comparison which you very naturally instituted between the healthy looks and burly frame of Mr. S. and my own appearance at that time. But how soon the Lord laid His afflicting hand upon him, and how he, too, was silenced for a time as I then was. So it is not health, nor the appearance of it, which promises any endurance; for as the worm Jacob can, with God's help, thresh the mountains, so, without His supporting aid, the strongest faint and the healthiest fall. How many strong, vigorous men have I, within these last thirty years, known to fall into the grave like blossoms touched with a May frost; and here am I still maintained in life, who many no doubt years ago had pronounced unable to survive a few months or years. I have sometimes wished that it had pleased the Lord to take me to Himself thirty years ago, when I was laid aside with a serious illness, from which, indeed, I have never fully recovered. How many sins and sorrows should I have been spared! But such was not God's will, and if He has been pleased to make any use of me by tongue or pen since that period, I have every reason to adore His inscrutable wisdom and His matchless mercy. I little thought then that I should have to occupy the position which the Lord seems to have assigned me in His providence and grace. I never sought it, and have only been maintained in it by a connection of circumstances which seem to have combined not only to put, but to keep me in a position from which many a time I would have gladly escaped. Some persons seem naturally fond of pushing themselves before men, which makes quiet and obscurity to be their torment; and others appear animated with a spirit of strife and contention, so that, like a sea-gull, they never seem so happy as in a storm. But I can say for myself that peace and quiet have always been to me naturally an object of greater desire than to occupy any prominent position, or to be engaged in contention and strife. But the fact is, that if a man, from the dictates of an honest conscience, and from the teaching of the blessed Spirit in the heart, is led to contend earnestly for the faith once delivered to the saints, he necessarily becomes a man of strife. This was just the case with the prophet Jeremiah: because he was compelled to declare what God showed him, and what he knew to be true, he therefore became a man of strife to the whole earth. He did not seek war; but it was thrust upon him by those who hated him for the truth that was in him.

I hope, my dear friend, that the Lord has led both of us to know and to believe, as well as to love, His precious truth. Having therefore this knowledge, this faith in, this love to, His truth, we cannot frame to ourselves the enmity which is felt by those who are ignorant of it in its power and preciousness. It is this which stirs up the enmity of their heart, and this being the case, need we wonder at the enmity manifested by them against all who know and love the truth, and in a more especial manner against those who proclaim it by tongue or pen? I ought to be by this time pretty well seasoned to the attacks of men who oppose the truth from an ignorance of its power as experimentally felt. I do not know whether you have seen any of the late pamphlets which have been written against me by the opponents of the true and proper Sonship of our blessed Lord. As far as regards myself I pay but little heed to them. The truth of God is far beyond and far above us all, whether we defend it or whether we oppose it. The Son of God is like the natural sun, to which He is compared, as being called the Sun of righteousness. The rays of the glorious orb of day are not impaired by the bats and owls, which hate it and flee from it into their dark caverns; nor are they heightened by the thousands of gladdened eyes to whom they are a guiding and a warning light. In a few years those who have advocated and those who have opposed the highest title and most glorious name of our blessed Lord will alike have passed away; but He will still be what He ever was—the Son of the Father in truth and love. He does not need our advocacy to those who see Him by the eye of faith, any more than the literal sun needs our praise when after a cloudy or inclement season it shines forth brightly once more, as it has done this day. Yet are we glad, as opportunity serves, to set forth His worthy praise, and, indeed, cannot but do so when our heart is in any measure softened with His grace, and our lips touched with a live coal from off the altar. The tongue of mortals, and, indeed, of immortals, can but faintly show forth His praise; but it is our mercy to be on the side of His friends, and not be ranked amongst the number of His foes.

* * * * *

Yours very affectionately,

J. C. P.

CXXXVIII —To Mr. Jacob

Stamford, Feb. 6th, 1861.

Dear Friend,

I was sorry to learn from your letter that the Lord has been pleased to visit you and your family with such heavy strokes.* There are few things more heartrending to a parent than to have his children torn from him by death; but we see that this was the appointed lot of some of God's most eminent saints. Look, for instance, at poor Jacob, whose grey hairs he felt would be brought

* Mr. Jacob lost a son and two daughters by scarlet fever.

down in sorrow to the grave by the loss of his beloved Joseph; for, though he was not really dead, yet he was such as much in his father's feelings as if he had actually seen his dead body torn to pieces. And look also at David. How deeply he felt the loss of Absalom, so that he would, in his feelings, gladly have died for him. There is only one way whereby one who fears God can be reconciled to such painful dispensations, and that is by submission to the sovereignty of Him who cannot err. This will not indeed heal the wound, but it will prevent it from rankling, and from what is worse than any affliction, viz., rebelling in our feelings against so kind and gracious a God as has watched over us with such care and tenderness for so many years. It is a great mercy that the Lord has so constituted us that time has a great effect in softening the grief that is felt under family bereavements; and thus, by degrees, the heavy weight of the affliction passes off the mind. I hope that it has pleased the Lord not only to give you submission, and your wife also, under these afflicting strokes, but also to make them, in some good measure, a blessing to your soul. From whatever quarter affliction comes it has a voice; and if we have but ears to hear, we shall find God speaking in it. This is the grand difference between those who fear God and those who fear Him not, that the former see God in everything, and the latter see God in nothing. Thus affliction brings no benefit whatever to the one, but often yields the greatest blessing to the other; and even if the child of grace do feel at times much rebellion under the stroke, yet usually sooner or later, when the soul has been humbled thereby, the Lord appears and sanctifies the affliction.

I am glad to learn that you are so comfortable under Mr. Gunner's ministry, and hope that you may find more and more reason to bless God that you have been brought under it. There is nothing so precious to a believing heart as the truth, when applied to the soul by the power of God. The Lord ever will bless His own truth; but how can we expect Him to bless error, or that He will make a lie to be profitable?

I believe that the end will show that there will be no reason to regret the controversy which has been so warmly carried on about the Sonship of Christ, especially in the metropolis. The effect will be to draw a clearer and sharper line of distinction between the men who hold the truth and those who have drunk in the error. You probably have heard or seen some of the pamphlets which have been launched against me on the subject. I have just looked at them, but no more, as I soon saw enough of their spirit to throw them aside. When men manifest such carnality and such bitterness we want no other proof that they are not taught of God. They cannot see it themselves, nor can their admirers see it in them, but those who know the truth by divine teaching and by divine testimony see at a glance where such men are, and know that they are not under that holy anointing which teacheth all things, and is truth and no lie. But as I have sent forth my little book on the subject I shall not take the trouble to answer the various pamphlets that erroneous men may write against me. I am, through mercy, better in health, and hope that the Lord may be pleased to continue to me that inestimable blessing, both for my own sake and those amongst whom I labour. My love to, and sympathy with, yourself and your wife under your afflictions and trials.

Yours affectionately in the Lord,
J. C. P.

CXXXIX —To Mr. Grace

Stamford, March 1, 1861.

My dear Friend,

I am sure that the friends at Oakham will have great pleasure in receiving the word of grace and truth from your lips, and may the God of all grace come with you there to bless your own soul, both out of the pulpit and in it, and to make the word a blessing to His people. There are remarkable instances sometimes of the Lord's special grace at such opportunities. Often a servant of God has gone in His providence to a strange place, and the Lord has directed a special word on such an occasion to some one's heart, who then either for the first time heard the truth, or, if not so in the letter, heard it for the first time then with power. Our dear friends Gadsby and Warburton were much blessed in this way, going as they did from place to place. A blessing often rests upon the servants of God in this way, of which they never hear. Indeed, the Lord in mercy often hides from them the good they do, lest they should be puffed up by it and think themselves something when they are nothing.

It would seem a great blessing if the Lord would raise up more ministers to feed the churches; for, indeed we may say "the harvest is great and the labourers few." Everything looks very dark and gloomy just now. This sad error has infected very many, and its advocates seem more and more bold and daring. But the Lord reigneth. He can and will maintain His own truth. It has always met with the greatest opposition, and yet it has come out triumphant over all. Grace be with you and peace from God the Father and our Lord Jesus Christ.

Yours very affectionately,
J. C. P.

CXL —To a Friend

Stamford, March 8, 1861.

My dear Sir,

In replying to your interesting letter I feel that I must, for various reasons, confine myself chiefly to one point; and it is that on which you have consulted me, viz., the meaning of the word αἰώνιος in classical authors. I do not, however, attach much value to the meaning of words in classical Greek when transferred thence to the pages of the New Testament. Language can only be the reflex of a nation's thoughts and knowledge, for it is the vehicle whereby they are mutually communicated to the members of that community. Thus, if from ignorance of the idea of eternity, the thought was not present to the Greek mind, or if present was only so in a dim shadowy form, then the word communicative of the idea would possess the same uncertainty and obscurity, for language can never rise beyond thought. The Greek lived only for time; eternity was not in his thoughts as it is in ours; and though he spoke of immortal gods and of an Elysium for good men after life, yet it was rather a negative idea of something beyond death than such a positive one as we now entertain from the fact of possessing an inspired revelation. I merely throw out these hints to show you how uncertain all deductions must be which are founded upon the meaning of the word in classical writers. We must look for the derivation of the word αἰώνιος to a higher source than the Greek. It is derived from a Sanscrit verb "ay" which signifies "to go, to pass by." This root we find in the Greek verbs ἴω, εἶμι and the Latin "eo." From this original root comes the Sanscrit word "âyus" signifying "time," whence are derived the Greek words "αἰές," "αἰών" and the Latin "ævum" which itself is derived from the Æolic form "αἰϝών" in which is the ancient digamma. The idea, then, is of something that is ever passing on—flowing forward, as it were, into the future. This is the reason why the word bears the two significations attached to it both of time and of eternity—each being viewed as something flowing onward, without any reference to the termination or non-termination of the period. Thus when a Greek thought or spoke of eternal life he did not attach to it necessarily the idea of an unceasing duration, but of an undefined something that flowed on out of sight. He viewed time, so to speak, as a river flowing by, and his idea of eternity was the flowing on of that river till it was lost out of sight. This idea seems confirmed by the other Greek word which is used in classical authors and also in the New Testament to signify everlasting, viz., ἀΐδιος, which signifies "unseen;" as if the Greek looked forward into the dark womb of eternity as something hidden from sight.

I cannot, therefore, furnish you with any decisive passages from the classics by which you may either substantiate or overthrow the meaning which you attach to the term; for if the word itself is shadowy and uncertain the context in which it is found will partake of the same character. Plato, for instance, uses the word in connection with glory, but his view of eternal glory was very different from the Apostle's, 2 Cor. iv. 17; for the Greek philosopher looked not beyond the limits of this time state, whilst the saint and servant of God could look up to the bliss arising out of the pleasures which are at God's right hand for evermore.

I conceive, then, that the only safe way of ascertaining the truth is by carefully examining, under the light of the Spirit's teaching, those passages in the New Testament in which the word occurs. And I cannot but think myself that as the same word is applied by the blessed Lord Himself to the punishment of the wicked and to the life of the righteous, Matt. xxv. 46, the duration of the one must run parallel with the duration of the other.

I am sorry to read of the distress through which your mind has passed on this subject, but if you have a sweet evidence in your own breast that you have passed from death unto life and shall no more come into condemnation, it will be your wisdom and mercy to bow with all submission to the sovereignty of God, knowing that the Judge of all the earth must do right.

I can only conclude with my best wishes that you may enjoy the Lord's presence and be led by Him into all truth.

I am,

Yours very sincerely for truth's sake,

J. C. P.

CXLI—To Mr. S. S.*

Stamford, March 22, 1861.

DEAR FRIEND,

I must confess that I feel much difficulty in giving you a suitable reply to your letter; for, on the one hand, I do not wish to say anything that may hurt your mind, or, on the other, to advance anything contrary to the feelings of my own conscience. Besides which, I have long felt that one man is a very unfit and incompetent judge of the leadings of God with another, especially in matters of providence. But while I say this, and therefore wish to judge very tenderly and cautiously of your present position, I cannot conceal from myself, and therefore should not conceal from you, that you are placed in a very trying and difficult position, in which, if I mistake not, you will find it extremely hard to act consistently with your principles and your profession. This difficulty you have in some good measure incurred by withdrawing yourself from the communion of the Church of England, and making a public profession of your faith in Christ in the ordinance of baptism. Now if you depart from your profession by acceding to the bishop's wishes to take the sacrament in the Church of England, how inconsistently you will be acting with that profession, and what guilt and trouble you may thereby bring upon your conscience. You were in some measure free to do this, except

* To Mr. S. S., when butler to the late Bishop of Carlisle.

as held back by conscience, before you joined a Particular Baptist church. But having once done so, it seems to me that you are bound by the very profession that you have made not to receive the sacrament in the Church of England. And I think you might very respectfully and yet very firmly name to the bishop the circumstances under which you are placed. He is perhaps not altogether aware of the firm and decided views which the Particular Baptists have about not partaking of the communion with unbaptised persons, and especially with such a mixed multitude as receive the sacrament in the Establishment. I cannot but think that if you were to lay before his lordship that this is with you a matter of conscience, and would explain to him the strong views and feelings which those have with whom you are connected upon the point, he would hardly press it.

I do feel myself strongly upon this point; and it is one on which I think all should stand firm who have ever made a public profession of their faith in Christ by being baptised in His holy name.

It must also be a great trial to you not to be allowed to go to chapel when you are in the country; but on this I cannot speak so decidedly, as much must be left to a man's own conscience.

If the Lord has indeed, as you hope, led you to your present situation, I hope He will guide and direct you how to act for His glory and your soul's own good.

I am sure you must be in a very trying position; and I have often thought that no persons are placed in greater difficulties than the higher class of servants who have been accustomed to live in high families.

Yours very sincerely,
J. C. P.

CXLII—To Mr. Grace

Stamford, April 12, 1861.

My dear Friend,

We shall be happy to see you to dine with us on this day week, and I hope we may have the sweet presence of the Lord in our mutual communication. There is a meeting together for the better and a meeting together for the worse, and usually when it is not for the one it is for the other. There is such a thing as carnalising each other's mind, and with God's help and blessing there is also a spiritualising of it. Paul desired to come to Rome that he might impart unto the people a spiritual gift, not only to the end that they might be established, but that he also might be comforted together with them by the exercise of their mutual faith. Those that feared the Lord in ancient times "spake often one to another;" and the Lord graciously heard and put them down in the book of His remembrance. There is very little real spiritual conversation in our day; and one would hardly think that persons had heaven much in their hearts who have the things of heaven so little in their lips. It is a sad mark of the cold and lifeless state into which the Church of God has sunk, that whilst there is so much bitterness and strife there is so little real union and love. It is said of Naphtali that "he giveth goodly words;" but why? Because he was "satisfied with favour and full with the blessing of the Lord;" for though many years separated the blessings pronounced upon him by Jacob and Moses, yet he was the same character in the eyes of each, as instructed and inspired by the Holy Ghost. I hope that you may come up from Brighton with Naphtali's experience as "a hind let loose," and may give goodly words both at Oakham and Grantham.

Yours very affectionately,

J. C. P.

CXLIII —To Mr. Tanner

Stamford, May 3rd, 1861.

My dear Friend,

I have no doubt that you have been expecting for some time an answer to your kind and affectionate letter. Indeed, my own conscience has not been slow in reminding me of my neglect. But in this, as in many other instances, to will has been present with me, but how to perform that which was good I found not. You are well aware how much occupied my time is, and what a hindrance in the way of work is a weak tabernacle. Thus the combination of these two things—much to do and little strength to do it, has a great tendency to throw one's work sadly into arrear.

I am sorry to say that just now I am labouring under one of my chest attacks which prevented me preaching here last Lord's-day, and will prevent me preaching on the one now approaching. Still, as I am mending, I hope it may please the Lord soon to restore me to my former work. I sometimes think I will make no more engagements to go from home, as it is often a matter of uncertainty whether I shall be able to fulfil them. Still, hitherto, the Lord hath helped me, and though occasionally I have been obliged to disappoint expecting friends, yet upon the whole I have been strengthened in my work far beyond all my expectations; and this encourages me not to give up until absolutely compelled. . . . . . . I hope that our mind when we are under any sweet influence from above, is led up into higher and more blessed things than anything which time and sense can afford. There is something very peculiar and very distinct in the operations of the blessed Spirit upon the heart. Those who know nothing of divine things by divine teaching are easily satisfied with a name to live and a mere form of godliness; but this will not and cannot satisfy any one who really possesses the life and power of God in his soul. But what different persons we are according to the influence of the flesh and the influence of the Spirit! and how we find these two principles ever opposing and conflicting one with another! But how totally different they are in their origin, nature, and end! How I look round sometimes and see how men are lost and buried in the poor vanities of this earthly scene, without perhaps one desire heavenward! How they all seem to live as if man were but like a beast whose life was for ever finished when death cut the thread! How totally unexercised about their eternal state and their fitness to stand before a holy, just, and righteous God! On the other hand how exercised is a Christian, sometimes nearly all day long, with divine realities —sometimes up and sometimes down, sometimes full of unbelief, and sometimes able to believe with a loving heart; sometimes as dark as midnight, and sometimes favoured with divine light in his soul; sometimes as dead and lifeless as though he were altogether dead in sin, and sometimes feeling the springing up of divine life like a brook. But there is one thing which I seem to see and feel, viz.—how little any one, even the most highly favoured, really sees or knows of the kingdom of God. No doubt in this time state very little can be really seen or known of it; but even so far as faith is privileged to enter into the things revealed in the word of truth, how little comparatively is seen, felt, and known. What deep mines of truth there are in the word of God which seem at present not broken up or brought to view, I mean so as to become coined into money for the enriching of the soul. And how we need the blessed Spirit to break up for us these rich mines, and thus to give us an inheritance of these deep treasures! But I am sure that we require a spiritual mind to understand and enjoy the word of God, and that is the reason why it is so little prized, believed in, and loved. We need a subjection of mind to the word of truth, what the Scripture calls the "obedience of faith," that we may take it, in the simplicity of a childlike spirit, as our guide and rule, as our instruction and consolation, as bringing eternal realities near to our minds, and lifting us up into a vital apprehension of them. But as we attempt to do this there ensues a conflict, so that we cannot do the things that we would. Unbelief, infidelity, reasoning objections, strong suspicions, subtle questionings, spring up in the mind; and sometimes rebellion, blasphemy, hardness of heart, and desperate enmity against what is revealed, so that in the dust of battle all believing views seem lost, and all the soul can say is, "I am full of confusion." My friend, I believe, is no stranger to these conflicts, and no doubt finds them a maul upon the head of pride and self-righteousness, as well as giving him the tongue of the learned and enabling him to speak a word in season to him that is weary. I do think that an unexercised minister is little else but a plague and a burden to the living family of God. These want their exercises entered into and the work of the Spirit traced out upon their heart; and not only so, but with that life, power, and freshness which alone spring from the soul of the minister being kept alive in the path of trial and temptation. When we were together we used sometimes to exchange thoughts upon these subjects, and I believe we saw for the most part eye to eye upon them.

Illness has often been made a profitable season to my soul. The Lord knows best how to deal with us, what burdens to lay upon our back, and through what afflictions to lead us to His heavenly kingdom.

Yours very affectionately,
J. C. P.

CXLIV —To Mr. Tiptaft

Stamford, May 15, 1861.

My dear Tiptaft,

It is not often that you have been at Allington at this season of the year. I hope that these warm sunny days, and the green leaves spreading themselves over the trees, are emblems of a better season, and represent the springing up of life and feeling in your soul and in your ministry in Wilts. Winter is no pleasant season either for body or soul, and though I have written a sermon to prove that it comes afore harvest, yet I cannot say that it is a season which I like, either in nature or in grace. But as in nature it is necessary to break the hard clods and prepare the earth for spring showers and May sunshine, so, I believe, it is necessary in grace to break to pieces the hard clods of the heart that there may be a tilth for the seed of life to spring up and grow. Few things are more mysterious to a Christian than the revivings of the work of grace upon his soul. Judging from myself at times all feeling religion seems lost and gone. At such seasons one wonders how the scene will end. But the Lord does from time to time revive and renew His work upon the heart, and there is a fresh acting of faith, hope, and love, with every other grace and fruit of the Spirit. I believe it to be a very good and a very needful thing to have the soul well and continually exercised on the things of God. I hope I can say for my part that eternal things are ever uppermost in my mind, either in a way of exercise or else in some actings of faith upon the blessed Lord.

You have, perhaps, heard that I was not able to preach for two Lord's-days; but, through mercy, I was permitted to get out again last Lord's-day. I preached twice, and administered the ordinance afterwards, and did not feel worse, except a little extra fatigue. I hope, therefore (D.V.), to go to Leicester on Friday. As I disappointed them last September I should have been sorry to be obliged again to fail in keeping my engagement. . . .

We live to see great changes, not only in men's affections but in men's opinions. It is good amidst all changes, without or within, to have the heart established by grace, and not like children to be tossed to and fro, and carried about with every wind of doctrine. It is a mercy to be in any way delivered from looking to man and to be enabled to look to the Lord as our all in all. I am very sure that I never got any good from looking to man, whether saint or sinner. If we expect much from our friends we are almost sure to be disappointed. In our greatest straits they can do us no good, for they cannot give us the light of God's countenance, or apply any sweet promise to the soul.

Thus, though I wish ever to walk in love and affection with my friends in the Lord, yet I never want to put them in the place of Christ or to look to them for what I know they cannot give me. And, as regards my enemies, I desire to bear all their attacks and their calumnies, knowing that it is my contending for the truth that stirs up their enmity.

I had a few lines the other day from Mrs. Isbell. She names in it that a minister, with whom you were preaching in Devon thirty years ago, was breaking up in constitution, and says of himself that he is looking for his great change. She says that when she heard him preach last she felt convinced that if she were taught of the Spirit so was he, and she believed that it would be well with him when called away. . . . Persons look to us as leaders in the same way as the soldiers look to their officers. And if they see us wavering and undecided, what a discouragement it is to them, and what confusion it is likely to create! So, for my own comfort, and for the sake of others, I feel myself obliged to stand separate from many persons who I dare not say are destitute of the life of God in their souls. It seems very plausible to be united to all who love the Lord Jesus Christ, and so, in fact, we internally are if we have any measure of His love in our heart. But as to walking in outward union with some, how is it possible to do so with any degree of consistency? But this they consider so narrow-minded, so bigoted, so exclusive, and to manifest such a proud and self-righteous spirit. Unless the trumpet give a certain sound, who is to prepare himself for the battle? I want no new doctrines, nor any new religion, as I want no fresh Bible and no new Lord; all I want is to live more daily in the sweet enjoyment of them, and to manifest more of their power in heart, lip, and life. We are no longer young; life is, as it were, slipping from under our feet; and, therefore, I desire to spend the rest of my days, be they few or many, in serving the Lord, walking in His fear, enjoying His presence, preaching His gospel, contending for His truth, and living to His glory. It is a poor life to live to sin, self, and the world; but it is a blessed life to live unto the Lord. I only wish that I could do so more and more; but I have to find that the good I would I do not, and the evil I would not that I do.

You will see the new house at Allington rising upon the ruins of that which you saw burning. I hope, when our dear friends move into it, it may be consecrated by the Lord's presence.

Yours very affectionately,
J. C. P.

CXLV—To Mrs. Peake

London, June 17, 1861.

My dear Friend,

. . . I think I never came to London weaker in body and soul than this time. I much dreaded yesterday, and would have almost written to Mr. Brown to take my place. But I never found the promise more true, "As thy day, so shall thy strength be," for I was brought through most comfortably in body and soul, and preached to a large and most attentive congregation with a strength of voice surprising to myself, and in the morning had sweet liberty of soul. On Saturday I could scarcely, from lumbago, walk round Mr. C——'s garden, and yet stood up for nearly three hours, at two periods yesterday, without much pain or inconvenience. As there were a great many strangers and friends from the country my non-appearance would have been a disappointment. "Bless the Lord, O my soul."

I hope you are enjoying not only the refreshing sea-breezes, but a sweet gale of heavenly grace from off the everlasting hills. Poor Mrs. —— has much felt this painful dispensation. May it be sanctified to the sufferers. It is sad when the pruning knife gives the branch no fruitfulness. But we need all our afflictions. You are not the only sufferer among the family of God. 1 Tim. v. 5 well describes "a widow indeed."

Yours very affectionately,
J. C. P.

CXLVI—To Mr. Tanner

Hampstead, June 20, 1861.

My dear Friend,

Once more am I in this great metropolis, being, through infinite and most undeserved mercy, spared to proclaim again salvation by grace in Gower Street pulpit. It is about twenty-five years since I first opened my mouth in London, and I have but once or twice since then failed to come up every year; but I think I never in all those years so much felt my weakness in body and soul as on the present occasion. When the train which brought me up was passing through the last tunnel, I could have wished it was taking me out of London instead of bringing me to it. But the Lord was better to me than all my fears, for I was scarcely ever brought more comfortably through. "Strength made perfect in weakness" has long been my experience, and so I found it then. I had been suffering for more than a week with an attack much as that I had at your house, so that I could scarcely walk a hundred yards without pain and labour; yet I was enabled to stand up in the pulpit, so that few would have seen that anything ailed me. Is not this wonderful? and to whom does the praise belong but to the Lord? I never expect to be free from trial, temptation, pain, and suffering of one kind or another whilst in this vale of tears. It will be my mercy if these things are sanctified to my soul's eternal good, and the benefit of the Church of God. I cannot choose my own path, nor would I wish to do so, as I am sure it would be a wrong one. I desire to be led of the Lord Himself into the way of peace, and truth, and righteousness, to walk in His fear, live to His praise, and die in the sweet experience of His love. I have many enemies, but fear none so much as myself. O may I be kept from all evil and all error, and do the things which are pleasing in God's sight, walk in the light of His countenance, be blessed and be made a blessing. Our days are hasting away swifter than a post; soon with us it will be time no longer, and therefore how we should desire to live to the Lord and not to self!

My dear friend, I do not feel able to preach twice at Cirencester on July 25th, and should prefer 6.30 p.m., as I think we should have more people in the evening, and I rather prefer that time of day. The Lord's-day at Abingdon generally much tires me, and so do my labours at Allington; then there is (D.V.) the Calne anniversary on the 30th. I shall be pleased to stay at your house (D.V.) from the Tuesday till the Friday, and renew our friendly and affectionate intercourse.

Yours affectionately in the truth,

J. C. P.

CXLVII.—To Mr. Tanner

Stamford, Sept. 12, 1861.

My dear Friend,

This day year, for the first time, I came under your roof, and preached at Cirencester, though to-morrow will be the anniversary according to the day of the year. I little thought when you met me at the station that I should stay so long in the ancient town of

Cirencester; but as it was the Lord's will that I should be laid up with illness, He very kindly located me under your roof, that I might have those kind attentions which mitigated, if they did not remove, the trial, and opened a way whereby we should become better acquainted with each other, and have, I trust, an enduring union in the solemn realities of eternity.

Once more, then, am I returned, after my wanderings, to my own home, but as usual only it seems for the purpose of going out again, as I shall be leaving it for Leicester in a day or two. I wish that my time now permitted me to write to you at greater length, and above all that the Blessed Spirit would supply me with gracious thoughts and feelings, that I might communicate something that might be to edify. But, alas! I daily find that in me, that is, in my flesh, dwelleth no good thing, and that though to will is present with me, yet how to perform that which is good I find not. Perhaps were we sitting together you might be enabled to draw more out of me than now seems rising in my heart; for a man of understanding, which I take you to be, can draw water out of the well even if it be deep, and this you do by letting down the bucket of your own experience, or as it is some times done when the pump does not act, by pouring down a little water into it.

I certainly have been much favoured this summer with a measure of health and strength in going about to preach the gospel; and I have found not only natural strength given according to my day, but I trust also my spiritual wants supplied both for myself and the people out of the fulness that is in Christ. But now I seem drooping, not being so well in body, and but lean and barren in soul, so that I am somewhat like the poor harvest labourer who has had strength given him to cut down and gather in the corn, but feels wearied with so much harvest work. Ministers are labourers, and according to the Lord's own figure, harvest labourers, for he bade His disciples pray that the Lord of the harvest would send labourers into the harvest. But in the spiritual as in the natural field, *labourers* not *loiterers* are wanted; and when the crop is heavy, the sun hot, and the day long, the labourer must needs feel weary and worn. But as he will not grudge his labours if they have gathered the corn well in, and he has received his harvest wages, so the spiritual labourers must not repine if their labours are blest to the gathering in of immortal souls, and they receive the rewarding testimony of the Lord's approbation in their own bosom. As a nation we have been highly favoured this harvest. You will recollect your drive one evening to hear poor Mr. Shorter, when you had to pass through flooded lanes, and saw the corn drenched with wet in the fields. But had I come amongst you this year, all your crops would long ago have been safely secured before the anniversary of my former visit. Many hearts were trembling, and many anxious eyes were scanning the appearance of the clouds of heaven when I was in Wilts, as all bore in remembrance the harvest of 1860, and would have sunk at the recurrence of such a calamitous season. It is often so in grace as in nature. The trials and afflictions of the past make us dread a recurrence of them. Our coward flesh shrinks from the cross, and though we cannot deny that we have received benefit from the suffering, yet we dread to be put again into the same furnace. Besides our usual trials, we had heavy ones last year—I in my affliction under your roof, and you shortly afterwards in Seymour's leaving you for a foreign shore. Could we wish to have a recurrence of these trials, even though we hope they were in a measure over-ruled and sanctified to our soul's good, and perhaps to the good of others? But the Lord does not consult us either as to the nature or the time of those trials and afflictions which He is pleased in sovereign wisdom to lay upon us. It is our mercy when we can see His hand, not only bringing them on, but supporting us under them, and carrying us through them. If we had no personal trials, temptations, or afflictions, we should not do to stand up before the Lord's people, for they, for the most part, are painfully tried, and many of them sorely afflicted. It would be, therefore, impossible for us to enter, with any feeling, into their tried cases, unless we ourselves knew something experimentally of the path of tribulation. It is a great mercy if the Lord be pleased by His dealings with us in providence or in grace to keep our souls not only alive but lively. There is such a tendency in us to slide down into a state of carnality and ease, to get away, as it were, from the burden of the cross, and as Job speaks, to swallow down our spittle—alluding, I presume, to the difference between doing so at ease in the cool shade, and having a throat parched with travelling through the hot wilderness. How needful it is with the Lord's help and blessing to have our loins girt about and our lights burning! How soon we sink down into carnality and death, and like a rower plying against the stream, at once fall down with the current when we cease to ply our oars. These oars are prayer, reading, meditation, and heart examination, and without them too soon we slip away from the harbour to which we hope we are bending our course. And yet we daily find that we cannot use these oars to purpose except the Lord be pleased to put strength into us. We may, indeed, attempt to use them, and should not cease to do so. But, alas! of how little avail are they unless He who teaches the hands to war and the fingers to fight, teach us also their use, and give us power to use them in His strength, not our own.

I am glad to hear that the Lord was pleased, in some measure, to bless my labours at Cirencester when I was there last I certainly did not expect such a congregation on so wet a day, and so rainy an evening; but it seemed to show that the people came from a real desire to hear the word, and disregarded all natural hindrances. It is a sweet satisfaction, after we have laboured in the Lord's name, to have some evidence that our labour has not been in vain in the Lord.

Yours very affectionately,
J. C. P.

CXLVIII—To Mr. Crake

Leicester, Sept. 19, 1861.

My dear Friend,

The obituary, concerning which you have written to me in your usual kind and affectionate way, has just been forwarded to me. When I first cast my eye over it I thought it would do for the wrapper, but when I came to examine it a little more carefully, and especially when I read the closing scene, I felt that the body of the work was a more fitting place. Most of our readers much prefer a good obituary to be placed in the body of the work than put upon the wrapper, as the type being smaller and the paper less clear, there is often some difficulty in reading it; besides which, the wrappers are lost when the work is bound. But if placed in the body of the work some delay must occur before it can appear. Perhaps you will explain this to the aunt of the deceased, intimating at the same time that we shall hope to insert it as soon as our space admits.

I should be very sorry if you thought that the union in heart and spirit which, I trust, has existed between us for so many years, were weakened by time or distance. There are not many, speaking comparatively, with whom I have a real union of spirit; but where it has been once formed, it is not with me lightly broken. Of course want of intercourse will to a certain extent diminish, but it never will break asunder a union which the Spirit has once created, and at my time of life new friends are not easily made, nor new friendships entered into. I hope, amongst the evidences which I possess of being a partaker of the grace of God, is love to those who love the Lord, and, opposed as I am by so many enemies, I feel to cleave all the more earnestly to real friends. I have long felt that, with all the minor differences which often divide the living family of God, that their union is far deeper than any circumstances which can arise to cause disunion. No doubt Satan is continually at work to separate even chief friends by working upon the corruptions of our nature, and filling the mind either with suspicions or stirring up miserable jealousies. May we have grace to resist Satan in this matter, and to cleave in affection to those with whom we have felt any spiritual union, or with whose religion we have found any inward satisfaction!

Yours very affectionately,
J. C. P.

CXLIX.—To Mr. Tanner

Stamford, November 22, 1861.

My dear Friend,

*   *   *   *   *   *

Our coward flesh shrinks from every affliction and trial, and even though we may have proved in times past that there has been a blessing couched in them, yet our heart murmurs and frets under the weight of the cross. But the Lord, like a wise parent, does not consult us as to where, when, or how He may lay on the chastising stroke. It is best, therefore, to fall into His hands, and to lie at His feet begging that He will sanctify to us every afflicting stroke, not lay upon us more than we can bear, and remove the trial when it has done its appointed work. Of one thing I am very sure, that it is far better to suffer from the Lord than to sin against the Lord. There is no evil which we need really fear except sin; and, though the Lord, in tender mercy, forgives His erring, wandering children, yet He makes them all deeply feel that indeed it is an evil and a bitter thing to sin against Him. I myself have no opinion of that religion, let it be called by what name it may, which does not make the conscience alive and tender in the fear of God. The blessed Lord gave Himself for our sins that He might deliver us from this present evil world; and the fountain which was opened in His bleeding hands, and feet, and side was to wash away not only guilt and filth from the conscience, but to sanctify the soul. Holy John saw blood and water gush from the Redeemer's side when it was pierced with the Roman spear; and thus blood to wash away sin, and water to purify the heart, lip, and life flowed together from the wounds of the pure humanity of the Son of God. I only wish that I could live more in the enjoyment of those two rich and unspeakable blessings—salvation and sanctification. But we shall always find it to be a fight of faith, a struggle against the power of temptation and corruption, a conflict between the spirit and the flesh, and one in which by strength no man can prevail, for the weak take the prey, and the race is not to the swift, nor the battle to the strong. In myself I can truly say I have neither help nor hope, but am obliged, every day of my life, to look out of myself to the blessed Lord that He would manifest Himself to my soul, and shed abroad His love in my heart by the Holy Ghost. I am not one bit stronger in myself with all my long profession, and, I hope, possession of the life of God; but, on the contrary, have a more sensible feeling of my weakness, sinfulness, and helplessness than ever I had before. At the same time I hope I have learned more deeply and thoroughly whence all my strength, wisdom, righteousness, and sanctification are to come, and thus to look more to the Lord and less to self.

I hope you find the Lord with you in your attempts to exalt

His worthy name, and that you find yourself encouraged in the work. Sometimes it is most going on when we see it least, and when we feel most desponding as to any good being done, that is often the very season when the Lord is most at work. To be blessed with signs following is the greatest encouragement that a minister can have.

Yours very affectionately,
J. C. P.

CL.—To Mr. Hoadley

Stamford, Nov. 26, 1861.

Dear Friend,

I am glad that you still bear in affectionate remembrance, and I trust in some measure in soul profit, what I was enabled to deliver in your hearing at Gower Street Chapel. I always think that it is a sign of hearing to profit when there is an abiding of the word in the heart. Our blessed Lord says, "Abide in me and I in you;" and again, "If ye abide in me, and my words abide in you," John xv. Now this shows that there is no real fruit unless there be an abiding in Christ, as His words abide in us. It is this abiding of the word in the heart which makes it take root downwards and bear fruit upward. It is indeed very blessed when, as the apostle speaks, "The word of Christ dwells in us richly in all wisdom," Col. iii. 16; for it is through His word applied with power to the heart that Christ makes Himself known and precious.

I wish I could give you any information or any counsel concerning which you have written to me. Mr. W—— is quite a stranger to me both personally and by report, and therefore I am not able to say one word about him, good or bad. But this I know, that the true servants of God are very scarce, and that it is very easy for a man to profess a certain line of truth, just to serve a purpose of his own, when he is not acquainted with it experimentally, or indeed may be secretly opposed to the power of those very truths which he professes to hold. Nor do I know any servant of the Lord whom I could recommend. Perhaps, however, Mr. Brown, an old friend of mine, formerly of Godmanchester, but now residing at 3, Egremont Place, Brighton, might be enabled to come for a Lord's-day or so, as he has no fixed place at present, and supplies sometimes at Pell Green and the Lower Dicker.

I do not see that you need condemn yourself for taking a part in the service of God when you have no preaching. Somebody must do so that fears the Lord and who can in public call upon His name. As long as you do this with a single eye to the glory of God, and with a desire for your own soul's profit and that of the people, there can be no just ground of accusation against you;

and if you find reading the sermons profitable to your own soul, and the people feel the same, I would not advise you to give it up, but go on with it, as the Lord gives you grace and strength. I cannot now add more. The Lord guide and keep you.

Yours affectionately in the truth,

J. C. P.

CLI—To Mr. Crake

Stamford, Nov. 27, 1861.

My dear Friend,

I am much obliged to you for the very interesting letter of Mr. M—— which you have kindly sent me. I have read it with much pleasure and interest, and should much like to insert it in the *Gospel Standard*, if Mr. M—— has no objection.

I have not yet been able to look over the obituary sent me at the same time, but shall hope to do so when I can get a little quiet leisure. I believe Mr. Gadsby intends to enlarge the *Gospel Standard* wrapper in the coming year; and in that case there will be more room for various things which seem hardly worth a place in the body of the work. I find it to be a matter of great difficulty, and one that requires both much grace and much judgment, how to carry on the *Gospel Standard* most for the glory of God and the profit of His people. I am well convinced that its influence has been great, and I have no doubt for much good. It has opened a way for bringing before the Church of God much that otherwise would have been altogether lost. Many sweet and savoury letters of departed saints, and many obituaries of those who lived and died in the fear and love of God, have been preserved and brought before the saints of God; and we may well hope that the blessing of God has rested upon such testimonies. It affords also a kind of rallying point for the scattered saints of God throughout the land, who from time to time find their experience described and their views of truth which have been taught them by the Holy Spirit sweetly confirmed. We live, too, in a day full of error and evil, so that we need some one to lift up the voice for truth in its purity and power. I feel myself indeed very unfit and very unworthy to conduct such a work; but, as hitherto the Lord I trust hath helped me and given me strength according to my day, I hope to go on still in His name if the Lord spare my life and give me the needful grace and strength.

I desire to sympathise with you and your wife in all your troubles and afflictions. You have found the benefit of them and a blessing in them, and I trust are still realising the power of God to support you under them and the grace and presence of the Lord to bless you in them.

Yours affectionately,

J. C. P.

CLII —To Mr. Grace

Stamford, Nov. 27, 1861.

My dear Friend,

My time this evening is limited, and I can therefore only send you a few lines to express my affectionate sympathy with you in your trials and afflictions, and my hope that at evening time there will be light. It is indeed truly distressing to see those who are near and dear to us fading like a leaf, and to have daily before the eyes such a sad and solemn testimony to the Adam fall. What but the grace of God which bringeth salvation can gild with light the pillow of death, and cast a ray through the dark valley of that shadow through which all must pass! I hope it may please the Lord to give you some token that poor Lydia's soul is safe before she is called to resign her last breath. O how vain and fleeting are all things here below! What is the pride and fashion and all the worldly gaiety of that town in which the Lord has fixed your abode when viewed in the solemn light of a dying hour? What a description has the Holy Ghost given to us of God's view of these matters in Isaiah ii., iii., and how His hand is put forth in anger against all who are found exalting themselves against Him. May our lot, living and dying, be with the saints of God whom He has redeemed with the precious blood of His dear Son, whom He has called and quickened by His grace, and to whom He has made known the blessed mysteries of His kingdom as set up in the heart by the power of the Holy Ghost. Time and life are fast passing away with us; but we hope that through distinguishing grace we have not lived altogether to sin and self, but have endeavoured, very weakly, indeed, and imperfectly, yet in the main sincerely, to serve God in our day and generation, to seek the good of His people, to be blessed and be made a blessing. To live a life of faith upon the Son of God is indeed a blessing beyond all price; and such a life here will prepare for a life of eternal and unalloyed enjoyment hereafter.

I was glad to learn that upon the whole you enjoyed your visit at Leicester. I had a few lines the other day from our friend Mrs. S——, who speaks warmly and affectionately of your visit. She is one of those who are looking for the power, the dew, the unction, and savour of truth in the heart, and she is not satisfied as hundreds are with the bare letter.

I can only now add our united love and sympathy to Mrs. Grace and yourself.

Yours very affectionately,

J. C. P.

CLIII —To Mr. Brown

Stamford, Nov. 29, 1861.

My dear Friend,

I hardly recollect at this present moment on which side the debt of a letter lies between us; but I shall assume that I am your debtor, and if I be not it will not much matter, as correspondence between friends does not stand upon the same rigid terms as a banking account or a tradesman's ledger.

You will be glad to hear that through mercy I continue quite as well in health as I can expect at this season of the year, being enabled to attend to the labours of the ministry, as well as those no less difficult and responsible labours which devolve upon me in earnestly contending for the faith once delivered to the saints by my pen. One reason, however, why I now address you is that I am endeavouring to make my arrangements for going from home, if the Lord will, next summer. I have undertaken, if the Lord give health and strength, to be at Gower Street for six Lord's-days commencing June 8th, and when I have fulfilled my engagement there, I purpose (D.V.) to go into Berks and Wilts for July and part of August. Now, I should be much pleased if you could undertake to give me some aid during my absence from home. As you so well know the friends here and at Oakham, and they so well know and so much esteem and value you, I need say nothing upon that point. I shall leave it therefore with the Lord and yourself to come to a decision upon the subject. It is indeed a long way to come from Brighton, and your infirmity of eyesight makes travelling a greater difficulty to you than to many; but the Lord hitherto has given strength according to your day, and enabled you since you have left a permanent charge to go from place to place without injury if not without inconvenience.

I think that your obituary of Mr. Crouch will be read with much pleasure and interest in the forthcoming *Standard*. When I was younger in years and more favoured in health I used sometimes to preach for him at Pell Green, but we never had much conversation upon the things of God. I have indeed rarely met with a gracious man and minister who seemed more bound up in conversation. It was not from want of divine matter in his heart, and probably arose either from natural shyness, or from being at the time much bound in spirit. Ministers are sometimes afraid of one another, as I have often felt myself, and where this feeling prevails it shuts up that free communication in the things of God which is so sweet and refreshing. At the time I took the fault more to myself than ascribed it to him; but I have since heard from our friend Mr. Grace that he was often bound up in spirit, or at least had not that door of utterance with which some are favoured. But he was a man deeply led into a knowledge of self, and when he took his pen was able to express himself with a freedom as well as an originality of thought and language which seemed to be denied him in conversation. My going down to Pell Green arose from my connection with one of his deacons, old Mr. Walter, who was in the habit of coming up to London to hear me on my annual visit to the metropolis. I do not think that I have often met in my life with a man so deeply and continually exercised about his state and standing as good old Mr. Walter. He has at various times much opened his mind to me, and I believe was blessed on one or two occasions under my ministry.

One of the most painful, and I might almost say alarming features of the present day, is the removal of the servants of God, and that so few are raised up in their place. On every side error seems to prevail, and were we to believe their own testimony there is no lack of ministers of the gospel. But where are those to be found who preach it with the Holy Ghost sent down from heaven? Where are those who can set forth the truth with the sweet savour, unction, and dew of the blessed Spirit attending it to the hearts of the hearers. I should be glad indeed to see the Lord raising up men after His own heart, pastors, who can feed the Church of God, and ministers who need not to be ashamed as rightly dividing the word of truth. But I much fear that things will go on from worse to worse, and though the Lord will always have a seed to serve Him and servants of His own equipping and sending forth, yet their number may be very scanty, and their gifts and graces very limited. What makes the matter to my mind more perplexing is that there is a spirit of hearing in the churches if there were ministers raised up to feed the people with sound gospel food. Our race will soon be run; may it be our earnest desire to spend the rest of our appointed days here below to the glory of God and the good of His people. This world has done little for us, and must every day do less and less. We owe it no thanks, and desire to live separate from it, and heed neither its smiles nor its favours. The Lord make us faithful unto death that we may inherit a crown of life. I hope that as long as the Lord gives me a tongue to speak or a pen to write, I may use both to His glory.

Yours affectionately in the Lord,

J. C. P.

CLIV —To Mr. Godwin

Stamford, *Nov.* 30, 1861.

My dear Friend,

I just drop you a line before I start for Oakham, as you will perhaps want to make your arrangements (D.V.) for the coming year. If the Lord gives me health and strength I am likely to be out from home a good deal next year. . . .

I received a letter the other day from the deacon of a church at ——, giving an awful account of the conduct of a minister there. He wrote to me to ask my advice whether he should withdraw from his ministry, and my advice was that he had better do so under the circumstances, and had better meet together with a few friends by themselves for reading the word and prayer, than stand a deacon and lead the singing under such error and such evil as had come to light. I have received letters from other places expressing how the poor children of God are robbed and spoiled under these letter ministers, and bidding me still to go on to lift up my voice and pen against them. My own conviction is that very few of them have had the fear of God planted in their hearts, or know anything of Jesus Christ by any personal discovery of His person and work to their consciences. They are, for the most part, bitter enemies of experimental truth, and hate those who contend for it with a perfect hatred. The letter, which I will send you some day, mentions the wrath of these men against the *Gospel Standard* and the editor. But I hope I can say that none of these things move me. I see where the men are, that they have a name to live when they are dead, a form of godliness whilst they deny the power thereof; and many of them I firmly believe are held fast in some sin, either covetousness or drunkenness, or something worse, not to speak of their enmity and malice against the saints and servants of God. It is a mercy of mercies to be separate, not only in person but in heart and conscience, from such men, and to cleave in love and affection to the real saints of God, and to all who know divine realities by divine teaching and divine testimony. I only wish that I could live more in the sweet enjoyment of the truth of God, and make it more manifest by my lips and by my life that I am in vital and unctuous possession of that truth which indeed maketh free. But I have to lament a body of sin and death which is ever striving for the mastery, and the painful recollection of many departings from the Lord makes the chariot wheels run heavily. But still I struggle on as I best can, looking up to the Lord for continual supplies of grace and strength, and having no hope nor help but in His mercy and love as made known to the soul by the power of God.

We have just lost Mrs. C., one of my hearers ever since I have been at Stamford. I did not know much of her, but Mrs. B——, was very intimate with her, and has no doubt of her safety.

Yours affectionately,

J. C. P.

CLV—To Mr. Tips

Stamford, Dec. 9, 1861.

My dear Friend,

I am truly sorry to hear from your kind and affectionate letter that you have been and still are sick. The Lord, my dear friend, has seen good to take this way of afflicting you, and to lay upon you His chastising rod. It must have been a very great trial both for yourself and your dear wife; but I am truly glad to find that the affliction is working in you the peaceful fruits of righteousness. Good King Hezekiah was laid upon a sick bed, and, as it appeared, a bed of death. But he cried unto the Lord; the Lord heard his prayer, and by giving him a blessed manifestation of pardoning love cast all his sins behind his back, and thus healed his soul as well as his body. This made the good old king say, "O Lord, by these things men live, and in all these things is the life of my spirit: so wilt thou recover me, and make me to live" (Isa. xxxviii. 16). Illness is often made use of by the Lord as a furnace in which He tries the faith of His children. Job could say when he was tried, "I shall come forth as gold" (Job xxiii. 10). And I hope that my dear friend will find it so. The refiner of gold does not keep the metal in the furnace longer than is absolutely necessary. He knows exactly when the dross is separated, and when it is time to remove the pure metal out of the fire. So, I trust, the Lord will deal with you. You will find it good to be much engaged in prayer and supplication at a throne of grace; to read, study, and meditate over God's holy word; and to examine His gracious dealings with your soul. It is a great blessing to be spiritually-minded, for that indeed is life and peace. When a Christian man is taken aside from his worldly business, and has to spend much of his time in the quiet solitude of a sick room, it separates him in heart and spirit, as well as in body, from the world. He meditates on the solemn realities of eternity; the salvation of his soul is felt to be his chief concern; and if the Lord is graciously pleased to draw him near unto Himself, and to commune with him from off the mercy-seat, he has a sacred pleasure which none can know but those who have experienced it. He sees and feels how time is passing away, how soon he must stand before the bar of his righteous Judge; and this makes him feel that nothing is worthy of a moment's comparison with being saved in the Lord Jesus Christ with an everlasting salvation. It is in these seasons that we learn lessons which we have never learned before, or, at least, not so deeply or effectually. It is a good thing to see and feel how short we come of being what we should be, and how little we really know of the grace and glory, love and blood, beauty and blessedness, suitability and preciousness of the Lord Jesus Christ. "He is the way, the truth, and the life, and no man cometh unto the Father but by Him" (John xiv. 6). "He of God is made unto us wisdom, righteousness, sanctification, and redemption" (1 Cor. i. 30.) But we cannot believe in Him to the saving of our soul, nor receive Him into our heart and affections, unless the Holy Spirit takes of the things of Christ, and reveals them unto us. We should, therefore, be ever praying to the Lord to send forth His Holy Spirit into our hearts that He may reveal

Christ in us, intercede in and for us, and enable us to cry, "Abba, Father!"

Your affectionate Friend in the Gospel,
J. C. P.

CLVI—To Mr. Grace.*

Stamford, Jan. 10, 1862.

My dear Friend,

I sincerely desire to sympathise with you and Mrs. Grace in the trying affliction and painful bereavement which you have just sustained, in the removal of your beloved daughter. From what you have named of her experience, particularly toward the last, I think there is every ground for a good hope that she was amongst the number of those favoured souls who were redeemed by the blood of the Lamb, and made alive unto God by regenerating grace. Considering her age, mode of bringing up, and natural disposition, there was hardly reason to expect a very marked and conspicuous work of grace upon her soul. We hardly know how feeble and faint may be the measure of saving grace in a truly quickened soul, especially if there be great fears of making an insincere profession. It was not as if she had the way of truth to learn for the first time; or any self-righteous profession, which had to be pulled down with a strong hand. There could hardly be, therefore, that clear, marked, and decided work which we see in persons who have been brought out of the world by a mighty hand and an outstretched arm; nor was there, so to speak, that necessity of being taught terrible things in righteousness, which in some cases seem to be almost necessary to burn up the wood, hay, and stubble of a legal righteousness. She was evidently sensible of her danger, had often heard the way of salvation pointed out, and the blessed Lord ever held up as the only hope and help for the people of God. We cannot say then how secretly or mysteriously the Lord might have begun or carried on the work of grace upon her soul.

Last evening I happened to open the Bible in the chapel upon Mark iv. 26, and following. I just glanced my eye over the parable, and as I saw something sweet and experimental in it, I expounded it before prayer and preaching. While doing so, I was struck with the expression of "a man sleeping and rising night and day, and the seed springing and growing up he knoweth not how." Whether "a man" be a minister, the sower who soweth the seed, or whether he be a believer in general, it seems plain that the lesson which the Lord meant to teach was that man had

* This letter appeared some years ago in "A Short Account of the Peaceful Death of Lydia Grace." Brighton: C. Verrall.

nothing to do with the matter, and that whether he slept or whether he awoke, he could not contribute one atom to the germination of the seed or the growth of the plant. The earth, by which I presume is meant the heart of man, or, rather, the new heart promised, bringeth forth fruit of herself, independent of the care of man, but wholly dependent upon the rain and sun which come from God. But the blessed Lord goes on to tell us that the work of grace upon the heart resembles the growth of wheat in having first the tender blade, then the ear, then the full corn in the ear.

Now I am not going to give you a sermon upon that text, or even to say what I understand by it, but the parable strikes my mind as having some bearing upon poor Lydia's case. You could hardly tell when the seed was first sown in her heart. Most probably it was sown by your own hand. But you slept, and you rose night and day, and the seed sprang and grew up you knew not how. You might and did supplicate the Lord on her behalf, and many others did the same; but neither you nor they could contribute one mite to the germination of the seed, or the growth of the plant. Her heart, made honest and sincere, we hope, by the grace of God, brought forth fruit of itself. You were watching to see the seed spring up and grow, and in due time you saw a little tender blade, which grew up you knew not how. I much love tenderness in the things of God. Josiah's heart was tender, and the Lord took blessed notice of it. From all I have heard about poor Lydia, there was a tenderness in her religious feelings. She was afraid of presumption, hypocrisy, and making a profession without the power. All this looked well as far as it went. But as long as there is only the blade, you can scarcely tell a wheat field from a grass field. Something more is wanted to prove it to be corn, and not grass. There is the ear, which seems to be some formation of Christ in the heart; for, as in the literal figure, the corn is formed in the ear, though still green and milky, so in grace, when the blessed Lord is in any measure revealed to the soul, and embraced by faith, He is then in substance all He ever will be. It is true the corn has to be ripened, but this has little to do with the shape of the grain. So I trust your poor dear girl had a sufficient discovery of the Lord Jesus Christ to give her a saving faith in His blood, and obedience, and a love to His name. I like what she said to her mamma about the passage from Micah, and we would hope that as the Lord "delighteth in mercy," and she "delighted in mercy" too, her will was melted into the Lord's, and that being joined to Him, through faith in the promise, she was one spirit. I think also that the words which were made sweet to her at the beginning of her illness, were very suitable, and we know if they came from the Lord He will be faithful to His own word of promise. It must have been a very painful trial to you both, and the care, labour and anxiety of nursing must have fallen very heavily upon your poor dear wife. If you have travailed more for her in soul, your wife had to bear the heavier burden in ministering to her poor afflicted body. But it is an unspeakable mercy for the saints and servants of God, that by these things they are instructed. A fool (I use the words in a Scripture sense) learns wisdom from nothing; but a wise man learns wisdom from everything. The beauty and blessedness of the grace of God is, that it is always sufficient for the state and case of the soul that is a partaker of it, and generally speaking, the deeper the trial, the greater is the strength communicated under it, and the more profitable the lesson learnt from it. A minister without trials soon becomes a dry breast to the tried and tempted family of God. Thus I trust that your heavy trial will be blessedly sanctified, not only to your own soul, but to the spiritual profit of your people also.

Yours very affectionately,

J. C. P.

[I need scarcely say that the above letter was written by me without the slightest expectation of its ever appearing in print. As, however, a wish has been expressed that it should be appended to the foregoing little Memoir, I did not think it right to object, especially as when I wrote it it was with some measure of life and liberty. It also gives me the opportunity of adding that, to my feelings, the most satisfactory evidence of the poor dear girl's eternal safety arises from the words which were spoken to her before her departure—"This night thou shalt be with me in Paradise." If that assurance were enough for the dying thief, was it not enough for Lydia Grace?—J. C. P.]

CLVII—To Mr. Parry

Stamford, Jan. 22, 1862.

My dear Friend,

It is not often that our letters cross. It was, therefore, kind in you not to wait until I wrote again. Friends should not stand upon ceremony; but you are not fond of writing, and my time is a good deal occupied with work that will not stand still. I believe that the Address is generally very well liked. If I may be a judge of my own composition I have written better and worse; I therefore consider it about an average; but if I may say so I think it is written in a good spirit. One thing I am very sure of—that whether it be preaching or writing, I have no power to do either to any purpose except as I am specially enabled. It is surprising what a difference I feel in the power of conceiving gracious thoughts or giving them spiritual utterance by tongue or pen. It is easy enough to use words, but what are words if the life-giving power of the Spirit be not in them? There is almost as much difference between a living man and a corpse as between words animated by the Spirit and words in which there is only the breath of man.

But in this, as in everything else, the Lord is a sovereign, not only as to those on whom He bestows the unction of His Spirit, but also as to the times and seasons when He grants it. Private Christians know this from the difference of their feelings in prayer, hearing, reading the Scriptures, meditation, and Christian conversation; and if called upon to pray in public, they know it also from the different way in which they are enabled to exercise their spiritual gift. I have often thought and said that, though from education and long practice I may be able to speak or write so as not to be altogether confounded, yet as regards liberty, life, power, or feeling I am as dependent upon the Lord in the exercise of my ministry as any of my poorer and less educated brethren. Indeed, sometimes every gracious thought and feeling, with every good word and work, seem utterly gone, just as if I had never known any one divine truth, or as if the Bible had never come before my eyes or with any power into my heart.

I think you have done well upon the whole in establishing a prayer meeting; but, like most other things, it is easier to begin than to go on. I was very much struck with an expression made by a gracious friend of mine some time ago. Speaking of a minister whom you do not know, but who stands high in the professing Church, he said, "He has no prayer in him." Well, it struck me in a moment, Where or what must a man be if there be no prayer in him! I almost fear that his judgment was correct, for he had often heard him pray and preach, and judged him from the feelings of his own soul. So I would say of those who pray at a prayer meeting, if there be no prayer in them it will be but a poor dead lifeless service, but if there be prayer in them it will come out of them, to their own refreshment and to that of the hearers. But you well know, my dear friend, that the Holy Spirit alone can bestow the spirit of grace and of supplication, and that this blessed Intercessor intercedeth in and for the saints with groanings which cannot be uttered. Mr. Huntington was against prayer meetings, I suppose from seeing how they became preaching nurseries; but surely if prayer be good in private it should be good in public, and there is no more reason why a gracious man should not pray spiritually in the pew as well as a godly preacher in the pulpit.

We have been spared to see the beginning of another year; the Lord knows whether we shall be permitted to see its close. This time, thirty-one years ago, I was staying under the roof of our friend William Tiptaft, then Vicar of Sutton Courtney, and so weak and poorly was I at that time that I did not go out of doors for the months of December and January. Most probably those who knew me then did not think that my life would be prolonged up to this time. Poor Mrs. C. for one used to think that I was doomed to an early grave; but I have lived to see her and her sister, too, taken away before me. Truly could David say, "My times are in Thy hand." The blessed Lord holds the keys of death and hell; and as He has thus far preserved my life He can, if He will, prolong it still. My desire is whether it be long or short that I may walk in His fear and live to His praise, enjoy in my own soul His manifested favour and be made a blessing to the Church of God. I have had many persecutions and many enemies, but here I stand, at this day, unharmed by them and much more afraid of myself than I am of them. It is a mercy that though I have never been strong in body, and now begin to feel the infirmities of advancing years that my mental faculties have been preserved. I cannot, indeed, study and read as I once did, but am still enabled to get through the work that lies before me, both in preaching and writing.

I am glad that the testimony of poor Edward Wild was well received in your parts. I think it has been generally liked as a simple narrative of the Lord's work, and one stamped with sincerity, if not with any great depth.

No doubt you and yours, in common with us all, have sympathised with our poor afflicted Queen. You know that I have always been what is called a loyal subject, having no sympathy with radicals and republicans, but I believe that the whole country has felt for her from the palace to the cottage. What a mercy it would be for her if the grace of God would but sanctify the afflicting stroke to her soul's immortal good!

I continue, through mercy, much as usual, though this last frost has rather pinched me. I preached, however, twice on Lord's-day. Time is advancing with us all. O that when it shall be said to us "Time no longer," it may bear us into a blessed eternity!

I am,
Yours very affectionately,
J. C. P.

CLVIII—To Mr. Leigh

Stamford, Feb. 14, 1862.

My dear Friend and Brother in one Common Hope,

I should be very glad if I could give you any counsel upon the point concerning which you have written to me; but I have no doubt that you have long proved, as I have had to do, that in all matters connected with the things of God "vain is the help of man." Nor do I know, for the most part, a more difficult point as regards acting in the fear and love of the Lord, than how and when to join one's self to the visible Church of Christ. Not that I mean that to my mind there is any difficulty as to what a Church of Christ is, for according to my view that is clearly laid down in the New Testament; the difficulty is in forming a personal connection with a church. For there are so many things to consider, even when the question is fully settled in one's own mind as to what a Gospel church is. There is, first, the consideration whether it be the will of God that I should join a church at all. Some of the best Christians whom I ever knew either did not see the ordinance of baptism, or did not see their way to be baptised. Then, secondly, one has to consider the church which presents itself to our view upon which the question arises;—do I feel a spiritual union and communion with the members of it? Then, thirdly, there is the ministry in that church which might not altogether be commended to my conscience, or be made a blessing to my soul. Then, fourthly, there is the question whether I am of such a natural temper and disposition, or whether grace has so subdued my carnal mind that I am fit to be a member of a Gospel church. I know, at this present moment, several persons, both male and female, undoubtedly partakers of grace, and some of them well taught in the things of God, who, from infirmity of temper or a contentious spirit, are not fit to be members of any church. I once saw a church torn to pieces and almost broken up by one member, but in a remarkable way the Lord appeared and the member resigned. Since then they have had peace, and it is a church as much favoured with the power and presence of God as any that I know. Now all these things have to be well considered, to be spread before the Lord, and not taken up except as He is pleased to guide and lead. The privilege of being a member of a Gospel church is great indeed. It is a high honour to make a public profession of the name of Christ, to sit down at His table, and to be joined in fellowship with those who fear God and walk before Him in the light of His countenance. But in proportion to the greatness of the privilege is the necessity of being led every step by the Lord Himself. Nothing is more easy than to be baptised and join a church. It is done by hundreds, the whole of whose religion stands in the flesh. But a spiritual man cannot move forward in such a carnal way, for if he do he will find afterwards nothing but bondage and condemnation.

You will think, and that justly, that I have given you very little help in this matter. And the reason is, because I wish you to be led by the Lord alone. From what I have said in the former part of this letter some might think that I consider it a matter of indifference what a church of Christ is, or whether it be right in a Christian to become a member of it. But to think so would be a great misapprehension of my meaning. Indeed it lies just the other way. It is because I have such a view of what a church is, and of the blessedness of being a member of it under divine teaching, that I have written as I have done. It is not from indifference, but from seeing the spiritual character of the whole matter, that so many difficulties arise in my mind. As a proof of this, in my ministry I scarcely ever touch upon baptism or a Gospel church, not that I do not hold both with as firm a hand as those ministers who are always bringing it forward, but because I wish for the Lord Himself to lead His people to see it for themselves, and to be persuaded by His own sweet and invincible power. . . .

The *Gospel Standard* is not what I could wish it to be. Like its editor, it falls very short of his own standard of real vital godliness. But his desire and aim are the glory of God and the good of His people, and that the sweet and sacred unction of the Holy Ghost may spread itself through what is written and what is inserted. It is quite a fight of faith, for there are many adversaries, but the Lord still holds up my hands. . . . It is a mercy that the Lord did not suffer your foes to triumph. The Lord will fight for His redeemed. I was reading this morning 2 Kings ix., and could not but see from it what a dreadful thing it is to sin against God.

I am pretty well, through mercy, in health, but not likely again to visit Liverpool. I thank you, however, for your kind invitation.

Yours affectionately, in the Lord,

J. C. P.

CLIX —To Mr. Hoadley

Stamford, March 4, 1862.

Dear Friend,

Amidst all my labours for the profit of the Church of God, the various trials and temptations with which I am exercised, and the numerous enemies, internal and external, against whom I have to contend, it is a sweet satisfaction to find that the Lord is pleased to bless to any of His people what I send forth in His holy name. However the Lord's people may differ from each other in station, education, abilities, and other mere natural circumstances, yet are they all blessedly united in one spirit to the Son of God. Therefore they love the same truth, feel the same power, live the same life of faith, and eventually die to enjoy in substance what they have tasted in shadow. In writing the address for this year my desire was to edify and profit the Church of the living God. This, I knew, could only be done by the power of God resting upon my pen; for in myself I am a poor, blind, ignorant, destitute, and unfeeling wretch, who cannot even think a good thought, much less write a good word or perform a good action. It is a mercy then that not only you, but others also, have felt a measure of sweetness and savour in what then dropped from my pen. To the Lord be ascribed all the glory.

I was sure that you would find Mr. Brown an honest, gracious, and experimental man. In giving him out to preach here, or speaking of him, I have called him sometimes "Good Mr. Brown." He has gone through a good deal of trial and trouble, and this, by the grace of God, has softened and meekened his spirit.

I have often thought that those who are placed at the head of a little cause in the country are put into a very trying situation when they are brought to see the emptiness of all profession and preaching which do not stand in the power of God. It is to me a grievous sign in the present day that there are so few men raised up who preach the Gospel with the Holy Ghost sent down from heaven. There is no lack of ministers, such as they are, and men, too, who hold the truth, at least in the letter. But some hold it merely in the head, and others, it is to be feared in unrighteousness. But, oh, how few are enabled to preach it feelingly and experimentally under the savour and blessed unction of God the Holy Ghost. The Lord seems taking away His servants. You have lost within about a year four in your own county, Mr. Vinall, Mr. Crouch, Mr. Cowper, and poor old Mr. Pitcher. Oh, that the Lord would raise up men who know the truth, love the truth, preach the truth, and live the truth!

I am much obliged to you for your kind invitation to come and pay you a visit when I come to London (D.V.) in the summer, but I do not think that I shall be able to avail myself of it. You must therefore come up and see and hear me, as you did last year.

The Lord bless thee and keep thee.

Yours, in Gospel bonds,

J. C. P.

CLX.—To Mr. Parry.

Stamford, March 19, 1862.

My dear Friend,

I am truly sorry to learn from your last kind letter that you have been so unwell from that trying and weakening complaint—influenza. I am glad, however, to find you are somewhat better, and hope that the return of these chilling eastern breezes may not bring back so unpleasant a tenant of your earthly house.

As regards myself I am thankful to say that I have been unusually favoured this winter in exemption from those attacks on the chest, to which for many years I have been so liable. Not that I believe I am really any stronger in constitution, but it has pleased the Lord to preserve me from taking cold. Through His goodness and mercy I have preached, without intermission, since I left Allington, both on the Lord's-day and the week-day, with the exception of one evening, when I had a slight touch of lumbago, and the weather being cold and wet I thought it most prudent to stay at home. It has had a favourable influence upon the number of my congregation, for when there is an uncertainty about the pulpit being supplied it deters persons from coming from a distance, especially if the weather be unfavourable.

I have at length succeeded in making my arrangements for what I call my summer campaign. I think I can promise you the last Lord's-day in July, and the first three in August. I am sorry that my visit to Allington should fall in with the harvest; but I had no alternative, and therefore you must do with it the best that you can. Our esteemed friend Mr. Tiptaft has kindly consented to supply for me all July, which enables me to leave home with greater comfort. You will be sorry to hear that he has been very poorly from a cold in his chest and cough, and I understand he looks ill, though better. You will be glad to see him next month, and to hear his voice in your little chapel. You will find him the same man as ever.

I am glad to find that in your illness you have not been altogether left of the gracious Lord. It is but rarely that we can see at the time itself what benefit there is to spring out of sickness and affliction. Our coward flesh cries out for ease, we want to get better, and dread being worse; and as illness usually fluctuates, we are raised up or depressed according to circumstances. But indeed it is an unspeakable mercy when the affliction is truly sanctified to our soul's good, when we can submit to the Lord's will, lie passive in His hand, and know no will but His. When, too, a little measure of meekness and softness is communicated with faith and hope, in exercise upon the blessed Lord, it seems to reconcile the mind to the affliction. When, too, we can read the Word of Truth with sweetness and pleasure, are enabled to call upon the Lord with a believing heart, and are in any way blessed with that spirituality of mind which is life and peace, then we can say, "It is good for me to have been afflicted." All the saints of God have ever acknowledged that it was in the furnace of affliction that they learned their deepest lessons and got their greatest blessings. Some, if not many, of the usual trials of the Lord's people you are in good measure exempt from; but as each must bear his cross, yours, and, I may add, mine also, has been bodily affliction. Persons who are healthy and strong may think lightly of it; but those who know what it is by painful experience feel that it is no small an affliction, especially when it is more or less permanent. It is a good thing, however, to be thus daily reminded of our latter end, and, as the apostle says, thus to die daily. It has a good effect in loosening the heart and affections from the poor perishing things of time and sense, and impressing deeply upon our minds that this polluted world is not our rest or home. We take much to uproot us, for our carnal heart strikes deep root into earthly objects—much deeper than we are aware of until we find how closely we cleave to things which we thought had scarcely any hold upon us. James gives good advice where he says, "Is any among you afflicted? Let him pray." You will find it a great mercy if you are enabled in your affliction to call upon the Lord; for, though He may seem to hide His face and delay to answer, yet He puts the tears of His saints in His bottle, and writes their prayers in His book.

I am glad to find that our friend Mr. Tanner was heard profitably and acceptably by the friends at Allington. I shall never forget their kindness to me when I was laid up by illness at their house. It was a singular providence that it should be so ordered, but no doubt there was a purpose in it. It is in my mind to look in upon them (D.V.) on my way from Abingdon into Wilts. I much value him as an honest, upright man, and one who fears God above many. In this day it is a great thing to find a man in whom we can place dependence as firm in the truth from an experimental knowledge of it. In a few days (I think the 23rd instant) I shall have left the Church of England twenty-seven years. That is a long space of time—much longer than many thought I should have lived when I came out. I cannot say much in favour of either my words or works; but, perhaps, what I have said, written, or done during that interval may not have been altogether without fruit. No one exactly knows what influence his words, especially if he be a public man, have on the minds of others; nor, indeed, are those persons altogether aware of it who feel the influence, for it is usually very quiet, gradual, and imperceptible. The operation of truth upon the heart is like the light of day, gradual and yet effective, or like dew and rain, which soften and fertilise the ground, we can scarcely tell how. So divine truth in the lips, or written by the pen of a servant of God, often has a very gradual influence upon the mind; but this influence, though imperceptible, is not less real, for it is due not to the man but to the truth which he proclaims, and which the blessed Spirit seals with power upon the conscience. The Lord has placed me in a position which I never sought or desired; but, being in it, I do not see my way to retire from it as long as I have grace and strength to execute it. It costs me at times a great deal of mental labour, as you would see from the writing which I have monthly to produce for the *Gospel Standard*, and all this in addition to my ministerial labours. I wonder sometimes that my poor brain can sustain so much work, for sometimes on the Lord's-day, after two laborious services, I write a good part of the evening. Still, as strength is given me, I go on, desiring not to live to myself, but to the glory of God and the good of His people. I only wish that I could enjoy more myself of the precious truth of God, and feel more of its liberating, sanctifying influence upon my own heart, lip, and life.

Yours, very affectionately,

J. C. P.

CLXI —To Mr. Parry

Stamford, May 23rd, 1862.

My dear Friend,

I have been very desirous to send you a few lines ere this, but, as usual, have been prevented by a press of needful writing and correspondence, besides my ministerial labours.

Mr. Godwin would tell you how I am as regards the poor body—just helped through day by day without any reserve of strength to fall back upon, like the balance of a rich man at his banker's. He would also tell you of the congregations which we had at Godmanchester. There certainly is an increased spirit of hearing in that place and neighbourhood which I have now known for some years past; and I trust from what I saw and heard that our friend T. G. is where the Lord would have him to be, and is blessing his labours among the people. I suppose such a congregation was never before seen in the chapel. Some said there were 1,000 people present, and others 1,300. It took more than half an hour in the afternoon to get them seated. It is a large commodious chapel, without galleries, and very easy to speak in. I cannot say that I felt much at liberty on the Lord's-day, but on the Tuesday evening was more indulged, and I hope we had a good time.

The period is rapidly drawing near when I shall be leaving home (D.V.) for what I call my London campaign. Hitherto I have found the promise good, "As thy day is, so shall thy strength be." I trust, therefore, that once more I may be enabled to raise up my Ebenezer. Most probably I shall have large congregations, and I shall need all the bodily strength which the Lord may give me. But this, though most desirable, falls very short of being blessed in my soul, and blessed also to the souls of others. Next to the salvation and sanctification of one's own soul, there can hardly be a greater blessing than being made an instrument of good to the Lord's family. But, oh, how we need the special power and blessing of the Spirit that any good may be effected by the words of our mouth! What strongholds of Satan we have to pull down; what arrows of conviction to launch; what balm of consolation to administer; what strong hearts to break; what broken hearts to bind up! And who is sufficient for these things? How the whole first and last is of the Lord! So that if the least good be done, or the least blessing imparted, the praise and honour of it must all be freely given to the God of all grace. I was never more convinced of this in all my life than I now am. Ever since you have known me you can bear witness that I never gave any strength to the creature, but ascribed the whole of our salvation, first and last, to the God of all our mercies; and the longer I live the more I know of myself, and the more I see of others the more am I convinced that the Lord must have the glory of the whole. Indeed, I do see so much of the fall of man, and what I am as a poor, vile, filthy, guilty, and helpless sinner, that I am too glad and too willing to be saved wholly by sovereign grace, and wonder sometimes whether that amazing grace can ever indeed have reached my breast. At one time of our lives we may, perhaps, think that it is very easy to be religious; but when we have been well drilled in the school of temptation then we begin to see that it is the hardest thing in the world, so hard, indeed, that nothing short of a miracle of free grace can work in us that religion which shall save the soul. When I have, with God's help and blessing, finished my London labours, I hope to set my face towards Wilts, taking in my way Abingdon and Cirencester. Should the Lord permit me once more to come into Wilts I hope it may be under the teaching and testimony, work and witness, of His most blessed Spirit. If I think of myself, and myself alone, I could not dare to entertain such a hope; but in spite of all my weakness and worthlessness we have now had the experience of nearly twenty-seven years to afford us some little testimony that the Lord has condescended to meet with us in our attempts to worship Him in spirit and in truth, as well as to preach and fear His holy word. We know that there are those now dead of whom we have no doubt that they were blessed in the house of prayer, and who will be raised up one day out of their lowly tomb in which they rest in hope, so that your little graveyard will send forth a company of glorified bodies when the great trump sounds. As, then, you pass by their sleeping dust and look upon their graves with affectionate remembrance, it gives you to hope that they have not borne away all the blessings, but that there are living souls yet who come in for a share, too, of the same grace which was richly bestowed upon them. How often you pass by the graves of poor old Farmer Wild, our dear friend Dredge, the two sisters, poor Ed. Wild, and others, of whom you have a well-grounded hope that their souls have passed into rest and peace. And we, too, my dear friend, must one day follow them and be laid as low in the grave as they are now. O that the Lord would smile upon our souls and bless us with a sweet manifestation of His love, that when our time comes we may lay down our head in peace with a blessed testimony that the Lord is our God. It sometimes seems as if it were too great a blessing to expect. How base have been our backslidings—at least I may say so of my own! How little we have lived to the glory and honour of God! And still how weak our faith, and hope, and love! How many years have I preached and written, and, I may say, considering my health and strength, how much have I laboured! And yet how little, how poor, how insignificant it all seems. And yet I hope at times I have not laboured in vain nor spent my strength for nought.

Yours very affectionately,

J. C. P.

CLXII —To Mr. Tanner

Bottesford, May 29, 1862.

My dear Friend,

I named to Mary that I might send you a few lines, and this I now attempt to do in my own handwriting, which I cannot often employ, as I seem to have almost worn it out, like an old soldier with hard service, until it has scarcely a sound eye to see with, or a firm foot to stand on. Tongue and hand are well employed when each is used for the Lord's glory and His people's good; but both in me are crippled and lame—one from weakness of the chest, and the other from inability to trace quickly and legibly those characters whereby truth is conveyed to the eye as by words it is carried to the ear. Still He who makes His strength perfect in weakness has hitherto enabled me to employ both tongue and hand in His most blessed and self-rewarding service.

How time slips away with rapid wing! Revolving months have brought me against the eve of my summer campaign, when I leave my quiet home, my wife, family, and my books, to sojourn for a while in the busy metropolis, and then turn my face towards the swelling hills and green downs of Wilts. But before I once more (D.V.) see their broad backs and undulating line, I hope to visit that ancient town where He who fixes the bounds of our habitation has cast your earthly lot, and there, with the Lord's help and blessing, renew those ties of friendship and affection, all laid, we trust, beforehand on a right basis, and cemented during that eventful season which I spent under your roof in the autumn of 1860. In our day there is but little union or communion between those who profess the same truths and who preach the same gospel. The reason of this is that there is so little union and communion with the blessed Lord; for wherever there is union and communion with Him there must be the same with His people. Where, too, humility is wanting, and where pride, ambition, or covetousness prevail, there cannot be real union and communion, for that monster Self steps in between to intercept it. But when we are made willing to take the lowest place, and to esteem others better than ourselves, there seems to be some foundation laid for Christian union. Such is, I trust, my feeling wherever I see real grace. Gifts may be useful in their way; but it is grace, and grace alone, which unites the soul to Christ, and to those who are Christ's. If ministers, instead of seeking after gifts and popularity, were hungering and thirsting after larger communications of grace for their own souls' present and future benefit, and for their people's, there would be more union among them. But we are poor, fallen creatures, and I have no right to censure others where I am so deficient myself.

I cannot at present fix the exact day when I shall hope to see you, but most probably it will be either Tuesday, July 22nd, or Wednesday, July 23rd, if the Lord grant me health and strength to carry out my London and Abingdon engagements. I should not object to speaking on the evening of the Thursday in the same hall as before, if you think there would be a sufficient congregation to warrant our meeting there instead of the chapel. I still carry about with me a weak tabernacle, having often much cough to try both body and mind. Still, hitherto I have found strength equal to my day, and been helped through my labours so as not to break down, though often very weak before, and in, and after them. No doubt I need all the ballast I carry to steady my ship, for there is no safe sailing without it. You, too, have your cares and trials; bodily cares, family anxieties, business perplexities, ministerial troubles, and no doubt besides, and beyond all these, that most pressing and most present of all—the heavy weight of a body of sin and death hampering and clogging every movement of the soul Godward and heavenward. Under the pressure of all these trials and temptations, what a poor, empty thing does the world appear, how transitory and vain our present earthly life; and, indeed, all things within and without with which we are surrounded. Sin and death seem visibly stamped upon them all. But though we thus seem to get sick of earth, sin, and self, yet we feel the need of divine communications of life, light, liberty, and love, to raise up the heart and draw the affections heavenward. Hunger is not food, weariness not rest, and sickness not cure. How we need the blessed Lord to appear for us, and in us, that we may find in Him that rest and peace, that happiness and consolation, which none but He can bestow. How poor, how empty, how needy am I without His grace; how unable to think, say, or do any one good thing! How dark my mind, how cold my heart, how earthly my affections, unless He be pleased to move and stir my soul toward Himself. Thus I daily find and feel that without Him I can do nothing, and that He must be my all in all. In private, in public, whatever I do, or wherever I am, from Him is all my fruit found. Amongst the professors of the day how few know and love the truth, and amongst the preachers how few preach it from any sweet experience of its power! I am afraid of myself, and I am afraid of others; so powerful is unbelief, and so deceitful the heart, so strong is Satan, and so mighty is sin. May the Lord Himself teach and guide us, bless us and hold us up—for then, and then only, shall we be safe.

I have written a sad stupid letter, but it will show you how dark, barren, and unprofitable I am without the Lord's especial help.

Yours affectionately in the Lord,

J. C. P.

CLXIII—To Mrs. Peake

Stamford, Sept. 11, 1862.

My dear Friend,

I need not tell you how disappointed I was at not being able to come to Oakham for last Lord's-day, especially after so long an absence, but my voice was almost wholly gone, and therefore even if I had come and got into the pulpit I could not have made myself heard by the congregation. How true it is that disappointment and vexation attend all our earthly steps. I have not been better in health I think for many years than during my absence from home, and have laboured harder in the ministry than since the year 1847. Just then, as I was hoping to give my friends at home a little of my renewed strength, this stroke has come upon me which seems to bring back all my old feelings of tenderness and weakness. . . . . I feel very unworthy that any of the dear family of God should be looking to me for instruction and edification when I want so much for myself, and daily feel my own deficiency in everything spiritually good. Still, if the Lord be pleased in any way to make use of me for the building up of the Church on its most holy faith, to Him must be ascribed all the praise, for I cannot take an atom of it to myself.

I return you Mr. Grace's letter. You probably know that we met in Wilts at the Calne anniversary, and that I got him to preach there to the satisfaction of a large number of spiritual hearers. As I expected to find him much pulled down by his illness he did not seem to me to be looking at all more poorly than I expected to see him. He had come that morning more than twenty miles in an open vehicle, had risen at four o'clock, and had not slept all night. But in spite of all this he seemed to be strengthened in body, soul, and spirit, to preach to a very large and attentive congregation, and did not seem to suffer much afterwards.

Yours very affectionately,

J. C. P.

CLXIV—To Mrs. Tanner

Stamford, Sept. 15, 1862.

My dear Friend,

I desire very sincerely to sympathise with you and your family in the heavy trial through which you are all now passing in the severe illness which it has pleased the Lord to lay upon my dear friend Mr. Tanner. I truly hope that the persuasion which you have that he will be still spared to yourself, his family, and the church, will be realised; but after so severe and prolonged an attack, recovery, if the Lord be graciously pleased to grant it, must be slow. I am sure that he has the desires and prayers of all who know him in the Lord that he may be spared. Prayer is a powerful weapon in the hands of the Lord's family, and thus we hope that it may please the Lord to hear prayer on his and your behalf, and to spare his valuable life.

We felt it very kind in Mary giving us so accurate and detailed an account, keeping back nothing, and yet at the same time giving us some good ground of hope that he might still be raised up from his bed of sickness and affliction. There seems now some reason why you should have been lately so much favoured. The Lord saw the trial which was coming upon you, and He therefore prepared you for it. I am sure that you must need all the faith that He may have given you, and all the support which may be granted for both body and soul. It must indeed be a most anxious time with you all, and you no doubt see now the mercy of your son's return. Thus you see mercy mingled with judgment and strength and support graciously given when most needed. We all have to learn that it is through much tribulation that we must enter the kingdom. Trial after trial, like wave after wave, rolls over the family of God; and the more that the Lord favours and blesses them in His grace, the deeper and heavier for the most part do their trials become. The day of adversity is ever set against the day of prosperity; and wisely so, that we may learn our dependence upon the Lord and know more of His goodness and grace.

I shall be very anxious to have fresh intelligence how your dear husband really is. May the gracious Lord of His infinite mercy spare my dear friend's life, support and bless his soul under the affliction, and comfort and support your heart. My love to him if he can receive the message. Two years ago, just at this time, I was under your kind and hospitable roof. Had it been this year what an additional load it would have been to your mind. How wisely, how kindly does the Lord dispose all events!

Believe me to be, my dear Friend,

Yours with much sympathy and affection,

J. C. P.

CLXV—To Mr. Brown

Stamford, Oct. 29, 1862.

My dear Friend,

I was sorry to hear that you were suffering from the effects of your naturally gouty diathesis, and had not the free use of your lower limbs. You must feel it much being so often called from home, and having to travel by such various conveyances. We must all have our daily cross. My tender chest has long been one to me, and deprivation of the free use of your hands and feet has been and is still one to you. But we trust that this cross has not been without its profit. The Lord saw that we could not be trusted with health. Like an unbroken steed, full of high courage and spirits, it might have run away with us had we been placed upon its back; and what might have been the consequence? A broken neck or a fractured limb. I was sitting some time ago by the bed-side of a woman who has been more or less confined to her bed for thirty years. I said to her, "You don't know what sins you have been kept from by being confined here." The thought seemed to strike her as one with which she had not been conversant, and she named it afterwards as an unseen benefit of her affliction. So lame feet may keep a man from running into evil, and make him walk, if not more easily and comfortably, more in the strait and narrow path. Our unseen mercies may be greater than our seen. The prophet's servant did not see the horses and chariots of fire round about the mountain. But they were there, though he saw them not. We need many trials, and a long course of them, to meeken our spirit and give us patience; for tribulation worketh patience, as patience worketh an experience of the mercy and goodness of the Lord, and as an experience of past and present support worketh a hope of support for the future. Trial of some kind or other is indispensable to a Christian man, and especially to a Christian minister. The Lord's people are a tried people, and therefore need a tried experimental ministry.

I feel much for the appalling distress in Lancashire, and look forward to the coming winter with great apprehension, knowing the general sequel of previous famines. I have been apprehensive from the very first lest there should be a breaking out of fever, which now seems to be the case at Preston.

I travelled from Leicester to Oakham with Dr. S——, and I put the question to him whether such a fear might not be justly entertained. He was clearly of that opinion; and I should not be surprised if we had a repetition, at least on a smaller scale, of the Irish Famine in 1847. I am doing what I can to help the brethren, and obtained at Oakham a collection of £41 when I was last there. But my want of local knowledge is a hindrance to my satisfactory distribution of the money sent me or collected by my own exertions. I am therefore obliged to let Mr. Gadsby take that part of the good work upon himself. You would probably hear from Mr. Grace his account of his northern visit, but a mere passing view cannot give an adequate idea of the depth and extent of the calamity. Its physical evils are and will be increasingly dreadful, but I much fear that its moral evils will be even greater and more permanent. It has already reduced to the same level the provident and the improvident, the industrious and the indolent. This is one moral bank already swept away; and if it pauperise Lancashire, it may next sweep away that other noble bank—the stout-hearted independence of Lancashire men. Still He who sits upon the water-flood can keep back the waves; and He whose prerogative it is to bring good out of evil can make even this calamity a blessing. The two greatest public calamities which we have known, the Irish Famine and the Indian Mutiny, have been made of the most signal service to both those countries. We may add to this, perhaps, that other third calamity, the Crimean War, which swept away a whole host of abuses. We may hope, therefore, that a blessing will come out of this cotton famine, and, indeed, I understand a more dreadful crash, if possible, must soon have come from over-production had the present cause of suffering not intervened. I greatly fear from all I have seen and heard that the northern churches are at a very low ebb in vital godliness. Who knows but that this heavy affliction may be a means of stirring up the suffering people of God in the north.

I am through mercy pretty well in health, though by no means free from my almost constant companion, a troublesome cough. But somewhat singularly, which I must attribute to the goodness of the Lord, it does not much trouble me in preaching.

I hope that you had a comfortable visit amongst my people. I was absent from them a long time, but they felt that my place was well supplied. I do not know that I have preached so much for fifteen years as during the last summer, especially in Wilts.

Yours affectionately in the Lord,

J. C. P.

CLXVI —To Mr. Tanner

Stamford, Dec. 19, 1862.

My dear Friend,

I have often thought of you during your long and heavy affliction, and have endeavoured to put up my poor prayers on your behalf, that the Lord would be pleased to spare your valuable life for the sake of your dear wife and family, and the Church of God. And I do trust that the Lord will go on to strengthen your poor weak body until He restores you to a good measure of your former health. I can well sympathise with you, for I know full well what a deep and heavy trial bodily affliction is. But what a rich and unspeakable mercy it is when the affliction, though so painful and trying to the flesh, is sanctified to the soul's profit. We want something powerful to pull us out of our carnal besetments. It is not a little thing which will bring down our proud heart; and heavy and repeated blows seem needful to knock us down and keep us down. But, oh, how kindly and graciously does the Lord make the bed in all time of sickness—not laying upon us more than He gives us strength to bear; and, as we have proved, surrounding our bed with the kindest and tenderest of nurses, and providing every earthly means of relieving the poor body. Mary was kind enough to tell me of a sweet view which you had of the adorable Lord at the right hand of the Father, ready as it were to receive your ransomed spirit had it been His holy will to have called you unto Himself. It is these views of Jesus by faith which raise up the tried and exercised soul to see Him as all its salvation and all its desire; and such gracious visitations of His presence, and such believing views of His person and glory, have a most blessed and sanctifying effect upon the soul and make most durable impressions.

Should the Lord, as I hope and trust, restore you again to the work of the ministry, it will give a power and a force to your testimony on behalf of the crucified, risen, and glorified Son of God. Oh, may we believe in Him more firmly, love Him more strongly, and cleave to Him more closely.

Yours very affectionately,

J. C. P.

CLXVII.—To Mr. Tanner

Stamford, Jan. 6, 1863.

My dear Friend,

I am sorry to learn that you are still suffering from your old complaint. I greatly fear that you will never be free from it, and that it is one of those crosses which the Lord sometimes binds fast round the shoulders of His people that they may carry it to their dying day. My best wish is that it may be richly blessed and truly sanctified to your soul's good, and that you may reap the peaceable fruit of this painful affliction as one who is exercised thereby. But feeling some sympathy with you in your affliction, and some moving of affectionate desire toward you under it, it has come into my mind to drop you a few lines, which you will take as a token of my love, if there be nothing in them worthy of your perusal. We would, if we could, spare our friends the trials and afflictions under which we know they groan, being burdened, and yet we are well aware that it is the will of the Lord that they should be thus afflicted that they might become partakers of His holiness. But our coward flesh shrinks from suffering, whether it be in our own persons or in those of our friends. So Peter, if he could have had his fleshly will, would have prevented the redemption of the Church by the blood of the Son of God. That his dear Lord and Master, the Son of God, in whom he believed by a special revelation of His Divine Sonship, that He, co-equal and co-eternal with the Father and the Holy Ghost, should be nailed to a cross, and there die in shame and agony, he could not endure. He therefore put forth his feeble hand to stop the work which the Father had given the Son to do, and by so doing was actually, though unwittingly, an accomplice of Satan. So we would spare our friends from the nails of crucifixion, not seeing, by so doing, we should, if we could succeed, rob them of that suffering with Christ which is necessary, that they should be glorified together. I will not, therefore, do you the injury of wishing your sufferings less, but would desire instead that as the sufferings abound so also may the consolation. What no doubt you chiefly feel next to the pain of personal suffering, is the hindrance which it is to the work of the ministry. Still even there the Lord can blessedly over-rule it for your good and the good of the people; and even if you preach less you may preach with more savour, unction, and power.

We are entered, my dear friend, upon a new year, and whilst I wish the best blessings to rest upon you and yours during the year, yet no doubt we shall find it, if we are spared, full of trials and temptations; and it will be our rich mercy if deliverances and manifestations of the Lord's goodness and mercy at all keep pace with them. You and I are going down the hill of life. We shall no longer possess the health and strength of years gone by, even in that minor measure which was allotted us compared with many of our brethren in the ministry. It is my desire, when at all favoured with a sense of the Lord's presence, to walk more in His fear, and to live more to His praise than I have ever yet done. I feel it to be a mercy that my mental faculties are preserved to me without much sensible diminution or decay; and as, without my seeking, the Lord has placed me in a position to speak far and wide to His people, my desire and prayer are that He would give me His grace, not only to keep me from evil that it may not grieve me, but to feed the Church of God, as far as He enables me, with such savoury meat as their soul loveth. I feel, I hope, an increasing desire to contend earnestly for the faith once delivered to the saints, to live myself in the enjoyment of the power of God's truth upon my own soul, and to bring before the people such divine realities as are made known to my heart and conscience. As you know, I have no one to help me in this lawful strife but the Lord. Indeed, perhaps I could not bear a partner in the firm, and therefore find it best to work alone.

* * * * * *

Yours very affectionately in the truth,

J. C. P.

CLXVIII—To Mr. Jacob Blake

Stamford, Jan. 29, 1863.

My dear Friend,

Not having heard of you or from you for so long a period, and having forgotten your address, I hardly knew whether you were still a sojourner in this vale of tears. This was the reason why I put the notice on the wrapper of the *Gospel Standard*, and I am very glad to find that you are still spared to be a witness for truth in this dark and cloudy day, when the sun seems much to have gone down upon the prophets. It is a mercy, therefore, that you are still spared to contend earnestly for the faith once delivered to the saints. The Lord has graciously promised, "That a seed shall serve Him"; and though the Lord's people are too often like two or three berries on the top of the uppermost bough, yet His promise still holds good.

I was much pleased and encouraged by the testimony contained in your letter, that the Lord graciously condescends to make use of my sermons and writings for the good of His dear people. Many of the Lord's people walk in great darkness, the reason often being that the way to the city is not clearly cast up. When, therefore, they can see that the path in which they are walking is the strait and narrow way which leadeth to life eternal, they gather up a sweet hope that the Lord Himself has put their feet into it, and will never leave them or forsake them, but will bring them off more than conquerors through the blood of the Lamb. I was much struck with what you said about the effects of my sermon at Langport, for I must confess that my mind that evening felt very much confused. But the Lord is a sovereign, for you were not the only one blessed that evening; Mr. D. had a special blessing. It has happened to me sometimes, in my experience as a minister, that the Lord has in a very particular manner attended the word with a divine power from my lips.

Yours affectionately in the Lord,

J. C. P.

CLXIX.—To Mr. Tanner

Stamford, February 6, 1863.

My dear Friend,

I was glad and yet sorry to see your well-known handwriting—glad to perceive that you are able once more to put pen to paper, sorry to think that you should have overtasked your strength to do so kind an office. One of the most painful effects of protracted illness is the exhaustion of mental power, especially when the mind is naturally active and has been long accustomed to expend its energies without sensible fatigue. This exhaustion of mental energy you seem much to have experienced, and it may be some time before you recover the free use and easy exercise of all your mental powers. But it is an inestimable mercy when, in the absence or suspension of mental energy, the soul can quietly and softly repose on the bosom of mercy. And, indeed, this is one of the choicest blessings of the covenant of grace, that it gives rest and peace, quietness and stillness in the assurance that the work of Christ is a finished work, that nothing remains to be done, and that all is secured in the person of the Son of God, in whom the Father is ever well pleased. If we had to work out our own salvation where could we begin and where could we end? What could we do on a bed of sickness, amidst racking pain, restless nights and wearisome days? How blessed, then, is a salvation without money and without price, that meets the soul in all its wants and woes and sustains it by the mighty power of God.

My dear friend, you have been deeply afflicted in body, have suffered greatly, and been brought down to the very chambers of death. And yet what goodness and mercy have been displayed on your bed of languishing! What kind, tender, watchful, and unwearied nurses you had to anticipate all your wants, and smooth, as far as it lay in their power, your restless pillow. Nothing has been wanting which the thoughtful heart or loving hand could supply; and all that medical skill could do to alleviate your symptoms, check the disease, and restore you to health has been done. You name the great kindness which has been manifested on all sides in sending you grapes and other things often very acceptable in a sick-room. In answer to prayer, as we hope and trust, the Lord has thus far raised you up; but all this is the least display of the tender mercies of the God of your salvation. The sweet assurance which He gave you of His everlasting love when you were first compelled to take to your bed is the greatest blessing of all, and well worth all the sickness and suffering which followed. But now you must expect to find and feel more than ever the workings of that corrupt nature which is indeed the seat of every foul abomination, and which, to our shame and sorrow, is uncured and incurable. No amount of past mercy or sweet enjoyment of the goodness of the Lord can heal that corrupt fountain which is ever manifesting itself in some evil thought, base desire, or corrupt imagination. And sometimes Satan takes advantage of bodily weakness to stir up peevishness, fretfulness, self-pity, rebellion, and discontent—evils which seem to lie in the marshy lowlands of our nature as distinct from the higher grounds of pride and self-righteousness which Satan chooses for his stronger fortifications. You will find many things opened up to you in a clearer light than you ever saw them before, when, at least, you get a little respite from the workings of self, and can, as it were, sit before the Lord with solemnity of mind, viewing His dealings in providence and grace with an enlightened eye. You will also find a clearer, broader, and brighter light shining upon the word of truth; will sometimes wonder that you never saw the things of God so plainly before; and will think that if you were enabled to stand again before the people of God you would preach to them almost in a new way, and urge truth upon their consciences as you think you have never done before. You will also have clearer light and deeper views of those two grand subjects for thought and meditation—the depth of the fall, and the height of the recovery. You will see also more of man's dreadful condition by nature with all his miserable sinfulness and helplessness; and you will see more of the beauty and blessedness, grace and glory of the Son of God. You will also see more of the wretched profession of the day; how low the Church is sunk; how torn with strife and confusion; how weak in faith, and hope, and love; and how woefully deficient in all those fruits of righteousness which by Jesus Christ are to the glory of God. You have already seen how feeble is the ministry of the present day, what little work is really going on, and how few the Lord seems raising up to preach the Gospel. But with all these things you will feel a greater love to the truth, and to the dear people of God for the truth's sake, than you ever seemed to have felt before; and will be firmly convinced that, in spite of all their weaknesses and infirmities, they are the excellent of the earth in whom is all your delight. But I must not fill up my paper with my preachings, though you and I have sometimes talked these matters over, and see, I believe, eye to eye in most points; and it is for this reason, and in this confidence, that I have thus freely written. I sincerely hope and trust that it may please the Lord, in His own good time, to restore you to the enjoyment of comfortable health, and enable you once more to go forth in the work of the ministry, that your bow may abide in strength, and the arms of your hands be made strong by the hands of the mighty God of Jacob. I have been, for the most part, pretty well, through mercy, during the winter, but just now am suffering under a slight attack of my usual complaint, which has laid me aside for the last Lord's-day, and will, I fear, prevent me going out on the coming Sabbath. Still I trust, through the goodness of the Lord, it will pass off, and that I may be enabled to go forth once more preaching the word of life.

I have been making my arrangements, if the Lord prosper them, for the coming summer, and hope, with God's blessing, to come into Wilts, but this year not before the beginning of August. I should also much like to see you, and would endeavour, if possible, to make some arrangement for that purpose, but at present you must take the expression of my wishes and intentions. Should the Lord prosper my way toward you I hope that I may find you much restored.

I am, my dear Friend,
Yours very affectionately in the Lord,
J. C. P.

CLXX—To Mr. Grace

Stamford, March 18, 1863.

My dear Friend,

The friends here would have been very glad if your strength had permitted you to preach among them the word of life on April 15th, but as I know from experience how fatiguing and exhausting it is to preach two successive evenings, I will not press it. I hope the Lord will be with you at Oakham, and crown His word with that blessing which makes it so sweet and precious when it comes home with a divine power to the heart. This is what we want, both privately and publicly, and what I am from time to time sighing after, especially when exercised with temptations or burdened with trials. "He sent His word and healed them;" this is what the soul longs to feel, as it is sensibly afflicted with that grievous malady, sin, which makes the whole head sick and the whole heart faint. I believe that the truth is never really known, valued, or prized, except as we feel the desperate state into which sin has cast us, and feel something of the liberating, comforting, sanctifying power and influence of truth upon the heart. Every truth connected with the Person and work, love and blood, grace and truth, power and glory of our blessed Lord becomes sweet and precious as it is really believed in and experimentally realised to be spirit and life. It seems as if we were sometimes obliged to hang upon the Lord's words as a matter of life and death—as if the soul would bear its whole weight upon His words, to see and try if they are sufficient to sustain the weight, almost as a man struggling in a deep swamp, which seems as if it would engulf him, will fling himself upon a dry tussock that he may stand upon it firm. Temptations are most trying to the soul, and I think there are few which I have not in some measure tasted of; but their effect is, when the storm has passed, to establish and endear the truth of God more to the heart. This, I suppose, is the reason why James bids us count it all joy when we fall into divers temptations, and why Peter tells us that the trial of our faith is much more precious than of gold, though it be tried with fire. As a matter of experience and observation we find very few of the Lord's people exempt from trials and temptations, and those who are are generally as unsavoury as the white of an egg. All must have their daily cross. You have yours and I have mine; and though we find it hard to carry, galling to the shoulder and depressing to the spirit, yet we know what we should be without it.

I am sorry to find that your health is not as strong as it was, and, what seems almost a new feature, that you cannot bear the cold winds as you used to do. They are very bracing to the constitution when the chest or frame is sufficiently strong to bear them, but when they give cold or chill the limbs I know from experience that exposure to them is hurtful. I endeavour myself to secure a walk every day, if the weather at all admit, as I am well convinced that without air and regular exercise the bodily functions cannot be sustained in health, and by keeping too much indoors a susceptibility of cold is induced. But we begin to find that sixty is no more forty than forty was twenty, and we may expect, if our lives be spared, that every year will more sensibly bring with it infirmities and sensible tokens that with us soon it will be time no longer. When we look around, how we see men whom we have known departed from the scene! How many you have seen removed from the stage of life! You and I, often weak and poorly, and, in a sense, dying daily, in deaths oft. What lessons do all these things speak, and how they remind us how fleeting is time, how short and uncertain is life, how lasting eternity, how nothing desirable here below but a precious testimony of an interest in the love and blood of the Lamb!

I quite agree with you in your comparison between Goodwin and Hart. At the same time I think that Goodwin's "Mediator," though it may be the deepest is not the most unctuous of his works. I prefer some of his shorter pieces, and his "Exposition of Ephesians." But to read him requires almost as much attention as a mathematical problem. His writings are too deep, too laboured, and too prolix for the present age. I have been reading lately Huntington's "Rule and Riddle," and have felt it very instructive and edifying. You have perhaps heard that Mrs. L., who gave me Bensley's edition of Huntington's works, is dead. She was confined to her bed with paralysis for many months, but made, I understand, a good end.

It is rather more than three years ago (March 6th) since you, Mr. Tiptaft, Mr. Pickering, and Mr. Brown met in my room. You then said that most probably we should never meet all again together. How rapidly have these three years fled. On that very day poor Mr. Isbell breathed his last. We still are spared. Oh may we be blessed and made a blessing! This sums up all.

Yours affectionately in the Lord,

J. C. P.

CLXXI —To Mrs. Peake

Stamford, April 23, 1863.

My dear Friend,

I take it very kind of you sending me some account of Mr. Grace's sermon and of your visit to our two afflicted friends. I hope it may please the Lord to bless the word which Mr. G. was enabled to speak. I fully believe that he loves the Lord, His truth, His people, and His ways; and what he speaks, he speaks out of an exercised heart. The Lord will bless by whom He will bless, and He has His own time and His own way of blessing.

I am glad you have been to see both the C——s. I——'s illness, and its fatal nature, have come upon us quite suddenly. I highly esteem him and believe him to be a man taught and blest of God, and right as well as ripe for eternity. If I am spared to come amongst you again I shall miss no hearer so much as him, as he was so attentive to all that was said; ever sitting in the same spot, and a pillar of the truth. I shall, indeed, miss him very much. He would often come into the vestry when he had heard well to greet me with his friendly smile and his cordial shake of the hand. He has been a hearer of mine ever since I came into these parts, and we have always been much united in spirit, if not always in judgment.

I am sorry that I cannot give you a very encouraging account of myself, though, through mercy, I am somewhat better. But my medical attendant says that it will be at least a fortnight before I shall be able to go out of doors, and at least a month before I shall be strong enough to preach. Indeed, he says I ought to have two or three months' rest, as this last attack has so much pulled me down. We cannot foresee things, but I can now see that it was very rash and imprudent in me to come to Oakham the last time. The exposure to the cold, and the exertion of preaching, fixed the attack upon the lung which was going off previously.

I felt what you said about the love which subsists between the members of the mystical body of Christ. I hope I feel it. To be laid aside is to me a very heavy trial in more ways than I can now mention; but to have it sanctified to my soul's good would be worth all the suffering. Love to all the friends.

Yours very affectionately,

J. C. P.

CLXXII —To Mr. Crake

Stamford, April 30, 1863.

My dear Friend,

As I send this from a sick bed, to which I am almost wholly confined, by a severe attack of one of my usual chest complaints, and am forbidden much exertion of mind or body, I can only acknowledge very briefly your kind communication and its enclosure. I have the pleasure of personally knowing Mr. L., as some years ago, when I was at Brighton, he wished to be introduced to me, having, I believe, been favoured in reading some of my writings. I did not see much of him, but my own observation, and Mr. Grace's testimony of him, much agreed with the account that you have given of him. Indeed, the narrative speaks for itself, and is fully commended to my conscience as a simple, truthful, unexaggerated, at the same time sweet, savoury, and unctuous account of a very special blessing. I particularly felt it, as since my affliction I have had very much of the same fervent spirit of prayer and supplication of which Mr. L. speaks; and I hope it may be the forerunner of a similar blessing, for I find more and more that nothing short of direct blessings from the Lord's own mouth can satisfy my soul. When put into the furnace it makes us examine matters from beginning to end; as Mr. Hart says, and I find it true,

> "Afflictions make us see
> What else would 'scape our sight."

What a view does the furnace give of the sins of which we have been guilty. As Mr. L. says, "Our whole life since a profession seems one great sin." With this comes confession and a seeking unto the blood of sprinkling with a desire that the conscience might not only be purged thereby from guilt, filth, and dead works, but also made alive and tender in the fear of God.

I shall have great pleasure in inserting Mr. L.'s narrative in the *Gospel Standard*, and believe it will be commended to the consciences of many who truly fear God.

As reports are apt to get about magnifying sometimes attacks of illness, I think it right to say that my doctor fully believes the attack will go off; but I expect it will be some time before I shall be able again to preach, as I am much brought down and scarcely hope to be able to fulfil my London engagement.

I am,

Yours affectionately in the truth,

J. C. P.

CLXXIII—To Mrs. Pinnell

Stamford, May 11, 1863.

My dear afflicted Friend,

I desire to sympathise both with yourself and your bereaved children in the great and irreparable loss which you have sustained in the removal of your beloved and lamented husband, and their most tender, thoughtful and affectionate father. Nor should I have delayed to write to you immediately on the receipt of the distressing intelligence, had I not been so very unwell as to be prohibited from exertion of mind or body. I have been suffering under inflammation of the chest, which has been very obstinate, and though, I trust, now giving way, yet still not removed.

How well I remember poor dear Mr. Pinnell coming with yourself and dear John, then a babe, to Newington House in 1835. Then it was that I first came really to know and value him, though it was not my first introduction to him; and ever since that period I have been pleased to renew my acquaintance, and I hope, I may add, real, sincere, Christian friendship with him. He was not a man who talked much; but in all he said there was a sincerity which much commended itself to my conscience and won my affections. Indeed I do not know that we ever had the slightest difference or coolness, though from circumstances we did not see much of one another. For many years he used to come to Abingdon with the late Mr. Godwin to hear me on my annual visit; and when he could not do so, as of late years, I have been privileged to renew our friendly intercourse by visiting him at his own house. I was fully purposing to do the same this year, if health and strength allowed; and had fixed in my own mind the very time, which was to be at the expiration of my London engagement. But, alas! his lamented decease has concurred, with my illness, to defeat my plans. How deeply will you and your family miss his wise and affectionate counsel and protection. But I trust that the Lord will appear on your behalf and theirs. The anxiety of sorrow which he sustained through poor John's illness and death, humanly speaking, brought him to his end. Dr. C. told me that Mr. S's. heavy trial was doubtless the cause of his affliction and death. So poor Mr. P. almost seems to have lost his life with his beloved son's.

I have only just left myself room to sympathise with your daughters and sons. May the Lord be a father to them and a husband to you.

Yours very affectionately,
J. C. P.

CLXXIV—To Mr. Tanner

Stamford, May 16, 1863.

My dear Friend,

I am much obliged to you for your kind and affectionate inquiries about my health, and though I am forbidden to dictate too much, I cannot forbear sending you a few lines just to tell you how I am. We can sympathise with each other in these heavy trials, though you have been a greater sufferer in body than I. But we know not only the weight of bodily affliction but also of being laid aside from the ministry.

I truly rejoice that you have been restored to your beloved work; and though you may not see in yourself the effects of the furnace, it may be visible to your people. In reading your letter this thought came over my mind, that we must be brought down in soul before there can be any union and communion with the Lord or with His people. It is only in the valley of humiliation that there is any sensible communion with the Man of sorrows or His broken-hearted contrite people. And all other union is not worth a straw.

The Lord seems cutting Israel short. We have almost in a fortnight lost three of our most esteemed members; but they all made a good end, and departed full of faith, and hope, and love.

Yours affectionately in the Lord,

J. C. P.

CLXXV—To Mrs. Peake

Stamford, May 29, 1863.

My dear Friend,

As I am sure you will be very desirous to know how I am progressing, I will send you a few hasty lines, and am happy to say, then, that with the blessing of God I am much better. My medical man much wishes me to go somewhere for change of air; but I cannot at present see my way to do so. If all had been well, I should this day have reached London. I cannot but feel the trial being laid aside so long, and sometimes it makes me fear that the Lord has a controversy with me. I feel, indeed, quite to deserve His displeasure from many, many acts of disobedience, and am fully sensible that if He should utterly cast me aside as a vessel in which He hath no pleasure, I should have my just desert. I am very sensible of all the sin and imperfection which hath cleaved to me, both as a man and as a minister; and I am very confident that nothing but rich free and sovereign grace can superabound over these abounding sins. Still I hope that in His own time and way the Lord will restore me to the work of the ministry, though at present I cannot say when.

I am sure you will all feel much concerned that our dear friend Tiptaft should be obliged to take rest from his beloved work. I feel that we cannot ask, or indeed allow him, to fulfil his engagement in July, though I hope that he will come on a visit to Wharflands, where he would enjoy quiet and rest.

How everything serves to remind us that we are all passing away, but it is through much tribulation that we enter the kingdom. We cannot choose our own trials, nor our own afflictions; all are appointed in fixed weight and measure, and the promise is that all things shall work together for good to them who love God.

Yours very affectionately,

J. C. P.

CLXXVI—To Mrs. —— and Miss ——

Stamford, June 9, 1863.

My dear Friends,

I cannot forbear sending you a few lines written in my own hand to acknowledge your most unexpected and undeserved kindness and liberality. I am afraid, however, of saying too much or too little; but let me assure you I much feel your kindness and the Christian love and affection which I am sure prompted it. I do not often speak of the Lord's providential dealings with me, but I have seen them in a remarkable manner. He enabled me, many years ago, to give up all my prospects in life, and has most blessedly fulfilled a promise which once He made sweet to my soul (Mark x. 29, 30). I left all I had in possession or in prospect, and have I not received "houses?"—I live in one of my own; "and brethren?"—have I not many? "and sisters?"—are not you and many others? "and mothers?"—yes, mothers in Israel; "and children?"—literally and spiritually; "and lands?"—for even that I have; "with persecutions?"—and have I not had them? and now the last and best is still to come—"eternal life."

And you, dear friends, how you, too, have seen the Lord's providential hand. He has given you beyond all you hoped and expected during your former days of trial, and has given with it what is far better still, a free liberal spirit to minister most unweariedly to the necessities of the saints.

I am thankful to say I am much better, and walked nearly to Tinwell without fatigue, and enjoyed the beautiful fresh air. How good the Lord is to those who desire to fear His great name, and live to His glory. I begin much to feel my absence from the courts of the Lord's house, and hope next Lord's-day (D.V.) to meet with the people, even if I take no part in the service. . .

Your very affectionate and obliged Brother and Friend,

J. C. P.

CLXXVII—To Mr. Brown.

Stamford, July 2, 1863.

My dear Friend,

Various circumstances have prevented my answering your kind and affectionate letter at an earlier period. My time, you know, is generally much occupied, and I have had of late the additional hindrance of illness and bodily weakness. I cannot, however, leave home without sending you a few lines just to keep up our friendly and brotherly intercourse, which is apt to drop if all correspondence be suspended. You will perhaps be surprised to hear that I am going to London (D.V.) to-morrow to supply at

Gower Street for July. I go there very unwillingly, and I almost fear unwisely, as I am by no means fully recovered from my late attack of bronchitis, but trusting that the Lord will make His strength perfect in my weakness. . . . Time is rapidly passing away with us all, and I should be sorry to depart this life divided from any who, I hope, truly fear God.

I fear, from all I hear, that you are still a cripple, and can scarcely move from place to place without the aid of crutches. Thus it seems to be the will of God to afflict us both in our earthly tabernacle, though in such different ways. But no doubt He who is all-wise has selected for us both that peculiar way which He knows is best for our good—a way by which our pride may be effectually humbled, and our helplessness best taught us, and yet mercy mingled with the dispensation. Thus, like the psalmist, we have to sing of mercy and judgment, and such, no doubt, has been the character of our experience for many years, as it is the general character of the Lord's dealings with all who fear His great name. Some time ago I was conversing with a dear saint of God, Elizabeth Holloway, of Devizes, who has been, if not quite confined to her bed, yet quite a cripple from an injured spine for nearly thirty years. I almost casually made the remark that perhaps she scarcely knew from what evils she had been kept by her long affliction. She paused for a moment, and seemed struck with the thought. As she afterwards told me, it was never presented to her mind before—at least, not so clearly, and she saw in it fresh proof of the mercy and wisdom of God. Thus you can hardly tell from what evils you have been preserved by your affliction. Nor again can we always or often see what sympathy and affection, as well as prayer and supplication from the God of all our mercies, are drawn forth on our behalf from the family of God, who witness the various afflictions with which the Lord is pleased to visit us. Thus, besides the more visible blessings which spring out of our afflictions and trials, there may be others less manifest, but not less real or less important. Time with us is fast passing away, one or another of our friends keeps dropping off, and we who survive for a time may soon be numbered with the dead. It will be our mercy to be found with our loins girt about, and our lamps burning, and we waiting like good servants our Master's return. There is a blessed promise to those found so watching and waiting.

I trust that you find the Lord present with you in the work of the ministry, and that you have continued proof that you are where He would have you to be.

Yours affectionately in the Lord,

J. C. P.

CLXXVIII—To Mr. Grace

Stamford, July 3, 1863.

My dear Friend,

Will you kindly thank Mr. L—— for his donation of £1 for publishing works of truth in Holland, as I have not time to write to him. I have just heard from Mr. Los, Gz. He tells me that through the aid of the donations of English friends he is bringing out a cheap edition of Huntington's "History of Little Faith," and intends from time to time, if the Lord enable, to bring out other works of the immortal coalheaver; I should think his "Bank of Faith," or his "Posthumous Letters," would be very suitable. He seems to be a man of a warm heart, and an earnest contender for the faith once delivered to the saints.

I am glad to find that your health is so much restored. It is indeed a precious gift of God, but, like most others, never really prized until lost. Of all men ministers seem most to need strong bodily health, having so much labour to perform of body and mind. But the Lord knows best how to deal with us both in body and soul.

I go to London in great weakness, but have often found the Lord's strength made perfect in it. I preached twice at Oakham last Lord's-day to one of the largest congregations I ever saw in the chapel—as large, I believe, as you saw there. I was comfortably brought through, and afterwards administered the ordinance. We all seem much to feel the loss of those members who have been taken out of our midst. I never seemed to realise their loss before. As they were aged, experienced men, we shall much miss their counsel and their prayers. I would gladly see more of the young raised up to fill up the place of those who are passing off the stage of life.

We had a pleasant visit at Leamington; I derived much benefit from the change, and could I have been there another fortnight should, I believe, have more sensibly felt it. I spoke there on the Lord's-day, in a lecture-room, to about fifty people.

Yours affectionately in the Lord,

J. C. P.

CLXXIX—To Mr. Tanner

Allington, July 28, 1865.*

My dear Friend,

I am glad there is some hope of seeing you at Calne. May we meet in the spirit, as well as in the flesh, and find and feel the presence and blessing of the Lord resting upon us in

* This letter has been inserted, by mistake, out of its proper order.

public and in private, in our intercourse with the Lord, with His people, and with one another. I trust I feel thankful in being so far better as to be able again to speak in His blessed name. I have laboured now for ten continuous Lord's-days, eight of them at Gower Street, and am not worse for my labours—indeed, rather stronger than when I began them. How good the Lord is to poor unworthy me. May a sense of it lead me to walk in His fear and live to His praise! I was well attended at Gower Street Chapel, and my last Tuesday evening congregation was quite a usual Lord's-day one. I felt encouraged that eight Lord's-days had not worn out my ministry amongst them.

I feel for you in your trials and afflictions, so various, painful, and multiplied. But dare I wish you free from what the all-wise, all-gracious Lord lays upon you? Could He not in a moment remove them all?

Yours affectionately in the Lord,

J. C. P.

CLXXX—To Mr. Grace

Allington, Aug. 3, 1863.

My dear Friend,

I reached here last Friday evening after a month's sojourn in London, where I had a very comfortable, and, I hope, profitable visit. I was with my dear friends Mr. and Mrs. Clowes, whom the more I know the more I value. I was favoured, for the most part, with liberty in the pulpit, and my health, instead of suffering, was improved up to the end. Indeed, London air at this time of the year, always suits my chest. There is a warmth and dryness about it which exactly suits my breathing apparatus; and I have almost reason to believe that London, as a residence, except, perhaps, at the foggy portion of the year, might suit me better than our northern exposure. Your air would be too keen, and too loaded with moist saline particles.

We had yesterday our usual attendance, almost as Hart says:

"Gathered from all quarters,"

and I hope the Lord was with us.

To-morrow is Calne anniversary, where, if spared to go, I shall meet one of the largest gatherings of the seed royal that is well known. You may have something like it in Sussex, but we have nothing like it in Lincolnshire or Leicestershire. I hope that we may have the Lord's presence and power in our midst. It is not often that you have shaken hands in one day with so many honest palms. I have said sometimes that it has almost made my hand ache after it has been grasped so much, and often so warmly, by hands hardened, not like a reprobate's conscience by God's judgments, but by honest labour. Hard hands and tender hearts are far better than soft palms, or smooth tongues, and seared consciences. I find a great difference in my preaching here and in London; not that there is any change in doctrine or experience, but a rustic population requires a more simple and almost familiar mode of utterance than suits a London congregation. It is not that I study my style, or seek to adapt it to different classes of people; but the thing comes, as no doubt you have felt, almost intuitively, without study or forecast. It is like sitting down to converse with my old almshouse woman and Mr. S. of W. We naturally necessarily drop into that style of speech which adapts itself to the person we converse with. And I am well convinced unless a minister can in this sense be all things to all men it will much limit his usefulness. We need not be low, we need not be vulgar, we need use no word which would offend the most fastidious ear, and yet be perfectly intelligible to the fisherman on the beach or the woman that cleans the chapel. I have often admired our Lord's discourses from this point of view, independent of their solemn weight and power. What dignified simplicity, what exquisite clearness! Intelligible to the lowest, and yet, in their depth, unfathomable to the highest capacity. Blessed Lord! May our desire and delight be to exalt Thy worthy name; for Thou art our all in all! All divine truth is in Jesus, comes from Him and leads to Him. He is the Alpha and the Omega, the beginning and the end, the first and the last. To know the only true God and Jesus Christ whom He hath sent, is eternal life, and all knowledge short of this is but death—as deadly in its consequences as the fruit of the tree of knowledge of good and evil.

Yours affectionately in the Lord,

J. C. P.

CLXXXI—To Mr. David Beattie

Stamford, *Oct.* 16, 1863.

Dear Sir,

I sincerely wish that I could with the blessing of God write you anything that might afford relief to your troubled mind, but I feel how helpless I am in this matter

Your case, as you describe it, is truly pitiable; but it is what many have passed through before you, who afterwards had reason to bless God for the fiery trial. We have all by nature a great deal of vain confidence and self-righteousness which have to be burnt up in all who truly fear God; and the Lord often sees it necessary to show His people terrible things in righteousness that they may learn experimentally somewhat of the depth of the fall and the need of being saved by the free sovereign grace of God. Besides which the Lord has to make His people see and feel the exceeding sinfulness of sin, that they may truly loathe it and themselves for it. Now when the soul is under these painful exercises, it cannot tell what the Lord is about nor how the scene will end. Sometimes it hopes and sometimes it fears, but its fears are usually much greater than its hopes; and so it goes on, often it may be sinking lower and lower until the Lord appears. You will find in this month's *Gospel Standard,* and in the forthcoming number, an account of exercises even greater than your own, in the first piece, called "A Mirror of Mercy," so that you have no need to despair. And you will find in "Grace Abounding," by Bunyan, an account of his deep troubles and almost despair.

If I could give you any advice, it would be to continue as far as you can reading the word, and above all plying the throne of grace with earnest prayers and entreaties that the Lord would pity your case, have mercy upon you, and reveal to you a sense of His pardoning love. The great thing is not to give way to despair, nor give up what little hope you may have that the Lord will in due time appear for the deliverance of your soul. The blessed Lord is able to save to the uttermost all that come to God by Him, seeing He ever liveth to make intercession for them (Heb. vii. 25). And the same gracious Lord has said, "Him that cometh to Me I will in no wise cast out," John vi. 37. You will find it good to plead with the Lord His own promises, such as the one I have just quoted, and that also, "Come unto Me, all ye that labour and are heavy laden, and I will give you rest," Matt. xi. 28. The blessed Lord came to seek and to save that which is lost, Luke xix. 10; and thus there is hope for every poor sensible sinner who feels himself in a lost condition.

That the Lord may soon graciously appear for your deliverance is the desire of

Yours very sincerely,
J. C. P.

CLXXXII—To Mr. Grace

Stamford, Nov. 10, 1863.

My dear Friend,

Circumstances are always occurring to prevent that free and frequent communication with our friends which we desire in order to maintain with them friendly and brotherly intercourse. Sometimes we lack the time and sometimes the inclination; sometimes engagements to preach or travelling, with its various hindrances, prevent our sending the intended letter, and I for my part am sometimes deprived of the ready aid of my secretary, without whom I do not now often write letters to my friends. Please then to accept these apologies for my delay in communicating with you by letter.

We should have been glad to see you here had you been able

so to have arranged it; but the King's business must always take precedence, and supersede everything else. I am glad that you have found an open door at Helmsley, and that you feel encouraged to go into that distant and almost unknown region. It is in grace sometimes as in nature—new, fresh soil gives better and healthier crops than that which has been so much worked. I was struck with your expression of "breathless attention." That is not a feature often seen in congregations which have long heard the word of life; though, I believe, in such places at least where the Lord manifests His presence and His power, there generally is a good share of solemn attention if the preacher has anything really worth hearing.

Ministers sometimes complain of the want of attention in their hearers when the fault is in themselves; for who cares to hear a cold, dry, dead sermon which is merely a repetition of what has been heard over and over again? All preaching and all hearing that really profits the soul must be of the Lord. I feel for myself an increasing desire that the word might be blessed. Life is passing away and the shades of evening are being stretched out. I desire, therefore, that during the time when I may be allowed to preach and write, the blessing of God may rest upon my labours more abundantly than it ever yet has done. Both of us have had our threatenings, and may be looking forward to the time of being laid up or laid aside. May we work then while it is day, for the night cometh when no man can work.

Yours affectionately in the Lord,

J. C. P.

CLXXXIII—To Mr. J. Blake

Stamford, Dec. 21, 1863.

My dear Friend,

Your post office order came safely to hand, and will be paid to the secretary at the end of this month. I see so much good done by the Aged Pilgrims' Friend Society, and so much thankfulness manifested by the poor old pilgrims, that I am very glad to support it myself, and to see others doing the same. Satan will always oppose that which is good; and he will sometimes work upon our covetous heart to make us grudge giving anything to the Lord's cause, or the Lord's people. But what is the consequence if he get the better of us, and shut up our hearts and hands? We get into a cold bondage frame, in which there is no comfort for ourselves, and no doing any good for others. Besides which, by shutting up the bowels of our compassion against the Lord's people, we provoke the Lord to shut His hand against us. I wish that I could have my heart and hand more open to the

Lord's poor, but having family expenses I cannot do all that I would. It is a great mercy to be kept looking to the Lord for the continued supplies of His Spirit and grace; for without it we soon sink down into carnality and death. Oh, that we might live more a life of faith in the Son of God, in the sweet persuasion that He loved us, and gave Himself for us! This is the happiest and the most blessed life that a man can live on earth; but none can do so except by the special help and continued grace of God.

May you and I be enabled to walk tenderly in the fear of God, and to live to His glory.

I am, my dear Friend,
Yours affectionately in the truth,
J. C. P.

CLXXXIV—To Mr. Grace

Stamford, Jan. 18, 1864.

My dear Friend,

I am quite sorry that you will not be able to look in upon me on your way to Oakham. It is not often that we meet; and yet I trust we have generally found it good to do so, for as iron sharpeneth iron, so a man sharpeneth the countenance of his friend. On most points, I believe, we much see eye to eye, and, I trust, feel heart to heart; so that when we have met there has been neither bar nor jar between us, and we have met and parted with desires for each other's welfare in the best sense of the word.

I am obliged to you for sending me S.'s sermon; I may, perhaps, review it, but have not quite made up my mind on the subject. If I should do so I shall endeavour to take an impartial view of the sermon, and the general character of such preaching, which is much fairer than running a man down unmercifully without giving him one good word.

My two favourite authors from whom I may say I have derived more instruction, profit, and consolation, and, I may add, more heart-searching examination than many others, are Dr. Owen and Huntington. I am now reading, as far as time and opportunity allow, the doctor's Commentary on the Hebrews, which I purchased some time ago, (the original edition in four folio volumes.) That epistle has always been a great favourite of mine, and Dr. Owen is truly great in those deep and important subjects which are there handled—as, the Person, sacrifice, bloodshedding, and death of our great High Priest, with His present intercession within the veil. These are the divine realities which form the food of faith. But how little are they received and believed in, even by some of whom we would hope better things. Most seem satisfied with hoping that they are the children of God because their feelings tally with what are described as marks of grace from the pulpit. But the Lord Jesus Christ, as the object of their faith, with the anchorings of hope and the flowings forth of love toward His dear name, with the various exercises whereby this faith in Him is tried, they seem to know so little of, and, what is almost worse, do not seem aware of any deficiency. But a faith of which our once crucified and now glorified Lord is not the subject and object scarcely seems to be such a faith as the Scripture speaks of. Look, for instance, at John's first Epistle! What a stress he lays upon believing in the name of the Son of God; and how he separates all men into two classes, those that have and those who have not the Son of God. He does not lay down a certain number of ever-fluctuating feelings as sure marks of heavenly grace; but comes at once to the three Christian graces, faith, hope, and love, —faith and love in almost every verse, and hope in 1 John iii. 3. I am also reading, as occasion serves, Goodwin on the Ephesians; but I cannot get on so well with him as I do with Owen. In some deep points of truth he is perhaps more profoundly versed than Dr. Owen, but there is so much repetition and such long unwieldy sentences that after I have read them I scarcely seem edified or profited by what I have read. How different is the immortal coalheaver! How at once he comes to the very marrow of his subject, and in his original, inimitable way throws off from his pen living words of the truest and most gracious experience, from the beginning of a work of grace up to the highest point of divine attainment. Like a master musician he runs up and down the chords of the heart, and strikes off without the least effort passages of consummate truth and beauty. It almost seems as if the book of the human heart, with all its deceitfulness and baseness, the book of the new man of grace, with all its varied pages, and the book of the word of God were all equally familiar with him, and that he turns alternately from one to the other with all the intimacy that a merchant has with his journal and ledger, and finds in a moment what order to write, or what sum to pay. I must confess that no writer knocks the pen so completely out of my hand as the poor coalheaver, whose very name must now hardly be whispered in the professing Church.

My daughter gave me your message about the sermon from Job viii. 11, 12, but it is not in my possession, nor, indeed, am I very clear that it was ever published. When my sermons go from me I rarely see or read them again. If they are made useful to the Church of God I hope to be able to give Him the praise; but I leave it entirely in His hands to do with them what seemeth good in His sight. I have not the slightest pecuniary interest in them, though I think it right carefully to revise them that no error or mistake may go forth.

Yours very affectionately in the Lord,

J. C. P.

CLXXXV—To Mr. Tanner

Stamford, February 19, 1864.

My dear Friend,

. . . . I see more and more what an afflicted people the Lord's people, or, at least, the best of them, are. What sufferings in body, what trials in mind, what afflictions in family, what perplexity in circumstance, what trials in the Church, what foes without, what fears within, are the most spiritual of the Lord's people exercised with. But how by these afflictions they are separated from the great mass of dead and worldly professors with which the visible Church is filled; and how through these tribulations the work of grace is deepened and strengthened in their soul. We can look back to ourselves, and we can see in others how many wares were taken into the ship, which, in the storm, had only to be thrown overboard. I can see even in those gracious friends to whom my heart is knit that many things were cleaved to, if not actually indulged in, from which the furnace of a later period in life has purged them. The Scripture well and wisely speaks of grace in our heart as gold; but this gold gets mixed with dross and tin, not that gold is dross and tin, but, as in the natural ore, the gold lies as if in streaks and in veins embedded, as it were, in worthless matter, so the grace of God in a Christian's heart lies, as it were, in thin veins, surrounded with the mass of nature's corruptions. This is why we so need the furnace, for its hot fires discover and separate everything in us which is opposed to the grace of God. Thus I have observed in those Christians who have passed through the deepest trials, and been most exercised in their own souls, more simplicity, sincerity, uprightness, godly fear, consistency, and fruitfulness; and yet with all this we find them continually lamenting their barrenness, deadness, and unprofitableness. Why so? Because the light which shines into their mind reveals, and because the life which is moving in their heart makes them feel those deep and abiding corruptions which are never purged away in their being though they may be in their power and prevalence.

I was much pleased with what you said about having your mind more fixed upon our blessed Lord, as having died and risen from the dead, and gone up on high. I have long seen and felt that our faith, if it is to work by love and purify our heart, must have an object—a divine and heavenly object to whom it can look, on whom it can hang, and with whom it may have to do. There is a great tendency in the mind, and one, I must add, often encouraged by the ministry of the day, to look too much at our evidences instead of looking to Christ. It is a delicate subject to handle, and I should much like to talk it over with you in the fear of the Lord, and in that exercise of our enlightened judgment and spiritual experience which makes conversation profitable; and, I believe, as we see eye to eye in these matters, we should not differ nor dispute. The great difficulty is to avoid getting on one wrong ground in our anxiety to get off another. We see, for instance, many preachers speaking in very bold language of always looking to Christ, and shooting arrows of contempt against the poor tried children of God for being so much bowed down with doubt and fear, and against the ministers who, they say, encourage them in them. Now, how grievous it would be to join, even in appearance, with such men, for we feel confident that the faith of which they speak is for the most part presumption. But then, on the other hand, there may be an error in leading the poor child of God to look too much to the work within instead of the work without, and make his feelings to be his Christ. Now we know that all our hope centres in the blood and righteousness of the Son of God, and we know that our faith, if it bring any peace or consolation with it, only does so as it receives the Son of God as of God made unto us wisdom, and righteousness, and sanctification, and redemption. To take Christ out of our sight is like taking the sun out of the sky; and to look to one's self for light is like substituting a lucifer match for the light of day. What we want is for the blessed Lord to come into our soul in His dying love, in His risen power, in His free, rich, superabounding grace, in the manifestations of His glorious person, and in the sweet assurance that He loved us and gave Himself for us. This is the doctrine—the heavenly doctrine which Paul preached, and which he prayed that the saints might enjoy (Ephesians i. 12—23; iii. 8—21), and this was his own experience (Gal. ii. 19, 20). Though so deeply favoured and so richly blessed he was not looking to, nor leaning upon, his own experience, even though he had been in the third heaven, but was looking to, and leaning upon, his blessed Lord. How this shines, as with a ray of light, through his blessed epistles, and oh, that we might be taught by the same spirit, have the same in measure, experience, and preach to others the same glorious Gospel, holding forth the word of life that we may rejoice in the day of Christ that we have not run in vain, neither laboured in vain.

You complain of your want of ability, &c.; but all our ability is of the Lord, and not of ourselves. One man may have greater natural ability, more clearness of thought and power of expression, or his spiritual gift may be larger, as one servant in the parable had five talents given to him, and another two. But "Well done, thou good and faithful servant," was said to both. The great thing is to labour with a single eye to God's glory according to the ability which the Lord gives us. It is the Lord's word, not our own, which we have to preach, and what the Lord blesses is not what we speak, but what the Lord speaks in and by us.

How mysterious are the Lord's dealings with His people, and

often how inexplicable; but it almost seems as if the Lord had a controversy with Zion in taking away or laying aside His servants, and raising up so few to fill up their place. It will soon be with us time no longer. Oh, that we might be enabled to say when the time comes, "I have fought a good fight; I have finished my course, I have kept the faith."

Yours very affectionately in the truth,

J. C. P.

CLXXXVI—To Mr. Grace

March 30, 1864.

My dear Friend,

The friends, I am sure, will be very glad to hear you as they have had so little preaching lately. It is trying to be so much in the furnace, and to be so often laid aside from the work of the ministry; but I hope it may be sanctified to my soul's good. But no chastisement we read for the present is joyous, but rather grievous, nevertheless afterward it yieldeth the peaceable fruit of righteousness unto them which are in exercise thereby.

I have been reading, during my illness, Bourne's Letters and Vinall's Sermons, and have found much in both agreeable to my own experience of the things of God which has been both confirming and encouraging. It is in the furnace that we learn our need of realities, our own helplessness and inability, and yet find there is a movement of divine life Godward—a reaching forth after the Lord Jesus, His person and work, His blood and righteousness, and dying love. It also brings to our mind the shortness of life, how vain all things are here below, and what a solid reality there is in the things of God as embraced by a living faith. I have felt much union with the poor afflicted family of God, and seen the blessedness of true humility of mind, brokenness of heart, contrition of spirit, godly sorrow for sin, separation from the world, and living to the glory of God. These are things which will abide when head knowledge, pride, and presumption, will be driven like the chaff before the wind.

Yours very affectionately,

J. C. P.

CLXXXVII—To the Members of the Particular Baptist Churches in Stamford and Oakham.

Stamford, April 2, 1864.

Dear Friends and Brethren,

As it has pleased the Lord again to lay upon me His afflicting hand, and thus to prevent my coming amongst you in the ministry of the word, I have felt disposed to send you a few lines by letter to show you that I still bear you in affectionate remembrance.

I need hardly tell you what a great trial it is to me to be thus afflicted, not only on account of the personal suffering of body and mind which illness almost always brings with it, but because it lays me aside from the work of the ministry; for with all its attendant trials and exercises, and with all my shortcomings and imperfections in it, I have often found it good to be engaged in holding forth the word of life among you, and have been myself fed sometimes with the same precious truths of the everlasting gospel which I have laid before you. But if it be a trial to me to be thus laid aside, it is no doubt a trial also to those of you who have received at any time any profit from my labours now to be deprived of them. In this sense, therefore, we may be said to bear one another's burdens; and so far as we do so in a spirit of sympathy and love, with submission to the will of God, we fulfil the law of Christ.

But as nothing can come upon us in providence or in grace but by the Lord's will, and as we are assured that all things work together for good to them that love God, and are the called according to His purposes, among whom we have a humble hope that we are, there is, doubtless, some wise and gracious purpose to be accomplished by this painful dispensation. I have, as you well know, long held and preached that it is through much tribulation we must enter into the kingdom of God; that the Lord has chosen His Zion in the furnace of affliction; that it is the trial of our faith, and therefore not an untried but a tried faith, which will be found unto praise, and honour, and glory, at the appearing of Jesus Christ; and that no chastening for the present seemeth to be joyous but grievous, yet that afterwards it yieldeth the peaceable fruit of righteousness unto them which are exercised thereby. Now I have to learn for myself, experimentally and feelingly, the reality and power of these truths, as well as ministerially set them before you. Indeed those of us who know anything aright, are well assured in our own minds that none can speak experimentally and profitably of affliction, and the fruits and benefits of it, but those who pass through it and realise it.

But besides you, my immediate hearers, I have a large sphere of readers, to whom I minister by my pen. There seems, therefore, a double necessity that I should sometimes, if not often, be put into the furnace, that I may be able to speak a word in season to them that are weary. Marvel not, then, nor be cast down, my dear friends and brethren, that your minister is now in the furnace of affliction, but rather entreat of the Lord that it may be blessed and sanctified to his soul's good, so that should it please God to bring him out of it, he may come forth as gold. Peter speaks of being in heaviness for a season, if need be, through manifold temptations (1 Peter i. 5); and James bids us "Count it all joy when ye fall into divers temptations" (James i. 2). The words "manifold and divers," though differently translated, are the same in the original, and the word "temptations," as I have often explained to you, includes trials as well as temptations in the usual sense of the term. . We may expect, therefore, that our trials and temptations should not only widely differ in kind, but be very numerous in quantity. Now as to temptations, in the usual sense of the term, I think I have had a good share, for I believe there are few, whether external, internal, or infernal, of which I have not had some taste, and of some more than a taste. But I cannot say the same of trials, for some severe trials have not fallen to my lot. Though I have had losses, and some severe ones, I cannot say I have had experience of painful business trials. Though when I left the Church of England, I gave up all my present and future prospects, and sacrificed an independent income, yet, through the kind providence of God, I have been spared the pressure of poverty and straitened circumstance. I have not suffered the loss of wife or children, and have been spared those severe family trials which so deeply wound many of the Lord's people. But of one trial, and that no small one, I have had much experience—a weak and afflicted tabernacle. Though my life has been wonderfully prolonged, yet I have not really known what it is to enjoy sound health for more than thirty-three years, and for the last seventeen have been liable to continual attacks of illness, such as I am now suffering under. Thus I have had much experience of the furnace in one shape, if not in some of those which have fallen to your lot. But this I can truly say, that almost all I have learnt of true religion and vital godliness, has been in the furnace, and that though ill health has been the heaviest natural trial I have ever experienced, yet I trust it has been made a blessing to my soul.

But I will now tell you, my dear friends and brethren, a little of what I have felt under my present affliction, for you will feel desirous to learn whether I have gained any profit by trading. I cannot speak of any special blessing, and yet, I trust I have thus far found the affliction profitable.

1. I have been favoured at times with much of a spirit of prayer and supplication. This I count no small favour, as it has kept my soul alive and lively, and preserved it from that wretched coldness, barrenness, and death into which we so often sink. We must feel the weight and power of eternal realities, and highly prize spiritual blessings before we can sigh and cry to the Lord to bestow them upon us. If I did not covet the Lord's presence, and the manifestations of His love and blood, I should not cry to Him as I do for the revelation of them to my soul.

2. I have seen and felt the exceeding evil of sin, and of my own sins in particular, and been much in confession of them, and especially of those sins which have most pressed upon my conscience.

3. I have seen and felt much of the blessedness of true humility of mind, of brokenness of heart, and contrition of spirit, and what a choice favour the fear of God is as a fountain of life to depart from the snares of death! You all know how, for many years, I have stood forth as a preacher and as a writer, and yet I feel as helpless and as destitute as the weakest child of grace, and a much greater sinner, as having sinned against more light and knowledge than he.

4. I have felt my heart much drawn to the poor afflicted children of God, and especially to those who manifest much of the mind and image of Christ. I never, during the whole course of my spiritual life, felt the least union with the vain-confident doctrinal professors of the day, but have always cleaved in heart and spirit to the living family of God. But I have never felt more drawn than now to those of the people of God, who live and walk in the fear of the Lord, who are spiritually minded, who manifest the teaching of the blessed Spirit, and whose souls are kept alive by His continual operations and influences. I lament to see any who profess to fear the Lord carnal, and worldly, and dead, do not covet their company nor envy their state.

5. I have been reading during my illness Mr. Bourne's Letters, Mr. Vinall's Sermons, and Mr. Chamberlain's Letters and Sermons, and am glad to find myself joined with these men of God in the same mind and in the same judgment. I have found their writings profitable, sometimes to encourage and sometimes to try my mind; but as, in the main, I feel a sweet union of spirit with them, I trust it is an evidence I have been and am taught by the same spirit.

One of the most trying circumstances of my illness is that any exertion of the mind increases the complaint and retards the recovery. I need perfect rest of mind and cessation from all mental labour; and yet I am so circumstanced that, with the exception of preaching, I am obliged to work almost as hard as if I were in perfect health. I have, however, this consolation, that I am working for the good of others, and that I must work whilst it is day, for soon the night will come when no man can work.

I have spoken thus far and thus freely of some of my own trials and the effects of them; and now I wish to add a few words upon my present affliction in its peculiar bearing upon yourselves as a church and congregation. Everything connected with vital godliness has to be tried. My ministry among you; the cause of God and truth as ours professes to be; the faith and patience, hope and love, of those who fear God in the church and congregation; the mutual union of minister and people, and of the people with each other, have all to be tried as with fire. (And it seems that the Lord is now trying us in all these points. We have lost by death during the past year some of our oldest, most established, and valued members, and by their removal the church has become proportionately weakened.) My own ill-health, for the last few years, has left you for weeks sometimes without the preached word. And as we know that a congregation is first brought together and then kept together chiefly by the ministry of the word, this circumstance has a great tendency to thin and weaken our assembly. Many will come to hear preaching who have no real knowledge of or love for what the minister preaches; such hearers, therefore naturally fly off when there is no minister in the pulpit. But these very things which naturally weaken a people as a people, and try the strength of a cause as a cause, try also the reality and vitality of the work of God among them. The ministry of the gospel, when owned of God, is no doubt a great blessing to a people, and the deprivation of it will be deeply felt by those who derive profit from it. But this very deprivation may have its attendant benefit. You may see more clearly and feel more deeply thereby that you must get your blessings, your encouragements, your tokens for good, your helps by the way, your sips and tastes of the Lord's goodness and mercy, more directly and immediately from Himself. And this will help to put the ministry in its right place—to be highly prized as an ordinance of God, and yet not to be made almost a substitute for those other means of grace, such as prayer and supplication, reading the word, private meditation, and meeting together among yourselves, all which the Lord can bless as much, if not more, than the ministry itself.

If my ministry has been owned of God to your souls, it will stand. The blessings which you have received under it, whether many or few, little or much, will abide and be rather strengthened than diminished by my present suspension from my labours. If all I have preached in your ears for more than twenty-five years is merely in the letter, and you have never received the least blessing nor felt the least power from my ministry, all you have heard will fall away from your mind and memory, like last autumn's leaves from the trees. Now then is the time to prove, by the effects left on your spirit, whether my word has been to you only in the letter, or has been attended with some power to your soul. Many people's religion goes no deeper and reaches no further than hearing and approving of what they hear. They may at the time seem interested, or instructed, or even moved, with what they hear; but nothing is carried home with them to sink deep into their heart and to work with a divine power in their conscience. These are well described by the Lord as coming to hear His word as His people come, and sitting before the prophet as His people sit, and hearing His words but not doing them. So to some, if not many of you, I may have been as one that hath a pleasant voice, and can play well on an instrument; and with your mouth you may have shown much love, but your heart has gone after your covetousness (Ezekiel xxxiii. 30—32).

Now when the voice is silent and the sound of the instrument not heard, such people's religion seems to die away. The Lord, then, may be purposely trying your religion by suspending the ministry for a time, to show the difference between those who have a living spring in their souls independent of and distinct from the preaching, and those whose religion lies almost wholly in the use of the outward means.

We often speak of our weakness. It is a part of our creed and of our experience that the strength of Christ is made perfect in weakness. But what a very painful and trying lesson this is to learn, whether individually as Christians or collectively as a Christian Church! Now that is just the very lesson which you are learning now, and which I believe you will have to learn more and more. It is not often that living churches are what is called flourishing churches—that is, in the usual acceptation of the word. Large congregations, an abundance of respectable hearers, a continual accession of members to the church, flourishing circumstances, and a great flow of such prosperity as the worldly eye can measure, is not the appointed lot of the true churches of Christ. All this we may seem to see and to believe, but it is only trying circumstances that can really convince us that when we are seemingly strong then we are weak, but that when we are weak then we are strong.

But I will not weary you longer. I shall, therefore, only add that, as the Lord through undeserved mercy is gradually restoring my health and strength, I trust that after a little time I may be given to your prayers. Meanwhile I commend you to God and to the word of His grace, which is able to build you up, and to give you an inheritance among all them which are sanctified.

Brethren, pray for us,

Your affectionate Friend and servant in the Lord,

J. C. P.

CLXXXVIII—To Mrs. Peake

Stamford, April 26, 1864.

My dear Friend,

I am much obliged to you for your affectionate and very interesting letter. As I was reading it the words came to my mind—

"Love all defects supplies."

But before I enter into its contents it may perhaps be as well just to tell you a little how I am. Through mercy, then, I am gradually, though very slowly, regaining strength, and I still hope with the help and blessing of the Lord, if the weather continue fine, to be enabled to come to Oakham on Friday. Till then I must reserve all arrangements about the chapel; but I certainly do not expect to be able either to preach or to have a church meeting.

All I could do if the friends wished it, and the day were favourable, would be to administer the ordinance.

I much liked the account which you gave of our dear friend, Mr. Grace's testimony amongst you. It was quite commended to my conscience as simple, spiritual, and suitable. There was nothing in it, as it seemed to me from your account, too high or too low, but such a line of things as would meet with the average experience of the Lord's family. He told me when here that the text from which he hoped to speak at Oakham had been presented to his mind, and I said to him that I had generally found that such seasons were favourable. I expected therefore that it would be a good season. I hope I can rejoice in the Lord's blessing the labours of other good men. It is indeed a sad spirit when ministers are jealous of each other, and would rather cavil, and, what I call "nag at" each other, instead of desiring that the blessing of God might rest upon them and their labours. Every sent servant of God has his own peculiar gift and line of things, in which he is strong, and out of which he is weak. Now it matters little what be a man's gifts or abilities, it is only what the Lord blesses which is of the least worth or value. I have long seen and felt this, and I hope an experimental feeling of it has much kept me from exalting myself and despising others. Oh, that miserable spirit of detraction and envy which would fain pull others down that we might stand as it were a little higher upon their bodies! Where is there any true humility of mind, simplicity of spirit, brotherly love, or an eye to God's glory when this wretched spirit is indulged? But I have rather wandered from my subject. I hope that a permanent blessing may rest upon the seed which our dear friend was enabled to sow.

I can assure you, my dear friend, that I always receive your letters with very great pleasure. Our dear friends at the Wharfland are unable from various reasons to communicate what I so much wish to hear from Oakham when I am absent. The Lord has given you the pen of a ready writer, and thus I have to look much to you for those communications in which I take so deep an interest. What you say about church meetings is most true. We have lost our senior, and therefore weightier members, and though I through weakness of health feel less and less able to hold the reins, yet, as it is necessary that there should be some presiding head, I hope the Lord may strengthen me for that purpose.

I hope I may be enabled to go to Leamington. We have already engaged the same lodgings which we had last year. My medical man thinks that the change will, humanly speaking, do me good, as he says that all I need now is strength. We shall therefore, the Lord willing, if weather permit, come to Oakham on Friday on our way thither if the Lord should prosper our journey.

Yours very affectionately,

J. C. P.

CLXXXIX.—To Mr. Tanner

Stamford, April 27, 1864.

My dear Friend,

Afflictions and trials, when they are made to work together for good, much draw the family of God nearer and nearer to each other. I have used this figure sometimes—Put together two pieces of cold iron, there is no uniting. Put together one piece glowing hot out of the furnace and another cold piece, still no union. Bring together two pieces, both out of the furnace, and let the heavy hammer of affliction fall upon them both together, there is a welding, a union, they become one. The application will suggest itself without any explanation. I have felt, since I have been myself in the furnace of affliction, much more drawn to and united with the suffering family of God than when I am out of it. I have no doubt, dear friend, that you have felt the same in your afflictions and trials, and that they give you more feeling for, more union and communion with the suffering members of the mystical body of Christ than when you are not so much in the furnace. The humble, the simple-hearted, the tempted and tried, the afflicted, the broken in heart and contrite in spirit, are not these the choicest of the Lord's precious jewels? And why? Because they are more like Christ, more conformed to His image, more manifesting the power of His grace. I never was, since I made a profession, one in mind and spirit with the heady, bold, daring professors; but though for many years I could not clearly discern where they were wrong, yet I had an instinctive feeling of disunion and of separation from them in heart. I think from the very first, where there is what our blessed Lord calls the light of life, there is a spiritual discernment both of the truth of God and of the children of God. By the first we are in good measure kept from error, and by the second from becoming mixed up with ungodly professors. Not but what we often make great mistakes; but this is more from want of judgment than from wilful error. The Lord therefore graciously pardons such errors in judgment, as He knows that they are not done out of malicious wickedness.

How mysterious is the life of God in the soul. It seems like a little drop of purity in the midst of impurity. When I was a boy in London there was exhibited in the window of some eminent watchmaker a very curious movement, if I may so term it. If I remember right there was a flat plate of glass or metal, I forget which, suspended horizontally on a central pivot. In this plate there were cut, what I may call, perhaps, little paths or roads communicating with each other, top and bottom, and a large globule, as it seemed, of quicksilver kept perpetually coursing up and down these paths, depressing alternately each side of the plate as a kind of pendulum. I may, perhaps, describe it wrong, as more than forty years have passed since I have seen it, but it just struck my mind as a representation of the new man of grace in the heart, coursing up and down so bright, shining, and spotless, and yet giving movement to and regulating the whole machine. Please to forgive me if my figure be wrong.

I have had a severe attack of what I may almost call my constitutional malady—bronchitis. Through mercy all the inflammatory symptoms have been removed, and now my chief ailment is great weakness and tenderness. Still, I am thankful to say that I am daily mending, and, being able now to get my walks when the weather admits, I hope I may, with God's blessing, be after a little time restored to my usual health. It is very trying to me and to my people that I should be laid aside as I so often am; but they bear it with much kindness and patience, and I doubt not there is a secret purpose of wisdom and goodness to be accomplished thereby. "What I do thou knowest not now; but thou shalt know hereafter." It is a part of true Christian wisdom, of living faith, of real humility of mind, of submission to the will of God, to be content to believe what we cannot see. "He leadeth the blind by a way that they knew not." A sense of this blindness will lead us to commit our way unto the Lord, to trust in Him that He may bring it to pass. But we have to mourn over our ignorance, darkness, unbelief, infidelity, and that wretched want of submission to the will of God, which adds so much to the weight of every trial. If we could but believe, and be firmly established in the belief, that our various trials, whether bodily, or family, or mental, or connected with the church, were for our own good, how much would it lighten their load. But to grope for the wall like the blind, and to grope as if we had no eyes, leaves us to carry the burden alone, and you know what poor fainting work we make of it when we have to carry the load with our own arms. The sweet persuasion that the Lord has sent the trial, will support us in it, and will bring us out of it, wonderfully lightens every trial, however weighty it may be in itself.

You have now a trial before you. You are going to London, weak in body and suffering various ailments which seem to need the especial care of home. Amidst all these ailments you have to stand up before a London congregation, amongst whom there may be some choice children of God, and very many sharp-eyed, keen-eared critics. You are looking, perhaps, to what you think is your want of education or ability to set forth the precious truths of the everlasting Gospel. You do not consider how the Lord can strengthen you in body, mitigate your ailments, alleviate your pain, take away the fear of man, and give you a door of utterance which may not altogether satisfy yourself, and yet may be satisfying to the hearers—at least to that part of them who alone deserve the name of hearers. I have long seen, and see it more and more, that it is not gifts and abilities that the Lord blesses, but His own word in the heart and mouth of His sent servants.

As to gifts and abilities, they are something like what Mr. Huntington says of female beauty, scattered upon some of the worst of men. The letter ministers are far beyond the experimental in abilities, and, in their way, far greater preachers. But what are all their gifts and abilities but to build up themselves and their hearers in a graceless profession? A few simple words in the mouth of a simple-hearted servant of God, like David's sling and stone, will do more execution than all Saul's armour, or the spear of the Philistine like a weaver's beam. Be content then to go simply in this thy might, with what the Lord has done for you, and what He may speak by you; and if Mr. Pride gets a wound in the head it will not be the worse for the grace of Humility. If you have but a single eye to the glory of God, He will bring you through safely, and, it may be, successfully and honourably.

One trying feature with my illness has been my inability to exercise my mental powers, or even my vocal; so that writing and dictating could only be carried on with great fatigue and bodily injury. But now, through mercy, as I am gradually regaining strength, I feel more mental energy and somewhat stronger in body, not only to walk, but to speak and dictate.

Yours affectionately in the Lord,

J. C. P.

CXC—Mr. J. Davis, of Melbourne, Australia

Leamington, May 18th, 1864.

Dear Friend,

Your letter enclosing a P. O. order for £5, (which I will pay to the Aged Pilgrims' Friend Society), has been forwarded to me from Stamford to this place, where I am staying for the benefit of my health by the advice of my medical attendant. It has pleased the Lord to lay upon me His afflicting hand, so that for two months I have been unable to stand up in His holy name. I trust, however, that through mercy I am gradually, though slowly, recovering, and hope that it may please the Lord to raise me up again and restore me to my work.

I am glad to find you have been spared to return to your adopted country, and found your family in health. You have been spared to pass over many miles of wide sea since we met last year at Allington. I am glad to have seen you, and both I and the friends, Mr. Parry and Mr. Tuckwell, whom you saw at Allington, felt a union with you in the things of God, and liked your spirit. I am sure you must feel it to be a trial to have so few with whom you can feel sweet communion in the things of God where you are now, more especially as there seems to be strife and division even amongst the few who meet together. Few things more show the low state of the life of God in the present day than that spirit of strife and contention which seems to rend asunder most of the churches. What little life and power there must be in the soul when people are ready to quarrel almost about a straw. How quick they are to see faults in others, and how slow to see faults in themselves. I find myself much more exercised about myself than about any other people. The great thing is to be right one's self, to have some testimony from the Lord that we are His, that we may walk in His fear, and live to His praise. We shall have plenty to do to look well at home, to watch the movements of our own heart, to be seeking the Lord's blessing, and to strive after union and communion with the blessed Saviour of poor, lost, guilty sinners. If those who profess to fear and love the Lord were more brought down in their own souls, were more humbled, and stripped, and emptied, and laid low, there would be less strife, less contention, less backbiting, and more love, tenderness, and affection towards the people of God.

I thought that I could see in you at Allington a spirit of love and affection to the Lord's people, and a great unwillingness to rip up their faults and failings. And it seemed to me that you had tasted, felt, and handled the goodness and mercy of the Lord in your own soul, which made you long after a renewed sense of His favour and loving-kindness, which is better than life itself. I desire, therefore, that you may be blessed and favoured in your own soul, made and kept very little and very low in your own eyes; and may the Lord keep you from a spirit of strife and contention, from getting entangled in the world, or being overcome by sin and Satan. You are called to stand firm, not only for living truth, but also to make it manifest by your life, conduct, and conversation, that you know its power and blessedness in your own soul.

My love to Mrs. Charlwood, and to all who love the Lord.

Yours affectionately in the Lord,

J. C. P.

CXCI—To Mr. E. Walter

Stamford, June 15, 1864.

My dear Friend,

I am sorry to say that it will not be in my power to accept the kind invitation which you have sent me to come down to preach at Wadhurst, or Tunbridge Wells during my anticipated visit to London.

I should much like once more to see your aged father, with whom in times past I have taken sweet converse in the precious things of God, and who for many years used to come up to hear me when I was in London. I do hope that the Lord has blessed his soul with more consolation than he used at that time to speak of, and that his last days may be his best days. He always had since I knew him much of the manifest fear of God in living exercise, but did not enjoy much of that sweet liberty which some of God's saints are favoured with. But I never doubted his case or state, and fully believe it will be well with him whenever the time shall come to cut the mortal thread.

The reason why I cannot come is the state of my health. I have been confined to the house for March, and a good part of April, through bronchitis, which has left me very weak; and though I am venturing to go to London in the strength of the Lord, yet it is in much weakness. I am therefore unable to accept any invitations, beyond my engagement at Gower Street, and have already refused several.

I am glad that your poor aged father still bears me in affectionate remembrance. He has seen many of his old friends gradually decline and drop—amongst them his pastor, Mr. Crouch. But what a mercy it is that though man dies, Jesus lives, and that He is full of compassion, mercy, and truth to all those who fear and love His great name! The path in which your father has been led so many years is a safe way, though a rough and rugged way. But the end will make amends for all.

My sincere Christian love to him and to all who love the truth.

Yours very sincerely,

J. C. P.

CXCII —To Mr. Tanner

Stamford, June 22, 1864.

My dear Friend,

On looking over your letter this morning to refresh my memory, I was reminded of one of Bunyan's master traits, where, in describing the clothing of the women in the House Beautiful, he says, "They could not see that glory each one had in herself which they could see in each other. Now therefore they began to esteem each other better than themselves," &c. So I could see—don't think I am flattering—that grace in you which I cannot see in myself. You have had not only a long and trying affliction, but have had trial upon trial from almost every quarter—in your family, in your business, in the church, in your soul, and continually in your poor afflicted body. Your sympathising friends would, if they could, take all these loads off your back, and all these pains and infirmities out of your body. But the same hand which took away the affliction would with it take away the consolation, and by giving health to the body would remove health from the soul. You have not only a better but a wiser Friend than we poor mortals could be to you, even with our best wishes, and tenderest sympathies; and that all-kind and all-wise Friend will not lay upon you any more than His grace enables you to bear; and though the profit of it may not appear to yourself, it is seen and felt by others. No one but he who has had an experience of it knows what a heavy trial an afflicted tabernacle is, and especially when to weakness is added almost constant pain. Of the former, as you know, I have had much experience; but of the latter I have had less, perhaps, than many of my friends, for my illnesses have not usually been attended with bodily pain and suffering. But, through the goodness and mercy of the Lord, I am very much better, and entertain a hope that, with the help and blessing of the Lord, I may be brought through my London labours without breaking down. I have proved again and again that the strength of the Lord is made perfect in weakness, nor do I expect that I shall have any other experience of His strength but as made known in the same way. You know, my dear friend, that it is very blessed to feel the strength, but very painful and trying to learn the preceding weakness. But can the two be separated? If the strength of the Lord is to be made perfect in it, weakness must be as indispensable for that perfection as the mortice is for the tenon.

I was sorry to hear of your dear wife's affliction. But how kind and gracious was it of the Lord to give her such a rich blessing! Oh, how mysterious are His ways, and His dealings past finding out, and yet what goodness and mercy are stamped upon them all! How true it is that whom the Lord loveth He loveth to the end; and that He never leaveth nor forsaketh those in whose hearts He has planted the grace of godly fear. But oh, how in long seasons of darkness, all His past mercies seem buried and forgotten. I have often thought of a remarkable expression of Bunyan's in his "Grace Abounding," where he says "that when he had lost the feeling that though God did visit his soul with never so blessed a discovery of Himself, yet that he found his spirit afterwards so filled with darkness that he could not so much as once conceive what that God and what that comfort was." How true is this that there seems to be through darkness and unbelief such a clear and clean sweep of everything tasted, handled, and felt, that it seems even as if the very conception of them was gone. But it is in such spots as these that we feelingly and experimentally learn the depths of the fall, and how thoroughly and entirely destitute we are by nature of either power or will. Now what should we do, or what could we do, under such miserable circumstances, unless the Lord of His own rich, free, and sovereign grace, revived our spirit! What poor, unprofitable creatures should we be in the pulpit and in the parlour, in the church and in the family, on our knees or with the Bible open before our eyes, if the Lord did not come of His own free grace. It is this thorough in-wrought feeling and experience of our own miserable helplessness and of the freeness and fulness of sovereign grace, which enables us to declare as from the very bottom of our heart what man is by nature, and what he is made by grace ; and as all the dear saints of God have a similar experience, both of darkness and light, of nature's miserable destitution, and of the Lord's almighty grace and power, it enables us, according to the measure of our grace and gift, to speak to the heart and conscience of the living family of God. I see more and more that what the Lord blesses is His own word and work,—that it is not great gifts or abilities in opening up the word, but that it is what the Lord in His sovereignty blesses. I have long seen this in a remarkable way in our dear friend, Mr. Tiptaft, now laid aside. His best friends could not say that his gifts were very great, or that he was an able expositor of the word of truth. And yet how much has his simple testimony been honoured and blessed, far beyond that of men who have outshone him in ministerial gifts. No doubt he has been tried sometimes at his want of variety and ministerial ability, but has been strengthened and comforted by the testimonies which he has received of the blessing of God resting upon the word preached by him.

Yours affectionately in the truth,

J. C. P.

CXCIII —To Mrs. Isbell

London, August 3, 1864.

My dear Fanny,

. . . I think of moving to Croydon, as there is a place of truth there, and the climate is dry and warm. My year at Stamford and Oakham expires in October, and then I think of resigning my care of the two churches and congregations. I shall much feel the step every way, and shall have to sacrifice my salary, which I can ill afford with my family. But it is better to stop in time and not sacrifice my life, which I shall do if I continue labouring as I have done. My dear wife and our son Charles are gone down to Croydon to-day, to see about a house. It is a large place not far from London. It is much warmer than Stamford, with a dry soil.

I think this last attack has brought matters to a crisis. If it please God to restore my health I should not lay down the ministry, but supply occasionally. It is the continuous labour, and in all weathers, which tries me ; but I am deeply tried in various ways, as it is a most important step, and I cannot see plainly the will of the Lord. I need much faith and patience, and for some consolation to be mingled with my afflictions. I shall have more trials in providence as well as in grace, and a rough and thorny path every way. But the Lord is all sufficient.

I hope the review has not hurt your mind. If I write at all, it must be *honestly*; and I thought a few hints might be useful to others. Let failings be tenderly touched, but not wholly passed by, as if a person were a perfect character. The accounts of saints in Scripture mention the bad as well as the good; and I should have been accused of partiality if it had been wholly praise. But I should be sorry to hurt your mind. . . .

Your affectionate Brother,

J. C. P.

CXCIV.—To the kind Friends who have contributed to the Testimonial presented to me by the Church and Congregation meeting at Providence Chapel, Oakham

Croydon, October 11*th*, 1864.

My dear Friends,

I accept with much thankfulness and sincere gratitude the liberal, I may indeed say, noble, testimonial which you have given me of your esteem and affection. It is much beyond both my wishes and expectations; but I have long known your liberal minds, and that to your power, and beyond your power, you have for many years shown me similar proofs of your love. I deeply regret that I am compelled by my failing health to sever the tie which has so long bound us together. But so far as we are united by the more enduring and endearing bond of the spirit knitting our hearts together in mutual love and affection, distance and absence will not separate us in spirit, if they separate us in the flesh. We shall still desire and pray for each other's spiritual good, and meet at the throne of grace. The blessed Spirit may also sometimes bring to your mind and memory portions of the word of God's grace which I have for so many years preached among you; and this will remind you not only of me, but of those days when we were wont together, in the house of prayer, to find the presence and power of the Lord in our midst.

Great and many have been my infirmities and deficiencies, both as a minister and as a pastor, some perhaps arising out of my weak state of health, and others from a body of sin and death. But my desire and aim have been to preach to you faithfully and experimentally the gospel of the grace of God.

And now, friends and brethren, farewell. Accept my love in the Lord; and as we have so often met below, in the earthly courts of His grace, so may we meet above in the courts of His heavenly glory.

I am, my dear Friends and Brethren,
your late attached Minister and Pastor, and still
your affectionate Friend and Brother,

J. C. P.

CXCV—To Mr. Tanner

Thornton Heath, October 14th, 1864.

My dear Friend,

I have been for some time desirous to send you a few lines, but, as usual, have been prevented by many hindrances. But the main cause has been that I have had so much occupation of mind, and so little strength of body. Indeed I have hardly had a heart to do anything beyond what was absolutely necessary. Each day brings its trials, each evening its labours, and almost every moment its weakness. I keep, therefore, putting off this and that letter until I almost forget that I have letters that ought to be answered.

I came here last Friday, after a sad parting with many attached friends and hearers among whom I have laboured for so many years. The Lord mercifully gave me strength to preach at both places twice on the Lord's-day, and at Oakham on the Tuesday evening before I left them. I have given them the best part of my life, and spent upon them my health and strength. God grant that it may be manifested that I have not laboured in vain, or spent my strength for nought. Nothing but my failing health would have induced me to leave them ; but both they and I were well convinced that I was not fit to carry on my continuous labours. We parted therefore, I trust, in mutual love and affection, as well as mutual regret. I unhappily took cold the day before I left Oakham, and have been poorly ever since—not having crossed the threshold of my new abode since I entered into it. I have much desired to experience here the power and presence of the Lord, that I may have His approbation upon the step, and His sanction of my pitching my tent in this place. I desire to be ever watching His hand, both in providence and in grace; to acknowledge Him in all my ways, that He may ever direct my steps. I have been so often laid aside from preaching, and that for weeks and months together, that I do not feel the trial so great as might be anticipated. I live also in hope that it may be the Lord's will so far to restore me that, during the summer months at least, I may be enabled to go forth in the Lord's name. At present I am seeking rest, though, as usual, it is hard to obtain it, for much work lies before me ; and if my tongue be still, my pen apparently will not lie idle. Indeed I have never for many years sought indolence, but have found a willingness to labour as far as the Lord has given me strength. The meridian of life with us is gone by. The Lord has seen fit to lay his hand upon our poor bodies, and we may expect the rest of our lives to be more or less invalids, scarcely hoping for any length of time to be free from those attacks which we must expect rather to gain strength with declining years. I think sometimes of you, our dear friend at Allington, and myself. We all seem to have before us a trying path, and I believe our desire is to find in it submission to the will of God, and to have every trial sanctified and blessed to our soul's profit. No doubt we need a great deal to bring us down. "He brought down their hearts with sorrow." We desire to have a broken heart and a contrite spirit, a humble mind, a tender conscience. We desire to live and walk in the fear and love of the Lord, to be kept from evil that it may not grieve us. We also covet the presence and blessing of God in our souls, in the manifestations of His love and mercy. We desire also to see His good hand stretched out in providence, that we may have reason to bless and praise His holy name for His kindness and goodness to us; and yet with all this what coldness, deadness, and darkness often beset the mind! Unbelief and infidelity, doubt and fear, surmises and misgivings, possess the mind, so that the life and power of real religion appear almost gone. Thus we have many changes, and these will ever keep us from being settled on our lees and being at ease in Zion. The flesh, it is true, loves an easy path, and, left to ourselves, we would almost barter eternal life for better health, greater strength, and a larger amount of earthly good. But it is our mercy that we cannot choose our own way, our own will, or our own cross, but that all is appointed for us—what to do and what to suffer, what to be, and what not to be. I wish I could be more spiritually minded, which is life and peace, walk more in the enjoyment of the love and favour of God, feel more of the preciousness of the Lord Jesus Christ, and have a stronger faith in Him. We cannot always nor often tell how our trials and afflictions are working for our spiritual good, nor how they are answers to our prayers for more humility of mind and to know more of the power and blessedness of eternal realities. It takes a great deal to wean us from the world, to humble and mortify our proud heart and break our stubborn spirit. We should like to have it done quietly and gently, by a secret, spiritual, and supernatural influence resting upon the mind, without any affliction of body, trial of mind, or crucifixion of the flesh. We should like Jesus to be manifestly our All in All, without walking in a path of exercise or suffering. We tell people from the pulpit what is the right way of getting at spiritual blessings, and yet are ever seeking or desiring them to come to ourselves in some different way. At least I find it so to be the case with me. It is a great thing to be made spiritually upright and sincere, to be ever seeking the blessing of God as a felt internal reality, and to desire nothing so much as His sensible favour and approbation. But it is a hard struggle to get at this and into this in the right way, especially when the Lord seems to hide His face and turn a deaf ear to our petitions. Still we must keep on seeking His blessed face till He turn the shadow of darkness into the morning. . . .

Yours affectionately in the truth,

J. C. P.

CXCVI—To Mrs. Peake

Thornton Heath, Oct. 24, 1864.

My dear Friend,

I was beginning to feel very desirous, I may say anxious, to learn how matters were proceeding with you at Oakham when your kind and affectionate letter came to hand to relieve my anxiety. I read it with very great interest, and I hope some feeling, not only on account of the expression of your affection towards, and continued interest in, my unworthy self, but as giving me some account of what I wished so much to hear—what was doing as regards the settlement of a minister and pastor among you. . . . . May the Lord guide His servant to do that which shall be most for His people's good and His own glory; and I hope that my dear friends at Oakham and in the neighbourhood will unite their supplications that the Lord would make His will clearly known; for without that no real blessing could be expected. It is as much for the interest and comfort of the church and congregation that it should be the manifest will of God to bring Mr. K. among you as it can be for his. His coming might seem at first to settle matters quietly and comfortably; it would remove the trouble and anxiety about procuring acceptable Supplies; and all for a time might seem to go on prosperously. But unless the blessing of God rested upon his settlement among you, storms would arise in the apparently settled sky, and there would spring up difficulties and perplexities of a most trying nature. But if it were the manifest will of God that he should be settled over you, then whatever difficulties might arise, the power and presence of God and His blessing would overrule and overcome all. There is no use, therefore, trying to settle such an important matter in a hasty, I might add, fleshly way, nor to tempt him, as it were, to decide such a point, by offering worldly advantages.

I always foresaw that if it pleased the Lord to remove me, it would open a door for much perplexity how to get my place supplied. Not that I wish to attach any value or importance to my labours among you, but as knowing the extreme difficulty in procuring acceptable Supplies. It was with the greatest difficulty that I could get my pulpit supplied when I went out. All these things have been present to my mind for years—in fact, ever since I have been strongly pressed to go to London. I have always felt that I would stay with you as long as health and strength were granted, and nothing but most painful and trying necessity would have compelled me to leave you. I feel, therefore, deeply anxious that Mr. K. should be settled over you by the will of God, and that His blessing might rest upon every step which has been taken in His fear to promote it.

I shall not soon forget my last days among you; for surely I was helped both in body and soul to speak to you in the name of the Lord at my parting farewell. I have just finished revising the sermon which I preached from Phil. i. 5, 6, and I seem to think that it will be acceptable to the friends when it comes out in print, as I felt some sweetness and savour in revising it. I should much like to have my three farewell sermons put together in a little cover when the third has been published in the "Gospel Pulpit," that they may be a little memorial of my ministry among you, and may show both to friends and enemies what it has been. I would prefix a little preface, if thought desirable; and Mr. Ford probably would be willing to strike off some extra copies. I certainly had no wish that they should be taken down, but I now seem pleased that they have been; and may the Lord condescend to bless them abundantly. I should not have named this subject, had you not been the person through whom it was brought about. . . . . .

At this critical time all who love the Lord and His truth, and feel knitted to the cause of God at Oakham, should join heart and hand, to tide, as it were, the ship over the present waves,—you, dear friend, and others who can pray in secret, and the male members who have the additional privilege of praying in public. My poor prayers are put up for you all, that the Lord would bless you, and appear for you in this trying hour. I much liked the quotation you made from some good man about the uniting power of prayer. Oh, that we might know much more of it.

I am getting tolerably settled in my new abode. I have much coveted the special presence and power of God upon my soul as a testimony of His approbation; but though I have been favoured with a spirit of grace and supplications, and at times some nearness of access to the throne, I have not realised, as I could wish, the coveted blessing. I have been reading with much pleasure, and, I hope, some profit, "Huntington's Posthumous Letters." The more I read them, the more I seem to see the fulness and blessedness, and the varied experience of God's living truth, as set forth in them. Indeed, they are most choice and profitable reading. I should like you, dear friends, to read sometimes in them during the winter. They are short and sweet; you can take them up and lay them down without their requiring any stretch of thought, or continuous reading. I am so much occupied myself in writing, that I have not much time to read authors. What, therefore, I read, I like to be of the best; and I find no writings suit me better than those of the immortal coalheaver.

At present I have seen none of the friends, except Mr. Covell, who is very attentive and friendly.

Our united love to yourself and your dear sister, our dear friends at Wharfland and the Terrace. Mine to all the dear friends. I shall not soon forget our last church meeting. Greet them all by name, and indeed all who love the Lord.

Yours very affectionately in Him,

J. C. P.

CXCVII —To Mr. Whitteridge

Thornton Heath, Nov. 11, 1864.

Dear Friend,

There is much in your letter which I like, and it seems commended to my conscience as written by an honest man. You speak of yourself as one who has not had much education; and yet your letter evidences that you must have taken much pains with yourself, and after all even where, as in my case, a good foundation has been laid by early and long instruction, a man, to know anything aright, must very much educate himself. I speak of this, of course, only in reference to natural education; for, as you well know, we must be taught of God if we are to know anything as we ought to know. Any knowledge which I may have of the only true God and of Jesus Christ, whom He hath sent, must have come from the anointing which teacheth of all things, and is truth, and no lie, if indeed it save or sanctify my soul. But I have had to learn for the most part what I know, and what I teach by tongue and pen, through trial and temptation; for it is through much tribulation that we must enter the Kingdom.

But I now come to the main subject of your letter—the wish expressed in it that I could render some help in the way of counsel to plain, uneducated men. In the first place, I hardly know whether I am competent to give it, or whether, if given, any one would be willing to take it. I find for the most part that men ask for advice when they mean approbation. But, apart from this, neither time nor health would allow me to undertake such a task. My health is of late weakened, mainly with hard labour and exercise, and employment of mind. I want rest both of body and soul—for thought, tongue, and pen. My medical attendant told me a day or two ago he should like, if he could, to cast me into a six months' trance, meaning, I suppose, that I wanted perfect rest for that period of time. I could not, therefore, in addition to all my present work with the *Standard*, and much correspondence, put a fresh burden upon my back. I consider that in writing for the *Standard*, I communicate for the most part what I am taught and know.

I thank you, however, for your kind and friendly letter, and wish it were in my power to give you or any other sincere, simple man any such counsel as might be offered and received in the fear of the Lord.

Yours very sincerely for truth's sake,

J. C. P.

CXCVIII —To Mr. Grace

Thornton Heath, Nov. 15th, 1864.

My dear Friend,

It is indeed now a long time since I wrote to you, but it is our mercy that union and communion, if ever we have felt it, with any of the Lord's people, does not depend upon the post office, or, indeed, any other communication, but that which is maintained with our mutual Head. In Him all the members of His mystical body have both their being and their well-being; and thus their union and communion with each other still abide, however little there may be of present communication. There is one spot where all the regenerated family of God meet in spirit, viz., at the mercy seat; and there is one Object on which they all fix their eyes, viz., the Son of God at the right hand of the Father. Lovers sometimes have fixed for both to look at the moon at a certain hour, that they may feel that their eyes, though distant in body, are viewing the same object. But those who love the Lord have a higher love and a better object than either moon or star, for they look, and sometimes from the ends of the earth, to the Sun of Righteousness. I am well convinced that there is a secret union amongst the living members of the body of Christ; and surely next to union and communion with the Lord Himself is union and communion with His dear people. May it be our blessed portion to enjoy a larger measure of both, for they wax and wane together; and he that loveth Him that begat, loveth him also that is begotten of Him. How sweetly does holy John treat of brotherly love, both in its source and in its streams; and how decisively does he lay down its presence and its absence, as sure marks of life and death! But alas! in our day the love of many is waxed cold; and indeed it ever must be so where there is so little faith which works by love and purifies the heart.

Since I have been in my new abode, I have had much in various ways to exercise my mind. Illness of itself is a heavy burden to carry; and though I must not call myself positively ill, yet I have much weakness and indisposition, which has much of the same depressing effect upon the mind. I have come also to a strange place and to a strange house, in most respects very inferior, though the rent is higher, than my own house at Stamford. I have also been much exercised in my own mind upon many things which I cannot altogether name, but which have served to cast me down, and at times to bring a cloud over my soul. And yet I hope in and by all these things the life of God has been maintained and kept up more than it would have been in a path of ease. I am well satisfied from Scripture, from observation, and from experience, that it is only through much tribulation that we enter the kingdom of God, either really or experimentally. And I also believe that in very many, if not most, cases, trials and afflictions increase rather than diminish in the later stages of life. At least I expect this will be my case, and I have seen it also in others.

About ten years ago you gave me a volume of Mr. Huntington's "Posthumous Letters." This volume I make my daily companion—not that I mean I am always reading it, but generally do so at some part of the day. And I must say the more I read it, the more pleasure, and I hope I may add the greater profit, I derive from it. There is scarcely a point of Christian experience, from the lowest depth to the greatest height, which the immortal coalheaver has not touched upon, and indeed handled, with his masterly, unrivalled pen. Nor is there an exercise of the soul, nor a secret lust, nor hidden corruption, that he has not dragged to light. It is, indeed, a most precious and valuable legacy to the Church of God, and I could wish that it were more widely spread and better known. The two authors from which I have gained the greatest profit, and the soundest as well as most savoury instruction, are Dr. Owen and Mr. Huntington. I am a writer myself upon the things of God, but these two men above all others, and the latter especially, knock my pen out of my hand.

I am glad to find that, though I am laid aside, at least for the present, from the work of the ministry, you are still employed in the service of the great King. It is, indeed, a great honour for poor vile worms of earth to be employed as ambassadors for the King of kings and Lord of lords; but in these matters, as in all others, God is a sovereign, and as such I desire to submit to His holy will. It is a trial for me to be separated so much from my own former people; but I feel fully convinced that neither health nor strength were sufficient to allow me to continue ministering among them.

We shall be glad to see you if you can make it convenient to give us a call on your way to London. I gave your message to "brother Frank." He generally comes to see me once a week, and I find him both a pleasant and profitable companion. He is very friendly and very unassuming. At present I have not been able to get out to hear him, nor have I seen anything of his people. Dr. Corfe tells me that my chest is much better than it was when in London, and gives me every hope that I shall preach again.

I am, my dear friend,
Yours affectionately in the truth,
J. C. P.

CXCIX.—To Mrs. Peake

Thornton Heath, Nov. 24th, 1864.

My dear Friend,

We have been anxious to hear how Miss —— is, but no fresh tidings make us hope she is better. . . . I believe that affliction, especially when long continued, has a sobering effect upon the mind, for we learn in it our deep need of vital realities; and these, as they are felt and apprehended, put to flight all enthusiastic notions and mere visionary views and delusions.

I am very fond of a sound mind in the things of God, for this is what God gives with a spirit of power and of love (2 Tim. i. 7). In the things of God and in vital experience there is a holy soberness; for as in believing the truth we have not followed cunningly devised fables, so an experience of the truth brings with it a solemn, sober conviction of their truth and reality. In times of trouble, temptation, sickness, and death, we want something firm to support the mind, and this we have not in airy notions, but in the word of God, as made life and spirit to the soul. Few things have more discredited a profession of our most holy faith than the wild notions and still wilder expressions which some have indulged in, giving to the word of God all sorts of strained meanings, and thus perverting and distorting it from its divine simplicity. But I must not run on in this strain, lest I send you an essay instead of a letter.

I have rather got over the trouble and exercise which I had about the testimonial. I think perhaps that your view was the right one; and I dare say my pride was as much touched as my better feelings were pained. Good often comes out of evil, or, at least, it comes sometimes in a way in which we would not have it come. In this way, therefore, I desire thankfully to acknowledge the good hand of God in this very testimonial, though had it been left to my option, I should at once have stopped it.

The weather hitherto has much prevented me from getting out, and I much fear that I shall be a prisoner a good part of the winter. We cannot choose our own trials, but to be restricted from the enjoyment of free air and exercise I find to be very trying.

We much like Mr. Covell. He generally comes to see me once a week, and sits some time. We agree very well on most points. I find his conversation spiritual and profitable, without any affectation and cant.

Mr. Tryon came down to see me about a week since. He was very kind and friendly, and gave me some account how matters were going on at Stamford. Though absent from you, I still feel present with you. My desire is that the blessing of God may rest upon His church and people at Oakham and Stamford. I should not have left you, or at least not given up my charge, had the Lord given me health and strength to go on with it. But it is the mercy of the people of God that their edification or consolation does not depend upon man, but that the Lord Himself has undertaken both to comfort and to build up Zion. We may expect as we advance onwards, if our lives be spared, to be ever meeting with new trials and afflictions; but the Lord has promised that His grace shall be sufficient for us, and to this alone can we ever look as able to support us under them, and to bring us off eventually more than conquerors. It is a fellowship in affliction and trial, and a fellowship in the grace of the Gospel, which forms the tie between the members of Christ's mystical body. And why, but because it gives them fellowship with their common Head? (1 John i. 3; 1 Cor. i. 9.)

I much value your kind, sympathising, and experimental letters; and I hope sometimes, when strength and opportunity admit, that you will favour me with them. I must look to you, and almost only to you, to give me some account how you are going on as a church and people, and for that information also about the friends, and our own special friends and relatives, which is so interesting. . . . There is no greater temporal blessing than health, and indeed, without it, earthly happiness there is none. But no doubt it is good to be weaned from this poor wretched earth, and have our affections more fixed on things above. . . .

Yours very affectionately,
J. C. P.

CC—To Mr. Grace

Thornton Heath, Dec. 23, 1864.

My dear Friend,

I cannot find amongst my books the last volume of Mr. Huntington's Posthumous Letters; but I have four volumes published by Bensley in 1822. The last letter in the fourth volume is DCCXXXV., whereas the volume which you gave me ends with DXCII. I conclude, therefore, that I possess the Letters which you were kind enough to say you would get for me. Taken as a whole, one may say that they contain the very cream of vital godliness. Not being controversial, there is the absence of that sharpness which marks some of his other writings; and being struck off, as one may say, at a white heat according to his various feelings at the time, there is a freedom and a warmth about them, a reality and a power which much commends itself to one's conscience. It will be a sad day for the Church of Christ in this country when the writings of the immortal coalheaver are forgotten or utterly neglected, and there seems to be much fear of it, for there are only a few comparatively who read and value them. From no two authors have I derived such instruction and edification as Dr. Owen and W. H., S. S. They have both condemned me, reproved me, cut me up, sifted, and almost emptied me, and also brought comfort, encouragement, life and feeling into my heart. We have no such ministry now, take it for all in all, nor can we expect that matters will get much better—at least if Mr. Huntington is a true prophet. Still, I believe that the Lord has a goodly number of those who fear His name; but they are, for the most part, in a low place as regards faith and godliness, and those who seem to be more blessed and favoured are for the most part heavily weighted with trials and afflictions. I must say for myself that the path in which I am now walking is the roughest and most trying road which I have travelled for a good many years. If Mr. Hart be right,

> "That traveller treads the surest here
> That seldom sees his way,"

I am not out of the path; for, indeed, this has been, and is, my chief trial. I hope you may never be obliged to give up the ministry, or have to leave your own people, and your own home. The Lord, I hope, keeps me continually looking up to Him to make every rough place plain, and every crooked thing straight; but it is one thing to be waiting, asking, and begging, and another to be blessedly receiving. Mr. Huntington tells us that, "the soul that has life may take comfort in the furnace;" but this is hard work, though I do believe that a living soul would sooner have the furnace than be at ease in Zion.

I have been very busy with my Address; but with all my labour I cannot say much about it. No man and no thing are more than God makes them to be.

Yours affectionately in the truth,

J. C. P.

CCI—To Mrs. Peake

Thornton Heath, Jan. 2, 1865.

My dear Friend,

Let me wish at the opening of another year to you and your dear sister, and all whom we love in the Lord from personal intercourse with them, every mercy and blessing which the God of all grace may see fit to bestow upon them for both body and soul. May this year, if we are spared to witness its revolving course, be one marked with special mercies, and may every discovery of the Lord's goodness and grace endear Him unto us, and make us more desirous to walk in His fear and live to His praise.

I am very much obliged to you for your kind, affectionate, and interesting letter. I could not help saying, as I read it, "What should I do without Mrs. Peake?" For, I am sure, there's no one of our friends but yourself who is so well able to communicate what I wish to know of the spiritual movements in my late church and congregation. . . . My desire, both for myself and for my people, has been for many years not form but power, not letter but spirit, not gift but grace. In fact, from what I have seen and heard of gifted men I am frightened at them; for though gifts, when sanctified by grace and used for the Lord's glory, are made a blessing to the Church of Christ, yet I see so little grace in many gifted men that I am afraid of them. The only thing which does us any real good is what the Lord is pleased to do for us, and in us, by the blessed Spirit; and nothing will abide the fire, which is to try every man's work of what sort it is, but His own grace in the soul.

As the Lord, we hope, has brought Mr. K. among you, you will now have, as a church and people, to watch and wait for what He may speak to your hearts by His servant. You and all our dear friends who know something experimentally of the kingdom of God, which is not in word but in power, will be looking out and feeling for the power which may rest upon his word; and if he feel the power and blessing of God in his soul and ministry, and the Lord's people find and feel the same, it will be a confirming evidence that the Lord has sent him among you. I do hope that he may be more blessed in the calling and comforting of the Lord's people than I was, and that there may be a union of esteem, love, and affection betwixt him and the people. No doubt there will be trials, and you will have to bear and forbear with one another's infirmities; but if the blessing of God be in your midst everything else will be of little account. May the Lord keep you as a church and people from any root of bitterness which, springing up, may trouble you.

I feel that you are quite right in the gentle hint which you have given me springing out of Mr. ——'s letters. I am sure it is best, if we can, to leave those matters which have such a tendency to ruffle the mind. Much self-pity, fretfulness, and rebelliousness are caused thereby; and it is not well to have one's spirit chafed and angered, as it is a self-eating sore which will not heal if it be continually rubbed. It is not for us, if we are oppressed, to fight our own battles. It is best to leave these matters with the Lord, who has promised to make every crooked thing straight. . . . .

In my long observation of the people of God, and, I may add, also in my own experience, I have seen that the Lord does not usually or often thus lead His people. It is, I know, a very delicate and difficult point, as your late dear husband has often felt and said, to distinguish between real, divine leadings and impressions upon the mind. We can hardly think the Lord led Miss ——. All these circumstances teach us to watch and wait, and see what the issue of such things may be. I see that in Scripture much is said of a sober and sound mind. See 1 Thess. v. 6—8; 1 Tim. iii. 2; Titus i. 8, ii. 4; 1 Peter i. 13, iv. 7. v. 8; 2 Tim. i. 7. This sobriety of mind, especially when it springs from being sobered by afflictions, trials, and temptations, and by the solemn dealings of the Lord with the soul, is a blessed preservative, not only from levity and frivolity in the things of God, but also from delusion and enthusiasm. We see sometimes how easily some who, we hope, fear God are lifted up and cast down by some transient impulse. There is nothing weighty, spiritual, or broken in their communication; but a wildness, and very often a vain, confident, presumptuous assurance, which finds no entry into a heart exercised with Divine teaching. How narrow is the path that lies between truth and error, the teaching of the Spirit and the delusions of the flesh. We may well say of it, in the language of Hart, "The distinction is too fine for man to discern, therefore let the Christian ask direction of his God." How continually, at all times, and under all circumstances, we need to be looking up to the Lord Himself to teach, guide, and lead us. And have we not His own gracious promise that, if we acknowledge Him in all our ways, He will direct our paths? "I will guide thee with mine eye."

You were not the only person who has objected to my answer on the wrapper of the *G. S.* But I think perhaps it has been a little misunderstood. It has been thought from it that I hold with the practice of what is called naming children. This is not the case, for I see many evils attending it, though not wrong in itself could it be done in the fear of the Lord. But my main object was to testify against that spirit which will not suffer the least deviation from our own path. For instance, Mr. Covell does two things which I never have done, and which, I dare say, if I had attempted to do at Oakham, it would have caused a stir. 1. He returns thanks for women after childbirth, and asks for a blessing upon mother and offspring. 2. He prays, and often at some length, for our children, begging of the Lord to bless them, and if it be His will manifest them as His. Now this does not offend my ear, though I never do it myself and have often refused to do the first in London. Now, suppose that without any public ceremony, for my remarks were more addressed to private than public prayer—but suppose that a gracious couple, having had a child born to them, should, in simplicity and godly sincerity, kneel down before the Lord, and ask Him to bless the babe, mentioning it by its new name, could that be condemned? And suppose that their pastor were to kneel down with them, thank the Lord for His mercy unto them, and call the babe by the name which its parents had given it, with a petition for the Lord's blessing upon it, must that be summarily cut off and cut down as a work of the flesh? It is what I never did myself, but it was rather my carnality than my spirituality to which it might be attributed. This then was the point at which I aimed—not to tie up matters of this kind with our own string; but to allow good men a liberty of action where the Scripture did not condemn it. All this is quite different from infant sprinkling. But enough of this.

I am glad to hear about ——. You will not require now so many praying members. P—— tells me in her letter how much she enjoys the prayers of the friends on the alternate Lord's-day, and especially those of R. H., whose confessions so suit her. I think she, with others, prizes the reading meetings on the ground that otherwise these good men's prayers would not be heard in your midst, and therefore not the same union felt.

You will be pleased to hear that I feel better in health, and had a very nice walk to-day. Near our house is what is called a park, consisting mainly of nicely-gravelled walks, and so much out of the town that one scarce meets in it a single person. I find it very pleasant, and it leads to a beautiful cemetery. The air here is cold, but dry, and has not the same biting, nipping feeling as that at Stamford. Still, I much miss my own comfortable house, as this is very small, draughty, and smoky. Poor Mr. G. was depressed to see me in it.

I sympathise with your dear sister in her illness and weakness. None know its heavy weight but those who bear it. It is her mercy, like mine, that she has the attentions of a willing and affectionate nurse.

Though I have written so much, I have much more to say.

Yours very affectionately in the Lord,

J. C. P.

CCII—To Mr. S

Thornton Heath, Jan. 3, 1865.

My dear Friend,

. . . You are not ignorant of the path in which I have been called to walk since we parted at ——; and no doubt you saw from the weak state of my health there that I was not fit for the continuous labours of the ministry. In fact, I fear I presumed too much upon fancied strength, for finding myself much better after my visit to —— I made an engagement to preach in London, which proved too much for my bodily strength. I felt myself, therefore, compelled to give up the care and charge of my two churches and congregations, amongst whom I had laboured so many years, and seek to obtain, if it were the Lord's will, some benefit from total rest. It has been a trial to me to have to leave my own people and my own comfortable home; and what has added to it is that I cannot see the Lord's hand in it as I could wish. It is true that the Lord promises He will lead the blind by a way that they know not; but until He is pleased to clear up their dark paths they cannot believe that they are being rightly led. But amidst all this darkness I feel myself both driven and drawn to look to the Lord alone, seeking continually His face and begging of Him to speak a word with power to my heart. In all our straits and difficulties, in all our trying circumstances, whether in providence or grace, we have been taught I trust to look only to the Lord, to hang upon Him, and to cleave to Him with purpose of heart. I find every other refuge, hope, and help to fail; and this I am learning almost as a beginner in religion, to feel my helplessness, and look to the Lord as if I had never looked before, and to hang upon Him as though it were for the first time in my experience, after all I have seen, felt, and known Him to be.

I am, dear Friend,

Yours very affectionately in the truth,

J. C. P.

CCIII —To Mr. E. Walter

Thornton Heath, Jan. 17, 1865.

Dear Friend,

I was very glad to get a few lines from you, and to hear the account which you have given of your poor dear old father. I was always sure that sooner or later the Lord would break in upon his soul, for I do not know that I ever knew a man more deeply or more continually exercised about eternal things than he, or who had more of the fear of God, a sense of the weight and reality of eternal things, or more earnest desires for the manifestations of Christ to his soul. It is now many years since I first knew him, and ever since our first acquaintance we have been united in spirit; and now he is proving that the things he has so long professed are divine and blessed realities. I am sorry to hear of his afflicted body; and yet, as the poor earthly tabernacle must come down to the dust, it is a mercy that the Lord is for the most part taking it gently down. It is a mercy that, though so weak in body, he has all his mental faculties, and, above all, that the Lord is pleased sometimes to favour his soul with His sweet presence. The dear old man is now reaping what he has so long sown; and as he has sown to the Spirit so will he of the Spirit reap life everlasting.

I am glad to find that you and your wife are so kind to him in his old age. The Lord will bless you for it; and though you may feel at times the trouble, you will never repent having shown him that kindness which his necessities now require. I shall much prize the likeness of my dear old friend, and send one of my own in return.

It has been a great trial to me to have to leave my own people and my own home, and to lay down the work of the ministry. But I am thankful to say, in answer to your kind enquiries on the part of your father, I am better in health, and entertain the hope that when the weather becomes warmer I may be able to preach again, though I never expect to be fit for much work. Still, I am spared to employ my pen, and I hope the Lord will give me grace to use it for the good of His people. I am glad that your father liked my Address. It has, I believe, been well received.

Give my love to your good old father. I shall always be glad to hear how he is, both in body and soul.

Yours affectionately in the truth,

J. C. P.

CCIV—To Mr. J. Blake

Thornton Heath, Jan. 23, 1865.

Dear Friend in the Lord,

. . . I was much pleased with your experimental letter, and should be glad at some future opportunity to put it into the *Gospel Standard*, if not in the body, which being limited is much taken up, on the wrapper. It is indeed many years since you passed through the things which you have mentioned, and yet living experience is always fresh; there is something ever new in it, and this makes it refreshing to the saints of God. It is a mercy when the Lord keeps reviving His own work upon the soul, and does not suffer it to sink down into coldness, carnality, and deathliness. I have known those who many years ago seemed from their own account to have had a true and gracious experience of the things of God in their own soul; and yet, as years advance and age creeps on, appear to lose all its sweet savour, and to differ little from the dead professors of the day. And I believe this will be always the case unless they are well exercised with trials and afflictions, and corresponding mercies, so as to keep their souls alive and lively. It is a sad thing to be allowed to drop into a cold, dead state—especially if a man stand up in the name of the Lord to preach to saints and sinners. If he be cold and lifeless in his own soul, how can he instrumentally communicate life and warmth to the souls of others? And again, how is our inward life to be maintained but by prayer, meditation, reading the Scriptures and the writings of good men, and all connected with inward exercise through affliction and temptation? But how good is it of the Lord of His own free and sovereign grace, of His own pure mercy and eternal love, to revive His work upon the heart. It is this which gives us submission to His holy will, resignation to His afflictive dispensations, and a sensible feeling that there is nothing worth desiring, nothing worth living and dying for, but the enjoyment of His favour and love.

Wishing you every enjoyment of the Lord's goodness and mercy, such as you have felt in times past,

I am, dear Friend,

Yours affectionately in the truth,

J. C. P.

CCV—To Mr. J. Davis

Thornton Heath, Jan. 25, 1865.

My dear Friend,

I received safely your kind letter, with the enclosed bill for £5, which I will endeavour, as the Lord may enable, to give away from time to time amongst the poor saints of God. I have what I call my charity purse, which is supplied from time to time by kind friends, and this, with what I am enabled to add to it from my own, allows me to help sometimes the poor saints of God. I shall therefore put your money into my charity purse, and as opportunity offers, shall give a little here and there to the poor saints whom I know, or who come before me. This, I think, is better than giving it away all at once, for when that is done, the money is sometimes given where not so much needed, or, at least, not so seasonable. If, indeed, a little of the superfluity of your land of gold and wool could flow amongst the poor suffering saints of God in this country, what a blessing it might be to them, without injuring the donors. But the Lord only can open heart and hand, and make any one feel that it is more blessed to give than to receive.

You will perceive from the change in my address that I have left Stamford. Indeed, I have been obliged from failing health to give up the charge of my two churches and congregations at Stamford and Oakham, where I had laboured for more than twenty-six years. Through mercy I am better in health, but never expect to be able to labour as I have done in the work of the ministry; though I hope the Lord may enable me to preach a little from time to time when the weather is warm, as I much feel the cold, and cannot expose myself to it.

I hope you are favoured from time to time in your soul with a sense of the Lord's goodness and mercy. This I know is what your heart is after, and without which you cannot feel satisfied. O may nothing ever content us but the blessing of the Lord, which maketh rich; and if we are favoured with this, we shall not covet the miser's gold, or be satisfied with a portion in this life. I well remember your visit to Allington, and felt a union with you, which time and distance do not break. Mr. Parry and Mr. Tuckwell are both of them afflicted in body, but I hope alive in soul. Mr. Godwin is quite well, and labouring hard in the work of the ministry. I hear Mr. Covell, the minister here, very comfortably. He is a good man, and a good preacher, contending for experimental, saving realities.

The Lord bless you, and keep you in His love and fear. My very kind regards to your son Aquila, Mr. Huntley, and all enquiring friends.

Yours affectionately in the truth,

J. C. P.

CCVI.—To Mr. Parry

Thornton Heath, Jan. 27, 1865.

My dear Friend,

Though I am always glad to hear from you, yet you need never apologise for your delay in writing to me. When you were a better horseman than you are now, you used to say that "you would sooner ride twenty miles than write a letter;" and if so when comparatively body and mind were alike active, how much more unwilling must you be to take your pen now when it has become a more laborious task. I believe I should find quite as much if not more difficulty in corresponding with my friends than you, if I had not the advantage of being able to dictate instead of write.

I was very sorry to hear of our esteemed friend Mr. T.'s illness, but hope it may not be really serious. Oh, when I look round upon my friends, especially those who like myself are advancing in life, I see how affliction is falling upon them one after another. How true the words that "Whom the Lord loveth He chasteneth, and scourgeth every son whom He receiveth." And what a mercy it is when we can bend our back to every stroke of His chastising rod, and believe that all is meant for our spiritual good. These afflictions produce, under divine teaching, exercises of soul before God, shake us out of the miserable lees and dregs of carnality and self, and make us long for and desire those gracious visitations which alone can preserve our spirit. How sad it would be for men at our time of life, and with our long profession, to be at ease in Zion, and never be emptied from vessel to vessel. Except to fall under the power of temptation, which is the worst of all possible cases, few things are worse for a Christian than to drop into carnality and sloth; to have little or no heart for secret prayer or reading the word, but to be ever like a spider spinning out some filthy web, shut up in a dirty corner of carnal security. Even if we do not get much, and only have, so to speak, our daily bread, it is far better to have the heart drawn out toward divine things than be shut up in worldliness, fretful murmuring, and peevish discontent with ourselves and others. There is nothing which draws the heart out and up to divine realities as some inward view of the glorious Person and work of our most blessed Lord. We may not perhaps enjoy much of His sensible presence; but still He is the Object of our faith and hope; and as by night and day our thoughts and desires are mounting up toward Him as He sits on His throne of mercy and grace, there is some separation wrought thereby of heart and affection from this wretched world. Nay, even if we can only confess our dreadful sins committed before and against His holy Majesty, and seek for the application of His precious sin-forgiving blood to our consciences, there is some spiritual good wrought thereby, some separation from carnality and death, and some spirituality of mind in which alone is life and peace. I look back sometimes through my long profession, and feel condemned at the wretched carnality and worldliness, not to say worse, which have possessed my mind; how little I have walked and acted in the fear of God, and how little I have lived to His glory. It is indeed a humbling retrospect; and nothing but the precious blood of Christ, which cleanseth from all sin, can wash away the blots and inconsistencies of a long profession. Thus we come into the spot of the poor publican and the thief upon the cross, having no hope but in the superabounding grace of God in the Person and work of His dear Son.

I am very sorry to hear of your illness. Perhaps your anxiety about our esteemed friend, Mr. T., may have partly brought it on. With the Lord all things are possible; but the cause at Allington seems, humanly speaking, to hang upon you two. When you both shall have passed away, as we hope and believe to a happy eternal home—an event, I trust, yet distant—and your bodies lie mouldering in the little chapel yard, where you have so often stood, who will hold up the cause of truth as you two have done? Your house has long been a welcoming and welcomed home to men of God; but—I cannot bear to think of the future, and therefore stop. I have spent many pleasant times in your company, and under four distinct roofs, where I have been your guest; and while life lasts I shall always gratefully remember your liberal and affectionate Christian hospitality. Let us hope that we may be spared to meet once more in the summer, as I should like, even if I could not preach much, to see you and my other Wiltshire friends again. It will be thirty years on the 7th of next June since I opened my commission, preaching in the morning from Zeph. iii. 12, 13, and in the afternoon from Romans ii. 28, 29. I hope I then proclaimed the same divine truths as I do now, though, like the apostle, I might have used sharpness. But is not the word of God, if properly handled, "quick and powerful, and sharper than any two-edged sword"? You and others found it so; and was that not a proof that it was the word of the Lord to you? "The entrance of Thy words giveth light;" "Blessed is the man whom Thou chastenest, O Lord, and teachest him out of Thy law." Blessed are those chastenings and those teachings which bring us to the feet of Christ, and by which He is made precious to the soul. This is the end of God in all His doings and dealings with His people, to strip and empty them wholly of self, and to manifest and make His dear Son feelingly and experimentally their all in all. In Him and in Him alone can we, do we, find either rest or peace.

Through much mercy my health continues pretty good, and when the weather is fine, I endeavour to get a little walk. We have near our house a kind of park, with well-gravelled walks, and where one meets scarcely a single soul. Here I usually walk, and find it both pleasant and profitable. As we live a mile and a quarter from the chapel, I am obliged to have a fly, and generally go but once,—in the morning. I hear the minister, Mr. Covell, very comfortably. He is a good man, and has a good experience, with a very fair gift, having a great knowledge of Scripture, and much readiness in quoting it suitably and appositely. He is very friendly, and generally spends an hour with me once a week. It certainly is a relief to my mind not to have the burden of the ministry and the cares of a church and congregation upon my shoulders. Still, you may depend upon it, I am not without many exercises of mind, which, I trust, serve to keep my soul alive in the things of God; and if I cannot speak of any special blessings, I am thankful to find a warm spirit of prayer and supplication is often felt in my breast. I have no doubt, my dear friend, that if our secret prayers and ejaculations for these many years could be numbered, they would amount to many thousands, may I not say tens or more of thousands. One mark of the elect is, that they cry unto God night and day; and though our petitions may often seem unanswered, yet the word of truth gives us to believe that, so far as they are indited by the Spirit, they enter the ears of the Lord of Sabaoth. Depend upon it, a man must be very dead in his soul when there are no such movements of his spirit upwards. The Lord keep us from sinking into carnality and death. But only He who quickened can keep alive the soul; and it is our mercy if we ever find any revivings and refreshings from His gracious presence. I trust that in your last affliction you have felt something of the same blessing which you had before.

Yours very affectionately,

J. C. P.

CCVII —To Mrs. Peake

Thornton Heath, Feb. 2, 1865.

My dear Friend,

. . . . I think I have in this and my last letter answered most of your inquiries. I thank you for the excellent advice of Miss —— which you have kindly sent me. It is a most needful word of caution, and I hope I may have grace to beware of the snare which she so truthfully lays before me.

I hope the Lord will give me grace so to write upon the precept as not to swerve from those discriminating truths which I hope I have been enabled so long to contend for. I quite see, with you and her, that many legalists would gladly lay hold of what I might say upon the precept, unless grace and wisdom were given to me to handle it aright, to make it appear as if I favoured their legal views. So far from that, I can assure you that I never more felt the necessity and blessedness of sovereign free grace than I do at this present moment, and was never further from creature strength, wisdom, and righteousness. My heart is and ever has been with those only who look to, hang upon, and exalt the glorious gospel of the grace of Christ; but as I do see a beautiful harmony of promise and precept, grace and truth, love and obedience, in the person and work of the Son of God, I have felt led to lay these things before the Church of God. . . . In my walk yesterday in our quiet North Park, I seemed to have for a few minutes a very sweet and blessed view of the harmony of promise and precept, and indeed every Gospel truth, in the glorious Person of the Son of God. It is in Him, my dear friend, that all truths harmonise. He is the centre in which all gospel truth meets and unites; and out of Him, as an ever-flowing, overflowing fountain of life, of grace, and truth, the whole gospel, as a complete revelation of the wisdom and love of God, flows down into the hearts of His dear family. He is the Head and they the members; and as in our natural body there is a union of will and power which cannot be separated, so it is in the mystical body. Now all this is very different from taking the precepts as so many dead and dry commands. Depend upon it, we can never see and feel the beauty and blessedness of gospel truth, except as we see it by faith and love in the person of the God-Man. Severed from Him and the power and influence of His spirit and grace, the precepts are but burdensome commands.

Poor Mr. T., like us all, has his trials. But unless he needed them, they would not be sent. Wherever I turn my eyes I see affliction is the lot of the family of God; and I observe that the nearer they advance to their end the heavier do these afflictions become. My poor friend Mr. P. has had another severe attack, and now Mr. T. is ill. My sister too, Mrs. Isbell, has been quite ill, though now mercifully better. How true, then, it is "whom the Lord loveth He chasteneth," &c.!

What you have said about the new chapel at Oakham has quite satisfied my mind, and I hope the Lord's hand is in it. I fear you will all be disappointed in the Address, as it falls very short of what I could wish it to be.

I sincerely wish you and all my dear friends in Oakham and the neighbourhood every blessing of the new year, and may we all prove the goodness and faithfulness of God, both in providence and in grace.

Yours very affectionately,

J. C. P.

CCVIII —To Mr. James Churcher

Thornton Heath, Feb. 10, 1865.

Dear Friend in the Lord,

I do not think you can feel any real objection to the insertion of the last two or three lines of your letter in this month's number of the *Gospel Standard.* I did not, indeed, recollect to what your words "a very remote period" alluded; but I took it as the affectionate expression of your desire that my life might be spared for the good of the Church.* You have given me an interesting account of your late visit to our esteemed friends Mr. and Mrs. Church. It is good for those who love the Lord to meet together and speak of His precious name, as, no doubt, you have found at Gower Street; and the Lord speaks of hearkening and hearing the spiritual conversation of those that fear the Lord and that think upon His name. "Then they that feared the Lord spake often one to another: and the Lord hearkened, and heard it, and a book of remembrance was written before Him for them that feared the Lord, and that thought upon His name." Malachi iii. 16.

I should be glad to see the MS. book of which you speak. Though I attend the chapel at Croydon when weather and health admit, I have not yet seen Mrs. A., but I often hear of her from those who know her; nor have I yet made the acquaintance of W. G. Indeed I live much alone, and am very slow to form fresh acquaintances, though I ever desire to love those who fear and love the Lord.

My dear wife will be very happy to give you one of my likenesses. It is a matter in which I myself take no part. But as many of my friends like to see the outward man as well as the inward man of J. C. P., she has had some taken. But you must come some day, when the weather is more favourable, and see me here, and you can then take away with you the representation of my poor body—looking to my writings and preaching for the likeness of the renewed soul. I am thankful to say that, through rich mercy, I am somewhat better and stronger in health than in the summer. Still I shall never be again what I have been, and during the cold weather I keep much within doors. My desire is that every stroke of the Lord's afflicting hand may be blessed to my soul's good. It is through much tribulation that we enter the kingdom; and God will take care that all His children shall be more or less conformed to the suffering image of their great Head.

Wishing you, my dear friend, the enjoyment of every spiritual blessing,

I am, yours affectionately in the truth,

J. C. P.

* The letter here referred to will be found in the supplement of the *Gospel Standard,* February, 1865, the last few lines of which we here quote:—

"Dear Editor, may a double measure of your divine Master's spirit rest upon your warfare and wayfare; and that at a very remote period may you enter into the joy of your Lord is the desire of your loving correspondent,

"JAMES CHURCHER."

CCIX—To Mr. Tanner

Thornton Heath, Feb. 16, 1865.

My dear Friend,

I am truly glad that you did not repent of your journey to Croydon. It is good for those who fear God, and have some measure of spiritual union, to meet together for a little converse upon those things which belong to their everlasting peace. It is pleasing to the Lord (Mal. iii. 16), and strengthening to the faith and love of those who thus meet (Rom. i. 11, 12). I should be glad indeed if you lived a little nearer, that we might from time to time communicate more freely and fully than is possible by pen and ink. This John felt (2 John 12, 3 John 13, 14), for though to communicate by pen and ink is a privilege, yet it falls far short of communication by friendly and gracious conversation. But, no doubt, there are wise reasons why those who fear God and feel union with each other are often deprived of Christian converse. It may be a fact through the weakness and depravity of our nature; but it does not fall in with the gospel truth of one body and many members, and that they all are baptised by one Spirit into one body, 1 Cor. xii. 12, 13. My eye or ear, hand or foot, would not flourish most the more distant it was from, and the less united with, the other members. But alas! many blessed truths are weakened or broken asunder by the infirmity of the flesh. Yet of one thing I am sure, that where love is deficient there is a sad want of every other Christian grace.

"Love all defects supplies."

It is sweet to feel it, and a misery to be plagued with its opposite. But I am writing a letter to a friend, not preaching a sermon or writing a meditation.

I have often thought that though there is in our day so much strife and division, yet there is a real and close union amongst the living family. How many kind affectionate friends has the Lord given to me; and my desire is to walk with them in union and communion, and, as far as I can, to avoid everything which may tend to separation. Next to loving the Lord and His truth is loving His people; and how sweet it is to feel the flowings forth of love and affection to the Lord's people for His sake, and for the image of Christ which we see in them. The want of this love in our day stamps it with one of its worst characters.

No doubt you have heard of the serious illness of our friend Mr. Grace. He has been so reduced through weakness as to be scarcely capable of thought. But, upon the whole, he has been favoured with a calm and sweet reliance upon the faithfulness of a covenant God, and been able to lie peaceably and passively upon those everlasting arms which are underneath. He has not now his religion to seek, but enjoys the benefit of what in past seasons he has tasted, felt, and handled, of the pardoning love of God. Much prayer has been made for him by his church and his numerous friends, and much interest and affection shown on all sides. In one of the churches (Mr. Clay's) he was prayed for publicly. But the Lord seems taking home or laying aside His ministering servants. Good old Mr. Chandler, in Kent, is upon a sick, and, probably, dying bed. We look around, and how few there seem to be being raised up to take the place of those who have stood hitherto upon the battlements of Zion. And what sickness and affliction seem to fall to the lot of our personal friends. But, of course, as we advance in life we must expect both affliction for ourselves and for others; and, if not ourselves summoned away, to see those taken from us with whom we have walked in Christian union, and taken sweet counsel together. We know not how soon it may be with us "time" no longer. I was truly sorry to read the account you give of your son's affliction. You have indeed, my dear friend, affliction upon affliction, trial upon trial, wave upon wave; but not one too many, nor too heavy, if we can but believe that they are all sent in number, weight, and measure by a kind and loving Father, and only wise God.

You will see as I advance in the subject what are my views of the precept. I hope they may coincide with yours, but shall be very willing to receive and consider anything that you may say where you differ from them. It is indeed a trying spot to write what so many read, and amongst them so many of the excellent of the earth. I see no reason why you should not put pen to paper upon those blessed truths, such as the work of the Holy Ghost, into which you seem led feelingly and experimentally. No doubt, writing is a gift as much as preaching, and practice, too, is requisite in order to express ideas clearly and fully. But gold is gold, whether wrought with art and skill, or roughly and unartistically. And as the roughest workmanship in gold is far more valuable than the finest workmanship in plated metal, so sound experience and gracious teaching, however roughly wrought, will ever outshine all the lacker of mere creature eloquence when the substratum is base metal.

Yours very affectionately in the truth,

J. C. P.

CCX—To Mr. A. Hammond

Thornton Heath, Feb. 23, 1865.

Dear Friend,

If my advice can be of any service to the church at —— I shall feel very happy to give it; but I wish you and the friends to bear in mind that I can only give you counsel upon general grounds, as I am quite ignorant who the person is about whom you make the inquiry.

Now, to be candid with you, I must say that I have very little confidence in ministers who advertise their services. As far as I can see there has not been for many years a greater demand for real men of God than at the present time. It has pleased the Lord to call some of His dear servants home, and to lay others aside by sickness and infirmity. There are very few settled pastors anywhere; and yet there is a great desire in many places for real experimental preaching. Now it seems to me that a man really taught of God and able to feed his church with food convenient for them, need never advertise his services; for not only can God find him out in his obscurity, but God's people will find him out too. I never, therefore, feel satisfied with an advertising minister, as I think there must be something in the background, such as want of grace, want of gift, or want of character, which keeps him hidden in a corner. It certainly seems a taking advertisement for poor churches; and not knowing the man I cannot say that he may not be a gracious man with a small gift so as to prevent his general acceptability, and yet might be serviceable in a small way. If, therefore, you still think about the man who thus advertises himself, I should advise the church to move very cautiously and very warily, and to make very strict inquiries, not only of the man himself, but of any references which he may give to other persons.

You may depend upon it that it will be far better for you to go on as you are, either with your broken state, struggling to keep together in the fear of the Lord, than get a man amongst you who might bring in error, have only a letter knowledge of the truth, perhaps be a bad character, and bring nothing upon you but trouble and disgrace.

There was a time with you when the Lord seemed to smile upon your cause, when you had gracious and godly members, some of whom I knew, now gone home, and when the Lord blessed the word in your midst. Oh, how grievous it seems to be to look back to times past, and with Job to remember the days when in the Lord's light you walked through darkness, and the rock poured out rivers of oil. Oh, that those amongst you, and my good old friend Mrs. W. amongst them, might be stirred up to seek the Lord's face in prayer and supplication, that He would turn your captivity, and appear for you as a church and people.

If I can be of any service to you in this matter I shall be willing to do so; but you quite hurt my mind when you talk of paying me for it. Freely ye have received, freely give.

Yours very sincerely for the truth's sake,

J. C. P.

CCXI.—To Mr. Godwin

Thornton Heath, Feb. 28, 1865.

My dear Friend,

I have been desirous for some time to answer your truly kind, affectionate, and experimental letter, which I read with much sweetness and pleasure. When I read how the Lord had favoured your soul, and the sweet and blessed feelings which you had under it, the words came to my mind, "Love all defects supplies." When your letter came I had just been reading 1 Sam. xx., and I thought verse 23 was very suitable to the feelings of mutual union and affection which had been betwixt us for so many years in spite of all that sin and Satan, friends or foes, professors or possessors may have tried to break it. What you said also about the precept and the desire which you felt as the Lord blessed your soul to keep it, very much fell in with my own views and feelings, and with what I had been writing the day before. When walking in the North Park, a few days before, I had, for a short time, a very sweet and blessed view of the meeting of all doctrine, precept, and practice in the Person of our dear Lord—for so I must call Him as I believe He is dear to both of us, though you may have been more favoured than I. I am not fond of referring anybody to my poor writings, but if you will just read a few lines in page 94 of the March *Standard*, beginning with "All doctrine" down to "acceptable service," you will see what, for a few moments, seemed presented to the eyes of my faith. Now this was much the strain, though you were favoured with a larger and more abiding measure, of what I seemed to see and feel upon these points. When, then, your letter came, it so met my feelings, and so dropped into my experience, that it quite did me good to read it. And as I should like others to feel the same, I want to ask your permission to put it into the *Standard*.

This, my dear friend, is the right way to keep the precept. You were keeping it in the railway carriage. There was no wandering eye or wandering heart; no listening to the conversation; no going out after the things which feed pride and covetousness; nay, I dare say you did not want to look out of the window of the carriage. Love is the fulfilling of the law—love to the Lord, love to His truth, love to His people, love to His doctrines, love to His ways, love to His ordinances, love to His precepts. And I am well convinced where this spring is wanting there is love to neither doctrine, experience, or practice. Oh that I were more favoured with it in my own soul. I should want then no whip and no spur. But where there is not a spiritual mind and a love for the Lord and what comes from and what leads to the Lord, religion, call it by what name you will, is but a burdensome, legal, and unacceptable service. I like much what the Holy Ghost says by Paul, Gal. vi. 15, 16. Our best rule is the new creature—that new man which, after God, is created in righteousness and true holiness, Eph. iv. 24. And can we not say, dear friend, with Paul, "As many as walk according to this rule, peace be on them, and mercy, and upon the Israel of God." And if we are blessed with the possession of this inward rule, and the Holy Ghost shine and act upon it, we shall find it sweetly harmonise with the precepts as the outward rule. But there are very few, speaking comparatively, in the professing Church of God who can receive or bear this. When you began to insist on practice at W—— you know how it was received, and what a storm and confusion it created. Now, I believe that men can bear the precept, if it be handled in a legal way, though they themselves are walking contrary to it. But when a man thinks he can when he likes alter his ways the precept does not touch him, because he believes that if he is not fulfilling it now he can and will do it one day. But when it comes out of a gospel heart, is preached by gospel lips, and handled by gospel hands, then none will receive it but those who have felt the inward life and power of the Gospel with its effects in the soul. But I must not fall to preaching; you know these things better than I; and it is our mercy if we have been taught by the Holy Spirit to know anything for ourselves, either of doctrine or experience, either of promise or precept.

You have no doubt heard of the dangerous illness of Mr. Grace. But he has been spared to his wife and family, and to his congregation also, as I hope, though I understand it will be probably some time before he will be able to resume his place. He was comfortable in his mind during his illness, not favoured with any great manifestations but with a calm reliance on the faithfulness of God, and with some sweet communion with the Father and His Son Jesus Christ. He felt himself that he should die and was quite resigned.

You will be glad to hear that, through much mercy, I am better in health than when you were here, and hope now that it may please the Lord to restore me in some measure to the work of the ministry, though I hardly expect ever to be fit for much continuous labour.

Yours very affectionately,
J. C. P.

CCXII —To Mrs. Peake

Croydon, March 4, 1865.

My dear Friend,

You may perhaps have already received the sad tidings communicated in the accompanying letter. I call them sad, not for Mr. Grace's sake, poor dear man! who is sad no more and never will again know what sadness is; but sad to his family, to his church and congregation, to his personal friends, amongst whom we indeed were, and to the Church of God at large. At his age indeed, and with an attack so severe, it was almost to be anticipated that he might sooner or later sink under it; but I understand that he himself, whatever might have been his feelings at first, had lately anticipated recovery, for in a letter received this morning by Mr. Covell, from one of his leading men, it is mentioned that but a short time before he sank into the arms of death he had been speaking of preaching again. I wrote to him a few days ago, and I now feel glad that I did so, as it seems that he was pleased with my letter. Its chief drift was the sweetness and blessedness of calmly relying on the faithfulness of God, and lying like a little child in the arms of eternal love. It was not with him as if he had for the first time to find pardon and peace. That had been long ago sealed upon his heart. All that he then needed was to die in faith as he had lived in faith, and to receive the end of his faith, even the salvation of his soul. It will be an irreparable blow, humanly speaking, to his poor widow and family, and to his church and congregation. Indeed I know no one who could at all take his place over them. I should say that no man whom we have known was more generally respected, both in his personal and ministerial character, especially at Brighton, where he had lived in the eyes of the people so many years, and from his former connection with Mr. H. was almost as widely known by the world as by the Church. We shall never see his friendly countenance or hear his cheerful voice again—at least not in this life—nor shall we ever converse with him as we have done on the precious things of God. He is gone, and we must soon follow, and may our last end be peace, if not joy, in believing.

The Lord comfort, bless, and be with you both, and with all the Church of God. Our love to all our dear friends.

Yours very affectionately,

J. C. P.

CCXIII—To Mrs. ——.

Thornton Heath, April 19, 1865.

My dear Ann,

I fear you will begin to think that I have quite forgotten my promise to write to you; but you know how much my time is engaged, and, even were it not so, that to will is often present with me, but how to perform that which is good I find not.

What a mercy it is for us that, if indeed we belong to the Lord, nothing can ever separate us from His love, so that neither time, nor distance, nor circumstances can cut the bond of union.

Though we feel so often at a distance from Him, He is never at a distance from us; and as a proof of this there are from time to time revivals of faith, and hope, and love. And what a mercy, too, that the whole work of grace, from first to last, does not depend upon ourselves or upon anybody else, but depends altogether upon His faithfulness who cannot lie. But why do I say all this? To encourage you and all my dear friends from whom I have been separated in body, but not in spirit, to trust more in the Lord's goodness and mercy and less in themselves or in one another.

I was glad to find that you and my dear friends at B—— still cleave close to one another in love and union. Next to enjoying the Lord's presence, and having union and communion with Him, the greatest favour is to have union and communion with the dear family of God. And how painful it is instead of finding this sweet union to find little else but strife and division. But even this sometimes, though so painful and wounding to the feelings, works together for good—for it drives the soul from looking to and resting upon man, to look more to the Lord and to rest more upon Him. Thus when the spirit is wounded and distressed with what is seen of strife and division, if it make one look more to the Lord and seek more after a feeling sense of His goodness and mercy to the soul, it works for good though so trying and painful. I have always found that the worst effect of strife and division is to ruffle one's own spirit, and communicate that very spirit of strife to one's own mind which we so lament to see in others. It is in this way that strife leads to strife, and one evil begets another until every gracious and godly feeling seems withered and gone and nothing to remain but guilt and confusion.

It seems to me a great mercy that the Lord should have raised up Mr. —— to go in and out before you, as I hardly know what would have been the consequence had you been left without a man of God to keep you together and feed you with the bread of life. He is a man who has gone through much conflict and deep exercise in his own soul and enjoyed also blessed seasons of deliverance, so that he is able to speak a word in season to those that are weary. Those who receive benefit from his ministry, and esteem him as the servant of God, should seek to hold up his hands not only by prayer and supplication on his behalf, but by maintaining, as far as they can, a spirit of love and union towards him. I know from painful experience how the hands of a minister are weakened when, instead of pulling with him, the people pull against him. But this union of love and affection requires much self-denial and mastery over one's own spirit; for it is only by pride that cometh contention, and if the soul were well humbled in the very dust then there would be a spirit of sweet humility, and with that humility there would be forbearance and love.

I truly desire that every blessing may rest upon all who fear God and love the Lord Jesus Christ not only at —— but everywhere. And my advice to all my dear friends, both at B—— and ——, is to live and walk, as far as they can, in the fear of God, looking unto and hanging upon the Lord Jesus Christ, and living in a spirit of love and union with His dear people.

Give my love to all who remember me in the love of the Gospel.

Yours affectionately in the Lord,

J. C. P.

CCXIV—To Mrs. Peake

London, June 27, 1865.

My dear Friend,

I have no doubt that a few lines from me just to let you all know how I am, and how I am going on, will be acceptable to you and to our dear friends at Wharflands.

I came back much wearied by my labours at Oakham and Stamford, and was not at all well on the Saturday evening. Still I went to chapel on Lord's-day, and preached twice to large and attentive congregations, and on the whole, though weak, was comfortably brought through. On Monday I was better, through mercy, and preached on the Tuesday evening quite comfortably. And last Lord's-day I was still much better, and was helped in body and soul through both services. Mr. Ford was not there, which some regretted, as I was favoured with some life and liberty in speaking. My texts were Luke xxiv. 25, 26, and Heb. xi. 13. I showed from the first our folly, and mainly in four points. 1. Looking at external appearances, and judging our state and case from them. Here I named the gloomy cloud which hung over me last year in my illness, leaving an attached people and my own comfortable home, and how the cloud seemed gradually breaking. 2. Trusting to our own reasoning minds. 3. Crediting Satan's lies. 4. Being led by other people, and not looking to the Lord for guidance. I then showed the slowness of our faith to believe all that the Scriptures have spoken, and the necessity of the sufferings of Christ, and His entrance into His present glory. As I felt some liberty of heart and mouth to open these points, I almost wished that the reporter had been there. But I may (D.V.) have an opportunity of again speaking from the words, when they can be taken down, though I may not have the same door of utterance. A good man told me what a blessing my sermon on a similar subject from Psalm cvii. 17—20 (which you will find, I think, in the *Zoar Pulpit,*) had once been made to him, and that the blessing had been renewed that morning. Thus the Lord does not leave His poor unworthy servant, but helps him still in body, soul, and spirit. The heat was trying on Lord's-day, but we got all the air we could. I hope the good Lord will bring me through my London labours, and bless them. In the evening I dwelt much on the three marks of faith. 1. Seeing afar off. 2. Being persuaded of the truth and blessedness of the promises. 3. Embracing them with love and affection. I also spoke much of our being strangers and pilgrims on earth—how felt and how confessed—confessed in life and conduct, as well as in words. And I spoke of dying in faith, and dwelt on the life and death of our dear friend, William Tiptaft, as a remarkable example of both. I trust, on the whole, that we had a good day.

I had two nice walks yesterday. We are not far from Primrose Hill and Regent's Park, and I walk much in both. There are seats here and there, nice grass, and trees, so that I can sit and meditate quietly, and then walk on again, and rest again, and thus take air and exercise without fatigue. London air also at this season, and in this part, suits me well, as being warm and dry. I could not but bless and praise God yesterday evening, as I sat and walked in Regent's Park, for His goodness in thus far restoring my health. Last year, I could hardly walk a mile, and now I feel so much stronger in my walks. Praise the Lord, O my soul, and for enabling me once more to speak in His name.

An old lady (aged 85), whom I have known many years, Mrs. Wilds, a member of Mr. Huntington's church, was hearing me on Lord's-day, and told me how she had felt for and prayed for me in the winter. She is straight as a dart, and has all her faculties, being only a little deaf.

I am rather tried whether I have done right in coming to Gower Street for Sept. 3 and 10, instead of Oakham and Stamford, still there may be a purpose in it, which time will unfold. I do not give up, if I change the time of my coming. Mrs. P. and the children seem to like the new house. May the Lord bless and sanctify it with His presence. It is a mercy to have a home to go to, and one's own.

Yours affectionately,
J. C. P.

CCXV—To Mrs. Peake

Croydon, Oct. 23, 1865.

My dear Friend,

. . . . . I am sorry to have to mention a sad event, which took place on Saturday. I was sitting quietly in my room before dinner, when Mr. George Covell, the brother of the minister, came up to ask me to preach as yesterday. His brother, I am grieved to say, had broken a blood-vessel that morning after breakfast, and had brought up a considerable quantity of blood. Dr. C., his medical man, had been sent for, and had ordered him to bed, to be kept very quiet, and indeed had enjoined that course of treatment which I knew was usual in such cases. I felt much grieved at the circumstance, as he has been so kind a friend to me, and as I knew well what a grave symptom it was. I therefore said immediately that I would preach once for him, taking the morning service, but that I could not do more in my present weak state. My services, of course, were gladly accepted; and so yesterday morning, in the midst of a most driving rain, which lasted all day, I went in a cab to the chapel, and was, on the whole, helped through better than I could have expected. The incessant rain much thinned the congregation; still we had a goodly number, and I was very glad to do what I could to alleviate the blow, both to himself and the congregation. I am glad to say he is going on well. It was only on Friday that he came to see me, and, as the day was fine, wished to take me a drive into the country. He was very cheerful, and seemed to be in the best of health. When he has come to see me on a cold, wet, or snowy day, I have sometimes said to him, "Happy man, not to know or care whether it is cold or hot, wet or fine;" and now see, he is lying on a bed of sickness, bidden not to speak, and I, the poor invalid, standing up in his room. I have not felt anything for some time which has so truly grieved me; and I look forward with pain and fear to what may be the result. He is much loved by his church and congregation, and it will be to them a most severe blow. I cannot do much for him and for them, as at this time of the year my winter cough is often very troublesome; but still I hope to render what little help I can. Oh, how uncertain is everything here below! How often have I coveted his health and strength; and yet how all may be dashed in a moment! He has been much blessed in his soul of late, especially on a Lord's-day or two back, and for the most part enjoys a sweet assurance of his interest in the love of God, and the blood of His dear Son.

We still continue to like our new abode, and, I may say, our new town. I have found a nice dry walk, very retired, and very pleasant, which quite makes up for the park I have lost. One very nice feature of this place is the great dryness of the gravel walks, so that even after heavy rain, a day or two gives you a walk where you scarcely soil your feet. . . .

Yours very affectionately,

J. C. P.

CCXVI—To Mrs. Peake

Croydon, Dec. 29, 1865.

My dear Friend,

I quite reciprocate your kind wish that, instead of communicating by letter, we could exchange our mutual thoughts by an hour's conversation; but as this is for the present impossible,

I am glad to have recourse to the more imperfect mode afforded us by the post. . . .

Through mercy I continue pretty well, not having breakfasted once in bed this winter, whereas during the last I scarcely got up once before breakfast. I preached here last Lord's-day morning, from Hebrews vi. 18, 19, and took four leading points—1. The characters—those who had fled for refuge, &c. 2. Their strong consolation. 3. Its foundations, the two immutable things, God's word and oath. 4. The nature of their hope. I was brought comfortably through, and did not suffer afterwards. It is probable that you may see the sermon which I preached here December 3, as a young man took it down, and a wish has been expressed that it should be published in the *Gospel Standard*.

You will be glad to hear that my dear friend Mr. Covell is wonderfully restored, and seems almost as well as before. I wish you could have heard his opening address the first time he preached after his illness. He gave a testimony which might well make many of us blush or hang our heads down for shame. He said that for many months previously he had never once gone to bed dry-eyed—that is, as he explained it, without having shed tears during some part of the day, either of contrition or melted by mercy. He also said that, in reference to this, the words of Psalm cxxvi. 5 were much upon his mind, and that the interpretation which he gave them was the glimpses of joy which he felt on these occasions; but when he was laid upon his bed, that then he saw that this reaping in joy had a much greater fulfilment, for that he swam, as it were, in a sea of love, enjoying so much of the presence and power of God. I cannot tell you half that he said, and much wish that it had been taken down. The chapel was very full, and it might be said the people rejoiced with trembling, fearing his exertions might bring on another attack. But he seemed not at all the worse for it next day, and has now resumed his usual labours. I am (D.V.) to speak again for him on the morning of January 7, as it is ordinance day, and thus he has more than his usual labours. I feel quite willing and desirous to do what I can to help him, and as I have a cab to and fro, and the chapel is easy to speak in, I can do so without much risk.

30th.—I am sorry to find you have not been well. Where one naturally possesses an active mind, to have our energies lowered is in itself a suffering, especially where we have so many calls upon both body and soul. You have many cares, not only from the anxiety and burden necessarily attending your waiting upon your dear invalid sister, but from the weight with which church matters and church trials rest upon your mind. It is, indeed, a blessed mark of divine teaching to have sympathy with the cause of Christ and His afflicted members; but it adds much to the burdens which the true follower of the Lamb has to carry.

Where the conscience is tender in the fear of God, and the Lord's people much loved in Him and for His sake, it must open up a path of peculiar suffering, for it is a part of the fellowship of the sufferings of Christ which the Apostle longed to know. Those who are wrapped up in carnality and self, escape many of the trials and sufferings which befall the family of God; but if they escape the suffering, they also escape the consolation, and what is more, that conformity to the suffering image of Christ to which God has predestinated His people. It is a mercy that we have some left who love Zion, who feel bound up in her welfare and interests, and who can say with the Psalmist, Psalm cxxxvii. 6. Praying souls hold up a minister's hands; nor, indeed, can any others rightly expect to derive a blessing from his ministry.

I am glad to find that Mrs. B. made a good end. She always seemed a very attentive hearer, and one of the afflicted followers of the Lamb, as her countenance bore marks of care and suffering. How often it is that at eventide it is light! Mr. Lightfoot, who used to visit the sick a good deal at Stamford, has met with several instances of a blessing being given on the bed of death to exercised souls who sat for years under my ministry. It is encouraging to find how faithful God is to His own word and work.

Two good men, twin brothers, Moses and Aaron B——, called on me the other day, and both of them testified how much my published sermons had been blessed in Sussex. They had been on a visit to Mr. Godwin, and brought back a good account of his health, but a sad one of the ravages of the cattle plague, which has swept away nearly all the cows of the poor freemen who make the cheese at Godmanchester. Who can tell what the end may be, and what we as a nation may have to suffer? for we are so bound together that the loss to one is injury to all. But what few signs of national repentance! . . .

Yours very affectionately,
J. C. P.

CCXVII —To Mrs. Peake

Croydon, Jan. 24th, 1866.

My dear Friend,

I am just now in the thick of my sermon for Mr. Ford, which takes both time and care to bring out in a clear and acceptable way. I am making, I am sorry to say, very slow progress with the memoir of our late dear friend William Tiptaft; but I can only do a certain amount of work, and get so weak and jaded if I exceed it, that all the freshness of my writing seems faded and gone. I generally spend an hour after breakfast in reading the Scriptures, chiefly for the most part in the original, as far as time admits; and then, when my mind is fresh, address myself to my *Standard* work. After dinner I rest, and in the evening comes correspondence, and reading again the Scriptures before bedtime. And yet how time slips away, and what little real good seems to be got or done! At times it quite disheartens me to find so little progress made, if any at all. Still we must go toiling and suffering on, and not get weary in well-doing, but commit our ways and works to the Lord. I have often thought that the standard in my own mind both of preaching and writing is set rather high, and that is one reason why I seem sensible of so many failures. I never could be satisfied, even as a natural man, with anything mediocre or commonplace, and was always aiming at some knowledge or attainments beyond the common level. The same feeling perhaps accompanies my spiritual mind, so as never to rest satisfied with anything which does not bear the mark and stamp of God.

I was out on Lord's-day morning, and heard Mr. Covell from Heb. i. 8, 9; but he only got as far as the first clause of verse 8. He was very solemn and affectionate, said he was a dying man, and spoke to the people as such. I heard him very well till just towards the end, when the oppressive atmosphere of the chapel—not a single ventilator open—well-nigh overpowered me. . . .

Yours very affectionately,

J. C. P.

CCXVIII—To Mrs. Peake

Croydon, Jan. 29, 1866.

My dear Friend,

. . . . I need not tell you that in making engagements to preach I feel more and more my dependence upon the Lord to enable me to fulfil them. The friends, therefore, of course will bear this in mind, and I hope it may stir up prayer and supplication, on their and my behalf, that the Lord would grant our mutual desire to meet once more in His gracious and blessed name. We may, indeed, expect that every year, not to say month, may work a change in those of us who are advancing in the vale of years. I look round sometimes, and think how many are fallen asleep of friends and brother ministers, whose life, humanly speaking, seemed better than my own. Your poor dear husband, Isbell, J. Kay, and our dear and valued friend William Tiptaft. How I have seen them taken, and I left. Our friend Mr. Grace, too, Mr. M'Kenzie, Mr. Gadsby, and Mr. Warburton, besides private Christians whom I have known. How loudly these things speak, and seem to bid us sit loosely to the world, have our loins girt, and our lamps burning, not knowing how soon the message may come personally to us. I was much struck with what you said about the year 1866 being a marked epoch. . . . When I look round upon this miserable world, and see it so overflowing with sin and sorrow, God so provoked, His people so afflicted, wickedness so rampant, godliness so low, it gives room to some inquiring thoughts, "Lord, how long?" But I forbear expressing all that I think and feel, contenting myself with this, that the Judge of all the earth must do right, that He will avenge the cause of His elect, and that it shall be well with those who fear God. We read, I think, that there is a time when the mystery of God shall be finished, as He hath declared to His servants the prophets. Then there will be a full clearing up of that great mystery, which now so sadly puzzles us, why things are as they are in this sin-disordered world, and all things will be made clear to the glory of God, the praise of Jesus, the salvation of the saints, the destruction of sinners, and the confusion of Satan. Our present portion is to suffer with Christ that we may be also glorified together, believing that if we be dead with Him we shall also live with Him. Our wisdom and our mercy will be to be ever looking unto Him, hanging upon Him, and cleaving to Him with purpose of heart, fighting the good fight of faith—that fierce and daily battle which we have to carry on against sin and self, Satan and the world. I don't know any other way of getting on, or getting through our daily host of enemies without and within, but by believing in the Son of God, and looking to Him for the continual supplies of His grace; and this we are obliged to do, there being no other way open to us, and being shut out by law, conscience, guilt and fear, weakness, sinfulness, and helplessness from walking in any other path but where Jesus stands at the head of the way. It is like a person in a dark night on a lonely moor eyeing a light at a distance, on which he fixes his eyes, and to which he directs his steps. How graciously He says, "I am the way; no man cometh unto the Father but by Me." This seems sometimes our only direction, like the light of a lighthouse across the sea to guide the ship unto the desired haven.

But I am writing a letter, not preaching a sermon, and must therefore pause in the full current of thought. I was at chapel on Lord's-day morning. Mr. Covell preached from 2 Chron. xxxiii. 12, 13, but did not get much beyond "The Lord is God." He spoke very nicely upon affliction, and its effects in Manasseh's case. I heard him very comfortably, and could follow him very nicely in the path he laid down. I am (D.V.) to speak for him next Lord's-day morning.

I send you, by book post, the report of a benevolent society in active operation among our dear friend the late Mr. Grace's people. My reason for sending it is this: the committee applied to me to write an address to accompany the report, as they wished something by way of head to it. I therefore wrote the address, which they accepted unanimously, and as I thought you and our friends might like to see it I send you one. It arose, in the first instance, from Mr. Grace visiting a poor woman of the congregation, and, finding her so miserably destitute, he named the circumstance in the pulpit, observing, I believe, at the same time that there were doubtless many similar cases quite unknown to the congregation. The people were much moved by his words, and the result was, calling a meeting and starting the society. Every needy case may now be investigated and relieved. I so much liked the plan of the society that I felt induced to point out in the address its peculiar advantages. Abuses of course may and will arise; but if well managed, it seems to me a very useful and excellent plan—especially for a large and well-to-do congregation in a place like Brighton, where the poor are much hidden from view. The committee seem pleased with the address, and I hope it may lead to a wider development of the society.

I am glad to find that you, as well as others of our Oakham friends, were pleased with the Address in the *Gospel Standard.* It is encouraging sometimes to find that what one writes with a desire for the edification of the people of God is well received by them. It is, in fact, as in the ministry, the main reward of their cares and toils. I have hardly decided what subject I shall next take up for my "Meditations," but have some thoughts of writing upon the work of the ministry. It is a delicate and difficult subject to handle, but it is one which has exercised my mind for some years, and one on which I hope I can say I have had some long personal experience, it being now many years since my mouth was first opened to speak in the Lord's name. There are some points in it which, to my mind, are as difficult to handle properly as they are important; but I trust I may have wisdom given to me rightly to divide the word of truth, and write to edification.

Please to present my truly Christian love and affection to all my dear friends amongst whom I laboured so many years—and I hope not in vain in the Lord—including, of course, our dear friends at W., &c.

Yours very affectionately in the truth,

J. C. P.

CCXIX —To Mr. Hoadley

Croydon, Feb. 16, 1866.

Dear Friend in the Truth,

We have to thank you for a very fine hare, which you have been so kind as to send us through your son. These little marks show that you still bear me in affectionate remembrance. It is, indeed, one of my mercies that I have many friends among the dear family of God who love me for the truth's sake; and may I never say or do anything to forfeit their esteem and affection, but be enabled still to labour in word and doctrine according to the ability which the Lord may give me. I consider it a great privilege that I am still enabled to go on contending earnestly for the faith once delivered to the saints, and my highest reward is that the Lord should condescend to bless to His people anything which drops from my tongue or pen.

I hope the Lord still continues to strengthen you in standing firm for His truth; and you will find, as it is opened up to your heart with greater sweetness and power, a firmer standing in it and bolder contending for it.

I am, dear friend, yours in the Lord,

J. C. P.

CCXX—To Mr. S

Feb. 24, 1866.

My dear Friend,

* * * * *

You ask me a question, and inquire for a recipe which I can by no means give, and which, if I could, would neither satisfy nor be of any service to you. I believe that we can neither obtain nor maintain the presence of God, that His visitations are as sovereign as His grace, but are directed by infinite wisdom. There is an expression in the Ephesians well worth considering. "Wherein He hath abounded toward us in all wisdom and prudence" (Eph. i. 8). His abounding is in the riches of His grace; and yet it is guided by wisdom and directed by prudence. So that He knows how and when to give out of these abounding riches.

I hope you still continue your little meeting together. I found it good to be there when at ——

Yours affectionately in the truth,

J. C. P.

CCXXI—To Mrs. Peake

Croydon, March 22, 1866.

My dear Friend,

I was purposing to send you a few lines, even before your last kind and affectionate letter came to hand. You must not call it "poor and worthless," for I found it very interesting and acceptable. Indeed, I have to look to almost you alone for information on those matters which must ever deeply interest me, as having gone in and out so long among you. We are all glad too to learn how our dear relatives are, and you alone furnish us with the desired information.

I am glad that the two proposals made upon the wrapper of this month's *Gospel Standard* met with so ready an acceptance among you. As regards the Oaths Bill, I greatly fear that nothing effectual can be done. You are perhaps aware that Government accepted a small amendment proposed by Mr. Disraeli; but refused to receive a paragraph from him, which would have more fully denied the Pope's supremacy. The reason why the Government measure was carried on the first reading by so large a majority (the minority being only five) was because both sides of the House in the last Parliament seemed agreed to have one uniform oath for all the members. But the majority by which the second reading was carried was only fourteen, which is a much smaller one than the Government can bring up on most party questions. The only hope now is, that the House of Lords may throw it out on the second reading, though this seems doubtful, as it has been read for the first time in that House without opposition. In the next *Gospel Standard* there will be some little explanation on the subject of the oaths, as I have thought it might be as well to give our readers some little trustworthy information on the subject; and I have some thoughts of taking up the whole matter in a few papers in the supplement. Very few of our readers are in a position to learn the real nature of the subject; and at this crisis it seems desirable to state the matter in a simple, intelligible way. But I must not take up all my space with these matters.

It will be no disappointment to me if I am not the person to open the new chapel. Indeed, I was not aware till lately that any such thought or plan was entertained by the friends. Whoever opens it, and whenever opened, may the presence of the Lord fill the house, and thus a gracious token be afforded of His approbation.

I am sorry to learn that Mr. K. is suffering from a bad cold. He labours hard in the ministry, and will find, as others have found before him, that so much continuous exertion, with all the trials and exercises attending the ministry, tells upon the bodily strength. Most of our laborious ministers have been men of large make, wide and deep chests, and much bodily strength; such were Huntington, Gadsby, Warburton, and Mr. Kershaw. Our dear friend also, William Tiptaft, was a strong made man, broad and sound in the chest. O what a blessing health is, and what a trial is the want of it! How it has crippled me nearly every day of my life for many years, though I have been spared already to live longer than many once expected. I have also been favoured with much activity of mind; and if I have not been able, like many of my brethren in the ministry, to go about preaching the word, yet with my pen I have laboured hard, and perhaps never harder than at the present time. The older I get, and the more I see and feel the solemn importance of the truth of God, the more do I desire and seek to put forth nothing by mouth or pen which is not instructive or profitable to the souls of men; nor did I ever more, if so much, desire to keep very closely to the word of inspiration, and to advance nothing which is not in the fullest harmony with the Scriptures. I have read them a good deal this winter, and find them more and more full of holy wisdom and heavenly instruction. All I want is to believe them with a stronger faith and more sensibly, warmly, closely, and affectionately embrace the gracious and glorious truths revealed in them. It is for want of this faith simply to receive what God has revealed, that they are read for the most part with so little profit; unless they are mixed with faith, as the apostle speaks (Heb. iv. 2), they cannot profit the soul. I am now reading the earlier chapters of Isaiah, the beginning of Leviticus, and the Epistle to the Colossians, studying them as far as I can in the original, and seeking to enter into the mind and meaning of the blessed Spirit in them. If we read the early chapters of Leviticus with an enlightened eye, how much there is in them to illustrate the one great sacrifice of our gracious Lord. In Him we see the burnt-offering as offering Himself without spot to God, the sin-offering as bearing our sins in His own body on the tree, the trespass-offering as especially applicable to sins of commission, and the meat-offering as representing Him to be the food of our souls. Christ is the sum and substance of the Scriptures. Without Him they are a dead letter, full of darkness and obscurity; but in and with Him they are full of light and blessedness. The apostle says, "Let the word of Christ dwell in you richly in all wisdom" (Col. iii. 16), by which, I suppose, he means the word which testifies of Christ, and holds Him forth to our faith, and hope, and love. This is to dwell in us, not to be a passing visitant, but an abiding householder, and that "richly," so as to supply richly every want, and "in all wisdom," so as to make us wise unto salvation, and be ever guiding our thoughts, words, and ways. But oh, how short of all this do we come, our house being rather like an inn, or a London lodging-house, with all sorts of guests, and all better lodged, and better cared for, than the owner and master! Nothing more shows our desperate case by nature than the open doors and windows of our house, giving admission day and night to all manner of rackety guests, who care for nothing but their own convenience and enjoyment.

March 23.

I am glad to learn that dear Mr. Keal has taken so much to read the writings of the immortal coalheaver. I have often felt that no writer knocks the pen more out of my fingers than that wonderful man. And there is this great advantage in his writings, that though full of divine thought, they do not require any strong exercise of our mental faculties. Thus many can read Huntington who cannot read such writers as Owen, Goodwin, and Charnock. His great gift is opening up a living experience, in which he excels in clearness, fulness, and variety, and, I may add, in savour and unction, all other writers that I am acquainted with. He also throws great light upon the Scriptures, for no man ever had a greater knowledge of them, or a clearer insight into their spiritual meaning.

I am sorry to say that I am getting on very slowly with the memoir of William Tiptaft. Indeed, I can only give just the few last days in the month to it, and that only partially, for no sooner is the *Gospel Standard* off the wheels than I have Ford's sermon to attend to, which takes some time to bring out in any suitable way. As I may calculate on more than 2,000 readers, besides the many more who hear them read, I wish to bring them out in some measure suitable to so large and doubtless choice an audience. To do this properly requires both time and care. But besides this, there is such a lack of materials to build up the memoir with. In his latter days he was very silent about himself, and as I am working now upon the earlier part of his life and ministry, I have to trust chiefly to a memory which has to go more than thirty-five years back. But I hope when I have cleared the ground, and come to his letters, I shall be able to make more rapid progress. I have some thoughts of sending what I have thus far written to our dear friends at Wharflands, to have the benefit of their corrections, if I have made any mistakes in narrating the events of his earlier days; and in that case you will be at liberty to read the MS. The most valuable part of the memoir will be his letters, especially the earlier ones. I merely furnish the thread on which to string the pearls. His friends seem impatient for it to come out, and have undertaken to guarantee me from any pecuniary loss; but the chief difficulty with me is how to write the memoir so as to leave out nothing which is important or interesting, and yet not overlay it with useless matter. The letters will also need revising and curtailing, which will demand wisdom and patience. All this makes me at times quite despair of executing the task.

I was at chapel yesterday; the text was Exodus iii. 7, 8. I heard Mr. Covell very well.

Yours very affectionately,
J. C. P.

CCXXII—To Mr. Parry

Croydon, June 20, 1866.

My dear Friend,

It seems to be your lot never to be free for any long time from your affliction. This is painful for the present, and not very encouraging for the future. But what can we say to these things? If we believe that all things are arranged by infinite wisdom and eternal love, and can believe our own interest in these wise and gracious arrangements, it will reconcile us to the dispensation, though so trying and painful to the flesh. But I am well satisfied that we may see and believe all this as a matter of doctrine, and yet be utterly unable to take any comfort from it, or obtain any rest in and by it. Our head believes one thing and our heart feels another. Nothing, then, but the almighty power of the Lord in a way of support, and His goodness and mercy in a way of experimental feeling, can reconcile our poor fretful, wayward minds to the weight of a daily cross. And what adds to it is continual fear of doing or neglecting something which may bring on an attack of any complaint to which we are subject; so that we seem to move about in a kind of trepidation, fearing lest this cold wind, damp day, or some such circumstance may bring on what may be an attack. Through mercy, I do not usually suffer from pain, even when I am most ill; but to feel the weakness produced by it is in itself a suffering, and since I have known myself what the feeling of bodily weakness is, I have much sympathised with those of the dear family of God who suffer from great bodily weakness, and much more so when pain is added to it. It must have been very trying to you to have been laid up when Mr. H. was with you.

I am thankful to say that I am, through mercy, somewhat better in health, and am going to make the attempt of preaching at Gower Street next Lord's-day. I go up in much weakness and with many fears; but I know that the Lord can make His strength perfect in the one, and graciously dispel and disperse the other. I have often gone up to London weak and feeble, and yet been mercifully strengthened and left London stronger and better than when I entered it. There is something in the dry air at this time of the year which suits me there. But be it so or not, I must look higher and trace the good hand of the Lord in giving me strength according to my day. I felt for the deacons at Gower Street, and the church and congregation generally, as they have such difficulty in getting supplies, and my being unable to go last month much put them about on account of the shortness of the notice. I hope to be under the roof of my dear friends Mr. and Mrs. Clowes. I expect to see my good old friend every year more aged. But we must expect that others, like ourselves, feel the pressure of advancing age and infirmity. Nor need we wish ever to live in this miserable world. The grand thing is to have a good hope through grace, and to be blessed, when our appointed time comes, with dying faith in dying moments, and be carried safely through the dark valley of the shadow of death. It is a mercy in many respects that the time and mode of our dismissal is hidden from our eyes. Thousands who have dreaded the last stroke have found, when it came, it was not a stroke of wrath, but one of tender love, and longed to be gone before the thread of life was cut. I am very sure that nothing short of sovereign, superabounding grace, pure mercy, atoning blood, and dying love can meet our case, silence doubt and fear, open the gate of heaven, close the door of hell, and make the grave sweet. I was struck with a passage that I met the other day in good Dr. Owen. "I know not how others bear up their hearts and spirits; for my part, I have much ado to keep from continual longing after the embraces of the dust, and shades of the grave, as a curtain drawn over the rest in another world." We have stood sometimes over the grave of a departed friend, and have thought within ourselves, here is a rest for his poor worn-out body; here will it be safely kept till the resurrection morn. Some one, perhaps, may think or say the same thing over us.

I sincerely hope, with the help and blessing of God, that we may be spared to meet once more this year. I hope I might be able to speak a little in the chapel; but even if not, I must invite myself to pay you a visit, as we cannot expect now many years will be our portion upon earth.

I feel well satisfied, upon the whole, with my change from Stamford to this place. How the twenty-six years which I was there seem to have passed away, almost as a dream in the night! But if any good were done, any souls called or blessed, *that* does not pass away, *that* abideth. This is sweet in the recollection, and will one day be seen shining forth with a glory of which now we know but little. Do not trouble yourself to answer this. I would not leave home without sending you a few lines, as, for the want of a secretary, it may be some time before I can write to you again.

Yours very affectionately,
J. C. P.

CCXXIII.—To Mrs. Peake

Croydon, June 21, 1866.

My dear Friend,

Unless I take the present opportunity of sending you a few lines, I fear it will be some time before I can again communicate with you by pen. It would have given me much pleasure to have renewed our mutual friendship and affection by that personal intercourse which we have had in days gone by. You have always been a firm and faithful friend, and have never manifested that wavering and uncertain spirit which I have witnessed, painfully witnessed, in some others; and I trust the reason is that your friendship and affection are based upon a spiritual foundation, which is not, therefore, moved here and there by every wind, but has that stability in it which springs out of the security of the foundation itself. We have lived to prove the uncertainty of all earthly things; and the various trials and exercises of body and mind through which we have passed have well convinced us that all here below is stained by sin, spoiled by infirmity, and ever subject to change. But what a mercy it is that the foundation of God standeth sure, that those whom He loves He loves to the end—the words will recall to your mind a funeral monument, where you have shed the silent tear—and that none can pluck out of Jesu's hand the objects of His all-victorious grace! It would, I hope, have rejoiced the hearts of many if, as we see eye to eye in the things of God, so we might have seen each other face to face in the flesh. But such was not the will of God, and though I feel His trying dispensations, yet I desire to submit to His heavenly will. No doubt there was a purpose in it, though at present it may be hidden from our eyes. But I will not dwell longer on this subject. The time may come when I may once more see my dear friends face to face, but when I cannot say, as if I were to mention a time, it might only cause a fresh disappointment. I will, therefore, leave that matter to the disposal of the Lord, who can bring it about in His own way. When you receive this, I shall, if the Lord will, be in London under the roof of my old and attached friends Mr. and Mrs. Clowes, with the hope and expectation of preaching at Gower Street on the coming Lord's-day. I go up to London in much weakness and in much fear. May the Lord graciously make His strength perfect in the one, and remove and dispel the other. I have proved both in times past, and have sometimes left London stronger than when I entered it. At this season of the year the dryness of the air seems to suit my chest; nor do I feel the exertion at Gower Street so much as might be expected from the size of the place. It is the bad ventilation in chapels which hurts me more than the physical exertion of preaching, and had I stood in the new pulpit at Oakham, I should have looked round narrowly to see how the ventilation was managed, and might have longed to have the same command of a window as I was indulged with at the old chapel. How freshly sometimes has the breeze come in when I have almost fainted with the pent-up breath of so many hearers! I used to tell you I loved the pure breath of heaven both in nature and grace, though I admit that often the keen breezes chilled my frame. How we look back sometimes upon days that are passed, and how all seem now to have passed away as a dream in the night! But if God has in His mercy done anything for our souls, or if I instrumentally have been of any service to His afflicted family, that does not pass away; for what God doeth He doeth for ever, and the work of the Holy Spirit upon the heart is as firm and lasting as the finished work of the Son upon the cross. We look around, and see how this and that friend or neighbour is passing away. We think perhaps of those whom we have lost. But they are not lost, though we have lost them. They are safely housed in the mansions above out of the reach of every storm; and what a day will that be when the Lord comes to make up His jewels, when He will present them before the Father and say, "Of all whom thou gavest me I have lost none!" Oh, may we, and those with whom we have walked in friendship and affection, be found amongst them! That happy day will make amends for all suffering and sorrow felt here below.

You have, no doubt, long before this looked over what I have written—I dare not call it a memoir—of our esteemed and lamented friend William Tiptaft. R. H. is quite of opinion that it is not worthy of the man, and says that if God or man do not enable me to write something better, throw it aside. But, as I said before, I have no materials, nor am I likely to get any. You know how little he used to speak of the first dealings of God with his soul, and I have often thought him a remarkable instance of a person in whom the first work was but feeble, who afterwards shone forth with a bright lustre. But the children of God generally, into whose hands the work might come, would naturally be expecting something deeper and clearer than I can furnish them with, or than probably he himself experienced. Nor even do I think that his letters would fully satisfy their mind. They breathe great sincerity, and the early letters are full of warmth and zeal; but still they are below the man. It was his life and conversation which chiefly distinguished him. I fear, therefore, lest even his letters would be disappointing; and my own view is, it would be better to let him rest as he is, in the esteem and affection of the Church of God, without putting forward anything that might rather diminish than increase his claims upon their love and esteem.

I fear the present warm weather will much try your sister. You not only have to sympathise but to suffer with her, and this adds to the weight of your own trials. You are often called upon to act in various matters, and what would be easy with a fair amount of strength and energy, becomes a burden when the body is weak and the frame languid. How much, I think sometimes, I could do, how much more I could read, how much more write, how much more preach, if I were favoured with that superfluity of health which some might, so to speak, easily spare without feeling the loss! But the Lord, who doeth all things well, knows exactly what we are and what we need, and could give us an abundance—yea, a superabundance of health and strength, if it were for our good and for His own glory. To this point we must come, nor will all our fretfulness or unbelief alter it, that He must do with us according to His own will, and that our own happiest and safest spot is to be nothing, that He may work in us all the good pleasure of His will, and the work of faith with power.

A line will always be acceptable when you find leisure, though I cannot promise you an answer, as most probably I shall be deprived of the needful services of a secretary, to which I am now so much accustomed that I feel quite dependent upon them.

Accept our united love, &c.

The Lord be with you all on the coming Lord's-day, and give

His blessing to the ordinance and the candidates. I rejoice to hear of Mrs. R. H.

Yours very affectionately in the Lord,
J. C. P.

CCXXIV.—To Mr. James Davis, of Melbourne

Croydon, Oct. 18, 1866.

Dear Friend in the Truth,

I received safely your kind letter and the draft for £5 which it contained, and ought to have acknowledged its receipt by the last mail; but the day slipped away almost before I remembered I should have acknowledged it. Forgive me this wrong. My mind was much occupied by preaching and writing, and various engagements. As you kindly gave me the option I have just put down £2 10s. to the account of the Aged Pilgrim's Friend Society, and the other £2 10s. I keep as a little fund from which to relieve poor saints, of whom I know and see many in my various movements here and there. I am not able to do as much for them now as I was before I gave up my two chapels, and lost with them all the income which I had from them. I am glad, therefore, of any little help to enable me to give away a little to the poor saints of God.

Through mercy I have been pretty well during the summer, and was enabled to preach sixteen continuous Lord's-days, and once in the week, and sometimes twice besides. This I consider a great favour, and I hope that the Lord not only brought me through the work, but was with me in it. I was eight Lord's-days at Gower Street Chapel, and visited Wilts, being at Allington three Lord's-days, and preaching at the Calne anniversary, where I think we had the largest attendance which I have ever known. Our poor friend Mr. P—— is still a good deal afflicted, but was able to get out on all the Lord's-days that I was there. I fear, poor man, he will be afflicted for life; but his pains and afflictions seem to be sanctified to his soul's good. We are sorry to see our friends suffer, and yet what can we say when we see their afflictions sanctified to their soul? We cannot love them, nor feel for, and sympathise with them as the Lord does; and yet He sees fit in His wisdom and mercy to afflict them, and we know that He would not do so unless it were for the good of their soul. What can we say then? All we can do is to beg of the Lord that He would support, comfort, and bless them; and this we shall do, as we are led to feel for them, and sympathise with them in their afflictions and troubles.

You would see in this month's *Gospel Standard* the account which you sent of your departed friend. I think it will be read with much interest, as there is so much in it that is very striking, and such an experience, both of law and Gospel, as one does not often meet with in these days. What a proof such an account affords of the wondrous sovereignty of God, and the exceeding riches of His superabounding grace! It is such things which show us the Lord Jesus Christ is the same yesterday, to-day, and for ever, that He still deals with the souls of His saints, at least with some of them, as in days of old, and that true religion and vital godliness are ever the same as wrought in the soul by a Divine power. But how is the fine gold become dim, both in minister and people! Where are there now such ministers as Mr. Symons and Marriner, whom you used to hear at Bristol?

The work of God upon the soul is almost everywhere at a low ebb, and though there is in this country, and especially in Wilts, a spirit of hearing, yet there is but little power either in the pulpit or in the pew. It seems to be the same with you in Australia as with us—great profession, but very little Divine life and power. Error abounds, and is wrapped up under such specious shapes that it is very hard to detect it. But you will always find that where error is there will be pride and contention. It is only a knowledge of the truth, attended with divine unction and power, which will produce brokenness, contrition, humility, meekness with faith, hope, and love, godly fear, a spirit of prayer, separation from the world, and that sweet spirituality of mind which is life and peace.

I hope that the few among you who love the Lord and His precious truth will keep close together in love and union, avoiding all things which cause strife and contention. You may be few in number, and may be derided as a little knot; but it is better for a few to meet together and walk together in love and union, seeking the glory of God and His blessing, than to be mixed up with a number of people who have neither part nor lot in the matter of eternal life.

Please to give my love to Mrs. Charlwood, and any of the friends who may know me from my writings, and feel union with them, and with me for them. I hope Aquila is well, and your wife; kind remembrances to them.

Yours affectionately in the truth,

J. C. P.

CCXXV.—To Mrs. Peake

Croydon, Oct. 25, 1866.

My dear Friend,

I feel it to be a mercy to have been brought through all my travellings and labours, and to have reached my own home in peace and safety. To be preserved in our going in and out, and to find the Lord a shade on our right hand is indeed a mercy, and especially to one who feels his need of preservation from many things which do not affect the health or comfort of others; and besides all this, to have been allowed to fulfil all my engagements, and blessed, I hope, in fulfilling them, gives, or should give, an additional ground of thankfulness. I was enabled to preach during the past summer for sixteen continuous Lord's-days, besides speaking on the week evening, and in no one case disappointed the people, or broke an engagement. And I would fain hope that amidst all my weakness, sinfulness, ignorance, and infirmity, that the Lord was pleased sometimes to bless the word which I was enabled to preach in His name. If I have learnt anything by advancing years, and a long experience of the ministry, it is my own insufficiency to every good word and work; and that, even were I enabled to preach the Gospel with all clearness, faithfulness, and consistency with the word of truth; yea, were I just such a minister as I seem to see what a minister should be, even then all my words would fall to the ground, except so far as the Lord Himself were specially pleased to bless them to the souls of His people. Whilst, then, I am thankful for any little help given to preach the word of life, yet I would be far more thankful to find that a blessing rested upon the word. When, too, I consider what man is as a fallen creature, and what my heart is naturally, how hard, impenitent, obdurate, and unbelieving, and know that my heart is only as if a copy of all other hearts, how sensibly it makes me feel that the whole work, first and last, must be of the Lord, and that if He withhold the blessing, Paul himself might plant, and Apollos water, but there would be no increase. If, then, any blessing may have rested on my labours during the summer, I may well retire into my winter quarters with a feeling of thankfulness that they have not been in vain in the Lord. I am glad I have been to Oakham and to Stamford, not only once more to see my dear friends in the flesh, but also to unite with them once more in the house of prayer, and to feel some renewal and revival of the love and affection which never can be extinguished when once it has been kindled by the power of God.

I had some nice conversation with S. C. and her niece, also with others. At Stamford I was not able to see much of the friends, but was well attended, and felt comfortable in speaking amongst them.

I sincerely hope that you and your dear sister may derive benefit from your sojourn at L. It certainly was very beneficial to me both times that I was there. I am, through mercy, pretty well, and preached last Lord's-day morning and also on Wednesday evening. My texts were Jer. xxxi. 11, 12, Lord's-day morning, and Wednesday evening Heb. x. 36, 37. From Jer. xxxi. 11 I showed that there were six things stronger than Jacob, whom I took as a typical representative of a child of God: 1. the law; 2. sin; 3. Satan; 4. the world; 5. death; 6. hell, all which I worked out. Then the redemption by the Lord Himself by price and power, first price, and then power; then the effects as manifested to the soul in coming and singing in the height of Zion, on which Jesus now sits enthroned, and flowing with a melting heart to the goodness of the Lord to feed upon Gospel bread and Gospel wine, the unction of the Holy Spirit, the Paschal Lamb, and the fatted calf. I hope we had, upon the whole, a good time.

I spoke on Wednesday evening, as my friend Covell was gone to the anniversary at Cranbrook, and I had quite a good congregation. . . .

Yours affectionately in the Lord,
J. C. P.

CCXXVI—To Mr. Whitteridge

Croydon, Oct. 25, 1866.

My dear Sir,

* * * * * *

I am obliged to you for your kind invitation to preach in your chapel when I am in town; but you will perceive from personal observation that my physical strength is but small, and, indeed, I find that my labours at Gower Street are quite as much as I can accomplish. I could not, therefore, undertake to accept your invitation, as I find that to preach more than once in the week besides the Lord's-day is more than I can do without suffering, and the hazard of laying myself up altogether. It is many years since I have suffered from weakness of the chest, and indeed was compelled by it to give up two chapels and congregations, amongst whom I had laboured for more than twenty-six years. I feel it therefore a mercy that I am allowed during the summer months to speak a little in the name of the Lord, and gladly would I do more for His name's sake if His glorious Majesty did but give me the power.

To preach the Gospel is a very important, and, I may say, an arduous task. Rightly to divide the word of truth, to take forth the precious from the vile, to preach the Gospel with the Holy Ghost sent down from heaven, by manifestation of the truth to commend ourselves to every man's conscience in the sight of God. Well may we ask, Who is sufficient for these things? I feel myself most insufficient, but I know that the Lord maketh His strength perfect in weakness, and this encourages me to cast myself on Him, and seek help from His gracious hands who has said, "My grace is sufficient for thee."

I am, dear Sir,
Yours very sincerely, for truth's sake,
J. C. P.

CCXXVII —To Mr. Parry

Croydon, Nov. 23, 1866.

My dear Friend,

I was sorry to learn from your last kind letter that the Lord had again laid upon you His afflicting hand; but it was your mercy to find profit from the furnace, and that the painful trial was sanctified to your spiritual good. We are such poor, stupid, cold, lifeless wretches when things are smooth and easy with us, that we seem to need trial and affliction to stir us up, and bring us out of carnality and death. The word of God is written for an afflicted and poor people, and they alone understand it, believe it, feel it, and realise it. How often you had read Micah vii. 8, 9, and yet did not enter into its sweetness, suitability, and blessedness as you did in your late affliction. There is a sermon of mine from it in the *Gospel Pulpit*, No. 77, which you can look over, but I dare say you could preach a better sermon from it than I did if you could tell out all that you felt in the sweet application of it. Luther used to say that before he was afflicted he never understood the word of God. This witness is true. There is no real place for it in our conscience or affections. And yet how hard it seems and trying to the flesh to learn our religion in such a painful way; but any way is better than to miss the prize at last. And if we are favoured to reach the heavenly shore we shall forget all the perils and sufferings of the voyage. I hope, however, that you will take all due care of yourself at this trying season of the year, as you cannot stand the damp and cold as you once could. I have not been very well myself the last week, but with this exception I have, through much mercy, been more than usually well during the autumn. This has enabled me to get most days my usual walk, without which I rarely find myself in tolerable health.

I preach here sometimes, but more to assist my friend, who, though much recovered, is not I think very strong, than for any other reason. He is a very good preacher, much better than most that I know; and what is better than good preaching, his whole heart and soul seem in it. He has been very much kept during a long profession, nearly as long as mine, and been at times much blessed and favoured. This gives much life and power to his ministry, but at the same time makes it very searching. Last Lord's-day morning he spoke from 2 Kings xviii. 6, 7, and was very close upon cleaving to the Lord, and departing not from following Him. I could not find, alas, that I had cleaved so closely to the Lord, and not departed from following Him as he drew the line. But it is good sometimes to be searched, that we may see our sinfulness, confess and forsake it. The ministry of the day is for the most part so loose and lax that it is good to have a closer if not stricter line of experience drawn out, if it be not too strongly insisted on for the casting down of the tried and tempted. I remember how you once were much tried by a sermon which I preached from Romans xii. 1, 2, more than ten years ago (in 1856), though I believe I advanced nothing in it but what you would fully agree with. We need castings down and liftings up, sometimes to be searched and exercised about the reality of our religion, and sometimes to be strengthened and encouraged so as not to be utterly cast down. It is those who have no changes that fear not God. All who walk in the ways of truth and righteousness will find changes within, though we know that there are no changes without, for with God there is no variableness nor shadow of turning. Though we do not like these changes for ourselves, yet we have little union or communion with those who have none. The Lord we trust has opened our eyes and hearts too to see and feel what true religion is; and though we seem at times to have so little of it, and almost none at all, yet in our right mind nothing can satisfy us but what comes from and leads to the Lord. Growing years have not made us grow more in a good opinion of self, or the goodness of the creature. If we have grown in anything it is in a sense of the suitability, blessedness, grace and glory of the Lord Jesus Christ.

But I need hardly write in this strain. You well know from my sermons and writings what my views and feelings are; and I can only express privately what I do publicly, for I have not two kinds of religion, one for the parlour and the other for the pulpit, and you know I never had. . . .

Yours very affectionately,

J. C. P.

CCXXVIII—To Mr. Alfred Hammond, Minister of the Gospel

Croydon, Dec. 17*th*, 1866.

Dear Friend in the Lord,

. . . I am glad to see how the Lord keeps alive His sacred work upon your heart, though I doubt not that like most others of those who fear God you have your changes. Indeed I believe, for my part, that the soul, when once made alive unto God, can no more be healthy than through air, food, and exercise, in the same way as the body. Breathing out desires, and breathing in the breath of the Spirit, hungering and feeding upon the bread of life, movements and exercises of each spiritual grace as faith, hope, love, patience, repentance, and godly sorrow for sin, meekness and humility, quietness and resignation, a falling into the hands and before the face of God, the renunciation of all our own wisdom, strength, and righteousness—these and similar exercises keep the soul alive and prevent it settling on its lees or being at ease in Zion. These are the lessons which I am daily learning, and have been trying to learn for many many years, but seem to have learnt very little to profit. Still I have learnt something of what I am, and something of what the Lord is; and I have learnt in this school how vile I am, and how good is He. I feel myself utterly unworthy to occupy the position in which I am placed as a writer and preacher; still I desire to be faithful according to the measure of my light and grace. In this dark and gloomy day stewards need to be faithful, as I have every reason to believe you are.

The Lord bless your aged father, yourself, and all near and dear to you by natural and spiritual ties, with every needful blessing.

My love to you all.

Yours affectionately in the truth,
J. C. P.

CCXXIX—To Mr. Clowes *

Croydon, Dec. 17, 1866.

My dear Friend,

I was quite concerned to learn from my dear wife that you do not progress in any advance to health and strength, and that you yourself did not look forward to any great amendment. I know from experience with what a heavy weight bodily afflictions press, not only upon our mortal tabernacle, but upon our soul, and how depressing they are to the mind and spirits. I can, therefore, feelingly sympathise with you in this painful trial, and indeed all the more, as just now passing through it myself. But all we can say is, "It is from the Lord, and He must and will deal with us as seemeth good in His sight." You have had for many years a good measure of health and strength, and though rarely free from your stomach affection, yet you have been spared to a good age. You cannot expect to have now that health and strength which you had in younger days, and it will be your wisdom and mercy to bow down before the will of God, and submit with patient resignation to the strokes of His afflicting rod. He has often in times past blessed, relieved, and comforted your soul, and though through the power of unbelief you may at times call in question all He has done for you and in you, yet all your doubts and fears do not affect the reality of His work nor the exceeding riches of His superabounding grace.

I was glad to learn, from a few lines received from Mr. G., that you felt your feet upon the rock. May the Lord give you grace and strength there to continue fast and firm, and not be

* Thomas Clowes, Esq., died at Haverstock Hill, London, on Feb. 17, 1867, aged 78. See obituary in *Gospel Standard* supplement, June, 1867.

moved from your standing by the assaults of Satan and the flesh. But I know from painful experience that it is only as the Lord is pleased to give and strengthen faith that we can fight in this battle. We think of our sins, backslidings, inconsistencies, infirmities, the little fruit that we have borne or are bearing, and the few marks that we seem to have of the grace of God being in us of a truth. Unbelief is a dreadful foe to the soul's peace, and Satan takes every advantage of working upon our natural feelings to bring us into bondage and confusion. Bodily weakness also much helps him on, as we seem to have no strength of mind or body to resist him. In such extremities there is only one way of getting help and relief—to fall down before the Lord in all our weakness and sinfulness and beg of Him to undertake our cause, that the sighing of the prisoner might come up before Him, that He would save those who are appointed to die.

But I hope my dear friend has obtained some gracious answer from Him who is able to save to the uttermost all who come unto God by Him; for it is this alone which can give any solid comfort or abiding relief. You have for many years been learning your own sinfulness, weakness, and helplessness, and have often been brought down in your soul before God as having in self neither hope nor help. And there have been times and seasons also when you have had discoveries to your soul of the goodness and mercy of the Lord, which have enabled you to believe in His name, hope in His mercy, and cleave to Him in love and affection. Now all these things are so many pledges and foretastes of His unchanging and unchangeable love; and I hope that you may be enabled to hold firmly what the Lord has given graciously, and not give way to Satan and unbelief. We are miserable sinners in a miserable world. All around us, within us and without us, is a wreck and ruin. Sin, horrid sin, has utterly defiled both body and soul, and stained and polluted everything that is of the earth. Amidst all this wreck and ruin which we daily feel, there is only one ray of light to guide our feet through this tangled maze of sin and sorrow, and this light beams forth out of the Son of God as once crucified, but now risen from the dead and gone up on high to appear in the presence of God for us. He has destroyed death and him that had the power of death, even the devil, who through fear of death hath so often brought us into bondage.

I was glad to hear from my dear wife the message that you sent that you had no fear of death. He is the last enemy, and if his sting be taken away, then the victory is won. The sting of death is sin; but if that sin be pardoned and put away, then the sting is taken out, and to die is only to fall asleep in Jesus. I believe, for the most part, God makes His people willing to die before He takes them to Himself, for they feel there is no other release from trouble and sorrow.

I should much like to come up and see you, but am not able, as at present I feel very poorly. I sympathise much with your dear wife and son, both of whom love you so tenderly, and would gladly see you restored to your former health. I will not trouble either you or Mrs. C. to answer this. You will both of you accept my Christian love, and

Believe me to be,

Yours very affectionately in the Lord,

J. P. C.

CCXXX.—To Mrs. Peake.

Croydon, Dec. 20, 1866.

My dear Friend,

As a general rule, I believe it is best to answer a letter soon after its receipt, as the subject is then most fresh upon the mind of both writer and reader. But this is not often feasible, and has not been so in the instance of your last kind favour. . . . You know how interested I am in all that concerns the spiritual welfare of the church at Oakham. I am truly glad, therefore, to find that as the Lord takes with one hand, he gives with the other. You must expect to see every year increasing gaps made in your midst. For many years our ranks were but little thinned; but, as you know, my later days witnessed the removal of some of the chief pillars and ornaments of the church. My own feeling was much against widening the gate of the church, or we might have had numerous accessions. But my desire was quality rather than quantity—jewels which would one day shine in the heavenly kingdom rather than what might turn out reprobate silver. But we are liable to extremes, and, therefore, I do not say that we might not have kept out some who might well have come in. It is a very difficult and delicate point, and one which requires very great judgment, discernment, and wisdom from on high, united with the spirit of love and tenderness. All I can say is, that I hope your new members may be to the church both for its strength and ornament, and that neither you nor they may ever have any cause for grief for their admission among you. I am also glad to find that the Lord gives His blessing to Mr. K.'s ministry; and I hope that as he becomes increasingly united to the church and people, he will find a corresponding increase of light, life, and power to minister amongst them the word of truth. A church and its pastor should be like private friends, who know each other increasingly, through length and intimacy of intercourse, and are thus enabled better to understand and feel for, and sympathise with each other. The great point is *reality*, that a minister should be a real partaker of the grace of God, and be enabled by the Spirit's teaching and power to deal spiritually and experimentally with the word of truth, and with the heart and conscience of the people of God. If a man be right, all in the end will come right, and be made right; and if he is in his right place, that also will be made manifest. God will ever acknowledge His own grace, His own work, His own cause, His own people, and His own servants. Clouds and darkness may rest upon them all, but the true light will arise, and shine them all away. A minister, therefore, need well be assured of three things. 1, his own standing; 2, his ministerial commission; 3, that he is ministering to a people over which God has set him. Doubts and fears may and will try his mind upon all these three points; but only so far as he is in some good measure established in them can he find faith and confidence in doing the work to which he has set his hands. . . The loss of Mr. Lightfoot at Stamford will be, humanly speaking, irreparable. He and I did not quite see eye to eye on every point, but I very much esteemed him, and indeed, as a deacon, he was quite my right hand. No man in the church or congregation was, I believe, so much esteemed by the people generally; and from his great amiability of disposition, he had but few enemies. I fully believed he would make a good end, as I have seen for some years much growth in him of life and grace, and he was a man who increasingly loved and feared the Lord, bringing forth fruit in his old age.

I am at present very poorly from one of my chest attacks, and though not severe, it is very lingering. It is very depressing both to mind and body, but I trust I am reaping some spiritual fruit from it.

"Afflictions make us see," &c.

The world in my eyes is full of sin and sorrow; and happy are they who are safely landed out of it all on the heavenly shore. It is through much tribulation, &c., and I look for little else. Whatever come, I richly deserve every stroke of the chastening rod. I have written but a poor address; but I feel unless the Lord supply me, my cruse is empty.

I was pleased with what you said about our friend ——. He is a man whom I esteem for the grace of God, which I have seen in him. In the present dearth of ministers, we are glad to see any godly men raised up to preach the word of life. But we may expect things to get darker and darker in the visible Church of Christ, and the ministry of the word proportionately sink in power and efficacy. . . . .

Yours very affectionately in the Lord,

J. C. P.

CCXXXI—To Mrs. Peake

Croydon, Dec. 31, 1866.

My dear Friend,

The sad tidings contained in your letter came upon me quite with a sudden shock, as I had no idea that there was any serious danger connected with poor Richard's illness. Being accustomed to see him enjoying so much health, I could scarcely bring my mind to think of him as seriously ill. But oh, what lessons we have to learn of the brevity and uncertainty of human life; and how those seem taken away to whom we looked forward as pillars and supports of the cause of truth, when older heads should be laid low. I feel very much for the poor widow, with this heavy aggravation of all her afflictions, and I feel for the church and congregation, who have lost a most valuable member. There are few men with whom I have had more conversation or communion on divine things. We saw, I believe, eye to eye in the things of God, and he always treated me with great respect and affection. We cannot at present see the reason of this mysterious dispensation. Time only can unfold what is wrapped up in its bosom; and I cannot just now convey to you what thoughts have sprung up in my mind respecting it. Our dear friends at W. have troubles in their old age, and are likely to have more, but they have this satisfaction, as well as his poor dear widow, that he is gone to enjoy what his soul loved and longed for.

I was thinking this morning, as I was getting up, that there could be no real happiness or peace whilst in this poor body of sin and sickness. But we cleave to life; yet none of those who have dropped the body to be with the Lord would ever wish to take up again the miserable shell of humanity. How broken, how contracted, what a miserable tabernacle of sin and death must it appear to their enfranchised spirit—worse to them than a beggar's cast-off dress would be to us. My cold is, I hope, passing off. I was not able to get out yesterday. Mr. Covell preached from Rom. viii. 38, 39.

We unite in kind love to our dear afflicted friends, &c.

Yours very affectionately in the Lord,

J. C. P.

CCXXXII—To Mrs. Peake

Croydon, Jan. 16, 1867.

My dear Friend,

I have been much occupied with writing, but I take the first opportunity of sending you a few lines to express my sympathy with you all under those trying afflictions which have fallen with so heavy a weight on those whom we so much esteem and love. I feel very much for you all, and especially for poor dear E. in her distressing bereavement and the heavy pressure of her own personal affliction. I cannot say that at present I feel at all reconciled to the loss of our dear friend R. H. Indeed, excepting Mr. K., there is scarcely one whom I should miss so much if I were with you. He seemed so calculated to stand in the gap, and fill up the place of those who in time must have to give way to infirmity or old age. For many years our losses by death in the church at Oakham were but few. But oh, in these last few years what gaps have been made, especially amongst our male members, who are so much needed in the church. God is able to raise up others to supply their place, but no man having drunk old wine, &c. New members can never be to a church what old members are; for they lack the experience and the wisdom which the dealings of God bring about, in an exercised conscience and a matured judgment. You will much miss our departed friend's prayers on the reading days, for I have frequently heard how honest he was in his confessions, and how earnest and sincere in his petitions. He was possessed also of a good experience, and for the most part pretty sound in judgment, with a right apprehension of living realities, and a desire to glorify God by his life and conduct. I have had much conversation with him at different times, and I believe we always met and parted in sincere friendship and affection. We could communicate very freely in divine matters, and well understood each other's minds in those points of exercise and temptation, where hints are sufficient, and to go beyond which is to venture on unsafe grounds. He always treated me with great respect and affection, and if he did not agree with me on all points, would not make it a matter of dispute. When I have seen him looking so strong and healthy, I little thought that I should be the survivor. How often have I looked from my window on a winter afternoon, on my return from chapel, and seen him and his poor wife hurrying off through the cold air to go home amidst the dark night, when I was glad to keep close to the fire. It grieves me to hear that his poor widow is worse. Daily do I beseech the Lord that He would comfort her heart, give her faith and patience, and sanctify to her soul's good every stroke of His afflicting hand. Nor do I forget to ask the Lord that He would sanctify the stroke to her aged parents, who have had so many family trials of late years. I hope the Lord will abundantly bless Mr. K.'s ministry to the sorrowing church, as well as to the friends and relatives of the deceased.

I quite approve of the purchase of the ground at the cemetery. It is an odd word to make use of, but I have often said, "How very comfortable it is to have a cemetery where the people of God can be buried by their own minister, and lie together till the resurrection morn." You would more deeply prize the spot where you have placed a monument to your late dear husband, were his remains beneath it.

I was much interested in the account you gave of the funeral. I thought much of you all that day, the snow lying so deep, and the weather so cold. It must have been a very solemn and affecting scene; and the numbers who attended it, showed what great respect they had for his memory. I do hope the solemn event may be blessed and sanctified to the church and congregation. Such heavy strokes seem sometimes to stir up the soil, and fit it for the reception of the word. "Ye received the word in much affliction, with joy of the Holy Ghost." Deep affliction and the joy of the Holy Ghost going together make the word received not as the word of man, but as it is in truth the word of God, which effectually worketh in them that believe. I am always glad to get a few lines from you, as I have scarcely any other means of obtaining any intelligence, either temporal or spiritual, of what is going on amongst you at Oakham; and you may be sure that having been amongst you for so many years, you all still live in my affections and remembrance. I feel a great comfort in my own mind that, amidst all the trials which have befallen you, Mr. K. is with you to comfort your hearts by the word of life; for I hardly know what you would have done had the pulpit been vacant, and you left merely to supplies.

We unite in love, &c.; and please assure the church for me that I still bear it in my heart, and desire that the blessing of God may abundantly rest upon it.

I am, my dear friend,
Yours very affectionately in the Lord,
J. C. P.

CCXXXIII —To Mr. Copcutt

Croydon, Jan. 24, 1867.

My dear Sir,

* * * * *

The United States are a wonderful country, and possess in the largest abundance every natural gift of heaven. But unless God show great mercy in the gifts of His grace, and raise up a people in your midst to fear His great name, all your wealth and power, and all the capabilities so largely possessed of furnishing everything in the shape of wealth and abundance, may only prove sources of sin and eventual misery. Amidst so widespread a profession, one would hope that God has, here and there, some whose hearts He has touched by His grace; but there is a sad want of a preached gospel, and of ministers who take forth the precious from the vile, and so are as God's mouth. As the editor of the *Gospel Standard,* I get letters sometimes from various parts of the United States, and in almost all of them I find the same complaints of the want of a sound experimental gospel ministry. Gracious persons also, who have emigrated, send back the same report; so that I am forced to come to a conclusion that the truth as it is in Jesus is but little held and little preached.

I have the pleasure since I have lived here of sitting under a very sound, experimental, and much-favoured servant of God, Mr. Francis Covell. During, indeed, the severe weather, I have been much confined to the house, but greatly prize his ministry, as his soul is much alive in the things of God. In prayer especially he is most warm and fervent, with great sincerity and simplicity of petition, much humble confession of sin, and great earnestness in wrestling for heavenly blessings. In his preaching, also, though not what is called eloquent, yet his sermons are sound in doctrine, clear and savoury in experience, and strictly practical in all fruits of Christian obedience.

Your various journeys, both at home and abroad, must bring to your mind many pleasant reminiscences as well as striking contrasts. You have seen the palms and tropical vegetation of Cuba, the pine forests of Canada, the glaciers of Switzerland, and the green fields and well-cultivated lands of Bucks, besides, no doubt, a large acquaintance with the scenery of your adopted country. The face of nature thus affords many pleasant recollections; but how man has ruined every thing and every place which he has touched! What sin, misery, and wretchedness meet the eye and grieve the heart on every side! Violence, injustice, cruelty to man and beast, oppression, falsehood, selfishness, and disregard of everything but the cravings of aspiring ambition, show themselves everywhere; not to mention those grosser evils in which man seems to sink to a lower level than the beasts. There is one feature in this country which is especially admirable —the supremacy of law. No one, from the richest peer to the most abject pauper, can set himself against the law, and as our judges are men of great ability and sterling integrity, and are upheld and supported by all the power of public opinion, their decisions are final. Law is our grand protection, without which neither property nor person would be safe; and where there is in a nation a respect for law, liberty flourishes under its shade.

You are favoured in your children. We have a pleasant recollection of them. It is a great mercy when children are obedient and affectionate, well-disposed, and untainted with the evils of the day.

Our very affectionate regards to Mrs. C., yourself, and all your family.

Yours very sincerely,
J. C. P.

CCXXXIV.—To Mr. Parry

Croydon, Jan. 25, 1867.

My dear Friend,

. . . We can hardly expect to pass through life, and especially the latter stages of it, without trials and afflictions; for if they do not come in one shape they will in another. The Lord means to make us sick and weary of everything but Himself; and I believe that most of His people are made willing to depart before the final stroke comes. It is the want of sweet manifestations of His love and mercy, the sense of what we have been, and what a wreck and ruin sin has made of us, with the various exercises of mind that spring out of it, which so often make the prospect gloomy. But this stirs up many an earnest sigh and cry for the Lord to appear and to speak a word with power to the soul, that we may enjoy a blessed testimony to our acceptance in the Beloved. How much one is led to see and feel of the dreadful evil of sin! how loathsome it is in the sight of a holy God! what vile wretches we are in ourselves! and what a mighty work the gracious Lord had to do to save us from death and hell! I never saw so much of the evil of sin, and of my own evil case as a sinner, as I have seen and felt of late; and I do beg of the Lord, not only to manifest and reveal Himself with power to my soul, but to give me godly sorrow for sin, with a broken heart, a contrite spirit, and a humble mind. These things many overlook, and some despise, but they are choice gifts of God, and highly prized by those who know their value. Seclusion and solitude give time and opportunity to look over the past; and I am sure the reflection is anything but comfortable. Oh, what heaps of sins are brought to view, and how little we seem to have lived in the fear of God, to have sought His will, or been fruitful branches in the only True Vine! Men speak sometimes of looking back upon a well-spent life, but I cannot; I have to cast myself wholly upon the superabounding grace of God. No doubt advancing life and frequent indisposition make us see things in a very different light from that in which they are viewed by the young and healthy. But the question after all is, Which is the right view? Is the world a happy or a miserable one? Is life to be lived to self, spent in carnality and ease, or should we seek to live unto God? David could say, "Before I was afflicted I went astray, but now I have kept Thy word." It will be our mercy if afflictions have taught us the same lesson. But I must not sermonise, though I have no doubt that in these points we see and feel alike.

Allington must have presented but a cold and chilling appearance during the late frost and snow; and I can readily believe that the north-east winds, which were felt keenly here must have swept from off your downs with terrible force. But the snow must have been a great protection to the young wheats, and thus we can see mercy in that severe snow-storm which was so widely prevalent. I spent two winters at Allington, 1835-1836 and 1837-1838, and my reminiscences of it are of great cold without, whatever warmth and cordiality there was within, especially when the big blocks sent a roaring fire up the drawing-room chimney, aided by the draught of the middle door, left open by the present master of the house, then a little pale-faced boy. We have seen great changes since then, but, I believe, we may say that our mutual friendship and affection have not changed, but rather expanded as the little boy into the stout well-grown man.

Many friends have we seen removed since June, 1835 ; and the list of ministers who have stood in your pulpit since the chapel was opened, who have been removed by death, forms quite a long catalogue. Poor old Mr. S. is another added to the number. As my life is thus far spared, I desire that what still remains of it may be spent in the fear of God, and for the good of His people. I did not think, when I first knew you, that I should have written so much or been so widely known; but I have been led on, step by step, seeking neither praise nor popularity, but content to do what lay in my path and what I felt called upon from time to time to execute. The *Gospel Standard* and the sermons take up much of my time, and it is sometimes a weariness to the flesh; but they occupy my thoughts and exercise my mind upon divine things, which is better than indolence or distraction. I can hardly, however, get time to attend to the memoir of our late dear friend William Tiptaft, as the press, like the two daughters of the horse-leech, is ever crying "Give, give."

You will be sorry to hear that our poor friend Mr. C. is confined to his bed, and I should fear there is little hope of his ever leaving it. He is waiting anxiously for the Lord to appear and once more visit and bless his soul; but I believe the good old man has no fear of death. Poor Mrs. C. is almost overwhelmed with trouble.

Yours very affectionately,
J. C. P.

CCXXXV—To Mrs. Clowes

Croydon, Jan. 26, 1867.

My dear Friend,

I desire, sincerely, to sympathise with you in your present deep trial and heavy affliction, and I wish that I could offer you some consolation, or, at least, some hope, under the weight of your trouble. But I know well that none can give you any support or consolation but the Lord Himself. And oh, that He would kindly and graciously speak a word with power to the soul of your poor afflicted husband, and that he might be blessed with a feeling sense of the Lord's love to his soul. We do not doubt but that he is all right for eternity. We know, and he cannot deny, that the Lord in times past has been very gracious unto him, and has manifested His love and mercy to his soul. But he wants to hear again His blessed voice and to feel the certainty of His pardoning love through the application of His atoning blood to his conscience. Oh that it might please the Lord to give him one sweet smile, to break in upon his soul, and say, "I am thy salvation," break all his bonds asunder, and reveal peace with power to his heart. But even should this be withheld the Lord has already mercifully taken away his fear of death; and thus it may not please His gracious Majesty to grant him the blessing which he desires and we also desire for him. The Scripture says but little of the dying experience of God's saints; and sometimes we look too much for what the Lord has not especially promised—that is, any great manifestations of His love and mercy. He has promised to make their bed in all their sickness, never to leave them or forsake them, and that He would love them to the end. And all this He will fulfil in and for our dear friend.

I am glad that you have Dr. Corfe. You will find him a sympathising Christian friend, and his skill may alleviate, if not remove, his complaint. I wish you could have some one to help you to nurse him, as I fear it will overtax your strength, and you should, for his sake, keep up as well as you can. I would come up to see him, but, at present, cannot leave the house. Give him my affectionate love. He has my prayers that the Lord would appear for him. We unite in love, with most kind remembrances to Mr. L. I feel for him as well as for you.

Yours most affectionately,

J. C. P.

CCXXXVI.—To Mrs. Tanner

Croydon, Feb. 14, 1867.

My dear Afflicted and Widowed Friend,

But for much occupation I should have written to you immediately that I received the tidings of your late beloved husband's departure, that I might sympathise with you in your troubles and sorrows. I had heard of his illness, but was not aware till the day before he died that it was of so serious a nature. But now, poor dear man, he is released from all his sufferings, both of body and mind, and is in the fruition of that perfect happiness to which he so often looked forward during the latter stages of his pilgrimage here. Having so sweet an assurance of his eternal happiness, and knowing what a life of suffering his was, it would indeed be selfish and cruel to wish him back. You well know what he had to suffer with his many trials from so many quarters, and though you may deeply miss him, and weep at the thought that you will never in this life see his face nor hear his voice more, yet I am sure that you have every reason to rejoice rather than mourn. Still, nature will have its course, and it is often a great relief when the tears can freely flow, and grief find its appointed vent. It was a great mercy also that you and your daughters were able to minister to his wants and comforts in his last illness, and to have the sweet satisfaction of witnessing the sweet peace that he enjoyed in his soul. What an infinite mercy it also is that the Lord has blessed you with the consolations of His spirit at various times; and I do hope that as your afflictions abound, so also may your consolations.

I believe you know that we were much united both in heart and judgment. Indeed, I had great esteem and affection for him; and I am sure he always treated me with the greatest kindness and affection. I should be glad if you could put together some little obituary of him, as he was so much esteemed and respected by all who knew him, that there might be some record of him in the *Gospel Standard*.

With our united kind love to yourself and Mrs. W.,

I am,

Yours affectionately in the Lord,

J. C. P.

CCXXXVII —To Mr. Parry

Croydon, Feb. 16, 1867.

My dear Friend,

And so our dear and esteemed friend Joseph Tanner is entered into his eternal rest. For him there is no more pain or suffering, but an eternity of bliss and blessedness in the presence of God and the Lamb. We shall miss him greatly, especially you, who have lost in him not only a valued and affectionate friend, but a choice and acceptable Supply. We shall never see his face or hear his voice upon earth any more. He was younger than both of us, but from his many bodily afflictions more advanced in constitution than in age. He has left a good name behind him, which is a wonderful mercy, considering the snares and temptations to which he, in common with others, was exposed. Even his own family could scarcely have wished him to live when they saw him so continually racked with pain and suffering. It must have been a satisfaction to him to see his eldest daughter comfortably settled in life before he was taken away. Thus he could sing both of mercy and judgment, and the combination of these two makes in divine things the most harmonious music. I believe he had a very sincere and warm esteem and affection for you, and had a good union with the friends generally at Allington. How one after another is passing away, and if our dear friend W. T. had been alive he would have been reckoning up how many ministers, who had occupied the Allington pulpit, had been removed by death. I have no doubt that many thoughts have crossed your mind in connection with the removal of our esteemed friend, and many desires and petitions have gone upward that when your time shall come you may find the Lord to be the strength of your heart, and your portion for ever. I have no doubt your prayers will be abundantly answered.

I am, through mercy, pretty well, and got out for a walk yesterday, besides being at chapel on the previous Lord's-day. At this season of the year I find myself for the most part best within doors, for though I much enjoy a walk, yet I pay dearly for it if it give me cold. It seems very hard to be deprived of that air and exercise which we once enjoyed, and which we see others still enjoying, but if it be a trial laid upon us by the Lord we must submit to it with other afflictions from His all-wise hand.

I do not like to make any positive engagements, but, as far as I can foresee events, I think I might be with you, if the Lord will, and give health and strength, for the month of August; and, without promising, I should like to give you, if I could, the four Lord's-days of that month. I cannot expect to be able to go on preaching year after year, even if my life be a little longer spared.

Yours very affectionately,
J. C. P.

CCXXXVIII—To Mrs. Clowes

Croydon, Feb. 25, 1867.

My dear Afflicted and Widowed Friend,

I should have written to you before this to express my deep and affectionate sympathy with you under your distressing bereavement if I had not thought it best to wait a little until the first gush of your sorrow had found vent. When sorrow is so very recent and so pressing, there is no room in the heart to receive any word from a friend; and none but the Lord Himself can either console or support the troubled spirit. Knowing how all your affections, and almost your life, were bound up with my dear departed friend, I am sure that your grief must be very great. But I do hope that the Lord may not only impart some sweet consolation to your troubled heart, but give you also some submission and resignation to His holy will.

I should be glad if you could bear in mind how many mercies have been mingled with your bereavement. He was spared to you for many years, and was permitted to live to a good old age, possessing all his faculties both of body and mind to a remarkable degree. Was not this a mercy for you both? The Lord also took his earthly tabernacle gently down, and thus gradually prepared your mind for his final removal. Was not this a mercy? How much more deeply you would have felt it if he had been taken away suddenly! How united also you both were both in natural and spiritual love; and what a kind, tender, and affectionate husband you always found him to be. The recollection of this, I know, only increases your grief, for you keep thinking upon all that you have lost in him. But is it not a great mercy that you can look back upon the years of your married life with satisfaction, and without any regretful recollection? You were also enabled to nurse him tenderly and affectionately to the last, and do everything for him which his illness and infirmities required. Was not this a mercy that sufficient health and strength were given you to do this?

But the mercy of mercies is that you have so good a testimony that he is gone to his eternal rest. It pleased the Lord, indeed, for His own wise purposes to keep him for many months in a low place. Poor dear man! He was so afraid of presumption, vain confidence and hypocrisy, that he almost misjudged his own state and standing. Having been blessed in days gone by with clear manifestations of the Lord's love to his soul, he could not rest satisfied unless they were renewed. I never doubted him, though he often doubted himself; for not only his past experience, but his life, conduct, tenderness of conscience, godly fear, true humility of mind, separation from the world, and Christian spirit, clearly manifested his possession of the grace of God. In all my long intercourse with him I never received from him anything but the greatest kindness and affection. A man of more tender spirit I never knew, or one who boasted less of himself, or in any way put himself forward. I much feel his loss, and shall always think of him as long as I live with the highest esteem and affection.

I much regret that my health did not allow me to come up and see him, and to comply with your wish that I should pay the last tribute of affection to his remains. I was glad to learn that the Lord shone upon his soul before He took him hence, though, had it even not been so, I should not have been shaken in the least as to his eternal happiness.

And now, my dear friend, I do hope that you will not abandon yourself too much to your great sorrow. You cannot recall him; nor would you in your right mind wish so to do. Resignation and submission to the will of God are very desirable for you; and when you can say "Thy will be done" it will bring you relief. May the Lord sweetly shine upon your soul, and give you a word to comfort your heart. I endeavour to pray to the Lord that He would give you resignation to His holy will, comfort your heart, and grant you faith and patience. If you could drop me a line just to let me know how you are, and especially anything about the last days of my dear departed friend, I should esteem it a favour.

Please present my kindest regards to Mr. L——; I feel for him as well as for you. He has lost, indeed, a most kind and affectionate father.

My dear wife unites with me in kind love and sympathy.

Yours most affectionately,

J. C. P.

CCXXXIX—To Mrs. Peake

Croydon, March 6, 1867.

My dear and esteemed Friend,

I am not surprised that our friend O. should feel as he does towards our dear departed brother R. H., or wishes to put on permanent record those traits of Christian uprightness which he has mentioned. I will think over the subject, and, as far as space admits, either in the next number, or at some other opportunity, will endeavour to record them in the *G. S.* The simple fact is, that being pressed for space we can only allot a certain portion for the obituary, and are therefore obliged sometimes to divide, and at others to curtail, the accounts that are sent us. But I am sure that in this day we want testimonies to vital godliness, and real, powerful, practical religion; for this is that in which there is, and, I suppose, always has been, so great a defect in the Church of God. I have often thought of, and sometimes quoted, the words of Bunyan where, speaking of Talkative, Christian says, "The soul of religion is the practic part," meaning, doubtless, that where there is no practice religion is but a lifeless corpse. But nothing commends it more to the consciences of all men, whether natural or spiritual, than to see the fruits of godliness made manifest, especially when they are directly opposed to self-seeking and self-interest.

The providence which removed him is indeed mysterious. We seem to understand, and be reconciled to the removal of the aged and infirm, especially of those who bore the heat and burden of the day, like the two Coopers and other members of your church; but to see the young, like R. H. and your own dear husband, taken away, whose lives seemed so valuable both to the church and their families, makes us sometimes wonder at the Lord's dealings. And yet we know how many sorrows and sufferings they have been spared, and the very circumstance that they were taken away in the very prime of life and usefulness casts round their memory a more tender and sacred halo. I believe that the obituaries in the *G. S.* are generally very acceptable and very profitable. Mr. ——, of Nottingham, has frequently mentioned to me how good he has found the obituaries, and we find sometimes how persons on their deathbeds have spoken of the encouragement which they have met with in reading them. In a sense, we may say of the departed saint whose experience and words are thus recorded, "By it, he being dead, yet speaketh."

We are deeply grieved to hear of poor Eliza's sufferings. Seeing nothing before her but pain and suffering, and having, we hope, a good testimony of her eternal safety, it will be almost a relief if the Lord would give her a parting smile and take her to Himself. When I left Oakham in 1864 I left them both, as it appeared, in the full enjoyment of health and strength, and now one is gone, and the other fast following. I pray the Lord to sanctify the affliction to her aged parents, that they may see in it the frailty and uncertainty of all things here below, seek more earnestly to know and live unto the Lord of Life and Glory, and submit with resignation to His holy will. My daily prayer for poor Eliza is that the Lord would comfort her heart, alleviate her pain, give her faith and patience, with submission to His will. Poor Richard is spared the suffering of seeing her suffer, which he could ill have borne, and all those anxious cares which would have been entailed upon him by her illness. We know not from how much death saves, and still less what it gives. Could we see with the eye of God we should see wisdom and goodness marked upon every movement of His hand.

You probably know that my dear friend Mr. Clowes is gone to his eternal rest. He was very much tried through the whole of his illness, and sank very low, fearing at times that he was lost; but about two hours before he died the Lord broke most gloriously in upon his soul. I will endeavour to let you see Mrs. Clowes's letter. She is indeed a mourning widow, for I think I scarce ever saw a woman whose almost every thought seemed to be to and for her husband. He was indeed a most kind and affectionate partner, and, as a Christian, blessed with a good experience, with great tenderness of conscience, and much circumspectness of life. We were much attached to each other, as I have known him for more than thirty years, and, being with him every summer since 1855, of course I have seen a good deal of him. He was a man of very tender feeling, and never parted from me without shedding tears of true affection. I shall much miss him when I go again to London, if spared to fulfil my engagement at Gower Street Chapel.

Yours affectionately in the truth,

J. C. P.

CCXL —To Mr. Parry

Croydon, March 27, 1867.

My dear Friend,

I have no doubt that you were shocked, though perhaps not surprised, at the tidings of poor Mrs. R. Healy's death. The case, indeed, was hopeless from the first, and nothing could be looked for but a long, suffering illness, of which death would be the close. At last she sank away, passing off quietly, and the last few days scarce able to speak audibly or intelligibly. But we have every good ground of hope that her soul was saved in the Lord with an everlasting salvation, as she had had at various times many sweet promises applied to her heart, and many encouraging words spoken with power. Her religion was, indeed, not so deep and clear as her poor husband's; but there was great sincerity and sweetness stamped upon what she said. It will be ten years on the thirtieth of next month since I married them. Looking at them then there was every promise of their life being long; but how mysterious are the ways of the Lord! They now lie side by side in the Oakham cemetery, yet could the question be put to them they would not change their present state of happiness and peace with any others who might be named as enjoying everything which this world can give; and were you their father I believe you would look at their grave with a sweeter satisfaction than if, in the full enjoyment of life and health, they were walking after the course of this world. I was much united in heart and spirit to poor Richard. As far as he had opportunity when I was at Oakham he would often come up to my sitting-room for the sake of a little undisturbed spiritual conversation, and very sweetly would he speak of the things of God and His dealings with him. I have often envied his health and strength, as he was a stout, strong young man, caring little for wind or weather, though there was something in his countenance which at times betrayed a native delicacy of constitution. But here I am still in the wilderness, having survived him and many others whose prospects of life, humanly speaking, were much greater than my own. We think of bringing out a little memoir of him, which will, I believe, be found interesting and edifying. He was a man who carried out his religion into practice. Some instances will be named in the memoir; but I will just mention one now. One day during the cattle plague he was struck with the fact that his beasts had been preserved. "Well," he said, "Thy poor people, Lord, shall reap the benefit," so he sent Mr. Keal £20 to be distributed among the poor members of the church and others who feared God in the congregation. I much doubt whether many professing farmers whose herds were spared have acted in a similar way.

With you and me, dear friend, the bloom of life is utterly gone, and we may almost say, "We would not live alway." There is nothing for us as regards us personally to look forward to but increasing years and infirmities until we are brought down to our native dust. Our chief desire and the longing of our heart is to be favoured with some sweet manifestations of the Lord's love and mercy, and no doubt your heart, like mine, often goes up to His blessed majesty that He would take pity on us in our low estate, compassionate us, and speak a word of peace and consolation to our inmost soul. He has taught us, we trust, to fear, revere, and adore His great, and glorious, and holy name, and to believe in His dear Son, looking to Him alone as all our salvation and all our desire. We have seen and felt a little of the evil of sin, and desire to repent of it with real godly sorrow, brokenness of spirit, contrition of heart, and true humility of mind. We would desire also to be more separated from the world in heart, spirit, and affection, to be spiritually minded, which is life and peace, and to know more of that holiness without which no man shall see the Lord. And though we find sin still working in us, and sometimes as bad as ever, yet our desire is to have it subdued in its power as well as purged away in its guilt and filth. We have lived to see what the world can do for us, and found it can only entangle, and what sin can do, which is to please for a moment and then bite like an adder. And we have seen also a little of the Person and work, blood and righteousness, grace and glory, blessedness and suitability of the Son of God; and He has won our heart and affections so as at times to be the chief among ten thousand and the altogether lovely. But with all this we want more clear visitations of His gracious presence, more precious words from those lips into which grace is poured, and more sensible discoveries of Himself in the light of His own countenance and the words of His own application. Am I an interpreter? Do I read some of the desires and feelings of my friend's inmost soul and express the breathings of his heart toward the Lord at various seasons by day and night? I tell my friend Covell sometimes that I want "realities," and that if he did not preach them I could not sit to hear him. How I see men deluded and put off with a vain show, and how few there are, whether ministers or people, who seem to know anything of the transforming efficacy of real religion and vital godliness. Here I have been about forty years, for it is just now forty years since eternal realities were first laid upon my mind, groping and feeling, as it were, my way to the true light and to the true life, to the vital power and divine reality of the kingdom of God. And yet, after all my thousands of prayers, looking and crying to the Lord for His teaching and blessing, and all my reading, writing, preaching, and professing, how little do I seem to know of the kingdom of heaven as set up in the heart by the Holy Ghost! Only just enough to show me what and where I am, what I want, and the miserable state of all who are destitute of the life and power of God in the soul.

I hope what I am writing from Ephesians i. may be made a blessing. I have seen much in that wondrous chapter, and if I can but a little lay bare its glorious riches it may comfort and encourage some of the dear family of God. Thus I may hope to preach from my study, if not from the pulpit.

Yours very affectionately,

J. C. P.

CCXLI—To Mr. King *

Croydon, April 2, 1867.

Dear Sir,

I am sorry that you should take the trouble of reading such books as that from which you have sent me an extract;

especially as you acknowledge that the reading of it produced much hardness, barrenness, coldness, and deadness in your soul. Indeed to my mind the title of the book is itself sufficient to condemn it. Predestination as a divine truth is not to be calmly considered from principles of reason, being in a christian point of view wholly a matter of divine revelation. The great Apostle of the Gentiles who has laid it down so clearly and fully (Rom. ix.), does not attempt to reason about it; but, in answer to one who does, says, "Nay but, O man, who art thou that repliest against God?" and in Romans xi. 33, shuts the whole matter up in the words "O the depth of the riches both of the wisdom and knowledge of God!"

I do not feel disposed, therefore, to examine the extract which you have sent me; though, as far as I have looked at it, it seems to me both erroneous and sophistical. Thus he speaks of the existence of sin being in consequence of the sovereign appointment of God. Now I do not believe that this is Scripture doctrine, nor do I know a single passage even bearing that way. I fully believe that the entrance of sin into the world, and of death by sin, was according to the permissive will of God, for without it it could not have entered; but not appointed by Him in the same way as what is good, for such an assertion, reason how we may, would make God the Author of sin. I think, also, that all his reasonings about sin being a creature and such metaphysical subtleties are mere sophisms. Two things are very evident; first, that sin is a most dreadful evil, hateful to God, and calling down His displeasure and righteous punishment; and secondly, that there is no remedy for this dreadful evil, except through the incarnation and bloodshedding of the Son of God. Here I rest, not being willing to trouble my mind with daring reasonings of men destitute of godliness, and here I advise you to rest too.

Yours very sincerely, for truth's sake,

J. C. P.

* Mr. King having sent Mr. Philpot an extract from a publication entitled "Predestination, Calmly Considered from Principles of Reason," &c., Mr. P. sent the above reply.

CCXLII—To Mrs. Peake

Croydon, April 16, 1867.

My Dear Friend in the Lord,

I am very glad that the memoir of our late dear friend, William Tiptaft, so far as written, has given satisfaction to yourself and my Oakham friends. I have had to steer a kind of middle course which is always very difficult to maintain. On the one hand I wish to write an interesting biography, and on the other to make it as far as I could spiritual and profitable. I think readers generally, and I may include amongst them spiritual readers, take much interest in the narrative of circumstances which, if providential, have yet a bearing on what is spiritual, for, generally speaking, the dealings of God with us in providence and in grace are so connected that they cannot be separated. Take, for instance, the way in which you and your dear sister were brought to—What an influence it has had upon your subsequent life, and I may truly add has been made a blessing to others as well as yourselves. So my connection with William Tiptaft, through our meeting together at the clerical meeting, has had an influence on all my subsequent life. It was for this reason, therefore, that I thought it well to give so much place to mere narrative. I did not wish even to name myself beyond a passing notice; but I felt almost compelled to do so by the circumstances of the narrative, and I am glad you think I have not said too much.

W. T., in his later days, was much more reserved about himself than when I first knew him. This, I think, arose from his great cautiousness lest he should in any way commit himself. But the effect has been much to diminish the narrative part of the memoir, and if my memory were not in some things rather tenacious I could not have gathered up what I have written upon the early days of our friendship. But his letters, however good, needed a little relief as well as explanation, as it is somewhat wearisome to read a series of letters, and unless explained they are often obscure. I hope, as far as I may be favoured with help from on high, I may go on with the memoir, but the *Gospel Standard* takes up so much of my time, and when that is finished my sermon for the "Gospel Pulpit," that I have only a few days at the end of the month to attend to the memoir. I may also add that I have not now the strength of body and mind which I once possessed, so that I soon get weary and flag, which makes writing not only a burden but what I write heavy and dull. Still I must go on, I suppose, like the ox labouring in the furrow till worn out with toil, and if my labours are blessed of God it is my best reward.

Dear Richard's letters to his poor afflicted wife have been read, I understand, with much feeling and interest. There is *heart* in them. Like Paul's, in a sense, they were written out of much affliction and tears. The dear man knew what he wanted for himself and her, pressed after and at times enjoyed divine realities and cast aside, in the earnestness and almost agony of his spirit, the rags and wraps of a wordy profession. There is also great tenderness of spirit and strong affection in them towards his poor suffering partner.

I do hope that his memoir, when it comes out, may be profitable to the Church of Christ, and, if spared, I shall hope to write a little Preface to it and to insert what would otherwise have appeared in the *Gospel Standard*. . . .

Yours very affectionately in the Lord,

J. C. P.

CCXLIII —To Mr. James Davis, of Melbourne

Croydon, April 18, 1867.

Dear Friend in the Truth,

Your handsome rug and the two muffs came safely to hand on the second of this month, and we beg to express our thanks for them; one of the muffs I have given to my dear wife, and my daughter begs to thank you very kindly for thinking of her and for sending her so pretty a present.

Your last kind letter came to hand this morning. I am always sorry that anything should appear in the *Gospel Standard* which can stumble any mind or hurt the feelings of any child of God, especially when it has any reference to the glorious Person of our adorable Lord. There certainly is no evidence that the blessed Lord ever actually wrought with His own hands, nor is it implied in the expression, "Is not this the carpenter's son?" which was but the expression of scorn and contempt in the mouth of the ungodly; and I am sure anything that in the least degree touches upon the holy humanity of our gracious Lord makes one who loves His name to shrink, and, as you say, shudder lest anything should be said derogatory to Him.

I am fond myself of Berridge's "Hymns," but there are many expressions in them, as in his other writings, of which I by no means approve. When, therefore, I edited, in 1842, his "Songs of Zion," though I did not feel warranted to alter much, yet I struck out some expressions or omitted some verses of which I could not altogether approve. But, dear friend, where shall we find anything like perfection in the creature? or any writer in whom there will not be expressions that we cannot approve of? I am very sure that I have written things, especially in times past, or rather dropped expressions, which I should not do now; and I dare say sometimes when you think of expressions that you yourself have made use of you have had to wish that you could recall them. Indeed James tells us that "if any man offend not in word the same is a perfect man," which, I am sure, neither you nor I ever profess or expect to be.

I am glad that the Lord does at times encourage you still to go on speaking in His name. He accepts what a man hath and does not look for great gifts in setting forth His truth. A few broken words, which He is pleased to apply to the soul with a divine power, will be made a lasting blessing when all wordy eloquence falls to the ground like water spilt. The great thing is to have a single eye to the glory of God, a love to His dear people, and to know experimentally the things contended for. All the saints of God have to a certain extent the same teaching, the same experience, and the same feelings. Some indeed are more blessed and favoured, but all in their measure are led into the same precious truth in the same blessed way. When, therefore, they hear a servant of God contending for those divine realities of which they have felt the life and power, it often sweetly revives the work of grace upon their heart, and encourages them to hope and believe that they are rightly led and taught. But you justly observe that the chief thing is to have the inward witness, and I am well satisfied that there is no real satisfaction without it. The want of this makes many a poor child of God sigh and cry, and when he gets it makes him rejoice.

I am sorry to find from your last letter that you are complaining of your chest. I thought that in your beautiful climate you had not those complaints in the chest which we have in this damp, foggy country.

I am sorry to hear Mrs. C. is not well; please give her my love. How is Aquila? I wish the Lord would send you a real servant of His, but I have little hope of it. We are fast losing our best men here and none are raised up to take their place. What a world it is of sin and sorrow! Oh to be saved from it and out of it with an everlasting salvation!

Yours affectionately, in the Truth,

J. C. P.

CCXLIV—To Mr. Parry

Croydon, May 18, 1867.

My dear Friend,

We were much concerned this morning to learn from your daughter's letter the sad tidings of Mr. H.'s serious illness. I do hope that the Lord will be pleased to compassionate his case, and for his own sake, his dear wife's sake, and his family's sake, to spare his life. I seem to have a good hope that he will struggle through. C., when speaking about inflammation of the lungs one day, said that by far the greater majority of cases recovered, especially when there were health and youth on the side of the patient. I had it most severely at college, and Dr. Bourne, a physician who attended me, told one of our tutors that he had rarely seen a worse case, and yet I was brought through, though for three days and nights I lay bathed as it were in a sea of perspiration. It is at such times and on such occasions that we seem to see the infinite worth and value of the grace of God which bringeth salvation. We shall be anxious to hear how he is.

As regards myself, you have been rightly informed, for I have had an attack of my old complaint, from which I am but slowly recovering. Mr. Gadsby expressed a great wish for me to marry his daughter at Gower Street Chapel; and as I had known her from an infant, I did not like to refuse. I took, however, the precaution of having a brougham to take and bring me back, hoping I should in that way escape cold. But it was a remarkably cold day, the wind being in the east, and when I went into the vestry there was no fire there, and I seemed struck with a sudden chill. There was a large congregation to witness the ceremony, and I must say that I was much helped in conducting the service, and the whole was carried on in a very proper and becoming manner. I took the opportunity of showing at some length that marriage was a divine institution, and in giving an address to the newly-married pair, I took the opportunity of showing what were the mutual duties of husband and wife, addressing myself as much to the married in the congregation as to the bride and bridegroom. My wife and elder daughter were with me; we lunched with a friend, and came home directly afterwards. Unhappily, however, I took cold, and it has been rather a severe attack, so that I have been obliged to defer my visit to Gower Street for two or three Lord's-days, and, indeed, have had great fears whether I should not be obliged to give up all my engagements for the summer, and yours amongst them. But I am, through mercy, slowly recovering, and hope that it may please the Lord so far to restore me that I may not wholly disappoint the friends.

How, on every side, we see the strides which death is making. In March, 1860, I was very ill, and, as I was slowly recovering, a letter came one morning announcing the decease of our friend Isbell. About the middle of the same day our dear friend William Tiptaft, who was supplying for me, came to see me. He had not been long seated before in came Mr. Grace, of Brighton, bringing with him his friend Mr. Pickering. Whilst we were conversing together on the best things, Mr. Brown, of Godmanchester, who was then staying in Stamford, also came in. Mr. Grace was struck with the circumstance, and said, in a very solemn manner, "We four ministers will never meet again together in one room. Let us, before we part, read and pray together." This was of course done. William T. read and Mr. G. prayed. It was a solemn season with us all, and when we parted it was, I believe, in love and affection. Now since that date William Tiptaft, Mr. Grace, and Mr. Pickering have entered into their rest, and I heard yesterday, from good authority, that Mr. Brown is not expected to live. What a voice these dispensations have, and how they all say, "Be ye also ready!" How they call upon us to be as men whose loins are girt and lamps burning, and to be waiting for the Lord's coming. My desire is to have every stroke of affliction sanctified and blessed, and to hear the voice of God speaking in every dispensation, especially those which are trying and afflictive.

I hope that the Lord may bless Mr. Hazlerigg's visit, both publicly and privately, and that much of the presence and power of the Lord may attend his testimony. You will give him my love, and my prayers and desires for the blessing of God upon his visit.

We unite in love and sympathy with your family circle.

Yours very affectionately,

J. C. P.

CCXLV—To Mr. Knight

Croydon, May 21, 1867.

Dear Friend,

It is very difficult to give advice upon any point unless one is well acquainted with all the circumstances of the case. But as far as I can understand the matter which Miss Jacques and you have laid before me it comes pretty much to this. In whom does the governing, controlling power lie? In the church or certain individuals who set up an authority against it? I do not enter here upon the point whether the superintendent is an eligible person or not. It appears from your note that the teachers formerly chose him subject to the approval of a committee; and that the late one having resigned, the teachers have chosen another, of whom the committee do not approve, and recommend another person whom they consider more eligible. And it appears that the teachers having rejected this person, and this having caused strife and contention, the whole matter has been placed in the hands of the church. I consider this to have been a very proper mode, and that when the teachers and the committee could not agree about the superintendent, and a contention arose between them, it was quite right to bring the matter before the church that they might decide it.

Now, as a general rule, I think it is not well for the church to interfere too much in the management of the school; and if it can confide in the teachers, to allow them a certain liberty in managing their own concerns. But then the teachers must not abuse this liberty or set up an authority of their own, distinct from that of the church. But I wish to know in whom does the power and authority rest. Is not the school in connection with the church and congregation? Does it not meet in a building belonging to the church? Are not the teachers members either of the church or of the congregation? How, then, can the teachers set up an authority of their own and act in defiance to the church?

I hope, however, that the teachers may be better instructed and learn what is their becoming place. And I hope also that the church will deal very kindly and leniently with them, for they are useful and valuable persons, and are much to be respected for the trouble they give themselves in teaching the children as long as they keep in their place and confine themselves strictly to their own duties. For see the consequences of the church giving all power out of its hands and allowing teachers or superintendents to act as they please, introduce such books as they think right which might be erroneous, and thus really teach doctrines inconsistent with those which are held by the church.

I should also name that in my opinion the pastor should have a voice in this matter as well as the church; for he is the shepherd of the flock, and surely the lambs, so to speak, should be under his guidance in some measure. In fact, in most churches the pastor exercises a general superintendence of the Sunday school, visiting the classes, and by his personal presence strengthening the hands of the teachers and encouraging the children in their attendance.

But yours is not the first church in which I have seen the pride and self-will of the teachers, and their claiming for themselves an authority inconsistent with the word of God and their own position as members of the church and congregation.

I hope, however, it may please the Lord to bring the teachers to a right mind, and at the same time to bestow upon the pastor and members of the church a kind, conciliatory, and affectionate spirit, that the matter may be settled in the fear of God, and without the school receiving permanent injury.

I hope also that the teachers may see how much of the good and prosperity of the school depends upon them and their personal conduct, and that as they expect the children to listen to and obey them, so they set them the example of listening to and obeying the voice of the church.

Yours affectionately in the truth,
J. C. P.

CCXLVI—To Mrs. Peake

Croydon, Oct. 17, 1867.

My dear Friend,

. . . . I feel thankful to have regained my own home in peace and safety, and to have been preserved during my absence as well as favoured with a sufficient measure of health and strength to fulfil all my engagements and to preach for fourteen Lord's-days continuously. I hope also that I may say without presumption that the Lord helped me in soul as well as in body, and enabled me to set forth His truth as I have received it. I was glad to see my old friends, and to speak to them once more in the name of the Lord; and I hope there were those amongst them who felt the power and savour of the word of truth which I was enabled to bring before them. No one I believe is more convinced than I am that nothing but the power of God accompanying His word can make it effectual either to kill or make alive, to wound or to heal, to pull down or build up. And from whomsoever's mouth words of grace and truth drop, whether educated or uneducated, whether learned or unlearned, the power is the same. Some despise learning and some despise the want of it; but the people of God know what power is when they feel it to accompany the word; and those who know not what that power is are no judges of the matter. It is a day of small things well-nigh everywhere, and those who have life seem much overborne by darkness and the death that is in their carnal mind.

I had a pleasant and I hope profitable visit to Nottingham. The room was very full, and on the Tuesday evening we had quite a large congregation. Some young clergyman sat close to the pulpit. What he thought of my discourse I can hardly conjecture, but he seemed to listen very attentively. One does not know what good is done on such occasions, or how it may please the Lord to bring His word home with power to some thoughtless sinner's heart. I never saw Mr. —— in better health, and we had some short but very sweet conversation upon the things of God. He is truly a spiritually minded man, and to be made and kept spiritually minded our dear friend W. Tiptaft used to say was one of the greatest blessings which we could have. The Memoir* is nearly sold out, but I hope the second edition which is passing through the press will shortly appear. It seems to have been generally very well received, and the letters highly prized. By them, he being dead, yet speaketh; for I hear it often remarked, "How vividly they recall the man."

My visit to Oakham seems almost like a dream, and you perhaps feel the same. It came and went; but I hope, unlike a dream, it has left some traces of its real existence.

Yours very affectionately,

J. C. P.

CCXLVII—To Mrs. Brown

Croydon, Dec. 14, 1867.

My dear afflicted and widowed Friend,

I desire sincerely to sympathise with you under your most distressing bereavement. It has indeed not come upon you unexpectedly, and thus your mind must have been in some good measure prepared for this desolating stroke. You have also the unspeakable consolation of knowing that your dear husband has passed away from this world of sin and sorrow to be for ever with that dear Lord whom he so sincerely loved and faithfully served

* Memoir of William Tiptaft.

when here below. Still, with these sources of consolation, when such a bereavement comes, though they alleviate the shock, yet nature must ever feel the pain and grief of the loss; and, therefore, there is no use in friends trying to make a burden light which cannot but be from its nature heavy. Under such circumstances no one but the Lord Himself can administer support and comfort; and His way often is to allow the stroke to be deeply felt, giving just sufficient support under it, that it may do its appointed work. You may, therefore, not at present receive that strength and consolation for which you might look; but if the Lord grant you faith and patience, He will in due time appear for you and fulfil every promise which He has given to the widow, and to her especially who is a widow indeed and desolate.

Few men have died more in the esteem and affection of God's saints and servants than your late dear husband. His great sincerity and uprightness of character, boldness and faithfulness in the declaration of truth, and the sweet spirit which more especially of late years accompanied his ministry, much endeared him to all who knew him, especially to those who sat under his ministry. I always found him a sincere and affectionate friend, and could only regret that for the few last years I have seen so little personally of him. But I most highly esteemed him for his work's sake.

The Lord support and comfort you in your affliction.

Yours affectionately in the Lord,

J. C. P.

CCXLVIII—To Mrs. Peake

Croydon, Jan. 10, 1868.

My dear Friend,

. . . . How we seem to stand, as it were, amid the dead and dying! How many of those with whom we have walked and talked on the things of God have passed away; and how, as each one is removed, it speaks as a personal warning, "Be ye also ready." But we know well that all our readiness must be in Him and from Him who gave the precept. What a gradual unloosening there is of the ties which bind us to life. And I believe for the most part the Lord makes His people willing to depart before He calls them up from this world of sin and misery.

I desire to sympathise with you both in your path of trial and affliction. Your dear sister has had a long and painful experience of an afflicted and suffering tabernacle, the trials of which those who enjoy health and strength have no idea of. And as regards yourself, such a weight of care, labour, and anxiety has been laid upon you as to tax to the utmost all your powers of mind and body. But in the world, and especially in the Church, there must be those who are willing and able to work and spend their energies on tasks laid upon them for the good of others; and, though sometimes they rebel at having so much cast upon them, yet they are made willing to work when they see and feel it is for the glory of God and the good of His people.

I am very sorry to hear so sad an account of poor Mrs. P——. No doubt she needs all the heavy strokes which have been laid upon her. She is a woman of good and choice experience, and has had greater manifestations of the Lord to her soul than most can speak of. The faith thus given her has to be tried by fire, and I have no doubt that she will come out of the great Refiner's hands with her dross and tin purged away. I know perhaps more of her experience than most do, and the remarkable way in which my writings, and especially "Winter afore Harvest," were blessed to her soul, when she did not know whether I was alive or dead, and then her being brought under my roof and ministry in a special way of providence have much knit us together. The Lord will surely regard the work of His own hands, and it will be well with her in life and death. I also much respect her husband, as I have long marked his consistent Christian conduct and bearing under very trying circumstances.

I am glad that you like the Address. It is very difficult year after year to write what shall be edifying and instructive to so many of the family of God, and so varied in circumstances, character, leadings, and experience. But my desire was to lay before them such things as I know from experience harmonise with the Scriptures of truth and the teachings of the Holy Spirit. This I believe the Lord will ever bless.

My Christian love to all who love the Lord.

Yours very affectionately in the truth,

J. C. P.

CCXLIX.—To Mrs. Peake

Croydon, Jan. 30, 1868.

My dear and valued Friend,

. . . I feel much obliged to you for your kind feeling towards my ministry among you, and could say much upon the point if I could do so without seeming self-exaltation. The blessing of a sound, healthy ministry is little appreciated, because, like our food, its influence upon the whole system cannot be always distinctly traced. To be kept from error which is so rife and so deadly, to have the eyes, heart and feet guided and directed to the only true object of real faith, hope and love, to have all that is good in us by grace nurtured, strengthened and encouraged, and all that is evil in us, worthless and unprofitable, to be exposed to view, beaten down, cast aside, or subdued; to have weak things strengthened, feeble things confirmed, and the grace of God and what we are by grace brought out of and disentangled from all creature admixture—this peculiar feature of a sound, wholesome ministry is only valued by a few who know that in it is their life. My desire and aim from the very first of my ministry, with all its weakness and shortcomings, have been and are to exalt and trace out the special grace of God as manifested in and by the Three Persons of the glorious, undivided, and indivisible Godhead. And you, dear friend, in looking at and over my testimony, whether preached or written, from the earliest days in which I stood before the Church of God, will be able to see that there has been a unity in it from first to last, whether by tongue or pen. Suffer me to add that our dear friend W. T. used to say that my writings would be more valued when I was gone. But I am sure of this, that if there be any value in them it is because the Lord was pleased to show me from the very first, and to impress deeply upon my mind, the grand distinction between nature and grace.

The first sermon that I ever preached was from Romans vi. 23, at South Morton church, in Berks, and a gracious, godly woman, the late wife of Mr. Doe, who happened to be present, and was considered a mother in Israel, I am told, said of me after it, "That is a good man, and he will leave the Church of England." She lived to witness the truth of her prediction, and has often heard me at Abingdon Chapel. Excuse this much about myself.

* * * * * *

Yours very affectionately,

J. C. P.

CCL—To Mr. Hoadley

Croydon, Feb. 24, 1868.

My dear Friend,

I am much obliged to you for your kind remembrance of us in sending us your acceptable present, and I should have been glad to have thanked you in person, had you given me the opportunity yesterday, or looked in upon me this morning.

Like many others, you probably did not expect to see me in the pulpit yesterday, and indeed, as I then said, I would much sooner be a hearer than preach myself. I hope, however, you were not disappointed, or at least, if you were, that it was made up in the evening. My dear friend Mr. Covell and I fully, I believe, understand each other, and that our mutual desire is the profit and edification of the people of God. We are not striving which should be the greater, but believing that in the mouth of two witnesses every truth shall be established, are made willing so far to work together that the people of God may have all the profit, and the Lord all the glory. I told our dear friend when I first came to Croydon that my desire was to avoid all party spirit with all strife and contention, and that I would, for my part, much sooner never step into his pulpit than be the least means of causing or strengthening any spirit of division or disunion.

I am, my dear Friend,

Yours, I trust, in the best bonds,

J. C. P.

CCLI—To Mr. Parry

Croydon, March 20, 1868.

My dear Friend,

I hope the obituary of our late dear friend will be acceptable next month. It is not exactly all that I could wish, but I have done my best. The letter which he wrote to our friend T. G., giving an account of the special blessing with which he was favoured last June, will, I believe, be much commended to the conscience and affections of the living family. He certainly was a man of clearer and deeper experience, and more tried and exercised, as well as more blessed and favoured, than I was aware of. I have often felt union with him when he has spoken upon the things of God, but he was for the most part reserved and shy, and not favoured with the gift of utterance as some are. Among the letters which he wrote to our friend T. G. there is a very good one describing the deathbed of R. D., and the feelings he had in not having been allowed to return blow for blow, and stripe for stripe. What bondage the poor man was in, almost trembling to see the cart coming over the brow of the hill! But they were both good men, lived and died well, and now sleep not far from each other. You have had encouraging testimonies that the little chapel has had the blessing of God resting upon it. This is what you have ever desired and prized above everything else for yourself and others. The memory of the just is blessed, and I hope that what appears in the *Gospel Standard* will spread the fragrance of his memory beyond the narrow precincts of the little hamlet in which he lived and died, and the little knot of people by whom he was personally known, esteemed, and loved. When the wicked perish, though they die in the multitude of their riches, the more they are remembered the more their memory stinks; but the righteous, the more they are remembered in death the sweeter their memory is.

I am, through mercy, much as usual, but feel it best to keep chiefly within doors, though I manage to get to chapel, and sometimes to speak once for my friend Covell, which I suppose I shall do if the Lord enable to-morrow morning.

* * * * * *

Yours very affectionately,

J. C. P.

CCLII—To Mr. Godwin

Croydon, March 20, 1868.

My dear Friend,

I have been so very busy of late that I have been obliged to neglect my correspondents, and amongst them my old, faithful, and affectionate friend, to whom I am now endeavouring to send a few lines. Writing, however, is but a very imperfect mode of communicating with our spiritual friends. There is always something which we should like to say, but cannot, and which we could impart so much better in seeing them face to face. I feel this especially with respect to one or two things which you have named in your last kind letter. We have to be tried about ourselves, and we have to be tried about others, and for much the same reasons —that there are things in them and things in ourselves which we cannot make altogether straight with conscience and the word of God. And I am well persuaded that none but He who makes crooked things straight can make these things straight either as regards ourselves or others. And there's another thing which you know as well as I do, that the more we know of persons and the more we see of them, as well as the more we know of ourselves and see of ourselves, the less grace do we seem to see in ourselves and them. Now what does this bring us to but highly to value the least mark of real grace; and I am sure it rejoices us to be able to find in ourselves and others any clear testimony that God is with us of a truth. I am glad therefore that you were able to speak so confidently at O—— of a dear and old friend of ours, and I hope it may have a good effect. I quite understand an unwillingness to see friends when one is ill, for I have had, and still have, much of the same feeling myself; though when I have been enabled to break through the feeling I have been cheered and comforted by their company and conversation.

The memorial of our late dear friend Richard Healy is just published, and I think will be read with feeling by the Lord's family. I should like to insert in the *Gospel Standard*, as opportunity may occur, some of our late dear friend Carby Tuckwell's letters. The one which he wrote to you, giving an account of the special blessing with which he was favoured last June, will appear next month in the obituary. I have often felt much union to him when we have got upon the things of God, and much esteemed and respected him; but he was, as you know, rather reserved, and not gifted with utterance of speech, as many are. We are losing our choice friends and companions, and where shall we find others to take their place?

Our dear friend at A. would deeply feel his doctor's death. What a mercy to be kept by the mighty power of God! What debtors we are to Him, both in providence and in grace, both for body and soul, both for this life and that to come. My chief, my daily grief is to have sinned against so good a God, and my desire is ever to walk in His fear, and to live to His praise. It is His goodness which leads to repentance, His mercy which melts the heart, His truth which liberates and sanctifies the soul, and His grace which superabounds over all aboundings of sin. What have we now, dear friend, to live for, but during our short span of life to know and enjoy more of His presence and love, and have clearer testimonies of what He is unto us and in us?

I am, through mercy, much as usual. Our good friend wishes me to take his place next Lord's-day morning. His annual collection on the 8th inst. was £166 3s. 1d. You would think there must be both will and power in his congregation. But he sets a noble example of liberality, and the Lord honours him.

Yours very affectionately in the truth,

J. C. P.

CCLIII —To Mrs. P—— and Miss M—— *

Croydon, March 25, 1868.

My dear Friends in the Lord,

In my prayers for you both I feel led to ask of the Lord to give you faith and patience, for these two graces you much need in active and daily exercise. But that you may have them brought into your heart and there maintained with a divine power, tribulation is needed, for tribulation worketh patience (Rom. v. 3), as well as the trial of faith (James i. 3). And this patience must have her perfect work that you may be made perfect and entire, wanting nothing. If, then, you had no trials or perplexities, no tribulation or temptation, you could not have your faith tried as by fire, and there would be no patience accompanying it, working with it and perfecting it. Nor, again, would you have it made manifest to yourselves or others that you are possessed of the grace of love, for that beareth all things and endureth all things (1 Cor. xiii. 7). I was thinking the other morning about Christian love, and I seemed to see that it was the first of all evidences and the last of all graces. Let me explain my meaning. Love to the brethren is the first scriptural evidence of having passed from death unto life. But this love, as we journey onward, and have to do more and more with the crooked ways of God's people, is the last of all graces, as well as the greatest, as having to live and thrive under well-nigh everything which serves to damp or quench it. As patience, then, is useless without burdens to bear, and trials

* This letter appeared in the *Gospel Standard*, September, 1868, and is again published at the request of a friend.

and temptations to encounter, so love is useless unless it has to be maintained under all those circumstances, and all that chilling opposition which seem so contrary to it. If the people of God were all we could wish them to be, and for ourselves to be, kind, forbearing, forgiving, affectionate, unsuspecting, open-hearted and open-handed, prayerful and spiritually-minded, love would flow out so toward them, that it would not be a matter of any difficulty. But to love the people of God for what we see of Christ in them, in spite of all their crookedness, perverseness, ignorance, obstinacy, ill-temper, fretfulness, and deadness in the things of God—this is the difficulty. But the Lord does not bestow His graces to lie idle in the bosom; but to manifest their presence, their activity, and their power by what they have to do. If, then, you are to be blessed with the graces of faith and love and patience, you must expect burdens, exercises, afflictions, perplexities, annoyances, and a variety of circumstances most contrary to your natural feelings and expectations. But if, in the midst of all these painful and perplexing circumstances, faith credits the word of promise, patience quietly and meekly endures its load, and love is still maintained in exercise in word and deed, you will find the approbation of the Lord in your own breast, and will sooner or later prove that He ever honours His own grace and His own work in the soul. The great thing that we have to dread is the giving way to, and being overcome by, our own spirit; or, what is worse, mistaking our own spirit for a right spirit, and our own will for a right will. In these things we need to be instructed by the Holy Spirit, the promised Teacher, that we may have not only a right judgment in all things, but be enabled to speak, live, and act as He would have us to do. I think I know something of your perplexities and difficulties, and can see that to support you under them, and bring you through them, you need faith and love and patience, and this is the reason why I have ventured to lay before you a word of friendly counsel and encouragement, and I shall be very glad if you may find it suitable and supporting. I have endeavoured to show you such a path as I should desire, if grace enabled me, to tread myself if placed in a similar position. But, alas! it is one thing to give advice, and another to act upon it one's self. I remember, how many years ago, the words of Eliphaz (Job iv. 3, 4, 5) came to my mind as sadly applicable to my case. But we have to learn our weakness, as well as where and in whom our strength lies, and the Lord is very merciful and gracious, never leaving us, nor suffering us to be led into any path in which His grace is not sufficient for us, if sought and looked to; for we have to confess that when it has been otherwise, it has been because we did not look to Him, nor lean upon Him; but looked to self either for strength or indulgence.

Yours very affectionately in the Lord,

J. C. P.

CCLIV—To Mrs. Peake.

Croydon, May 8, 1868.

My dear Friend,

* * * * * *

I walk every day when I can, and usually to the same spot, which is more than a mile from my house to the top of a gentle hill, where there is a seat under a wide-spreading oak, and commanding a lovely view of hill and dale, the latter wooded, and there I sit in the warm sun, sometimes meditating or otherwise engaged, perhaps not unprofitably, with soul matters, whilst the lark is singing just above me, or the thrush giving out its shrill sweet note. I think I never saw so much of the glory of God, and, I may add, His goodness and beauty as manifested in visible creation. I was thinking in my walk to-day, when I looked round upon the beautiful face of nature, how beautiful must He be who has stamped so much of it on this present world; and yet what is all this beauty compared with the riches of His mercy, grace, and glory as manifested in the Person and work of His dear Son! (2 Cor. iii. 18; iv. 6). How grievous it is ever to sin, rebel against, disobey, or displease such a God; and it is my desire to walk in His fear, live to His praise, and to glorify Him by knowing His will, and doing it. There is no peace, rest, or happiness anywhere else, nor is it possible for God to make a man happy except by making him holy, sanctifying him by the power of His spirit and grace, and conforming him to the image of the Son of His love. When this is perfectly done he will be perfectly happy; but as long as sin remains in him, and it will do so to his dying day, he will ever find something to mar his peace. . . .

Yours affectionately in the Lord,

J. C. P.

CCLV—To Mrs. Isbell

London, July 2, 1868.

My dear Fanny,

I am sorry to find from your letter that you are still so afflicted in body. I was in hopes you were gradually recovering health and strength, and, though weak, were able to come down stairs, or even get out into the open air. Unless much favoured and supported bodily illness is a great affliction; but you know where to look to for strength, and who has graciously said, "I will never leave thee, nor forsake thee." In times past He has been your stay, and "He is the same yesterday, to-day, and for ever." To be so weak and helpless is a great affliction; but it is sent to wean you from this world, make life burdensome, and death desirable. You have had a long life compared with most, and for the most part a healthy one, and you cannot wonder if growing years bring with them growing infirmities. How many have we seen younger than we borne away, and we still remain. It is nearly twenty-one years ago since I came to Stoke from Malvern. Dr. S., your dear husband, and many others, little dreamt that I should survive them. But here I still am, "faint yet pursuing," in body and soul. . . .

The Lord support you under your trials and afflictions.

Your affectionate Brother,

J. C. P.

CCLVI.—To Mrs. Peake

Allington, Aug. 19, 1868.

My dear Friend,

Having now a little respite from my labours, and an opportunity not being likely soon to recur to write to you again, I send you a few lines according to your request.

You will be desirous to know how my health is, especially as the season has been so very trying. In common, then, with most who are weak I much felt the great heat, especially as being obliged to preach to large congregations at the very time when it was at its greatest height. I was, however, mercifully brought through my labours in London, and have now completed my engagement here. I trust I found the strength of the Lord made perfect in my weakness, in soul as well as in body, and that He gave testimony to the word of His grace. But, for the most part, the things of God are at a very low ebb everywhere, both in town and country, and the churches seem much sunk into a cold, lethargic, and apathetic state. There are, indeed, a few souls which seem kept alive, and are sensible of their own state and the state of others, and these the Lord seems from time to time to revive under His word. There are some of these whom I know at Gower Street, and who spoke of the revival and renewal which they experienced under what one of them called the "sweet droppings of the Gospel." I cannot say that I felt any peculiar or extraordinary power resting upon my spirit as I have sometimes experienced; but upon the whole I was favoured with some good measure of life and liberty. Some of the sermons were taken down; some perhaps of the best, and two especially, were not, as Mr. Ford was not there. I may, however, take the same words again when he is present, though, without special help, I shall not be able to handle them as I did then.

We had, I believe, on the whole, a good day at Calne, and the collection on behalf of the Aged Pilgrims' Friend Society was more than £30. Some of the friends said they had never heard me speak with greater power there. But the place was so full, the ventilation so imperfect, and the heat so great that I much felt the exertion, and did not get over it for several days. Mr. Taylor was not able to come on account of illness, which was a great disappointment.

I hope it may please the Lord to give me health and strength for the work which still lies before me; but this extreme change in the weather, from drought and heat to cold and damp, makes me feel very poorly. We are poor, dissatisfied creatures. When it was so hot I was impatiently waiting for the cold; and now the cold is come I could almost wish the heat were back. We have been favoured in the weather as regards the Lord's-day, and I hope we have been favoured also in the house of prayer, especially on the last Lord's-day, when the Lord, I trust, enabled me to speak with some life, feeling, and power. We had a large congregation, and gathered from distant quarters, some having come twenty miles, and there was a large collection of vehicles. . . .

Yours very affectionately in the truth,

J. C. P.

CCLVII.—Addressed to the Congregation in Providence Chapel, Oakham.

Sept. 13, 1868.

Dear Friends,

It is a sad disappointment to me, and I doubt not will be so to many of you, that I am not able, from bodily indisposition, to stand up before you this morning and speak to you in the name of the Lord. But it has pleased the Lord to lay upon me one of those attacks of cold on my chest which so often, in times past, laid me aside, and which not only used so much to try my faith and patience but yours also. Having been favoured for thirteen Lord's-days to preach His word, I was greatly in hopes that health and strength might have been given me to speak once more to those who were so long my own people, that our union and communion in the Lord might be strengthened and renewed, and that meeting once more in the house of prayer we might realise the power and presence of the Lord in our midst. But we live to prove that our thoughts are not the Lord's thoughts, and that disappointment upon disappointment attends all our plans, even when they are made, as we hope, for the glory of God and the good of His people. You were looking, perhaps, too much to the instrument, and expecting that from the man which the Lord keeps in His own hands, the blessing which maketh rich. It is a great trial to me that I cannot, as I hoped and expected, meet with you once more in the house of prayer, that heart might unite once more with heart in prayer and supplication, that I might preach to you again the word of life, that our faith, hope, and love to the Lord might be strengthened, and our esteem and affection for each other renewed. It is, however, a great alleviation of my trial that our dear and esteemed friend Mr. K. has so kindly determined to forego his engagement and preach in my stead, and may such a blessing rest on him, and the word of God by him, that all disappointment may be removed, and you well reconciled to the will of God in this trying dispensation.

The Lord be with you and bless you.

Your affectionate Friend,

J. C. P.

CCLVIII.—To Mrs. Isbell.

Oakham, Sept. 21, 1868.

My dear Fanny,

It is now some time since I sent you a few lines, but we often hear of one another through the correspondence of our dear relatives. I was sorry to learn that the Lord had laid upon you His afflicting hand; but that is what we must expect at our time of life, and if these afflictions are blessed and sanctified to our souls' good, as we trust they are, they are rather marks of the Lord's favour than of His displeasure. But I know well that the poor coward flesh is fretful and impatient under the affliction, and would fain have a smoother, easier path. I have myself been suffering for nearly a fortnight under one of my old attacks, and am not yet recovered from it. I was carried through thirteen Lord's-days, besides preaching in the week; but the great heat and exertion in London seemed at last too much for me, and when the weather turned suddenly cold the great change affected my chest and brought on one of my attacks. Being, however, not severe, and hoping it might pass off, which it does sometimes, I came down here to fulfil my engagement. But to my great disappointment, and that of the people, my complaint increased so that I was not able to preach here, as engaged on the 13th. There was a large congregation gathered to hear me; but Mr. Knill very kindly consented to stop and preach, which much alleviated the disappointment. Nor was I able to go to Stamford for the 20th, being at present confined to the house, and indeed to my two rooms up-stairs. I shall try, however, if I am able, to go to Leicester, as I have several times before disappointed the friends there from illness. I long much for my own home, and what I call my winter quarters, when I am not obliged to preach, or even leave the house if the weather be unfavourable or myself indisposed. I was greatly in hopes that I might be suffered to fulfil all my engagements; but it was not the Lord's will and I must submit.

It must be a great comfort to you to be with your niece and so be relieved in good measure from those domestic troubles and anxieties which you must have had in a house of your own. I view it, therefore, as a special providence on your behalf, and doubt not that you, at times, have seen and felt it to be so. But such is our unbelieving infidel heart that, though we may see the Lord's hand at first in a circumstance, yet when difficulties and perplexities arise we get into a state of darkness and confusion, and almost fear it has been a wrong step. Wherever we go, and wherever we are, we must expect trials to arise; but it will be our wisdom and mercy to submit to what we cannot alter, and not fret or repine under the trial, but accept it as sent for our good. You have had a long and trying affliction, but I hope you see at times mercy mingled with it. To be taken aside out of the world, to have opportunity for meditation, that after you have done the will of God, which is as much by suffering as by doing, you may receive the promise. Do not give way to fretfulness, murmuring, impatience, self-pity, hard thoughts of God, unbelief, doubt and fear, and other such evils of the heart which obscure the light of God's countenance and bring confusion and darkness into the soul. Those whom the Lord loves He loves unto the end, and as you have had many proofs and marks of the Lord's love to your soul, let not Satan and unbelief rob you of your faith and hope. I commend you to His grace, believing that He will be with you to the end. My own path is often dark and cloudy, but I daily endeavour to do what I have been counselling you to do.

Accept my brotherly love in every sense of the word. Though I do not often write to you, I think of you and endeavour, in my poor way, to ask of the Lord to support and bless you and give you faith and patience to hold out and hold on.

It is more than thirty-two years since I first came to this place, and about four since I was obliged, from failing health and strength, to leave it. In the lapse of those years I have seen great changes. Many, very many, have died since I first preached to them, and most of those who professed to fear God, and believe in His dear Son, have died well, but their decease has left great gaps in the church and congregation, not likely, I think, to be filled up, at least not with equally gracious people. . . .

Your affectionate Brother,

J. C. P.

CCLIX—To Mr. Parrott

Oakham, Oct. 1, 1868.

Dear Friend in the Truth,

It was a great disappointment to me not to be able to fulfil my engagement at Stamford on the 20th ult., and I have no doubt it was so to others who, like yourself, in times past have been blessed and favoured in that house of prayer, and were looking forward for a fresh discovery of the Lord's goodness and love to their souls under the preached word. It is very difficult to read the mind of the Lord in these dispensations of His providence. As regards myself I feel willing and desirous to preach His word, so far as I understand it, feel the power of it, and taste and handle its sweetness and blessedness; and I know there are those who desire to come under the sound of the word as thus preached, from seeing eye to eye with me in the things of God, having felt, as we hope, the same divine power and seeking after the same spiritual blessing. I know well that it is not a man's gifts or abilities which can profit or edify the Spirit-taught family of God. These may please and attract outer-court worshippers, but those who have seen the beauty of the Lord in the sanctuary want His presence, His power, and His blessing. This is what I am ever seeking after both in my own soul and in my ministry, for I am well satisfied that all short of this leaves us full of unbelief, darkness, guilt, and bondage. But the blessing of the Lord, it maketh rich, and He addeth no sorrow with it.

I am glad to find that you have been brought out of your long captivity. The Lord is faithful, and where He has begun a gracious work He will fulfil it until the day of Christ. What a mercy it is to have a faithful covenant-keeping God, and a gracious, compassionate High Priest who can sympathise with His poor, tried, tempted family, so that however low they may sink, His pitiful eye can see them in their low estate, His gracious ear hear their cries, His loving heart melt over them, and His strong arm pluck them from their destructions. Oh, what should we do without such a gracious Lord and most suitable Saviour as the blessed Jesus. How He seems to rise more and more in our estimation, in our thoughts, in our desires, in our affections, as we see and feel what a wreck and ruin we are, what dreadful havoc sin has made with both body and soul, and what miserable outcasts we are by nature, as helpless and forlorn as the poor babe spoken of (Ezek. xvi), "Cast out in the open field, to the loathing of its person, in the day that it was born." But oh, how needful it is, dear friend, to be brought down in our soul to be the chief of sinners, viler than the vilest, and worse than the worst, that we may really and truly believe in and cleave unto this most precious and suitable Saviour.

Can we not say that we have laid at His sacred feet thousands and tens of thousands of earnest petitions, prayers, supplications, and importunities, that He would come into our heart with a divine power, speak to us words of peace, and commune with us from off the mercy-seat? And when He is pleased in any measure to discover the wondrous mystery of His Person and work, blood-shedding and obedience and death, and to give us to know the power of His resurrection in raising up our souls from death unto life, and secretly inspires faith, and hope, and love toward Himself, as the glorious and glorified Son of the Father in truth and love, what then are all earthly things, compared with Him? . . .

Yours affectionately in the Lord,

J. C. P.

CCLX.—To Mr. James Davis

Oakham, Oct. 1*st,* 1868.

My dear Friend,

Your kind, friendly, and experimental letter was safely received, enclosing a bill for £5 for the poor saints of God, and would have been answered sooner, but the mail was gone before it came to hand. I am much obliged to you for the money which you have sent me, and will endeavour to do my best with it. I often meet with cases of need amongst the dear family of God, and sometimes I am enabled to add a little myself to what I call my poor relief fund. In this way I can sometimes give a larger sum than I could unassisted, and I endeavour to spin it out and make it go as far as I can.

I am sorry that you should have experienced so heavy a loss; but I have found myself more than once, when I have been calculating on some increase of income, or some temporal advantage, that a sudden stroke has come and swept it away. We are thus taught not to trust in uncertain riches, which make to themselves wings and fly away, but trust in the living God, who has helped us so many years, and not suffered us to lack any good thing. Those words of our Lord, Mark x. 29, 30, were once made very sweet to me, for I could see them all fulfilled in my experience; but the sweetest of all was, "and in the world to come eternal life." That crowns all. We might have all the gold that ever was dug up in Australia, and what would that profit us on a dying bed, or in the great day, if gold were our god, and we had no other to look to, believe in, or love?

It has been with us a summer almost unparalleled for heat and drought, the thermometer being for several days at 92° and in some places 94°. The whole country was burnt up, and the grass fields almost as brown as the road. I very much felt the heat and the exertion of preaching, and it very much prostrated my strength. I was at the Calne anniversary, and it was one of the very hot days, though not the hottest of the season. The heat of the chapel was very great, as it was much crowded; but I was much helped in speaking, and many of the friends spoke of it as having been a blessed time to their souls. My text was Jer. xxxii. 14, and I endeavoured to show from it the two kinds of evidences, which we must have to know that we are redeemed—

sealed evidences known only to the happy possessor, and open, which are to be known and read by others. I said that these were put into an earthen vessel—our poor, frail, mortal bodies, and that they are in a sense buried with us, and will rise with us in the resurrection morn. Your old friend Hicks was there, and friends from Bath, Castle Cary, Malmesbury, and a long way round. It was at the anniversary that I first saw you, as no doubt you remember. Our friend Mr. Parry was better this visit, and able to hear me each Lord's-day. He sadly misses our dear friend Mr. Tuckwell, and indeed all do who knew him and esteemed him for the truth's sake. He made, indeed, a good end, and, as dear Tiptaft used to say, was well laid in his grave. I saw there many old friends, but it was the middle of harvest, and that and the great heat kept some away.

I hope you find the Lord with you in speaking to the people. You would find it a great trial to be laid aside.

* * * * * *

Yours affectionately in the truth,
J. C. P.

CCLXI —To Mrs. P. and Miss M.

Croydon, Oct. 12, 1868.

My dear Friends,

I should have written to you before had I not been so very poorly, as well as much occupied with *G. S.* work; and even now I hardly know whether I shall be able to send you more than a few lines.

We were highly favoured in our journey home, not only in the day, but in the comfort of the transit, being by ourselves all the way, and passing from Leicester to London by the new line without once stopping. Still I felt very tired before I reached my own home, and though preserved from taking fresh cold yet I have felt greater weakness than when at Oakham. I trust, however, that through mercy the attack is passing off, though I expect it will be some time before I regain that measure of health and strength, never very great, which yet enables me to go through the various tasks that lie before me with some tolerable comfort.

I do not think I ever felt the disappointment so great as being laid aside on this present occasion. I wished so much to be allowed to speak once more in the Lord's name to those who I knew were desirous again to hear my voice. It is, indeed, to me a mysterious dispensation, and yet, I hope, it has in some measure been sanctified to my soul's good. I have felt, through infinite mercy, much of the life and power of divine truth in my heart, have had much of a spirit of grace and supplications, and not been suffered to drop into carnality and death, or be filled with murmuring, fretfulness, self-pity, or rebellion. The flesh, indeed, has felt, and sometimes almost fainted under the burden, but the spirit has been made willing, has cleaved to the Lord with purpose of heart, and hung upon Him, and Him alone, as a nail fastened in a sure place. It has been with me a sowing time, and I hope in due season to reap if I faint not. It is very sad in old age to sink into worldliness, carnality, carelessness, and deadness; and though the flesh may writhe under the afflicting strokes of God's hand it is a mercy to have the life of God stirred up thereby, to be separated in heart and spirit from carnal, earthly things, and to have the affections set where Jesus sits at the right hand of God.

I felt anxious to know about Leicester, and am glad to learn from Mr. Knill's letter that the Lord was with him, and granted him a sweet sense of His presence, with an opening of the heart and mouth to speak in His name. The Lord very frequently overrules these disappointments, and not only displays in them the sovereignty of His will, but also the power of His grace.

You will be glad to hear of my son's recent success. . . . Surely I have much reason to be thankful that at present my family turn out so well—especially when I look around me and see what a trial unruly children have been and are to gracious parents.

I am, my dear friends,
Yours very affectionately in the Lord,
J. C. P.

CCLXII —To Mrs. Peake

Croydon, Oct. 28, 1868.

My dear and much esteemed Friend,

My impression certainly was that —— had ceased to be a subscriber to the A. P. F. Society. I had not heard that the subscription was paid through you. I have often admired the spirit in which Mr. —— acted when he had to curtail his expenses. He said the question was whether he should lay down two extra carriage horses, or give up his subscriptions for various religious and benevolent objects, and he at once preferred the former course. What we are enabled to give to the Lord's cause and the Lord's poor sanctifies, so to speak, the whole of the rest, and no one can expect to see the hand of God in providence stretched out in his behalf who from a spirit of covetousness or self-indulgence diminishes, unless actually compelled, what he has thus consecrated to the Lord's service. I have proved again and again, in providence, that the Lord will abundantly make up any sacrifice that we may make, or any act of kindness and liberality that we may show to the members of the mystical body of Christ.

I was much pleased and struck with E.'s letter. There is so little in our days of that sweet communion with the Lord of which she speaks, that I have thought that its insertion in the *G. S.* might be both a stirring up, as Peter speaks, of the pure minds of others, as well as a tacit reproof and rebuke to the cold and carnal state in which Christians are for the most part so deeply sunk. . . . .

The feeling of weakness, when one has so much to do which demands energy and strength, is in itself a severe trial. Only those who know how exhausting mental labour is can form an idea of the trial which there is in weakness even where there is no pain; but when pain is mingled with it, it makes the trial severe and the burden of the daily cross heavy. But I trust I am deriving some spiritual benefit from it. We need trial upon trial, and stroke upon stroke to bring our soul out of carnality and death. We slip insensibly into carnal ease; but afflictions and trials of body and mind stir us up to some degree of earnestness in prayer and supplication, give a force and reality to the things of God, show us the emptinesss and vanity of earthly things, make us feel the suitability and preciousness of the Lord Jesus; and as we taste any measure of sweetness and blessedness in Him He becomes more feelingly and experimentally all our salvation and all our desire. The Lord has His own way of dealing with us. None can lay down lines for Him, and though His dealings with each seem to differ widely, and few at the time can read His purposes, for He brings the blind by a way which they knew not, yet in the end all His ways are found to be ways of mercy, truth and peace—all stamped with the impress of infinite wisdom, and tender mercy and love. . . . .

Yours very sincerely and affectionately,

J. C. P.

CCLXIII—To Mr. Parry

Croydon, Nov. 5, 1868.

My dear Friend,

You have been very kind in communicating to me the tidings of our dear friend Miss Wild's death. It has taken place somewhat sooner than I had anticipated, but considering that the winter is coming on, which would no doubt have severely tried her weakened frame, I cannot but view it as a mercy that she is removed to that happy land of which "the inhabitants shall no more say 'I am sick.'" She was one of the honestest persons that I ever knew in my life, and though there was a roughness or rather abruptness in her manner, yet it was so mixed with good feeling, as well as softened by grace, that there was nothing in it repulsive or annoying. I always liked her from my first acquaintance with her when I used to go to S., and afterwards to the farm on the hill. She was a very tender and affectionate daughter, and she and her poor mother, with many points of roughness in each, yet were much united in the things of God, and were, I believe, especially in latter days, a comfort to each other. There was one thing very satisfactory in her religion—that you could depend upon all that she said, and that she would rather keep back the marks and evidences of God's manifested favour than put them forward, or wish you to think well of them. I consider that the Lord was very gracious to her in the latter portion of her life; and though she had a rough and thorny path, yet her afflictions and trials were much blessed and sanctified to the good of her soul. I wish there were more like her, whose religion bore so clear a stamp of being a divine work, and one which the Lord so owned, crowned, and blessed.

I hope, through God's mercy, I am slowly recovering from my late attack; but though not severe it seems to have laid deeper and firmer hold of me than almost any one that I have had since I left Stamford. I think the heat and exertion of preaching during the last summer had enfeebled my frame, and therefore when I took cold it seemed to lay firmer hold of me. I much feel being shut up so much in the house, as I have not been out of the gate even to chapel since I came home. I hope, however, that the affliction and trial has not been sent altogether in vain, and that I have reaped some small measure of spiritual profit from it. Hart well and wisely says:—

> "Affliction makes us see
> What else would 'scape our sight."

It seems to bring us to book, to make us consider our latter end, to wean and separate from the world, to give power and reality to divine things, to stir up the grace of prayer and supplication, to show us the emptiness of all natural and creature religion, to make us look more simply and believingly to the blessed Lord, to feel how suitable He is to every want and woe; and that in Him, and in Him alone, is pardon, acceptance, and peace. It also discovers and brings to light many past sins, and working with the grace of God brings us to confession, self-abhorrence, contrition, brokenness, and humility before Him against and before whom we have so deeply and dreadfully sinned. We cannot choose our own path, or our own trials; and usually do not know what the Lord is doing with us by them until after light discovers them. He bringeth the blind by a way that they knew not, but sooner or later He will make every crooked thing straight, and every rough place smooth. When we look back upon the way by which we have been led, how many things we see which should, indeed, humble us into the very dust. And yet how wonderfully has the Lord at various times appeared for us, and in various ways stretched forth His blessed hand. My desire is, and never was stronger in my life, to walk in the fear of God, and to have the manifestations of His mercy, goodness, and love. There is a divine reality in true religion, as our dear friend Miss Wild found upon a dying bed; and if we have not a little of this divine reality we have nothing. For this, you will bear me witness, I have always contended, from the day when you first saw my face and heard my voice in Stadham church; and it was this which gave me a place in your esteem and affections, because you had a testimony in your own conscience that it was a solemn and saving truth, and that in it lay the sum and substance of all vital godliness. You have had many testimonies to the power and reality of this real religion in those at Allington, who have lived and died in it as our dear friend Mr. T., and many others; and I consider your little place highly favoured that the Lord should have had many living witnesses, that His eye has been upon it for good, and that He has honoured, owned, and blessed the word of His grace preached therein. It is a sweet confirmation of the past, and a blessed encouragement for the future; for Jesus Christ in whom we believe is the same yesterday, to-day, and for ever.

Yours very affectionately,
J. C. P.

CCLXIV—To Mr. Godwin

Croydon, Nov. 19, 1868.

My dear Friend,

. . . I have often thought what a mercy it is that the people of God are not dependent upon one another for the supplies of grace whereby they live unto God. The ministry is useful, the conversation of friends is useful, correspondence by letter on the precious things of God is often useful, and from each and all of these we have derived or communicated profit. But how soon these cisterns may become dry, and indeed, unless supplied immediately from the Lord Himself, all the water contained in them is soon dried up and gone. What a mercy then it is for our souls that there is a most gracious Lord in whom it hath pleased the Father that all fulness should dwell, that we might receive of His fulness and grace for grace! How blessedly suitable He is to every want and woe, and how the poor soul is ever looking unto, longing after, hanging upon, and cleaving to Him as all its salvation, and all its desire. Friends live apart, those whom we have known and loved are taken home, there are few opportunities for union and communion amongst Christian friends; but the Lord is ever nigh, ready of access by night and by day, full of pity and compassion to poor sin-sick souls, and able to save to the uttermost all that come unto God by Him. He never disappoints any who trust in Him, is more willing to hear than we to pray, and more willing to give than we to ask. The great, the only real grief of the soul is that it should sin against Him, be denied His presence, not get a word from His lips, a smile from His face, or a touch from His hand.

We, my dear friend, are fast travelling down the vale of life; our lease will soon be run out, and after that every year is beyond Scriptural limit of the appointed life of man. My desire is that my last days may be my best days, and I much dread sinking down into carnality and death. I have many things to try my mind—indeed, some things, I may say many things, which try me most I have never named, and probably shall never name to any living soul. Every heart knows its own bitterness, and the wormwood and the gall which lie at the bottom of the heart do not always or often come to light; and yet it is felt that nothing but a word from the Lord can purge them out or sweeten them. But I have proved this, that trials and exercises of body and mind keep the soul alive unto God, and thus I hope I have reason to bless Him, among other mercies, that He is pleased to keep my soul more or less alive unto Himself, and that chiefly through circumstances which in themselves are painful and distressing. Among the wonderful mysteries of the kingdom of God this is not the least—the way in which He makes even those very sins which cause shame and sorrow to work together for our spiritual good. It is a wonderful thing to be a Christian, and the longer I live the more I see how few there are, and what little real grace the very best Christians possess or manifest. In this life it is as it were the bud; the full fruit is reserved for a state of glory.

I do not seem at present to recover as much from my late attack as I had hoped and could wish. I think the last Lord's-day morning that I preached at Gower Street I spoke as strong as I had done for some years, and the friends remarked how well I was looking. But no doubt the heat of the season and my labours were telling their tale upon me, so that when a cold attacked me it took a deeper hold. It was a great disappointment to me, and I believe to many of the friends, that I could not fulfil my engagements—especially as they had been looking forward to see and hear their old friend and minister once more. I was enabled indeed to speak once at Oakham on the following fortnight, but I think it much threw me back.

We are all, through mercy, pretty well.

Yours very affectionately in the truth,

J. C. P.

CCLXV —To Mrs. Clowes

Croydon, Nov. 23, 1868.

My dear Friend,

I have often reproached myself with not writing to you, and I fear you must have thought it not only neglectful but ungrateful on my part, and a poor return for the great kindness and hospitality which I have received at your hands. But you know, my dear friend, how much my time is engaged, and that my silence does not spring from any want of gratitude or affection. I take, then, the opportunity of a little leisure to send you a few lines. . . .

Now, my dear friend, as regards yourself. You found things at Y——, some of which gratified and some of which pained your mind. You were glad to find there was a pleasing recollection of your deceased brother, and yet how many things recalled to your mind the memory of the loved one whom you have lost. It was his native county, and I have always observed that Norfolk men have a singular affection for the place of their nativity. It was the case with your dear husband, who, though so long separated from it, still retained a good deal of his native affection for it. When you sat upon the pier, looking out on the wide sea and inhaling the healthy breeze, how you longed to have him again at your side, and the silent tear trickled down your cheek, or a convulsive sigh burst forth at the recollection of the past, and the feeling that you would never again in this life see him more. But you have found that the sorrow of this world worketh death. A heart devoid of feeling and affection is repulsive and disgusting in all, but in none more than in a widow, who, in losing her husband, has lost her earthly all. But this earthly sorrow is, for the most part, so often mingled with self-pity, murmuring, fretfulness, unthankfulness, creature-idolatry, and hardness of heart towards God, that it is often, if not sin, yet an occasion for sin. And I would ask you if, after you have had one of your fits of sorrow and passionate grief, whether, unless the Lord has blessed and supported you under them, you have not found darkness of mind, hardness of heart, and unbelief to get sensible prevalence. This is what the apostle means by telling us that the sorrow of this world worketh death, as opposed to that godly sorrow which worketh repentance to salvation not to be repented of. Do not think me unkind in writing thus. I know and feel for your desolate state; but that is the very reason why you should not, by brooding over your sorrows, increase their weight and make you feel every day more desolate still. I do hope that the Lord will draw you near unto Himself, and, using this affliction as a means of weaning you from all earthly happiness, will fix your heart more upon Himself. If you could see it you have many mercies to be thankful for, and would even find that there was a blessing couched in your bereavement.

. . . As regards myself I hope I may say I am better; but my recovery has been very slow. At present I continue in the house, and fear I shall be a prisoner most of the winter.

My dear wife and daughters unite with me in love.

Yours very affectionately,

J. C. P.

CCLXVI.—To Mrs. P. and Miss M.

Croydon, Dec. 22, 1868.

My dear Friends in the Lord,

I must plead my usual excuse for delay in writing to you —occupation in connection with my labours for the benefit, I trust, of the Church of God; and as you, amongst others, will read what has come forth, I trust from my heart it will be almost as if I had communicated directly with yourselves.

I am thankful to say that I feel somewhat better than when I wrote last. Twice I have been for a little walk, and was able last Lord's-day to go to chapel for the first time since my return home. I was glad once more to meet with the people, and they seemed glad also to welcome me again in their midst. The text was from Isaiah xii. 2; but I did not hear my dear friend quite so well as I hoped, and as I have sometimes heard him. But we well know how much we vary in our hearing, and how dependent we are upon the Lord to make His word spirit and life to our souls. The disciples who heard the gracious words that fell from our Lord's lips in the days of His flesh knew and felt but little either of their meaning or their power. It was only after His resurrection and His ascension on high, when He sent the promised Comforter and Teacher, that what they heard Him speak was brought to their remembrance, its meaning unfolded, and its truth and power impressed upon their souls. Not only must the seed be good, but there must be a prepared and good soil for it to fall into; and even then showers and sun are needed to make it spring up, and grow, and bear fruit. It is a great mercy when those words of the apostle are fulfilled in us, "Let the word of Christ dwell richly in you in all wisdom." Our heart must ever be full of something—either sin, worldliness, vanity and folly, or the solemn realities of eternity. And it is according as our mind and thoughts are occupied with one or the other that we are what we are, either before God or man. If sin, carnality, worldliness, and all that is vain and foolish, occupy and possess our minds, the growth of these weeds choke what there may be of the life of God in the soul; and we are barren, unfruitful, unbelieving, and worldly-minded, both inwardly before God and in our conversation, walk, and conduct before men. But when the word of God strikes deep root in the soul, then, as by it alone do we know anything of divine realities, there is more or less of fruitfulness before God and man. All the truth that we know profitably and savingly, all the experience that we have of the things of God, all the acquaintance, union and communion that we have or can have with the Father and the Son in this time state can only be through the word of truth as opened by the Spirit to the enlightened understanding, and applied by His power to the heart and conscience. And there is this great blessedness in the sanctifying light and life, which come into the soul through the word, that they draw the heart upward into heavenly things, and thus subdue and keep out the power of those worldly things of which our mind is naturally full, and in which our carnal nature lives. But the wonder is, what strange and sudden changes and mutations take place in the mind; so that in one half-hour we may seem so under the power of eternal things, as if there were nothing else worth seeking or desiring, and yet in the next half-hour we may seem in our feelings as carnal, worldly, sinful, and sensual, dark, ignorant, and unbelieving, as if there were not, and never had been, one grain of grace or godly fear in the soul. But amidst all these changes it is our mercy that we have to do with the Father of Lights, with whom there is no variableness, neither shadow of turning, and with His word, which endureth for ever. May we highly prize it, read it with profit and pleasure, feel its power and influence, be cast into the mould of it, and ever find it to be a lamp to our feet and a light to our path. It is a treasure of which nothing can deprive us, and though we should ever highly prize a preached gospel as being an ordinance of God, and be thankful for having our lot cast under it, yet the Lord may be pleased to feed our souls in private as much, if not more, by reading and meditating upon the word of His grace. Nor does this at all interfere with, or militate against the preached word, for the best hearers are those who are best instructed out of the word in what they get alone, and their souls when watered by private reading, prayer, and meditation are most fit to receive the word in its public ministration. Next to being quickened and made alive is to be kept alive and lively in the things of God; and this cannot be by negligence, sloth, and carelessness, as if God would give the blessing independently of our seeking or desiring. But I will not run on further in this strain, lest the whole of my letter should be too much on one subject.

I send you some letters, amongst them one from the French lady whom I named to you. I had asked her to spend a part of her holidays here, and at the same time expressed my wish that she would write down some of the dealings of God with her soul, and I told her that she might write to me in her own language if she felt more liberty in doing so. This will explain some things in her letter. I have often thought of several things which she named in the account that she gave of the Lord's dealings with her soul. There was something in it so real and sterling, so original and fresh, so evidently the teaching and work of the Lord, that it made a deep impression upon my mind, and her manner was so simple, humble, and modest, that what she said commended itself so much to the conscience. Most of us old professors are so covered over and muffled up in a kind of traditionary religion that when we meet with one who has been led in a peculiar, and yet unmistakably gracious path, it seems to come with a peculiar weight and freshness to the mind.

And now, my dear friends, I wish you the enjoyment of all those blessings which are connected with the season of the year—assuming that it was the season in which the Lord came into the world; and may we never forget why He came, for it is most suitable to us. "This is a faithful saying, and worthy of all acceptation," and therefore of yours and mine, "that Christ Jesus came into the world to save sinners," and can we not add—I am sure I can, and that with great reason—"of whom I am chief." And, again, "The Son of Man came to seek and to save that which was lost." And were we not lost, to all intents and purposes, completely ruined without hope or help? And have we not a thousand times over destroyed ourselves so as to need above most Him in whom is all our help? I am well satisfied that a knowledge of sin and of the depths of the fall is necessary to any right view or feeling of salvation by the blood of the Lamb.

I am, through mercy, quite as well as I can hope to be at this season of the year, when I am so much confined to the house; and live in hope that when warm and dry weather comes I may once more breathe the beautiful fresh air.

In writing to you, my dear friends, I feel myself to be addressing also others of my dear Oakham friends. Accept my love for yourselves and them.

My family are all around me, and, through mercy, pretty well.

Yours very affectionately in the Lord,

J. C. P.

CCLXVII—To Mr. Copcutt

Croydon, Jan. 8, 1869.

My dear Sir,

* * * * * *

You speak in your letter of a sermon by the late Mr. M'Kenzie. He was, indeed, a very gracious, godly man, and was for several years co-editor with me in conducting the *Gospel Standard.* He died in the year 1849, comparatively a young man, was much esteemed by the Church of God as a minister of truth, and was taken away, as appeared to us, just in the midst of his usefulness, making a very good end, and leaving behind him a cherished memory.

Mr. Tiptaft was indeed a most remarkable man, and my memoir gives but a very imperfect account of the life of self-denial, separation from the world, devotedness to the work of the ministry, nobility and liberality of mind which he displayed ever since I first knew him. It is remarkable how the Lord owned and blessed his ministry. No man in my day was so much owned, both to the calling of sinners and the consolation of saints. He was not highly gifted as a minister in the ordinary sense of the term; but what he spoke was with authority and power, as what he knew for himself by divine teaching and spiritual experience, and it was so backed and confirmed by the power of his life and his upright godly walk. He was thus a striking instance that it was not by might or by power, that is of the creature, but by the Spirit of the Lord of Hosts, that all real work is done. What is effected by mere eloquence only touches the flesh and passes away; but what God does in the soul by the power of His grace is saving and permanent.

I should like you to see some of the back volumes of the *Gospel Standard*, published now many years ago, as there are many papers, letters, obituaries, &c., in them, which are very edifying.

Yours very sincerely,

J. C. P.

CCLXVIII.—To Mrs. Peake

Croydon, Jan. 27, 1869.

My dear Friend,

In the persuasion that a few lines from me will not be unacceptable, even if not strictly demanded in the way of debt, for I think I wrote last, I feel disposed once more to communicate with you by pen. Christian intercourse is often profitable; and, where this cannot be obtained by personal communion, it may be kept up by letter. Not that I am able in myself to send you anything that may be for your spiritual profit; but as the Lord has sometimes kindly deigned to use my pen in His service, I am encouraged thereby thus to communicate with those whom I know and love in the truth.

In all who truly fear God and believe in His dear Son; in all in whose hearts the blessed Spirit is graciously at work both to bring down and raise up, lay low in their own eyes and make Christ precious, show the evil of sin, give them repentance for it, creating a love for true holiness and spirituality of mind, with meekness, simplicity, sincerity, tenderness, brokenness of heart, and contrition of spirit—I say, where the blessed Spirit is thus at work, there and there only will there be true union in the solemn things of God. True union lies deep, and its foundations are out of sight. There is nothing in it earthly or carnal; and, as what is earthly and carnal in us ever floats, so to speak, at the top, everything truly spiritual, holy, and gracious, being weighty and solid, lies at the bottom. If you will examine your heart, as seeing light in God's light, you will see that the best part of your religion lies the deepest. No man, therefore, can know anything of the mysteries of true religion and the secrets of vital godliness who is not well brought down in his own soul. And thus a Christian, to his wonder and surprise, finds that the lower he sinks in himself, the more that he is abased, humbled, and brought down in his soul before the Lord, the nearer he is able to approach Him. In this way a sight and sense of our dreadful sins, the evils of our heart, the iniquities which are more in number than the hairs of our head, when attended with a feeling of the infinite forbearance of God, his tender mercy in Christ, the riches of His superabounding grace, the depths of His wondrous love, are made most profitable. Until we are really humbled and brought down before God, with a view of His mercy and grace in Christ Jesus, we cannot bear to deal honestly with ourselves, or for others to deal honestly with us. It 'is our pride, our self-righteousness, our presumption, and our hypocrisy, our double dealing with God and our own consciences, which make us shrink from being searched by His word and the light of His Spirit. As long as a man stands in his own strength or goodness, all the curses of God's law strike at him as a sinner; but when he falls flat, as it were, on his face, confessing his iniquity, loathing himself in his own eyes for his baseness, and looking up in faith, hope, and love to the Lord of life and glory, as putting away sin by the sacrifice of Himself, then all the storm is ceased, and the blessings, promises, and mercies of the gospel fall upon his soul like the still small rain and the refreshing dew. And as these mercies enter into his heart, they bring forth in him every gospel fruit. Prayer, and sometimes praise, spirituality of mind, love to the Lord and His truth, earnest desires to walk in His fear and live to His praise, separation in heart and spirit from an ungodly world, an understanding of the heavenly meaning of the Scriptures, and a stretching forth of the cords of love and affection toward the dear family of God—these and other fruits spring up and grow in the heart which is truly brought down by grace. On the contrary, where the evil of sin is little seen or felt, where there is no abasement of spirit or humility of mind before the Lord, as being so utterly vile, and no corresponding sense of the infinite mercy and goodness of God, there religion for the most part is only in name. In that soil pride, self-righteousness, presumption, hypocrisy, worldliness, carnality, and covetousness, a spirit of strife and contention, a name to live when dead, a trifling with God and conscience, an indulgence of secret idols, and walking in many things which are highly displeasing to the Lord, will be found rife and strong. Be not afraid, therefore, dear friend, of seeing the worst of yourself. You have not seen half or a tenth part, I may say a hundredth part, yet. With all your experience of many years, and all the sight and sense which you have had of the evil that is in you, you have really seen and known but little of what a fallen sinner is in the sight of God. Indeed none of us could bear to see it. The sight would sink us into despair unless specially held up by the power of God. But I would say to you and to all my friends in the Lord, Be not afraid of sinking too low in your own eyes. Dread presumption, pride, self-righteousness, vain security, a dead assurance and empty formality; but covet sweet humility, brokenness of heart, contrition of spirit, tenderness of conscience, spirituality of mind, meekness and quietness; and above all things covet earnestly precious manifestations of the Lord to your soul, sweet glimpses of His person and work, and breakings in of the light of His countenance, and of what He is in Himself as the Son of God, and as the Mediator between God and men, the risen and glorified Intercessor, who is able to save to the uttermost all who come unto God by Him. The Lord means to teach us that grace is grace, and that we can be saved in no other way. It is a lesson easy to learn in word, but to know it in its blessed reality and truth is no such easy matter; for it can only be known by knowing experimentally the depths of sin and guilt out of which it saves. When, then, we are being led down into these depths there seems to be little before the soul but ruin and despair. It does not see that this sight and sense of sin is a needful preparation to know what grace is and what grace can do, but when grace is manifested in its fulness and its superaboundings, then the wonder is that grace so rich and free should ever be extended unto or should ever reach a soul so vile.

I send you some letters in which you will see some expression of the writer's with reference to my Address. Most writers are but imperfect judges of their own compositions, though they know the feelings under which they were written, and the subject which they handle. Readers also are imperfect judges unless they have been led into the same or similar paths. You will see how this bears upon the Address. Those who have not had some experience of the path there traced out cannot well understand or follow it; but those who have painfully known what it is to have declined from the right ways of the Lord, and then have been brought up and brought back, may read in it much of their own feelings.

I cannot say much of myself, except that I am thus far preserved from illness; but my cough is often troublesome and my breath short, and I feel I have not the strength which I had even a few years ago. It may, perhaps, with God's help and blessing, be a little better when the warm weather comes and I can walk out more.

Our united love to you both. Mine to the dear friends.

Yours very affectionately in the truth,

J. C. P.

CCLXIX —To Mrs. Clowes

Croydon, February 16th, 1869.

My dear Friend,

I have felt desirous to send you a few lines of affectionate sympathy on the recurrence of the mournful day which took from you the delight of your eyes; and though I would not wish to encourage you in feeding that sorrow which often worketh death, yet would I wish to feel for you and with you under the weight of your distressing bereavement. How rapidly has time passed away since that dark and gloomy day, and I trust that it has mitigated the keen edge of your sorrow, though the only true balm is to be found in those sweet consolations which can bear the soul up under the heaviest load. As I trust the keenness of your sorrow has been thus mitigated you will be able to see with clearer eyes, and to feel with more abounding and abiding gratitude the unspeakable mercy that your late dear husband left behind him so sweet a testimony of his interest in the precious blood and righteousness of our gracious Lord. This is an enduring consolation when you can realize it by faith, and is the best remedy against all murmuring and rebellion under the painful dispensation.

Great and many are your mercies if you could but clearly see and realize them. How many poor widows have deep providential trials from which you are exempt. How afflicted others are in body or mind, and how many godly women have no clear evidence that their husbands died in the Lord. Nor are you without some sweet testimonies and gracious visits of the Lord to your soul, all which are or should be matter of thankfulness and comfort.

Yours very affectionately,

J. C. P.

CCLXX —To Mrs. P. and Miss M.

Croydon, March 3rd, 1869

My dear Friends in the Lord,

As you will be expecting a few lines from me, I will endeavour not to disappoint you, though I feel very unable at the present moment to send you anything really worth your perusal; still such is your kind and affectionate feeling that I am sure you will bear with me and the unprofitableness of my communication.

Among the trying and painful parts of our experience we have to learn the dryness and deadness of our souls when not under any felt divine influence, and that at such seasons if we attempt to speak or write upon the things of God, barrenness and death seem to rest upon all that proceeds from us. Truly our gracious Lord said, "Without Me ye can do nothing." He is and ever must be everything in us as well as everything for us, and everything to us. Without His divine communications we can neither pray, nor read, nor meditate, with any faith in living exercise; and therefore as all our springs are in Him, and as all communication from Him is through faith, the suspension of His gracious influences through the Spirit leaves us dark, barren, dry, and as if dead. But what a mercy it is for those who have an interest in the love and blood and grace of the Son of God, that He changeth not, but rests in His love, is of one mind and none can turn Him, and is the same yesterday, to-day and for ever! When we take a review of all the temptations, trials, sins, backslidings, wanderings and startings aside that we have been guilty of, all the hard thoughts, peevish and rebellious uprisings, with all the sad unprofitableness, backwardness to good, proneness to evil, determination to have our own will and way, and all that mass of inconsistency which sometimes seems to frighten us in the retrospect lest we be deceived altogether,—I say when we look over these things, what reason we have to cling close to the precious blood and righteousness of the Christ of God, that we may find in Him a refuge from our sinful, vile and guilty selves! It seems sad that after so many years' experience of the goodness and mercy of God, and after all we have seen, known, tasted, felt and handled of the Person and work of the Lord Jesus, of His suitability, beauty, blessedness, grace and glory, we should still find so much sin, carnality, unbelief, infidelity, and every other evil, alive and lively within. How it shows the depth of the fall, and the incurable corruption of our nature, that neither time, nor advancing years, nor bodily infirmity, nor any other change of circumstances can alter this wretched heart, turn it into a right course, or make it obedient and fruitful; but that like the barren heath, no cultivation can bring out of it either flower or fruit. But on the other hand, what a rich and unspeakable mercy it is for those who are born of God, that they are possessed of a new and divine nature in which there have been planted by an Almighty hand, the precious graces of faith, hope, and love, with everything which can qualify and make them meet for the inheritance of the saints in light. Perhaps, as we advance in life and become established in the truth, we see and feel more clearly and distinctly the difference which separates these two natures, and look with almost equal surprise on the dreadful depravity of the one, and the spiritual character of the other, grovelling in the one in all the dregs of earth, and I might say, all the sins of hell, and rising up in the other to all that is holy, heavenly, and good. Mr. Huntington says that he was three men, though but one coal-heaver: 1, as a man; 2, as having an old man; and 3, as having a new man. This witness is true. We have our natural body, which often makes us sigh under the sicknesses and infirmities which attend it; then there is that corrupt nature which has so long been, and still is, such a plague; and then there is that new and divine nature, we trust, which is born of God, and which sinneth not, dwelling as it does in the midst of sin and corruption. Now as the natural body is sustained by food, and our corrupt nature is fed and strengthened by all that is evil, so the new man of grace is sustained by the pure truth of God, and especially by communications of grace and life, out of the fulness of the blessed Lord. It is to Him that the new man of grace looks, listens to His voice, hears His word, delights in His Person and work, longs after the visitations of His presence, and the manifestations of His love, and oh, how at times it longs for, presses after, and cries out for His visits, "Oh, when wilt Thou come unto me!" and how gladly, as Hart says, would it entertain Him, and give Him the best room! But how soon again all these earnest desires and pressings forward seem to droop and die; and our wretched heart again grovels in the dust just as if there never had been, nor was one grain of grace or one spark of divine life. How earnestly at times do I desire and pray for the Lord to rend the veil, break in with His own most blessed and glorious light, and come Himself into my heart in His risen power and glory. There is much truth in Mr. Hart's words and the connection—

"We pray to be new-born,
And know not what we mean."

But what an unspeakable mercy it is for us that the Lord changeth not as we change, and that He views us not as standing in all our rags and ruin, all our filth and folly, but in the Person of His dear Son, in whom He is ever well pleased.

I desire to commend you both, with all whom we know and love in the Lord, who worship among you with your dear pastor and his wife, the deacons and members of the church, to the Lord.

Yours very affectionately in Him,
J. C. P.

CCLXXI.—To Mr. Tips

Croydon, April 19, 1869.

My dear Friend,

I am happy to tell you that I am alive, and that the report of my death is not true. It has pleased the Lord, however, for the last few years to lay upon me His afflicting hand, so that I am not able as before to carry on the work of the ministry, except sometimes in the summer when the weather is warm, as my complaint lies chiefly in the chest, so that I am not able to go out much when the weather is cold or damp. I have been obliged, therefore, to leave Stamford, as it was too cold for me, and to move to a somewhat warmer climate. I am still able, however, to use my pen, and every month there is published a sermon of mine in the "Gospel Pulpit," published by Mr. Ford of Stamford, which he took down from my lips as I preached them in London.

I dare say you have not forgotten your visit to Stamford, and what you saw and heard there, though we were not able to converse so much as we could have done if we had understood one another's language. But I hope we understood a better language —even the language of Canaan. I have no doubt you have had your share of trials and afflictions since we parted, and I hope that they have been blessed and sanctified to your soul's spiritual good. It is through much tribulation that we enter the kingdom of God, and many are the afflictions of the righteous, but the Lord delivereth him out of them all. This makes all the difference between the afflictions of the righteous and of the ungodly, that to the one the afflictions are a blessing and to the other a curse; for they soften the heart of the one, and they harden the heart of the other. In the case of the righteous, they instrumentally bring forth prayer and supplication to the Lord, and wean the heart from the world; but in the ungodly they only produce sullenness, self-pity, and rebellion. What a mercy it is to have a God to go to, and to know that we have a merciful, sympathising High Priest at the right hand of the Father, who is touched with a feeling of our infirmities, and is able to save to the uttermost all who come unto God by Him. When we look at the majesty, holiness, justice, and purity of God, and seeing light in His light see also our own sinfulness and depravity; when we think of the numerous—yea, innumerable—sins and crimes which we have committed in thought, word, and deed; when we see also our helplessness and inability to save or deliver our souls from the wrath to come, the sight and feeling of all these things is enough to sink our souls into despair. But when we see by the eye of faith what a Saviour God has provided for poor lost sinners in His dear Son, what a mighty Redeemer, ever-living Advocate, and all prevailing Mediator, then it raises up sweet hope and blessed encouragement, and the heart goes out after this divine Mediator in faith and love as feeling how suitable, how precious He is to those that believe. We thus learn that there is no salvation but by sovereign grace, that the Son of Man came to seek and to save that which was lost. We are very unwilling to see, much more to feel ourselves to be sinners, but it is only as sinners that we can be saved, for "this is a faithful saying and worthy of all acceptation, that Jesus Christ came into the world to save sinners."

Yours in Christian affection,

J. C. P.

CCLXXII.—To Mrs. Peake

Croydon, April 21, 1869.

My dear Friend in the Lord,

The tidings contained in your letter of the removal of Mrs. Prentice from this vale of tears were somewhat sudden, but not altogether unexpected, for your last kind communication prepared me to anticipate such a change. It would, indeed, be a blessed exchange for her, for her sufferings during the last few years have been great and complicated, and perhaps she was not constitutionally able to bear suffering as some oan who are similarly afflicted. I consider her, viewing what God did for her soul and the circumstances under which it was done, as one of the most remarkable instances of the power of God that have come under my personal observation. My memory is not what I may call a verbal one, which I have often regretted; that is, I cannot distinctly remember the exact words of a conversation related to me; but if I could do so the relation which she gave me of the dealings of God with her soul would indeed be very marked and memorable. I have always considered her deliverance as the greatest that I ever heard with my own ears, and for clearness and power very little short of what was vouchsafed to Hart and Huntington. But it was something to this effect: she was in very deep distress of soul, and went into a dark closet where she threw herself flat upon her face. All of a sudden the dark closet was lighted up as if with a heavenly glory; she looked up astonished at the sight, and it seemed to her as if she saw God the Father sitting upon His eternal throne, and He spake to her these or similar words, "Thou canst not be saved by the works of the law. Out of my dear Son I am a consuming fire; but for His sake I have forgiven thee all thy sins, past, present, and to come, and thou shalt be with Me for ever; live to My glory." This is the substance, and, I think, very near the exact words. I need not tell you what a wonderful revolution they wrought in her soul; but what seemed to make almost the deepest impression was the words, "Live to My glory," for there she found the great difficulty, and her inability except by special grace. But it made, and kept, her conscience tender, and was ever set before her as the guiding rule of her life. I think it was after this that she got so dreadfully entangled in legal bondage through sitting under a legal ministry, that she almost lost sight of this great deliverance. I believe it was about this time that my sermons first fell into her hands, and one of them, I think it was "Winter afore Harvest," was the means of bringing her out of this legal bondage. I have heard her say that the first time she read it, it seemed to her as if a light from heaven shone upon one special page, and from that was reflected into her heart. So blessed was this sermon to her soul, and so fond was she of it that she carried it in her bosom till it was quite worn out. I have seen it, and tattered it was. She had no idea that the writer was alive, but thought he had been dead many years ago and, to use her expression, was with Abraham. Through her master's son, who, I believe, heard me in London, she learnt that the writer was still alive, and that there were more sermons to be had by him. Some of these she somehow procured, and finding they were preached at Eden Street sent me a letter directed there which somehow reached me. I cannot go through the remarkable steps in Providence whereby she came first to Stamford, and then under my roof; but Mrs. W. knew all the circumstances and could tell you, and very probably remembers much of her experience which I have forgotten. Like most others she had her defects and failings, and these often obscured the work of grace; but, taking her as a gracious character, I consider that there are few amongst you who were so well and deeply taught in the things of God, or who knew so much of the power and reality of the thing she professed. I had much union of spirit with her, and believe I can say I never heard her drop a word on the things of God which was not commended to my conscience. As regards spiritual things we never had a jar, and she always treated me with great respect and affection. But you know as well as most that generally there are trying circumstances when master and servant both profess, and, we hope, possess the truth and fear of God. I have heard her say, however, that she found it profitable to her soul to be under my roof, and, though I dare hardly add it, that my example was good for her soul.

You will be glad to hear that I am, through mercy, somewhat better, and have had a nice walk to-day, enjoying, as much as I can enjoy anything earthly, the pure fresh air, which is very pleasant here, and the sweet return of spring. You will remember it was the season that your dear husband so much loved. But often with me it has been marred by attacks of illness.

I enclose a letter of Mr. Parry's, which you will hardly understand from not knowing the persons of whom he speaks. I am utterly unworthy, and ever was, of such a favour and such a distinction; but I should lie against my right if I did not believe that God had wrought by me, and at one period very specially. This is the time of which Mr. P. speaks, when I first went to Allington. There was a power put forth at that time inferior, I admit, but almost similar to that shown at Oakham when William Tiptaft first preached there, and the effects of that power are visible to this day, though nearly thirty-four years ago.

Yours very affectionately in the truth,

J. C. P.

CCLXXIII—To Mr. Parry

Croydon, May 31, 1869.

My dear Friend,

I have reason to believe from all I have heard that the obituary of the Wilds has been generally well received. What people want is something real, something genuine, something that they can depend upon; and you will find that, for the most part, it is not great things which comfort and encourage the people of God, but that peculiar line of trials and exercises every now and then lightened up and delivered from by the Lord's appearing, such as is marked out in the obituary. There is also some biography connected with the spiritual part which always gives an interest to obituaries, and when connected with the experience throws a light upon it.

I am not surprised that you look back sometimes to those former days, going on for 34 years ago, when certainly there was a marked power attending the word at Allington. Besides those whom we remember with so much affection, some of whom you have named in your letter, there were doubtless others powerfully wrought upon, of whom we knew little or nothing; for the work was not confined to a few years, but was spread over many at my annual visits when we used to have such gatherings from all parts. I have had and still have many exercises both about my personal standing and my ministry; but I cannot doubt that the Lord has wrought by me, and indeed, on several occasions, in a very marked way. I have often thought of the words of the great apostle, 1 Cor. ix. 27, latter clause; and indeed but for sovereign and superabounding grace should find it so. I often tell the Lord what a theme of thankful praise, what a debt of eternal gratitude I shall owe Him for saving my soul. People say, but I can more than say, I am sure that no greater sinner will enter heaven.

Mr. Hazlerigg was here on Wednesday evening, and preached from Phil. iii. 10, 11. I am glad to say that I heard him very sweetly. He preached not only a very able but a very experimental and faithful sermon—indeed, a superior sermon, and with a good deal of real vital experience, and such things as I could set to my seal were not only sound gospel truth but the real feelings of a living, exercised soul. It happened to be what is called the Derby day, and the cab which I ordered did not come till 7.20, so that I only got in after he had begun prayer, in which I thought him very nice. He called in the afternoon, when he spoke of the late Mrs. ——, and was well persuaded of her safety. He visited her in her illness, and said that on one occasion when he left her she had spoken with so much brokenness, contrition, and with such sweetness upon the dealings of God with her soul, that, to use his expression, "he had never left a sick room more exhilarated or persuaded of the reality of the work." We both felt that what once looked well in her had been sadly buried by prosprity, &c., but, as he remarked, the Lord would not let her enjoy this world, for she had little else but bodily suffering, and I believe at the last very great. I understand that on one occasion she was so blessed that not being able to sing herself from weakness, she had her maids into her room and made them sing for her. What a sovereign God is, and how, as poor Mrs. Wild said to Mary, the work of the Lord upon the soul can never be extinguished, however weak it may seem for a time to appear.

I have been obliged to give up going to Gower Street for the last three Lord's-days in June, not feeling sufficiently strong for two full services. Indeed, this cold spring and these terrible east winds have much tried me, and much prevented my getting out for a walk, as I cannot face them, and find it better to keep indoors during their continuance. I hope I may be able to go to Stamford and Oakham in the beginning of July, but even that, at the present, is uncertain. I should like to come to you for the first three Lord's-days in August; and even if not able to preach, or to preach but little, I should be glad to pay you a visit for old friendship's sake. The Calne anniversary is fixed for August 4th, and Mr. Kershaw and Mr. Taylor were expected; but I have heard to-day that Mr. Kershaw is seriously ill, and that his impression is that "his work is done," and I almost fear whether his impression may not be true, as when men of his advanced age begin to sink they often pass away.

Yours very affectionately,

J. C. P.

CCLXXIV—To Mrs. Peake

Croydon, June 3, 1869.

My dear Friend in the Lord,

I have been so much occupied with preparing for publication my little work on the "Advance of Popery," that I have scarcely found time to attend to my private correspondence. This must plead my excuse for not taking earlier notice of your kind and interesting letters. I have now, however, nearly finished it, and hope to be able to get it out before the end of the month. It has cost me some time and trouble, as I had both to re-write some parts and re-arrange others; and, after all, having been written at various times and in detached articles, I fear it will be found to want unity of thought and language as well as arrangement, and to have too much repetition.

I have received several communications like your own requesting me not to abridge the sermons, and therefore I feel bound to listen to what seems to be the general feeling and voice of its readers. The Lord works by whom He will work, as He sends by whom He will send; and thus, if His Gracious Majesty is pleased to make use of my printed sermons for His people's good and His own glory, what can I say? I did not commence their publication, nor have I derived the slightest profit from them. All the labour that I have bestowed upon them, in revising and preparing them for the press, has been on my part wholly gratuitous, so that I have had nothing for my trouble but the pleasing thought of their being made profitable to the Church of God, which is far better pay than all that gold or silver could bestow.

I am glad that you as well as others have read with such interest and feeling the account which I have been enabled to give of the Wilds. They were, indeed, most worthy and excellent people, so honest and sincere in word and deed, so afraid of presumption and hypocrisy, and so deeply tried and exercised in almost every way—body, soul, family, and circumstances. I should think there was scarcely a trial or temptation, come from what quarter it may, which poor Mrs. Wild had not some experience of. But perhaps the account of her trials and sufferings, which I have recorded in the *Gospel Standard*, may be made a means of comforting and encouraging others who are called to walk in the same path of tribulation. She was a very sensible woman, and, if I may say so, was very much attached to me and my ministry, indeed much more so than I could publicly mention. It is at Allington as at Oakham, the old wine is better than the new. Though there are still many gracious people in that church and congregation, there is not now the life and power that there was in years past, nor the gatherings from all parts which there used to be in my former annual visits. But it seems to be everywhere the same. There is a gradual declension of the life and power of godliness. The work of grace upon the people is not so deep, clear, or decided, nor is the power of the Lord so present to heal as in days gone by. And I fear it will go on getting worse and worse till, according to the prophecies of the last days, men will have the form of godliness whilst they deny the power thereof. The way of the Cross is hateful to flesh and blood, and therefore a smooth, easy path securing, as they think, the benefits and blessings of salvation without self-denial, mortification of the flesh, painful exercises, and many trials, is eagerly embraced and substituted for the straight and narrow way which leadeth unto life. And by this, or some other deceit of the flesh or delusion of the devil, all would perish in their sins, unless the Lord had chosen a peculiar people in the furnace of affliction and predestinated them to be conformed to the image of His dear Son, here in suffering, and hereafter in glory. They, like all the rest, would gladly, as far as the flesh is concerned, stretch themselves on a bed too short and wrap themselves up in a covering too narrow, and thus make a covenant with death and hell that they might be disturbed by fears of neither. But this the Lord will not suffer, and therefore lays judgment to the line and righteousness to the plummet, and then they find that they have made lies their refuge, and under falsehood have they hid themselves. Now until this covenant with death and hell is broken up, there will be no view by faith, no being brought unto or building upon the foundation which God has laid in Zion, even that stone, that tried stone, that precious corner-stone on which the Church is built. We may thus bless the Lord for every conviction, pang, trial, exercise, sorrow, distress, or temptation, which may, so to speak, uncase us of our self-righteousness and hypocrisy, and bring us to cleave to the rock for want of a shelter. And this not only at first, as if when peace was obtained by faith in the Son of God there were no more convictions of conscience or distress of mind to be undergone, but it was through more or less the whole of the divine life, one may say, to its very close. I have been reading lately, and indeed read most evenings, Bourne's weighty letters, and I find them profitable as pointing out so clearly the way of tribulation with its benefits and blessings. I should like you and your dear sister to read sometimes these truly experimental letters, and believe you would find them instructive and profitable. They and "Huntington's Posthumous Letters" are, with the Scriptures, my chief reading.

I hope that we may be spared to meet once more, and to commune upon those things which make for our peace. Our intercourse with the family of God in this life is not only very imperfect through the weakness of the flesh, but broken into and interrupted by distance of the body and local separation, where there is no distance in feeling, or separation in spirit. Like, therefore, communion with the Lord, all communion of saint with saint must in this life be transient and broken. Still, it is real, and so far is a mark of life, and a pledge of a higher and fuller communion in the life to come.

I still hope that I may be allowed to come among you in the beginning of July, if you are willing to take the risk of my not being able to preach, or at least of having only short services. I shall probably be in London, at my dear friend Mrs. Clowes's, for a week or ten days, on my way to Oakham, if enabled to come.

Give my Christian love to all my friends in the Lord.

Yours very affectionately in the truth,

J. C. P.

CCLXXV —To Mrs. Kershaw

Croydon, June 11, 1869.

My dear Friend,

I am sorry to find from a letter just received from Mr. Gadsby, that dear Mr. Kershaw is gradually sinking into the arms of death. But O, what a mercy and a blessing it is for him and for you, and may I not add, for all his friends and the Church of God, that he is so favoured in his soul, and that the blessing of God rests like the dew upon the branch. It is, indeed, a fitting crown to his long and laborious life, a sealing testimony of the Lord the Spirit to the precious truths which he has so long preached, and a confirming evidence that the Jesus, whose name, blood, righteousness, and dying love he has so long laboured to exalt, is now smiling upon His aged servant before He takes him home to Himself.

Amid all your present cares and anxieties, and the fatigue of nursing the dear invalid, I could not ask you to drop me a line how he is, but if S. J. would but write me a few words I should feel much obliged. Truly she said in her note to Mrs. G. that his removal will be an indescribable loss to you and her. But oh, my dear friend, what a blessed thing it is for you to have such a testimony on his behalf, and though when the stroke comes you may feel as if it were tearing body and soul asunder, and may sadly mourn your desolate state after so many years of wedded happiness and spiritual union, yet it will be a sweet balm to your bleeding heart that he whom you so long and so justly loved is for ever with his dear Lord. Please to give him my Christian love. We have always walked in love and union for many years, and no cloud has ever come across our intercourse with each other.

Yours very affectionately in the truth,

J. C. P.

CCLXXVI —To Mr. Tips

Croydon, June 18, 1869.

My dear Friend in the Lord,

You have asked me to write to you very soon after I should receive your kind and affectionate letter, but my time is very much engaged, and I have been lately very busy in bringing out a little work upon the "Advance of Popery in England," which has taken up time and attention; besides which, my health is not good, and I cannot labour with either tongue or pen, as in days past. I was not able therefore to comply with your request.

It is, indeed, a wonderful mercy to have divine life communicated to the soul, to have any living faith in the Lord Jesus Christ, any hope in God's mercy, or any love to Him who is the altogether lovely, or any affection to His people as bearing His image and belonging to Him. This hope, faith and love, the Lord seems to have given you, my dear friend; and it is because He has wrought these graces in your heart by a divine power that you love His truth, His ways, His word, and those who faithfully preach and write it. It never was an honour that I sought to be made a blessing to His people by my sermons and writings; but it was the Lord's will, and the Lord's work. Nothing belongs to me but sin and shame. I have no good works to plead, but, on the contrary, have to confess my sins which have been great and grievous, and have no hope but in the precious blood of the Lord Jesus Christ, which cleanses us from all sin. Most probably we shall never meet again on earth, but it will be the greatest of all our mercies to arrive safe on the heavenly shore; and I am very sure that it must be the free, rich and superabounding grace of God which alone can bring us there. We live in a world of sin and sorrow; our wicked hearts are continually entangling us in sin and evil. It is very easy to depart from the Lord, but very hard to return to Him. Repentance, reconciliation, pardon and peace are the free gifts of His grace, and indeed, it is a mercy that the Son of Man, who is the Son of God, came to seek and to save that which was lost.

I am not able to preach much now as my chest is weak and tender, and I am unable to bear cold and damp, of which we have had much this spring.

My love and best wishes to you and yours, and all who love the Lord Jesus Christ amongst you.

Yours in the love of the Truth,

J. C. P.

CCLXXVII —To Mrs P. and Miss M.

London, June 24, 1869.

My dear Friends in the Lord,

Now that I write with my own hand, I cannot send you so long or so legible a letter as when I use the pen of my secretary; but you shall have, as you deserve, my best.

I reached my dear friend Mrs. Clowes's house safely, through mercy, on Saturday, and trust I took no cold by the way. She gave me a most warm and hearty welcome; and as we are much united, both from our long friendship and spiritual communion, and the house affords every comfort that I can require, I am at home here in every sense of the word. All I want is a little more bodily health and strength, and above all, more of the felt presence and power of the Lord.

I took the whole morning service at Gower Street, last Lord's-day, and was comfortably brought through, feeling life and liberty, both in prayer and preaching. Text, Isai. iv. 2, 3. I meant at first to take also verse 4, but found on meditating on the subject that it was, so to speak, covering too much ground. The reporter was there, and thus you will, D.V., see what I was enabled to preach. I may perhaps take verse 4 another day, as there is much deep experimental truth in it if I could bring it forth. I was tired and exhausted afterwards, but this is only what I must expect. I had reason to be thankful that I scarcely coughed the whole time, and my voice was clear and strong.

Mr. Kershaw is on his dying bed, but, to use his own words, "as full of heaven as he can hold." It is a fitting termination to his long, laborious and godly life. I send you some letters which will tell you how he is or was, both in body and soul. He has a strong constitution, but I greatly doubt whether he will be here many days.

Mr. Garner is supplying at Gower Street. The friends admire his kind feeling toward me in not being jealous, because I take a service as if over his head. I told the people Lord's-day morning that he had been a hearer and transient member of mine for several years, and had always shown me great esteem, respect and affection, and that I could, therefore, without hurting his feelings or wounding his dignity, take his place, but that there were very few ministers to whom I could even propose such a thing.

I hope I may come among you in the fulness of the blessing of the Gospel of Christ. But do not look to me, or you will surely be disappointed. The Lord is a jealous God. I fear you will see me weaker in body, as I have never really got over the attack I had last September, and the cold, wet spring has robbed me of my grand tonic—my walks. My daughter S. who is at Plymouth, gives a poor account of Mrs. Isbell; she reads to her twice daily and is, I doubt not, a comfort to her. My sister has found a blessing in my meditations on 1 Pet. i., especially about the incorruptible inheritance, and has had them read three or four times to her. With kind love to all my dear friends,

I am, yours in the Lord,

J. C. P.

CCLXXVIII—To Mrs. P. and Miss M.

London, July 19, 1869.

My dear Friends in the Lord,

You will be desirous to hear how I am and how I was brought through my labours yesterday. It was very hot and the congregation large, but on the whole I was brought comfortably through. My texts were, Jude xx. 21, Jer. xvii. 7, 8. Mr. Ford was there both times. I felt dry and shut up in the morning, but was more at liberty in the evening. I slept but little from fatigue and heat, but on the whole am pretty well to-day, and have had a nice refreshing walk. I preached at Stamford from Heb. iv. 1, and spoke much of what the rest was, "my rest," *i.e.* God's rest, what it was to come short of it, either for a time only, or fully and finally. There was a good congregation, and great attention paid to the discourse. I felt liberty in speaking, and had some solemn feelings which, I think, showed themselves in the sermon. I should like you to have heard it. The reporter was there. I was quite comfortably lodged and well waited upon, and treated with the greatest kindness and affection.

Many thanks, dear friends, for your kindness to me and mine. The Lord repay it a hundredfold into your own bosom. I am not sorry for my visit, and the friends here tell me how much better I am looking.

Yours affectionately,
J. C. P.

CCLXXIX—To Mrs P. and Miss M.

London, July 27, 1869.

My dear Friends in the Lord,

I received and have acted on your kind orders for the books to the three places, which will no doubt be executed with the usual care and punctuality.

I was helped through last Lord's-day, though the heat was great and the congregations large; my texts were, Rom. vi. 21—23, Ezek. xxxiv. 15, 16. Mr. Ford was there both times. I cannot say much about the sermons, but they were listened to with great attention. We had a collection for the Aged Pilgrim Friend Society, and raised, I think, about £47. I contrasted the meanness of some of the collections (see page 97 of the "Report") with the liberality of others, and named my dear people of Oakham as standing third or fourth on the list. The secretary told me that in some of the Church of England collections the expenses swallowed up the whole or nearly the whole amount.

Dear Rebecca! I felt much for and with her, and could weep with those that weep—at least in some measure. How much better her state than a dead calm. I cannot add more as I have to preach this evening, and expect a large congregation.

The Lord bless you both with much of His manifested presence and love.

Yours very affectionately in Him,
J. C. P.

CCLXXX—To Mrs. Peake

Allington, Aug. 6, 1869.

My dear Friend,

. . . . . .

We had, I trust, a good day at Calne Anniversary on Wednesday. The large chapel which was lent to us was thronged with people, and the collection for the Aged Pilgrim Friend Society was £30 12*s.* 4*d.*, reduced by necessary expenses to £27 17*s.* 6*d.* Mr. Taylor preached an able and faithful sermon from Micah vi. 8. I had preached from the same text at Gower Street this visit, and W——, who heard both sermons, said how much we ran in the same track. I preached from my old text, part of Jer. xv. 19, and had some life and liberty. My texts here on Lord's-day were, John xvi. 33, Exod. xxxiii. 15, 16. It was generally considered a good day, one of the best we have had at Allington for some time. I may, D.V., preach from the texts in London that they may be published, as I had some sweet thoughts and feelings on and in them. I seemed to see, as I never saw before, the connection between our dear Lord's overcoming the world and the path of tribulation.

Tell dear —— that, in overcoming the world, the Lord has overcome *all* in it, therefore her *bodily* tribulation, which He holds in His hands as a conquered foe and lets out just enough of its power to afflict but not overwhelm.

Such a desire was expressed at Calne for the publication of my "Meditations on the Ephesians," that I think of doing so. I found the same feeling in London.

Yours in love,
J. C. P.

CCLXXXI—To Mrs. P. and Miss M.

Croydon, August 27, 1869.

My dear Friends in the Lord,

In reply to the kind inquiry I am thankful to be able to say that through mercy I am recovering from my late attack, which indeed was brought on more by fatigue and over-exertion than from taking cold. As then I have obtained a little rest, it has been blessed to my relief. I need not tell you that it is a great trial to me to be again obliged to disappoint the friends who in various places were looking forward in expectation of once more hearing my voice. It was, however, so widely made known that I could not come to Abingdon, that there was not so much disappointment there. The chief difficulty is how my place is to be supplied at Gower Street on so short a notice. . . .

I wish I could send you a favourable account spiritually to counterbalance what I have said of myself naturally; but I have felt very flat and lifeless during this last visitation, with more peevishness and fretfulness under the weight of the cross than last year, when there seemed to be much more life and feeling under its pressure than now. This want of divine support and the movements of divine life makes me less able to bear the cross with submission to the will of God. It also very much spoilt my visit at Allington, for I could neither walk nor talk, and spent most of my time alone after the first fortnight. It teaches me, however, my dependence for every spiritual movement upon the Lord, and that without Him I can do nothing. I preached only on two Lord's-days at Allington; but they were days to be remembered, especially the first, and the blessing of God upon the word was somewhat remarkable from its being so generally felt by the spiritual part of the congregation. The second Lord's-day was very wet and cold, and I preached twice, with my chest in pain, and was much exhausted afterwards. But I believe it was a good day for the people, as my mind was much weighted and solemnised by the load I was carrying. I feel thankful I have reached my own home; though in this large town, we are almost as quiet and as retired from noise as if we were far in the country.

Yours very affectionately in the truth,

J. C. P.

CCLXXXII.—To Mrs. Peake

Croydon, Sept. 16, 1869.

My dear Friend in our Gracious Lord,

I feel much obliged to you and your dear sister for the kind and affectionate wishes and prayers for me; but I must say that I feel also utterly unworthy of your kind opinion of me, for I think if you knew me such as I see and know myself to be, it would alter your judgment. Still, if the Lord is pleased in His sovereign grace to make use of me in any way for the good of His Church and people, to Him be all the glory.

The obituary in this month's *Gospel Standard* is certainly a very marked instance of the power of sovereign grace. Dr. D., of the "Gospel Magazine," was so blessed in reading it that he wrote to me a letter which you will see in our next number. Surely it is very gracious of the Lord, and shows His tender care over His people that He should give the *Gospel Standard*, with all its infirmities, such acceptance and such a wide circulation amongst those who fear His name. Our Lord said, "That which ye have spoken in the ear in closets, shall be proclaimed upon the house-tops." And thus letters like those of Miss V., and the experience of E. W., come abroad and reach the ears and hearts of thousands. I am sorry to say that I still continue very poorly, and do not seem to shake off my complaint or to regain strength. It appears as if there was some irritation going on which makes me very short-breathed, and at times feverish. But C., who listens very carefully to the sounds of my chest, thinks it is gradually subsiding. At my age, and after so many attacks of the same complaint,

I must naturally expect slower returns to convalescence. I was enabled to get through my sermon for Mr. Ford before it came on, and the obituary for *Gospel Standard*, which I could hardly have attended to otherwise. One trying effect of illness is that it weakens the mind as well as the body, impairs the power of close thought and attention, and but for special help seems also to weaken faith and waiting on the Lord.

Had my visit to Oakham been deferred to this month, it would have been impossible for me to come among you. There was, therefore, a mercy so far that I was enabled to visit you at a more favourable season, and when I was better and stronger.

I was much pleased to hear that Mrs. S. had been blessed lately in hearing our dear friend Mr. K. It was what she had much longed and prayed for, but felt that it was not in her power nor his to bring the desired blessing. I have much union with her in the things of God, and much admire her general spirit, singleness of eye, and spirituality of mind. I wish there were more like her; but God is able to raise up, both at Oakham and Stamford, a fresh crop when the present shall have been gathered into His garner. But no man having drunk old wine straightway desireth new, for he saith the old is better; and I do not think we shall ever feel the same union with the new as we have had with the old members and saints, so many of whom are now gone home.

Yours very affectionately in the Lord,

J. C. P.

CCLXXXIII —To Mr. W. Harrodine, late Servant to Mr. Robert Pym

Croydon, Sept. 29, 1869.

Dear Friend in the truth,

I can only send you a few lines in answer to your kind and interesting letter. I remember very distinctly your speaking to me in Gower Street vestry, for I was struck with what you said about hearing Mr. Pym speak of praying over the Bible, and what conviction it wrought in your mind. I have frequently thought that Mr. Pym's last few letters contain some of the sweetest and clearest Gospel truths that I know; he had such clear and blessed views of the Person, glory, and work of Christ as are rarely met with, but which found a blessed response in my heart. Of all the Church of England ministers in these last days who preach the truth, I think he was the clearest, soundest, most separating and experimental.

But I must now answer your two questions:—1. As regards the sermon which I preached at Gower Street from Heb. x. 35—37; it was not taken down, nor do I remember at this moment whether it is to be found in any other of my sermons published by Paul or Justins. 2. As regards my health, it is not very strong at this present time, as I have had an attack lately of my old complaint, a kind of chronic bronchitis, which has pulled me down a good deal, and made me very susceptible of the least external cold. But all these things I desire to take as so many warnings that my race will soon be run; at present my mind seems very dark, but I am still looking up to the Lord that He would shine upon my soul and dispel every dark cloud of night.

I cannot add more this evening; but wishing you the enjoyment of every new Covenant mercy,

I am,
Yours affectionately in the truth,
J. C. P.

CCLXXXIV —To Mr. James Churcher

Croydon, Oct. 15, 1869.

Dear Friend in the Lord,

I had not heard of the removal of your late partner in life until the receipt of your kind and affectionate letter. You have indeed sustained an irreparable loss, but you have the sweet satisfaction of knowing that she is with that dear Lord whom she believed in and loved whilst here below. I will, as far as my health and time admit, look over any account which you may send to me of the Lord's dealings with her in providence and grace. I shall then be able to form a better judgment how far it may be desirable to insert it in the *Gospel Standard*. You can, if you like, write copiously, though I think for the most part that a concise account is preferable, as many things which may appear of importance to relatives may not appear so to general readers, and it is difficult to abridge and suppress a long account, not only as requiring judgment and giving trouble for the pen, but also as breaking the links which often connect the whole into one chain. Though, therefore, I have said you might if you like write copiously, yet if you could compress the best parts of her life and experience into a smaller compass it would be desirable. In fact, most writers are too lengthy and prolix, and spoil what is really good by mixing up with it what is of little value; for it is in writing, and indeed in religion and in everything else, that what is most valuable is most scarce, and lies usually in a very small compass.

Give my love to all the friends with whom you stand in union.

Yours affectionately in the Lord,
J. C. P.

CCLXXXV.—To Mrs. P. and Miss M.

Croydon, Oct. 20, 1869.

My dear Friends in the Lord,

You will perceive from the handwriting that I have got back my junior secretary, and very glad we all are to welcome her home after her long absence; nor could I have spared her so long had it not been for the sake of my poor invalid sister, to whom she was a great comfort in reading to her out of the Word of God, Bourne's Letters, &c. She is quite confined to her bed, and says that she has little wish to live. She has at times been much favoured with the presence of the Lord, and, taking her experience throughout, has known more of His gracious visitations, applications of the word with power, marked answers to prayer, &c., than many have enjoyed. She has not, indeed, much to live for, though much attached to her relatives and taking great interest in their welfare.

But you will be desirous to know a little about myself. During the warm weather I got out most days, and though the heat was somewhat oppressive, yet the fresh air and exercise were very beneficial. But this sudden change has somewhat tried me and given me a little cold, which I trust, however, may pass off by keeping closely within doors till the weather is warmer. I have just finished my *G. S.* work and revising the sermon, and generally feel for two or three days afterwards a need of almost absolute rest. The mind, and its organ the brain, will not endure more than a certain amount of labour, and to go beyond that, sooner or later, is sure to tell upon it. I have, so to speak, husbanded my mind for many years, never pushing it beyond a certain point, and then by exercise, or rest, or sleep, endeavouring to fit it anew for fresh labour. By doing this, and the blessing of God resting upon it, I have been enabled to do a great deal of work, and to do what I have done carefully and thoughtfully, without which nothing can be really well done. I am sure, my dear friend, you can sympathise with me in this, as your own mind being so much occupied is often jaded and worn out and needs rest.

But of all rest the best is that when we can rest where God rests—in His dear Son; to cease from our own works and rest wholly and solely in the blood and righteousness and finished work of the blessed Lord. And how graciously and tenderly He invites us to do so! Matt. xi. 28, 29. We are often poor, restless creatures, looking here and there and everywhere but to Him who hath said, "O Israel, thou hast destroyed thyself, but in Me is thy help." And we well know that all the rest and peace that we ever have got in times past, or get now, is by believing our interest in Him, and in what He has done and suffered to save poor sinners from death and hell. How suitable He is to all who from sheer necessity cleave to Him, and find at times a blessed sweetness in looking to Him and leaning and hanging upon Him!

There often is for a long time a contention in the soul against God's way of salvation, either from self-righteousness or gloomy despondency. We are unwilling sometimes to see the worst of ourselves, or to believe we are as bad as Scripture and conscience tell us; and then, again, when some light shines into the mind to show us what we are, the greatness of our sins and the dreadful nature of sin generally, then it seems as if there was scarcely ground for hope. Sometimes unbelief, or infidelity, or impenitency, or rebelliousness, and various other startings up of the carnal mind stand as obstacles to salvation, which nothing can remove but the power of the Lord subduing the heart into faith and repentance. When, then, we can come out of our wretched selves and receive God's salvation as a free gift of His unspeakable and superabounding grace, then, and then alone, is there rest and peace.

I have been obliged rather to curtail my "Meditations," as I wished to finish the chapter by the end of the year, and shall therefore have to pass over much that otherwise I should like to unfold at greater length. But it is not well to tire readers, for long meditations are like long sermons, which weary when they should edify.

My little work on Popery is, on the whole, going off pretty well. There have been some favourable reviews of it, one of which, in the *Morning Advertiser*, I send herewith, and as I think you do not see the *Gospel Magazine*, I will also send that.

I hope that dear Miss M. continues pretty well, and that you, my dear friend, are enabled to bear up against all discouragements.

Yours very affectionately in the Lord,

J. C. P.

CCLXXXVI—To Mr. Copcutt

Croydon, Oct. 25, 1869.

My dear Sir,

I should have written earlier to acknowledge the receipt of your long and interesting letter had I not thought that the fulfilment of your order for the books, which I attended to immediately, would have shown you that it had come safely to hand. I hope, therefore, that the parcel reached you safely. I added to your order one or two books which you had not named, and instead of sending you Berridge's "Christian World Unmasked," sent you the whole of his works as I thought you would find them interesting. Though there is a great deal of quaintness and almost levity in most of his writings, he was a man well taught in the things of God, and a burning and shining light in his day and generation. His "Songs of Zion" I consider peculiarly valuable as containing so much true Christian experience, and unfolding both sides of the question,—I mean what we are by nature, and what we are by grace, with the varied phases of the life of God in the soul. They were written during various illnesses, when he could not get out to do his beloved work of preaching the Gospel; and though they were written out of his heart, and have proved such a treasure to the people of God, yet he himself thought so little of them that he was minded again and again to throw them into the fire. England has no such men now as appeared in that day; for we are sadly sunk in all that pertains to vital godliness, and I fear much resemble the state of that Church of which we read that it had a name to live but was dead. The most active men in the Church of England, or the Established Church, are the Ritualists, who, in fact, are disguised or rather undisguised Papists, and who would very gladly join the Church of Rome, if they could be received on equal conditions, or take their preferments with them. But I think there is almost more danger to be apprehended from a small but powerful party called the Broad Church, but who, in fact, are secret infidels, as doubting the inspiration of the Scriptures, the miracles, the prophecies, and everything in the Word of God of a supernatural kind. These men avail themselves of every discovery in science, to oppose thereby the Word of God as a divine revelation; and as infidelity is deeply rooted in the human heart, and their views and arguments are very plausible, there are very many no doubt who are deeply tainted with this infidel spirit, who for various reasons dare not give full expression to their inward sentiments. In fact, true religion is as much a matter of divine, inward revelation as the Word of God of divine, outward revelation; and thus where there is no spiritual work of God's grace in the heart, there there is no real means of proving the Word of God to be His inspired revelation. But it is impossible for an enlightened mind and a believing heart not to see that the historical and supernatural parts of God's Word are so blended and intertwined that they must stand or fall together. And indeed, I may say that the same spiritual light which discovers the emptiness and hollowness of a mere ceremonial religion, such as Ritualism, discovers also the fearful character of infidelity; and thus the Christian finds no rest except in believing God's testimony in the word, and through the word in his own heart. But I almost forget that I am writing a letter and not an essay, though as you are surrounded by the same or similar evils, you may perhaps find something not uninteresting in the above remarks.

We have had, on the whole, a fine spring and summer. I was staying during the harvest at Allington, Wilts, of which some mention is made in the obituary of the Wilds (in the *Gospel*

Standard, for last April), under the roof of an old friend whom I have known for more than thirty years. Though for a part of the time I was very unwell, yet I enjoyed the quiet of a retired village after the noise and bustle of London. I was at Gower Street Chapel for two Lord's-days in June, and in the early part of July paid my annual visit to my old friends at Oakham and Stamford. They received me with much affection, and I preached to large congregations; the sermons were taken down by Mr. Ford, and will in due course be all published. I do not know whether my sermons are sent you, but you are no doubt aware that one is published every month, and they have a wide circulation.

You ask me if I know when Mr. Huntington's first wife died. I do not know, though I have often tried to obtain it from his works. She never rose with him, if I may use the expression, but always continued in mind and manner an uneducated woman. He, on the other hand, was one of nature's gentlemen, and in advanced life quite courteous and dignified.

I was at Stadham from the year 1828 to 1835, preaching there and at Chislehampton, a village near. I have had hearers there from eighteen different parishes, counted as such, besides others, probably, unknown.

Mr. Abrahams made a good end. He was sound in the truth, especially on such grand points as the Trinity, the Sonship of Christ, &c. He suffered a good deal in his last illness, but was much supported and often spoke of the wondrous grace of God in bringing him, a poor Jew, from Poland to this country, and calling him to a knowlege of Himself.

I have just published a little work on the advance of Popery, consisting chiefly of articles which have appeared in the *Gospel Standard*, but partly rewritten, and much rearranged. It is selling pretty well; but there is a general apathy in this country about the advance of Popery, which seems likely much to favour its progress. It is coming in chiefly through the medium of the Established Church; hundreds, probably, of its ministers being deeply infected with it.

We are glad to hear tidings about your family, for we have a very distinct and pleasing recollection of them all. You appeared when we knew you to be a very united family, and that pleasing sight is unhappily rare.

I hope you have not suffered from the storms and floods, both in the pecuniary and physical world, of which we have read so much. The various journals and communications from your side of the Atlantic gives us much interesting information. What a country it is! How vast its elements of material wealth; and how wonderful the energies of the people! Oh, if the grace of God did but work mightily in that vast field, what a harvest would it render! But all accounts seem to tend the same way, to show the general absence of spiritual vital religion. But it always has been the case that only a remnant, according to the election of grace, loved and served God.

I was much interested in your account of the life and death of your old friend who saw so many vicissitudes. We must come to the end of our race in the appointed time. May we finish our course with joy! My dear wife and family unite with me in affectionate regards to Mrs. Copcutt, and all your family, wishing them with you the best of blessings.

I am, my dear Sir,
Yours very sincerely, for truth's sake,
J. C. P.

CCLXXXVII —To the Rev. Dr. Doudney

Croydon, Nov. 5, 1869.

My dear Sir and brother in one common hope,

I feel sorry to be obliged to return the MS. which you have kindly sent me for insertion in the *Gospel Standard.* I do so reluctantly, but there are various reasons which have induced me to come to this conclusion; and I trust that I shall not in briefly naming them say anything which may wound your mind or hurt your feelings.

1. And first let me drop a few remarks upon the communication itself. I cannot at all understand, or at least see, with you in the first case which you have brought forward as a victory over death. The lady whom you name as so smiling before the king of terrors, was evidently not doing so under the smiles of the Lord, as her experience, if it be worth the name, was but at least a faint hope in God's mercy; and I can hardly understand how she could say, "I am very low-spirited," and acknowledge her want of more faith, and yet smile and almost laugh at death. At any rate, I feel that I could not bring it before my readers as a proof of triumph in death, whatever secret encouragement it may have administered from other causes to your soul.

2. But apart from my objection to the insertion of this particular article, I have other reasons which I trust will not pain your mind when I say they have induced me to decline its insertion.

I have hitherto for many years maintained a separate position from all other religious periodicals, and chiefly for this reason, that I have felt to obtain thereby greater liberty in thought, word, and action. I inserted your last communication as a matter of simple equity and justice; but if I were to go on inserting your communications, however excellent they might be, it would appear to many like a coalescing with you, and to do so would seem to involve on my part a sinking of many and wide differences which still exist between us, and would so far almost nullify, and as if stultify, not only those differences, but much of what I have publicly said and written connected with my secession from the Establishment.

3. I have therefore to consider also my numerous readers, and that large body of churches of truth, including both ministers and members, of which the *Gospel Standard* is the usually recognised representative and organ, many of whom might thereby be much led to feel that I was departing from that peculiar and separate position which I have so long occupied, if I kept inserting pieces by editors of other magazines, and especially of any connected with the Establishment.

At present we have each our own peculiar work to do—each our own circle of readers—each our circle of friends and adherents; and in that circle we can move with more freedom than if we went out of it to unite with any other under the idea of Christian union, which often involves, if not a compromise of principle, yet a sacrifice of freedom of action. I feel, therefore, that I must not do anything which would at all imply that I am abandoning my present ground to occupy one different from that on which I have so long stood.

I greatly fear that I shall not succeed in conveying to your mind my exact feelings upon this point, and that what I have written may seem to you to spring from an unchristian narrowness of spirit, or even an exclusive "stand-by-thyself" feeling which is very foreign to my inmost mind. Thus I may wish a man well in the name of the Lord, and desire that the blessing of God may rest upon him and his ministrations, with whom on other grounds I could not unite. Take, for instance, the late Mr. Pym, or the late Mr. Parks. There are very few men with whom I have felt more union of soul and spirit than with the former, some of whose letters I consider to embody in the sweetest experimental way the precious truths of the Gospel. On such a man I could wish with all my heart that the blessing of God might rest both in his own soul and in his pulpit ministrations; but I could not unite with him as a minister in the Establishment without falsifying all my own experience when I was in it, and by which I was brought out of it. They, like you, had their special work to do, and God owned and blessed them in it. Nor, would I if I could have done so, brought them out of the sphere of their labours by a move of my hand, though I would not myself have done what they did, and as you must do, by continuing ministers in it. In their own sphere of labour they were most useful, and met with the usual reproach of faithful labourers. As such I honoured and esteemed them, though I could not unite with them; and, in a similar way, I desire that the blessing of God may rest upon you and your ministry, both by tongue and pen, though I could not unite with you in either.

After this, which I fear may be to you a somewhat painful explanation, allow me to add that I am very glad to recognise in this month's "Gospel Magazine" various indications which to my mind prove that you have received much benefit from your late painful and trying experience. I was especially glad to read what you say on page 563, upon the Lord's servants being "called to encounter dark and dismal depths, in order that a clearer, closer, deeper, more scriptural line of teaching and personal experience should be the more earnestly and perseveringly insisted upon." It is from want of this searching ministry that there has been so much dead and dry doctrinal preaching in men professing truth, without that "deep, heartfelt, experimental, testing-and-trying, probing-and-proving" ministry of which you have so well spoken. It is surprising what a deal of dross, hidden from ourselves, is purged away in the furnace of temptation, and I can well sympathise with what you say at the top of page 563, where you speak of a temptation of which I have known, and even now know, so much, but by passing through which many years ago, I was first taught the difference between that faith which is natural and notional, and that faith which is the expressed gift and work of God.

Wishing you, my dear sir, every blessing of the new and everlasting covenant ordered in all things and sure, and thanking you for your kind sympathy with me and desires for me,

I am, yours very affectionately in our gracious Lord,

J. C. P.

[Note.—The above letter to the Rev. Dr. Doudney, editor of the "Gospel Magazine," was published in that periodical, January 1870, and in the *Gospel Standard* for June, 1870. The reader will easily glean from the letter itself the circumstances which led to its being written.]

CCLXXXVIII.—To Mrs. P. and Miss M.

Croydon, Nov. 22, 1869.

My dear Friends in the Lord,

I fear that you will think me very neglectful in taking no earlier notice of your kind communications, especially as they contained so much connected with the severe and painful trials of our dear friend Mr. K. But I have been more than usually busy with the *Gospel Standard* this month, both as regards the obituary and the meditations. The great difficulty with the former was the number of letters from which I had to choose, and the long account which the poor husband had written of his wife's sufferings which it was necessary much to abridge; and the difficulty was what to take and what to leave, as the whole was exceedingly interesting. But I trust that though I have been obliged to condense and abridge the account, I have preserved the most interesting and profitable part. I hope also that the short account which Mrs. S. has furnished us of the experience of the late Mrs. B. will appear in the supplement; and I have appended to it a few observations of my own as a testimony to the weight and worth of her Christian character. A few notes have been sent me from Stamford of the experience of the late Mrs. K., but I have deferred their insertion as hoping to be able to glean up from some of the friends a fuller and clearer account. Had her obituary been inserted there would have appeared in one number the death of three of my old members; two at Stamford, and one at Oakham. How loudly and strongly do these things speak to us, "Be ye also ready." But, alas! how can we prepare ourselves for our great change? The Lord alone can make us meet for the inheritance of the saints in light, and when the time for our dismissal comes favour us with dying faith in dying moments.

I have not yet answered our friend S.'s letter. I am very doubtful whether he can ever reap much advantage from attempting to read the New Testament in the original. It is a most difficult language to acquire to be of any value, and must be learnt in youth when the memory is active and strong. If he is fond of reading and wishes to study I should much rather recommend him to read our great and godly Puritan writers, such as Owen, Sibbes, Charnock, &c. But study even of these writings is often more apt to make a man book-learned than feed his soul and put life into his ministry. This must have been the result of the dealings of God with his soul, a knowledge of sin and salvation, a prayerful study of the word of truth, and a living under the teaching and testimony of the blessed Spirit. I have been, and still in good measure am, a diligent student of the word of truth in the original languages, and a reader of the writings of godly men; but all this I have found very insufficient in the day of trial and temptation, and of very little benefit as regards the ministry. Nothing but the work and witness of the blessed Spirit through the word of his grace can bring any life or feeling, power or comfort to my heart, or enable me rightly to divide the word of truth and speak or write effectually to the hearts of God's people. My learning, therefore, such as it is, is but of little use in seasons of affliction and trouble to speak peace to a burdened conscience, or assure my soul of its interest in atoning blood and dying love.

I am thankful to say I am pretty well in health, but much confined to the house. Indeed I rarely get out except on the Lord's-day to chapel, which I usually do when the weather is not too cold or wet. My sons are living in London together, in lodgings, and thus the younger has the benefit of the older's instruction, and the older the younger's company, and as they are much united in brotherly affection it adds much to the comfort of each.

They generally come down here every Saturday, returning on Monday.

I have not heard much how the obituary of poor Mrs. Prentice has been received, except the two letters which I forward; but I have no doubt from my own feelings that it has made a deep impression upon many hearts. What the people of God want is reality and truth, life and power, simplicity and godly sincerity, not confused, indistinct, laudatory, "cooked" accounts, but something which speaks for itself that God was in it. It was this feature which made the account of the Wilds so acceptable, and good old Mrs. Freeman, and the same is stamped, I think, more clearly still on the words and experience of Mrs. P. It may be a fulfilment of the words which were spoken to her, "What thou doest, do to My glory." This may now be done in the glory brought to God by her striking account of His work upon her soul and the letters which I insert this month.

Yours most affectionately in the truth,

J. C. P.

CCLXXXIX.—To Miss Richmond

Croydon, Nov. 22, 1869.

My dear Friend,

. . . . You enquire very kindly about my health. It is, I am thankful to say, better than it often is, though I am much confined to the house, and rarely get out except on the Lord's-day, when, if the weather be tolerably fine, I usually manage to get to chapel, which I feel to be a privilege as well as a benefit. It is, indeed, my mercy, and I hope for many others also that though laid aside from the active work of the ministry, I am yet enabled to use my pen in the service of the Lord; and I am thankful to say that I have had many sweet testimonies of the blessing of God resting on what I have been enabled to put forth in His name. And I hope the Lord may enable me still to contend earnestly for the faith once delivered to the saints, and still attend it with His power and blessing.

I had not heard of the death of your dear little nephew, nor that your school was broken up in consequence. It must have been a great trial to you in every way, but I am glad to find that that you were favoured with resignation to the Lord's will, and had some words to assure you that it was not in anger but from His dear covenant love. How different might it have been with you if the Lord had suffered the rebellion of your heart to rise, and how much more it would have added to the weight of the trial! It is indeed a mercy when we can fall into the hands of the Lord, and see and feel that—

"He is too wise to err,
Too good to be unkind."

I am glad to hear that you have peace and union in the church, and that the Lord still is adding to you such as shall be saved.

With regard to my coming to Abingdon for two Lord's-days next summer, I fear it will not be in my power to do so. Indeed, I often think that my preaching days are over, as I have not strength for the work, and you know that this summer I was not able to fulfil my engagement, nor do I think it likely that I shall be able to go to Gower Street next year, as I have done for so many years. At any rate I could not make any promise of coming to Abingdon, though I should be very glad to see my friends there once more. It is now many years that I have known some of them, and it is a mercy that amidst so many storms of sin and Satan, temptation and trial, we have been able thus far to stand. None but the Lord can hold us up, and I trust that he will do so even to the end.

I am sorry to hear of poor John Hatt's trial, and will endeavour to bear him in mind, though I have so many applications of a similar kind that I greatly fear I shall not be able to get him on the society. My last nomination was of Sarah Adcock, of Uppingham, who has kept her bed for more than thirty years, suffering at the same time almost continual pain. How true it is that through much tribulation we are to enter the kingdom of heaven. And I trust that your afflicted sister at Stadham may find it so, and that her afflictions may be blessedly sanctified to her soul's good. We unite in affectionate love to you and with my love to all the friends,

I am, yours very affectionately,

J. C. P.

CCXC.—To Mr. S

Croydon, Nov. 24, 1869.

Dear Friend in the Truth,

I have not been able for several reasons to reply to your interesting and affectionate letter, and even now fear that my answer will fall very short of my wishes, as I cannot take up the various points which it has opened up.

But, first, let me notice that I am truly glad you should have found the experience of Isabella Prentice so much commended to your conscience, and that the blessing which my sermon "Winter, &c." was made to her, found a response in your own. I wish you could have heard her tell out her experience yourself, for there was something so marked and original in her expressions, and such life and power stamped upon them. I have usually found that where persons like her have been brought up in perfect ignorance of the way of truth, that when the Lord is first pleased to shine into their soul, it leaves a mark upon them which we do not find in ordinary Christians in whom the light has been more gradual. And I have observed also that those whose lot has been cast under a legal ministry, and who have had to grope and groan under hard burdens, usually come forth into the liberty of truth with greater clearness. But I need not dwell on these points as no doubt you have observed, and I may add, experienced in your own soul the truth of what I have thus stated. I come now therefore to the point on which you have asked my advice, viz.—will it be desirable for you to attempt to study the New Testament in the original language. Now, at your time of life, with your delicate health, and your ministerial engagements, I greatly doubt whether you could ever attain to such a knowledge of Greek as would be of any real service to you. You might learn enough to compare passage with passage, and this might interest you, as for instance, to discover that in 1 John ii. 24, where we have in our translation three distinct words, "abide," "remain," and "continue," it is but one and the same word in the original; but beyond this you would not reap very much benefit, for a critical knowledge of the language requires very great study, a powerful memory, and a cultivated intellect. . . . .

I do not wish to discourage you too much, though I greatly doubt whether you will derive as much benefit as you anticipate. Still you might make the trial, and if I can be of any service to you in giving you directions how to go on, if you name to me your chief difficulties I will endeavour to help you. Your mention of good Mr. Fowler called to my mind what he once said to me in conversation, "Do not give up your Greek Testament." But though I have given you what directions I could about your study of the Greek Testament, yet I think myself that you would derive more real benefit from studying such books as Dr. Owen's various doctrinal and experimental works, Sibbes, and Huntington, than wasting your time and strength on attaining a knowledge of Greek. But I need not tell you that the word of God under the teaching and application of the blessed Spirit must be the food of your soul both privately and ministerially; and you will find that prayerful meditation upon it, and seeking to enter into its divine and spiritual meaning, will often sweetly feed your soul and will fill you at times with such holy admiration of the wisdom and grace of God in the word of His truth, that you will say, "Thy testimonies are wonderful: therefore doth my soul keep them. The entrance of Thy words giveth light; it giveth understanding unto the simple;" and as your soul is under these sweet impressions of the truth and power of God's word, you will reproach yourself for not reading it more in the same way. But when you try again so to read it, and so to feel it, you will find it all gone; darkness and confusion will cover your mind and even a disinclination felt to reach the Word of God at all.

I hope you may be encouraged in the work to which you set your hand. If of God, as I hope it is, for I well remember our little meetings at ——, you will find encouragements as well as discouragements. Do not seek for or expect great things, which are usually very deceptive, but seek after real things, to feel the life and power of God in your own soul, and a sweet flow of his unction and grace for the souls of others. You will then have the satisfaction of a conscience made tender in God's fear, and his approbation to rest upon your spirit.

Your wife is in a safe though not a happy place. The time will come when she will say "Thou hast loosed my bonds."

Yours very affectionately in the truth,

J. C. P.

CCXCI —To Mrs. Isbell

Croydon, Nov. 25, 1869.

My dear Fanny,

I am sorry to learn that you are so depressed both in body and mind; but the two are probably much connected with each other, and therefore I trust that as you obtain some relief from your present indisposition you may find some corresponding change for the better in your mind and spirits. But you have lived long enough in this vale of tears, and have also learnt in soul experience, that it is through much tribulation we enter the kingdom of God, that trials and troubles do not come upon you without the gracious permission and are under the wise regulation of the Lord. And it is your mercy that in times past, even if not now, you have found Him a very present help in time of trouble, and that He can by His presence and His power support the soul under the heaviest load. Now it is a most blessed truth, whether you can lay hold of it or not, so as to feel the comfort of it, that those whom the Lord loveth He loveth unto the end, and that neither life nor death nor any other creature is able to separate that soul from the love of God which is in Jesus Christ our Lord. I hope, therefore, that amidst all your depression of spirits and darkness of mind you may be able to hold fast by the faithfulness of God. He has in times past given you many sweet promises, manifestly answered your prayers, been with you in providence, and blessed you in grace. Now, therefore, when you are come to those days of which the wise man says that "the grasshopper is a burden," I hope the Lord may appear for and shine into your soul. It is an infinite and unspeakable mercy that the work of our gracious Lord is a finished work, that He has put away sin by the sacrifice of Himself, that our salvation is not a work for us to perform, but that those who are saved are saved in the Lord with an everlasting salvation. And you will find that the more you are enabled to believe and realise this and can look to and hang upon the Lord alone for salvation and every other blessing, the more peace of conscience you will feel, be more reconciled to the will of God, and have more submission to all that He may see fit to lay upon you.

Our time in this life cannot now be long; we have outlived the rest of our family; and whichever of us is next taken away, the survivor will be the last. As regards this life there is not much in it to make us desirous to live, and yet there is a natural shrinking from death, and even a fear how it may be with us in that solemn hour. But all we can do is to cast ourselves upon the rich mercy, the free, sovereign, and superabounding grace of God, and to look to the Lord to be with us in His blessed presence that we may fear no evil when called to pass through the dark valley of the shadow of death.

I have no doubt that you will much feel the departure of Captain and Mrs. S.; and much pleased indeed am I with the account my daughter gives of his great kindness and attention to you. But it seems as if it were the Lord's will to cut in some way or other every tie which binds you to earth. You have lost your husband, the free use of your bodily faculties, the society of many affectionate friends, the benefit of a gospel ministry, and many privileges once enjoyed; but you have not lost your God. And if all these painful bereavements make you cleave all the more closely to the Lord of life and glory, so as to find all your happiness, rest, peace, strength, help, and hope in Him, you will find a blessing couched in all these losses and sufferings. I do not often write to you; but I do not the less feel for and pray for you, desiring of the Lord that he would bless your soul with His presence and promises, and grant you faith and patience even to the end.

We are very glad to have dear S. back, and indeed I greatly missed her, not only on account of her usefulness in writing, but her affectionate attentions.

I am, through mercy, pretty well, but keep much to the house, except on the Lord's-day, when, if the weather be tolerable, I get to chapel.

We are all, through mercy, pretty well, and unite in love to yourself and our dear relatives.

Your most affectionate brother,

J. C. P.

APPENDIX

APPENDIX

It has been found necessary to gather into an appendix a few selections from Mr. Philpot's writings, and some short communications from friends, which, while they were too important to be omitted, could not well be included in the memoir or among the letters.

The two annexed letters were written by J. C. Philpot in reply to a Resolution passed by the Baptist Church, meeting at Zoar Chapel, Great Alie Street, at a Special Church Meeting, held December 11, 1860, and sent to all the ministers who supplied their pulpit. The following is the resolution:—

"It was resolved, 'That this Church hold the faith which they believe to be the faith of God's elect, and revealed to their souls by the power of the Holy Ghost, and in the written Word of God, that our Lord and Saviour Jesus Christ is, and ever was, the eternal Son of God, in his divine nature and person, from all eternity; that had He never taken our nature upon Him, had no worlds been formed, angels created, or Church chosen, God the Eternal Father, God the Eternal Son, and God the Eternal Spirit, would have self-existed in co-equal and co-eternal union, essence, nature, persons, and relationship, in one all-glorious God, and that the same glorious Person, who now sitteth at his Father's right hand, glorified with the glory He had with Him before the world was, and clothed in a body like our own, in His two-fold nature and complex person, is the co-eternal Son of God, the immortal Son of man.'"

"To the Church of Christ assembling for the worship of God, at Zoar Chapel, Great Alie Street, London.

"Dear Friends in the Lord,

"I do not know that I have any right to address you upon the subject of your late Resolution, by which you have expressed your faith in the true, proper, and eternal Sonship of our most blessed Lord; but as I have been invited to do so in the letter which contained a copy of that resolution, I feel induced to do so for the truth's sake.

"I consider that the time is fully come for the Churches of truth in this land to speak out with decided voice. And, indeed, if the churches professing the truth in its experience and power are silent upon such an important point as the Sonship of our blessed Lord, what an encouragement does their silence give to ministers or members who hold error! Such a step may seem at the time to produce contention and confusion, and to cast the Church into much trouble and perplexity. Besides which, as decision in favour of truth is necessarily offensive to those who hold error, it is sure to raise up much enmity and opposition; and as the spirit of erroneous men is almost always a spirit of bitterness and wrath, those who speak out boldly in favour of truth often get much wounded in their feelings by the harsh speeches uttered against them. But let not these things move you. They are the sure and invariable effect of truth speaking with decided voice. I must say that your Resolution does you great credit as a church and people professing the truth as it is in Jesus. Enemies may cavil at it, may criticise its language, and may attempt to overthrow the statements contained in it. But I call it a noble Resolution, bold and faithful, clear and decided, and for the most part expressed in plain, simple, unmistakable language. You have not sheltered yourselves under ambiguous expressions, but have boldly declared what you believe to be the faith of God's elect, and what is revealed to their souls by the power of the Holy Ghost, as contained in the written word of God; and you have in very plain and clear language declared your belief that our Lord and Saviour Jesus Christ is, and ever was, the eternal Son of God in His divine nature and person; and you cut to pieces that erroneous view that He is the Son of God only by virtue of His complex person, by plainly declaring that had He never taken our nature upon Him, God the eternal Father, God the eternal Son, and God the eternal Spirit, would have self-existed in co-equal and co-eternal union, &c.

"It was absolutely necessary for you, dear friends of truth, to have drawn up your Resolution in such clear and decisive terms as to allow no loophole for error to creep in; and by so doing you have shown, as a church, great firmness and decision.

"It now remains with you to be as firm and decided in carrying out your Resolution as in drawing it up or in passing it. I have no authority to dictate to you, or to anybody else, what is your or their duty under such circumstances. But my former connection with you, and, I hope I may say, my love for the truth itself, warrant me in reminding you that all should be of a piece; that it will not do for the Resolution to speak one language and the pulpit another, for then indeed the trumpet would give an uncertain sound. I hope and believe that the Lord will stand by you.

The Lord himself has said, 'He that honoureth not the Son honoureth not the Father which hath sent Him' (John v. 23); and therefore he that honoureth the Son may be said to honour the Father. You will, no doubt, have many trials and perplexities, and may even witness a breach and separation. But the Lord will be with you and that to bless you. Be firm, be steadfast, do not sacrifice the truth of God for any fancied advantage or false peace; but abide by the truth of God as commended with power to your consciences.

"Wishing you, dear friends, the enjoyment of every spiritual blessing,

"I am, yours affectionately in the Lord,

"J. C. P.

"*Stamford, Jan.* 4, 1861."

"To Mr. Lake,

"*Stamford, Jan.* 5, 1861.

"My dear Friend,

"I enclose a letter herewith which I have written to the church of which you are a deacon, which you can, if you like, read to them. I do not think that I should have ventured to do so had you not intimated, when you sent me the Resolution, some desire that I should offer any remarks that I might feel inclined to do upon it.

"Our friend Mr. G. has since sent me what I may call the counter-statement, drawn up by those who are held fast in the error condemned by the Resolution. I have expressed in my letter to the church my opinion upon the Resolution itself. I did not feel myself called upon in that letter to express my views of the counter-statement which has been circulated in opposition to it; but I think I scarcely ever read a more confused piece of writing or one in which there was a greater jumble both of thought and expression. It is easy for men to cavil and censure and ridicule the most solemn mysteries of our most holy faith. But it is perfectly absurd for men to attempt to overthrow the faith of God's elect by such weapons as are there used. I have not time, nor indeed inclination just now to take it to pieces and expose its confusion and its errors; but it is in some sense a good thing for the cause of truth that erroneous men manifest themselves to be so full of confusion and uncertainty.

"I hope that the Lord will give you grace to be bold, firm, and faithful. You are placed in an important post, and great firmness and decision are required of you at this present moment. I do hope that you may be kept from your own spirit and from imitating the bitterness and hostility which they display who are on the opposite side. We are to 'earnestly contend for the faith which was once delivered unto the saints;' but not angrily or bitterly. 'The wrath of man worketh not the righteousness of God.' And the servant of the Lord, whether minister or deacon, should not strive, but be gentle to all, in meekness instructing those who oppose themselves, 'if God peradventure will give them repentance to the acknowledging of the truth.'

"It is not improbable that there may be a separation from you in consequence, and your natural mind may seem to shrink from it, for you may fear that its effect would be to weaken the cause and injure Zoar. But such considerations should not have any influence upon your mind. At best it is but carnal policy to seek to retain enemies of truth in a church which professes it in its life, experience, and power. Such persons are really enemies in disguise, and so far from strengthening the church really only weaken it. They are like bad mortar or rotten bricks in a building, which may add to its size but are rather sources of weakness than of strength. The grand difficulty will be about the pulpit. I do not know who now has the control of the Supplies, but I hope whoever has will take care as far as possible that there be no discordant sound, for it would seem very inconsistent for a church to have drawn up and passed so clear and decisive a Resolution, and then to sit under any minister who holds and preaches views in direct opposition to it. I hope the Lord will guide and direct you. You will much need His support and presence, but a good conscience and the smile of His approbation will support and comfort you under every opposition from without or from within.

"I am, dear Friend,

"Yours affectionately in the Lord,

"J. C. P.

"To Mr. Lake,

"*Deacon of the church at Zoar Chapel,*

Great Alie Street, London."

The following short extracts are selected from sermons and other writings by Mr. Philpot, and will, we are sure, prove acceptable to our readers, for they speak of his inner life, the life of God in his soul:—

The Lot of a Preacher

A.D. 1849.

"It has been my experience in dark and trying moments again and again to envy anybody and everybody who has not to stand up and preach. Sometimes a sense of my unworthiness and unfitness, sometimes a natural repugnance to appear in a public capacity, sometimes deadness and darkness of mind, sometimes a feeling of my many wanderings and general unprofitableness, sometimes powerful temptations and fiery darts, and sometimes the persecutions I have endured, have made me feel the lot of a preacher to be of all the most hard. There are but two seasons when I feel any satisfaction in carrying the seed basket, 1, when I have bread to eat, and corn to sow; and 2, when I hear of instances that I have not carried the seed basket in vain."

The Wilderness

A.D. 1850.

"When I was a Fellow of my College at Oxford, soon after I felt the weight of eternal things, I have sat in the Common Room after dinner with the other Fellows, and amidst all the drinking of wine, and the hum and buzz of conversation, in which I took no part, have been secretly lifting up my heart to the Lord. But I could not go amongst them after I got into the wilderness. The reason was, I was not fully brought out; though there was a blessedness felt in the things of God, yet the evils of the world were not clearly manifested; temptation was not powerfully presented; and therefore, the danger of it was not felt nor feared."

The Cross

From the *Gospel Pulpit*, No. 6.

"And who has not found, in the first approaches of God to his soul, in the first dealings of the blessed Spirit with his conscience, great mountains and hills in the way? Some of these are from natural, but not for that less trying, quarters. How our relatives and friends oppose, perhaps persecute us; how our temporal interests often stand in the way of our conscience, and how, as was particularly my own case, all our worldly prospects and all our long and deeply cherished plans stand as a mountain in the way of taking up the cross and following Christ. My first stroke was the cutting down of all my worldly prospects, for those who could and would have advanced me to emolument and honour were deadly enemies to the truths of the Gospel which I had embraced. The second was sharper still, for it took away my all, and almost stripped me to my last penny. When I was in the Church of England, I thought nothing could bring me out, for I dreaded the prospect of poverty and sickness, as I was at that time in a bad state of health. Oh, what a mountain this was before my eyes! The very thought of leaving, how it worked in my mind, until conscience knocked at the door again and again; and the voice of conscience at last obliged me to listen and obey. But so different was the prospect from the reality, that the day after I left was one of the most comfortable I ever had in my life; and truly wonderful, for more than twenty-three years since, have been the Lord's providential dealings with me."

God's Method of answering Prayer.

From a Sermon preached at Zoar Chapel, June 10, 1841.

"Now there is sometimes in men's minds a kind of confusion in this matter. They are in a certain path, from which they want to be extricated; they are under a trial, from which they want to be delivered; they call upon the Lord to deliver them; and they ask some manifestation of Himself; some going forth of His hand, some divine leading which they are to follow. But the Lord may be working in a very different way from what they think; and they may really be inattentive to the internal voice of God in their conscience, because they are expecting the voice to come in some other way. It was just so with myself. When I was in the Establishment, burdened with all the things I had to go through, and troubled and distressed in my mind, I was calling upon the Lord to deliver me, to lead me out, to show me what to do, to make the path plain and clear. Now that was my sincere cry; but I expected some miraculous interposition—to hear some voice, to have some wonderful leading; and in waiting for that, I was waiting for what the Lord never meant to bestow. And I was brought at last to this internal conviction: suppose I were living in drunkenness, suppose I were living in adultery, suppose I were walking in known sin, should I want a voice from God to say to me, 'Leave this drunkenness, come out from this adultery, give up this sin?' Should I want some divine manifestation to bring me out of a sin, when my conscience bore its solemn witness, and I was miserable under the weight and burden of it? No; the very conviction is the answer of God to the prayer; the very burden which the Lord lays on us is meant to press us out of that in which we are walking. So I reasoned with myself: 'If I am living in sin, if it be a sin to be where I am, if I must do things which my conscience tells me are sins, and by which my conscience is burdened as sins, the very conviction, the very distress, the very burden, is the answer. It is the voice of God in the conscience, not the voice of God in the air, not the appearance of God in the sky, but the voice of God in the conscience, and the appearance of the frown of God in the heart.' And on this simple conviction I was enabled to act, and never to this day have repented it. I have, therefore, been led to see by experience, that we are often expecting wonderful answers, mysterious answers, and the Lord does not mean to give those answers."

Secession from the Church of England, and Ministry at Allington

From the *Gospel Standard*, for April, 1868.

"In March, 1835, after some years' conflict of mind, and prayer and supplication to the Lord, I was enabled to secede from the Church of England, both as a minister and a member, and cast in my lot with the poor despised people of God. At this time, I had no place or people in view among whom to minister; for I went out almost like Abraham, not knowing whither I went; nor, indeed, could I well expect any such door could be opened to me, as my health at that time was so weak, and my chest so tender, that I could not preach twice on the Lord's-day without suffering from it for some days afterwards. But for some time previous to my secession, though at the time unknown to me, a remarkable spirit of prayer had been poured out on a leading member and deacon at Allington, since a dear and valued friend of mine, who had heard of me through my dear brother, the late William Tiptaft, and who knew, through him, the exercises of my mind, that I might leave the Church of England, and come and preach there. He has often since told me how suddenly and unexpectedly (for never having seen me, and having only heard of me through report, he could not himself account for it) this spirit of prayer came upon him; nor could he find any rest in his mind until he had come up to Stadhampton, in Oxfordshire, where I was then residing, that he might hear me preach and form my personal acquaintance. I hope to be excused if I add, that, having accomplished this desire, the spirit of prayer in him was much strengthened and encouraged, though it was more than a year and a half afterwards before I was enabled to secede. Upon this point, however, I do not wish to dwell, or mention other circumstances, all of which worked together to the same point; but I believe that if I could fully detail them, my readers would feel with me, that my going to Allington was one of the most remarkable answers to prayer that are often recorded.*

* I cannot forbear, however, giving an extract from a letter, received a short time since, from the dear friend to whom I have thus alluded:—

"Your coming to Allington was at a most suitable time; and it must have been the Lord's hand and the Lord's will, as the sequel has proved to be. If ever a spirit of prayer was given to me for any one thing, it was on that point, viz., that the Lord would be pleased to send you to Allington. I felt constrained in my feelings at that time, so that it was somehow a pleasure to beg of the Lord that he would answer my prayer. But what the end would be I did not know, or whether I should ever succeed or not. But I am sure of this one thing, that my thoughts at that time were more about you than all my business and everybody else put together—perhaps more than I thought about my own soul's standing. It has been brought very much of late to my mind afresh, and I remember how, when I used to walk about the orchard, my thoughts used to be running about making preparations for you, if you should come, contriving sometimes one plan

"In June, then, 1835, I paid the friends there my first visit, and was with them for five Lord's-days. Having been for some years somewhat sharply exercised in my own mind, not only as to my continuing in the Church of England, but as to my own personal experience of the truth of God, as well as my state and standing for eternity, I may freely say my ministry was at this time of a very separating, searching, and, I believe I may add, cutting character; and having much zeal and warmth as most young soldiers have, I used to cut away right and left, without fearing foe or sparing friend if I thought him wrong. In this spirit, and with this ministry, I went to Allington, where I found a people, both there and in the neighbourhood, who had been accustomed to smoother tidings than those which I brought, and, as I thought, sunk into a dead and flat state of soul. This put a fresh edge on my sword, and I dare say I cut pretty sharply at a lifeless profession. But I have every reason to believe that my going there, and my ministry at that time, judging from the effects, were of the Lord. It is difficult to speak of one's self, and therefore I shall only say that the impression made upon the people by my ministry was very marked. Some fell under it, others fought against it, and some did not know what to make of it, partly because it was a sound to which they were unaccustomed, and partly because they misunderstood my meaning and drift. Amongst these latter at that time was Carby Tuckwell. He treated me with the greatest kindness and respect; but as I spoke sometimes pretty freely of the state of things at Allington, declaring from the pulpit that I believed the deacons were in some measure to blame for it, he was induced to think that I set myself almost personally against him, that I suspected his religion and tried to uproot it as not being genuine. This was not the case, but still such was the impression on his mind. He, however, cordially joined in inviting me to come again, which I did in the following September; and as my ministry became better understood and more fully received by the people, I continued with them not only all the winter, but remained with them, though I always declined their repeated wish to be settled over them, until in the autumn of 1838, when I saw my way to remove to Stamford, though I have never failed visiting them every year, generally for a month, from that time to this."

and then another. Sometimes, I thought, if you would never come here, I would move to wherever you settled. Still I could never move back from calling upon the Lord that you might come here, though often questioning whether I was right. Nor was I ever easy till, after my begging and entreating, he made a way open and answered my cry. Let whatever will take place, I know there was a real spirit of prayer for you on me then, and I feel satisfied that your coming to A. was wholly of the Lord.

"J. P."

Man's Vileness and Helplessness

"I was not stripped, nor brought down for several years after, as I trust, the Lord quickened my soul, though from the first I was led to strive more or less after lawful objects, and could not do without an internal religion. But thorough soul poverty had not laid hold of me; shame and confusion of face had not covered me. I had not then felt what a vile monster of iniquity I was, nor loathed and abhorred myself in dust and ashes. Man's utter helplessness was to me more a doctrine than a truth; I was not acquainted with the mighty overwhelming power of sin, nor had the ploughshare of temptation turned up the deep corruptions of my heart. I, therefore, strove unlawfully. When I fell, as I fell continually, I had some secret reserve in self, some prayers, or repentance, or hopes, or resolutions, to help me out of the ditch."

"I have stuck unto thy Testimonies."

"I know by soul experience that sticking to God's testimonies has kept me from many errors. When I have been placed, years back, before my mind was established in the truth, in circumstances of great trial; when I have seen dear friends fall around me, on the right hand and on the left, some into one error and some into another, and my own mind was driven to and fro by these winds and gusts, it was this solemn conviction that made me stick to that testimony which God had dropped into my heart, not to go into things which I had not known, nor to rush into doctrines which I was not spiritually taught. I have seen some friends dropping first into Arianism, then into Socinianism; others I have known to become Irvingites; some going into one error and some into another. And what then kept me? Why, this solemn conviction, which I trust the Lord himself had implanted, to stick to God's testimony, to cleave to what I had felt, to abide by what I had known, and to hang upon that as the only link which held me up from making shipwreck altogether. And thus the Lord kept me by this powerful though invisible tie, when those who seemed to know more than I departed on the right hand and on the left. Therefore, by soul experience I can, in some measure, say, 'I have stuck unto thy testimonies;' and since then I have felt the solid benefit of sticking to God's testimonies in my conscience, though it has cost me many sacrifices, and often made me on the right hand and on the left to encounter friend and foe. But to stick to God's testimonies will bring peace at last."

The utter Poverty of Man

From a Sermon, preached at Brighton, Aug. 14, 1856, from 1 Cor. ii. 12.

"In the beginning of my experience in the things of God, which is now more than twenty-nine years ago, I had this truth impressed upon my conscience, as I have reason to believe, very powerfully and very distinctly, by the finger of God—that I could know nothing, but by divine teaching; have nothing, but by divine giving; and be nothing, but by divine making. And this truth thus impressed upon my conscience, so far from being erased by any subsequent experience, either of myself or of the Lord, has only been more and more deepened from that time to this. I think I can at times see the wisdom, as well as the goodness, of God, in tracing that truth on my heart in the first beginnings of grace; for I can perceive several benefits springing out of it. Just at that time my natural mind was very strongly bent upon human knowledge, for I had spent many years in various studies; and had it not been counteracted by divine teaching, I might have attempted to make myself a Christian, as I had previously made myself a linguist. Again, it set grace as a divine jewel in my heart's affections, and compared with it, everything else in my eyes was but dung and dross. A third benefit which I see at times to have sprung out of it, was, that it brought me to admire grace in others, wherever I might see it. It not only brought me down to stand on a level with the most ignorant and uneducated who possessed grace, but very often in my soul's feelings sunk me very far below them; for I could see in them clearly that grace which darkness of mind had often hidden from myself. Grace, in the first instance, having thus been commended to my conscience, it has taught me ever since so to esteem, admire, and love it, wherever I can recognize it. Nor do I think that I should be very far from the mark, if I say that the apostle Paul, though I would not be so presumptuous as to compare myself for a moment with him, was not of a different mind; for who so much as he exalted the grace of God, and the teaching and testimony of the blessed Spirit?"

Eternal Life

From the same.

"With God's blessing we will look at a few of these things freely given!

"1. One is Eternal Life. Has your soul ever anticipated in any degree the pleasurable sensation and prospect of eternal life? I remember when I was in the Church of England, and, be it known, I was neither a dead man nor a dead minister then, for if I have the life of God in my soul now, I had it then; and I have living witnesses that my ministry then was blessed to the quickening of souls; but when in the Church of England, I had one day to bury a little child, one of the sweetest children in the poorer walks of life that I ever knew. The funeral being a little delayed, I stood at the grave till they brought the corpse for me to bury; I was very poorly in body but favoured in soul: I looked into the grave, and felt, 'Oh, how sweet to lie down there! I never shall be happy in this life; it is but a scene of affliction and sorrow, and I never shall have a body free from sickness and sin till I have a glorified body.' How sweet to look forward to a happy eternity! What a glorious prospect, when realized by faith—eternal bliss in the presence of God; joy for evermore in that happy, eternal home!"

Life given for a Prey

From a Sermon, preached at Salem Chapel, Landport, Portsmouth, from Jer. xlv. 5, August 22, 1841.

"So spiritually, in all places whither the living soul may come, in whatever state or stage of experience it may be, life is given unto it for a prey. Is the child of God sinking in doubts and fears, and well-nigh overwhelmed with despondency, fearing lest 'of faith he make shipwreck,' and go down into the billows of endless woe? His life is given him for a prey. *Despair* is now seeking to prey upon it; but 'it shall not be given as a prey to its teeth' (Ps. cxxiv. 6). Or has the Lord lifted up upon him the light of his countenance? Even then his life is still given him for a prey. *Presumption* may attack the soul that has been thus favoured, or *pride* make its insidious assault; thus, in either state, an enemy is at hand. If in doubt and fear, despair may open its mouth; if blessed with confidence, presumption or pride may 'war against his soul.' Thus, in whatever state or stage a spiritual man may be, whether a new-born babe, a child, a youth, a man in Christ, or a father or mother in Israel, his life is still given him for a prey; and, in every stage, he has just so much grace given as is needful for him, and only just so much. Thus, the deeper a man's religion is, the more powerful are the enemies that attack him. The babe has little grace and few enemies; the man in Christ and strong in the Lord has enemies proportionate to his strength; the greater the grace, the more the trials; the stronger the faith, the heavier the burdens; therefore, be his state or stage what it may, '*in all places* whither he shall come,' be it the barren sand or the green pastures, the land of great drought, or fountains of living waters—moments of sweet communion, or of guilt and self-condemnation—sorrow after an absent Lord, or enjoyment of a present Jesus; in whatever state or stage of Christian experience he may be, it is still true, 'life is given him for a prey.'

"This then, my friends, is a short epitome of vital godliness. In my right mind, in standing up in this pulpit, or in any other where the Lord's providence may call me, I have, in my right mind, but one object; not to make proselytes to my creed—not to draw together a congregation—not to work upon your natural feelings; but to contend for the power of vital godliness, so far as I am acquainted with it. So far as I am under divine teaching, my desire and aim is not to deceive souls by flattery—not to please any party—not to minister to any man's pride or any man's presumption; but simply and sincerely, with an eye to God's glory, with His fear working in my heart, to speak to the edification of His people, to do the work of an evangelist, and 'to commend myself to every man's conscience in the sight of God.' And depend upon it, that a minister who stands up with any other motives, and aiming at any other ends than the glory of God and the edification of His people, bears no scriptural marks that he has been sent into the vineyard by God Himself; nor will the Lord own his labours, or bless his testimony.

"So far, then, as I have been taught the mysteries of vital godliness, this is the truth that I believe and preach, that spiritual life is the sovereign and free gift of God to his elect—a covenant blessing, given freely in the appointed season; and that this life is maintained by the invincible energy of God the Holy Ghost, as an irrevocable gift, and to shine throughout an endless day. And yet though so freely, so irrevocably given, and so inviolably preserved, yet 'given for a prey'—with difficulty preserved, so to speak, in the midst of enemies. It thus agrees with those words, 'If the righteous *scarcely* be saved;' not 'scarcely' as implying any deficiency in the power of God to save, nor any risk of fatal or final miscarriage, but 'scarcely' on account of the temptations, snares, hindrances, and obstacles with which he is beset.

"If the Lord, then, has been our teacher, He has taught us something of these lessons; we have learned the *sovereignty* of the gift by seeing so many passed by, and us, the most undeserving, visited therewith; its freeness, by knowing our thorough ruin and helplessness; its preservation, by its being kept alive unto this day; and *the manner of its preservation*, by feeling the fangs of so many cruel enemies, and, though cast down, not destroyed. And thus we may set to our seal, that though a rough and rugged —a strange and mysterious way, that yet it is a right way, and one that leads to 'the city which hath foundations,' where there are 'pleasures at God's right hand for evermore.'"

The only-begotten Son of God—Co-eternal and Co-essential with the Father

Extract from Mr. P.'s preface to his tract on "The True, Proper, and Eternal Sonship of the Lord Jesus Christ."

"And now for a few words why I send forth this little work. It is because I wish to leave on record my living and dying testimony to the true and real Sonship of Jesus, and that in a more convenient and permanent form than could be the case were it confined to the pages in which it first appeared. It is a truth which has for many years been very precious to my soul, and one which I trust I can say the Lord himself, on one occasion, sealed very powerfully on my heart. From the very first moment that I received the love of the truth into my heart, and cast anchor within the veil, I believed that Jesus was the true and real Son of God; but rather more than sixteen years ago God's own testimony to his Sonship was made a special blessing to me. It pleased the Lord in November, 1844, to lay me for three weeks on a bed of sickness. During the latter portion of this time I was much favoured in my soul; my heart was made soft and my conscience tender. I read the word with great sweetness, had much of a spirit of prayer, and was enabled to confess my sins with a measure of real penitence and contrition of spirit. One morning, about 10 o'clock, after reading, if I remember right, some of Dr. Owen's 'Meditations on the Glory of Christ,' which had been much blessed to me during that illness, I had a gracious manifestation of the Lord Jesus to my soul. I saw nothing by the bodily eye, but it was as if I could see the blessed Lord by the eye of faith just over the foot of my bed; and I saw in the vision of faith three things in him which filled me with admiration and adoration—1, His eternal Godhead; 2, His pure and holy Manhood; and 3, His glorious Person as God-Man. What I felt at the sight, I leave those to judge who have ever had a view, by faith, of the Lord of life and glory, and they will know best what holy desires and tender love flowed forth, and how I begged of Him to come and take full possession of my heart. It did not last very long, but it left a blessed influence upon my soul, and if ever I felt that sweet spirituality of mind which is life and peace, it was as the fruit of that view by faith of the glorious Person of Christ, and as the effect of that manifestation. And now came that which makes me so firm a believer in the true and real Sonship of Jesus; for either on the same morning or on the next, for I cannot now distinctly recollect which it was, but it was when my soul was under the same heavenly influence, I was reading the account of the transfiguration of Jesus (Matt. xvii.), and when I came to the words, 'This is my beloved Son, in whom I am well pleased; hear ye Him,' they were sealed with such power on my heart, and I had such a view of His being the true and real Son of

God as I shall never forget. The last clause, 'hear ye Him,' was especially sealed upon my soul, and faith and obedience sprang up in sweet response to the command. I did indeed want to 'hear Him,' as the Son of God, and that as such He might ever speak to my soul. Need any one, therefore, who knows and loves the truth, and who has felt the power of God's word upon his heart, wonder why I hold so firmly the true and real Sonship of the blessed Lord? and if God indeed bade me, on that memorable morning, 'hear Him,' what better authority can I want than God's own testimony, 'this is My beloved Son'? For 'if we receive the witness of men, the witness of God is greater: for this is the witness of God which He hath testified of His Son. He that believeth on the Son of God hath the witness in himself.' (1 John v. 9, 10.) But if he has not this inward witness, and for the want of it listens to carnal reason, need we wonder if he make God a liar? Truly did the blessed Lord say in the days of His flesh, 'All things are delivered unto Me of my Father: and no man knoweth the Son, but the Father; neither knoweth any man the Father, save the Son, and he to whomsoever the Son will reveal Him.' (Matt. xi. 27.) It has long been a settled point in my soul, that 'a man can receive nothing, except it be given him from heaven' (John iii. 27), and therefore, if the Son of God has never been revealed with power to their heart, how can they receive Him as such? Happy are they who can say, by a sweet revelation of Him to their soul, 'And we know that the Son of God is come, and hath given us an understanding, that we may know Him that is true, and we are in Him that is true, even in His Son Jesus Christ. This is the true God, and eternal life.' (1 John v. 20.) May I ever hear Him and Him only, and may He speak not only *to* me but *through* me to the hearts of His dear family; and as He has enabled me thus far to defend His dearest title and worthiest name, may He now smile upon the attempt to give it a more enduring form, and to Him with the Father and the Holy Ghost, Israel's triune God, shall be all the glory."

The blessedness of Divine Chastening

From "The Zoar Pulpit," No. 149.

"The Lord sees fit to chasten some in body. In speaking of the case of Hezekiah he says, 'He turned away from all human help, and fixed his eyes wholly and solely on Him who is able to save.' It is in sickness and affliction oftentimes that the Lord is pleased to manifest Himself to our souls, bless us with His presence, and stir up in us a spirit of prayer. I myself am a living witness of it; the greatest blessings I have ever had, the sweetest manifestations of the Lord to my soul have been upon a sick bed. Illness is often very profitable. Bodily afflictions separate us from the world, set our hearts upon heavenly things, draw our affections from the things of time and sense, when the Lord is pleased to manifest Himself in them. And yet there are other times and seasons when we are laid upon a bed of sickness, and yet no blessing is given. I remember once, after the Lord had blessed my soul upon a bed of sickness, when I got a little better and the blessing had worn off, this thought crossed me, 'Oh, your spiritual state of mind was not the effect of grace; you were sick and afflicted; it was that, and not anything specially from God that brought those feelings.' Soon after, I was laid upon a bed of sickness again; had I then the same blessed feelings, the same views of Christ, the same spiritual-mindedness in my soul? Quite the contrary; all was hard, dark, dead, and barren. Then I saw that it was not the sickness that could make Christ known, loved, or precious, but the power of God made manifest in it. And thus, sometimes, we learn from our very barrenness, hardness, and deadness profitable lessons, and are convinced thereby that we are utterly unable to raise up one spiritual feeling in our souls."

Definition of a Christian

Written by Mr. Philpot when at Stadham, in Bunyan's "Grace Abounding," a book belonging to one of his young parishioners.

"Christ is all (Col iii. 11).
E. Ellen Bobart.
July 31, 1832.
1 Cor iv. 20. Heb xiii. 20. 21.

"A true Christian is one that is born of God (John i. 13); believes in the Son of God (John ix. 35); has the kingdom of God within him (Luke xxvii. 21); lives a life of faith in Jesus (Gal ii. 20); has fellowship with the Father and the Son (1 John i. 3); suffers for Christ's sake (Phil. i. 29); is hated by the world (John xv. 18, 19); but is separate from it (2 Cor vi. 17); and fights and conquers every enemy (Rom viii. 37; xvi. 20; Rev. iii. 21)."

In answer to an inquiry from one of the members of his church as to the nature of the promises in the word of God, Mr. Philpot wrote the following excellent lines:—

"The Promises.

"That the promises should be characteristic is but an incidental circumstance, and only a small part, speaking comparatively, of their blessedness. This circumstance neither affects their source nor their character.

"1. Their source is the free grace and eternal love of God. Titus i. 2; 2 Peter i. 4.

"2. They are a part of the everlasting covenant, and are, therefore, separate and distinct from all circumstances and incidents of time. Heb. viii. 6.

"3. They are all 'Yea and Amen in Christ Jesus,' and therefore distinct from all the experience of the saints. 2 Cor. i. 20.

"4. Their foundation is the faithfulness of Him that cannot lie, and therefore independent of all the fruits and graces of the Spirit. Ps. lxxxix. 34—37.

"For promises not characteristic, see Romans viii. 32; ix. 15, 25, 26; xi. 26—29; Heb. xiii. 6; Isa. xi. 9; xliii. 25; xlv. 25; lx. 19, 20."

Posthumous Renown

"A desire not wholly in death to die, but after the mortal frame is returned to its native dust, still to survive in the mind and memory of those whom we leave behind, is evidently a feeling deeply embedded in the human breast. Nor is this desire confined to the individual heart, which seems to covet for itself an enduring remembrance even when it shall cease to beat; it is equally shared in by surviving relatives and friends. From the lowliest gravestone in the country churchyard, to the noble mausoleum in the nobleman's park, or the richly sculptured monument in Westminster Abbey, the desire is equally made manifest, as an all-pervading feeling, that the departed should not be utterly forgotten on earth.

"But of all enduring monuments, none abide the corroding tooth of time like those memorials which the deceased have reared to themselves by their own genius or their own abilities. Stone decays, brass rusts; and were it not so, names as names are soon forgotten; but the works on which genius has impressed its ineffaceable stamp live from generation to generation. This is true, not merely in nature but in grace, and applies not only to those works which are handed down by applauding hands from age to age as a nation's literary treasures, but to those writings also of gracious men which instruct and edify successive generations of the family of God. Many eminent saints have lived of whose former existence no trace now remains; many deeply taught and highly favoured ministers have preached whose very names are now utterly lost. But the same God of all grace, who wrought in their hearts to believe, prompted others of His saints and servants to leave on record either their experience or their testimony to His truth; and thus, though dead, they yet speak in their writings, to the Church of Christ. Their souls have long entered into rest, and their bodies have long mouldered into dust, but they still live in their writings, and their words, which otherwise would have perished with them, are even now as goads and as nails fastened in our consciences by the great Master of assemblies. Men who have lived to themselves all their lives, and never done any real service to God or man, as if they would grasp earth even when forced by death to leave it, seek to perpetuate their memory by monuments of stone or brass, for no living witnesses of their bounty or their benefits rise up to call them blessed; but the faded letters and mouldering stones soon testify that their memorial is perished with them. But where grace has sanctified genius or talent, and employed them in the service of the sanctuary, as labouring with the pen for the glory of God and the profit of His people, not only are the names of such writers embalmed in the memory of the righteous, but as long as their writings endure, God is glorified and His church edified by their works. There might have lived in the seventeenth century preachers as powerful as Bunyan, and ministers as deeply led into the mysteries of truth as Owen; but they have left behind no 'Pilgrim's Progress,' or 'Communion with God,' to instruct and edify the church of Christ for succeeding generations. In the last century, Hart was not the only reclaimed backslider; Newton not the only converted infidel; Berridge not the only Pharisee brought to Jesus' feet; but these men of God still live in their writings, whilst their fellow-sinners, and yet fellow saints, for want of such enduring memorials, are on earth remembered no more."

[Extracted from *G. S.*, Aug. 1860, being the commencement of review of "A Memorial of the late William Peake, of Oakham, Rutland, &c."]

Mr. Covell's Account of his Last Visit

From the *Gospel Standard*.

"Our dear and highly-valued friend, Mr. Philpot, was at chapel on Sunday, Nov. 21, though the weather was too cold for him to have prudently ventured out, on account of his weak chest; yet he was such a lover of God's house, His truths and ordinances, that when health and weather permitted he was sure to be there. When the morning service was over, he came as usual into the vestry, expressed his feelings as to what he had heard, shook hands, and exclaimed, 'Happy art thou, O Israel!'*

"When I called upon him on the following Tuesday, he said he thought he had taken cold. I said he looked so well on the Sabbath that I had been hoping he would take the morning service on the first Lord's-day in December, when he replied, 'I think my preaching is all over. I feel as if I shall not be able to preach again,' and after some further conversation I left him. From that

* Mr. Covell's text that morning was Deut. xxxiii. 29.

time he appeared very poorly, though nothing serious was apprehended, and when I called to see him on December 6, I found him confined to his bed. When I entered his room he said, 'I am very ill; one of my old attacks, but more severe.' I said 'How is your mind?' 'Dark and dead,' he said, 'and nothing short of a manifestation of Christ to my soul will do for me. Hart's hymn suits me well:—

> 'Come needy, come guilty,
> Come just as you are.'

I said 'God will teach us to the last our dependence on Him, for He knows the pride of our heart, that if we could do without Him we would. You remember the last sermon you preached for us—the sealed and open evidences? You have them now,' I said, 'the open ones.' When he answered, it was for the truth, and the truth brought him out from the Church of England in sincerity and faith; and as for the sealed ones, 'Oh,' he said, 'what thousands of prayers and tears have gone up from my heart to God in secret!' 'Then,' I said, 'there is honesty of heart, and the fear of God you are in possession of.' 'Oh! but,' he replied, 'my sins and the many things I look back upon with such shame and sorrow.' Then I said, 'This made Christ so fitting a Saviour that as we came to Him at first, so it must be to the last.—"Have mercy upon us; save, or we perish!" We should not get beyond it.' Knowing how weak he was, I said I would leave him; when he asked me to read him one of Mr. Hart's hymns and a psalm; and he said, 'How often, when you have been tracing out spiritual evidences, I have felt and been sure I possessed them, and how my heart has echoed to them, that I am sure we are of one spirit.' I read hymn 779, in Gadsby's Selection, and said, 'You know what these things are?' He looked and smiled. I then read Psalm xxxviii., and at various verses, oh, how he responded to them! After a few minutes in prayer, in which he responded so feelingly, we shook hands, never to see each other again in the flesh, to hear his voice, or to take sweet converse together.

"I mourn his loss, and feel that I have lost one of the kindest, wisest, and most prayerful of my highly valued and loved friends; but to him it is eternal gain. Blessed soul! Happy man! from sin and sorrow free! His praise is in all the churches; therefore I need say no more.

"FRANCIS COVELL.

"*Croydon, Dec.* 13."

The following letter, addressed to Mrs. Philpot by the late Joseph Parry, containing a graphic account of his early connection with her dear husband, cannot fail to prove interesting. It is a valuable testimony by one who, as his dearest friend, knew perhaps more than any other man of his inmost feelings, and had many opportunities of watching both his public and his private life :—

"*Allington, Nov.* 5, 1870.

"MY DEAR MRS. PHILPOT,

"In forwarding you your late dear husband's letters written to me years gone by, I cannot refrain from referring to a few of the exercises of my mind before I had the pleasure of personally knowing him in the flesh. My mind became impressed in a most remarkable manner through a conversation which I had with your late dear uncle, William Tiptaft, in the year 1832, relative to the state of soul experience through which dear Mr. Philpot, then in the Church of England, was passing. I was told that he was so tried and exercised by fears that he was doing wrong in remaining where he was, his conscience was so burdened with the forms and ceremonies he had to attend to, that he had, moreover, such a weak chest, that if ever he saw his way to leave the Establishment he would be unable to take a large place or congregation, and that it was such a trial to his weak state and troubled mind as few persons had ever gone through. After relating to me very many of his deep soul exercises, and telling me into what a humble, sweet state of mind he was brought down, Mr. Tiptaft said, 'I believe the Lord has so prepared him that he would be satisfied with ever so humble a residence, provided it were dry, not damp, and were wind-tight and water-tight, with a few poor sensible sinners to preach to, rather than remain with the fetters he has now to keep him in bondage. He said to me the other day, "Tiptaft, all that I can now feelingly say is, 'Lord, I am oppressed, undertake for me!'"'

"This conversation made such a deep and lasting impression on my mind that I could never get rid of it. It gave me some little encouragement to hope that as dear Mr. Philpot could not take a large place in a town or anything of that sort, who could tell but the Lord might direct his steps to our little, humble place? and a spirit of prayer and supplication was given me for nearly three years such as I never have before or since experienced for any particular thing, independent of my *own* salvation. I had no rest in my spirit until I had gone up to Stadhampton to see and hear this dear man of God in the church. In the month of October, 1833, my wife and I went; we found the church so thronged with hearers that there was hardly standing, much less sitting, room. I had never seen him in my life, but could not fancy the young clergyman standing there in the desk reading the prayers to be him, from the description our dear friend Mr. Tiptaft had given of him. At length, after the prayers were read, this young gentleman came down, went to what is called the squire's pew, opened the door, and helped the black gown on to a tall and handsome man, who seemed about thirty years of age. The young curate did it so kindly and affectionately towards our friend that it pleased me much to see it.

"Mr. Philpot soon ascended the pulpit, and gave out for his text 2 Cor. iii. 15, 16. I stood up all the time, listening to every word that he said, drinking it in like a thirsty ox. Amongst other deep and experimental things he said that he feared the greater part of his congregation were lovers of pleasure rather than lovers of God, and it was their village feast-day that brought so many to church. The veil of which he had been speaking was over their eyes and hearts, or they could never repeat all those responses they had repeated so loudly, turning and bowing to the east, while some of them were living in the open practice of the very sins they had asked to be delivered from, crying out, 'Lord have mercy upon us, and incline our heart to keep this law.' Whether it was the squire of the parish or the meanest pauper, unless they turned to the Lord the veil was not and never would be taken away. I had never heard such faithful preaching in the Church before.

"After the service was over I handed him a note of introduction which I had from Mr. Tiptaft; he received us very kindly, and at his request we accompanied him across the green to his apartments; and after a little conversation we prevailed on him to return with us in our covered conveyance to Abingdon, about eight miles distant. The old landlady, in whose farm-house Mr. Philpot had rooms, seemed quite astonished that he should think of going out after church time, in the month of October, and in the evening too; it was a thing she had never known him to do before. On the same evening we all went to Mr. Tiptaft's chapel to hear him preach, and a very encouraging, blessed time we had.

"After service I believe we all sat and wept together in Mr. Tiptaft's little room. Our two now dear departed friends appeared to be real brothers. We sat up to a late hour, while Mr. Philpot talked very freely of his troubles about continuing in the Church, saying that if he had more grace he should not do so, and it was the want of grace and faith that kept him in it. I remember his quoting from Jeremiah, 'He hath hedged me about that I cannot get out; He hath made my chain heavy.' 'The Lord,' he continued, 'has made me useful and acceptable to many at Stadham and in the neighbourhood, and how can I quit them without some very clear intimation and direction from Him? I know I cannot go back again into the world; but I cannot say I delight myself in the Lord. What a poor minister should I be to a people who have heard and known the truth for years; saddle myself on such I dare not. "Oh that I had wings like a dove! for then would I fly away, and be at rest." Nothing short of an answer that the Lord will be my guide, so that I might see the pillar of cloud going before me, will ever induce me to leave my present post. I should only be a darkener of the Lord's counsel by words without knowledge; for a man may be called by grace without ever being called to the work of the ministry.'

"When he afterwards came to Allington he used to say, 'Now I am come to reside with you just as long or as short a time as we suit each other and the church. I disclaim all priestcraft. I am a poor sinner, not a very *good* man, but a very bad one.' Yet our household can bear witness that a more consistent, honest, upright man never breathed. He, dear man, laid claim to the badness of his heart, but he could lay claim also to the grace God gave him, which pardoned him and justified him freely by the redemption of the Lord Jesus. He kept us all in place in the house, and we never once had a jar; all was regularity; and every one respected, loved, and, I may add, revered him.

"When first he came amongst us he was very close and searching in his preaching, and it was enough to make a living man tremble. The only way to become wise was to become a fool, and never to say more of one's self than what the Lord had taught and wrought in you; without Christ man can do nothing. He was made a great blessing to many souls around us, though at first some could hardly understand his line of things and thought him too cutting. I remember how our dear friend Dredge said to me, after one sermon, that he could have gone to the stake and have been burnt for the truths he had heard that morning rather than give them up. There was life indeed amongst us at that time as a people, and the neighbourhood all round used to flock to Allington from nearly all the different parts of the country, many walking twelve and fifteen miles to hear the word of life. Some when returning home, they have told me, would sit down on the road-side and say, 'Well, we can never stand this searching preaching, it cuts us up root and branch.' One of our old supplies came to chapel, one week-day evening, when Mr. Philpot was expounding in the table-pew from Lam. iii. 16, and said afterwards, 'Well, if the Allington people can stand this searching work, I shall think something of them after all.'

"Dear Mrs. Philpot, I am quite exhausted; I can go no further. I shall be glad if these reminiscences are of any use to you. Wishing you prosperity in the work you have undertaken, and with our united love to you all,

"Believe me to be,

"Yours very sincerely,

"JOSEPH PARRY."

THE CALNE ANNIVERSARY

In many of the letters frequent mention is made of the Calne Anniversary. Mr. Philpot's connection with Calne sprang originally out of his frequent visits to Allington, the two places being distant only ten miles. His first visit to Calne was in April, 1836, when he came over from Allington at the request of a few friends and preached in a chapel which was kindly lent for the occasion. At that time a chapel had already been commenced at Calne, and in May, 1837, this building was inaugurated under the name of Zion Chapel, by Mr. Philpot, assisted by Mr. Shorter, and Mr. Hooper of Devizes. As each summer recurred, the friends at Calne made it a custom to celebrate the anniversary of the opening of their chapel, and Mr. Philpot was absent only two or three times from these interesting gatherings. At first he supplied in conjunction with Mr. Warburton, of Trowbridge, but after the death of that good man, in 1857, he found an able coadjutor in Mr. Mortimer of Chippenham. An agreement was made between the Calne church and Mr. Philpot, that when the debt of the chapel had been cleared off, the annual collections should be devoted to the Aged Pilgrims' Friend Society, and now for many years that Society, and through it the poor saints of God, have reaped the benefit of the Calne Anniversary. Mr. Philpot was perhaps more widely known and more highly respected in the West of England than in any other part of the country, and the annual gathering at Calne was looked forward to by many hundreds of the Lord's people in those parts with pleasurable anticipation. Under God's blessing it was made the means of calling to repentance many a sinner, and of encouraging and comforting many a poor saint. Mr. Philpot looked forward to the annual event with as much interest as his hearers, and it was a great trial to him that on two or three occasions he was prevented by his weak state of health from being present at it.

LIST OF PUBLICATIONS BY THE LATE MR. J. C. PHILPOT

A Letter to the Provost of Worcester College, Oxford, on resigning his fellowship and seceding from the Church of England, in which the errors and corruptions of the Established Church, the principle and practice of the universities, as well as the congregations and preachings of the orthodox and evangelical clergy, are freely commented on. First edition published in 1835.

Secession from the Church of England Defended. Containing also remarks on the occasional services of the Prayer-book. First published in 1836.

Two Letters to the Editors of the "Gospel Standard." One on Strict Communion, and the other in answer to the question, "Were Christ's Disciples baptized?" together with a preface and testimonies from the ancient fathers, learned men, and ancient formularies, for strict communion and immersion. From the May and July numbers of the *Gospel Standard* for 1840, vol vi.

An Answer to the important Question, "What is it that saves a soul?"

The Heir of Heaven walking in Darkness, and the Heir of Hell walking in Light. A sermon preached at Stamford on Lord's-day morning, October 23, 1836, and published shortly afterwards.

Winter afore Harvest; or, the Soul's Growth in Grace. A sermon preached at Oakham on Lord's-day, August 20, 1837, and published shortly afterwards.

The True and proper and eternal Sonship of the Lord Jesus Christ, the only-begotten Son of God. Published in 1861.

Memoir of the late William Tiptaft. Published June, 1867.

The Advance of Popery in this Country viewed under both its Religious and Political Aspect. Published June, 1869.

In March, 1842, Mr. Philpot wrote a Preface to John Berridge's "Zion's Songs," published by Heydon of Devonport.

Mr. Philpot also selected the Hymns for the second supplement to "Gadsby's Hymns" and wrote a short Preface in 1845 or 1846. This was a work which employed much of his time and was no small labour.

In May, 1857, Mr. Philpot wrote a Preface to John Warburton's "Testimony," and in May, 1859, he wrote a Preface to the new edition of "Mercies of a Covenant God," by John Warburton.

In one of his letters it will be seen that he revised the manuscript of this work for his friend John Warburton.

Sermons in the Penny Pulpit, published by J. Paul, London.

Sermons in the Zoar Chapel Pulpit, published by the late E. Justins, London.

Sermons in the Gospel Pulpit, published by J. Ford, Stamford.